# ECONOMIC
# GROWTH
# AND
# DEVELOPMENT

# ECONOMIC GROWTH AND DEVELOPMENT

## BRUCE R. MORRIS

UNIVERSITY OF MASSACHUSETTS

*in cooperation with*

## C. WENDELL KING

UNIVERSITY OF MASSACHUSETTS

*Pitman Publishing Corporation*

NEW YORK / TORONTO / LONDON

ECONOMIC GROWTH AND DEVELOPMENT *is
one of a series of textbooks published in
cooperation with E. K. Georg Landsberger.*

*To my wife and family*

# *PREFACE*

One would like to write a text on economic development in which he could say to the student, "This is why countries do not grow and this is the exact sequence of steps they must follow in order to develop. Economic teachings say this is so." Unfortunately, there is no agreed-upon theory of development. Also, the problems in each country are different. Moreover, the amount of emphasis individual countries desire to place on economic growth instead of other possible goals varies. As a result, the policies that each country must follow also differ. Therefore, the emphasis in this book is on the presentation of a wide range of problems and solutions. A major thesis of the book is that the problems and the specific combination of remedies are unique for each country and must be studied specifically, if helpful proposals are to be made. Our purpose is to aid the student in knowing what to look for and in understanding the kinds of difficulties that have to be overcome. No one formula can be universally used to bring about development.

Mathematics and complex diagrams are not used in this book. Not that I think that mathematical formulations of growth models are unimportant and of no use. Quite the contrary. It is my experience that the student who is being introduced to the subject too often devotes his time to struggling with the mathematics and the diagrams and ends up learning very little about the problems and difficulties of the underdeveloped countries and the wide range of possible solutions. Once a student has studied the subject and has acquired a working knowledge of what is happening in underdeveloped countries, and understands what things might be tried, he is ready for a more mathematical treatment.

This book is written under the assumption that the student has had an introductory course in economics. Many subjects discussed here could well be given more extended treatment, but textbook pages are not unlimited, although the student may sometimes think so. Some lengthy, complicated subjects had to be condensed; some, treated lightly; some, only mentioned. To supplement this necessary curtailment, each chapter cites sources and additional readings that can be read profitably in conjunction with this book.

No claim is made that new theories are presented in these pages. Every author has his own personal viewpoints and emphases, but the main role of an introductory text is to present an outline of what is known and the general problems involved. No text can be complete in itself. Unless the student enters the library and seeks additional viewpoints and other materials, his knowledge will be incomplete. He must test various views and different prescriptions, and weigh these in an effort to reach valid conclusions. This is particularly true of a subject as incomplete as the theory of economic development.

Some topics seem to spring up in many places. Mostly this is so because a development effort is not an attack on one sector of the economy in isolation. There must be many points of attack, and measures are interrelated. Thus, it is difficult to write about one sector without referring to others or to measures which affect other sectors. Ideally, the student should read all chapters before studying each chapter individually. Because this is obviously impossible, an order of presentation must be chosen and cross references provided. No apologies are necessary for the order of presentation in this book, although other sequences could have been adopted equally well.

After an introductory chapter and a brief summary of theories affecting economic development, phases of the economic life are presented one after the other. The succeeding chapters discuss their importance in the development process, the problems involved, and some of the reforms that must be made to improve the contribution of each economic phase to the total development of the economy. Each reform requires capital. Chapters 14 and 15 complete the study of development by setting up guidelines for determining policy, once the specific conditions of a given country are known.

Two points have already been made. The first is that the combination of development measures applicable to each country is unique. The second is that a wide variety of more or less interrelated measures is necessary for development and that the all too scarce resources of the country must be allocated in a manner calculated to achieve the best results. A third point of emphasis is that economic development is not for economists alone, but requires attention to the human factor and to social and cultural phenomena. In fact, the author believes that the primary problem in economic development is the improvement of the human element, and it is this that should have priority in the investment program.

It appears that a writer on economic development must establish his pedigree of experience in underdeveloped countries. I spent two years in

Indonesia on a teaching assignment for the University of Wisconsin under a grant from the Ford Foundation, hence the many references to that country. Of course, neither the University of Wisconsin nor the Ford Foundation is responsible for any of the viewpoints of this book. I have also visited almost all of the Asian countries. Professor C. Wendell King, who contributed the chapter on Social and Cultural Factors, spent a sabbatical leave in Jamaica.

An author owes a debt to many people, either directly or indirectly. Thus, first of all, I wish to acknowledge my indebtedness to the unnamed many whose ideas I have unknowingly made my own. There are also the nationals of a number of countries with whom I have discussed development issues. I am especially indebted to Professor C. Wendell King, University of Massachusetts, for his chapter on an area where economists fear to tread. Various colleagues have read and contributed comments on various chapters, notably Professors Sydney S. Schoeffler, David Storey, and Norman Aitken all of the University of Massachusetts. Two graduate students, Father Raymond Cahill and Norman Cournoyer, read large sections of the work. My student assistant, Gerald Creem, worked long hours in running down library materials. Especially, I wish to thank the typists who followed the text through many wanderings and mazes to produce a final draft, namely, Misses Alice Morris and Alice Stosz, who typed the first drafts, and Mrs. Doris Holden, who prepared the final manuscript.

BRUCE R. MORRIS

# CONTENTS

# ECONOMIC
# GROWTH
# AND
# DEVELOPMENT

# CHAPTER
# I
# *Introduction*

Since World War II, economists, students of other disciplines, and the general public have been intensely interested in the problem of economic growth and development. Whenever man has faced problems, he has tried to solve them either by magic incantations or rituals, guesswork, or serious study. Today two-thirds of the world's population live in chronic poverty and this has become perhaps the most important problem that the world has to face. Chronic poverty of such dimensions is not a new problem, but for the first time, man en masse seems aware of it and realizes the necessity for solving it. As a result, the problems of economic growth have top priority in economic thought, if judged by the amount of space devoted to them in the economic literature. Students of the other social sciences are also devoting their attention to it, and it is now realized that economic growth cannot be explained solely in economic terms.

Economic growth is not a new topic in the field of economics, as we shall see in Chapter 2, where the theories of leading writers on the subject are introduced. From the beginnings of economic science, occasional writers have concerned themselves with the subject, and a few, including Adam Smith, who is considered the "founder" of the subject of economics, have made it the center of their discussion, but concentrated attention was only sporadic until the 1950's. Therefore, the intensive study of economic growth is virtually a new subject and is probably the area where economists are least sure of themselves. Economic growth, both at home and abroad, has become a top governmental policy issue for all nations. Unfortunately, the issues arose so rapidly that economists were not ready with a developed body of economic analysis. But need usually brings action, and today we have specialists who are concentrating on this field. Intensive study by specialists will hopefully lead to more precision in our theory, although we are perhaps too interested in immediate practical results to achieve the rapid results one would desire. As yet there is no generally accepted formula for ensuring growth, but there is much speculation and theorizing, with verification lagging. But this is the usual course in any serious study. Because conclusions are so tentative, the student should closely scrutinize each theory, hypothesis, insight, or policy injunction for reasonableness and compare it with other views. Most conclusions reached at this time can be only tentative and are dependent upon future verification.

Each era has a different dominant interest, depending on the major problem of the day. New problems may require new techniques to solve them, and this has been true in the study of economics. The problem of economic growth has given rise to new theoretical techniques. For almost the entire nineteenth century and well into the twentieth, the dominant problem was the efficient allocation of resources, and economists devoted their time almost exclusively to this. By the 1930's the public was concerned with depressions and security, and much of the effort of administrators and economists was devoted to making people secure—with social security, bank deposit insurance, minimum wage laws, and control of security sales, to mention a few of the issues in the United States. The fear of unemployment following World War II turned the people's attention toward maintaining full employment. Increasingly, economists became aware that full employment was not a sufficient goal and that, in addition, a country should strive for more goods and services.

For various reasons this concept of growth or development attracted the attention of the public as well as economists and other social scientists.[1]

1. The war and postwar tensions made it obvious that economic power is essential for military and diplomatic power. The weapons of modern warfare are costly and technically complicated. Only a nation with advanced production processes can afford to produce them. Poor countries only impoverish themselves if they try to buy them. Thus, because of the worldwide interest in national power, already advanced nations have become interested in growth so that they can stay ahead in economic and military strength; less advanced countries wish to avoid becoming militarily weak, and so try to develop economically.

2. Statistical information has become more abundant and it is obvious that there are wide disparities in standards of living among the various

countries, that the rates of growth among them vary considerably, and that, within individual countries, rates of growth have been different at different periods in their history. It is thus obvious that identifiable factors affect the rate of growth.

3. There has also been a growing belief that without suitable growth, countries cannot maintain continuous full employment and particularly cannot find jobs for their youth as they seek to enter the labor market.

4. Roused by these same forces and others, underdeveloped countries have adopted intensive programs to develop themselves. Stephen Enke[2] says that these countries have become aroused because the movies, improved communication, and better contact with outsiders have made them aware of higher living standards elsewhere; have accepted the Soviet propaganda that their poverty is due to Western exploitation through political and economic domination; have become cognizant of the ability of governments to force change.

Whatever the reason, previously poor countries have arrived at the conclusion that poverty is not necessarily inevitable and that something can be done about it. Actually, most such countries are now too optimistic about the prospects of growing and may find that their expectations cannot be fulfilled. Such countries now realize not only the possibilities of change, but also that failure to attain economic growth is associated with political dependence and an inferior status. They are thus determined to do something about it and are making efforts, whether effective or not.

These efforts have reacted on Western countries so that they have also developed great interest in the problems and the economic growth of the less advanced countries. Indeed, the term "economic growth" is usually associated with underdeveloped countries and not with the developed, although there is no reason why this should be so. For example, most college courses labeled "Economic Growth," or "Economic Development" deal with underdeveloped countries.

Why this interest on the part of the West? Unfortunately, much of its interest may be military. The so-called Free World is interested in persuading other countries to accept some form of democratic freedom rather than Communism, and believes that the newly emerging government entities are less likely to be democratic if they are poor than if they grow economically. It is impossible to buy their friendship, but assistance is essential so that they can develop economically and thus eliminate a basic cause of their becoming fertile fields for Communism. Although this outcome is not entirely an economic matter, one must realize that no country can live in isolation and that all countries do have an interest in the type of world in which they live.

Of more importance to economists is the prevalent theory that the growth of the poorer countries is necessary for the growth of the richer because such growth will make possible mutual trade and the exchange of raw materials and manufactured goods. General development will increase sales for the more advanced countries because the richer other countries are, the better customers they are likely to be. The growth of industry in other countries will lessen markets for some industries in the West and even destroy some, but other industries in which the advanced nations can be expected to have a comparative advantage will grow to take the place of obsolescent manufactures, provided these industries continue to advance technologically. Moreover, even though economic growth in the underdeveloped countries may temporarily divert their attention from the production and exportation of raw materials, development in the long run can be expected to exploit resources that are profitable and available for world trade. Thus, the West has an economic as well as a military interest in general economic development of these countries.

In addition, the West has a genuine humanitarian interest in such development. There is a surprising amount of concern about the rest of the world and not all the actions of the West are motivated by personal gain.

Moreover, the compression of the world's span in terms of travel and communication time has made all nations aware of the problems of underdeveloped countries, and they realize that events occurring in them are no longer remote and isolated affairs but can affect other parts of the world. In the interests of maintaining a peaceful and prosperous existence, the currently more developed countries have been forced to become interested in the underdeveloped portions of the world.

## Definitions and Concepts

It is the usual practice to refer to countries as being underdeveloped (or undeveloped) or advanced, although the terminology is not precise. In general, these words mean "poor" countries and "rich" countries, based on the amount of their per capita national output, with an arbitrary dividing line at around $500 per capita per year. Because there is a wide scatter of incomes (see Table 1.1), this is obviously a flexible classification. One of the aspects of terminology is a psychological one. The term "poor" country is unacceptable because of the connotation of inferiority. For a while the term "undeveloped" was used, but this seemed equally unacceptable. The term "underdeveloped" at least gave the connotation that development was possible. Now this term seems to have lost favor with some of the nations termed "underdeveloped," and the term "newly developing" or "newly emerging" is beginning to be encountered. Nevertheless, the word "under-developed" will be used here to refer to all countries with low per capita incomes, with no connotation that they are or are not currently growing.* Advanced countries will be classified as those with per capita incomes above $500.

The terms "economic growth" and "economic development" seem to be used interchangeably and refer to a rise in the per capita national output.† This usage will be followed here. Thus, a country will be considered to be experiencing economic growth if it undergoes a persistent increase in its national output of goods and services per capita over a period of years.**

The world is really interested in development or "progress" or "welfare," but these are too difficult and too subjective to define and discuss with any precision. A too materialistic outlook may not make for the best life and the happiest people, but the content of the "good life" is not easy to deal with. The basic function of a society is to provide what its people want, whether this is economic, spiritual, or otherwise, and a society should be judged on the basis of how it meets these wants. However, it is doubtful if we will ever be able to measure the increase in "welfare." In judging the performance of a society, one is forced to judge the progress of the immeas-urable nonmaterial values, as discussed below. Actually, because different peoples have different sets of values, each must decide for themselves the extent to which economic growth aids or interferes with the satisfaction of other values. Economists, as economists, are concerned with prescriptions

* One of the objections to the use of the word "underdeveloped" is that rich countries may be the most underdeveloped, compared to their potential. In fact, it is entirely possible that the richer a nation, the easier it is for it to grow, if it does not follow policies that hinder growth. It is unlikely that any nation is doing the best possible with its resources.

† But R. S. Shearer ("Concept of Economic Growth," *Kyklos*, No. 4 (1961, p. 499) advocates a distinction: *economic growth* to refer to an increase in the output of goods and services, and *economic development* to imply a more general development, including personal and social values. Thus, a country might be growing economically but failing to develop (or even may be retrogressing) because other values were being lost.

** It is, of course, possible to define growth in terms of any measure, such as population, accumulated wealth, productive capital, material goods, technological information, or quality of the people. However, many of these are unmeasurable, and the chief concern seems to be the goods and services available for use.

It would also be more realistic to measure economic growth as the relationship between the output of goods and services and the input of factors (the factors avail-able, even though not used), thus developing a concept of economic efficiency. How-ever, it makes as much sense to relate the output to the number of consuming units as to relate it to any single factor such as man-hours of labor or dollars of capital employed. Measures of a combined input of capital-labor-land are not yet practicable, especially as an international standard for comparison.

for economic growth, although in actual policy situations they cannot help but keep other values in mind.

The economist, then, while fundamentally interested in total welfare, concentrates on economic growth or an increase in the annual national output of goods and services. Although not synonymous with welfare, this is used as an approximation to welfare. Increased output may not represent progress, for the goods may be overabundant, may merely offset certain evils (as in the case of military expenditures), may be produced at too great a cost to other values, or may even be harmful to society.* Other goods might have been more useful or important.

Increased output is not the sole end of man, but it does aid in meeting other goals. It leads to possible greater leisure and thus to a possibility of greater cultural attainment and improved education, to better health, to military strength, and to other noneconomic goals. A nation that grows economically can take better care of the crippled, sick, and others unable to take care of themselves. It is less apt to be militarily and politically dependent on others. It is less apt to be subject to the revolution of the masses. At the very least, it increases the number of choices available to a people and thus increases the possibilities of attaining increased welfare.†

Thus, we are concerned primarily with the problem of enlarging the output of goods and services. In order to make this concept somewhat more relevant to welfare, economic growth will be considered as an increase in annual per capita output. Considerations of "real progress" and "welfare" must be discussed on a different basis.** It is possible to use total output as a measure of growth, for such output might be available for other uses, for example, the reduction of illiteracy or the decrease of disease. However, per capita output seems a better standard. This, however, must be interpreted with care; for example, the way the income is distributed has an influence on the well-being of a people.††

* The word "harmful" is as subjective as that of "welfare." Some individuals would list cigarettes or whiskey in this category, others would include the services of professional athletes, and there are those who would include religious services. Thus, no list of goods could be agreed upon so that the proper exclusions from national output might be made.

† W. A. Lewis (*Theory of Economic Growth*, Homewood, Ill., Richard Irwin, Inc., 1955, pp. 420-423) says that, although wealth may not make a people happier, it does permit a people to avoid slavery to a constant struggle for subsistence, provides a longer life, healthier children (and a more rested and prettier wife), and frees people from the worst consequences of some of nature's menaces, such as famine. He also adds that growth benefits women more than men.

** The problem of national objectives, economic and noneconomic, will be discussed in another chapter of this book.

†† Dr. Simon Kuznets suggests that one ought to deduct the personal costs involved in producing these goods, recognizing, of course, that this is unmeasurable.

The output of goods and services is measured by statistics of national income, the most commonly used in the United States being those calculated by the Department of Commerce and published regularly in the *Survey of Current Business.* Details of their construction are included in the usual elementary economics course and need not be repeated here. From country to country the method is roughly the same, although definitions may vary and the details of calculation and presentation may be somewhat different. The figure usually used to measure economic growth is the *gross national product* (GNP), which is the dollar value of the output of goods and services within the country during the year. But all this output is not available for consumption, some being used to replace capital goods that have worn out or have been destroyed. Some is used to pay government personnel for rendering services to business. Except for several other minor items, what is left is *national income,* which in some respects is a better measure of economic growth in that it represents the amount available after the capital equipment is left intact and certain governmental services for business rendered. It also corresponds to the income of all factors of production.

Output is measured in terms of money because it is the only commensurable unit for all goods and services. The fact of changing price levels makes this an imperfect measure, but it is the best we have for overall output. Besides changing price levels, other problems are encountered. For the most part we count only goods and services that enter the market, thus understating the amount of goods and services available, especially for the less developed economies where a smaller amount of total output enters the market. The monetary figures may be adjusted for nonmarket production, but this introduces into the figures an element of very rough estimate. For these reasons the published figures for different countries are scarcely comparable. E. E. Hagen[3] would compensate for this by applying varying factors to the calculated figures, the largest factors applying to those countries with the lowest incomes. This is, of course, a rough adjustment, but probably gives a more accurate relative picture than the published data. The statistical problems are complex and the resulting totals are subject to varying degrees of error, although not quite as much for the advanced countries where data and statistical techniques are more advanced. It may be noted further that international comparisons are difficult because techniques and definitions vary to some extent, and converting to a common monetary unit is not satisfactory. For example, exchange rates deviate in

("Measurement of Economic Growth," *Journal of Economic History,* supplement [1947], p. 24). As an example, one might mention the personal cost to the Russian peasant of shifting to the collective farm.

differing degrees from purchasing power parities, and people consume different things, so that comparisons of the prices of a common list of goods are not a good test of relative prices.

Thus, although our interest is in economic growth, we are working with a concept that expresses our goal in only a limited way and which cannot be accurately measured. Nevertheless, if the limitations are understood and our output figures are supplemented by other measures, we can make rough estimates of the economic growth of different countries.

Some partial measures have been devised, based on supposed differences between underdeveloped and advanced countries. M. K. Bennett[4] illustrates this by a comparison of a number of countries using nineteen such partial measures; namely, food calories per 100 pounds of humanity per day, proportion of calories derived from other than grain and potatoes, tobacco per capita, infant mortality, physicians per 1,000 population, consumption of cement, household energy, textile fibers used, school attendance, mail volume, moving picture theaters, freight carried by mail, inanimate energy used by railways and inland waterways, motor vehicles, telephones, energy in manufacturing, livestock, and climate. Not all these measures represent real differences between advanced and underdeveloped countries; for example, the number of calories consumed, and the procedure of combining this into an index is questionable, but the use of such measures is desirable. Other possible measures, whose relevance will become clear in Chapter 5, include various aspects of vital statistics such as fertility of the population, infant mortality, and composition of the population. J. Viner[5] suggests as a test the numbers of the population living in crushing poverty, which would be an excellent supplementary measure if the statistics were available. It is obvious from the foregoing discussion that accurate comparisons are not possible, but it is possible to obtain a reasonable classification of countries as advanced or underdeveloped.

## The Facts of Underdevelopment

Keeping in mind the inadequacies of our statistical data, Table 1.1 shows the great disparity in per capita income now prevailing in the world. Minor differences should be ignored, but the difference between per capita income figures of $2,691 for the United States and $73 for India represents a very real difference. It will also be noted that there is even great disparity among countries on the same continent. For example: In Africa, the per capita income in 1962 ranged from a low of $43 in Upper Volta to $554 in South Africa; in Asia, from $57 in Burma to $1,232 in Israel; in Europe, from

$352 in Portugal to $1,951 in Switzerland; in North America from $93 in Haiti to $2,691 in the United States; and in South America from $86 in Paraguay to $701 in Venezuela. If $500 is taken as the dividing line between developed and underdeveloped countries, twenty-four of the ninety-three countries included in the survey may be considered developed. Eighteen more had per capita incomes between $200 and $499, and fifty-one were below $200. Table 1.2 shows this division by continents.

Unfortunately, many countries are not included in Table 1.1, particularly the Communist-controlled economies. A rough comparison of their position can be seen in Table 1.3, which is calculated on a basis different from that for Table 1.1.

**TABLE 1.1.**

*Per Capita Gross Domestic Product at Factor Cost and Other*
*Measures of Growth for the Countries of the World.*
*(Expressed in United States Dollars)*

| Continent and Country | Per Capita GDP | | Physicians per 100,000 Population[b] | Number of Students in Higher Education per 100,000 Population[b] | Newspaper Circulation per 100,000 Population[b] |
|---|---|---|---|---|---|
| | 1953[a] | 1962[a] | | | |
| *Africa* | | | | | |
| South Africa | $ 429 | $ 554 | 49.8 | 187.6 | 61 |
| Algeria | 133 | 229 | 17.3 | 72.0 | 22 |
| Gabon | 114 | 203 | | | |
| Ghana | 135 | 187 | 4.7 | 15.6 | 32 |
| Libya | — | 186 | 7.3 | 52.4 | 7 |
| Rhodesia and Nyasaland | 158 | 178 | | | |
| Senegal | 162 | 165 | 1.8 | 54.2 | 6 |
| Morocco | 158 | 159 | 10.6 | 42.6 | 22 |
| United Arab Republic | 138 | 156 | 38.9 | 432.3 | 20 |
| Ivory Coast | 83 | 143 | 3.2 | 4.1 | 3 |
| Congo (Brazzaville) | 70 | 107 | | | |
| Congo (Leopoldville) | 92 | 100 | 1.7 | 4.3 | 2 |
| Nigeria | 98 | 96 | | | |
| Kenya | 75 | 85 | 7.8 | 3.9 | 14 |
| Dahomey | 83 | 80 | | | |
| Mali | 71 | 79 | 1.3 | — | 1 |
| Central African Republic | 69 | 78 | | | |
| Mauritania | 70 | 75 | | | |
| Togo | 80 | 73 | | | |
| Sudan | 62 | 72 | 2.8 | 29.6 | 4 |
| Madagascar | 68 | 70 | | | |
| Tanganyika | 50 | 68 | 5.9 | 9.3 | 4 |
| Cameroon | 50 | 62 | | | |
| Uganda | 66 | 60 | 6.6 | 14.0 | 8 |
| Chad | 49 | 60 | | | |

**TABLE 1.1.** *(Continued)*

| Continent and Country | Per Capita GDP 1953[a] | Per Capita GDP 1962[a] | Physicians per 100,000 Population[b] | Number of Students in Higher Education per 100,000 Population[b] | Newspaper Circulation per 100,000 Population[b] |
|---|---|---|---|---|---|
| Niger | 67 | 57 | 1.0 | — | 0.4 |
| Ethiopia | 38 | 51 | | | |
| Upper Volta | 34 | 43 | 0.8 | — | 0.1 |
| Tunisia | 154 | — | 13.2 | — | 14 |
| Guinea | 61 | — | 2.5 | — | — |
| Angola | 43 | — | 6.7 | — | 9 |
| Mozambique | 25 | — | 4.9 | — | 3 |
| *Asia* | | | | | |
| Israel | 558 | 1,232 | 24.0 | 526.7 | 210 |
| Japan | 217 | 551 | 106.8 | 810.3 | 416 |
| Singapore | — | 336 | | | |
| Turkey | 210 | 272 | 35.4 | 253.6 | 45 |
| Lebanon | 197 | 225 | | | |
| Saudi Arabia | 174 | 225 | — | — | 4 |
| Jordan | 101 | 223 | 17.3 | | 18 |
| Fed. of Malaya | — | 207 | 17.1 | 29.0 | 67 |
| Hong Kong | 130 | 188 | | | |
| Iraq | 100 | 162 | 19.6 | 226.5 | 10 |
| Iran | 97 | 153 | 27.8 | 104.5 | 15 |
| Ceylon | 108 | 137 | 27.2 | 68.9 | 37 |
| Philippines | 90 | 125 | 14.4 | 987.7 | 18 |
| China (Taiwan) | 78 | 121 | 73.7 | 323.7 | 66 |
| Syria | 117 | 119 | 21.7 | 217.3 | 19 |
| Korea, Republic of | 77 | 110 | 25.6 | 391.4 | 69 |
| Thailand | 91 | 106 | 13.0 | 166.5 | 14 |
| Pakistan | 56 | 74 | 11.4 | 161.6 | 7 |
| India | 65 | 73 | 17.7 | 21.0 | 11 |
| Indonesia | 60 | 73 | 22.0 | 51.4 | 11 |
| Laos | 57 | 68 | | | |
| Cambodia | 52 | 68 | 0.9 | 15.4 | 6 |
| Viet Nam, Republic of | — | 68 | | | |
| Afghanistan | 25 | 61 | | | |
| Burma | 42 | 57 | 8.3 | 75.3 | 12 |
| *Europe* | | | | | |
| Switzerland | 1,173 | 1,951 | 144.7 | 431.7 | 374 |
| Sweden | 1,177 | 1,833 | 91.9 | 435.9 | 477 |
| Norway | 1,066 | 1,608 | 120.7 | 292.5 | 384 |
| Luxembourg | 1,060 | 1,543 | | | |
| Denmark | 965 | 1,492 | 120.2 | 383.7 | 345 |
| United Kingdom | 1,028 | 1,454 | 90.5 | 362.4 | 506 |
| Germany, Fed. Rep. | 751 | 1,439 | — | 455.6 | 307 |
| France | 861 | 1,437 | 96.6 | 492.2 | 252 |
| West Berlin | 653 | 1,372 | | | |

TABLE 1.1. *(Continued)*

| Continent and Country | Per Capita GDP 1953[a] | 1962[a] | Physicians per 100,000 Population[b] | Number of Students in Higher Education per 100,000 Population[b] | Newspaper Circulation per 100,000 Population[b] |
|---|---|---|---|---|---|
| Netherlands | 780 | 1,250 | 131.2 | 695.4 | 278 |
| Belgium | 831 | 1,239 | 123.8 | 447.3 | 285 |
| Italy | 496 | 917 | 160.8 | 321.3 | 101 |
| Austria | 476 | 850 | 161.1 | 546.9 | 208 |
| Finland | 442 | 770 | 61.4 | 499.6 | — |
| Ireland | 513 | 755 | | | |
| Greece | 210 | 374 | 124.0 | 284.5 | 125 |
| Portugal | 205 | 352 | 79.3 | 239.4[c] | 81 |
| *North America* | | | | | |
| United States | 2,080 | 2,691 | 130.7 | 1,797.9 | 326 |
| Canada | 1,475 | 1,887 | 104.2 | 478.7 | 231 |
| Puerto Rico | 405 | 825 | | | |
| Panama | 287 | 429 | | | |
| Jamaica | 235 | 418 | | | |
| Mexico | 228 | 361 | 57.9 | 248.8 | 83 |
| Barbados | 206 | 323 | | | |
| Costa Rica | 227 | 260 | | | |
| Dominican Republic | 161 | 214 | 12.4 | 165.9 | 27 |
| Honduras | 160 | 194 | | | |
| Guatemala | 120 | 166 | 19.4 | 182.3 | 23 |
| El Salvador | — | 134 | 19.3 | 89.6 | 45 |
| Haiti | 83 | 93 | 3.9 | 28.7 | 11 |
| Cuba | 246 | — | 113.4 | 300.7 | 129 |
| *South America* | | | | | |
| Venezuela | 474 | 701 | 67.1 | 283.0 | 96 |
| Argentina | 390 | 462 | 151.4 | 774.8 | 155 |
| Chile | 364 | 422 | 63.0 | 257.7 | 134 |
| Colombia | 204 | 285 | 51.7 | 196.2 | 56 |
| Ecuador | 139 | 188 | 51.7 | 236.2 | 56 |
| Brazil | 116 | 179 | 43.0 | 143.1 | 54 |
| Peru | 133 | 173 | 48.8 | 240.7 | 76 |
| Paraguay | 83 | 86 | 73.7 | 248.2 | 37 |
| British Guiana | 271 | | | | |
| *Oceania* | | | | | |
| New Zealand | 1,324 | 1,860 | 140.6 | 665.2 | 383 |
| Australia | 1,127 | 1,843 | 114.2 | 675.7 | 376 |

SOURCE:

[a] United Nations, *Yearbook of National Accounts Statistics, 1963*, Statistical Office of the United Nations, Part D, Table 3B, pp. 327 ff. No allowance has been made for price changes between 1953 and 1962.

[b] United Nations, *Statistical Yearbook, 1962*, pp. 603 ff, 623 ff, 649 ff. The most recent year's figures available are used.

[c] University students only.

**TABLE 1.2.**

*Distribution of Countries by Amount of per Capita Income, 1962,*
*by Continent*

| Continent | Over $500 | $200-$499 | Under $200 |
|---|---|---|---|
| Africa | 1 | 2 | 25 |
| Asia | 2 | 6 | 17 |
| Europe | 15 | 2 | |
| North America | 3 | 6 | 4 |
| South America | 1 | 2 | 5 |
| Oceania | 2 | | |

SOURCE: Table 1.1.

**TABLE 1.3.**

*Per Capita Income[a] of Communist Countries and*
*Selected Other Countries, 1961*

| | | | |
|---|---|---|---|
| U.S.S.R. | $ 986 | United States | $2,790 |
| | | Switzerland | 1,010 |
| | | Sweden | 950 |
| East Europe | 825 | Belgium | 800 |
| Cuba | 516 | Puerto Rico | 771.6 |
| | | Mexico | 415.4 |
| Yugoslavia | 489.1 | Netherlands | 500 |
| North Korea | 211 | South Korea | 158.4 |
| North Vietnam | 199 | South Vietnam | 210.3 |
| China | 167 | India | 139.8 |

SOURCE: P. N. Rosenstein-Rodan, "International Aid for Underdeveloped Countries," *Review of Economics and Statistics* (May, 1961), pp. 118 ff.
[a] Per capita incomes have been translated into an estimate of the equivalent purchasing power of United States dollars in the United States.

One can note that rates of growth also have varied from country to country. Because the 1953 figures are given in 1953 dollar equivalents and those of 1962 in 1962 equivalents, all the problems of estimating international equivalents of national income statistics are increased. Nevertheless, a rough comparison can be made. Four countries and two other areas more than doubled their per capita incomes in the nine years (1953-1962): Japan, Afghanistan, Jordan, Israel, West Berlin, and Puerto Rico. All five showing decreases are located in Africa. Between these extremes was a wide variety, with some tendency for the wealthier to advance faster than the poorer. Especially those with incomes under $200 did relatively poorly. Inasmuch as the poorer countries are located in Africa and Asia, those continents did more poorly than the rest.

Many partial measures of welfare or progress could be cited, as previously observed.[6] Only three are presented in Table 1.1: physicians per 100,000 population, number of students in higher education per 100,000 population and newspaper circulation per 100,000 people. These reflect, roughly, the health standards, educational effort, and general literacy at a level sufficient to read a newspaper (and afford one). Although there is not a perfect correlation between national income and physicians per capita, there is a rough correspondence. A few countries appear to have far more physicians than one would expect from their incomes; for example, the United Arab Republic, Taiwan, Greece, Portugal, Argentina, and Paraguay. The striking feature is the great diversity, ranging from only 0.8 physicians per 100,000 population in Upper Volta to 161.1 in Austria and 160.8 in Italy. Similarly, there is a wide range in the numbers in higher education per 100,000 population. Many of the African nations are not represented, but even so, the range is from 3.9 in Kenya to 1,797.9 in the United States and 987.7 in the Philippines and 810.3 in Japan, the next two leading countries. There is again a rough correspondence between income and such students, but a number of exceptions exist. Similar statements can be made about newspaper circulation. Again, the variation is large, ranging from 0.1 per 1,000 population in Upper Volta to 477 in Sweden and 416 in Japan.

Food is the primary need of people and the first one to be met. One would not expect, therefore, as much variation in the total food consumed as in other less essential items or as in the protective foods. Table 1.4, however, reveals considerable variation in the per capita food supplies in the various countries. Most of the underdeveloped countries are not included in this survey. If they had been, the disparities would have been far greater. Although some of the differences can be ascribed to different food habits, and although in some countries the population eats to excess, the differences indicate real differences in the standard of living. The country with the lowest calories per capita had only 66.9 percent of that available to the average of all countries. The showing was even worse in the case of the protective foods, 10.8 percent in the case of vegetables, 4.8 percent in meat, 13.0 percent in eggs, 20.0 percent in milk protein, 56.0 percent in total protein, and 19.4 percent in animal protein.

Much more could be presented, but these facts are sufficient to indicate that there are great differences in the amount of progress in the various countries and that large numbers of them have fallen far behind the recognized advanced countries such as the United States, Canada, Northwest Europe, Oceania, and now the U.S.S.R. In general, the underdeveloped countries are found in Africa, Asia, and Latin America, especially Middle America. Using Rosenstein-Rodan's estimates for 1961, expressed in purchasing power of United States dollars in the United States, the averages for various geographical divisions show great diversity, as seen in Table 1.5.

## TABLE 1.4.

### Food Supplies per Capita Available for Human Consumption in Selected Countries, Latest Year 1960-1963

| Country | Calories | Cereals, kg | Starchy Roots, kg | Sugar, kg | Pulses & Nuts, kg | Vegetables, kg | Meat, kg | Eggs, kg | Fish, kg | Milk, kg — Fat | Milk, kg — Protein | Fats, kg | Protein (gr) — Total | Protein (gr) — Animal |
|---|---|---|---|---|---|---|---|---|---|---|---|---|---|---|
| Canada | 3060 | 63 | 59 | 46 | 6 | 81 | 78 | 15 | 8 | 8 | 9 | 20 | 92 | 64 |
| United States | 3090 | 65 | 47 | 41 | 7 | 96 | 97 | 19 | 5 | 8 | 8 | 21 | 91 | 65 |
| Argentina | 2860 | 89 | 106 | 36 | 3 | 50 | 103 | 9 | 2 | 4 | 4 | 15 | 84 | 54 |
| Brazil | 2790 | 105 | 160 | 41 | 27 | 7 | 27 | 3 | 3 | 2 | 2 | 7 | 65 | 18 |
| Chile | 2420 | 118 | 77 | — | 9 | 81 | 35 | 3 | 9 | 3 | 3 | 9 | 77 | 28 |
| Colombia | 2070 | 70 | 116 | 51 | 7 | 14 | 33 | 3 | 2 | 3 | 3 | 5 | 46 | 20 |
| Ecuador | 1970 | 75 | 133 | 26 | 9 | 31 | 14 | 4 | 5 | 1 | 3 | 5 | 50 | 16 |
| Honduras | 2340 | 132 | 11 | 22 | 11 | — | 13 | 4 | 1 | 4 | 4 | 6 | 58 | 15 |
| Mexico | 2650 | 136 | 17 | 30 | 23 | — | 23 | 6 | 3 | 2 | 2 | 11 | 75 | 24 |
| Paraguay | 2440 | 68 | 257 | 17 | 13 | 77 | 44 | 1 | — | 1 | 1 | 7 | 60 | 24 |
| Peru | 2170 | 100 | 147 | 24 | 9 | 39 | 17 | 1 | 8 | 7 | 7 | 17 | 54 | 12 |
| Uruguay | 2980 | 90 | 70 | 33 | 4 | 15 | 101 | 7 | 2 | 3 | 3 | 10 | 95 | 62 |
| Venezuela | 2340 | 96 | 111 | 34 | 12 | 43 | 26 | 3 | 6 | 1 | 1 | 4 | 60 | 22 |
| Ceylon | 1990 | 119 | 32 | 18 | 29 | 56 | 2 | 1 | 6 | 1 | 1 | 4 | 42 | 7 |
| Taiwan | 2290 | 157 | 58 | 9 | 10 | — | 16 | 2 | 14 | — | — | 4 | 58 | 16 |
| India | 2000 | 139 | 11 | 18 | 22 | 97 | 2 | — | 1 | 3 | 2 | 5 | 51 | 6 |
| Japan | 2280 | 149 | 68 | 17 | 16 | 16 | 9 | 7 | 27 | 1 | 1 | 4 | 70 | 23 |
| Pakistan | 1980 | 155 | 4 | 13 | 5 | 29 | 4 | — | 2 | — | — | 3 | 44 | 7 |
| Philippines | 1800 | 114 | 40 | 15 | 7 | 110 | 14 | 3 | 10 | 4 | 5 | 18 | 42 | 14 |
| Israel | 2850 | 117 | 36 | 32 | 8 | 152 | 41 | 20 | 7 | 1 | 1 | 18 | 87 | 36 |
| Jordan | 1830 | 96 | 9 | 26 | 9 | 100 | 10 | 3 | 1 | 2 | 3 | 5 | 50 | 9 |
| Lebanon | 2320 | 122 | 15 | 19 | 12 | 100 | 14 | 2 | 2 | 2 | 3 | 12 | 63 | 14 |
| Turkey | 3110 | 223 | 38 | 17 | 13 | 105 | 14 | 2 | 2 | 4 | 4 | 8 | 98 | 16 |

# TABLE 1.4. (Continued)

| Country | Calories | Cereals, kg | Starchy Roots, kg | Sugar, kg | Pulses & Nuts, kg | Vegetables, kg | Meat, kg | Eggs, kg | Fish, kg | Milk, kg Fat | Milk, kg Protein | Fats, kg | Protein (gr) Total | Protein (gr) Animal |
|---|---|---|---|---|---|---|---|---|---|---|---|---|---|---|
| United Arab Rep. | 2620 | 198 | 10 | 10 | 8 | 91 | 12 | 1 | 5 | 3 | 2 | 4 | 77 | 12 |
| Mauritius | 2430 | 136 | 12 | 38 | 12 | 44 | 6 | 2 | 6 | 2 | 2 | 12 | 49 | 12 |
| South Africa | 2820 | 166 | 14 | 41 | 4 | 36 | 44 | 3 | 9 | 3 | 3 | 5 | 80 | 32 |
| Australia | 3140 | 84 | 44 | 50 | 4 | 64 | 109 | 12 | 5 | 7 | 7 | 14 | 90 | 60 |
| New Zealand | 3510 | 86 | 62 | 40 | 4 | 86 | 113 | 21 | 6 | 11 | 11 | 20 | 112 | 77 |
| Austria | 2970 | 102 | 80 | 38 | 4 | 55 | 62 | 12 | 4 | 7 | 7 | 18 | 86 | 48 |
| Belgium-Luxembourg | 2950 | 81 | 123 | 28 | 4 | 76 | 64 | 12 | 5 | 5 | 6 | 30 | 83 | 46 |
| Denmark | 3370 | 80 | 118 | 46 | 6 | 65 | 69 | 11 | 16 | 9 | 9 | 28 | 94 | 58 |
| Finland | 3140 | 110 | 111 | 39 | 2 | 17 | 35 | 8 | 12 | 12 | 12 | 20 | 95 | 55 |
| France | — | 99 | 104 | 29 | 7 | 105 | 74 | 11 | — | 6 | 7 |  | 100 | 49 |
| Germany, Fed. Rep. | 2950 | 78 | 128 | 30 | 4 | 47 | 61 | 13 | 7 | 6 | 7 | 26 | 80 | 49 |
| Greece | 2910 | 155 | 41 | 14 | 11 | 118 | 27 | 6 | 10 | 5 | 5 | 19 | 94 | 32 |
| Ireland | 3430 | 106 | 141 | 48 | 3 | 65 | 64 | 16 | 4 | 8 | 9 | 19 | 90 | 55 |
| Italy | 2750 | 134 | 52 | 4 | 8 | 140 | 31 | 9 | 5 | 4 | 4 | 17 | 79 | 30 |
| Netherlands | 3020 | 83 | 96 | 42 | 4 | 69 | 50 | 12 | 4 | 8 | 9 | 28 | 81 | 46 |
| Norway | 2930 | 77 | 95 | 39 | 4 | 33 | 39 | 9 | 20 | 11 | 8 | 25 | 80 | 48 |
| Portugal | 2610 | 130 | 88 | 19 | 8 | 105 | 20 | 4 | 21 | 2 | 1 | 17 | 72 | 27 |
| Spain | 2790 | 111 | 125 | 18 | 17 | 134 | 21 | 8 | 11 | 2 | 3 | 20 | 76 | 22 |
| Sweden | 2990 | 72 | 84 | 41 | 4 | 31 | 52 | 12 | 21 | 10 | 9 | 23 | 84 | 56 |
| Switzerland | 3280 | 101 | 66 | 41 | 9 | 76 | 63 | 10 | 4 | 10 | 9 | 21 | 91 | 52 |
| United Kingdom | 3270 | 81 | 94 | 47 | 6 | 56 | 77 | 15 | 10 | 7 | 8 | 23 | 90 | 54 |
| Yugoslavia | 2940 | 185 | 64 | 18 | 11 | 55 | 28 | 3 | 1 | 3 | 4 | 10 | 99 | 24 |
| Lowest as % of Average | 66.9 | 55.8 | 5.3 | 13.4 | 21.7 | 10.8 | 4.8 | 13.0 | 13.7 | 20.8 | 20.0 | 22.0 | 56.0 | 19.4 |

Source: Food and Agricultural Organization, State of Food and Agriculture. Rome, 1964, pp. 224-229.

**TABLE 1.5.**

*Per Capita Incomes of Various Geographical Regions, 1961*

| Region | Per Capita Income[a] |
|---|---|
| *Developed* | |
| United States | $2,790 |
| Canada | 2,048 |
| Oceania | 1,513 |
| West Europe | 1,472 |
| U.S.S.R. | 986 |
| *Underdeveloped* | |
| South and Middle America | 425 |
| Middle East | 257 |
| Africa | 164 |
| Asia | 154 |

SOURCE: P. N. Rosenstein-Rodan, "International Aid for Underdeveloped Countries," *Review of Economics and Statistics* (May, 1961), p. 118.
a Expressed in United States purchasing power.

## Characteristics of Underdeveloped Countries

It is important to have an overall view of the typical characteristics of an underdeveloped country.[7] But because such countries are quite diverse in resources, population, and so on, no standard description can be evolved which will apply in its entirety to any individual country. Furthermore, no single characteristic is typical of an undeveloped country, nor is one characteristic limited to underdeveloped countries. As development programs have been implemented, these characteristics have changed, so that they are less and less indicative of deprivation. To the extent that they do change, a country may be developing. It is also important not to misinterpret common characteristics as the cause of underdevelopment, for they may be the result rather than the cause of poverty. The real problem is to distinguish the strategic variables that cause the lack of growth from those that are the result of it.

Although there are sparsely settled regions, the typical situation is either a densely settled population or a rapidly increasing one, with high fertility rates and high mortality rates, especially infant mortality. The result is a large proportion of children and short working lives. The high death rate is due to inadequate nutrition and the prevalence of infections and diseases, made more serious because of low standards of hygiene and sanitation and poorly developed public health facilities and medical services. Illiteracy is high and specific job training is low. Thus, there are too many people, and these are poorly equipped for meeting the problems of a modern world.

Production is characterized by a heavy reliance on primary production, especially agriculture, and these countries are usually unprogressive even in this area. A high proportion of the people, up to 70 or 80 percent, are engaged in agriculture, and a high percentage of these are in subsistence agriculture. Much of the overpopulation is in the agricultural areas, so that marginal productivity is low or even zero or negative. The prevailing family system is often the extended family in which several generations live together, thus concentrating the overpopulation on the farms and resulting in much underemployment and seasonal unemployment. Little employment opportunity exists outside agriculture except for a few handicrafts. Capital equipment on the farm is meager and crude; landholdings are usually of small size and often scattered; farming methods are primitive and perhaps unchanged for centuries; markets are poorly developed and getting goods to market is even more poorly organized; and there is much tenancy and indebtedness, so there is little incentive to build up the land. The picture of agriculture is one of poor productivity and little chance of improvement without help, for subsistence farming makes it virtually impossible to escape into improved agriculture, which takes capital and improved technical knowledge. Although most people live on the farm, overcrowded cities are likely to develop in the first stages of growth. It is there that the better wages and jobs and better educational opportunities are found, and of course cities are the seats of government. However, city populations are not stable. Many, especially young males, leave the village to try their luck in the city, may be unsuccessful, and soon return home after a while for various reasons, including the wish to rejoin their families or to buy land, or just because of dissatisfaction with the city. Others stay and eke out a precarious existence from odd jobs, begging, or possibly crime and vice. The result is often a modern city surrounded by shacks and swarming with a shifting and restless people.

Manufacturing represents a small part of economic activity, consists for the most part of the simple processing of primary products, and is carried on in the homes or in small shops under primitive methods with a labor force that includes the women and children. There is little capital in the form of modern industry, and savings are low. What little savings there are are usually invested in land or jewels or abroad. As a result most manufacturing is labor intensive. Entrepreneurs and innovators are a major shortage and businessmen tend to have a philosophy of monopoly, large profit, and small volume. Businessmen, in the larger sense, have little experience because all substantial business was previously foreign-dominated. This situation plus the onus placed on moneylenders who charged high rates has led in some areas to business being held in disrepute or at least in low esteem.

In contrast to the subsistence agriculture and small-scale manufacturing, a section of the economy may be geared to international trade, serving to increase the wealth of a few (often foreigners) and not to serving the wants of the people. Usually, exports consist of a few primary products, leaving the country vulnerable to price fluctuations and outside influences. Imports are mostly luxury consumption goods for the few. Balance-of-payments difficulties are common. Because much of the control over this output is in the hands of foreigners, usually from the advanced nations, who live together and establish conditions to which they are accustomed, a kind of new world grows up within the indigenous community, touching it only peripherally. The existence of this advanced sector next to the unadvanced has given rise to the term "dual economy."

Although most of the production is for direct subsistence, a small part does enter the market. The distribution system, for the most part, is as inefficient as the system of production. Much of the produce is sold in the local bazaar where price bargaining is the rule. Each producer brings a small amount to the market and patiently sits much of the day to sell it. On the other hand, much of the surplus in the villages may be gathered together by the moneylender, who accepts goods in payment for his loans and tends to exploit the peasant. Often the middleman is a foreigner. Goods are transported to market largely by human power, especially woman power, or by oxcart. In some areas, notably Africa, much of the exchange may be carried on under the obligatory gift system. The town economy is different. Here people work for money wages and purchase their needs in stores, which are usually one-family stores dealing in a limited variety of goods, or in the local bazaar to which sellers from the village have come long distances and in large numbers. The towns are thus money-oriented.

Economic institutions and social overheads, such as light and power, roads, and schools, are poorly developed. Credit facilities, taxation, transportation, education, housing, and health services exist only in rudimentary degree. A high degree of illiteracy persists. Inflation usually stems from inferior practices of government finance. Legal systems may be based on custom and not suitable to modern enterprise. Credit is in the hands of the local moneylender, who charges high rates.

There is generally maldistribution of income, with a poorly developed middle class. A few live in great luxury and tend to import foreign goods while the masses live in great poverty with inadequate diets (especially in animal proteins), inadequate housing, and the absence of almost anything that can be classified above a necessity. Most of the income of the masses is expended on food. However, as contacts with the advanced countries grow, there is a great desire to emulate their consumption and thus a demand for foreign goods, called the "demonstration effect."

Governments are often unstable, inexperienced, and authoritarian. In the past they have been dominated by the wealthy and have been uninterested in the general welfare. Today there are a variety of governmental forms, with many dictatorships, but because of a fear of revolt there is usually a greater responsiveness to the wishes of the people (or some organized group), sometimes inadvisedly so. Few are truly democratic in the Western sense. Initially, the competence and honesty of government officials might be questioned, but this is improving. Nepotism, however, is usual.

Many countries have recently been liberated from colonialism and suffer in two ways: first, from a reaction against any practices of the old master and, second, from a loss of the former's investing and directing classes. Reaction against past domination may affect the acceptance of foreign ideas and promote the retention of old customs and habits, which may be uneconomic.

Social and cultural patterns differ, but the following are commonly encountered: an inferior position for women; behavior based on custom, with tradition too strong for change or innovation; much expenditure on ceremonies; fatalism and extreme importance attached to salvation so that much time and money are spent in religious observation; superstitious practices in all phases of life; prestige systems based on other than ability (for example, birth or education), and with economic opportunity determined by this; a strong desire for children, for reasons of prestige, security, and religion; and extreme nationalism. These have great impact on the economic activities of the people.

Most of the underdeveloped countries are in the torrid zone or the frigid zone. Thus, their underdevelopment is sometimes blamed on their climate. At our present state of knowledge this seems true for those in the frigid zone but probably not for those in hot climates, for if it were true, there would be no hope for such countries. Temperate climates are no guarantee of success, as we have seen, for example, in Korea. Much of the coincidence between hot climates and lack of development happens because life is relatively easy and requires no great effort. Debilitating diseases have been typical, and are responsible for much low effort, but with modern medicine and increased desires, there is no reason why human achievement should lag in these countries. There may be problems with agriculture, as we shall see, but climate itself should not be a fatal bar. However, it does take extra effort to wipe away accumulated behavior patterns and the wide spread of diseases. Many have made only a small start in this direction.

One way to describe underdevelopment is in terms of "vicious circles." [8] One vicious circle may run from: people are poor; therefore, they have low savings. Low savings mean a lack of capital investment, which in turn means low productivity. Low productivity indicates poverty. Or a second goes from poverty to undernourishment, to poor health, to low work capacity, to low productivity, to poverty. A third is: poverty means small purchasing power and thus no incentive to invest; primitive production methods; low productivity; and poverty. The obvious solution is to increase incomes, but this results only in another vicious cycle: increased incomes lead to better health and more children, low income per capita, and poverty. One could make up as many "vicious cycles" as there are supposed "causes" of underdevelopment. These serve merely to emphasize the characteristics of underdeveloped countries and do not prove any causal relationship.

## Drives and Deterrents to Growth

Many factors may affect the growth or decline of an economy. These we choose to call drives and deterrents. Each factor may act as either, depending on the situation and on whether the variable is increasing or decreasing. For example, in some instances increased savings are a must for countries whose productive facilities are not sufficient to meet the demands of its people. In such cases savings, if followed by corresponding investment in productive facilities, would be a drive toward growth. In other situations where there is already excess capacity, additional savings and investment would result only in more excess capacity and would slow down growth. Paradoxically, in earlier times, such as in early United States history, increased population was an advantage. Today in many areas of the world that are trying to start their economic growth, increased population thwarts their efforts. Thus, no separate list of drives and deterrents is possible. As we proceed in later chapters we shall look at each factor.

Although the factors listed below will affect growth, we cannot say that any certain change will bring about growth, for any change takes place in a total institutional framework. In one case the situation may be favorable and in another, unfavorable. The same factors have not all been present in all countries that have grown, nor have they been present in the same sequence. Growth has taken place under a variety of institutional circumstances, in capitalistic United States and communistic Soviet Russia, in democracies and dictatorships.* But it has also failed to take place in capitalistic and communistic countries and in democracies and dictatorships. Thus, we must be modest about our claims for the success of any specific policy.

* It would be a good exercise to make a list of capitalistic and communistic nations that have grown or not grown.

It appears that growth is not due to any specific formula, but to the simultaneous appearance or improvement in a few strategic factors at the right time and under the right conditions. Thus, there may be a number of different formulations for growth, one of which is, of course, best for the particular circumstances. As yet we cannot define such formulations with any degree of confidence or accuracy. It is difficult even to envisage a "law of growth" in the sense that certain combinations of conditions must be present for growth to take place. Rather it appears that there may be a few "trigger" or "propulsive" factors, which will induce growth if they appear under the right conditions or if no strong deterrent bars the way. For example, innovations in production methods tend to trigger growth, but only if there is capital available and entrepreneurs are ready to exploit the innovation, plus a willingness of the people to accept change. Thus, a prescription for growth in any specific situation cannot be simple and must provide for a wide variety of changes.

The list of factors that can affect growth can be made very long, as long as any conceivable list of economic, political, social, and other factors. The problem is to find the most important and the main relationships. This is the task of economic theory, one thus far not well developed. The list given below is not exhaustive, but serves to indicate the magnitude of the job.[9] Succeeding chapters will discuss the most important of these. It will be noted that some affect the capacity to produce, others the means or desire to acquire or use these goods, and others the institutional arrangements that permit or bar change. Changes in all these are needed to induce economic growth. The way to economic growth is via an increase in productivity, a deceptively simple statement because getting increased productivity in many settings is not very simple. The thesis of this book is that economic growth depends on postponing some consumption so that capital can grow while simultaneously increasing the productivity of all factors of production in all areas of economic life. The method for accomplishing this, although following fairly general patterns, is peculiar to each specific situation. The formula for the economic growth of any specific country must be developed essentially on the spot. But general principles can be developed as guides.

It is possible to classify the following list of factors as "propulsive"; that is, those that create a spark for growth, or as conditions which must exist if the propulsive effects are to be realized—the tinder of growth.*

*Factors that affect the capacity to produce:*

1. The amount, quality, and availability of natural resources.
2. The state of agriculture.

* Try to classify these in your own mind at this point. At the end of the course compare your ratings.

3.  The labor force, including its quantity, training and education, skill, distribution, mobility, hours worked, and the amount of effort expended.
4.  The accumulation of capital goods, which depends on an excess of production over immediate consumption.
5.  The amount of innovation and technological improvement, including innovations in business practices as well as machines.
6.  The existence of progressive business leadership, either private or, if as seems necessary in some underdeveloped countries, government.

*Factors that affect the capacity and willingness to use output:*

1.  Consumer purchasing power as a means of absorbing the goods produced. This depends on consumers' desires and ability to spend or save, population growth, the distribution of income, and possibly the existence of a substantial middle class as being the most likely support to expanding markets.
2.  Investment opportunities and a willingness to invest. This can be influenced by business cycles and the degree to which economic activity is in balance.
3.  The balance of foreign trade payments, which is influenced by price levels, efficiency of production, government trade policy, capital flows, and the terms of trade.*

*Institutional arrangements that may permit or bar change:*

1.  Government activity, including the efficiency of the government, the state of the budget, the character of taxation, its attitude toward business, the character of the legislation that affects the operation of productive enterprises, and the degree of internal peace and harmony.
2.  The nature of the existing economic institutions such as the monetary system, banking and credit, and other financial institutions, the communications system, the existence of social overheads, the existence of a price system and monetary economy, and the nature of property rights.
3.  Cultural factors, including the attitudes of the people toward change and production, their social objectives, customs, religion, and other social institutions, and the attitude toward care of the unproductive.
4.  Whether the economy is growing or stationary, for there seem to be principles of inertia and momentum in our economic as well as our physical life.
5.  The amount of uneconomic activities, such as war and crime.
6.  The amount of flexibility or ability to adjust to new conditions in the economy, or conversely, the amount of immobility, monopolistic restrictions, or other restrictions, government, labor, or private, in the economy.
7.  The character of the people, including their education, freedom of thought, willingness to apply reason to social and economic questions, and their health.

As a general statement it may be said that the technical problems of production are more easily solved than the larger economic problems of deciding what technical problems need solving along with the social and

---

* This is the relation between an index of the prices of goods imported and the prices of goods exported.

political ones. On the technical side there are usually no serious obstacles to the expansion of production. Such problems can safely be left to the technicians.

## *The Place of Growth in a Country's Objectives*

It has already been stated that a country might be interested in some objective other than growth, or at least might be willing to sacrifice some economic growth for another goal. Before any policy can be devised for a country, it must determine what it wants; that is, what its real objectives are, and how much it is willing to pay in terms of effort to obtain these. The important thing is what that country deems as proper ends. One of the great dangers is to try to view problems from one's own philosophy and in one's own interests and not those of the underdeveloped countries.

The economist is presumed to be able to tell the effect of a given action on economic events, but he cannot prescribe what ought to be done because this implies an objective. Yet, the economist is a citizen and as such is entitled to views as to what society should be like, and he should be free to work toward such ends. Also, where society's objectives are stated, he is expected to prescribe an appropriate course of action to attain them. Thus, economic policy is closely entwined with social philosophy.

There is no objective standard as to what sort of society is good or bad, and there are no natural laws that will bring about the ideal society, as was assumed by the early classical economists. Man must decide what kind of world he wants and he must work to attain it. Moreover, actions that run counter to a nation's concept of what is worthwhile will have little chance of becoming adopted. For this reason, prescriptions of policy for economic growth must fit into a nation's beliefs.

All people have beliefs and these differ widely. What seems important to one in a given country may seem unimportant or incomprehensible to others. A review of some values cherished in the United States will indicate how different the beliefs of other countries may be: freedom of the individual, democracy, equality of opportunity, a social minimum or social security, rewards based on personal achievement, the individual to be judged on his own merits. Of course these are not realized in their entirety or, in some cases, even to any degree of satisfaction, but they represent ideals and must be considered along with the traditional economic objectives of efficient allocation of resources, reasonably stable prices, full employment, and economic growth.

Not all the foregoing and other possible objectives are consistent with one another, so that compromises may have to be made. One country may try a different combination than another. Later, the consistency of certain cultural values and economic growth will be considered more fully; as an example, it is questionable if excessive social security is consistent with growth in countries where savings are low. Some social security is helpful, but it is possible to be carried too far, in that funds taken for consumption might otherwise become invested, and incentives may be dulled. Similarly, a certain amount of time and money spent on religious devotion may aid economic growth by providing a less fearful and a more contented atmosphere. Conversely, excessive religiosity may absorb too much time and funds and produce an atmosphere of traditionalism that does not admit of change. Thus, a nation must choose, and it may have to sacrifice economic growth for something its people want more. The political situation may prevent a country from following what economists may recognize as sound strategy for economic growth. Moreover, the underdeveloped countries, or their leaders, may be more interested in national power and prestige than in economic growth. For example, it is doubtful if Indonesia's support of a large military establishment is conducive to growth, especially since much of the equipment has been financed by Soviet loans to be repaid later in goods which will be sorely needed. Likewise, the advanced nations with their aid programs may treat the problem as one of military or diplomatic power or as an aid to sales or the purchase of raw materials. The economist can prescribe what he thinks the best policy for economic growth, but in any specific case he must be aware of the compromises that must be made.

Economic growth is desirable, but nothing, least of all growth, occurs without costs in efforts and sacrifices sustained, dangers encountered, and in alternatives forgone.[10] These should be taken into account in considering any program for growth—and likewise, these should be weighed against the costs of failure to grow, for the lack of growth involves costs also. Thus, the analysis of proper policy is complicated and involves many subjective judgments, as a list of possible costs will indicate.

*Among the possible costs are:*

1.   The possibility of inflation will be ever present, especially if one insists on full employment as one of the conditions of a growth program. If full employment is also a goal, one loses a source of control over labor and industry, both of which may demand too large an income because the fear of unemployment and price competition has been removed. Later on we shall examine the effect of inflation on growth.

2.   Growth usually produces a situation of constant change, with resulting insecurity and losses for many. For example, it may be found by workers that their specialized skills are no longer needed and by some industries

that their products are no longer wanted. Growth will mean specialization and increased danger from change. Change may mean social, esthetic, ethical, cultural, family, and religious dislocation. Efforts of people to protect themselves against change may result, with a consequent drag on growth.

3. Growth will mean an increased pace of life, with a consequent increased mental and physical strain.

4. Economic instability as seen in the frustrating modern business cycle will become more possible. Underdeveloped countries have the instability of crop failures, but this is clearly understandable, whereas the phenomenon of men who are able and willing to work but have no jobs, even though people lack goods, is frustrating at best.

5. Government activity will probably be extended. Whether this will also result in a loss of personal freedom is debatable, but it appears likely in countries where democratic freedoms are not the tradition.

6. Growth has often led to policies that exploit and waste resources.

7. Leisure as well as present consumption must be sacrificed in order to provide for a buildup of capital goods.

8. In some cases, growth has been accomplished through the exploitation of some group; for example, workers through low wages or farmers through low prices for their products and heavy taxation. At the very best, one might expect an unequal distribution of the gains of growth.

9. Necessary for growth may be those attitudes and institutions that are not popular or do not fit into a people's concept of proper behavior or a desirable life. For example, there must be a striving after wealth; there must be a decline of acting in accordance with custom or authoritative rules and the substitution of action based on reason. Towns will surely grow and people will have to give up their village life for the uncertain advantages of urbanization.

*A lack of growth or a stationary or declining standard of living also has costs:*

1. Dissatisfaction with one's lot would be common, with consequent efforts to improve one's own position at the expense of others. This is the genesis of discrimination and exploitation, which is more likely to arise when there is little to share than when there is much or when jobs are plentiful.
2. Social and political upheavals would be a constant danger.
3. Lack of useful and productive employment (although there might not be much open unemployment), ill health, and general misery would be the lot of many; and this might be a threat to other values such as individual freedom and democracy, which might be traded for possible security.
4. Countries that fail to grow economically would be militarily weak and subject to possible aggression.
5. Humanitarianism, as expressed in social security provisions and other wel-

fare measures, would be next to impossible. Thus, many would suffer because they had no means of earning an income, whether because of unemployment, ill health, work accident, widowhood, or for other reasons.

Even after all these things have been considered and the conclusion is reached that, in balance, growth is "worth it," there are problems in that during the transition period, there will be many painful situations such as changing habits of work, upsetting social relationships and moral values, and seeing the benefits go to only a few.

## The Possibility of Growth

The question is sometimes raised whether the precarious world situation makes it impossible for new countries to grow. The present industrialized countries started off as industrial "islands" in a sea of underdeveloped countries and therefore did not have the competition with which the present underdeveloped areas are faced. These latter areas do have some greater difficulties than the present advanced countries did.[11] The economic level at which most of them are starting is much lower. Presently affluent countries in the Western bloc had a long period of slow expansion before industrialization started, and were considerably wealthier. Today the relationship between population and resources is, in many cases, less favorable. The rate of population growth is probably greater (since the introduction of public health measures) and the outlets for emigration are pretty well dried up. International capital markets are not so active, although government loans and aid have taken their place. Governments are not so stable. The social, cultural, and ideological traits are not so conducive to growth. A scientific revolution, with its demand on rationality, has not yet arrived; the calculating, materialistic, and profit-oriented attitude, which focuses attention on economic matters, is not so well developed; traditionalism is more usual. The market economy is not so well developed and education is not so well established. The scale of investment needed to compete is larger and more expensive; social capital, such as schools, is necessary before industrialization can be successful. It is harder to exploit labor or the farmer, and "the demonstration effect" draws off purchasing power, which might well go for capital goods.

Thus, the newer countries have considerable handicaps. But they also have assets that the advanced countries did not have when beginning development. First of all, they know that economic growth is possible, for they see examples before them. This also gives them the incentive to try to grow. Second, there is a great deal of accumulated scientific and technical knowledge which they can borrow. Of course the machines and practices of the

West cannot be taken over without change, but the principles of adapting ideas to specific situations are pretty well known. Lastly, there is access to the capital of the more advanced countries, through borrowing and economic aid.

Thus, one would not expect the new countries to follow the history of the West exactly. The situations are different, and growth, if it occurs, can be expected to be different.

## REFERENCES

1. Much of the material in this chapter is derived from MORRIS, B. R., *Problems of American Economic Growth*. New York, Oxford University Press, 1961.
2. ENKE, STEPHEN, *Economics for Development*. Englewood Cliffs, N. J., Prentice-Hall, Inc., 1963, pp. 3-7.
3. HAGEN, E. E., "Some Facts about Income Levels and Economic Growth." *Review of Economic Statistics* (February, 1960), pp. 62-67.
4. BENNETT, M. K., "International Disparities in Consumption Levels." *American Economic Review* (September, 1951), p. 632-49.
5. VINER, J., *International Trade and Economic Development*. New York, The Free Press of Glencoe, 1952, pp. 127, 128.
6. BENNETT, *op. cit.*
7. More detailed descriptions will be found in succeeding chapters. For other descriptions, see ENKE, *op. cit.*, pp. 16-39; SHANNON, L. W.,

ed., *Underdeveloped Areas*. New York, Harper & Bros., pp. 12-20; LEIBENSTEIN, H., *Economic Backwardness and Economic Growth*. New York, John Wiley & Sons, 1957, pp. 38-57.
8. NURKSE, R., *Problems of Capital Formation in Underdeveloped Countries*. New York, Oxford University Press, 1955, pp. 45, 57.
9. Other listings are in CLOUGH, S. S., "Strategic Factors in Economic Growth." *Political Science Quarterly* (March, 1955), pp. 19-27; and SPENGLER, J. J., quoted in W. W. Rostow, *Process of Economic Growth*. New York, W. W. Norton & Co., 1952, pp. 72-75.
10. BRONFENBRENNER, M., "The High Cost of Economic Development." *Land Economics* (May, 1953), pp. 93-104.
11. MYRDAL, G., *Rich Lands and Poor*. New York, Harper & Bros., 1957, pp. 100-106.

## ADDITIONAL READINGS

ALLEN, G. C., "Economic Progress, Retrospect and Prospect." *Economic Journal* (September, 1950), pp. 463-80.

BLACK, E. R., "The Age of Economic Development." *Economic Journal* (June, 1960), pp. 266-76.

BREWSTER, J. M., "Beliefs, Values and

Economic Development." *Journal of Farm Economics* (November, 1961), pp. 779-96.

DALTON, G., "Traditional Production in Primitive African Economies." *Quarterly Journal of Economics* (August, 1962), pp. 360-78.

ELLIS, H. S., and N. J. BUCHANAN, *Ap-*

*proaches to Economic Development.* New York, The Twentieth Century Fund, 1955, Chaps. 1 and 20.

ENKE, S., *Economics for Development.* Englewood Cliffs, N. J., Prentice-Hall, Inc., 1963, pp. 3-39.

JASZI, G., "The Measurement of Aggregate Economic Growth." *Review of Economic Statistics* (November, 1961), pp. 317-32.

LEWIS, W. A., *Theory of Economic Growth.* Homewood, Ill., Richard D. Irwin, 1955, pp. 420-35.

SMITHIES, A., "Rising Expectations and Economic Development." *Economic Journal* (June, 1961), pp. 255-72.

STALEY, E., *The Future of Underdeveloped Countries.* New York, Harper & Bros., 1954, pp. 92-95.

WILLIAMSON, H. F., and J. A. BUTTRICK, *Economic Development.* Englewood Cliffs, N. J., Prentice-Hall, Inc., 1954, pp. 3-21.

# CHAPTER
# 2
# *Theories of Economic Growth*

Although concentrated or mass attention has been given to the problems of economic growth and development only since World War II, economists have been concerned with this matter from the time economics became a special branch of study. Indeed, the early writers, such as the Mercantilists and Adam Smith, made economic growth or the wealth of nations (as Adam Smith termed it) the center of their attention. Later economists shoved the theory of growth into the background for various reasons, with occasional writers like Marx and Schumpeter breaking out of the pattern to discuss growth more intensively. In recent years much attention has been given this problem with respect to both underdeveloped and advanced countries. The latter have begun to realize that they have not solved all their problems of growth. Many writers have contributed ideas, which will be discussed in rather summary form, although their contributions deserve far more extended discussion and analysis. The serious student should read the writings of these pioneers in the study of growth. For the present, a working acquaintance with their ideas will be helpful in understanding the concepts emphasized in later chapters.

The theories put forth are often in dispute and have not been verified beyond a shadow of a doubt, but they do provide insights into the problems of development. At this point in the evolution of the world's concern with the problems of growth, there are few, if any, certainties; we are left with only insights, theories, and speculations to guide us. One writer after the other has seen something in the process of development which he has considered significant and has perhaps emphasized beyond its real importance. But learning often proceeds in this way, a new contribution being magnified out of proportion only to find eventually its proper place in the whole array of influences that bear upon a given problem.

Many of the ideas were developed with respect to the then advanced countries and may or may not be applicable to the present underdeveloped countries. The basic generalizations are apt to be valid, but the framework of institutions and attitudes may be so different that different emphases and policies may be necessary.

A review of the ideas of these men also will make it obvious that the subject of development runs beyond the confines of rigid economic analysis. Anyone interested in the problems of growth must consider the effects of social, cultural, political, and other forces as well.

As J. Viner[1] points out, theory is always simpler than reality and can be misused when applied to practical problems. The theorist sets up an abstract model of the real world and works from a few premises and with only limited objectives. His interest is in understanding the effects of a certain event or occurrence under ideal conditions so as to isolate and understand better its influence on the world in general. The real world is different and much more complex. There are many objectives, some of which are in conflict, but all may be legitimate goals. The influences acting in the world are many and varied, and they may have conflicting or interacting results. They take place and have their effects under many and varied circumstances. Thus, the determination of policy in the real world is difficult and subject to error, for it is difficult to discover all the factors at work, to assess their exact strength in the milieu in which they operate, and even to find the best compromise among all the objectives to be pursued. Nevertheless, the theorist's work is basic and progress comes from innovations in ideas and in learning as much as possible about each individual factor. The natural sciences have progressed far in this fashion, and it appears in fact that this is the only way to arrive finally at the "grand" solution. For example, physicists studied carefully the effects of gravity and the laws of falling bodies. But this was not sufficient to drop a bomb accurately. The influence of momentum, air pressure, wind direction and velocity, and perhaps other things had to be added before accuracy was possible. A more felicitous example is the attempt to land a man on the moon, which may even have been accomplished by the time this book is printed. Many individual pieces of research and much careful exploration of the individual factors involved are necessary before the actual final attempt can be dared.

One of the major concerns of man has been to find fundamental causes of phenomena to which he could devote his efforts and solve his problems, a sort of magic-formula approach. Man seems to try to reduce his problems to simple solutions. Often the approach to the solution of underdevelopment takes this form. However, P. T. Bauer[2] advances the thesis that a quest for a fundamental cause or causes of development is largely fruitless. He concludes that modern science began when the quest for fundamental causes was eliminated and we began to observe phenomena and find results that stemmed from specific occurrences. Economic development is a complex phenomenon, and many things impinging upon it do not appear in the same combination in different areas of the world. Fundamental ideas are necessary, but their effects and the proper combination of policies are unique for each area at each point in history and must be studied on the spot. The various contributions to growth theory have been concerned mostly, and properly so, with parts of the problem, and only a few theorists have attempted a total description of the whole process of development. The real problem is how to fit all the ideas into an appropriate policy for each specific area at the specific time under consideration.[3]

H. W. Singer[4] makes an interesting observation on the progress of thought related to the problem of development. He points out that, from Adam Smith to John M. Keynes, there was surprising agreement that economic growth of the already developed countries would sooner or later succumb to some obstacle or would reach its maximum, whereas in countries where development had not begun, conditions were good for its start. Today, he says, the obstacles to development are considered problems of underdeveloped countries, whereas there is great optimism about the developed countries, which are seen to be in a position to overcome almost any obstacle. Considerable pessimism is expressed about the underdeveloped countries because of the tremendous effort considered necessary to get the process of development started. Singer himself, however, feels the pessimism unjustified.

## The Mercantilists

A good starting point is the concept of development held by the Mercantilists.[5] These men wrote during the period 1400 to 1800, although similar views were expressed later and even occur today. The driving force behind these concepts was the rising industrialist and merchant classes who were anxious to advance their own fortunes through seizing new and promising business opportunities both at home and abroad. Spengler[6] calls the Mercantilist age a transitional system characterized by the breakup of medieval unity and medieval controls, the rise of self-interest and material values, and the establishment of the conditions prerequisite to the rise of liberalism (or early capitalism), and the replacing of religious virtues by worldly ones.

Of first importance to the efforts of the new business classes was security under which to undertake their activities. This required a strong national power and sufficient government interference in economic affairs to bring about a favorable business climate. Thus, they believed in a major role for the state in economic affairs. Private enterprise was emphasized only under suitable government regulations and encouragement. For example, exclusive grants to manufacture or trade were given, especially for trade in foreign areas, tariff protection was favored, and every effort was made to secure supplies of raw materials, labor, and so on at low prices. To further the interests of traders, internal trade restrictions such as tolls would be eliminated, national power and prestige would be built up in order to protect trade abroad, trade with controlled areas would be regulated to provide adequate markets and to reserve the profitable manufacturing enterprises for the home merchants, and a large population would be encouraged in order to keep wages low and so permit home manufactures to be competitive. Export trade and manufactures were thus considered the causal factors for growth and wealth, which were considered synonymous.

The Mercantilists perceived that the conditions of life were not static and could be changed and that man's desire for gain could arouse action. They realized, however, that these actions had to be controlled so as to serve the public interest.[7] Enterprisers were to be left free and policies that tended to limit them were frowned upon, but workers were not to be free. Wages were to be kept low, to discourage workers from seeking leisure, since the Mercantilists did not appreciate (until later) that the desire for additional goods could stimulate effort. Not until about 1800 was the advantage of an internal market realized, major reliance for a market being placed on the export trade.

Manufacturing and trading, especially foreign trade, were considered the strategic factors in growth, with agriculture following along under the stimulus of their development. Agriculture was to serve industry by supplying low-priced food, in order to keep wages low, and by producing the necessary raw materials cheaply.[8]

In other respects, also, they were interested in policies that would reduce costs. The opening of new lands would reduce rents and keep the price of raw materials down. Low interest rates would give a country a competitive advantage. Hence, they stressed personal frugality and saving, the importance of profits and rents as a source of savings, and the inflow of gold and silver, which could be readily invested and which would presumably keep interest rates low.[9] A growing stock of money was stressed in order to keep the rate of interest low, to satisfy the growing requirements of trade, to be used to employ unused workers, and to prevent falling prices.[10]

The Mercantilists saw the advantages of extending the country's economic boundaries by enlarging its areas of political control through establishing colonies, or granting trade concessions, or engaging in foreign trade. Trade was designed to bring in raw materials, precious metals, and other primary products that could not be obtained at home. The Mercantilists had a great concern with the balance of trade and the importation of precious metals, although the reasons are not quite clear. S. Enke[11] speculates on the possible motives for this emphasis. This could have developed because Mercantilists thought gold and silver were the more desirable goods, or because they saw the need for an increasing monetary supply to keep pace with the expanding trade or to finance a large military establishment and foreign wars, or because of the desire to substitute an investable item for luxury consumer goods. This emphasis meant importing only necessities and reserving to their own industries the markets they controlled. Larger trade balances could be obtained only by producing more, and this could be accomplished only by using the unemployed resources. Much of Mercantilistic practice was devoted to expanding markets for the country's manufactured goods and services, such as shipping. In other words, they wished to sell their labor services and receive in return primary products and precious metals. Colonialism, with the colonies destined to serve the mother country, was an important part of their program.[12]

The Mercantilists wrote in a period when two major innovations were being introduced: nation building and stamped money. Perhaps it was natural for them to overemphasize these. However, they did contribute some ideas that are current today. They created the concept that it is necessary to have a strong state if growth is to occur, and they built a case for state intervention to achieve economic ends. Their methods and policies were crude in the light of later knowledge, but they did recognize the power of the state as an agency for seeking a nation's objectives.

They recognized a need to absorb unemployed workers in newer and more productive occupations than agriculture, mainly manufactures and trading. They stressed the need of foreign markets if industry was to be built up. High wages, which would be necessary for an internal market, were thought to discourage industry and lessen savings. They saw that for industry to expand, there must be low costs and savings. They thus placed an emphasis on low costs, to be sure, by keeping wages down, and not by increased productivity, but they did see the importance of low costs. They also saw the necessity to limit imports to items that would promote the national interest.

However, the techniques were crude, the objectives were those of a minority, the masses were to be used for the benefit of a few, and a narrow nationalism neglected the interests of other peoples.

## Adam Smith

Following the Mercantilists was Adam Smith, who attacked their system vigorously, especially the emphasis on government controls, and substituted a system based on no government intervention except for providing economic overheads, defense, internal security, courts of justice, and other aids to private enterprise.[13]

Smith wrote at the time of the Industrial Revolution in England (1776) when he could observe that western Europe was developing and many other areas of the world were not. He was interested in development and made it the center of his thought. In fact, he called his book *An Inquiry Into the Nature and Causes of the Wealth of Nations*. He thought Mercantilism was stifling development, especially in the colonies, and that close government control was exercised in the interests of a few and in an ineffective manner.

He saw growth as the outcome of increased productivity, of which the major source was the division of labor that arises out of the propensity to exchange. Division of labor, in turn, was dependent on a widening of the market and the accumulation of capital, and thus dependent on savings. Hard work would also contribute to increased productivity. Although he mentioned the widening of the market as a factor in increasing productivity, his emphasis was on increased supply as a cause of development rather than increased demand. He seemed to count on international trade as the chief source of increased demand and the widening market, since he laid considerable stress on the advantages of international trade. Capital accumulation was necessary and would take place only if there were profits, for workers had no capacity to save. Only through capital accumulation could the level of technique improve, and in turn this increased profits. Thus, he might well have said that only growth permits growth.

Thus, once started, growth tends to be cumulative, partly because of the possibilities of large-scale internal and external economies for firms as market size increases. Increased productivity increases the possibility of savings and provides bigger markets, which leads to further specialization. Smith was generally optimistic about the prospects for growth, but expressed fear that a rise of wages might lower profits and so endanger capital accumulation and growth. It is difficult to say how he felt the process would begin. Apparently, he relied on a widening of markets and the proper motivation of individuals to start the process, which would then keep going.

Division of labor was considered better suited to industry than agriculture, so manufacturing received considerable emphasis. However, Smith did believe agriculture must develop at the same time, since in his view, development could not proceed without an agricultural surplus to feed the urban population, to release workers for industry, and to form the basis for a demand for manufactured goods.[14]

Of utmost importance in starting and maintaining the process of growth was the proper motivation of individuals. He saw growth encouraged by letting individuals follow their own self-interest, but thought that their actions needed restraint through the force of competition. This view was based on rather tenuous assumptions. He assumed that the individual was interested in himself and that his interest lay in making money or income. An individual would make the most where he served society best, for other people were interested in maximizing their own best interests and could take care of themselves adequately. In pursuing their own interests, they would patronize or hire another only if he offered his services on as favorable terms as anyone else. Everyone would be employed in his best use because he would tend to shift to areas where he would get the largest returns, easy mobility being assumed. No one could make excessive profits or wages, for others would rush in to share in his good fortune. Therefore, offers and demands would be coordinated through the market, and personal and social interest would coincide. Individuals, in an effort to increase their returns, would do things better and so advance society.

Monopoly and efforts to restrain trade were considered harmful to development and were to be eliminated. Smith particularly wished to limit the influence of the government because its record in his day was one of corruption, restriction, and ineptness. Techniques of control and the theoretical bases for development were not yet developed. Smith was not against government interference per se, but against bad government interference. Therefore, the way to national wealth lay in creating the right institutions of free enterprise, private profit, freedom of exchange, and private property, with individual efforts directed and coordinated through the free play of competition and the market. If the right institutions prevailed, it would be unnecessary to bother about growth because individuals would work, accumulate knowledge, and accumulate capital under the incentive of self-interest.

For Smith's time and place, his prescription for growth seemed success-ful. There were some bad spots on the record in England, the United States, and a few other countries, such as the failure to consider business cycles or the human costs involved, but development did occur in a select number of countries that substantially adopted his system.

It is questionable, however, whether this system is as applicable to pres-ent-day underdeveloped countries, whose economies are operating on a much lower level than that of the England of Smith's time. The underdevel-oped countries have large surpluses of population and limited markets so that the necessity and opportunity for division of labor is limited. More-over, capital, entrepreneurs, and trained labor are not available and eco-nomic overheads are undeveloped, so that there is limited incentive to enter new pursuits. The economies are generally so inflexible that the incentive of self-interest and control by competition do not produce the progress Smith saw arising at the stage of development he witnessed in England at the time of his writing. The institutions he saw as vital to successful development may be applicable at a later stage of development, but do not seem appro-priate in the situation in which many countries find themselves today.

## The Classical School

The members of the Classical school, of which Adam Smith was the foun-der, were interested in how economies develop. There was considerable var-iation among the members, of whom Thomas Malthus, David Ricardo, and John Stuart Mill are the best known, but their general attitude was one of pessimism. This pessimism was engendered by the twin obstacles of popula-tion growth, as described by Malthus, and Ricardo's law of diminishing returns. Each writer, like Malthus and Ricardo, emphasized one or two major deterrents to growth. Growth was looked on as a race between these deterrents and technological progress, with the ultimate result the stationary state. In general, technological progress was considered to depend on capi-tal accumulation, and in turn this was considered dependent on the rate of profits, which would decline under various circumstances.[15] Capital accumulation was thus the keystone of the Classical theory of development, but this was destined to decline until a stationary state was reached. Be-cause the stationary state was considered inevitable, the obvious policies were to promote technological progress and the most efficient allocation of resources, both of which would be best encouraged through a laissez-faire governmental policy and the encouragement of a free market, both internally and externally.

The concept of the stationary state is an interesting one. It was not that no activity would be going on but that the forces of growth and stagnation would be in balance at some point. Population increases would bring wages to a minimum of subsistence, defined as a sufficient amount to replace the existing population. Population increase would thus stop. Surplus profits would sink to zero as the preceding pressure of population would force rents to rise and wages to increase because the law of diminishing returns would force up the cost of subsistence. With profits decreased, all investment would be for replacement and not added investment. All labor would be employed in its superior use because of the force of competition, and there would be no incentive to change employment.

Disturbances, such as the opening of new lands or a new invention, might disturb this equilibrium, but economic forces would operate to restore a new stationary state.[16]

## THOMAS MALTHUS

Thomas Malthus[17] wrote at the turn of the eighteenth and nineteenth centuries. He saw growth as a separate problem and anything but automatic, and therefore necessarily requiring explanation.

He is best known for his theory of population, which he saw as a factor that discouraged growth and as the force that would limit economic growth by leading to a reduction in capital accumulation. He believed people possessed a strong sexual drive so that there was a tendency toward rapid population growth unless checked by moral restraint, meaning late marriage or abstinence within marriage. He had no great expectations that these would be adopted and so thought there would be a too rapid rate of population increase. He expressed these fears by his well-known statement that population tends to increase geometrically and food arithmetically, obviously not expecting rapid technological improvements in agriculture. As a result, population would tend to outrun food supply, resulting ultimately, if not checked otherwise, in restriction by the positive checks of famine, disease, and war. He appears to have had some idea of diminishing returns from land, which with the pressure of population could reduce the return from capital. However, he did not seem to use this as the reason for a decrease in profits and consequent capital accumulation. Population increases would result in low wages and might be expected to increase profits, but this in fact would not happen because of the lack of incentive to invest.

B. Higgins[18] credits Malthus with other fragmentary ideas that have been subsequently incorporated into discussions on growth. Demand could be a major obstacle to development. He recognized an optimum in the propensity to save, beyond which consumer spending would be reduced to levels that would endanger growth. He recognized the possibility of a backward sloping curve of effort; that is, that with higher wages, workers might reduce their efforts or their hours of work. He used this to explain the lack of development in some countries. Foreign trade would stimulate new demands and thus be an incentive to work. A lack of transport could prevent the division of labor necessary for economic growth. He urged land reform in order to increase agricultural output.

Malthus had something of a balanced growth theory* in that he believed each sector of the economy to be a market for the others, and that a failure of one to expand (for example, industry or agriculture) lessens opportunities for the others.

## DAVID RICARDO

David Ricardo,[19] too, appeared pessimistic about the prospects for economic development. He believed that capital accumulation was the major essential for development, and that this could be effected only through the savings of the profit-making class. It was this emphasis on the necessity for profits and capital accumulation that led to his pessimism, for he thought that profits tend to disappear. This would come about as the result of a rising population and his famous law of diminishing returns. He saw the proceeds of production as divided into three shares: wages, rent, and profits. As population grew, pressure would be put on the land and the output per worker would decline in accordance with the law of diminishing returns. This would necessitate higher wages to workers in order to maintain them at subsistence wages. At the same time, the increased pressure on the land would force the rise of rents as the less fertile lands had to be used or additional workers were used on the better lands. As a result, profits would decline until there would be no more incentive or opportunity to save and invest, and progress would cease. At this point, the economy would be at the stage that has come to be called "the stationary state." The only escape was by opening new fertile lands abroad and through technological improvement. Ricardo felt that the latter could check the situation only temporarily and would ultimately be overtaken by the superior forces of population pressure and diminishing returns.

In the meanwhile, the stationary state could be postponed by promoting the utmost efficiency in the use of resources. This led Ricardo to devote much of his effort to studying the laws of economic efficiency and to make this the center of the study of economics, an influence that lasted over a

* See the discussion about R. Nurkse in a later section of this chapter.

century and even into the present. He advocated laissez-faire because he believed government regulation interfered with efficiency in production, and favored free trade in order that countries could reap the benefits of comparative advantage and have access to new lands that would produce cheap food. In these ways, profits might be maintained and thus induce capital accumulation and development.

## JOHN STUART MILL

Succeeding economists extended, for the most part, the analysis already developed by Smith and Ricardo. John Stuart Mill[20] generally followed the same line as his predecessors, but made several innovations. He emphasized the role of noneconomic factors such as custom and other social and cultural phenomena, and advocated the need for removing barriers imposed by these. In particular, he condemned the wastage of output by the luxurious living of a few because it reduced capital formation. In order to increase capital formation and encourage greater effort, he saw the need for better government, security of property, moderate taxes, secure land tenure, improved education and training, and borrowing foreign technologies and capital. Along with his predecessors he felt it necessary for land and capital to increase faster than population, and was fearful of a too rapid growth of population that would ultimately bring growth to a halt as it used up all the land, which was the ultimately limiting factor together with the law of diminishing returns. The latter could be temporarily, but not permanently, offset by technological improvement. This pressure on the land would reduce profits and thus also the capacity and desire for savings and capital accumulation. Improvements in production could come through education, progress in science, specialization, better economic organization, and certain personal characteristics such as willingness to work hard, a propensity to improve methods, and honesty in economic dealings. Thus, a stationary state was likely, but could be postponed.

## NEOCLASSICISTS

The Neoclassicists were a group of men who introduced the marginal concept into economics during the period roughly from 1870 to 1914.* To them, growth seemed to be virtually an assured thing, although it was a gradual process and certainly not the problem it had been in Smith's and Ricardo's day. In general, they restricted the study of economics to short-run problems and the efficient allocation of resources. They treated such

* Notable names are William Stanley Jevons, John Bates Clark, F. Y. Edgeworth, Alfred Marshall, Leon Walras, Vilfredo Pareto, P. H. Wicksteed, A. C. Pigou, and Knut Wicksell.

subjects as population and technology as external to the economic system, although as affecting it. They placed considerable emphasis on capital accumulation and the role of interest rates, but did not really develop this into a theory of growth. Through their influence the study of growth virtually disappeared from economics until revived around World War II.

D. H. Robertson[21] divides this school into three groups, according to their models of the trend of capitalistic society. The first group (Marshall, Pigou, Cassel) used as a model a steadily progressive economy in which all factors increased at a uniform and constant geometric rate, but which was in other respects unchanging, although none saw this as realistic. The second group (Wicksell) is pictured as seeing capital equipment as increasing so much that its reward would sink to a minimum and further accumulation would cease and wealth would become stationary. The third group (Marshall, Cassel) was one of greatly increasing saving, but also of rapidly increasing demand for savings for the creation of machines, and a rapid increase of demand for goods so that investment would remain profitable. Their views were thus generally optimistic as to the prospects for growth, although the prospects of temporary setbacks because of business cycles came to be recognized.

Marshall also contributed a concept of "external economies," which has been expanded and is useful in analyzing development. He used this term to indicate the gains to a firm from the expansion of the industry to which it belonged or of the industries that supplied it. Thus, growth leads to further growth and the idea of "balanced growth" (to be discussed later) could be developed.

J. E. Meade[22] has reconstructed from these views how a Classical economy would grow. In general, growth occurs from an increase in capital and technical knowledge and is depressed by growth of population. Only if technical knowledge increases can growth continue, for otherwise diminishing returns to capital as it accumulates reduces output per head unless capital and labor are readily substitutable.

Thus, the major emphasis of the whole range of Classicists was on the importance of the accumulation of capital, with a recognition of the role of technological change but with a limited vision of its future impact and a fear of the deterring influence of population change. Their laissez-faire view of the role of government depended on certain favorable human and environmental conditions that are not universally applicable. This concept may thus be of dubious value to most underdeveloped countries.

## *Karl Marx*

Karl Marx, writing around the middle of the nineteenth century,[23] made the concept of development the core of his system of thought.[24] The following basic beliefs influenced his thought.

First of all, he believed in the materialistic interpretation of history; that is, that the method of production determines all relationships, including the economic and social ones. Thus, he may be classed as having a "stages" theory of development.* He thought that economic systems would pass through the stages of primitive communism, slavery, feudalism, capitalism, and finally to socialism and communism. In general, he believed there would be sharp breaks between stages and that the moving force was the class struggle. In each stage, one class would struggle against a dominant class and eventually triumph; that is, until the stage of capitalism was destroyed and the classless society would emerge.

The central concern to us is the evolvement, growth, and collapse of the capitalistic system. Marx recognized the capitalistic system as a powerful force for economic development, but saw contradictions in it which would bring about its collapse. He saw growth as coming primarily through capital accumulation and technological change, which would accompany and be dependent on one another. Capital accumulation would come through the savings of profit makers or capitalists who alone would save and would be sure to invest, for in Marx's view they had a compulsion to invest and a great desire for more and more profit with which to invest.

Profits would come from surplus value. Marx believed in the labor theory of value and substantially in the subsistence theory of wages, although he modified this somewhat. Thus, workers received enough to reproduce themselves, but the goods they produced would sell for the amount of labor embodied in the products. Thus, say, if a worker could turn out enough to maintain himself in six hours but had to work twelve, his surplus value would be six hours worth of production. Capitalists would try to increase the surplus value, and could do this by increasing the productivity of labor or working it longer hours. The chief means of increasing productivity would be through the accumulation of capital and improving technology.

An employer interested in increasing the surplus value would introduce some technological change, which would, in time, be imitated by others. The new change, being more productive (and obviously, by this reasoning, capital using and labor saving), would throw workers out of work and keep

* This type of theory will be discussed later in the chapter.

wages from rising. The spread of the change and the accumulation of capital would tend to reduce the surplus value achieved by any one producer, and each would strive to make additional technological changes, thus causing more and more unemployment. In time, firms would be forced to become larger and larger so that small employers would be squeezed out to increase the ranks of the unemployed. Eventually, producers would be unable to sell all they could produce and would tend to suffer one business crisis after another. This could be postponed by selling abroad, and there would be a race for foreign markets which the various nations would try to secure by establishing colonies and converting them into suppliers of raw materials and markets for manufactured goods. This, too, would fail in time, although exploitation would get progressively worse and the nations would engage in imperialistic wars to gain each other's colonies and enlarge their markets.

Capitalism would thus lead to rapid development because of capital accumulation and technological change, but would ultimately break down for one of three reasons, although Marx was not clear which one would actually be the cause. These three possible means of collapse were revolution by the oppressed unemployed, business breakdown under increasingly severe business cycles caused by the lack of purchasing power,* or imperialistic wars.

Thus, Marx came to the opposite conclusion from Smith concerning the benefits of the laissez-faire, free-enterprise society. He saw it as bringing rapid advance, but also as leading to exploitation of the worker, international competition with its concomitants of imperialism and war, and business cycles.

Marx made much of the exploitation of labor during development, which he blamed on technological change and the capitalist search for more and more surplus value. Few previous economists had paid much attention to unemployment, assuming that the operation of the price system would eliminate it. But Marx saw unemployment as permanent and increasing. The facts of the day exhibited increasing unemployment and misery, and he attributed this to the operation of capitalism. Workers seem to have a hard time of it in a developing economy, regardless of the type of economic system, but he attributed it to the system of his day. The U.S.S.R. has shown no less exploitation of the worker, for his living standard has been kept low by deliberate intent, although he may not be unemployed. Their system, thus, is avowedly exploitative of workers and peasants (whose consumption has also been limited). This may be necessary in any country that

* Only if the capitalist failed to reinvest his savings, inasmuch as everyone else would spend all his income, could this happen.

tries to grow rapidly, since large amounts of output must be diverted to capital accumulation from consumption, which workers would prefer. Capitalism, in its early stages, also depended on worker exploitation and, in addition, paid no attention to job security or other aspects of the worker's welfare. In the minds of theorists, such matters could not exist for long, and businessmen seized on this view to justify their practices. It was the resulting labor exploitation against which Marx rebelled and out of which he built his theory of development.

Thus, Marx contributed several ideas. He showed the power of capital accumulation and technological change in increasing productivity. He saw that capital accumulation and technological progress usually accompany and are dependent on one another. He emphasized the need for consumption to keep pace with productive capacity, if development is to continue. These ideas are important to keep in mind, even though his predictions as to the course of history have proved false.*

His ideas are scarcely applicable to underdeveloped countries, although the appeal of his ultimate remedy (eventual communism) may be. In the first place, the lack of purchasing power in these countries is obviously not due to technological advance, and the cause of their difficulties can hardly be blamed on rapid technological progress. Their population problems are also obviously not due to industrial unemployment arising from the rapid growth of industry. Nevertheless, his influence on the study of development has been tremendous, and his ideas concerning the necessity for capital accumulation and technological change appear in all theories of growth.

## The Protestant Ethic

The concept of the "Protestant ethic" is associated with the names of R. H. Tawney[25] and Max Weber.[26] Both, as did many others, saw a striking relationship between the economic development of the sixteenth and seventeenth centuries and the rise of the new religion of the time, and sought to explain this correspondence. These two men held essentially that a major force in the rise of capitalism was the new idea toward life engendered by the Reformation, which made it possible for businessmen to expand their operations and carry on successfully with social approval. The medieval church had discouraged the pursuit of profit and the accumulation of

* For example, the overthrow of capitalism did not take place in the most industrialized countries, workers in the capitalistic countries did not get progressively worse off, and the share of wages in total product has not fallen, unemployment has not shown the great rise predicted, and innovation has not reduced profits and has not been entirely labor saving.

wealth, and had forbidden the taking of interest. It had emphasized "just" prices and "just" wages, which were not favorable to the enterprising businessmen of the growing societies.

With the opening of the possibilities of increased trade and profit, a new concept was necessary. The Protestant Reformation, particularly the Calvinist branch, was said by Tawney and Weber to have contributed the ideas and "spirit" that made capitalism possible. Among these ideas were:

1. All occupations or "callings" were considered equally respectable as long as one did his job well. If one worked hard and did his best, no matter how humble his job, his work was just as sanctified and pleasing to God as was that of the higher callings. The worker could thus live a Godly life without withdrawing from the world, and was encouraged to work hard. As K. E. Boulding[27] put it, although one could not live the perfect life of Christ under any conditions, he could observe the minor virtues of thrift, hard work, sobriety, punctuality, honesty, fulfillment of promises, and so on. Such attitudes on the part of workers are conducive to productivity and the accumulation of wealth.

2. Thrift was emphasized, so that the acquisition of wealth was made respectable and a legitimate end in itself. This also stimulated capital accumulation. Interest taking was made acceptable.

3. There was an emphasis on individual responsibility for one's own life, including his religious life, and this carried over into the economic field and gave rise, in an extreme form, to the belief in "rugged individualism" and laissez-faire.

One writer said that these ideas broke religious life into small sects, which became small, closely knit groups that would help one another.[28] This gave rise to joint stock companies. The same writer adds that Protestantism was a cheap form of religion and so aided the accumulation of capital.

Considerable criticism has been made of this thesis. In the first place, the Protestant ethic has not proved to be a sufficient reason for development, as is illustrated by the lagging growth of Scotland, one center of the Calvinist theology, and in the South in the United States, one of the most Protestant sectors in that country.[29] Although this does not prove that the ethic had no influence, it does show that other factors are necessary if growth is to occur.

However, Weber and Tawney probably did overdo their thesis. Undoubtedly, other things were at work in sixteenth- and seventeenth-century England and in other areas. The time was ripe for enterprising men to undertake new ventures. The virtues of enterprise, thrift, and hard work, and the availability of capital are qualities designed to get the utmost out of a situation, and should not be overlooked in any list of factors favorable to development. That these are the exclusive property of Protestants today would be impossible to hold, as the progress of Japan illustrates, but in the sixteenth and seventeenth centuries, their rise corresponded with the growth of the new religion. Furthermore, religious persecutions drove such people over a considerable part of Europe and the New World, and thus brought cultural contact, which can be stimulating, and transferred skills and scientific knowledge to new areas. It may even be that the impetus to development was not due to the ethic at all but to the striving of a minority group seeking to gain status.

It is also possible that development brought about the Reformation and not the reverse. Religion is often a drag on change because of its emphasis on conformity. When changes break through, it is obvious that the old religion must either accommodate to the change or a new one must rise. In most areas, development brings all kinds of stresses, including those that are religious in nature. It may well be, and deciding this is a job for the historians, that the times demanded a new spirit and new ideas, which found expression in a new religion, a new law, a new philosophy, and a new economics. If this is true, developing countries can expect adaptations of their religions to the new situation or the breakup of these and the possible emergence of new ones. This does not appear to be an improbable expectation.

The value in this concept of the Protestant ethic is in emphasizing the role in development of valuations and ideals and of the social and intellectual environment.

## *Joseph A. Schumpeter*

Joseph A. Schumpeter[30] is usually credited with reviving an interest in economic growth in this century. He was strongly influenced by Marx, although he was a great admirer of the capitalistic system. He was convinced that it brought great economic and social progress, but was equally convinced that it would stagnate and break down.

In considering the causes of growth under Western capitalism, he was convinced that the causes of growth could not be separated from the causes of business cycles, that they were part of the same process. Thus, he saw development as coming in a series of waves or spurts, being borne along on the rising swell of the cycles.

The central idea in his theory of development is the role of the innovator. The entrepreneur's role was conceived as being split into three parts: the innovator, the manager, and the supplier of funds or capitalist. The innovator is the central figure. He is the man who seeks, in the pursuit of profits, to put into practice changes or innovations. These might include new goods, new uses for old goods, the opening of new markets, the use of new raw materials, the reorganization of production; in short, any new idea that changed economic practice. Schumpeter felt the innovators were likely to be the New Firm and the New Man and that their rise was to be encouraged.

In order to innovate, these enterprises must have access to funds, and these would usually come from credit. Innovations were said to be lumped, as the first sign of profitable possibilities during a slump would be a good time to innovate. Credit would be borrowed and the innovations made. If these proved successful, a host of more timid men would imitate the innovation and borrow to do so. The result would be a great spurt in investment and in the economy. Eventually, the cycle would turn downward as the new investments became productive and flooded the market with goods; debts would be paid off, thus reducing the credit outstanding; and the rate of investment would drop; and, in time, a lull would be reached. Eventually, another new opportunity for innovation would present itself and the cycle would be repeated. However, growth would occur because each cycle would start from successively higher levels. Without the innovator, the economy would settle down to a virtual stationary state, which Schumpeter called the "circular flow."

Eventually, however, the capacity of the system to grow would decline as innovators became discouraged because social action, in trying to improve the lot of the masses and redistribute income, would reduce profits; the prestige of the businessman would be attacked; entrepreneurship would become routinized; and trade unions would make the climate for businessmen less favorable. Any other situation that tended to reduce opportunities for profit would similarly defeat growth.

Schumpeter's theory did not deal directly with underdeveloped countries, but his stress on the importance of the innovator and the incentive to innovate are extremely important. His views do suggest that underdeveloped countries must search for new and improved means to produce (they can borrow many of these) and must encourage the innovational type of businessman, whether he be a private enterpriser or a government official.

## Harrod-Domar and Other Mathematical Models

R. F. Harrod and E. D. Domar[31] adopted the objective of making the Keynesian analysis dynamic. Keynes had analyzed the short-run relations among savings, investment, and employment; Harrod and Domar extended the analysis to the long-run or dynamic relationships. Basically, their analysis deals with the relationship between the growth of savings and investment and income under circumstances in which full employment would be maintained. Their formulas may be considered as the forerunners of more recent attempts to apply mathematical tools to the analysis of growth. Neither really developed a full model of growth, nor did he represent his formulation as such. Their aim was a more limited one: to express certain relationships that must be achieved if an economy is to grow smoothly with full employment. Others have developed more complicated models to express the basic factors they believe necessary for growth. Reference will be made later to a few of these.

Harrod's basic formula is $G = S/C$, in which $G$ is the geometrical rate of growth of income or output, $S$ is the fraction of income saved, and $C$ is the value of the capital goods required for a unit increment of output.* As an illustration, if a country saves 12 percent of its output and the marginal capital-output ratio is 4, the rate of growth is 3 percent. In this equation, $S$ depends on the level of income, and investment (which equals savings) depends on the rate of growth of income. For smooth growth these must maintain a proper relationship. Harrod[32] distinguished three different growth rates: $G_W$, the warranted rate of growth, was the rate that would leave "all parties satisfied that they have produced neither more nor less than the right amount." $G_N$, the natural rate of growth, was the maximum rate of growth allowed by the increase of population, accumulation of capital, technological improvement, and the work/leisure propensity schedule, supposing that there is full employment. $G_A$ is actual rate of growth.

In Harrod's model, if $G_A$ exceeds $G_W$ (that is, is greater than is warranted by the rate of savings, given the existing marginal capital-output ratio), there will be a shortage of capital equipment. Incomes will grow faster than is warranted by the capital investment, the system will be stimulated to further expansion, and $G_A$ will move farther from $G_W$. The reverse would also be true.

If $G_W$ is above $G_N$, there is a chronic trend toward depression. This simply says that if the savings ratio, given the current marginal capital-output ratio, is greater than the capacity of the country to grow, all the savings cannot be invested, and incomes will fall below the rate needed to maintain full employment. If $G_W$ is below $G_N$ and $G_A$, incomes will rise faster than actual investment, and there will be an incentive to invest.

The basic problem, as more clearly stated by Domar, is to determine the necessary increase in investment that will increase incomes sufficiently to

* Today this is usually termed the *marginal capital-output ratio*.

absorb the increased output made possible by the new capital without causing unemployment. He assumes a closed economy; that is, no outside trade, a full employment level of income, and a constant level of the propensity to save and the productivity of capital. His problem is to determine how an equilibrium rate of growth can be maintained. He proceeds by building up the increase in the supply side and the demand side of the economy's output, which, of course, must be equal if equilibrium is to obtain. The increase in output, or supply, equals $I\sigma$, in which $I$ equals total investment and $\sigma$ equals the amount of real income produced by one dollar of newly created capital, less the loss of production from replacing old equipment. On the demand side, the increase in income, $\Delta Y$, equals $(1/a)$ $(\Delta I)$, where $a$ is the marginal propensity to save and $\Delta I$ the increase in investment. This is the same as the Keynesian multiplier. For full employment growth, $I\sigma$ must equal $(1/a)$ $(\Delta I)$ or $\Delta I/I = a\sigma$; that is, the percentage increase in investment must equal the product of the propensity to save and the productivity of investment. In terms of the example given above, if the productivity of capital is ¼ (the reverse of a capital-output rate of 4:1) and the rate of saving is 12 percent, the rate of investment and growth of income necessary to retain full employment is 3 percent. To maintain full employment over a period of time, investment must grow at a rate equal to the marginal propensity to save times the marginal output-capital ratio.

It will be observed that three things (at least) may stimulate growth: an increase in the amount of investment in capital equipment, an increase in the productivity of capital, and an increase in the ability to consume products. The problem is to maintain a proper balance and not devote all increases in production to capital formation or income creation (unless, of course, an initial imbalance so dictates).

As added investments are made, two things happen: Productive capacity is increased and incomes are increased. In order for there to be steady growth with full employment, a certain rate of growth of capital formation is required, and incomes must increase correspondingly in order to keep the new capital fully employed. If incomes increase more rapidly than the output afforded by new investments, rising prices will result, and there will be a tendency to try to increase investments, usually by borrowing. If savings are large and are translated into investments to a degree greater than the potential productivity can be absorbed, the capacity cannot be utilized and layoffs will occur.

New investment not only creates productive capacity but also incomes. Incomes must increase at a percentage rate given by the two formulas. In order to maintain steady growth, however, investment must be greater in the next year and must be equal to $a\sigma$. The more one increases income in one year, the harder it will be to increase investment the next year, to maintain this income. Various factors thus affect the problem. A high propensity to save requires a large increase in investment. A large increase in the productivity of capital requires a large increase in income in order that the products may be absorbed. The more ambitious the desired rate of growth as determined by the amount of savings, the greater is the probability that the actual output will fall below the full employment rate; that is, spending will fall. The solution is then more investment. This leads to a paradox, for if all the product cannot be sold, capital seems to be excessive and one solution then is to increase investment.

Many questions can be raised concerning these formulas. In the first place, they assume that the propensity to save and the capital-output ratio remain constant, which is not necessarily true. If adjustment is necessary in an economy, a government might well adjust its fiscal policy so as to influence the economy's propensity to save. Even the capital-output ratio could be changed, although it would probably take an autocratic government to accomplish it. The U.S.S.R., for example, has postponed low-output investments such as housing and city services. Technological events could, of course, change this ratio.

Second, no allowance is made for the substitution of factors of production for one another. In actual practice, many combinations are possible. Also, many types of adjustment are possible in the economy, thus permitting the economy to adjust to full employment in various ways. One of these types of adjustment would afford the highest rate of growth while maintaining full employment. It is likewise possible, although not certain, that the highest obtainable rate of growth may be realized with less than full employment. In a heavily overpopulated country, this is a very likely situation.

Third, too many essential factors are eliminated for these formulas to be realistic or, rather, too many factors are gathered together into one variable. For example, many factors affect the capital-output ratio. Moreover, there has never been a long sustained period of growth with full employment to permit empirical testing of these formulas.

However, the formulas have been important in developing our concepts of growth in that they have called attention to certain factors that cannot be neglected. In the first place, they have emphasized the necessity for investment to grow in order that full employment may be maintained as populations grow. On the other hand, they have shown that incomes must also grow. In so doing, they have pointed out the need to consider ratios among certain quantities, such as the propensity to save and invest, and the productivity of capital and the growth of income. They indicate that it is possible for an economy to grow and not stagnate, but only if certain special conditions are met. The central issue they point to is not that of maximizing current output but of achieving the maximum attainable rate of steady growth.

Later models[33] have attempted to account for the more important variables in economic growth and to express these in a mathematical model, which is expected to be realistic enough to form a basis for policy determination. As D. H. Robertson puts it, they "attempt to hole out in one." [34] Tinbergen and Bos[35] express well the viewpoint of those advocating such models as "the essence of a model is precisely that of an orderly and, in a sense, complete administration of knowledge." They continue by saying that a model consists of a number of elements: a list of variables, known and unknown, exogenous and endogenous; a list of relationships specifying the links among variables; and coefficients. To be useful, a model must be complete: It must not overlook any important variable, it must be correct in that its coefficients must express reality, it must be manageable, and it must be understandable to those who use it. To express these conditions indicates their limitations. Tinbergen and Bos recognize the difficulty of solving all problems in one equation and suggest planning in stages or by successive approximations. A few strategic variables would first be discovered and others would be added later.

Normally, these models concentrate on capital investment and industrialization, which are without doubt critical factors. Such models are highly useful in expressing relationships and will become more useful as our knowledge increases and use of computers improves. However, they do present a number of problems today. First, most of them are based on rigid relationships, whereas adjustments among the many elements of the economy may be flexible. Second, in order to get simplicity into a model, too many factors have to be ignored. Many economists see the remedy for underdevelopment in one or two crucial factors.* Those who base their beliefs on these one or two crucial factors really have to assume that the neglected factors will be present at the right time, and this may not be so. For example, most formulations seem to assume that there will always be appropriate marketing institutions and governmental institutions, that people will accept the required changes, that entrepreneurs will exist, and that the right kinds of labor will be available. Primarily, the historical, social, and institutional factors are neglected.

Third, many assumptions or abstractions that are questionable are incorporated into the formulas. Some of the common assumptions made in published formulas are: a constant marginal capital-output ratio; a constant

---

* However, this type of view is not limited to those who use mathematical formulations, as our presentation of theories of growth shows.

consumption function and savings ratio, or a constant marginal propensity to consume and save; production consists of two goods, one consumption and one investment, or all behave alike at the average of all commodities; constant production functions; all units of the factors are universally available; time sequences are ignored, or it is assumed that all production needs are always met; international trade is ignored; monetary effects are neglected. It is generally agreed that these are to be ultimately reinstated when conditions permit, and eventually they can probably be taken into account.

Fourth, before a model can be established, one must know the strategic functional relationships, which are as yet unknown. The present ones are simple relationships, which give rough approximations but are not nearly exact enough to express reality. Fifth, statistical data are lacking and the models are difficult to verify empirically. As yet, none is widely accepted.

## *Leibenstein and the Critical Minimum Effort Thesis*

Harvey Leibenstein[36] sees underdeveloped countries as countries with stable equilibrium at a low level. If the equilibrium is disturbed, forces tend to restore per capita incomes to the previous low level. The process of economic change is one in which the outcome depends on a struggle between forces that promote growth and those that inhibit it. Underdeveloped countries are those in which the income-depressing forces are greater than the income-raising forces. Thus, ordinary or small changes do not induce growth. What is needed to start a country growing is a large effort to overcome the growth-depressing factors. This effort is called the "critical minimum effort."

Small efforts are ineffective for various reasons. Because most people have less food and other goods than they want and need, they consume any increased income rather than reinvest it. Increased incomes enable populations to grow, and this equalizes purchasing power at the old income level. Investments, especially in human beings, take time before they are profitable, and so are not appealing. The resistance to new ideas is not overcome by small changes. At this stage the capital-output ratio is large.

These beliefs have been challenged, but they are usually regarded as reasonable approximations to reality. The conclusion from this analysis is that development efforts cannot be gradual but must be of a certain size in order to increase incomes rapidly enough to permit rising consumption and rising savings at the same time, to overcome the rate of population growth, to encourage entrepreneurs to invest, to affect values and ideas, and to afford economies of scale.

Similar views have been held by others. R. R. Nelson[37] presents a picture of a "low equilibrium level trap." Maurice Dobb[38] implies that if growth is to occur, it must be rapid in order to take advantage of the economies of scale. P. N. Rosenstein-Rodan[39] says large investments are necessary in order to break through certain discontinuities or rigidities. A. O. Hirschman,[40] to be discussed next, argues for the "big push" in order to provide an incentive for additional economic undertakings to spring up.

## Balanced or Unbalanced Growth: Nurkse and Hirschman

A major theoretical dispute has centered on whether a country should attempt to grow by means of balanced or unbalanced growth. Ragnar Nurkse[41] is representative of the former and A. O. Hirschman[42] of the latter.

Nurkse was convinced that the only way for a country to grow was through a balanced growth. He reasoned that starting one industry would not increase purchasing power sufficiently to absorb all the products of that industry. However, if a number of industries developed at the same time, all their products could be absorbed by the incomes of the total number of workers added to the work force. Thus, the workers and other income recipients in the total complex of industries would become the market for each industry. For example, if only a shoe factory were started, the workers would spend only a small fraction of their income on shoes. The remainder would be spent on products that are inelastic in supply and would result only in raising prices of such goods. But, if a shoe factory, a clothing factory, a soda pop factory, a toy factory, and improved agriculture were all started at the same time, the added incomes would find added goods and all the new goods would have a market. It is to be assumed, of course, that the right industries would be chosen. It is particularly important that agriculture develop along with industry, for increased incomes will be spent to a large extent on food. As the industries develop and grow, specialties may be produced to take advantage of export trade opportunities, and this will encourage expansion.

Hirschman, on the other hand, believes that an economy can develop most rapidly by deliberately unbalancing the investment pattern in a way that will induce growth in other areas. The important thing to accomplish is to get local investors to undertake new enterprises. Hirschman feels that countries are underdeveloped largely because there is no incentive for people with capital to engage in new enterprises. Conditions are static and opportunities limited.

The correct strategy is not Nurkse's view of balanced growth, which offers only limited opportunities, but to concentrate investments in a few key places in such a way as to open up opportunities for further profitable investment. The key concept is "linkage." An investment may afford "forward linkage," that is, may encourage investment in more finished stages; or "backward linkage," that is, investment in prior stages of production. The strategy is to find the investment with the greatest total effect. In general, Nurkse felt, this meant that industries would be near the center of the production process. By overbuilding such an industry, a potential market would be created by the need for raw materials and supplies. Moreover, later-stage industries would spring up to take advantage of the excess capacity of the new industry. In addition, the resulting increased purchasing power would make possible other industries. Social overheads, such as transportation facilities, would have a high linkage factor, as would basic industries like steel. Agriculture would have a low linkage. Backward linkage is the most important because it builds up a pressure for supporting industries. Hirschman would permit imports of consumer goods "to spy out the demand." Ultimately, the imports would be replaced by domestic production. Industry generally must start with a liberal sprinkling of consumer goods, for there is at first no market for intermediate goods. Textiles, iron and steel products, and pottery are important products for underdeveloped countries to consider. The important strategy to effect development thus lies in the character and sequence of investment that accompanies the "big push."

The presumed advantage of this strategy is that it leaves the way open for investment decisions to be made by private enterprisers, for the most part. They would assess the market possibilities after the original unbalanced investment by government. Government would thus limit itself to investment-inducing financing, leaving the bulk of the investment support to be supplied by private funds and individual initiative.

## Rostow and Stages of Growth

W. W. Rostow[43] in 1957 introduced a concept of stages of development which was reproduced in summary form in the *Economist*. This gave Rostow's view wide currency and opened the way to vigorous comment and argument. Previous writers had identified stages of development, such as a change from self-appropriation to pastoral, to agricultural, to agricultural and manufacturing, and eventually to agricultural, manufacturing, and commercial. Or the sequence might be in terms of the medium of exchange: from commodity barter to money exchange, and from money exchange to credit. Or development might be expressed in terms of the progressive grouping of trade: households, town, national, international. Rostow explicitly states that his theory of stages is offered in opposition to that of Marx, who identified the stages of primitive communism, slavery, feudalism, bourgeois capitalism, socialism, and communism.

Rostow sees history as a set of stages of growth, which he identifies as traditional society, transitional society in which the foundations for change are being laid, the "takeoff stage," maturing society, and high mass consumption.

Traditional societies are not static, but the level of production is limited. Agriculture is the primary economic activity and the social structure is hierarchical, with little opportunity for vertical mobility. Wealth and power are concentrated in the landlords. Excess income is spent in nonproductive ways such as religious feasts and ceremonies, monuments, wars, and luxury consumption. Family and clan connections are important. Political power resides in regional groups rather than a central government. Many changes are necessary before growth can begin. Agriculture must be supplemented by industry, communications, and services. The people's outlook must be reoriented toward national and international problems. There must be a change from the desire for a large number of births to one of a desire for individual progress. Excess incomes must be directed into investment. Belief in fate must give way to rationality. As these get under way, a country is ready for the second stage.

During the transitional stage, the preconditions for growth must be established. The rate of investment must increase to outstrip the rate of population growth. This, in turn, depends on the willingness of a few to apply modern science to production, of some to assume the risks of leadership, and of others to lend for industry. The population must learn to meet the problems of change and to operate within large organizations. Capital formation requires not only a changed attitude toward science and risk taking but also an adaptable labor force. A major requirement is increased productivity in agriculture. A high proportion of the new investment must go to social overheads. A new leading elite must emerge.

The usual forces behind getting the needed changes have been a rising nationalism that seeks ways to protect the country from the foreigner, the existence of a colonial power that introduces the necessary changes, merchants who see the advantages of modernization, or intellectuals who seek ways to raise the standards of life and welfare. Thus, in this stage there must be major changes in the political and social structure and in cultural values as well as progress in economic matters.

The third stage, the "takeoff," has generated the most discussion and argument. This is a short period of two or three decades in which the economy transforms itself so that growth is more or less automatic. This period is marked by three important changes. There is a decisive shift in the rate of investment (Rostow places this as an increase from 5 to 10 percent of national income). One or more leading sectors with a high rate of growth must develop. A political, social, and institutional framework that exploits the opportunities must emerge. The higher rate of investment may come from shifting land incomes to the expanding sectors, from inflation that shifts funds from consumption to profits, from the development of a major export industry, or from foreign capital. Various industries have served as leading sectors; cotton textiles in Britain, railways, enlargement and modernization of the armed services, or applying modern processing techniques to raw materials and foodstuffs such as timber in Sweden and meat and dairy products in Denmark.

The beginning of the takeoff can usually be traced to a particularly sharp stimulus such as a political revolution that affects the balance of power and the values of the country, the character of the economic institutions, and the distribution of income; new inventions with large secondary effects and external economies; or a newly favorable international environment such as a rise in export prices.

The drive to maturity differs by the nature of the takeoff. For some it is characterized by the growth of a complex of industries stemming from the original leading sectors. For example, if railways constitute the leading sector, there is a demand for cheap steel, which opens the way for other industries. In others, new leading sectors show the way. In fact, the ability to shift to new leading sectors as the growth of the old ones tapers off is a necessity for continued growth.

During this period, growth brings pressures for humane modifications, such as factory legislation. The characteristic of the leadership shifts from the bold adventurer to the professional manager. Society becomes bored with the miracle of industrialization and has second thoughts about its objectives. But savings and investment remain high and modern technology spreads throughout society.

The age of high consumption is characterized by the desire to turn most of the productive efforts toward consumption goods, a large part of which do not serve basic needs. Societies seek a new balance among such objectives as the pursuit of external power, the welfare state, expansion of mass consumption levels, and leisure.

Rostow's presentation has been widely praised and attacked. Situations representative of all these stages can undoubtedly be pointed out, but the problem is to delineate the changes from stage to stage and to explain the crucial determinants that cause a transition from one stage to another. Rostow fails to do this satisfactorily. Nevertheless, he does present an interesting picture of a general course of development and makes one aware that policies must be appropriate to the circumstances of a country.

Other criticisms may be noted. There has been a questioning of the fact of "takeoff" and the orderly succession of stages everywhere. No criteria are given for identifying a "leading sector," and there is doubt that a few growing industries are sufficient to lead growth without a corresponding growth on a wide front.* One problem of the stage approach is that it tries to divide a process of growth into distinct periods based on some dominant characteristic. To do this, one must assume sudden distinguishable changes, which seldom exist. Various threads of change move through society and one period seems to blend into another except for random upsetting changes like war, the rise of an outstanding leader, or a technological breakthrough. There is also skepticism that history must repeat itself rather than be consciously changed by man's actions. The government interventionists reject this thesis outright. Rostow himself seems to imply that such interference to speed up the development process would impair democratic institutions and noneconomic values.

Rostow's presentation should be a warning, however, to the underdeveloped countries that growth does not occur suddenly but needs a long period of preconditioning. The writer's belief is that the greatest amount of attention should be given to the transitional stage. However, the emphasis in underdeveloped countries seems to be on the "takeoff," possibly because the exact conditions necessary for it are not discernible and the leaders are optimistic, at least publicly. The "takeoff" also justifies large investments and thus an excuse for foreign aid and an emphasis on industrialization. Such a view does not do Rostow justice. He would seem to emphasize more the long process of providing social and economic overheads, changing institutions and attitudes, raising capital funds, and improving agricultural productivity.

## Other Contributors

Many other writers have contributed ideas to the problem of growth and are well worth reading. Only a brief mention of their ideas can be given here. The reader is urged to read the authors' own work. Others could be added easily to this list.

E. E. Hagen[44] is representative of those who emphasize sociocultural in-

---

* This, of course, would be the view of those who believe in balanced growth.

fluences on development. To him the problem is how to explain the entrance of continuous technical advance into traditional societies. For this to happen, a number of things must occur: interpersonal relations must move from particularism to universalism, class structures that impede innovation must be dissolved, inappropriate cultural lags must be eliminated, and motivations must change. Change may occur through an accumulation of techniques which draws in many, but this is unlikely unless accompanied by social change. This is most apt to happen if a subordinated group has access to technical knowledge and can exert pressure to produce change. In Hagen's book, *On the Theory of Social Change,* he emphasizes the development of personality during childhood and the influence of personality traits on growth.

B. F. Hoselitz[45] gives an interesting classification of eight types of growth patterns based on certain characteristics of the different countries. Countries can be expansionist or intrinsic, dominant or satellitic, autonomous or induced. The different combinations make for eight patterns. The United States from 1830 to 1890 is classified as expansionist, dominant, and autonomous. The U.S.S.R. from 1928 to the present has been expansionist, dominant, and induced. East Europe in recent times is classified as intrinsic, satellitic, and induced, and so on. The proper policies to follow depend on the underlying circumstances of the country.

W. A. Lewis[46] has postulated a theory of development under conditions of an unlimited supply of labor. This requires drawing labor out of the subsistence society by using capital to employ labor in industry. At this stage, capital widening, or the employment of larger quantities of capital of existing types, is indicated and the worker experiences no gains. In time, as labor supply becomes limited, labor becomes more expensive, and employers turn to capital deepening, or the use of newer types of capital on a more extensive basis. Only at this stage is the worker helped.

G. Myrdal[47] has introduced the concept of cumulative causation in economic events. The philosophic basis of economics has been one of countervailing change; that is, one change brings into play other forces that counteract it. An example is the tendency of change to produce turning points, giving us a typical cyclical pattern. Instead, Myrdal believes that change is cumulative unless stopped by outside forces. The result is that free market forces lead to greater rather than lesser inequality among countries. The low-income countries must therefore rely on the government to develop policies that will bring economic development.

P. N. Rosenstein-Rodan[48] has introduced an emphasis on external economies as inducing investment. The creation of one industry, although not profitable in itself, such as an electric power installation, may create investment opportunities elsewhere.

## REFERENCES

1. VINER, J., *International Trade and Economic Development.* New York, Free Press of Glencoe, 1952, p. 12.
2. BAUER, P. T., *Economic Analysis and Policy in Underdeveloped Countries.* Durham, N. C., Duke University Press, 1957, p. 32.
3. GALBRAITH, J. K., *Economic Development in Perspective.* Cambridge, Mass., Harvard University Press, 1962, pp. 4-16.
4. SINGER, H. W., "Trends in Economic Thought on Underdevelopment." *Social Research* (Winter 1961), pp. 387-414.
5. The Mercantilists, a very diverse group of writers from various countries whose ideas were not entirely similar, are grouped for convenience according to their central views of development. For a description of the views of individual members, see Heckscher, E. F., *Mercantilism,* rev. ed. New York, Macmillan, 1955; and Spengler, J. J., "Appendix to Chapter 1," in B. F. Hoselitz, *et al, Theories of Economic Growth.* New York, The Free Press of Glencoe, 1960, pp. 299-334. The statement presented here is based on Spengler, J. J., "Mercantilist and Physiocratic Growth Theory," in Hoselitz, B. F., *ibid,* pp. 3-54; and Enke, S., *Economics for Development.* Englewood Cliffs, N. J., Prentice-Hall, Inc., 1963, pp. 65-69. An extensive bibliography can be found in the Spengler book.
6. SPENGLER, "Mercantilist and Psysiocratic Growth Theory," *loc. cit.,* pp. 4, 20.
7. *Ibid.,* pp. 19-22.
8. *Ibid.,* p. 25.
9. *Ibid.,* pp. 31, 32.
10. *Ibid.,* p. 34.
11. ENKE, *op. cit.,* p. 68.
12. SPENGLER, "Mercantilist and Physio-

cratic Growth Theory," *loc. cit.,* pp. 35-41.
13. SMITH, ADAM, *An Inquiry into the Nature and Causes of the Wealth of Nations* (1776), E. Canaan, ed. New York, Modern Library, Random House, 1937. Adelman, I., *Theories of Economic Growth and Development.* Stanford, Calif., Stanford University Press, 1961, pp. 25-42. Meier, G. M., and R. E. Baldwin, *Economic Development.* New York, John Wiley & Sons, 1957, pp. 20-25. Letiche, J. M., "Adam Smith and David Ricardo on Economic Growth," in B. F. Hoselitz, *et al., op. cit.,* pp. 65-75.
14. *Ibid.,* pp. 66, 67.
15. HIGGINS, B., *Economic Development.* New York, W. W. Norton & Co., 1959, p. 87.
16. For statements of the Classical position in diagrammatic or mathematical form, see *ibid.,* pp. 87-99, and Enke, S., *op. cit.,* pp. 85-88.
17. HIGGINS, *op. cit.,* pp. 99-106. McKinley, E., "The Theory of Economic Growth in the English Classical School," in B. F. Hoselitz *et al., op. cit.,* pp. 92-94, 102-110. Malthus, T. R., *An Essay on the Principle of Population.* New York, Ward, Lock & Co., 1890. Malthus, *Principles of Political Economy.* New York, A. M. Kelley, 1951. Glass, D. V., *Introduction to Malthus.* London, C. A. Watts, Ltd., 1953.
18. HIGGINS, *op. cit.,* pp. 101-105.
19. RICARDO, DAVID, *On the Principles of Political Economy and Taxation.* New York, E. P. Dutton & Co., Inc., 1962. Meier and Baldwin, *op. cit.,* pp. 25-45. Adelman, *op. cit.,* pp. 43-59. Hoselitz *et al., op. cit.,* pp. 75-88, 94-112.
20. MILL, JOHN STUART, *Principles of Political Economy,* J. L. Laughlin,

ed. New York, D. Appleton & Co., 1885.

21. ROBERTSON, D. H., *Growth, Wages and Money.* New York, Cambridge University Press, 1961, pp. 5-10.
22. MEADE, J. E., *A Neo-Classical Theory of Economic Growth.* London, George Allen & Unwin, Ltd., 1961.
23. MARX, KARL, *Capital,* E. C. Paul, ed. New York, E. P. Dutton & Co., Inc., 1930.
24. ADELMAN, *op. cit.,* pp. 60-93. Higgins, *op. cit.,* pp. 107-21. Meier and Baldwin, *op. cit.,* pp. 46-64.
25. TAWNEY, R. H., *Religion and the Rise of Capitalism.* London, John Murray, 1926.
26. WEBER, MAX, *The Protestant Ethic and the Spirit of Capitalism.* New York, Charles Scribner's Sons, 1958. *General Economic History,* trans. by Frank H. Knight. New York, Collier Books, 1961, pp. 258-70.
27. BOULDING, K. E., "Religious Foundation of Economic Progress." *Harvard Business Review* (May, 1952), p. 36.
28. CLARK, S. D., "Religion and Economically Backward Areas." *American Economic Review Proceedings* (May, 1951), p. 263.
29. *Ibid.,* p. 258.
30. SCHUMPETER, JOSEPH A., *Theory of Economic Development.* Cambridge, Mass., Harvard University Press, 1934. (First published in German in 1911.) Schumpeter, *Business Cycles.* New York, McGraw-Hill Book Co. Inc., 1939. Higgins, *op. cit.,* pp. 122-43. Meier and Baldwin, *op. cit.,* pp. 85-99. Adelman, *op. cit.,* pp. 94-108.
31. HARROD and DOMAR developed similar formulas independently and are usually linked in a discussion of mathematical models. Harrod, R. F., *Towards a Dynamic Economics.* London, The Macmillan Company, Ltd., 1948. Harrod, "An Essay in Dynamic Theory." *Economic Journal* (March, 1949), pp. 14-33. Harrod, "Domar and Dy-

namic Economics." *Economic Journal* (September, 1959), pp. 451-64. Domar, E. D., *Essays in the Theory of Economic Growth.* New York, Oxford University Press, 1957. Meier and Baldwin, *op. cit.,* pp. 100-118; Higgins, *op. cit.,* pp. 144-66.
32. HARROD, *Economic Journal* (March, 1939), *op. cit.,* p. 16.
33. The following articles list a number of these models: Kaldor, N., "A Model of Economic Growth." *Economic Journal* (December, 1957), pp. 591-624. Champernowne, D. G., "Capital Accumulation and the Maintenance of Full Employment." *Economic Journal* (June, 1958), pp. 211-44. Kahn, R. F., "Exercises in the Analysis of Growth." *Oxford Economic Papers* (June, 1959), pp. 143-56. Ara, K., "Capital Theory and Economic Growth." *Economic Journal* (September, 1958), pp. 511-27. Eisner, R., "On Growth Models and the Neoclassical Resurgence." *Economic Journal* (December, 1958), pp. 707-21. Ranis, G., and J. C. H. Fei, "A Theory of Economic Development." *American Economic Review* (September, 1961), pp. 533-65. Robinson, J., "Model of an Expanding Economy." *Economic Journal* (March, 1952), pp. 42-53. Solow, R., "A Contribution to the Theory of Economic Growth." *Quarterly Journal of Economics* (February, 1956), pp. 65-94. Swan, T. W., "Economic Growth and Capital Accumulation." *Economic Record* (November, 1956), pp. 334-61.
34. ROBERTSON, *op. cit.,* p. 13.
35. TINBERGEN, J., and H. C. Bos, *Mathematical Models of Economic Growth.* New York, McGraw-Hill Book Co., Inc., 1962.
36. LEIBENSTEIN, HARVEY, *Economic Backwardness and Economic Growth.* New York, John Wiley & Sons, 1957. Higgins, *op. cit.,* pp. 388-94.

37. NELSON, R. R., "Theory of the Low-Level Equilibrium Trap in Underdeveloped Countries." *American Economic Review* (December, 1956), pp. 894-908.

38. DOBBS, MAURICE, *Political Economy and Capitalism.* New York, International Publishers Co., Inc., 1945.

39. ROSENSTEIN-RODAN, P. N., "Problems of Industrialization of Eastern and South-Eastern Europe." *Economic Journal* (June-September, 1943), pp. 202-11.

40. HIRSCHMAN, A. O., *Strategy of Economic Development.* New Haven, Yale University Press, 1958.

41. NURKSE, RAGNAR, *Problems of Capital Formation in Underdeveloped Countries.* New York, Oxford University Press, 1955. *Equilibrium and Growth in the World.* Cambridge, Mass., Harvard University Press, 1961, pp. 282-336. "Some International Aspects of the Problem of Economic Development." *American Economic Review, Proceedings* (May, 1952), pp. 571-83.

42. HIRSCHMAN, A. O., *Strategy of Economic Development, loc. cit.* Higgins, *op. cit.,* pp. 401-408. Enke, *op. cit.,* pp. 320-28.

43. "Rostow on Growth." *Economist* (August 15, 1959), pp. 409-16; and (August 22, 1959), pp. 524-31. Rostow, W. W., *Stages of Economic Growth.* New York, Cambridge University Press, 1960. Rostow, "The Take-off into Self-Sustained Growth." *Economic Journal* (March, 1956), pp. 25-48. Rostow, "The Stages of Economic Growth." *Economic History Review* (August, 1959), pp. 1-16. Meier, G. M., *Leading Issues in Development Economics.* New York, Oxford University Press, 1964, pp. 3-47. Higgins, *op. cit.,* pp. 234-38. Enke, *op. cit.,* pp. 194-206.

44. HAGEN, E. E., *On the Theory of Social Change—How Economic Growth Begins.* The Center for International Studies, M.I.T., Dorsey Press, 1962. Hagen, E. E., "Process of Economic Development." *Economic Development and Cultural Change* (April, 1957), pp. 193-215.

45. HOSELITZ, B. F., "Patterns of Economic Growth." *Canadian Journal of Economics and Political Science* (November, 1955), pp. 416-31.

46. LEWIS, W. A., "Economic Development with Unlimited Supplies of Labor." *The Manchester School* (May, 1954), pp. 139-91.

47. MYRDAL, G., *Rich Lands and Poor.* New York, Harper & Bros., 1957.

48. ROSENSTEIN-RODAN, "Problems of Industrialization. . . ," *loc. cit.*

## ADDITIONAL READINGS°

ARNDT, H. W., "External Economies in Economic Growth." *Economic Record* (November, 1955), pp. 192-214.

† BOULDING, K., "In Defense of Statics." *Quarterly Journal of Economics* (November, 1955), pp. 485-502.

† ELLIS, H. S., "Conditions and Rates of Economic Growth." *Journal of Farm Economics* (December, 1955), pp. 807-20.

† FRANK, A. G., "Hirschman's Strategy." *Economic Development and Cultural Change* (July, 1960), pp. 433-40.

HARROD, R. F., "Second Essay in Dynamic Theory." *Economic Journal* (June, 1960), pp. 277-93.

KLEIN, L. R., and R. F. Kosobud, "Some Econometrics of Growth: Great Ratios of Economics." *Quarterly Jour-*

* The publications identified by daggers are of especial importance.

*nal of Economics* (May, 1961), pp. 173-98.

KURIHARA, K. K., *Keynesian Theory of Economic Development.* New York, Columbia University Press, 1959.

LEWIS, W. A., "Consensus and Discussions on Economic Growth." *Economic Development and Cultural Change* (October, 1957), pp. 75-80.

OHLIN, C., "The Rostow Doctrine." *Economic Development and Cultural Change* (July, 1961), pp. 648-55.

OSHIMA, H. T., "Critical Minimum Effort Thesis." *Economic Development and Cultural Change* (July, 1959), pp. 467-76.

ROBINSON, J., "Accumulation and the Production Function." *Economic Journal* (September, 1959), pp. 433-42.

ROTHSCHILD, K. W., "Limitations of Econometric Growth Models." *Kyklos,* No. 4 (1959), pp. 567-88.

SUBRAHMANYAN, P., "Ricardian Theory of Growth Reconsidered." *Indian Journal of Economics* (July, 1960), pp. 79-86.

# CHAPTER
# 3
# Social and Cultural Factors

For a sociologist to discuss the social and cultural factors involved in economic development is to take, like Robert Frost, "the road less traveled by." Sociologists, and anthropologists, too, have been apt to view social change as precipitated most often by economic factors. Knowingly or unknowingly, they have thus tended toward a Marxian outlook in matters of change. The early evolutionists, for example, saw the "progress" of societies in terms of technological stages: food collecting, hunting, fishing, herding, and agriculture. Max Weber's analysis of the influence of Calvinism on the emergence of industrial capitalism, while long admired as an elegant foray on social theory, has not served very much to weaken the idea of economic primacy. In part, this is because economic factors are actually often of enormous initiating importance. In part, the continued emphasis on economic influences may be attributed to the popularity of Ogburn's theory of culture lag.[1]

Ogburn did not employ Marxian terminology or political ideology, but he clearly conceived of economic elements as comprising the bedrock of culture, with noneconomic elements comprising a kind of superstructure. He emphasized the distinction between material and nonmaterial culture, the former being largely a technological dimension. Change, he contended, originated more often and took place more rapidly within technology.[2] Technological innovations were believed by Ogburn to spread rapidly between groups and between societies. From steel plows to cotton gins to modern automatic machines, technological innovations, he argued, eventually had tremendous impact on nonmaterial culture. This impact was selective. What he termed the "adaptive culture" responded much more sensitively than did the "nonadaptive culture." Indeed, in certain cases such as religious ritual or literary style, the nonadaptive culture might show little or no effect from technological change. The same was not true of adaptive cultural elements such as workmen's compensation laws and managerial organizations, but even these rarely responded immediately to material innovations. During the interim, maladjustments and problems of various kinds arose until cultural rearrangements provided some amelioration. To describe this time gap, Ogburn coined the term "culture lag." While the concept of lag has been occasionally subjected to searching criticisms, it remains one of the most frequently cited sociological notions, both in textbooks and in popular literature.[3] Perhaps more than any other concept it has helped perpetuate the assumption of technological, and hence of economic, primacy when sociologists have considered the matter of change.

Ogburn's theory of lag is understandably appealing. It is as readily documented by personal observation as by carefully collected facts. It is comprehensible and neat. Above all, it possesses the attraction of being relatively simple. Unfortunately, it is too simple to provide an explanation for so complex a process as change. More and more, social scientists have come to recognize that few social situations can be explained by a single factor or by a one-to-one relationship between two phenomena. A single change in a society is usually the result of several factors operating simultaneously or in turn. Identifying these factors is never an easy matter. Weighing their relative importance is even more difficult, often impossible. Without disparaging Ogburn's contribution, which was of major significance, we shall insist that "one factor" generalizations must be viewed with skepticism. In our exploration of social and cultural factors involved in economic development, we shall, it is true, often be emphasizing first one factor, then another. Such a procedure is entirely for convenience; no assumption is made that any single factor operates in isolation from others or is of exclusive significance in concrete cases of change.

## Culture, Society, and Change

As the title of the chapter implies, cultural and social factors are not one and the same thing. In any concrete situation or event the two are inextricably entwined, but for purposes of analysis a distinction may be made between them. Basically, a society is people—people living with each other in a variety of relationships. Culture, on the other hand, is the knowledge and beliefs that people possess, the values they hold, and the norms or rules of behavior to which they subscribe. The terms "culture" and "society" are used not only to refer to these universal conditions of human life, however. They are also used to particularize. *A* culture refers to a particular and somewhat distinctive configuration of norms. *A* society refers to a particular aggregate of people who possess a feeling of belonging and who share a common body of traditions.

Especially since the emergence of anthropology in the latter half of the nineteenth century, culture has been recognized as the element that distinguishes human from nonhuman existence. Culture is the guidepost and often the directive for human behavior. Unlike the instincts that largely determine the actions of lower animals, culture is learned and not biologically inherited. Men living together in a particular society evidence many common beliefs, standards of behavior, and values of worth; and this shared body of culture results in similar actions and reactions and lends regularity or pattern to their collective lives. Regularity is especially apparent in the relationships that tie individuals to each other in any society. Behind these relationships or modes of interaction lies, of course, culture. In a given society the way a man will behave toward his wife, for example, and the importance he attaches to their relationship are largely governed by cultural norms and values which he shares with other members of the society. At the same time, and without continuously referring back to these cultural elements, we can observe that, because the husband-wife relationship is as it is, the man's relationships with other people will take a particular direction: the way he interacts with his children, his own parents, his wife's parents, and the stranger who comes to visit. Thus, human relationships—the *social* factor to which our chapter title alludes—possess a significance of their own, however much their particular forms are culturally conditioned. Furthermore, culture rarely defines these relationships in every detail and the individual is left some leeway for determining their nature and implementation; he is never completely a creature of culture, an automaton who behaves exactly as instructed.

This brief discussion of culture and society suggests why both dimensions make for much regularity and stability in human living. Each new generation in a given society acquires cultural guides and prescriptions from its elders, both by indoctrination and by imitation. In morals, knowledge, and beliefs, it thus becomes something of a replica of its predecessors. Members of each new generation also find awaiting them sets of relationships, statuses, and roles designed to link them together in a network called society. Thus, the patterns of interaction of one generation appear very much like those of previous generations, just as the cultural and social attributes of one individual resemble those of his age mates.

But as no two individuals are ever truly identical in their physical features, neither are they ever exactly the same in their ideas and behavior. Despite the social and cultural resemblance between generations, a resemblance that lends continuity to a society, no generation is ever a carbon copy of its predecessor. In short, no society of people is ever completely homogeneous or completely static. Change is both pervasive and universal. In part, this generalization is true because of the nature of society and culture. In part, change becomes inevitable because of contact between unlike societies and because of the disturbances that accompany these contacts.

Two of the reasons for internal change have been mentioned previously: first, the possibility of improvisation by individuals in a frequent absence of precise cultural guides; secondly, the inability of any generation to create its offspring in an exact social image of itself because cultural training or socialization is never a perfectly effective process. Another reason for change lies in the relative lack of compulsion associated with certain cultural prescriptions or norms. For example, a particular type of dress may be culturally defined as preferable rather than required, and by implication other costumes are at least possible. In such instances, the sanctions or means for enforcing the norm are likely to be relatively weak, whereas, by comparison, the sanctions behind a rule against incest are severe to the extreme. Weak or erratic enforcement of norms is often a product of cultural inconsistency. Side by side with the ideal of a strong kinship system may exist a growing emphasis on individual freedom to choose whatever job one wants or to marry whom one wishes. Or the youth are instructed to respect the aged while changing economic conditions render obsolete the knowledge and skills possessed by the elders. The psychological and social conflicts that result from inconsistencies of this sort lead to a serious questioning of one set of ideas or the other. Some members of the society are led to flout the old beliefs and to support new standards, involving either drastic innovations or a compromise between two inconsistent elements of the culture.

Also conducive to internal change is the elementary fact of life that physical, social, and psychological needs of some individuals outrun society's resources for meeting these needs. For example, concentrations of wealth or power that, by local standards, are deemed excessive may provoke the deprived to institute changes. These efforts are directed very often not only at a reapportionment but also at the system that brought about the deprivations. Natural causes can create situations where need gratification becomes less and less possible for more and more people. Drought, flood, and pestilence striking at food crops or food animals can create such intense problems that new techniques in the food quest are tried or old techniques are drastically modified. Similar pressures for change have emanated from rapid spurts in population—one of the most urgent issues for many of the developing societies today. Even the most economically developed nations still pursue futilely the utopian ideal in which all men have all their needs gratified at all times. Hence, in every society may be found individuals to challenge some aspect of the social system, which they perceive as thwarting their aspirations or failing to provide the satisfactions to which they feel they are entitled. Because of ever-present needs, then, and because of the inherent attributes of social life, internal change appears at once to be "natural" and inevitable.

Except where revolution has occurred (and true revolution is rare), internally generated change has tended historically to be rather slow. Rapid change, on the other hand, has usually been a product of contact between unlike societies. Today, social contact is virtually a universal phenomenon, whereas in the past many of the newly developing societies lived in relative isolation. To be sure, some of these societies were exposed to outside influences for several centuries through colonialism, conquest, and trade. But because contact was largely at the discretion of the conqueror, it was directed and restricted to suit his own purposes.

Several things distinguish the current situation from the relationships imposed through colonialism and imperialism. In the first place, far from being imposed, contacts today are eagerly sought by the emerging nations with societies more industrialized than themselves. Parenthetically, this interaction is aided not only by welcoming the outsider with his ideas and techniques, but also by sending members of the developing society to be educated and trained in a donor society. These couriers of change constitute an added means of contact which scarcely existed a half-century ago. The positions of leadership that many have come to occupy upon returning to their own countries suggest the importance of this device in the development process. The second feature that distinguishes the mid-twentieth-century contact between the outer world and the developing societies is its "across-the-board" influence. This generalized impact stems, in part, from the absence of colonializing goals among many donor countries whose assistance is far more diversified than it was in the past. In part, it reflects the eagerness of the recipient societies to revamp numerous facets of their life patterns simultaneously. There is a rush not only to change political structures but also to move from agrarianism to industrialism, to educate the masses, to substitute scientific medicine for magical practices, to expand trade with other countries, to introduce modern transportation and communication. In short, the objective is to modify traditional beliefs and practices in all institutional areas when they appear inimical to the "great transition" which the new leaders so urgently seek to bring about.

All this eagerness to modernize indicates that the element of planning is prominent in the changes being sought by (and already occurring in) developing societies. And here lies a third distinctive characteristic of the contemporary scene. In the past, many of the intruding innovations came about as unforeseen—and frequently unwanted—consequences of social contact. Indeed, the contact itself was often undesired, though inescapable, during the age of exploration and colonial expansion. But even in instances where trade with a European power might be welcome, the subsequential appearance of missionaries and colonial administrators elicited something less than enthusiasm from the host society. Insofar as changes were deliberately planned, control of the situation lay in the hands of the intruder and was employed largely to serve his own ends. Today many plans for change are formulated and administered by the native leaders themselves amid a rapid flowering of newly independent nations. The shift in control, however, has by no means solved or even simplified the problems of these nations. They are quickly discovering what social scientists have known for some time; namely, that social change is an enormously complex process attended by a large list of unanswered questions.

Thus, the individual who attempts to plan and direct social changes, particularly large-scale changes involving many spheres of life in whole societies, finds himself in somewhat the same dilemma as Alice in Wonderland nibbling on nostrums to get through the keyhole. A bit too much of this remedy, and the mark is overshot with devastating consequences; a bit too little of another remedy, and the results are too slow or completely inadequate for attaining the goal that is sought. Hence, the freedom to plan a nation's future is a freedom to try to find one's way, like Alice, through a Wonderland often bizarre, relatively uncharted, and filled with unexpected surprises. But it is also the freedom to use such guideposts as exist and, in a succession of frequently random choices and decisions, to substitute one potentially effective tactic for another that has proved useless.

The remainder of this chapter will focus on planned change with the understanding that plans need not be so comprehensive as to encompass an entire society or all the dimensions of its culture. Often, planning is restricted to a single aspect of life in a single village or to a certain segment of its population. Also, the plans themselves may be so loose or limited that they deal only with how a specific innovation should be introduced, no attention being given to its possible consequences for other aspects of social life or for other people than those toward whom it is directed. Rarely are provisions made for sustaining the new item once it is introduced. Planned change is thus many things to many men. It is a term that probably implies too much, both with respect to the scope of objectives and with respect to available information on means for achieving such objectives. The term has come into such common usage that, despite some of its misleading connotations, there seems little point in trying to substitute other phrases, such as "deliberate change" or "organized change," for these, too, carry their own ambiguities.

Because we shall be concerned chiefly with planned rather than fortuitous change, several dimensions of planning should be explicitly identified. This is not to say that each dimension is quite separate from all others, for they are in theory and in fact closely related and entwined with each other. Their separation here is a matter of convenience. First, though not always most obvious, is the plan itself as conceived by those who wish to introduce a change.[4] The plan may be, for example, to increase productivity of ground crops in a particular village or collection of villages. It may be to improve housing conditions among migrants who have moved from the countryside into shacktowns on the edges of a city. Or it may be to hasten the transition of a nation from a largely agrarian economy to an industrial one. In any of these cases, a useful distinction may be made between the goals of the plan and the means by which these goals hopefully can be reached. Lack of agreement on goals among planners and other policymakers poses formidable problems for the planning of change. But even when consensus is achieved on ends, there may be troublesome disagreement on means to these ends. Assuming the best of all possible worlds in which means as well as ends are agreed upon, we must attempt to identify the elements that make for success or failure of the plan proposed. These elements comprise the second dimension of planned change; namely, the innovating situation.

The innovating situation will include at least some of the means visualized in the plan for change. It also involves elements that are not conceived by the planners as means and which may prove to be either obstacles or aids in the attainment of goals. Often, one of the most obvious elements in the innovating situation is the relevant physical setting: land, vegetation, buildings, and so on.* Two categories of people provide additional elements of the innovative situation: the agents of change and the recipients of change.† Recipients are those people toward whom the innovation is directed, the people whose lives are presumably to be altered in some way. Agents of change, as the term implies, are the individuals responsible for attempting to bring change about. The status of the change agent has in fact two aspects, which sometimes need to be distinguished in analyzing the innovating situation. One aspect is the innovator or individual who introduces the innovation. The other aspect is the advocate or individual who picks up the innovation and becomes its supporter. These aspects might more correctly be described as two somewhat different types of roles which change agents may play. Frequently, both are played by the same individual.

The dynamic, living quality of the innovating situation is a product, of course, of the actions of change agents and recipients. Many techniques are available to the change agent for communicating and demonstrating new ideas and practices. And many devices are used by recipients as they decide to redirect, resist, or sabotage the agent's efforts. The innovator proposes and the recipient disposes. The advocate pleads the case. Underlying these actions and interactions are a host of other social and cultural elements: motives, values, knowledge, beliefs, expectations, and relationships. These are the many-colored threads with which is woven the complicated fabric of all social situations, including situations involving social and economic change.

## The Cultural-Social Context

Planned change, we have pointed out, is a key process for the emerging nations and is recognized as such by their leaders. Efforts at generating change, whether made by foreign or native change agents, take place in some kind of cultural and social setting. We shall not attempt to maintain a nice distinction here between what could properly be labeled "cultural" and what could be termed "social." For some theoretical discussions the distinction is significant. But, as we pointed out earlier, these two kinds of elements are almost inextricably interrelated and, for our purposes, the two will be at times treated as a single, complex category. Our discussion of

* The term "relevant" is used here deliberately since the physical setting may be inconsequential for some innovations.

† "Recipient" is the term used by Niehoff and Anderson (Ref. 4). While not entirely satisfactory, since it implies eventual acceptance of the innovation, it nevertheless seems preferable to other labels such as "target" or "client."

such factors in development as knowledge, values, beliefs, and shared expectations will amount to an emphasis on the cultural side of the coin. When matters of status, role, relationships, and organizations are being considered, we shall be dealing with the social side of the same coin.

## KNOWLEDGE AND SKILLS

A people whose storehouse of knowledge grows very little is a people with scant likelihood of bringing much change into their lives. Knowledge —information about the physical and social world—and skills necessary for applying knowledge are fundamental components of culture. They are the components perhaps longest recognized by scholars in many fields as being vital to change.* A corollary of recognizing this linkage between change and knowledge has been a widely held belief in education as the cure-all for "backwardness" within developing societies.

Enlargement of the world's reservoir of information has, of course, occurred at an accelerating though not always constant rate, especially during the past two hundred years. Some societies were touched sooner and some later by this enlargement. Today, scarcely any nation remains totally unaffected.[5] But the quantity of knowledge within various societies has grown to different dimensions. One of the major tasks of technical assistance has therefore been seen by some as a task of feeding information as rapidly as possible into the less developed societies. As the information reservoirs of these societies grow, the possibilities of economic development are presumably enhanced. The streams of information feeding into the developing societies can and do encounter various kinds of blockages and diversions, however, as we shall see later. Even when the flow of information is free, new facts and ideas sometimes lie unused, or they may be employed awkwardly. Expanding knowledge within a society, then, carries no guarantee that change will automatically come about, yet the probability is high. Without such an expansion of knowledge, the chances for the economic and social development of a society are slight.

Contacts with other peoples have been the main means by which any society's resources of knowledge have been enlarged. During most of man's history (and all his prehistory), the seepage of knowledge from one society to another has been slow and haphazard. But for the past century or so, the flow of information has grown rapidly until it has become torrential, increasingly conducted through mass media of communication and entertainment. Still, such media for the most part transmit knowledge in bits and

---

* For example, a very commonly encountered (and quite vague) generalization states that, as the world's base line of knowledge has been extended, the slope of the curve of change or "progress" has steepened.

pieces. Formal education, however, remains the chief instrument for systematic instruction, systematic in the sense of providing an orderly progression of learning and an explicit relating of various kinds of knowledge to each other. The emphasis placed on schooling in the developing societies is thus logical and essential. Mass illiteracy is indeed a formidable obstacle to economic development. On the other hand, accelerated educational programs are no panacea in themselves.

Difficult issues are encountered in trying to assess the actual contribution of expanded education to the developing societies. In empirical studies, the closeness of the relationship between literacy and development, for example, depends somewhat on the indicators used to measure development. Bowman and Anderson[6] used per capita income as an indicator and found the correlation with literacy to be irregular. While incomes of $500 or more were found only in countries with literacy rates of at least 90 percent, some countries with incomes under $100 were as high as 70 to 80 percent literate. Furthermore, in countries with literacy rates between 30 and 70 percent, virtually no correlation with income was found. When elementary school attendance instead of mere literacy was used, interesting relationships appeared. Incomes in 1938 were more closely correlated with attendance in 1955 than were incomes in 1955 with school attendance in the 1930's; that is, higher incomes appeared to precede rather than to follow the schooling of more people. These findings point to an interaction of factors rather than to a simple one-way influence exerted on one factor by another. The authors rightly stress that it is difficult to isolate any single factor in the development process and that education must therefore be seen in a broad context if its part in economic development is to be accurately assessed. We do not yet know just how it enters into the process, with what other factors it interacts, and in what kinds of time sequences.[7]

Using employment in the nonagricultural pursuits as an indicator of economic underdevelopment, a much closer relationship with literacy has been found.[8] In countries like Egypt and Brazil, where inroads on literacy were relatively slight until the past few decades, recent trends have involved greater advances in education than in economic development. On the other hand, countries such as Puerto Rico, which have been extending literacy for some time, are the ones now moving more rapidly in the economic sphere.[9] These kinds of differentials support the widely held belief that literacy is indeed a significant contributor to economic development when measured by increasing employment in nonagricultural vocations. On the other hand, it also appears that a certain degree of economic development serves as a goad to education. Traditional agriculture has obviously been possible in the midst of illiteracy. Not only do subsistence farmers see little value in education for their children or for themselves, but they are reluctant to relinquish their offsprings' labor for time in the schoolroom. With the growth of industrial cities and an increase in jobs promising a higher level of living and prestige, education has come to be viewed as a "passport" to the good life.[10]

Two dilemmas plague the developing societies in this area of education. One is well known, especially to the leaders of these societies. The poorer, least developed nations are the very ones least able to provide public education for even a segment of their populations, let alone for the masses of school-age children who comprise the fallout of the population explosion. Meager national budgets are called on at once to provide roads, health facilities, housing, communications, care for the aged and unemployed, and financial support for native industries as well as economic enticements for foreign investments. The list goes on almost endlessly. How then to build schools and train and pay enough teachers to break the generation-to-generation cycle of illiteracy? A second dilemma has been only recently recognized in some countries and not at all in others. This is the problem of the distribution and type of education attempted. If mass education is not yet possible, who should be educated? What kind of and how much education should be made available to those who can be accommodated in order to speed up economic development? *

Some of the nations that achieved independence quite suddenly during the 1950's and early 1960's discovered that they lacked even enough educated persons to staff their political bureaucracies, to provide minimum health and legal services, or to administer their constabularies and lead their military establishments. At the same time, an educated minority is far from sufficient for the long pull upward, even though it may provide the structural floor without which economic development and political survival would become exceedingly hazardous. The advantages of having an educated elite may be rather quickly exhausted, and further economic development remains stymied until education can be more widely disseminated. One of the problematic consequences of such a situation can be the polarization of the society into the educated and the uneducated, with little communication between the two groups, limiting the stimulus of the education acquired by the few. Thus, an educated elite may remain only a potential rather than an active ingredient for development.[11] A second consequence of investing too heavily in education for the few is apparent in several developing societies in which a surplus of white-collar and professional people find themselves unemployed or underemployed. India and Egypt are instances of nations currently producing more university graduates than the

---

* This and other matters of investment in persons will be discussed further in Chapter 5.

economies can use. Also, many underdeveloped societies are pushing very hard to provide primary education for most of their children while still lacking the secondary schools into which they can move.[12] It is difficult to see how imbalanced programs of these kinds can immediately facilitate the rapid economic development to which emerging nations aspire.

Two proposals have been suggested for altering the trends toward an overeducation for an elite and a truncated education for the masses. One is to build incentives into the occupations most needed by a country so that, for example, being an agricultural specialist, a rural medical technician, or a skilled mechanic will carry as much prestige and income as being a bank clerk, an urban doctor, or a junior executive. A second proposal is less radical: on-the-job training. Here the burden of cost would be borne by private as well as public organizations. Vocational and trade schools are said to be too inefficient a luxury for emerging nations; technical, managerial, and craft skills can best be developed on the job and at less expense.[13] Such proposals cannot, of course, be applied as rules of thumb to all developing societies, but a reappraisal of education in all such societies is in order and is necessary, as is much research to determine what educational techniques and programs can best contribute to the economic growth of a given country at its particular stage of development. Otherwise, education can remain worse than impotent or ill-utilized in the urgent race for development. It can prove a source of bitterness and unrest by having infused higher aspirations and new needs in the people of these lands without magically producing the means for realizing their dreams and desires.

VALUES AND BELIEFS

Another vital dimension of culture embraces values and beliefs. These elements, like knowledge and skills, are perpetuated and colored by systems of formal education. Schooling, after all, is not only a technique for transmitting morsels of fact to successive generations. It can also be a means for changing a people's general view of man and man's relationship to the universe. In industrial urban societies the growth of science and technology has been accompanied by and has stimulated an outlook that may be called rationalistic. This is to say, there prevails the idea that "natural laws" of cause and effect operate in nature and even in society. Hence, procedures, techniques, and programs are assessed in terms of whether they constitute workable and efficient means for achieving certain ends; they are valued in terms of their practicality and utility. Furthermore, people in rationalistic societies usually operate on the assumption that nature and, to some extent at least, human society are subject to manipulation. Man is believed to be the master of his fate.

In the emerging nations one commonly encounters the belief that man is a plaything of fate or of other supernatural forces beyond his command. Linked with this world view is a heavy value placed on tradition as good for its own sake as the source of guidance to what should and can be done by man. Societies holding this view are therefore often characterized as traditionalistic as opposed to rationalistic—terms that are useful for suggesting one kind of difference encountered between developing and developed societies. This difference is relative and not absolute. Actually, no concrete society is entirely rationalistic or entirely traditionalistic. Indeed, opposition to economic change in traditionalistic societies is sometimes completely rational, given the goals and values to which the people are committed. Having considered the advantages and disadvantages of some new practice, natives find the disadvantages greater and reject it, much to the dismay of the foreign expert who may then judge that the recalcitrants are either stupid or irrational. For example, an improved maize seed was introduced in the Helmand Valley of Afghanistan; with better techniques of cultivation, it produced three times the yield of the old variety. Yet the farmers strongly resisted the innovation, mainly because they felt that the bread made from the new variety of maize was inferior in taste to the old-style maize bread.[14]

Referring to developing societies as traditionalistic does not mean that people in these societies never employ rationality in arriving at decisions. Yet the dead hand of tradition lies more heavily on them than on people in industrialized societies. They are, in fact, more inclined to stay with the old ways of doing things, partly because the old ways are valued for themselves rather than being objectively assessed for their effectiveness as means to an end. People in industrial societies are generally more receptive to change, more critical of the past. The cultures of rationalistic societies entail a positive value on the new; change is something good. The interest in novelty is evident in the manufacture and consumption of a host of continuously altered material things, from automobiles to toothpastes. The relationship between industrialism and a climate emphasizing change is probably much too close to be coincidental.[15] In most agrarian societies, by contrast, individuals are reared in such a way as to induce them to view novelties and change with skepticism; maxims are quoted to support traditions; and the potential social deviant is inhibited by fears of criticism or worse.[16]

Some of the more effective constraints against change in the nonindustrial parts of the world originate in the cultural spheres of religion and magic.* Where little is known of modern science, supernatural explanations are available to account for the otherwise inexplicable; the aleatory element in life is much too pervasive and threatening to be ignored. Good luck or ill,

* This is not to say that these restraints do not also operate in advanced industrial societies. In the latter, however, their influence is considerably muted.

catastrophe or triumph, all are ascribed to the operation of forces that may be highly personalized, as individual gods, or which may be conceived as abstract influences, such as manu or kismet. While it may not be quite accurate to characterize the members of traditionalistic societies as "impotent in the face of overwhelming forces around them," [17] the assignment of cause and effect to supernatural forces is conducive to a high degree of resignation, to the feeling that trying to change the traditional ways of doing things is at best futile and at worst risky.[18] The gods can be entreated, but they cannot be controlled. There is no sense of mastery over natural or social conditions.[19] Drought, flood, pestilence, and famine have struck again and again until there is little room for confidence that these can be ameliorated by man's own efforts. This kind of fatalism is often the immovable object that any proponent of change, both native and foreign, encounters with dismay. Until a people can be convinced that at least some degree of control over natural and social events is possible, the road of the innovator will be hard indeed, and his chances for success rather slight. Education and the extension of literacy will have, as they always have had, a shattering effect *in the long run* on supernatural explanations of natural events and on fatalistic attitudes toward privation, disease, and disaster. But we all live in the short run. Programs designed for immediate and rapid development must therefore take into account and deal with on an *ad hoc* basis the various kinds of cultural obstacles briefly described above.

## KINSHIP, AGE, AND OTHER ROLES

Shifting the emphasis from cultural to social or structural factors, we shall now be concerned less with underlying values and beliefs and more with statuses, roles, and relationships between individuals and groups. By status we shall mean the position that an individual occupies in some kind of social setting. Role denotes the expectations accompanying a given status, the norms that a person should observe in view of his status. For example, the status "father" may carry the right to direct his children—and perhaps his wife—in certain economic tasks; it also usually carries the obligation to provide for their subsistence. The father's rights and duties, then, define his relationship with other status occupants. Their rights and duties, in turn, serve as guides to interaction with him. Thus, statuses and roles comprise a more or less neat map of social relationships, which people can and are supposed to follow in getting on with the business of daily living.

The ability of primitive and peasant societies to survive successfully in the absence of efficient control over their natural environment—and sometimes with intensely disturbing tides of change lapping at their borders—lies partly in the close-knittedness of their internal relationships. These relationships come close to being "social imperatives." Options are few or absent; obligations are accepted without question. Despite differences of interest and some cleavages between groups, communities are highly integrated.[20] Commitment to traditional patterns of interaction is not entirely an emotional or ethical matter, however. When food is short, the breadwinner incapacitated, or death or disaster intrude, one can turn to kinsmen or to fellows of special friendship groups for help, security, and reassurance. These are role relationships that have utility; they really work. Commitments to and faith in them thus become reinforced through life experience.

Effective and specific as these relationships may be in a preindustrial society, they pose certain problems when the industrial transition is begun. For example, the change agent's assumption that financial incentives will be sufficient to induce men to shift from nonindustrial to industrial work appears rather optimistic. In making the shift, these people will have to forego the kinds of relationships (often based on kinship) that have traditionally assured them economic and psychological security.[21] From their point of view, the risks are high and the rewards by no means guaranteed.

Continued loyalty to traditional associations and continued commitment to long-established roles impede industrialization in several ways. For one thing, individual mobility is a vital ingredient of all industrial societies. Yet individual mobility, both physical and social, can be seriously hampered by close personal ties external to the industrial system, and largely irrelevant to it except in a negative sense. If a man is required to share his material success with an extended group of kinsmen, the appeal of individual wage rewards for subjecting himself to routinized work is considerably dampened. Exclusive enjoyment of the personal rewards of wages is thus a crucial matter. The inflexibilities and dullness of industrial work are not especially attractive to a man who, however hard he has labored in paddy or field, has been able to set his own pace and his own work schedule. Or if he has been a skilled craftsman in his village, then employment in a factory where no expression of his peculiar talents is permitted portends loss of respect in his fellows' eyes and loss of self-respect in his own. All this is to say nothing of the loss of personal satisfaction in the work itself.*

Additional aspects of labor recruitment are also affected by kinship and other traditionally important role relationships. Industrial societies recruit, place, and reward workers largely on the basis of universalistic standards. That is to say, the employee is hired on the basis of his training, skills, and

* The fact that workers in developed societies have found substitute satisfactions and sources of prestige in factory, office, and shop is of no great moment. They have had a century or more in which to make the transition, and they started from a somewhat different social situation in the first place. Similar accommodations may well occur in the developing societies, but they will not be made overnight.

experience, and is paid on the basis of his job status and hours worked or output of work, or both. In traditionalistic societies this is not often so. The pattern is particularistic. One is assigned to a task or brought into some enterprise on the basis of the position he occupies in a kin group. Age, sex, and other statuses, too, may be a consideration. In short, "new occupations simply do not fit traditional standards of prestige, or are valued negatively because they involve manual labor and merit placement irrespective of age, kinship position, caste, or other forms of 'ascribed' status." [22]

Thus, various kinds of traditional statuses, particularly those within closely knit kin groupings, can pose a serious obstacle to economic development. In many ways they discourage mobility in especially talented or ambitious individuals.* By so doing, they inhibit mass involvement in industrial patterns of production. An illustration may be drawn from the American Indian tribes. Although their long-standing plight is a consequence of many factors, including political and ecological ones, their family organization and obligations have produced a serious brake on internal change. In some tribes, such as the Navaho, it is said to be difficult, if not impossible, to succeed in any business if one's family is too near. Almost limitless demands are made on the entrepreneur to provide kinsmen with gifts and loans, which do not require repayment. Cooperatives, too, have failed because of the conflict between the demands of family and of modern business practices.[23]

The constraints on change and development resulting from age-defined statuses are in some respects quite obvious. In most preindustrial societies the elders are regarded as the repositories of all collective wisdom. They are customarily respected; they possess prerogatives and powers not available to the youth. Since the very traditions in which they are expert are a source of their own prestige and influence, their vested interest in the perpetuation of these traditions is evident. Their opposition to change is therefore practical, however sincerely ethical it may also be. Mechanization in farming and in the production of material goods, for example, often involves primarily the youth, who are intrigued by the intrinsic nature of machinery and are receptive to technological techniques that help equalize their economic status vis-à-vis their elders. The latter, conversely, oppose new techniques, which threaten their prestige as the possessors of lifelong acquired knowledge and which weaken their ability to direct the training and economic activities of their juniors. Their reluctance to acquire for themselves the new skills and information often stems from the widely held notion that schooling (and less formal modes of instruction) is for youngsters but not

* One might also wonder how many potential entrepreneurs, by Western standards, have been constrained by traditional role requirements.

appropriate for adults. Even in the areas of child care and health, these attitudes obstruct change, for mature women feel it would be unseemly to be taught like little children in classes. To have young females of their family attend clinics or be delivered by trained midwives is also seen as a reflection on their own wisdom.

If it is the elders who have the greatest stake in the *status quo,* it is usually the youth and younger adults who have the least to lose from a disturbance of customary social arrangements. Added to the youths' greater tolerance toward novelties, especially those that might enhance their own prestige and rights, is another relevant matter. The young are usually also the ones more likely to perceive and learn about new ways of doing things whenever contacts take place between their own society and another. It is they who go abroad as students, who travel away as laborers to other islands or countries or to the larger towns within their own country. It is they who interact with youngsters from other societies, either in local schools or in play-group situations when there is a resident foreign population. It is they who are often, though not exclusively, employed as yard boys, maids, and baby sitters by families immigrated from the outside world. These kinds of situations have been especially well documented for some of the Marshall Islands in the Pacific, but also with other islanders. The youth, exposed to and comprehending foreign customs, inevitably carry new ideas back into their own villages and homes. They thus become a source of infestation for others. "Even within the family, younger children tend to be more influenced by what they see and hear from older siblings than from parents because of their closer traditional association with older siblings." [24] Culture contact among the young clearly becomes a disruptive influence in the process of child training and in the efforts of the older generation to preserve even for themselves a traditional way of life within developing societies. It is a familiar pattern, recalling the experiences of first- and second-generation immigrants in the United States during the decades of heavy population flow from the Old World to the New.

Sex status appears to be a less important social factor in social and economic change than either age status or kinship. Or this may be an impression derived from the fact that sex differences have been less often explored in the context of change. One thing is evident, however: Where women remain completely excluded from decision-making situations and from participating in everyday public activities, their chance of exercising an influence for change is remote. One might speculate that, on the other hand, their exclusion from leadership roles and from all but the most menial economic tasks could have a seriously retarding effect on economic development. Such abridgment of their activities, with its wastage of human resources, was traditional in the higher castes of India and still prevails in some of the Moslem countries. Where females have been less restricted, their interest in change has probably centered around innovations affecting their roles as women in the husband-wife relationship, in education, in the labor market, and in the political arena.

Two instances may be cited in which innovations were opposed by women; in both cases they believed the changes would affect their roles adversely, either by adding obligations or by subtracting prerogatives. In a village development project in India, an effort was made to introduce sanitary latrines. The younger men were inclined toward accepting these devices, but their wives were opposed, since to them would fall the tiresome job of carrying water for the operation of the latrines. Too, they felt that the innovation would interfere with their morning and evening visits to the village bathing tanks where relaxation and gossip were customarily indulged in.[25] To cite a second illustration, in Jamaica new marketing techniques and the planting of certain crops were opposed chiefly by the women of the villages. The reasons given the present writer were thoroughly rational in the light of female-role prerogatives. Marketing vegetables and fruits by small farmers has always been largely a female task, the produce being carried on foot, by donkey, or by passenger bus to the town market, where the woman might stay for two or three days, visiting and gossiping with her friends, until the stock is sold. In addition to the pleasures associated with these visits, her economic role affords a measure of control over the family finances by giving her the chance to hold some of the profits for her own use and savings. Although these examples are not unique, tendencies to accept or resist change are not generally related to sex statuses, for the advantages or disadvantages of change are less commonly associated with sex differences than with differences in age. Whether sex status is a critical factor, then, depends not only on the position of the female in a given society but also on whether a particular change has direct relevance for those of her rights and duties that are sex-defined.

SOCIAL STRATIFICATION

Another structural factor is social stratification, a system for arranging people at different levels of prestige and privilege and one that often transcends statuses based on age or sex. While it exists in industrial as well as nonindustrial societies, the bases and rigidities of stratification systems that have evolved in nonindustrial societies over many centuries are often obstacles to the further development of these societies. Such systems are not geared to the requirements of modern economic development and are often inconsistent with these requirements, especially with industrial recruitment, training, and utilization of labor. Caste is the most extreme and rigid type of stratifying social system, the classic type being found in India. In other countries, castelike or sharply defined class groups have traditionally existed in the form of aristocratic, noble, bureaucratic, and other elites.

Two matters will be discussed in connection with caste and its implications for development. The first is fairly obvious and has to do with the fact that caste systems define role relationships in economic as well as in other kinds of situations. They determine not only whom one may marry or associate with, but also what kinds of work he may do. Members of a certain caste may be permitted only the most menial and perhaps defiling types of occupations, such as street sweeping or disposal of excretia; members of another caste may not be allowed to enter into commercial enterprises or become weavers or carpenters; members of high castes would be demeaning themselves by undertaking any of these occupations. When economic tasks are thought to be properly assignable only on the basis of these traditionalistic considerations, how can the total pool of labor resources of a community be recruited for construction or for factory work or for large-scale, mechanized agriculture? Retraining men and women for the jobs that need to be done will frequently violate caste restrictions which, in many instances, will also prohibit the lowest castes from working side by side with higher ones. Furthermore, the money and mobility incentives ordinarily useful in inducing a person to drop an old set of skills and learn a new set are seriously diluted where caste limitations preclude future occupational mobility with its rewards of greater prestige and pay.

Even in relatively simple projects aimed at economic and community development, the importance of caste can be enormous. A project in the Indian village of Barpali, for example, attempted to introduce better water supplies and an improved variety of poultry. In the matter of establishing wells, the problem was not only one of getting upper caste villagers to participate in the manual and menial labor required of a cooperative venture but also one of resistance to the prospect of ritually pure caste members using a well equally available to ritually impure persons. Poultry raising provided an equally awkward situation and an especially instructive one. This occupation was customarily regarded as unclean and as properly confined to several untouchable castes. Efforts by the project staff at developing chicken farming into a full-time and systematic occupation, partly by introducing a better breed, soon ran afoul of a process called "sanskritization." The untouchable weaving caste members who kept a few chickens could theoretically raise their status by taking on ritually clean behavior. But to get involved in poultry as a full-time occupation rather than as a sideline would threaten the possibilities of their moving upward by means of prescribed methods built into the caste system. Only two individuals permanently adopted the use of better poultry strains. These persons were securely located in a higher, cultivating caste, and therefore were able to seek prestige and profit by means of "Westernization" or techniques existing outside the caste system.[26]

The concepts of Westernization and sanskritization point to a second important implication of caste as a social factor in development. While the upper castes may resist certain changes they regard as eroding their privileges, they accept other innovations as means of enhancing their own level of living within the developing society. Perhaps it comes down to the ancient principle that those who are secure can afford flexibility. Furthermore, adopting practices and roles associated with industrial societies has long-range practicality in view of the irreversible trend in most of the world toward industrialization. For the elite, Westernization is not only palatable, it is nutritious. In a country like India, for instance, "it is always the economically and socially more secure castes or groups that most readily accept innovative programs." [27] Caste, then, is by no means wholly an obstacle to change.

Besides sanskritization, another drag on economic development arising out of rigid systems of stratification is the difficulty of communication and cooperation. When people are resigned to obeying their superiors who hold much authority and who expect unquestioning obedience from those below them, an exchange of ideas and a flow of information cannot take place readily. Americans going overseas as teachers or technical advisers repeatedly comment on the problem of eliciting opinions from instructors or extension workers when the latter's superiors are present. They are equally struck by the lack of association between occupants of differing levels in the same enterprise, except for contacts inescapable because of the enterprise itself.[28] University faculties as well as health, extension, and other services tend to operate as crystallized bureaucracies with directives and policies originating at the top and flowing downward, and with little or no chance for response and comment to move upward. When the element of caste also enters the picture, the possibility of "feedback" becomes nil. In Ceylon, for example, the agricultural extension worker will usually be of a higher caste than the farmer he is supposed to serve and help; both parties accept the rigid lines dividing them, and the farmer's opinions are neither solicited nor proffered.[29] In India, apart from caste considerations, government officials have customarily taken an authoritarian and aloof attitude toward villagers. Even when new types of government workers were sent out by departments of education, health, and agriculture, "they followed in the footsteps of the police and the tax collector in their behavior and attitude toward the villagers." [30]

A problem of greater primacy than communication between various social strata is the more obvious one of resistance by privileged groups to innovations seen as potential threats to themselves. At the same time, their cooperation in any attempt at development is vital, for they often control the means of transportation, the permits for launching new businesses, the bulk of arable land, and other economic elements basic to development. In the Middle East, for example, a small but powerful land-owning elite has opposed programs designed to benefit the peasants; and in Latin America similar resistance has occurred, especially along the line dividing Indians from non-Indians.[31] Under the feudal conditions that still prevail in many underdeveloped societies, the landlord can arbitrarily decide, if he feels it is advantageous, to prohibit the introduction of agricultural extension projects and even health and educational programs. The latter, of course, could be a crucial innovation, threatening the large landowner's control of local information and his ability to manipulate rumor and public opinion.[32] Powerful and change-retarding elites need not always be of the homegrown variety. In New Guinea, missionaries and planters have been able to exercise economic and religious sanctions to discourage natives from participating in cooperatives and other new programs. The hostility of these elites is directed not only at programs but also at the change agents personally.[33]

Thus, even if we assume that a given innovation has utility for stimulating economic development and if we assume, with equal optimism, a receptive attitude by the people toward whom the change is directed, a proposal can still be scuttled through the opposition of a powerful elite group—whatever its motives for opposition. One of the tests of a truly skilled agent of change, therefore, is his ability to recognize the significance of such elites and to muster their acquiescence, if not their support, in a new venture. Lack of success in this kind of tactic would seem to leave only two alternatives: blasting loose the opposition through the intervention of central government power or retreating from the skirmish with hope for another effort in a more propitious time or place.

The several facets of the social structures that have been described appear to pose formidable hurdles for programs in economic development. But to say that they are formidable is not to say that they are insuperable. No element of social structure is totally rigid, nor is it static. Changes are already taking place in traditional relationships throughout the world. As technologies alter, as mechanization and science diffuse between and within societies, these tradition-bound roles and strata will be further altered. Thus, in the long run, the way will be opened for still more social and economic innovation. But the critical issue, of course, is not whether obstructive systems of statuses and roles will eventually be modified by economic development. Rather, it is: How can innovations be adapted to local situations *as they now exist?* There are, unfortunately, no Baedecker's guides to this dimension of developing societies, no well-thumbed rule books on the process of development. But in view of the problems and complexities associated with social and cultural factors, two minimal requirements are apparent for introducing change. One is that the proponents of change have a full and precise stock of information about the society involved and about the local situation into which the proposed innovation will be injected. The second requirement is for careful planning in the light of that information. At the very least, this means that changes must be introduced in a specific sequence. It also means that more than the responses of the direct recipients of the innovations must be reckoned with. The reactions of other nationals who believe that the change will ultimately impinge on their positions and prerogatives also must be counted as part of the total picture and as an influence for success or failure.

To conclude this discussion of the social context of development, we shall consider briefly the sequence of innovations and the significance of organizations. In many situations a fair amount of groundwork appears necessary before one can hope for an innovation's success. This is especially true of innovations bearing upon economic development. What it comes down to is that, before the basic innovation can be attempted, one or more preliminary innovations must be introduced. We shall here consider industrialization a basic innovation—an ultimate goal.* Members of various professions who have been involved as consultants or technical assistants in developing societies have discovered in these societies a partial vacuum, a vacuum that has made their work enormously more difficult and more frustrating than in their domestic settings. This vacuum is left by the relative absence of organizations. Much has been made of the frantic American who belongs to a dozen or more organizations, rushing from meeting to meeting, caught in the tentacles of the PTA, Rotary, SPCA, the Library Building Committee, the Crestview Neighborhood Association, and on and on. Whatever these many organizations may mean for individuals who are addicted joiners, much of what gets done in a developed society is, in fact, accomplished through organizations. Some are economically oriented, some religiously, some politically, some educationally, and some recreationally.†

Organizations function frequently as means for achieving what the participant believes to be "improvements" or "progress." They are exceedingly useful as media of communication for the dissemination of new ideas and

* Reduction in the birth rate or in the death rate might similarly be considered basic innovations.

† It is interesting and a bit curious that even activities that seem to be entirely ends in themselves, such as square dancing and family camping, provoke Americans into setting up related organizations.

information. In developing societies, however, the proponent of change finds few or none of these kinds of organizations ready-made. Hence, a great deal of attention is being given to the need for organization building by people concerned with technical assistance and other aspects of economic development.

Perhaps the first explicit recognition of this need is found in a 1959 publication on professional technical assistance.[34] To refer to the necessity for building organizations in the emerging nations unfortunately implies that these nations lack organizations and institutions. Nothing could be farther from the truth. If organizations are conceived as patterned modes of interaction oriented toward an agreed-on goal, then the existence of organizations is a truly worldwide phenomenon. There are, however, several somewhat distinctive features of organizations found in nonindustrial societies. For one thing, they usually involve relatively small numbers of people. Often they take the form of a cooperative work group or a ritual group. An example commonly encountered is a collection of neighbors gathering together periodically to help each other in harvesting, land clearing, or house building. Another is a small group of old men who meet for religious purposes and who have charge of the village's religious objects, its public rituals, and instruction of the young in religious traditions. A second feature of organizations in the developing countries is that their objective is the preservation of the past, not the initiation of the future. They serve to pass along to each succeeding generation the traditional ways of doing things. They are the main local repositories of knowledge accumulated by word of mouth over centuries.

Thus, most people in these societies have had little experience with organizational activities that extend beyond the village or the district or, more importantly, with organizations whose purpose is to generate new ideas and instigate new procedures. When an attempt is made to introduce change, occasionally existing organizations can be utilized at some point in the change-making process. But more often it is necessary to ignore the old organizations, which were designed to preserve the past. New ones must be created, capable not only of promoting innovations once they have proved their worth but also of remaining themselves viable and flexible enough to accommodate and support future innovations.[35]

Because general, organizational participation is uncommon in emerging nations, developing new organizations is no easy matter. Besides financial limitations there is an absence of manpower trained in leadership and other skills relevant to organizational activities. It may well be also that there is little or no "propensity for moving quickly into an organizational situation and beginning to interact effectively so that the organization produces output quickly." On the contrary, people unaccustomed to acting within organizations "tend to protect themselves from the necessity of interacting readily with persons who perform complementary functions"; and it appears that they do this by "emphasizing hierarchal arrangements, by blocking communications, by strict observance of rules and regulations, by very carefully adhering to the language of job descriptions, and any number of forms of behavior which are not conducive to effective organizational performance." [36]

Labor unions, cooperatives, colleges, extension services, research centers, along with civic, professional, and other voluntary associations, are examples of the kinds of organizations that serve as vehicles of change in modern societies and which are relatively scarce in the developing areas of the world. The paper quoted above by Milton J. Esman identifies several "clusters of organizational variables" that are significant where planned change is to be initiated and sustained. These clusters encompass leadership activity; doctrine or the specification of goals; programs or alternative lines of action for achieving specified goals; financial, personal, and authority resources; and an internal structure, including provisions for developing morale and managing internal conflicts.

To repeat, the creation of complex organizations in societies that have had little previous experience with this type of agency is a challenging enterprise. Building into the organizations the elements that will assure their durability after they are created is even more difficult. Once the expert's guiding hand is withdrawn, and with it various external incentives for participating, newborn organizations often die immediately or wither away from neglect. Yet in the absence of other means for adapting and supporting innovations in an uncertain environment, organization building would seem to be at least as important for economic development as financial investment and the transfer of technologies. Indeed, unless all three are provided simultaneously, ongoing development is unlikely to be achieved at the rate needed to keep up with population growth or desired by national leaders. Even change agents who recognize the importance of organization building are confronted by troublesome problems. What investment of financial and technological resources will be best (or quite useless) in a country in view of the organizations available to carry out a particular plan? What organizations in a specific situation should be developed first and in what sequence should others be created? These are only two of the queries whose answers are urgently required by agents of change on many levels and in many diverse, developing societies.

## Innovation and Selection:
## Dimensions of the Change Process

Innovations have always occurred in vast array. Today the variety is greater than it ever has been in human history or prehistory, and the sheer number of innovations bombarding most societies is staggering. Factory and farm machinery, medicines and chemicals, household implements, business equipment—these and many other items comprise the category of material innovations. In the nonmaterial sphere, each decade—indeed, each year— spawns new skills, bodies of knowledge, values, and beliefs pertaining to every realm of human living. Simply counting, listing, or describing the items that constitute innovations tells us very little, however, about the *process of innovation.*\* It has two aspects. One is inventive, involving the creation of something that has never existed before in just that particular form. The other aspect has to do with introducing the new item to some group of recipients, invariably with the hope that they will adopt it and thus start it along the way toward still wider acceptance. This matter of *introducing* a novelty, rather than *inventing* one, is our concern here, and nearly all our illustrative cases involve diffusion across cultural boundaries.†

The previous section of this chapter has described the social and cultural context within which innovations are introduced, and special attention was given to features of that context as found in many developing societies. Important as is the sociocultural context of innovation, no single element of that context can rightly be regarded as determining the outcome of the innovative process.

Neither is its outcome dependent entirely upon the type of novelty introduced. Remarkably few unsuccessful innovations were inherently destined for failure. At the same time, none has carried within itself a guarantee of success. A critical issue has always been, and continues to be, the relationship between an innovation and the sociocultural context within which it is presented. This is the problem of "fit." The degree of fit with the natural environment is also, of course, a consideration. An illustration of the latter

\* Confusing though it may be, the term "innovation" denotes a process contributing to change, and it denotes also a new material or nonmaterial item.

† The first group of recipients is usually part of the society within which the invention took place. Sometimes the new item, if accepted at all, never spreads farther than its native society. In other cases, however, an item developed in one society, and perhaps long since adopted by it, is eventually introduced to recipients in another society, the very thing being done in many technical assistance programs. If members of the second society accept the item (often modifying it as they do so), diffusion is said to have taken place.

problem would be a proposal to divert Eskimo labor into agriculture. Limitations imposed by a society's natural setting are, however, usually quite obvious, and we shall touch on them only briefly in this chapter.

Introducing a new idea or a new gadget is really only the beginning of the broad process of change. Novel elements are clearly necessary if change is to be accomplished, but novelties carry no guarantee that anything will, in fact, be accomplished. Once a new item has been displayed before some portion of a society, the *process of selection* begins. Selection involves the weighing and assessing of any item and its ultimate rejection or acceptance. Acceptance and rejection are always functions of a particular group of people acting in the context of a particular situation. In the previous section we discussed some cultural and structural characteristics of developing societies which, for the most part, make for difficulty in bringing about planned change. Here we shall deal with certain variables affecting the process of selection in *any* society, industrial or otherwise. Illustrations will, however, be drawn from nonindustrial societies.

FEASIBILITY IN VIEW OF RESOURCES

Brief mention was made earlier of the natural environment. This environment is part of a group's available resources and determines the feasibility of an innovation. Available resources include not only such things as soil, minerals, and food supplies but also the people's material culture created from these natural elements. Further, it includes the people themselves, the total population and its structure; that is, the proportion of people in various age groups, the ratio between the sexes, the population's birth and death rates, and its general condition of health. Thus, available resources provide something of an essential underpinning, which helps to determine whether a given innovation is even feasible for adoption. In view of available resources, fishing is no more feasible for desert nomads than is farming for the Eskimo.

Many kinds of resources, it is true, can be manipulated and transformed. In a majority of the developing societies it is probably safe to say that their potential resources have scarcely been tapped. In certain countries, for instance, a more or less chronic state of malnutrition due to inadequate food supplies or poorly balanced diet in turn results in a relatively low output of energy by human labor; hence, a vicious circle makes for a limited amount of usable labor resources at a given moment. Basic technological changes calling for greater and more sustained expenditures of human energy are scarcely feasible until preliminary innovations can facilitate the use of such energy. Furthermore, it must be remembered that the bulk of the population in developing societies depends on agriculture for a livelihood, and it is said that many of the resources characteristically associated with agriculture are not transferable to other productive enterprises.[37] The relevance of this claim becomes especially apparent if the concept of resources is extended to include the skills of a population as well as its material equipment and land. On the basis of these contentions, a strong argument can be made that the need for agricultural development is at least as great as, and immediately greater than, the need for the development of manufacturing industrialization.

To move to more concrete and obvious considerations with regard to feasibility, let us examine the problem of changing the practices of the self-employed "little man." Attempts at introducing more efficient hand implements in certain farming groups came to nothing because the people simply lacked the physical strength and proper stature for their use.* In Jamaica, an outside expert's suggestion that tractors be introduced to hasten agricultural development failed to take into account the fact that one-third of the agriculturally used land is in farms of less than twenty-five acres, and most of these are less than five acres in size. Moreover, many of these farms are broken up into scattered parcels and are located on steep mountain slopes. In view of resources of this kind, mechanization is not highly feasible.†

Another example of the importance of feasibility in view of available resources is pointed up in an editorial comment on reasons for the rejection of certain agricultural plans.

Take any of the schemes, past or present, and see if it can be undertaken by the small farmer? . . . and if you are honest you will say NO. The bulk of small farmers in Jamaica own an average of under twelve acres of land and have to plant a variety of crops so that each, in season, can bring a small pay day. No big farmer would ever plant canes in his bananas, or coffee in his citrus, or yams, cassava, peas and sweet potatoes on the same hill or mound, as the small farmer does. But if the man has only a few acres, with a part reserved for cows, a few goats and pigs, what else can he do? [38]

### UTILITY

In addition to the availability of resources that make an innovation feasible, its demonstrable utility is also one of the variables operating in the selection process. Utility is not here used in an absolute but in a relative sense: Does the new practice or idea have utility in the light of needs felt by the recipients? Needs are a matter of more than raw biological drives such

---

* Personal communication from Professor John Zahradnik regarding his experiences as an agricultural engineer in Iran.

† Nor is its feasibility enhanced by the absence of mechanical skills and the inaccessibility of parts needed for the repair of farm machinery.

as hunger, sex, and avoidance of pain. The satisfaction of even these elementary requirements is everywhere defined by culture. Only certain foods are regarded as suitable; sexual gratification is permissible only under particular circumstances; and even pain is to be endured or perhaps induced for some purposes. Beyond that, in each society there is a wide variety of needs that are far removed from human biology, needs which people feel because they have learned to feel them. These needs, too, are usually satisfied through culturally prescribed channels, other modes of satisfaction being taboo. For example, the need to be respected does not require that every member of the community but only selected persons give indications of respect. The need for affection or response similarly is gratified within a defined and usually small circle of people.

In discussing development programs, an experienced observer has said that "one of the most puzzling and sometimes frustrating principles is that one should start 'where the people are' and 'with what they want.' " [39] It is not here assumed that this principle is an inflexible one, but there is a considerable body of evidence to support the idea that grave difficulties accompany an effort to bring about changes that are irrelevant to a people's needs. Anthropologists and sociologists have given great emphasis to values in any society, since values largely determine the needs that a people will feel and, moreover, the needs they will feel most intensely. Norms determine or suggest how these needs may properly and best be met. To discover a group's needs is one starting point in a program of development. A next step is to provide new means for need satisfaction, means that will have at least as much apparent utility as the means already employed; preferably, they should have more utility, and this should be demonstrable to the recipients.

Work may be used as one example of the utility problem. Moore has commented on the enormous complexity of motivation and has rightly insisted that "man will work for as many reasons as there are values to be served by such activity and will refuse to work where that serves his values." [40] The apparent acceptability of working for wages will depend on whether the goods and services desired are in fact available through market mechanisms, a principle that Moore goes on to remind us is a limiting one.[41] It is here suggested that the converse of this principle also applies; namely, that wage incentives to work depend on whether the goods and services available in the market are the ones that are generally desired. Some of the answers to the worker's wants may not be readily available by market mechanisms.[42] In weighing the proposal that he accept a new form of employment, which may differ drastically from his customary work, the worker presumably asks himself, "What will this get me that I really want?" or, "Will this get me what I really want better than the way I am used to getting it?" These questions become especially crucial when it is remembered that his wants are not satisfied entirely by economic goods, however important they may be. Respect and prestige are also among the rewards of labor, and frequently new forms of work (for instance, factory employment) are not part of the traditional scheme of values.[43]

As Thorstein Veblen pointed out long ago, the need for prestige can be gratified through rather devious and sometimes surprising patterns of behavior, many of them with economic implications. In some of the warmer climates, especially the Pacific Islands, corrugated iron roofs for homes have been adopted for their status value despite the fact that they transmit more heat to the inhabitants than do the traditional palm-thatch roofs. The significance of prestige is also apparent in cases where latrines have been accepted with no understanding of, or appreciation for, their sanitary value, but because their possession enhances the family's status in the community.[44]

Prestige can, of course, be a group and not just an individual consideration, innovations being accepted when they have utility as competitive advantages between communities; roads, water supplies, and other improvements have been built in areas of Africa and Oceania through an appeal to intervillage rivalries.[45]

Foster[46] contends that, although certain values may at times counterbalance economics in the selection of innovations, economic utility will prevail in the long run. Local tastes and prejudices may serve to delay adoption, but "sooner or later the economic pull seems certain to outweigh other factors." He cites cases in which some new crops were accepted by farmers for their cash value, but others designed for domestic consumption were rejected; food items grown for the market, however, ultimately come to be accepted for home use as well. The present writer suggests, however, that even when the long-run acceptance is determined by economic utility, the urgency for change calls for priorities in the short-run use: Can the situation await the *eventual* acceptance of innovations on economic grounds?

The point is also made by Foster[47] that a given need may be more intensely felt at one time than at another, and that therefore the timing of the introduction of novelties can be a crucial matter. In the earlier stages of development people do not see the utility of literacy, for example, so clearly as they do later on. If tangible benefits cannot be discerned, interest in education remains inactivated and literacy programs lag. There is the example of a great enthusiasm for learning to read and write among older Nigerians while their young men were away in military service during World War II. With the soldiers' return after the war, the need to communicate through writing was diminished; so also was the interest in continuing education.

This issue of sequence or timing would seem to be part of the broader problem of *crisis*. Human needs are extremely diverse and fairly compelling. Cultural and social arrangements provide means by which needs can be met. Such arrangements are never perfect, however. Hence, need gratification is a recurring problem. But that problem becomes enormously intensified when traditional means break down or lose even part of their efficacy. It is similarly intensified when new needs arise for which there are no prescribed avenues to satisfaction. These are times of crisis. At such times a people's sense of frustration becomes acute and their discontent is chronic, so that their receptivity to innovations is consequently heightened. New ideas and practices have a far better chance of being accepted even though they may conflict with values that would reject them if the sense of deprivation were less intense.

In modern societies severe economic depression, racial strife, and major military conflicts provide crisis conditions. In developing societies, plagues, pestilence, and drought are similarly critical. The case of a group of villages in India illustrates concretely the significance of crisis. At a time when outside efforts were being made to establish protected drinking-water supplies for these villages, in none of them could an expressed need for antidisease programs be discerned among the residents. A public well project was successful in some villages, but not in others; in all villages a proposal to install sanitary latrines was largely rejected. A number of cultural and social factors operated against the adoption of both latrines and wells. But the well program was by chance undertaken during the dry season when very little water was available in certain villages. A limited crisis thus existed. The inadequacy of traditional modes of supplying water was dramatized, and the utility of the new alternative was more apparent than it might have been otherwise. In the villages with water scarcity, the wells were accepted. In the other villages they were not.[48] To be sure, the utility of an innovation in the light of felt needs is rarely a sufficient determinant in the process of selection. But it may become sufficient when a crisis develops, as it did in this case.

MEANING

Obvious though it may seem, the variable of *meaning* is often overlooked by change agents attempting to secure the acceptance of innovations. The meaning of an innovation is, of course, usually quite clear to the individual who is introducing it, but that meaning rests upon his own culturally inspired pattern of thinking and behaving, upon the relationships to which he is accustomed and the experiences he has had. When the recipient's background is of a different order, different interpretations are likely, if not inevitable. Indeed, the whole purpose of a proposal may not be understood at all. Language differences naturally loom up as dangerous shoals on which communication is easily wrecked. Even when the agent of change and the recipient use the same language, diverse backgrounds can lead to misinterpretation. In English-speaking rural Jamaica, for example, the term "wife" is not limited to a woman to whom one is legally married, and the term "family land" frequently refers to land held by kinsmen who are related only through the female line. Exclusive of the complexities of language are other problems aplenty in this matter of meaning. Consider the field of health. Most societies recognize and practice ways of treating illness once it has struck. In many emerging nations, however, the notion of preventive measures is absent. For this reason it has been much easier to induce people to subject themselves to shots and pills once they are sick than to convince them that certain medicines and vitamins should be taken to ward off illness.

Even more directly related to economic development are certain other practices that are foreign to people in less developed societies. Keeping records of, and collecting data on, existing resources and activities in agricultural and business enterprises are essential for the development process. The effort to introduce such practices is, however, often met with apathy or resistance because their purpose is not understood. Even worse, they may be misinterpreted by individuals long subject to tight colonial control or to the snooping of local tax collectors. Similar problems of the meaning of innovations hamper efforts by newly independent states to induce their citizens to participate in savings and investments programs, the purposes of which are misunderstood. The lesson here should be clear: However obvious and rational an innovation may appear to the agent of change (whether he be an outsider or an educated member of the society), he should never assume that the people toward whom the innovation is directed will comprehend correctly the nature of an innovation, least of all its purpose.

CONGRUITY

Congruity is another variable in the process of selection. A change that conflicts seriously with established beliefs and behavior requires especially skillful handling if it is to gain acceptance. Much of the earlier section of this chapter on cultural and social factors suggested the kinds of inconsistencies to be found between elements of traditionalistic societies and elements that appear to be necessary for "modernization." A few more illustrations will serve to make this problem more explicit.

In Buddhist countries, pest control in agriculture is difficult to introduce because of the religious taboo against taking any life.[49] Programs to provide education for females as well as for males are a contradiction in some countries where there is a belief that women should be kept abjectly subordinate to men. Employment of women in clerical and other nondomestic occupations encounters opposition for the same reason. Mentioned earlier was the difficulty of recruiting and assigning labor on the basis of skills and availability in societies where tasks are assigned on the basis of age, kinship, or caste status. The latter problem is illustrative of the distinction between role relationships that are characterized by particularism as compared with those characterized by universalism (see page 78). Very frequently inconsistencies between innovations and traditions in emerging societies create a clash between universalism and particularism as bases for role assignments and relationships.

Inconsistencies between the old and the new are not always direct and immediate. An innovation may be rejected, not because it is directly incongruent with an established custom but because it (1) presupposes other changes which do involve conflicts, or (2) may lead to derivative, future changes inconsistent with traditions. The first type of conflict is illustrated in the selection of a mate. The Western pattern of relatively free choice is frequently an attractive one to non-Western young people. Even when the older generation is willing to forego its prerogatives in arranging marriages, however, free choice presupposes social freedom for becoming somewhat familiar with prospective spouses, a freedom which non-Western cultures often taboo. To illustrate the second type of conflict, consider a community development project designed to improve sanitation or irrigation, or to provide industrial facilities. The project's goals may not be inconsistent with local ideas. But one of its implications is the eventual need for cooperative efforts by all members of the community. Such communitywide undertakings are often quite foreign to the residents, or they may prove directly contrary to local beliefs concerning the impropriety of working side by side at equivalent tasks with people who are one's inferiors or who are for other reasons incompatible. Or, to take another example, a more hardy and productive variety of corn may result in food of less acceptable taste and texture, and these esthetics in turn are linked with food-preparation procedures, the pleasures of family meals, and the culinary reputation of women. The new corn is thus rejected because of its conflict-laden ramifications.

Culture linkages, then, are an important aspect, perhaps the most important aspect, of the problem of incongruity. Any custom or value is tied to others. The recipients of change may rightly assume that a given innovation will ultimately have undesirable repercussions, quite apart from its immediate effects or the purposes for which it was designed. The greatest likelihood of such indirect blockages to acceptance occurs where customs are very closely interrelated. Degrees of interrelatedness or cultural integration vary, of course, both between societies and within societies.[50] Blockages stemming from derived culture conflicts pose special problems for the agent of change in that they are not readily discernible or predictable; hence, he may be heavily committed to an innovation before conflict develops or is discovered.[51]

Some qualifying comments should be made in closing this discussion of congruity and incongruity. Since innovations by definition involve some departure from the *status quo,* and since all societies and cultures are dynamic rather than static, it is obvious that innovations are constantly being adopted. Even when these departures involve inconsistencies with the existing culture, the contradictions do not always raise insuperable barriers to acceptance. A proposed change that is deeply incompatible with the values of one subgroup within a society may be far less incongruous for another subgroup and may constitute no real conflict for still another. Where inconsistencies do exist between an innovation and an existing cultural element, the significance of the inconsistency may be less in one situation than in another. Furthermore, incongruities are more tolerable in some institutional fields than in others. For example, industrial societies condone and even encourage technological and scientific innovations that clash with certain established ideas and arrangements. In the fields of religion and the family, conflicting innovations meet with less receptivity. Even here, however, there is flexibility of response, though it is not limitless. Divorce is inconsistent with the monogamous ideals of Christianity, but it is not so incompatible as polygamy. Cultural consistency, in short, is a conditional but not an absolute factor in selection.

COST AND RISK

Another variable must be included with those of feasibility, utility, meaning, and cultural congruity. This is the variable of cost, a necessary measure in the hands of an economist when he is evaluating the efficacy of methods of development. Cost, however, is a separate study in itself, one that is far too complex to discuss in detail here. Therefore, cost and risk will be treated in this chapter only as they are affected by or linked with social and cultural elements.

The point was made early in this chapter that people in the developing societies tend to be tradition-bound. That is to say, they tend to make decisions more on the basis of past experience than on the basis of whether the decisions result in using the most effective means for achieving an end. It would be an exaggeration to claim that this kind of conservatism is always ideological, always a product of extreme reverence for existing values. It may, on the contrary, be a matter of "sensible reluctance to take dangerous risks"; if the risk can be removed, "the peasants' alleged conservatism lessens." [52] Even when there is no considerable risk involved in a new venture, the costs involved may be regarded as not worth the advantages—and the reasons behind such a decision are not necessarily apparent to an agent of change. Even with a fair knowledge of the culture, a change agent may not be aware of certain critical aspects of the local situation which determine the recipients' inclination to accept or reject an innovation.

An illustrative case is that of a Brazilian village in which careful planning had preceded the introduction of a latrine program to improve sanitation. Cement slabs were provided free to the villagers, whose responsibility was then to dig the pits and erect the shelters. But there were very few takers. The lack of acceptance was eventually explained, in part, by the fact that the local population was highly unstable. Many people had arrived quite recently and did not feel themselves permanent residents; they planned to move on, and they were uninterested in making improvements they probably would not enjoy.[53] Thus, however little or much the residents may have understood about hygiene, the planners seemed to have understood even less about the residents.

The case described above involves a situation in which the cost simply did not hold sufficient promise of reward to make for acceptance of the innovation. In other kinds of situations, recipients often perceive something more formidable; namely, investing their time, energy, or resources in unaccustomed undertakings whose outcome they feel they cannot control or foretell. These undertakings become a matter of submitting themselves to new experiences which carry an unpredictable degree of risk. In the villages of India, for example, the Western-style cooperative has made little headway. While risks will be assumed in individually owned businesses, villagers eschew enterprises in which responsibility and control are shared. Employment for wages is regarded as preferable to involvement in cooperatives.[54]

The notion that the poorer or more deprived a people are the less they have to lose by change (and, therefore, the more receptive they will be to innovations) is a fallacy that has led to abortive planning in industrial as well as in nonindustrial societies. This judgment that "the lower classes have little to lose" has invariably been made, of course, by the upper classes, whose conception of the risks involved is colored by their own position and resources. In truth and in fact, there is no reason to assume that the poor are any less likely than the rich to ask themselves, "If I try this, what are the chances that I may gain nothing and lose what I do have?" For the poor, a relatively small investment of resources in the wrong direction will have far more disastrous consequences than it will for the wealthy.*

* Proclivities for gambling among the poor would seem to belie a concern for

In developing societies, farmers are reputed to be especially conservative because agricultural innovations involve taking risks with their most important resources: their livestock and their land. Having very little of either, the farmer hesitates to risk them in new practices when well-established customs can provide a measure of security, even at a subsistence level. The writer learned, for example, that under a development program in Jamaica, government loans for farm improvements were available on very generous terms. Such loans required, however, that the small farmers surrender their land titles as a surety. Few were willing to gamble with an asset they regarded as the key to their independence. Diverting the farmer's own labor and that of his family from customary tasks to government-sponsored projects, such as ditching fields, planting grass barriers, and so on also met with apathy except when cash payment was made for the time invested. Quite apart from immediate risks, once customary patterns are altered in one practice, other changes may become necessary, and the farmer regards with anxiety the unforeseeable consequences of successive innovations. In short, as long as traditional means will serve his high-priority, short-term goals reasonably well, he will not risk in a strange venture such resources as his poverty provides.*

Observations concerning the reluctance of people in developing societies to assume risks for their own betterment have been made by several writers.[55] Risk taking, then, is a widespread and largely rational consideration on the part of change recipients. The process of sanskritization (discussed earlier with reference to the caste situations of India) may well be an ideological factor acting to reinforce traditionalism in the same disadvantaged groups that are likely to resist change because of the risks involved. In other words, we might expect to find people *especially* opposed to change when they value old practices because these are identified with elite groups in the society (and hence are sources of prestige) and when they also believe that new practices will endanger such resources and status security as are already in hand.

A note should be added here concerning a seeming paradox: In some developing societies the promise of greater economic success for a per-

---

risk; cock fighting, horse racing, and numbers games are well patronized. The possibility of a payoff from gambling is, however, in much more dramatic and much more concrete form than it is from some development program requiring continuous effort over a long period of time. In short, the bait is more tempting, and then, too, there are always well-known and often recounted cases of individuals who did make a killing by gambling.

* These and other observations about Jamaica are derived from an investigation of social change made possible by the assistance of a research grant from the Human Ecology Fund in 1960.

son may be viewed by him as a pointless possibility, even as a real risk. Reference was made earlier to societies in which role obligations require the successful individual to share his good fortune with predatory relatives. Thus, there is the prospect of having his rewards from new and more efficient economic practices wiped out. But more than that, success can be downright dangerous in the small community. Each man's new ventures are known to most of his fellows, and the outcome is watched carefully. Rather than being admired and congratulated, the person who achieves unusual success is envied and criticized. He may even become the subject of theft and black magic or be himself suspected of having resorted to these very practices to bring about his gains. There is the belief that "one man's rise is another man's fall: that is, the progress of one farmer is felt to threaten other farmers." [56] Hence, pressures are brought to bear on him directly or indirectly to conform with community patterns. To put it another way, members of peasant communities "react in the most effective way known to them to discourage a neighbor from tampering with the traditional division of the pie." [57]

## Predicting Selection

Looking back over the factors discussed as being relevant to the acceptance of innovations, one might ask if they are indeed such formidable obstacles to change that technical assistance programs and other devices for hastening the development of emerging nations should be abandoned. To agree that they should be is to offer a counsel of despair. Had such a view prevailed among the leaders of either the donor or the recipient nations, development of the latter would be far less in evidence than it is today. Most social scientists seem agreed that the difficulties in securing acceptance of changes will continue to be considerable. They are not agreed, however, on just how great the difficulties will be. Indeed, some are relatively optimistic, and they are inclined to single out one or another of the factors in selection as being the touchstone for success. One eminent rural sociologist has proposed the following hypothesis with respect to utility: "So-called tradition-ridden peasants will not be inhibited by their sanctions and taboos if they are approached with alternative ways of doing things which they are already doing, and the doing of which yields them immediate, obvious results." [58]

On the other hand, our previous discussion has emphasized that acceptance of innovations is a matter of more than demonstrated utility or of any other single consideration. One factor operating in favor of change may be counteracted by another exerting influence in the opposite direction. In still other situations it may be that all the major influences are negative, with rejection of the innovation almost inevitable. And by the same token, if all factors converge in a way to make the novelty both highly desirable and also palatable, acceptance is a strong probability. The nagging problem, of course, is one of prediction. How to identify the significant factors and how to assess their *relative* significance? To these questions we have as yet no satisfactory answers. One step in the right direction would seem to be some kind of explicit model, which the agent of change could use as a guide in preliminary explorations of the social and cultural milieu into which his innovation is to be projected. A general knowledge of or an intuitive "feel" for the recipients' culture is probably just not adequate. What is needed, rather, is a model identifying clusters of norms and institutions that are especially crucial in dealing both with customary behavior and with deviations from tradition. The manner in which these nodes are linked with other aspects of the particular social and cultural system should also be incorporated in the model in order to be of maximum use to the bearer of strange (and often suspect) gifts from other social systems.[59]

## THE AGENT OF CHANGE

Our discussion of selection has by no means exhausted the list of variables involved in the process, and has only pointed up some of the more important ones. A last factor, which must be considered, is the agent of change himself. Not until he enters the situation can other variables such as congruity and utility become relevant, because it is he who brings the innovation to the recipients for their assessment. If the people adopt his proposal, it may be for reasons quite different from those that the agent thinks should have moved them. If they resist, it may also be that, from his point of view, their resistance is inexplicable or due to sheer stupidity. Rarely is he prepared to anticipate, or even to admit in retrospect, that his own behavior could contribute to their rejection. Nevertheless, he is in fact an exceedingly important ingredient in the selection process. In making their assessment of new proposals, recipients react not only to the innovation and how it relates to their life conditions but also to *who* introduces the novelty, to *how* he introduces it, and to their own notions of *why* he is there. Facing the well-intentioned change agent is the problem, "How does one help villagers to believe they can improve their own situation if they have never before had a concept of improvement, or if changes have always before been precipitated by the external forces of natural hazards, the spirit world, military or police action, and the power of lords and governments?" [60]

The agent of change, especially if he comes from an industrialized society, assumes not only that planned improvement is possible but also that there are appropriate, rational ways of bringing improvement about. Whether he is a construction engineer, a business manager, an agricultural economist, or a public health specialist, he brings with him not only his expert knowledge but also the values of his culture and of his own profession. While his expertness is an asset in bringing about change, his values may not be. The well-known experience called "culture shock" has traumatized many a professional person working in a foreign setting and rendered him incapable, at least temporarily, of accommodating his own expectations and ideas to those of the local people. Less sensitive change agents have ignored local values and bulldozed ahead, following their own impulses. These men have left few monuments to their endeavors. There is the instructive case of the American sanitary engineer building public shower baths in Iran. In the interest of economy and the conviction that men should not hesitate to appear nude in each other's presence, he omitted partitioned stalls from the structure. But the villagers would neither accept his philosophy nor his public baths.[61]

The agent of change can rarely set the wheels of development going, least of all *keep* them going, simply by trying to graft onto another social body an item taken intact from his own society. Although the term "transfer" is often used by scholars and agents alike, the operation is more complicated than the term implies. Very often a practice, an idea, or even a material object must be modified in various ways before it will be acceptable in a new setting. It is the change agent who must first of all recognize this need for modification; next, he must devise ways for adapting the item to fit it to the particular situation. This action calls for ingenuity and inventiveness, and thus he needs to be truly an innovator rather than simply a carrier. He may well have to develop new varieties of cereals, new implements, new methods of communication, production, or administration which have no more of an exact counterpart in his own society than in the one he is attempting to change.[62] Some of these requirements recall the point made earlier, that the change agent often finds himself in the business of building organizations, if his impact is to have any degree of permanence.

Thus, the effective agent of change must have not only a stock of expert information and professional skills but also the insight and ability for using them in, and adapting them to, unfamiliar situations. He must, in addition, be able to communicate objectives and knowledge to those people whose lives he seeks to change. This is not simply a matter of language. While a knowledge of the local tongue is undoubtedly an asset, its advantage may be as much in gaining the respect of recipients as in communicating with them. Communication, furthermore, involves much more than verbal argument. The utility of an innovation, particularly in the economic realm, has frequently been communicated more effectively through a demonstration project than through persuasive oratory. An experimental farm plot sown with improved strains of vegetables or a small factory containing efficient machinery can win the day despite a change agent's dependence on language interpreters.

Communication is also directly related to the problem of adaptation mentioned above. The chances of inducing acceptance are maximized if a novelty can be communicated in relation to existing needs or if it can be linked or suited to the group's traditions.[63] The agent's problem is to convey the relevance of his proposals, not their substance alone. An additional burden is placed on him when he is confronting several subgroups, which may interpret his proposals differently. In one Indian village, for example, the Community Development Project was seen by one segment as a means for realizing certain Westernized goals, by others as a threat to their own status, and by still others as an avenue to association with upper-caste people.[64]

A different kind of question faces the change agent almost immediately as he assumes his role: Should he encourage an equalitarian relationship with recipients or should he assume an authoritarian posture? Again, there are no pat answers. In some societies there is a great social distance between educated individuals in positions of leadership and the masses of people. The artificiality of a sudden, imposed equality between a change agent and ordinary villagers will not be overlooked by them. Nor may they be able to discard their inhibitions and respond freely to his overtures. The American proclivity for forming committees, for providing each person with a voice, and ideally a vote, in affairs affecting himself, is by no means universally regarded as necessary or even wise. In many parts of the world, authority is highly respected even when it verges on tyranny, and the strong man, as has frequently been demonstrated in Latin America, rules not only through political and military devices but his very strength elicits popular support as well.[65]

Whether a change agent who is clearly an outsider can presume to operate in arbitrary fashion even in societies where authoritarianism is accepted and admired is, however, a moot point. The local people may not follow so meekly a man who is not their own. Furthermore, there are developing societies in which sharp inequality has been a matter of enforcement rather than emotional commitment; in other places, ancient, authoritarian traditions are being questioned. In such societies the barriers between leaders and masses are resented, and the change agent's invitation to recipients to express their desires, to make suggestions and comments concerning proposed changes, may elicit immediate responses and enhance eventual acceptance of appropriate innovations. Here a collaboration between agent and recipient can be of enormous value. Here the collaborative, as opposed to the authoritarian, approach has the advantage of reducing anxieties and resistance among recipients. It facilitates a two-way communication, which can provide both parties with the information needed to institute effective changes.[66] The more a change agent can learn about *to what* he is adapting and *to whom* he is interpreting, the better prepared he is to play his role. Also, without a collaborative relationship, he will find it difficult to undertake the basic function of organization building. Indeed, one viewpoint holds that planned change, unlike change in other guises, always is properly characterized by mutual goal setting by agent and recipient and that there is a 50:50 ratio of power between the two.[67] In the case of an agricultural project in India, inability to gain farmer support for new techniques was dramatically reversed when one set of change agents (aloof and authoritarian government officials) was replaced by another set, which secured the recipients' confidence and cooperation by treating them as equals and collaborators.[68]

The proponent of change may, of course, find it impossible to establish an equalitarian relationship with *all* recipients whose acceptance is sought. Indeed, if the project involves large numbers of people, he would be unable to have any kind of meaningful relationship with even a majority. In such instances, those who are attempting to introduce change find it necessary to first win over selected individuals among the local population. If these individuals are "converted," they, in turn, can serve both as models to their fellows and as active publicists of the innovation. They become themselves agents of change. Their role is somewhat different from that of the initiator of the proposal, however. In recognition of this difference it is helpful to distinguish between the two facets of change making by the terms *innovator* and *advocate*. The latter is an agent, usually a local individual, who has accepted or supports an innovation and encourages its acceptance among other members of the recipient society. He is not, however, responsible for its initial introduction on the scene. The innovator, on the other hand, may be either native or foreign and is the original instigator of the change. He often plays the role of advocate as well, particularly when planned change is attempted across cultural and national boundaries.[69]

The problem is, of course, to find advocates who will have a strong, positive influence in the selection process. Innovators are not always the most effective advocates, if only because of local attitudes toward outsiders. An old woman in an African village put it this way:

You Europeans think you have everything to teach us. You tell us we eat the wrong food, treat our babies the wrong way, give our sick the wrong medicine;

you are always telling us we are wrong. Yet if we had always done the wrong things, we should all be dead. And you see we are not.[70]

In the face of this kind of persuasive folk wisdom, it is helpful to have change advocates within the group willing to admit that faults exist in their own culture and to urge that new alternatives might prove more efficacious.

Sometimes it is possible to muster advocate support among the formal leaders of a community. When these leaders are apathetic or opposed to change, however, advocates must be sought among informal leaders, persons who lack official status but who are respected and esteemed and whose actions and advice will be followed by others. These are occasionally the very individuals most receptive to innovation because they have been away from their own community or have in other ways already been exposed to new ideas. Potential advocates can be found among people somewhat disenchanted with tradition because their talents and knowledge find no reward in the formal status arrangements of their society. The native advocate is thus the person very frequently whose own problems stem from the existing patterns of social life and who consequently feels he has more to gain by changing rather than by preserving those patterns. By no means does this deny that an advocate of change may also be motivated by altruism, by a realization that developments in economics, health, education, and other fields are desirable for his whole society. The benefits that accrue to him personally may be quite incidental to his central concern for the group's welfare. Gandhi would seem to have been such an individual.

In much recent technical assistance work in developing societies, this role of the native advocate has been explicitly recognized and utilized. When an American professional person goes overseas on a project, various organizations require that the host country arrange for a native counterpart. This individual should have technical training or interests, or both, similar to the Americans; it is his responsibility to acquire new knowledge and skills. He serves as a liaison person between the American and the recipients and (hopefully) continues acting as an advocate after the American's departure and himself becomes the innovator. Much of this activity among counterparts is concerned with building organizations that can sustain the innovations introduced and can continue to generate additional innovations. Nor is the counterpart arrangement confined to technical assistance supported by governments. It has been found invaluable in private enterprises undertaken by businesses and universities and in projects supported by foundations in such fields as health, education, and general community development.

Indeed, so well established has become the system of relationships between foreign experts and native counterparts that a "third culture" is said to have evolved around the relationships. As outsiders and host nationals continue to associate in common undertakings, "they incorporate into the ethos of their ingroup standards for interpersonal behavior, work-related norms, codes of reciprocity, styles of life, networks of communications, institutional arrangements, world views, and on the individual level, new types of selves. These composite patterns differentiate a third culture from the cultures it transcends." [71] This third culture thus provides guidelines for the interaction and collaboration between foreigner and host, a ready-made pattern of behavior and values within which they can work for whatever changes or proposals the goals of their enterprise require. It is something of a catalyst for the change process. It facilitates the work of the outsider, who enters the situation as both innovator and advocate, and of his counterpart, who is initially an advocate but who ideally will become an innovator as well. How well these two kinds of "men in the middle" play their roles will continuously and enormously influence the nature and number of innovations accepted in the developing societies.

## Persisting Problems

Our discussion of the social and cultural factors involved in the development of nonindustrial societies has tended to emphasize obstacles to change. The emphasis has been given partly because there are so many unanswerable questions regarding just how the various factors operate and which are of the greater, which of less, importance. The emphasis on obstacles has been given also as an equalizer for the optimism prevalent in many quarters with respect to accelerating economic development. Optimism is evident among both the leaders of the societies that proffer assistance and the leaders, or some of them, of the recipient nations. Each expert and each leader sometimes seems to have his own particular remedy. Some have suggested that, if only *enough* money were channeled in, development would follow, though the showers of dollars have still somehow not planted the crops or manufactured the goods as predicted. Some have assumed that educational crash programs would produce able leadership and supply all the needed skills. Some have put their confidence in population control, some in democratization.

Our intention here has not been to indulge in extreme pessimism, nor to imply a counsel of despair. Certain means for facilitating development have been described. But since no one influence determines whether change will be long impeded or accelerated, the multiplicity of factors involved has been stressed. The development process, let it be said again and again, is an exceedingly complex one with many dimensions, some of them still poorly explored and little understood.

Yet even the most confirmed pessimist cannot deny that economic and social development have been taking place with dizzying rapidity in nearly all parts of the world—industrial and nonindustrial. Unless halted by utterly devastating nuclear war, these developments will continue. The choice is not between development or no development. The alternatives have to do, rather, with the kinds of changes that will take place, the rates at which development will occur (and especially whether these rates will serve to meet growing population pressures), and the prices that will be paid for change—prices paid in the currency of individual freedom, in the wrenching and wracking of traditional patterns of life, and in conflicts within and between the societies. These alternatives are theoretical, however. We are at present incapable of directing change with reasonable precision at the rate we might choose, or of expanding and constraining it at will; nor are we even agreed on the choices that should be made, except for a very vague agreement that industrialization and progress are desirable and that they should be achieved quickly. Beyond this broad and shallow area of consensus, the specifics are well entangled and heatedly debated.

A last problem persists. Social scientists have recognized for more than half a century that purposes and consequences are of two different orders. It is a simple principle, perhaps more often forgotten than remembered. It is an especially relevant principle to the area of social and economic planning. Men devise intricate blueprints for altering their own or someone else's society and continue to be surprised when the outcome does not square with their intentions. Working with imperfect knowledge and imperfect methods, the most carefully designed project inevitably generates consequences that are unanticipated and sometimes unwanted. Whatever name is lent them, these unexpected results plague the heads of government, bureaucrats, corporation presidents, and village project directors alike. "As programs are implemented, they characteristically exhibit persistent tendencies to turn out differently than planned—sometimes more successfully than anyone hoped, oftener, more disappointing than anyone anticipated—and in all instances replete with surprises." [72]

Illustrations of these latent functions, as Merton called them, are well known and may be drawn from every nation and from many facets of each nation's life. There are the technical assistance programs intended to aid the masses in developing societies, and which have often ended by enriching the upper classes and widening the gap between the two. There are the heavy investments of capital and labor in programs to industrialize these societies, investments which have ended in reducing food production and draining national treasuries for the importation of cereals and other foods. There are the heroic educational projects aimed at banishing illiteracy and preparing the youth for productive work, programs which have produced white-collar workers beyond a country's capacity to employ them and youth who disdain to do the undignified work required in factory and field. There is industrialization itself, the greatly loved panacea for backwardness and poverty. With it has come an unprecedented rapid growth of cities in nearly all emerging nations—cities pulling in the rural dwellers like magnets. And there is scarcely one of these cities that is not ringed by a moat of fetid slums to house the ex-farmers, more impoverished and increasingly more rebellious than their brothers in the poorest villages.

But not all the consequences of planned change are unwanted and not all are unanticipated. Though rarely on schedule, an enormous amount of development is taking place as intended—a testimony to the knowledge man has accumulated and to his skill in its application. Nearly all the emerging nations are determined that this development shall continue and shall accelerate. Side by side with commitments to national independence and sovereignty are the commitments to attain ever-rising standards of material and social well-being. This irreversible trend has been referred to as a kind of worldwide unification which "is the single most successful conversion movement in the history of ideological diffusion." [73]

## REFERENCES

1. OGBURN, WILLIAM F., *Social Change.* New York, Viking Press, 1927.
2. This, by the way, is one of the first propositions on change listed in Berelson, Bernard, and G. A. Steiner, *Human Behavior: An Inventory of Scientific Findings.* New York, Harcourt, Brace and World, Inc., 1964, p. 615.
3. MACIVER, R. M., and CHARLES H. PAGE, *Society.* New York, Rinehart & Company, Inc., 1937, pp. 574-76. Sorokin and Pitirim, *Social and Cultural Dynamics,* vol. 4. New York, The Bedminster Press, 1962, pp. 302-20, 377-88. Gilfillan, S. C., *Sociology of Invention.* Chicago, Follett Publishing Company, 1935, pp. 134-39.
4. NIEHOFF and ANDERSON have suggested this as the starting point in the analysis of cross-cultural innovation, but they do not distinguish the plan's means and ends explicitly. Niehoff, Arthur H., and J. Charnel Anderson, "The Process of Cross-Cultural Innovation." *The Agricultural Development Council Reprint,* No. 2 (September, 1964), p. 1.
5. BOTTOMORE, T. B., *Sociology.* Englewood Cliffs, N. J., Prentice-Hall, Inc., 1963, p. 279.
6. BOWMAN, MARY JEAN, and C. ARNOLD ANDERSON, *Development of the Emerging Countries.* Washington, D. C., The Brookings Institution, 1962, p. 159.

7. *Ibid.*, pp. 153, 158.
8. GOLDEN, HILDA HERTZ, "Literacy and Social Change in Underdeveloped Countries," in *Underdeveloped Areas,* Lyle W. Shanon, ed. New York, Harper Bros., 1957, p. 112.
9. *Ibid.*, pp. 112-13.
10. *Ibid.*, p. 110.
11. BOWMAN and ANDERSON, *op. cit.,* pp. 160-72.
12. "Any Nation's Biggest Business," *Carnegie Corporation of New York Quarterly,* No. 2 (1964), p. 2.
13. *Ibid.*, pp. 2-3, referring to Frederick Harbison and Charles A. Myers, *Education, Manpower, and Economic Growth.* New York, McGraw-Hill Book Co., Inc., 1964.
14. FOSTER, GEORGE M., *Traditional Cultures: and the Impact of Technological Change.* New York, Harper and Row, Publishers, 1962, p. 76.
15. *Ibid.*, p. 65.
16. *Ibid.*, p. 66.
17. HAGEN, E. E., "A Framework for Analyzing Economic and Political Change," *Development of the Emerging Countries.* Washington, D. C., The Brookings Institution, 1962, p. 12.
18. *Ibid.*
19. FOSTER, *op. cit.,* p. 66.
20. *Ibid.*, p. 91.
21. MOORE, WILBERT E., "Motivational Aspects of Development" in *Social Change,* Amitai and Eva Etzioni, eds. New York, Basic Books, Inc., Publishers, 1964, p. 294.
22. *Ibid.*
23. FOSTER, *op. cit.,* p. 94.
24. MASON, LEONARD, "Culturation as an Integrative Process." An unpublished paper.
25. FRASER, THOMAS M., Jr., "Sociocultural Parameters in Directed Change." *Human Organization* (Spring, 1963), p. 98.
26. FRASER acknowledges Srinivas' authorship of these two concepts: *Ibid.*, pp. 97-100. See Srinivas,

M. N., *Caste in Modern India.* New York, Asia Publishing House, 1962, Chapter II.
27. FRASER, *op. cit.,* p. 100.
28. KING, C. WENDELL, and EDWIN D. DRIVER, *Report on a Retrieval Study of the Professional Person Overseas,* processed, 1964, p. 48. (This investigation was carried out with the assistance of Bruce R. Morris and Thomas M. Fraser, Jr., and was supported by a grant from the Ford Foundation.)
29. FOSTER, *op. cit.,* p. 117.
30. SINGH, RUDRA DATT, "The Village Level," in *Human Problems in Technological Change,* Edward H. Spicer, ed. New York, Russell Sage Foundation, 1952, p. 61.
31. GOODENOUGH, WARD HUNT, *Cooperation in Change.* New York, Russell Sage Foundation, 1963, pp. 416-18.
32. FOSTER, *op. cit.,* pp. 104-105.
33. GOODENOUGH, *op. cit.,* p. 416.
34. SANDERS, IRWIN, ed., *Interprofessional Training Goals for Technical Assistance Personnel Abroad.* New York Council on Social Work Education, 1959, pp. 48-49.
35. BEERS, HOWARD W., "Application of Sociology in Development Programs," *CECA Papers.* Council on Economic and Cultural Affairs (January, 1963), p. 7.
36. ESMAN, MILTON J., an unpublished paper presented at one of a series of programs on "The Professional Person Overseas," sponsored by the Ford Foundation at the University of Massachusetts during 1964-1965.
37. MOSHER, ARTHUR T., "Research on Rural Problems," *The Development of Emerging Countries.* Washington, D. C., The Brookings Institution, 1962, p. 74.
38. NEMBHARD, LEN, *Public Opinion.* Kingston, Jamaica (January 29, 1965), p. 3.
39. BEERS, *op. cit.,* p. 7.
40. MOORE, *op. cit.,* p. 297.

41. *Ibid.*, p. 298.
42. *Ibid.*
43. *Ibid.*
44. FOSTER, *op. cit.*, p. 149.
45. *Ibid.*, p. 154.
46. *Ibid.*, p. 151.
47. *Ibid.*, pp. 166-67.
48. FRASER, *op. cit.*, pp. 96-97.
49. FOSTER, *op. cit.*, p. 79.
50. SPICER, EDWARD H., "Conceptual Tools for Solving Human Problems," in *Human Problems in Technological Change*, Edward H. Spicer, ed. New York, Russell Sage Foundation, 1952, p. 287.
51. FRASER, THOMAS M., Jr. An unpublished manuscript.
52. BEERS, *op. cit.*, p. 5.
53. FOSTER, *op. cit.*, pp. 162-63.
54. FRASER, *op. cit.*, p. 102.
55. BEERS, *op. cit.*, p. 5. Foster, *op. cit.*, p. 170-72. Mandelbaum, D. G., "Planning and Social Change in India." *Human Organization* (Fall, 1953), p. 6. Marriott and McKim, "Technological Change in Overdeveloped Rural Areas." *Economic Development and Cultural Change* (December, 1952), p. 226.
56. EDWARDS, DAVID, *An Economic Study of Small Farming in Jamaica.* Mona, Jamaica, University of the West Indies, 1961, p. 90.
57. FOSTER, GEORGE M., "Interpersonal Relations in Peasant Societies," *Human Organization* (Winter, 1960), p. 177. Lopreato, Joseph, "Interpersonal Relations: The Peasant's View," *Human Organization* (Spring, 1962), pp. 21-24. (Provides additional evidence from an Italian community.)
58. TAYLOR, CARL C., quoted by Mosher, *op. cit.*, p. 100.
59. FRASER, *op. cit.*, pp. 102-103.
60. BEERS, *op. cit.*, p. 7.
61. FOSTER, *Traditional Cultures . . . , loc. cit.*, p. 181.
62. HOSELITZ, BERT, "Problems of Adapting and Communicating Modern Techniques to Less Developed Areas," in *Underdeveloped Areas*, Lyle W. Shannon, ed. New York, Harper Bros., 1957, p. 408.
63. BOTTOMORE, *op. cit.*, p. 285.
64. FRASER, *op. cit.*
65. FOSTER, *Traditional Cultures . . . , loc. cit.*, p. 181.
66. BENNIS, WARREN G., KENNETH D. BENNE, and ROBERT CHIN, eds., *The Planning of Change.* New York, Holt, Rinehart and Winston, Inc., 1961, pp. 12-13.
67. BENNIS, WARREN G., "A Typology of Change Processes," *ibid.*, pp. 154-56.
68. SINGH, *op. cit.*, pp. 55-67.
69. BARNETT, H. G., *Innovation.* New York, The McGraw-Hill Book Company, 1953, Chaps. X and XI. (An excellent analysis of advocates and their assets.)
70. FOSTER, *Traditional Cultures . . . , loc. cit.*, p. 181.
71. USEEM, JOHN, RUTH USEEM, and JOHN DONOGHUE, "Men in the Middle of the Third Culture." *Human Organization* (Fall, 1963), p. 170.
72. *Ibid.*, p. 172.
73. MOORE, WILBERT E., and ARNOLD S. FELDMAN, *Labor Commitment and Social Change in Developing Areas.* Social Science Research Council, 1960, p. v.

## ADDITIONAL READINGS

BARNETT, HOMER G., *Innovation.* New York, McGraw-Hill Book Company, 1953.
BENNIS, WARREN G., KENNETH D. BENNE, and ROBERT CHIN, eds., *The Planning of Change.* New York, Holt, Rinehart and Winston, Inc., 1961.
BOTTOMORE, T. B., *Sociology.* Englewood Cliffs, N. J., Prentice-Hall, Inc., 1963.
CLEVELAND, HARLAN, GERARD J. MAN-

GONE, and JOHN CLARK ADAMS, *The Overseas Americans*. New York, McGraw-Hill Book Co., Inc., 1960.

FOSTER, GEORGE M., *Traditional Cultures and the Impact of Technological Change*. New York, Harper and Row, Publishers, 1962.

GOODENOUGH, WARD HUNT, *Cooperation in Change*. New York, Russell Sage Foundation, 1963.

LERNER, DANIEL, *The Passing of Traditional Society*. New York, The Free Press of Glencoe, 1958.

McCLELLAND, DAVID C., *The Achieving Society*. Princeton, N. J., D. Van Nostrand Company, Inc., 1961.

McCORD, WILLIAM, *The Springtime of Freedom*. New York, Oxford University Press, 1965.

MEAD, MARGARET, ed., *Cultural Patterns and Technical Change*. New York, The New American Library, 1955.

MOORE, WILBERT E., *Social Change*. Englewood Cliffs, N. J., Prentice-Hall, Inc., 1963.

MOORE, WILBERT E. and ARNOLD S. FELDMAN, eds., *Labor Commitment and Social Change in Developing Areas*. New York, Social Science Research Council, 1960.

MOSHER, ARTHUR T., *The Development of Emerging Countries*. Washington, D. C., The Brookings Institution, 1962.

SANDERS, IRWIN, ed., *Interprofessional Training Goals for Technical Assistance Personnel Abroad*. New York, Council on Social Work Education, 1959.

SHANNON, LYLE W., ed., *Underdeveloped Areas*. New York, Harper & Brothers, 1957.

SOUTHALL, AIDAN, ed., *Social Change in Modern Africa*. New York, Oxford University Press, 1961.

# CHAPTER
# 4
# *Agriculture*

## *The Role of Agriculture in Development*

Ultimately, the decision must be made as to how the economic resources—land, labor, and capital—are to be allocated so as to contribute most effectively to economic growth and other chosen objectives. One of the major questions is whether, and to what extent, to emphasize industry or agriculture, or some other aspect of growth. This is an important matter, but consideration of it will have to be deferred until we understand the problems in each sector of the economy. Suffice it to say at this point that it is undoubtedly unwise to emphasize any one sector of the economy (typically, this would be the industrial sector) to the exclusion of others. All sectors are complementary. This is particularly true between industry and agriculture. Industrialization cannot proceed very far without a progressive agriculture. Agricultural development, in turn, depends on a progressive industry. It is no accident that the most progressive nations agriculturally are also the most progressive industrially. The growth of each has aided the other, as well as being the result of common causes such as industrious and well-trained people with a desire for growth.

Agriculture has sometimes been called the most essential industry, on the grounds that people must eat to survive. However, other pursuits are essential, such as seeing that the food gets to the people and in a form that can be eaten. It takes a combination of activities to support a civilization. We need say only that agriculture plays an important role in every society, although, because of different conditions, a role of variable quantitative importance.

Normally, as economic growth proceeds, the number engaged in agriculture will decline relatively in favor of industry, commerce, and services, including the professions. Table 4.1 shows the percentage of the population of various countries engaged in agriculture. This ranges from a low of 5 percent in England and Wales and 7 percent in the United States to a high of 93 percent in Nepal and 85 percent in the Congo (Leopoldville). A comparison with Table 1.1 shows a rough inverse correlation between the level of the per capita domestic product and the percentage of the population engaged in agriculture. A comparison for each of the countries in the table with the percentage in agriculture around 1940 shows a considerable decline in the proportion of the people devoting their efforts to agriculture. Only a few exceptions to this decline occur (Czechoslovakia, India, and Indonesia). Thus, as development proceeds, agriculture can be expected to decline as a source of employment relative to the other sectors of the economy. The more rapid the technological advance in agriculture, the more rapid the decline that can be expected, unless this results in a new export specialty. But this does not mean that the subject of agriculture should be neglected, for it is by the development of agriculture that this occupational shift becomes possible.

Nevertheless, the problem of the relative allocation of effort among the various sectors of the economy must wait until the problems in each sector are explored. Accordingly, the next several chapters will be concerned with the problems that arise in various areas and only incidentally with the relations among them. The first to be explored is agriculture, the subject of this chapter.

People must have a sufficient quantity of food, and food that supplies the right kind of nutrients if they are to survive. In addition, they would like a sufficient variety of food to make life interesting. The content of the food intake is one of the most important determinants of the scale of living. Today the total production of food in the world is probably enough for subsistence of the present population, particularly if the food and population were more evenly distributed, but it is probably not sufficient to provide a healthful and varied diet for all; that is, to provide a satisfactory standard of living. The world's food supply, moreover, is very unevenly distributed. Many do not have enough to eat, and others get enough calories but have an unhealthful diet.* In particular, many lack sufficient animal

* See Table 1.4.

# TABLE 4.1.

*Percentage of Population Engaged in Agriculture, circa 1960 [a] and 1940 [b]*

| Country | Percent in Agriculture ca. 1960 | ca. 1940 | Country | Percent in Agriculture ca. 1960 | ca. 1940 |
|---|---|---|---|---|---|
| *Europe* | | | *South America* | | |
| Austria | 23 | 36 | Argentina | 19 | |
| Belgium | 12 | 17 | Bolivia | 72 | |
| Bulgaria | 64 | 80 | Brazil | 58 | 67 |
| Czechoslovakia | 38 | 37 | Chile | 28 | 35 |
| Denmark | 23 | 29 | Colombia | 54 | 72 |
| Finland | 35 | 57 | Ecuador | 53 | |
| France | 26 | 36 | Paraguay | 54 | |
| Germany, West | 14 | 27 | Venezuela | 32 | 50 |
| Germany, East | 18 | 22 | | | |
| Greece | 53 | | *Asia* | | |
| Hungary | 38 | 53 | Ceylon | 53 | |
| Iceland | 38 | 57 | Taiwan | 50 | |
| Ireland | 40 | 49 | India | 70 | 66 |
| Italy | 26 | 48 | Indonesia | 72 | 66 |
| Netherlands | 11 | 21 | Iran | 55 | |
| Norway | 19 | 35 | Israel | 13 | |
| Poland | 48 | 64 | Japan | 40 | 48 |
| Portugal | 43 | 49 | Korea, Rep. of | 80 | |
| Roumania | 70 | | Malaya | 58 | 61 |
| Spain | 49 | 52 | Nepal | 93 | |
| Sweden | 17 | 33 | Pakistan | 65 | |
| Switzerland | 12 | 21 | Philippines | 58 | 73 |
| England, Wales | 5 | 6 | Syria | 50 | |
| Yugoslavia | 57 | 78 | Thailand | 82 | 89 |
| U.S.S.R. | 39 | 50 | Turkey | 75 | 82 |
| *North and Central America* | | | *Africa* | | |
| Canada | 11 | 26 | Algeria | 75 | |
| Costa Rica | 55 | | Congo (Leopoldville) | 85 | |
| Cuba | 42 | | Ghana | 58 | |
| Dominican Republic | 56 | 77 | Mauritius | 44 | |
| El Salvador | 60 | 75 | Morocco | 57 | 74 |
| Guatemala | 68 | 71 | Mozambique | 75 | |
| Haiti | 83 | | South Africa | 30 | 64 |
| Honduras | 66 | | Tunisia | 68 | |
| Mexico | 54 | 65 | United Arab Rep. | 57 | 71 |
| Nicaragua | 68 | 73 | | | |
| Panama | 46 | 52 | *Oceania* | | |
| United States | 7 | 9 | Australia | 13 | 19 |
| | | | New Zealand | 14 | 23 |

SOURCE: *Production Yearbook*, Table 5A, 1963, pp. 19 ff. Food and Agricultural Organization of the United Nations.
[a] Latest year available.
[b] 1940 or most recent year available.

proteins. Others have much more food than they need for their own good health, while even in such countries some have too little. Thus, there is hunger in a world where agricultural science has produced what seem like miracles in the ability to produce food. The spread of modern scientific methods to the agriculture of the underdeveloped countries is essential. In some countries there is too little food and the immediate problem is finding how to feed the people, especially since the population will also probably be an increasing one. As a whole, the world population increases by over 100,-000 people every single day.* A second problem is that of increasing the quality and variety of food.

Supplying food is a serious problem, although some (for example, Colin Clark[1]) believe the world can easily produce enough to feed much larger numbers than now exist—28 billion persons if the world could attain the Dutch level of efficiency, measured by output per acre. However, one can hardly be optimistic that such a standard will be reached. All land is not equally fitted to attain this level, and land, especially fertile land, and population are not well correlated. The efficiency of agricultural methods varies greatly. It will take hard work just to increase the efficiency slightly.

There are large areas as yet uncultivated [2] that can be cultivated, but the obstacles are great. These lands need irrigation, drainage, or clearing, and it will be costly to bring them into use. Moreover, people must be moved to them. This development will not come about without considerable capital and effort. There is also the notion of recourse to the sea for food, but this, too, takes capital and effort. Actually, the major solution to the food problem seems to be increased productivity on the existing farmlands.

We can anticipate only slow increases in output, despite advances in the method of growing food that are little short of miraculous. As we shall see, there are definite problems of adapting our knowledge to specific areas and of getting these methods adopted.

Thus far, the discussion has been in terms of food. It should not be forgotten that agriculture also supplies raw materials to industry. The food-processing industry obviously depends on it. Clothing and shelter derive many of their materials from agriculture, and almost every industry relies to some extent on agricultural products. The same problems of efficient production to produce a sufficient quantity and improved qualities exist here, especially in the underdeveloped countries if their industry is to develop on a competitive basis.

There has been a tendency in the past, especially among the leaders of underdeveloped countries, to neglect the development of agriculture for various reasons. This must be overcome before agriculture can be improved.

* The growth of population is discussed more fully in Chapter 5.

1.   There is a tendency to associate a predominance of agriculture with poverty and of industry with riches. Although heavily agricultural areas like Denmark, New Zealand, and Iowa show that it is not necessary for such areas to be poor, the situation in many other countries seems to confirm this. Actually, this is a case of confusing mutual existence with cause and effect. It is just as likely that because people are poor (because they are unproductive), they must devote most of their attention to meeting their primary needs. Thus, poverty may cause a predominance of agriculture instead of a concentration on agriculture causing poverty.

2.   There is also a tendency to feel that agriculture is somehow inferior to industry because the previously dominant countries and those militarily strong were industrialized. Agriculture is associated with colonial status and military weakness. The almost universal strong nationalism of underdeveloped countries and the desire to avoid inferiority may lead to a neglect of agriculture.

3.   There is a strong and persistent belief that increased productivity in agriculture will lead only to a population increase, thus making the development problem even more acute.

4.   A major part of any agricultural program is usually land tenure reform. In some countries, particularly in Latin America, landlords have great political power. Because they stand to lose by such reforms, they may oppose efforts to devise an agricultural program.

5.   Some fear to develop agriculture, at least to the point where agricultural exports constitute a substantial part of total exports, because they fear and expect bad terms of trade* for primary products, or at least difficulties with unstable prices. Whether the fear concerning worsening terms of trade is justified is debatable.† Past experience has shown that prices in the export market for primary goods can be unstable and cause considerable difficulty.

6.   Some tend to shy away from trying to develop agriculture because they see a massive problem of training large numbers of peasants in improved methods and, what may be more difficult, getting them to adopt the proposed reforms. Also, to develop agriculture may look hopeless until markets are created and roads and other utilities developed, not to mention

* By the "terms of trade" is meant the relationship between an index of export prices and an index of import prices. Thus, if export prices have dropped 10 points to an index of 90 and import prices have risen 20 points to 120, the terms of trade index will be 90/120, or 75.

† Theodore Morgan ("Long Run Terms of Trade between Agriculture and Manufacturing," *Economic Development and Cultural Change* [Oct. 1959], pp. 1-23), comes to the conclusion, after examining various data, that no trend in one direction or another can be proved. This will be discussed more fully in Chapter 9.

the need for considerable direct capital investment to be made in agriculture. Developing agriculture looks like a long, expensive task.

Despite these views, more and more it is recognized that considerable attention must be paid to the problems of agriculture, for improved agriculture has a significant role to play in development. The end product of efforts to improve agriculture is not agricultural development for its own sake but for total economic growth. Agriculture is one part of the total picture. For various reasons, then, agriculture cannot be overlooked. Some of these reasons are listed below.

1.  The great bulk of the people in underdeveloped countries make their living in agriculture.* From 50 to 70 or 80 percent of the people live on the farm, so progress there brings aid to the bulk of the people. Their health and happiness deserve consideration.

2.  Prosperous farmers can provide a market for the products of industry. If the factories could sell all their products to people in sectors other than agriculture, such as industry or commerce, or could sell their products abroad in return for things that are needed, including the necessary food and raw materials, developing agriculture would not be necessary. But the industry of underdeveloped countries is not likely to compete on an extensive scale in world markets, so that for some time to come it must rely on local markets. The bulk of this market must be the farmers. The farmers make up too large a proportion of the population to be allowed to remain in poverty, if markets are to develop. Any nation handicaps its economic activities if a substantial portion of the people are unprogressive economically.

Exchange between the farmers and the city leads to an increasing development of internal trade and the building up of roads and other means of communication. This, in turn, leads to diversification of the economic structure of the economy.

3.  Because it is unlikely that industry can earn enough abroad to obtain the necessary raw materials and food for its workers, a surplus production is necessary in agriculture. As industry grows and economic activity increases, purchasing power is made available to many, including the industrial workers and employees of commercial firms. The tendency is for these people to increase their expenditure almost to the full extent of their increased incomes. A major want is more food. If added food supplies are not available, the result will be rising food prices, which will result in pressure for increased wages and through this to generally rising prices. Thus, agricultural development is a major factor in slowing up the inflation that threatens most newly developing countries.

* See Table 4.1.

4. Agricultural surpluses may at times be used for export, thus building up foreign exchange balances and so enabling the country to import its needs, including industrial capital. Or increased productivity may mean that less food need be imported, thus saving foreign exchange.

5. Increased productivity in agriculture can, if one can keep the peasant from increasing his consumption or the size of his family, provide a source of savings. As we shall see, savings will probably not be voluntary, and those savings that are made will not be likely to find their way into industry. Any savings that are to come from the peasant will have to be extracted from him by taxation or forced sales of his output.

6. As productivity in agriculture grows, the workers who are needed in industry or other services can be supplied. All new economic activities require the release of workers from somewhere, from existing employment or from nonemployment. Moreover, if agricultural productivity increases and food prices drop, the real incomes of nonagricultural people will be improved.

7. A prosperous agriculture is often credited with affording political and social advantages. Politically, farm people are presumed to be conservative if they are prosperous and own their land. In such a situation, revolution is less likely. Where the peasant is not prosperous, there is a great source of tension, which the Communists find a favorable ground for the spread of their beliefs. Hunger and exploitation and peace are not compatible. Small owner-cultivated farms are also presumed to aid in the establishment of freedom and democracy.

Some favor emphasizing agriculture because this involves the least risk of failure, but not all programs are successful. Agricultural development is sometimes thought to involve the least amount of outside capital, but this, too, is doubtful if the job is done correctly. Politically, some effort must be made to help the farmer or he will resent what appear to be favors to the city workers, who probably earn more than he does anyway.

Thus, the problems of agriculture must be explored to see just what faces an underdeveloped country in this sector of the economy.

## The Agricultural Situation in Underdeveloped Countries

Agriculture is carried on under varying sets of circumstances throughout the world. Climatic conditions differ and various forms of land tenure are in effect. However, certain generalizations can be made about the agricultural characteristics of underdeveloped countries, and a list of often encountered problems can be made. The generalized problems discussed below may not give an accurate picture of any one country, but they will describe the situation in broad outline. In any specific situation, an exact description applicable to that locality would be necessary before a suitable policy could be formulated.

A large proportion of the population depends on agriculture for a living, and populations have usually grown beyond the best population-land ratio. This, of course, varies from country to country, Asia being far more "overpopulated," for example, than Latin America. Countries with a low density of population may be "overpopulated," in the sense that the land cannot support adequately the existing population. The number that can be supported by a given area depends on the character of the land, the crops raised, and the technology used. However, under current conditions, many of the underdeveloped countries have too many people on the land.

Table 4.2 shows the density of population per square kilometer in 1962. Care must be taken in interpreting this, however. In the first place, countries that are more advanced industrially can be expected to have a greater density of population. The problem lies in a dense population in those countries in which a large proportion of the population earns its living in agriculture and where agricultural methods are primitive. For this reason Table 4.2 presents separately those countries whose agricultural populations are more or less than 40 percent of the total. A second point to keep in mind is that in many countries the population is concentrated in a few areas and other areas are scarcely settled at all. Examples are Indonesia, Philippines, Malaysia, and much of South America. In the 1962 census, of a total population for Indonesia of 96 million, over 70 million lived in Java. The overall density was only 66 per square kilometer, whereas that in Java was roughly 600 per square kilometer. Lastly, the amount of land suitable for agriculture and the quality of land differ from country to country. Thus, only an acquaintance with the particular conditions in a given country would disclose whether there are too many people on the land. Nevertheless, a density of 100 means only 2.5 acres per person, which is a small amount of land under existing methods of cultivation, especially in dry areas or areas where only one crop can be grown per year.

In part, overcrowding on the land comes about because of the kinship system that leads to the retention of an uneconomic number on the land. Such overpopulation means that there is a great deal of unemployment, seasonal and concealed.* People may seem to be occupied and busy, but they may add little or nothing to total output. Most of the available labor may be busy at certain seasons, particularly planting and harvesting, so it is not at all certain that the crop would not be reduced if some labor were

* Unemployment is discussed in Chapter 6.

## TABLE 4.2.

*Density of Population in Selected Countries, 1962*
*(Population per square kilometer)*

| Country | Less than 40% of Population in Agriculture, Density | 40% or More of Population in Agriculture, Density |
|---|---|---|
| *Europe* | | |
| Austria | 85 | — |
| Belgium | 302 | — |
| Czechoslovakia | 108 | — |
| Denmark | 108 | — |
| Finland | 13 | — |
| France | 86 | — |
| Germany, West | 220 | — |
| Germany, East | 149 | — |
| Hungary | 108 | — |
| Iceland | 2 | — |
| Italy | 167 | — |
| Netherlands | 351 | — |
| Norway | 11 | — |
| Sweden | 17 | — |
| Switzerland | 137 | — |
| United Kingdom | 219 | — |
| U.S.S.R. | 10 | — |
| Bulgaria | — | 72 |
| Greece | — | 64 |
| Ireland | — | 40 |
| Poland | — | 97 |
| Portugal | — | 98 |
| Roumania | — | 79 |
| Spain | — | 61 |
| Yugoslavia | — | 74 |
| *North and Central America* | | |
| Canada | 2 | — |
| United States | 20 | — |
| Costa Rica | — | 25 |
| Cuba | — | 62 |
| Dominican Republic | — | 66 |
| El Salvador | — | 123 |
| Guatemala | — | 37 |
| Haiti | — | 157 |
| Honduras | — | 17 |
| Mexico | — | 19 |
| Nicaragua | — | 11 |
| Panama | — | 15 |
| *South America* | | |
| Argentina | 8 | — |
| Chile | 11 | — |
| Venezuela | 9 | — |
| Bolivia | — | 3 |

**TABLE 4.2.** (*Continued*)

| Country | Less than 40% of Population in Agriculture, Density | 40% or More of Population in Agriculture, Density |
|---|---|---|
| Brazil | — | 9 |
| Colombia | — | 13 |
| Ecuador | — | 17 |
| Paraguay | — | 5 |
| *Asia* | | |
| Israel | 111 | — |
| Ceylon | — | 159 |
| Taiwan | — | 315 |
| India | — | 148 |
| Indonesia | — | 66 |
| Iran | — | 2 |
| Japan | — | 257 |
| Korea, Rep. of | — | 269 |
| Malaya | — | 56 |
| Nepal | — | 68 |
| Pakistan | — | 102 |
| Philippines | — | 98 |
| Syria | — | 27 |
| Thailand | — | 34 |
| Turkey | — | 37 |
| *Africa* | | |
| South Africa | 30 | — |
| Algeria | — | 5 |
| Congo (Leopoldville) | — | 6 |
| Ghana | — | 30 |
| Mauritius | — | 1 |
| Morocco | — | 28 |
| Tunisia | — | 34 |
| United Arab Rep. | — | 27 |
| *Oceania* | | |
| Australia | 1 | — |
| New Zealand | 9 | — |

SOURCE: Food and Agricultural Organization, *Production Yearbook, 1963*, Table 5A, pp. 19 ff, and United Nations, Statistical Office, *Demographic Yearbook, 1963*, Table 1, pp. 123 ff.

taken from the farm. There is, however, a great deal of idle time,* which is not utilized in an underdeveloped state of a country because no outside employment is available. One problem, thus, is to obtain adequate labor at peak seasons while reducing unemployment at other seasons. Two solutions suggest themselves: one to provide supplemental employment and the other to undertake research to remove seasonal bottlenecks.

* A survey in Indonesia (*Report on Labour Force Sample Survey in Java and Madeira*. Indonesia, Ministry of Labour, 1961) reports that about one-third of the available labor time in the rural areas is wasted. For a more extended discussion, see Chapter 6.

# TABLE 4.3.

Ratio of per Capita Incomes in Agriculture to per Capita Incomes
in the Rest of the Economy, Average 1959-1961

| Country | Share of Agriculture in Gross Domestic Product (%) | Ratio of per Capita Incomes in Agriculture to Other Incomes |
|---|---|---|
| United States | 4 | 0.5 |
| Canada | 7 | 0.5 |
| Sweden | 9 | 0.5 |
| New Zealand | 11 | 0.6 |
| Australia | 13 | 0.9 |
| Switzerland | 5 | 0.4 |
| Denmark | 14 | 0.7 |
| Germany, Fed. Rep. | 6 | 0.6 |
| France | 10 | 0.5 |
| United Kingdom | 4 | 0.7 |
| Belgium | 7 | 0.6 |
| Norway | 11 | 0.5 |
| Venezuela | 7 | 0.2 |
| Israel | 12 | 0.6 |
| Netherlands | 10 | 1.0 |
| Finland | 21 | 0.6 |
| Austria | 12 | 0.7 |
| Puerto Rico | 12 | 0.3 |
| Trinidad and Tobago | 12 | 0.6 |
| Italy | 18 | 0.5 |
| Ireland | 26 | 0.4 |
| Chile | 14 | 0.3 |
| South Africa | 11 | 0.2 |
| Argentina | 16 | 0.6 |
| Panama | 23 | 0.4 |
| Cyprus | 22 | 0.8 |
| Japan | 15 | 0.3 |
| Greece | 30 | 0.5 |
| Spain | 26 | 0.4 |
| Mexico | 20 | 0.2 |
| Portugal | 25 | 0.5 |
| Malaysia | 45 | 1.0 |
| Colombia | 35 | 0.6 |
| El Salvador | 37 | 0.2 |
| Philippines | 34 | 0.2 |
| Honduras | 47 | 0.3 |
| Turkey | 41 | 0.4 |
| Guatemala | 32 | 0.2 |
| Ecuador | 36 | 0.4 |
| United Arab Republic | 31 | 0.3 |
| Taiwan | 32 | 0.5 |
| Thailand | 38 | 0.2 |
| India | 48 | 0.5 |
| Korea | 39 | 0.4 |

SOURCE: Food and Agriculture Organization, *The State of Food and Agriculture*. Rome, 1964, p. 69.

Partly as a result of the overpopulation on the land, agricultural workers' incomes are low compared with those of nonagricultural workers and are usually at or near subsistence level, although even in the high-income countries agricultural incomes are low compared with other incomes.

**TABLE 4.4.**

*Productivity of the Agricultural Population by Continents and for the World,[a] Prewar, and 1947-1948*

| Continent | Yield per Hectare | | | Yield per Person | | |
|---|---|---|---|---|---|---|
| | Prewar | 1947-48 | 1947-48 as % of prewar | Prewar | 1947-48 | 1947-48 as % of prewar |
| | (metric tons) | | | (metric tons) | | |
| World average | 1.24 | 1.30 | 105 | 0.42 | 0.42 | 100 |
| North & Central America | 1.07 | 1.50 | 140 | 1.80 | 2.57 | 143 |
| South America | 1.28 | 1.39 | 109 | 0.58 | 0.48 | 83 |
| Europe | 1.51 | 1.34 | 89 | 1.04 | 0.88 | 85 |
| Oceania | 1.06 | 1.20 | 113 | 1.94 | 2.38 | 123 |
| Asia | 1.26 | 1.20 | 95 | 0.24 | 0.22 | 92 |
| Africa | 0.77 | 0.73 | 95 | 0.12 | 0.12 | 100 |

SOURCE: Food and Agriculture Organization, *Monthly Bulletin of Food and and Agricultural Statistics,*
Vol. 2, No. 9 (September, 1949).
[a] Excluding U.S.S.R.

Table 4.4 shows for the immediate postwar period the low output per person in agriculture in South America, Africa, and Asia, where most of the underdeveloped countries are. More disturbing was the failure of output to keep up with the growth of population in agriculture. By 1963-1964, the indices of agricultural output per capita (which is a different method of measurement than yield per person in agriculture) compared with the 1948-1949 to 1952-1953 averages were: western Europe, 130.3 percent; eastern Europe and U.S.S.R., 131.5 percent; North America, 100.0 percent; Oceania, 111.1 percent; Latin America, 101.0 percent; Far East, 110.6 percent; Near East, 113.8 percent; and Africa, 102.1 percent.[3] Much of the increase in output in the underdeveloped areas was not due to increasing productivity but to enlarging the area under cultivation. The following increases have taken place in the crop area in the various regions[4]: North America, -3 percent; western Europe, -4 percent; eastern Europe, 6 percent; Oceania, 18 percent; Latin America, 41 percent; Far East, 24 percent; Near East, 65 percent; Africa, 50 percent. Although these statistics do not permit a direct comparison, it seems a reasonable conclusion that agricultural productivity is not increasing, or is increasing only slowly, in most of the underdeveloped world.

Table 4.5 further shows the differences in output among countries, per hectare and per man. In general, it will be observed that in both respects, output is lower in the underdeveloped areas than in the developed ones.

## TABLE 4.5.

### Output per Hectare and per Adult Male Engaged in Agriculture, Average for 1956-1960

| Country | Index of Output per Hectare[a] Italy = 100 | Output per Adult Male Engaged in Agriculture Italy = 100 |
|---|---|---|
| United Arab Rep. | 300 | |
| Netherlands | 280 | 319 |
| Taiwan | 270 | 47 |
| Belgium-Luxembourg | 230 | 379 |
| Japan | 215 | 41 |
| Denmark | 185 | 367 |
| Germany, Fed. Rep. | 160 | 291 |
| Malaya | 120 | |
| Korea, Rep. of | 120 | 17 |
| Ceylon | 120 | |
| Norway | 120 | 103 |
| Italy | 100 | 100 |
| Switzerland | 98 | 173 |
| Sweden | 95 | 244 |
| France | 90 | 204 |
| Austria | 85 | 153 |
| Finland | 80 | 107 |
| United Kingdom | 80 | 346 |
| Indonesia | 75 | |
| Portugal | 70 | |
| Philippines | 65 | 25 |
| Israel | 65 | 172 |
| Ireland | 65 | 162 |
| Pakistan | 60 | |
| New Zealand | 60 | 1380 |
| Spain | 55 | |
| Thailand | 50 | 21 |
| Yugoslavia | 50 | 53 |
| Burma | 45 | |
| Greece | 40 | 72 |
| United States | 40 | 869 |
| Chile | 40 | |
| India | 35 | 21 |
| Canada | 30 | 567 |
| Iraq | 30 | |
| Iran | 30 | 38 |
| Colombia | 25 | 49 |
| Turkey | 20 | |
| Peru | 20 | |
| Tunisia | 20 | 40 |
| Brazil | 20 | |

**TABLE 4.5.** (*Continued*)

| Country | Index of Output per Hectare[a] Italy = 100 | Output per Adult Male Engaged in Agriculture Italy = 100 |
|---|---|---|
| Honduras | 17 | |
| Morocco | 15 | 35 |
| Syria | 15 | |
| Uruguay | 15 | |
| Argentina | 13 | 224 |
| Mexico | 12 | |
| Algeria | 7 | 43 |
| Venezuela | 7 | 39 |
| South Africa | 7 | |
| Ethiopia | 5 | |
| Australia | 5 | 941 |

SOURCE: Food and Agriculture Organization, *The State of Food and Agriculture*, 1936, pp. 110, 117.
  [a] Estimated from diagram, for which figures are not given.

Population pressure is such that production is apt to be at the subsistence level on both good and poor lands. This may be illustrated by the curves in Figure 4.1. In the case of the good lands (solid lines), population grows to the point $P$ where everyone is at the subsistence level even though production has been carried beyond the point where marginal output has become zero. In the case of the poor lands (dotted lines), population similarly tends to move to the point where the average output just yields a subsistence living. In this case marginal output will be positive.

Although most of the farmers live at a subsistence level and are scarcely influenced by events in the outside world, in some areas there is an efficient agriculture geared to export or to sales to the commercial towns, also geared to export, which is usually developed by private capital from outside, often under a colonial system. This agriculture is generally organized on the plantation system and concentrates on a few key products; for example, rubber, coffee, tea, cacao, bananas, and copra. These are either owned by foreigners or the production is geared to the needs of foreign countries, and the fortunes of the owners are tied to the world market. The benefits of the trade accrue to a few and the masses benefit not at all.* The existence of this efficient section plus the market-oriented industrial centers alongside a subsistence agriculture is usually termed a "dual economy." † The pro-

* The reason for this is given in Chapter 9.
† S. Enke (*Economics for Development*. Englewood Cliffs, N. J., Prentice-Hall, Inc., 1963, p. 29) calls the economies "triple" economies: "the subsistence economy of the rural areas, the native market area in and around towns, and the foreign enclaves."

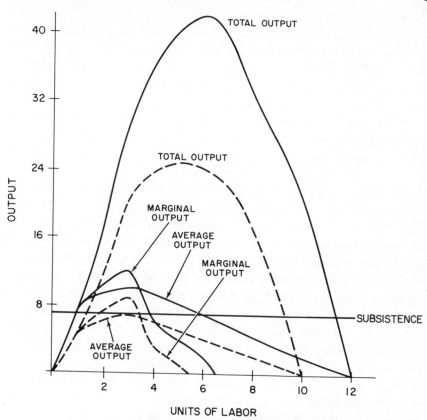

Figure 4.1    Effects of Population Pressure on the Land

> SOURCE: J. W. Mellor and R. D. Stevens, "Average
> and Marginal Product of Farm Labor in Under-
> developed Countries," *Journal of Farm Economics,*
> August 1956, pp. 780-91.
> NOTE: Solid lines represent good land, and dotted
> lines represent poor land.

duction of the export crops is usually on an efficient basis, but the subsistence section exhibits poor and primitive methods.

Not only is output per man low, but output per unit of land is also low,
although land is intensively cultivated. Table 4.5 shows the output per
hectare by continent. Asia and Africa are below the world average, although South America is above. William Brand [5] cites figures showing this
low production. In 1952 Japan produced 41.3 quintals of rice (1 quintal =
100 kilograms) per hectare; India, 11.8 quintals; Burma, 15.4 (1951);
Thailand, 12.9; and Indonesia, 15.8. In 1951 the United States output of
maize was 25.4 quintals per hectare; but Mexico produced 7.6; Colombia,

12.0; and Argentina, 15.1. In 1952 the United States yield of wheat was 12.3 quintals per hectare, but in Iraq it was 5.0; Jordan, 8.4; Lebanon, 7.4; and Syria, 7.3. Cultivation is intensive, but output is low because of a low expenditure of capital, poor technology, and inferior land that has been worn out from overcropping, and other reasons including all the defects listed below.

The agricultural structure, or the system of landholding or tenure, is often inefficient; that is, the size of the farms is not optimum, being either too small or too large; there is considerable tenancy with much exploitation; and in many areas there is insecure tenure.

Land may be held in various ways: by individual ownership of small plots, by individual ownership of large estates, or communally. The great majority live on small plots, sometimes under individual ownership, but just as often as tenants on the large estates. These plots tend to be too small to provide an adequate living under existing methods of cultivation and, in addition, are often fragmented. Holdings of small size result in a limited choice of crops and an inability to invest in capital equipment, fertilizers, and so on, which, when accompanied by low educational and training facilities, results in inferior techniques of cultivation. All this puts the producer in a poor bargaining position for purchasing and selling, especially when the farmer is in debt to the local middleman, supplier, or moneylender and must buy from and sell to his supplier. Because of excessive splitting of fields, because of inheritance laws or other reasons, even these small holdings may be fragmented. Fragmentation results in a waste of time and effort, an impossibility of introducing certain improvements such as irrigation by wells, prevents rational patterns of production, and increases the need for capital outlays or results in their failure to be adopted. The result of small fragmented holdings is a bare subsistence agriculture with little or no marketable output and no purchasing power.

Willard Thorp[6] sums up the situation by describing a typical peasant family. He reports the plight of the small peasant as: a family of six living on less than two acres, renting from an absentee landlord who may take up to two-thirds of the crop. The tenant has no security of tenure and may lose his land because someone offers the landlord more. He is badly in debt at high rates of interest. He works a worn-out soil with primitive tools and has never heard of commercial fertilizer; he uses some unselected seed saved from the previous crop. The two acres may be widely scattered, and he may have to walk as long as two hours to reach the nearest plot. He has no storage facilities, so he must sell what little surplus he has immediately and at whatever price is offered. He and his family work continuously, but their energy is sapped by malnutrition and bad health. It is a discouraging picture and there is no wonder the peasant cries for reform. It is also a poor base on which to try to build a program for economic growth.

On the other hand, land may be held in large estates. The characteristic feature of many of the Latin American countries is the excessive concentration of land ownership in large estates called *latifundia*. These are usually accompanied by tenancy and so afford no advantages of large-scale operation. Extensive grazing curtails the possibility of expanding food production, and the small farms are pushed into the hills so that considerable erosion takes place. Thus, there is reverse land use, with the hills cultivated and the valley floors grazed.[7] The concentration of ownership is extreme. In Guatemala, 0.15 percent of the farms represent 41 percent of the agricultural land. In Ecuador, 0.17 percent have 37 percent; in Venezuela, 74 percent of the farm acreage is in holdings over 1,000 hectares; and in Brazil, half of the farmland is held by 1.6 percent of the owners. Roughly, 90 percent of the agricultural land is held by 10 percent of the owners.[8] These *latifundia* include most of the best land, although much of their land also is uncultivable. Much of it remains idle. The owner usually lives in town, renting out the land to tenants or having it farmed by laborers who work a certain number of days for the owner in return for small plots of land they may cultivate for themselves. Cultivation generally is inefficient, and the excessive concentration limits the distribution of income to a level that is exploitive by modern standards.

In many areas of the world there are large estates or plantations, centrally managed and efficient, that use hired labor to produce crops for export. The most usual crops are rubber, coffee, tea, sugar, bananas, copra, and palm oil. These plantations have generally been productive, although small producers in some areas have been able to compete and supplement plantation supply. R. Kool [9] believes that estate agriculture offers a country a better prospect for rapid economic development than any other system because of its productivity and efficiency. It has the advantage of good management, modern methods, lower capital investment per unit of output, and less labor per unit of output. Estate agriculture, however, has handicaps. Usually, conditions of employment are unsatisfactory. The worker has no responsibility or chance to show initiative. The economy is dependent on world prices. When foreign capital and management leave, there is difficulty in getting efficient management. Lastly, estate agriculture may dominate the economy so that crop rotation is lessened and food production decreased. The dependence of Cuba on sugar is a case in point.[10] Few countries have been as dependent on one crop as was Cuba before the Revolution. Two-thirds of the cultivated land was in sugar, and sugar constituted four-fifths of the exports. One-third of the workers worked directly in sugar and many others were indirectly dependent on it, such as in processing, trade, and transportation. Sugar brought Cuba a relatively high per capita income, but made her vulnerable to outside price fluctuations and outside legislation, such as tariffs and quotas. The distribution of wealth and income was very uneven. The plantations were mostly foreign-owned, as were the utilities, transportation systems, banks, and insurance companies. Most farmers were landless or held small, insufficient plots. The lopsidedness of the economy was one reason for the Revolution there.

A third type of ownership is communal ownership. This has been more widespread in Africa south of the Sahara and is the most important form of land tenure there.[11] There, land has been held in various ways: tribal, village, or family. In parts of Latin America the Indians often hold land communally through the extended family.[12] Much of the work may be done communally, also. A third example is the Mexican *ejido,* where land is held by the village and allotted to the members of the village.

Several difficulties are inherent in communal ownership. To treat people fairly, the land is allotted to them in strips or fragments or is reallocated periodically, but this system provides little incentive for the individual to make improvements. Because ownership and control are by the group, it may be difficult to get improvements accepted. Also, because the individual does not own the land, he may have difficulty getting credit.

The size of holdings is uneconomic in most countries, and considerable tenancy exists with absentee ownership and high rents. The proportion of tenants varies from country to country, but is universally high in underdeveloped countries, even exceeding 50 percent.[13] Tenancy in itself is not bad, but as it has developed in the underdeveloped countries, it has not been consistent with either economic growth or social justice. Rents are high, rising to two-thirds of the crop in some areas, although the usual rent is one-half the crop, with the tenant and the landlord supplying various shares of the inputs.[14] Occasionally, money rents are charged, and in Latin America there are some labor rents. Rents are high and tenure is often insecure; that is, the landlord can remove the tenant any year he wishes, although he usually must wait until the crop is harvested. Accordingly, the tenant cannot afford to improve the land, for someone else may get the benefit of it; for example, another peasant may bid a higher percentage of the output to get such an improved farm. If the peasant invests in fertilizer to increase his crop, the landlord will get half of the additional produce, so that the increased investment may not pay the peasant. In fact, there is every incentive for him to mine the soil. The result is that no effort is made to maintain or conserve the soil or prevent erosion. As a result, much of the agricultural land of the underdeveloped countries is in poor condition.

In some areas,[15] "owners" have no legal title because there has never been a system of land registry. In the mid-East the legal position of the landowner is confused. Because rights are not certain, particularly in the case of water rights, the peasant may find he has no alternative except to sell his land to the large landowner.

Another major problem is that the peasant is poorly educated and poorly trained. Rural schools are often nonexistent or are poor at best when they do exist. The bulk of the rural population may be illiterate. In Indonesia[16] only 30.27 percent of the rural population has been reported as literate. This compares favorably with most other underdeveloped countries. Extension services and agricultural advice are likely to be nonexistent. Farming methods are custom-ridden and primitive, and provide little consideration for fertilization, weed control, and so on. Decision making may be a problem if the extended family exists, and innovation is difficult in the face of the tendency of the community to look with disfavor on innovations.

The small peasant lacks dependable markets and the necessary appurtenances to markets, such as adequate roads, transportation, storage, and processing facilities. The peasant must usually market locally, must sell when the crop is harvested, and often must allocate it to his creditor. His surplus is likely to be small and sold in the local bazaar to which the peasant (or more likely his wife) carries the produce on his back or head or with a carrying stick, traveling many miles to the point of sale. The seller may sit all day in the market to sell very little, perhaps a dozen eggs or a small amount of rice. Almost unbelievably, a score or more may come from the same village, each carrying an equally small amount. One suspects that the man-hours lost by inefficient marketing and transportation constitute a sizable fraction of the labor time.

The peasant lacks cheap credit with which to buy machinery or to adopt improved practices such as improved seeds, fertilizers, and pesticides. Credit is usually in the hands of the village moneylender or the merchant who buys the crop. The peasant is perpetually in debt, often to finance the customary celebrations of marriage, death, birth, manhood, and other occasions almost too numerous to mention. Interest rates are high, but the risk to the lender is high, also. A crop failure or the death of the farmer can easily end any chance of repayment.

Farmers are typically heavily taxed because land and products are visible, whereas it is difficult to administer an income tax. The tax systems of underdeveloped countries largely concentrate on commodity taxes.

The rural village is little developed. Water supplies are often unprotected and polluted, and sewage and garbage disposal is so haphazard that health hazards are usual. Communications with other villages are meager.

Agricultural conditions are not favorable in the tropics.[17] The soils have been neglected and are badly eroded. Rain and temperature combine to eliminate the best soil elements; unsystematic deforestation and cultivation on higher lands has caused erosion; intensive cultivation and poor soil maintenance has worn out the land; and population pressure has pushed the margin of cultivation onto the inferior lands. The tropics are favorable for the development of plant diseases, insects, and weeds. Pests, particularly rats, abound. Climatic conditions are often unfavorable. Rainfall may be irregular, with alternating wet and dry seasons. Natural elements play their part, as in the hurricane belt of the Caribbean. It was formerly believed that the climate in many areas was too hot for effective work, but this is probably not true. The past greatness of many of the underdeveloped areas attests to the fact that it is not impossible to be energetic in such areas. The introduction of modern medicines and diets has shown the possibility of overcoming the enervating effects of heat. The problem lies in the ease with which diseases can spread and with the difficulty of maintaining the soils properly.

Lastly, there is a problem of fluctuating prices and poor terms of trade for the export crops.* During World War II and the Korean incident, the demand for agricultural products and raw materials was high and the primary producing countries were prosperous. During the 1930's and after World War II, demands declined and prices fell greatly. These fluctuations arising from world conditions have a drastic effect, for the supply of these products is often so inelastic that decreases in demand depress prices badly, and vice versa. Whether the long-run terms of trade have been against these countries is a matter in dispute, but the disrupting effects of sudden changes in price is not. As prices fall, foreign exchange becomes short and financial difficulties arise. Development plans may have to be postponed because needed capital goods cannot be paid for.

Thus, the problems of agriculture are many and serious. Although not all are true of any one country, there is considerable uniformity. However, one should acquaint himself with the particular situation of the area in which he is interested. A brief description of the agricultural situation in various parts of the world will indicate the diversities and the similarities.[18]

The outstanding feature of agriculture in Latin America is the existence of large estates with many small farms, many of which are too small to afford a satisfactory living. The large estates are of two types. The first are the large centrally managed estates, called *latifundia,* devoted to the extensive growing of cereals or livestock operations and operated by paid labor or unpaid labor given in return for subsistence holdings. Argentinian wheat

* This will be developed in Chapter 9.

and cattle ranches are examples. The second type is the plantation, which is centrally and efficiently managed and which grows export crops, such as coffee and cacao in Brazil, sugar in Cuba, and bananas and coffee in Central America. Such large estates mean great concentration of land ownership and, in turn, an extreme maldistribution of income and a resulting concentration of political and economic power. In San Salvador, 4 percent of the owners own over two-thirds of the tillable land[19]; in Venezuela, 1.7 percent own 75 percent of the land[20]; and in Peru, 2 percent own 70 percent of the land.[21] A similar situation exists in most countries.

Land is abundant but much of it is wasted on the large *latifundia* so that little land is available to the small farmer. Much of that is fragmented. Productivity is low because the farmer is poorly trained, sufficient cheap credit is not available to the small farmer, and land holdings are of an uneconomic size. Concentration on export crops makes the area vulnerable to changes in world demand and price. Coffee, in particular, is now in oversupply, with large surpluses accumulating. Other problems arise from the communal land holdings of some Indian villages and from the system of unpaid hired labor previously mentioned.

In the Middle East there is considerable land in relation to population, but there is not enough water, without which the land yields nothing. Thus, the major limitation on output is water, the availability varying throughout the area. Egypt has the waters of the Nile to provide a narrow strip of cultivation, and Iraq and Lebanon have relatively more water than other countries in this area. In general, there has been concentration of ownership, with agriculture carried on under a tenancy system in which rents are very high and tenure insecure. Agricultural production is poor because of inferior implements and obsolete methods, resulting in low productivity. A special feature is the inadequacy of land registration and water rights. Israel represents a special situation in its public ownership of all land, with land being assigned more or less perpetually. It differs also in that it has a large-scale land settlement program and a highly developed form of cooperative holding called the *kibbutz*.[22]

Characteristic of African agriculture is communal tenure over large areas, deteriorating land, shifting agriculture, and poor methods except on the large plantations. Much of the land is owned by the tribe and is assigned by the chief, resulting often in fragmented plots or rotating occupancy, which is not conducive to proper maintenance. In addition, the tropical climate has a tendency to leach the soil and erode the land so that the land is poor. Clearing the forest exposes the land to the elements so that it is soon washed away. Because long fallow is needed, the agricultural sites shift constantly so that much land is needed per capita. Land is relatively abundant, but is expensive to clear. For the most part, primitive and traditional methods of culture are followed and agriculture is at a subsistence level. The exceptions, of course, are the large foreign-owned plantations that practice modern agriculture.

In Asia, the chief characteristics are a high density of the rural population which results in uneconomic small units, often fragmented, cultivated with labor-intensive methods, and a great deal of seasonal unemployment and underemployment. Antiquated farming methods, extremely high farm tenancy with high rents and heavy debt, decreasing soil fertility because of heavy cropping, inadequate credit conditions for the farmer, and farms clustered about the rural village all mitigate against a thriving agriculture. In some areas plantations are important; for example, rubber in Malaya and Indonesia, copra and sugar in Indonesia, tea in Ceylon, etc.

## Agricultural Reform

There is sometimes a tendency to think of agricultural reform as simply a change in land ownership, but this is too limiting a concept. Agricultural reform includes remedies for all the ills mentioned in the preceding section. It includes establishing farm units in the most economical size; providing security of tenure and controlling tenancy charges; providing clear titles to land and water; instituting adequate transportation and storage facilities; making adequate credit available at reasonable rates; providing efficient marketing methods, including the control of quality; seeing that taxes are equitable; improving agricultural techniques and equipment; educating the farmer generally and vocationally, probably in part through extension services; utilizing the land better; controlling floods and erosion; providing alternative employment opportunities in order to remove the excess workers; improving social and health conditions in the villages; regulating the conditions of the agricultural laborer; and even creating new land or moving people to unoccupied lands. Research to accomplish these reforms is a major part of any program.

It will be noted that some of these reforms are beyond the control of the individual farmer; for example, instituting the proper size of farm, providing clear titles, improving transportation facilities, preventing floods, and others. Although the individual farmer could undertake some part of the program, such as the use of improved techniques, it is a major problem to get him to do so. Thus, in all phases of the program the state finds itself involved. The biggest problem may be just to convince the peasant that it is desirable to work harder and that he can increase his scale of living.[23] He hesitates to change because he is close to subsistence and does not wish to take a chance on something new; he may be afraid to alienate the money-lender and the landowner; and he may even have to overcome the ridicule of his fellows who are bound to traditional practices.

Modern programs tend to be total plans and comprise a combination of measures.[24] Concentration on one program alone is of limited effect, for improvement along one line is soon limited if no improvement is made along others. For example, mere redistribution of land may not increase production. Along with it must go improved farming methods. The individual peasant is not likely to increase production without improved credit, transportation, storage, and improved methods, to mention a few. Small holdings and an independent peasantry put a great burden on the effort to improve agricultural practices, for increased knowledge and desire as well as the improvements must be transmitted to many individuals. Redistributing the land will not do this.

One difficulty is to decide what the objectives of an agricultural reform program should be. Various measures are possible, but the same ones may not be suitable for each program. For example, the peasant's desire for land ownership and the government's desire for efficient operation may not be compatible. Various goals may be: to maximize economic growth, to integrate agriculture into the general economy, to increase total food output, to become self-sufficient in food, to increase the efficiency of agriculture. Or they may be: to increase the output per acre or per man, to divide up the land so that the cultivator will be the owner, to improve land use particularly in seeing that unused land is used, or, as in the case of the Communist countries, to apply the Marxian doctrine of the evils of private ownership to agriculture.

Since there are seldom only a few objectives, desired programs are far from simple. Probably the prevailing motive in land reform movements has been that of justice, of which the chief means is redistributing the land. For purposes of inducing economic growth, the proper objective would be the most effective use of the factors employed, with a view to meeting the level of food and material needs consistent with the rest of the development program. Probably everyone would agree on maximum efficiency as a goal, but this might run counter to the cry of "to the tiller, the soil." Moreover, efficiency must be defined at a predetermined level of output. Even the most efficient combination employed to produce a level of output necessary for self-sufficiency may be inefficient because some part of the produce might be obtained, with a lesser expenditure of economic factors, by importation. The first decision is to determine the amount of agricultural activity which is to be sought, which will depend on the total development strategy.* After that is decided, the proper objective is the most efficient use of the factors of

* This will be discussed in Chapter 14.

production, modified by objectives of employment, widespread ownership, and so on, that a nation may desire.

A discussion of the general nature of reform programs will indicate what objectives are currently being followed and what is generally appropriate to increased efficiency. Again, one should be reminded that any program must fit a particular situation, for no two countries face exactly the same set of circumstances. There can be no standardized development program laid down for agriculture.

The first effort is usually to break up subsistence farming and to draw more and more farmers and more and more of the produce of each farmer into commercial agriculture. The extent to which this should be done is not easy to decide, for more is involved than economic problems only. As will be noted below, commercial agriculture involves, among other things, giving up kinship or extended family arrangements; establishing larger holdings than most reform measures contemplate; and requiring what might be unpalatable techniques for getting the crops into the market.

The first requirement, if agriculture is to be commercialized, is to break up the various forms of kinship arrangements or other communal sharing systems and to make each unit family dependent on its own efforts. With the kinship system, innovation is difficult, for it requires a group decision; there is a tendency toward overpopulation of a given area and a resulting great deal of seasonal unemployment through much of the year. The surplus population does not easily leave the security of the farm, and there is no particular incentive to work hard, for the product is shared by all.

The second requirement is to draw the individual families into commerce. Subsistence farming can and does exist on small individual farms with only occasional outside sales, unless efforts are made to draw the people into commerce. First of all, there must be a market, which will be found in export sales or in growing towns. Because most underdeveloped countries do not look with favor on increasing agricultural production for export as a primary development measure, the problem of finding markets is essentially one of increasing domestic markets. This is dependent on increasing urban jobs in industry, commerce, or services. Thus, agriculture cannot develop in isolation. Unless there are changes in the rest of the economy, commercial agriculture cannot develop. To take advantage of market opportunities, a host of service requirements must be met, such as transportation facilities, storage, possibly refrigeration facilities, an honest marketing system, and dependable sources of supply. Local processing plants would be helpful in serving as a market and would provide the beginning of industrialization. In particular, marketing practices as they now exist must be improved.[25] Forced sales to a supplier or creditor must be minimized.

Grades and standards must be established at least in an elementary way so that quality can be upgraded, standards of weights and measures maintained, and sanitary and health requirements provided.

A very real question is the speed at which a market will develop. This depends on the speed at which purchasing power will increase, either through rising incomes or increased population, and the income elasticity of demand for agricultural products. The commercialization of agriculture cannot proceed faster than the increase in demand for the products without depressing agricultural prices, assuming a relatively inelastic demand with respect to price. Therefore, it is likely that a substantial subsistence sector will be retained in agriculture for some time unless general economic growth is quite rapid.

If more products are to come into the market, the peasant must be induced or forced not to consume more himself, either in the form of a higher standard of consumption or larger families. Many peasants will not automatically respond to market incentives, but continue on the old subsistence basis because a change may be in conflict with tradition. Changing to a market economy will take time and probably will spread outward from developing towns. A number of techniques have been tried to get the peasant to part with his crop. Some of these may not be acceptable socially. In each particular case, a country may have to compromise between its economic and social objectives. Available techniques are: to increase the desire for nonagricultural consumption goods, thus increasing the peasant's desire for cash; requiring the peasant to sell to the government a certain proportion of his crop at a fixed price (if this fixed price is below the market price, there will probably be a problem of evasion and enforcement; if the price is much too low, the peasant may divert his efforts to another crop); levying taxes payable in money; permitting an unequal distribution of land, thus obtaining a surplus on the larger farms; adopting a substantial segment of plantation-type agriculture; encouraging farm indebtedness; if available, introducing easily applied and acceptable techniques that will increase the total crop quickly (although this is only a doubtful hope); or, as under the Communist system, instituting collective farms.

The third requirement, in part, for the commercialization of agriculture may be the necessity for peasants to introduce new crops and to undertake a certain degree of specialization. If the history of agriculture in the United States is a valid example, one can expect the nature of agriculture in any area to make a number of shifts. First comes subsistence agriculture. Second, there is a gradual growth with increased outputs of the same types, the surplus going to the cities. Then, one can expect the gradual movement of the more readily transported products (such as wheat in the United States) to less developed areas, with the older areas concentrating on the less transportable, and eventually, as the region industrializes or commercializes, concentrating on truck gardening, dairying, and other specialties. A developing country must be prepared for such transformation of agriculture and must be prepared to give the farmer the necessary technical advice and credit. Fortunately, the beginning step is probably to increase the output of existing crops, but specialty farming may not be far behind. This may create a problem for tropical agriculture, for specialization may require a greater effort to maintain the poor soils. Mixed agriculture is probably a better way to maintain soil fertility. This difficulty may impose a major barrier to development at some point.

A further problem of commercialized agriculture is that it will increase the demand for hired labor, with resulting problems of income and working conditions, especially if some large-sized farms are allowed to develop. These are sizable problems but commercialization of agriculture is a necessity. The question is how, how fast, and on what kind of farms.

The second aspect of an agricultural reform program is to get an acceptable form of land tenure. Two extreme solutions—breaking up the land into small holdings in order to provide ownership for the bulk of the peasants and the Soviet-type collective farm—and, in between, a considerable variety of modifications of these types, have been the result.[26]

"Land to the landless" and "To the tiller belongs the soil" are popular cries in many areas and programs. Various countries have instituted such reforms by forcing the dissolution of large estates and redistributing the land among small holders.*

The Japanese plan, promoted by the United States under the Occupation, was based essentially on establishing individual farms plus aid to make these farms efficient. The basis of the plan was the compulsory sale at fixed government prices of all the land of absentee landholders, of all land above 2.45 acres (1 cho) of resident landlords, and all holdings above 7.35 acres.† Payment was made in long-term government bonds at a low interest rate (3.2 percent). The value was the presumed capitalized value of the share of the land in the net income and was calculated by applying factors to the 1938 rental value of the various categories of land. The valuations were low and, owing to the inflation that occurred, amounted virtually to confiscation. The land was distributed in holdings of 2.45 acres or less to tenants and farm laborers at the purchase price, payable in thirty-year installments at 3.2 percent interest. Inflation made these terms very easy,

* The best known of the schemes of this type are probably those of Japan, Egypt, and India, but there are similar plans in all parts of the world.
† The latter two provisions were to be national averages and not absolute figures.

especially when compared with former arrangements in which the tenant gave up half or more of his crop for rent and paid excessive interest rates. In less than two years almost three million persons acquired land and 92 percent of the land became owner-operated.[27]

In addition, the program controlled rents, provided for cash rentals and secure tenure, and, later on, included the reclamation of undeveloped land, irrigation, watershed protection, afforestation, and the institution of a program to change the people's diet (for example, toward wheat, beef, and dairy products). An important feature of the program has been an effort to increase the productivity of the farmer, an effort that seems to have been successful. Japanese food production, for example, was at an index of 133 for 1962 to 1963, with 100 equaling the average output of 1952-1953 to 1956-1957.

There seems universal acceptance that the program has been successful. Two examples will indicate the degree of praise. Ladejinsky[28] describes the results as instilling considerable initiative in the Japanese farmer and his striving to improve and accumulate a large increase in investment, a great increase in productivity, an increased quest for education, a stronger political influence, and a rising market for Japanese industrial output. M. Kaihara[29] says the program minimized the social and economic chaos that followed defeat in World War II, contributed to industrial reconstruction through lower food prices, augmented agricultural output, and was the motivating power behind economic progress.

It seems obvious that the program proved a success for the time being. However, the small size of farms may now be a barrier to further progress. As reported in the *Washington Post*,[30] Japanese experts warned the nation that production was threatened by "the nation's inability to effect a transformation from 'farming' to the wider scope of 'agriculture.' " The article points out that 74 percent of the farmers were supplementing their incomes elsewhere and that only 30 percent of all farm households could be considered genuine farm families. The farmer has turned to machinery, but the farms are too small to use efficient machinery. The solution given was the development of larger farms.

The Egyptian program (1952) seems also to have been successful in maintaining productivity. It required the compulsory surrender of all over 200 feddans (approximately 200 acres), with some exceptions. In 1961 this was reduced to 100 feddans. The owner could also transfer 50 feddans to a child, but only a total of 100 feddans. He could also sell his land under some restrictions, but no more than 5 feddans to any one purchaser. He was compensated at ten times the rental value of the land, which was estimated as seven times the basic land tax—a low price. He was paid in thirty-year, 3 percent bonds, which was later changed to forty-year, 1½ percent bonds. Land was distributed in lots of two to five feddans, with the following order of priority: the tiller, large families, the less wealthy. The orchards were distributed to graduates of agricultural institutes. The payment price was the requisition price plus 15 percent for expenses, payable in thirty annual installments at 3 percent interest. An important feature was that all owners had to join an agricultural cooperative so that there could be production planning and adequate guidance. The operation of these cooperatives is described by K. H. Parsons[31] as follows: Usually each owner has three plots, each being an integral part of a larger field of fifty to a hundred similar plots. The whole village area is thus cropped in a three-field pattern. This permits a common rotational pattern, concentrates the crops that are to be sprayed, and protects the cotton from seepage from rice irrigation. For certain purposes (for example, deep tillage, fertilizer application, irrigation, and insect control) the village is treated as a single unit, the work being done at the direction of the central management and each landholder being charged the cost. Seeding, cultivation, and harvesting are performed by the individual. The cotton is marketed cooperatively and credit provided cooperatively. Parsons further states that incomes have been increased because of the retention of the incentive of individual ownership, a reduction in the annual cost of the land, maintenance of a high quality of technical management, cooperative purchasing of supplies at lower cost, and higher returns from cooperative marketing.

Other programs to establish small farms as the major agricultural unit have usually not been so far-reaching nor so successful.* In general, the programs are similar: A maximum amount of land which can be retained is set, usually without regard to the quality of the land or to the most economic size of the unit. Payment to the former holder is made at a low valuation in long-term bonds paying a low rate of interest. Distribution is in small plots, often too small to be efficient, usually to those already actually tilling the land—tenants and agricultural laborers. The cost is usually low and on convenient terms.

The general objectives of dividing the land—increased production and the effort to get political stability by satisfying the peasant's land hunger— may be inconsistent, depending on the economies of scale in agriculture. The present schemes have perhaps tried to satisfy the political objective rather than the economic in an effort to prevent revolution, eliminate the powerful and conservative landed aristocracy, and perhaps promote democ-

---

* Taiwan seems to have had a successful program. See Tsui Young-Chi, "Land-Use Improvement: A Key to the Economic Development of Taiwan." *Journal of Farm Economics* (May, 1962), pp. 363-72.

racy. Communists exploit the maldistribution of land and income, and redistribution relieves this at least temporarily. But, unless there is enough land to satisfy all, and unless the division is economic and permits an adequate living, resentment is apt to rise again. Thus, in the long run the real question must be whether redistribution into small plots is capable of permitting increased productivity. There is no evidence that this is so, and there seems to have been little consideration given in the usual program to the economics of farm size. There are just too many landless people to permit distribution to all in economically sized units. The immediate effect of redistribution is often to decrease productivity through loss of efficient direction and capital. Unless programs are undertaken at the same time to aid the farmer with respect to technical advice, credit, marketing, and so on, he may be worse off after redistribution and productivity may be down.

The redistribution programs, however, seem to operate on the unproven assumption that there are economies in large-scale agriculture, so that ways must be devised to retain the incentives of ownership, yet provide some way to combine these farms into larger units with better management. This is a recognition that only in exceptional cases, like Japan's, can small-scale farming be immediately successful. The barriers to training large numbers of small farmers to become good farmers immediately are too great.

The best size of farm and type of tenure is a debatable question and probably differs for each country. Therefore, it is necessary for each country to study its own situation and to decide on its program on the basis of facts. The important thing is the facts.* In considering this question some presumed advantages and disadvantages of large- and small-scale farms should be observed.

The possible advantages of large-scale operations for underdeveloped countries are: trained management can be afforded; the most advanced methods can be used, and there are means of enforcing their employment over a large area; more efficient machines may be available, and these can be more fully utilized; these farms have better means of yielding surpluses; better bargaining power in the purchase of supplies; credit is likely, and marketing techniques are apt to be better. Its chief advantages are more likely to be realized where the product must be marketed in large volume and must be graded or standardized, where returns on the investment are long delayed, and where large amounts of capital are needed.

The disadvantages of large-scale farming are: the lack of incentive to the workers; the inability to shift out of one product if the market becomes

---

* It should be recognized that the optimum size may change as incomes increase, technologies change, and so on. A reform movement that attempted to freeze the unit size and tenure once and for all would be unwise.

poor; the tying up of large amounts of capital; the lessening of democratic political control; often the necessity for relying on unstable foreign markets; and the possibility of foreign domination.

Small-scale peasant agriculture also has its advantages: The owner has an incentive to develop his land and work hard; political conservatism is likely; and less social distinction and a growth of democracy are likely. But farms cannot be too small or fragmented. K. H. Parsons[32] believes the most efficient size of farm is quite small, and E. L. Long[33] states that if the criterion of efficiency is taken to be "the gross value productivity per acre above variable capital costs," which he advocates as the proper standard for capital-poor, labor-plentiful countries, the early data for India indicate advantages for the small farm, although they do not prove this. The real need is to get the facts about the optimum size.

The extreme alternative is to eliminate the small farm as much as possible and adopt the collective farm system, as in the Russian *Kolkhoz* and in other Communist countries. The collective farm was expected to lead to increased production through mechanization and improved management. Soviet Russia and its followers seem to have a firm belief in the economies of large-scale agriculture.* The formation of collective farms has not notably increased food production, which is still the weak point in the Russian and Chinese economies, although accurate information to substantiate this is not available. The peasants do not seem to be any better off, especially in China, and they have no hope of attaining the status of owners. If collectives have not increased production, they have been efficient in extracting surpluses from the peasant and keeping down his consumption and income, which was the major problem with small-scale farming in Russia in the early period following the revolution. The collective and its methods represents development by exploitation, which is impossible without rigid state control. This is not acceptable to many peoples. On the other hand, for those who wish to impose a dictatorship, it is an aid in establishing control over the people. For Communists it is considered desirable, for private ownership of land does not fit in with their convictions. Thus, the decision to collectivize involves as many noneconomic considerations, which may interfere with efficiency, as does the opposing system of small private farms.

Various intermediate alternatives have been tried as a means of keeping large units but dividing the land rights.

A unique type is the *kibbutz* in Israel. Under this arrangement a large farm is owned and operated cooperatively by a group of families. Or rather

* B. A. Balassa ("Collectivization in Hungarian Agriculture." *Journal of Farm Economics* (February, 1960), pp. 35-51) describes the Hungarian experience of attempting large farms and extensive agriculture in a country which, he says, is suited for intensive agriculture. The results have been a deterioration in output.

it is operated communally, for the income is shared and even meals may be taken in common. The usual arrangement is for the election of a board of management, which assigns jobs and supervises the operations. These seem to have been successful, but successful communal living has not been a common experience among many peoples.

A second special type is the Mexican *ejido*.[34] Under the Mexican agrarian reform, land was assigned to the villages, which reassigned it collectively or to individuals who could keep it as long as they cultivated it. The individual could not sell or mortgage his land. Actually, the *ejido,* as it generally operates, has not preserved any advantages of large units or centralized direction. The land has been divided into small plots and progress is no longer great.

A plan that has experienced considerable success is the Gezira plan in the Sudan, a government-sponsored project.[35] This project was started in the early 1920's as a joint venture of government, a commercial firm, and the tenants, and covers over one million acres. In 1950 the government assumed the functions of the commercial firm. Originally, the tenant received 40 percent of the profits; the government, 40 percent; and the company, 20 percent. In addition, the tenant kept all the millet and lubia* he raised. Each tenant received forty feddans of land, ten of which he planted to cotton, five to millet, and five to lubia, while twenty lay fallow. The government provided the land through purchase or lease, built the dams and canals, and was responsible for the supply of water. The concession companies, and now the government, supplied the subsidiary canals; cleared and leveled the land; operated the ginning factories; supplied buildings and machines; managed and supervised the land and cultivation; collected, stored, and marketed the crop; and made loans to the tenants. The tenant was responsible for supplying the labor to grow the crops and for the preparation and maintenance of the field irrigation systems. The results have been impressively successful.

The Gezira scheme is the most productive sector of the Sudan economy and in 1954 accounted for nearly half of the country's total exports. At that time it gave full-time employment to 29,000 tenants and 2,000 employers; the average annual income per tenant was 222 Egyptian pounds, considerably higher than that of any other comparable rural population in Africa. Apart from the substantial increase in income, the Gezira scheme also succeeded in less than two decades in transforming primitive and seminomadic tribes into a community of educated farmers.[36]

A fourth alternative is the formation of producers' cooperatives.[37] These are voluntary organizations of farmers in which the management of certain functions is turned over to an elected management to be carried out for the

* These are the chief food grains of the Sudanese.

ECONOMIC GROWTH AND DEVELOPMENT

benefit of all. They may be single-purpose or multipurpose. They have on occasion been helpful in providing credit, purchasing supplies such as fertilizer, providing machinery, improving livestock, seed distribution, pest control, marketing, and processing. They may also supply technical assistance, but it is questionable whether they can do this as efficiently as government extension services.

Cooperatives have borne the hopes of many underdeveloped countries as the means to greater agricultural efficiency*; and many governments encourage them and give subsidies, special loan facilities, or tax exemption or reduction. However, cooperatives are advantageous only if the peasants will join them and if they have efficient management and adequate finances. The first two conditions have been the weak points of cooperatives. They do hold promise, but efforts must be made to train good managers and to promote their acceptance.

Puerto Rico has tried to solve the problem by operating the expropriated estates as public corporations. An effort is made to give the workers a sense of ownership by giving them a share in the profits. Productive efficiency seems to have been maintained.[38]

A last alternative is to maintain enough large estates to produce the crops that are necessary for growth and turn the remainder of the land over to small-scale agriculture.[39] This rests on the assumption (unproved) that estate agriculture represents a better chance than small-scale agriculture for increased production and rapid economic development. Presumably, efforts to aid the small farmers to develop efficiently could be a part of this program. Actually, this simply amounts to trying to develop agriculture section by section rather than all at once. Leaving out considerations of equitable treatment, this may be the fastest way to develop agriculture, that is, by spreading out good practices from the originally established efficient areas. In the meantime, subsistence agriculture could be used as a "dumping ground" for surplus labor until expansion could absorb it. In the developed countries, prosperity did not come to all simultaneously and there were always pockets of low-paid labor, especially in agriculture, sales and services, and domestic services. Growth has improved conditions in these occupations as labor has become short in supply. These same areas, with the addition of the local transportation industry, are also the areas of excess supply and low-wage employment in the present underdeveloped countries. This solution of expanding certain prime areas while leaving others stag-

* For example, Colombia, Costa Rica, Peru, Chile, Ecuador, Haiti, Puerto Rico, Surinam, Malaya, Thailand, Taiwan, Philippines, Indonesia, India, Japan, Egypt, Israel, Morocco, Sudan, and many other countries have programs to promote cooperatives.

nant does not present a happy outlook in terms of equity, but it may prove most efficient in increasing the total output.

There is no single answer. What is needed in every country is research to pinpoint the best form of landholding to meet the country's manifold objectives.

As part of the effort to reform land tenure, many countries exercise a control over farm tenancy.[40] These are concerned with two major problems: insecurity of tenure and excessive rents. Typical corrective measures are protection against arbitrary eviction, minimum lease periods, and the right to purchase the land at some multiple of the annual rent. Undesirable rent practices are curtailed by setting limits on the rent charged, prohibiting personal service as a means of rent payment, and providing compensation for improvements.

Tenancy under arrangements that are fair to both tenant and landlord is desirable, for tenancy is a useful transition to ownership.

Too small farms or fragmented farms in many parts of the world constitute one of the major obstacles to growth. Unfortunately, much less effort is devoted to combining such holdings into efficient units than to breaking up large units.[41] The chief measures used are commissions for voluntary land consolidation and exchange, and prohibition against selling or bequeathing land below a given limit. The new lands distributed are controlled by minimum-sized holding stipulations.

The third major reform effort is to train the farmer to improve his techniques and his equipment. Without this, commercialization of agriculture will not be very helpful and land tenure reforms will lead nowhere. Where holdings are small, a large burden is put on improving techniques. The best hope for progress lies in improving existing practices on existing lands. Opening new lands may be too expensive. Adding more labor by existing practices may add little or nothing. The potential for increasing production by efficient agriculture is great; for example, rice production in Japan is considerably greater per hectare than in other less developed countries (see page 125).

In many countries agricultural techniques have not changed essentially for centuries, although occasional improvements have been introduced. There is little knowledge of soils or plant nutrition or of the use of modern chemical fertilizers, weed killers, or pesticides. The potential knowledge is available, but the big handicap is getting the farmer to accept change because of the hold of custom. For example, the Indonesian woman harvester still cuts one stalk of rice at a time, although better techniques are available. On other occasions the barrier arises because the suggested change involves a long series of changes; for example, a new variety of food crop may require changes not only in cultivation but also in processing and preparation of the product for food. Also, the taste may be changed! Sometimes the suggested change may require too much capital; for example, the so-called Japanese method of rice cultivation requires more capital than the Indian method. Sometimes the improvement runs up against an irrational fear, such as the belief that vegetables will reduce human fertility.

What is badly needed is research on the most effective way of spreading good farming practices. We do know that the best chance for change lies in associating it with other changes or with the prevailing religion. Small improvements have the best chance of acceptance and can often pay large dividends, such as the introduction of the steel hoe in Africa. Improvements of *proven* value on the small farm are likely to be accepted.

The need is great. Much can be done to better agricultural practice. Because labor is usually plentiful, the primary objective is to introduce land-saving innovations rather than labor-saving innovations, at the same time being economical of capital. Examples of such innovations are improved fertilization,* larger yielding varieties, and shorter maturing varieties. There is much that can be done in improving simple tools and adopting simple mechanization, especially with cooperative use, in fighting plant diseases, killing rodents and other pests, practicing scientific breeding, killing weeds, increasing the efficiency in the use of water and land, and utilizing by-products such as animal hides. In some areas, just working harder and more systematically would help.

Advanced nations already practice improved techniques, but it is impossible to carry them over unchanged to the underdeveloped countries. For one thing, they are undoubtedly designed for a different labor-land-capital ratio. Scientific principles can be transferred but specific technologies cannot. Techniques, seeds, and crops must be adapted to local conditions. Therefore, the most important step is the development of a research program and a system of extension services. The most valuable experimentation is not likely to be in research centers but at the farm level to improve the farmer's existing practices. The farmer needs *proven* improvements and must see these in practice if acceptance is to be rapid.

Unfortunately, improvements usually require a combination of improved

* The use of improved fertilizers can yield large returns. Trials in India showed an average increase in paddy rice yield of more than 13 kilograms per kilogram of nitrogen applied as fertilizer. (See "Possibilities of Increasing World Food Production." *Basic Study No. 10,* Food and Agriculture Organization, 1963, pp. 103-108.) The cost of 1 kilogram of nitrogen fertilizer in India in 1956-59 was a little over 4 kilograms of rice. (See *How the United States Improved Its Agriculture. Study Foreign-76.* Economic Research Service, U. S. Dept. of Agriculture, 1964, p. 21.) Corresponding results for Japan were an increase of 10 kilograms of rice at a cost for the fertilizer of 1.3 kilograms of rice. The major problem, of course, is in securing the capital with which to finance the purchase of the fertilizer.

practices.[42] Each improved practice will help, if used correctly, but its full efficiency may depend on the application of the total combination. Even the application of one improvement like the use of commercial fertilizer requires skill, for the amount needed depends on local conditions and can be excessive or deficient. Illiteracy reduces the ability of the peasant to calculate the advantage of various alternatives, especially combinations of them, and to apply them efficiently, once he has decided to adopt them. Thus, a major stumbling block to rapid progress is the high rate of illiteracy in rural areas. Extension services can do much, but this requires efficient government administration and a large supply of technically qualified personnel. These, too, are apt to be in short supply.

The ingredients of a successful program to increase efficiency are the extension of educational opportunities to the rural areas, research and especially field testing, agricultural extension services with a trained staff, and soil surveys. These are apt to be quite expensive and long delayed. Only simple improvements seem feasible now, except in limited areas.

It has already been suggested that introducing improved practices requires certain supplies such as improved seeds and fertilizers and, most importantly, credit. Providing these is a fourth area of reform.[43] Unfortunately, efforts have lagged in all areas, although considerable attention has been given to credit.[44] To eliminate the hold of the village moneylender or merchant, credit must be supplied through special government banks or cooperatives. The production period of agriculture is too long to be suited to commercial banks.

Government agricultural banks are in the best financial position to make agricultural loans, especially long-term loans, and to provide competent advice. However, government agencies may be looked on with suspicion by the peasant and therefore their facilities may not be utilized.

Cooperative credit agencies overcome this latter objection, but have difficulty getting adequate funds unless subsidized by the government; they often lack trained personnel; the risk is great in a limited area; and they sometimes are too prone to grant consumption loans. Considerable tightening up of their operations is necessary.

A fifth phase of a program may be the creation of new agricultural lands or the transmigration of excess farmers from one area to a new one. Land in a sense can be created; that is, made to be productive, as were the reclaimed lands in Holland. Creating such land usually adds little to the total. However, substantial unoccupied land areas are available, but require a great deal of capital investment. The potential areas are mountain slopes, tidal lowlands, and jungles. Mere mention of these indicates the difficulty of development.

In some areas where there is a maldistribution of population, there is a temptation to resettle people on unoccupied areas; for example, Malaysia,[45] Indonesia, Philippines, Venezuela, and Brazil. It may be very costly to expand transportation facilities, clear the land, support the settlers until the first crop is produced, and teach the settler new techniques. Furthermore, the mobility of rural labor is not great, and it is difficult to secure the needed workers for the expansion.

For the most part, it is cheaper to increase the productivity on existing lands. The greater surplus will be more likely to enter the market to meet the growing urban needs in already existing communities.

A sixth part of a program, which may be nearly all-inclusive of the other parts, is included in a term called "Community Development." [46] It is an effort to improve the health and social life of the village and includes the modernizing "of all phases of life." A United Nations publication defines it as follows:

Community Development means the process by which the efforts of the people themselves are united with those of governmental authorities, to improve the economic, social, and cultural conditions of communities, to integrate these communities into the life of the nation and to enable them to contribute fully to national progress. The distinctive features of community development programmes are the participation by the people themselves in efforts to improve their level of living with reliance as much as possible on their own initiative: and the provision of technical and other services in ways which encourage initiative, self-help, and mutual help and make them more effective.[47]

Typical activities, in addition to those previously mentioned, are health and sanitary measures such as medical aid, midwifery training, malaria control, and sewage control; providing an adequate and uncontaminated water supply; promoting education, including adult education, and starting libraries; improving communications; encouraging better housing; and encouraging social and cultural activities, including entertainment, sports, and fairs.

The primary technique—and this is also its main purpose—is to get people to help themselves. National efforts to raise the level of economic and social life of the villages seem doomed to failure unless much of the initiative is taken over by the local people. Thus, the major effort is seen to be getting local groups to take on the task, supplemented by national resources. The goal is to develop potential leadership of the nation. This is the greatest hope of the movement; this would be its greatest triumph, if realized, but undoubtedly it is its greatest failure. Community Development projects seem to start off well in countries that try them. Schools and community centers are built, wells are dug, and cooperatives are started for banking, agriculture, and small industry. The problems seem to arise when there is an effort to expand such projects and make them nationwide.

Although efforts have been made for many years to improve community life, the Community Development program started with the Etawah project in India in 1948.[48] The idea caught on, and similar projects were extended to other villages through United States aid beginning in 1952. Soon India had a full-scale program, with an effort to extend Community Development to almost every village. Since then, similar projects have been tried by over fifty countries with varying degrees of intensity. The result of the Indian program was a bureaucratic organization with outside leaders sent into the villages. Some benefits in improved health, sanitation, and agricultural practices were realized, but the expected surge of local leadership does not appear to have developed. If the experience of a few villages is typical,[49] much of the budget has gone into administration buildings. More recent discussions indicate a disillusionment with the project. One suspects that the best result will be obtained by a slow spreading from one successful village to another, but this will be a long, drawn-out process. Spontaneous movements are quite apt to be successful; crash efforts are not. The latter tend to involve large numbers of incompetent personnel and appear to be imposed on the local people, and are therefore resented.

Various other complaints have been raised. One objection reported is that the old leaders and the rich tend to control the projects and to absorb the new techniques and the equipment so that the poor receive little help.[50] The same report points out that village society is not constructed to absorb aid and advice in equal fashion. The villages are hierarchical, and one can expect that the hierarchy will absorb the new resources as it did the old. On the other hand, if the administrators come from outside the village, the villagers have no confidence in them and even distrust them as state officials. The best course seems to be to work with the old hierarchy and hope that it will be broken down and replaced by more general control. This does not seem to be imminent in India.

Success seems associated with small projects and a variety of projects so that everyone gains something and takes an interest. Projects must meet felt needs of the community, although these may be created by proper conditioning. A preconditioning phase of education seems a necessary prerequisite in helping the villagers and in coordinating with the national plan. Or, as it has been said, the people must first be convinced that they have a problem.

Another possible objection lies in the effort to promote supplemental employment opportunities in the form of handicrafts or small-scale industries. Care must be taken that these are not uneconomical of capital or that they do not result in an effort by the village to become self-sufficient to the detriment of specialization and efficient production.

Nevertheless, the goal of community development remains a reasonable one, and efforts should be directed toward developing ways of realizing the goals of economic and social betterment and integration into the national life. Much concentrated study and research into the necessary techniques are required.

A difficult problem is the proper taxation of agricultural land.[51] Farmers typically have been heavily taxed, for land and the products of land are visible, while other taxes, such as income and corporation taxes, which have little import for the farmer, are not very feasible for underdeveloped countries. The tax structures of underdeveloped countries are largely concentrated on commodity taxes. From the standpoint of equity or justice, some lightening of this burden must be considered. But the dictates of fiscal expediency will probably continue relatively heavy taxation on agricultural products until other types of taxes can be made more productive and can replace them. Also, taxation may be necessary to help carry out the country's program of agricultural reform and economic growth. Taxes might be used to force better cultivation; for example, a tax on unused land or a tax based on optimum use and average yield could force land redistribution and better cultivation.[52] Taxation could also be employed to extract food surpluses from peasants or to supply capital funds for industrialization. Japan has followed the latter course. Kuznets[53] points out that in the past two decades of the nineteenth century the land tax provided over 80 percent of the central government tax revenues and that the ratio of tax to income produced was between 12 and 22 percent in agriculture and only 2 to 3 percent in nonagriculture. He also points out that agriculture contributed heavily to industrial capital in Russia through taxation, confiscation, and other measures. He says one of the crucial problems of modern economic growth is finding a way of extracting agricultural surpluses for the financing of capital formation without discouraging the growth of agriculture.

No one tax policy for all can be laid down. The tax structure will depend on the peculiar conditions of the individual countries and the objectives sought. If growth were the sole criterion, taxes on agriculture would undoubtedly be heavy, and the amount expended in return for the benefit of agriculture would be only as much as was necessary for its development. But as we have seen, even with this limitation, investment in agricultural growth may have to be substantial.

A number of reform measures have been outlined. No underdeveloped country could follow all of them to their ideal limit, for capital would undoubtedly be restricted. In any program there is always the problem of priorities and proportions, and these depend on the particular situation. This applies both to the choice of alternatives within the field of agriculture itself and also between developing industry or agriculture or any other sector. Presumably, some attention must be paid to all phases of the problem. Basic research is just beginning to investigate and outline the best procedures for developing agriculture. Various suggestions have been made as starting places. Innovations may be made within the context of present practices and the economic and social system.[54] This is really a "go slow" approach. The program may be limited to indirect and slow measures, particularly education,[55] which is an even longer-run approach. Improved management may be given priority.[56] There may be an impact program in limited areas[57] or regional development may be stressed.[58] In all these alternatives an important principle is to see that, whatever measures are devised, they encourage the farmer to take the initiative to improve himself. Only in this way can agricultural growth become self-generating.

As to the overall development of agriculture, it must make sufficient progress to meet the demand generated by the general development.

## REFERENCES

1. CLARK, COLIN, "Do Population and Freedom Grow Together?" *Fortune* (December, 1960), p. 138.
2. STAMP, L. D., *Our Developing World*. London, Faber and Faber, 1960, pp. 39 ff.
3. These figures are derived from Food and Agricultural Organization, *The State of Food and Agriculture* (1964), p. 16.
4. Food and Agricultural Organization, *op. cit.*, 1963, p. 101.
5. BRAND, WILLIAM, *Struggle for a Higher Standard of Living*. New York, The Free Press of Glencoe, p. 26.
6. THORP, WILLARD, "Land and the Future." *Land Economics* (November, 1951), pp. 367-72.
7. Department of Economic Affairs, *Land Reform*. New York, United Nations, 1951.
8. These data are taken from Carroll, T. F., "The Land Reform Issue in Latin America" in A. O. Hirschman, *Latin American Issues*. New York, The Twentieth Century Fund, 1961, pp. 163, 164.
9. KOOL, R., *Tropical Agriculture and Economic Development*. N. V. Wageningen, Neth., H. Veenman & Zonen, 1960, p. 73.
10. For a detailed account of the Cuban case, see Hirdingsfield, M. S., "Cuba, a Sugar Economy." *Current History* (March, 1952), pp. 150-55.
11. Department of Economic Affairs, *op. cit.*, pp. 28 ff.
12. CARROLL, *op. cit.*, pp. 167-68.
13. Department of Economic Affairs, *op. cit.*, p. 15.
14. *Ibid.*, pp. 15 ff.
15. *Ibid.*, pp. 25 ff.
16. *Report on Labour Force Sample Survey in Java and Madeira*. Indonesia, Ministry of Labour, 1961.
17. KOOL, *op. cit.*, pp. 27-37. Stamp, *op. cit.*, pp. 37-65.
18. Food and Agricultural Organization, *The State of Food and Agriculture* (Annual Issue). International Bank for Reconstruction and Development Studies: *Economic Development of British Guiana*, 1953. *Economic Development of Ceylon*, 1953. *Agricultural Development of Colombia*,

1956. *Basis of a Development Program for Colombia,* 1950. *Economic Development of Guatemala,* 1951. *Economic Development of Iraq,* 1952. *Economic Development of Jamaica,* 1952. *Economic Development of Jordan,* 1957. *Economic Development of Kenya,* 1963. *Economic Development of Libya,* 1960. *Economic Development of Malaya,* 1955. *Economic Development of Mexico,* 1953. *Economic Development of Nicaragua,* 1953. *Economic Development of Nigeria,* 1955. *Economic Development of Spain,* 1963. *Surinam,* 1952. *Economic Development of Syria,* 1955. *Economic Development of Tanganyika,* 1961. *Public Development Program for Thailand,* 1960. *Economy of Turkey,* 1951. *Economic Development of Uganda,* 1962. *Economic Development of Venezuela,* 1961. Department of Economic Affairs, *op. cit.* (1948-1950). Department of Economic and Social Affairs, *Progress in Land Reform.* New York, United Nations, I, 1954, pp. 19-49; II, 1956, pp. 6-12.

*Latin America*

Carroll, T. F., "Land Reform Issue in Latin America," *loc. cit.,* pp. 161-201. Ferrero, R. A., "Peru's Land Problem," *Americas.* (December, 1962), pp. 32-36. Parva, R. M., "Significant Changes in Foreign Agriculture" (Brazil). *Journal of Farm Economics* (December, 1961), pp. 1092-1102.

*Middle East*

Kristjanson, B. H., "Agrarian Based Development of Iran." *Land Economics* (February, 1960), pp. 1-13. Warriner, D., *Land Reform and Development in the Mid East,* London, Oxford University Press, 1962.

*Africa*

Ardener, E., *Plantation and Village in the Cameroons.* London, Oxford University Press, 1960. Marcus, E., "Agriculture and the Development of Tropical Africa." *Land Economics* (May, 1960), pp. 172-80.

*Asia*

Froehlich, W., ed., *Land Tenure, Industrialization, and Social Stability.* Milwaukee, Wisc., Marquette University Press, 1961. Jacoby, E. H., *Agrarian Unrest in South East Asia.* New York, Asia Publishing House, 1961. Klein, S., *Pattern of Land Tenure Reform in East Asia after World War II.* New York, Bookman Associates, 1958. van der Kroef, J. M., "Land Tenure and Social Structure in Rural Java," *Rural Sociology* (December, 1960), pp. 414-30. Renne, R. R., "Land Tenure Reform and Economic Development in Asia," in R. A. Solo, *Economics and the Public Interest.* New Brunswick, N. J., Rutgers University Press, 1955. Cohen, J. B., "Problems of the Economic Development of Asia," *Economic Development and Cultural Change* (October, 1952), pp. 196-208. Dantwala, M. L., "Land Reforms in India." *International Labour Review* (November, 1952), pp. 419-43. Dhami, S. S., "Rural Development in India." *International Labour Review* (May, 1954), pp. 452-73. Karan, P. P., "Land Utilization and Agriculture in an Indian Village." *Land Economics* (February, 1957), pp. 55-64. Karve, D. G., "Significant Changes in Foreign Agriculture" (India). *Journal of Farm Economics* (December, 1961), pp. 1081-91). Ladejinsky, W., "Agrarian Revolution in Japan." *Foreign Affairs* (October, 1959), pp. 95-109. Ohkawa, K., "Significant Changes in Foreign Agriculture" (Japan). *Journal of Farm Economics* (December, 1961), pp. 1103-11. Yanaga, C., "Japan: Asiatic Co-operation." *Current History* (November, 1953), pp. 269-73.

19. TORRES, A., "More from this Land," *Americas* (August, 1962), p. 7.
20. DELWORT, L. D., "Land for Venezuelans," *Americas* (August, 1961), p. 27.
21. FERRERO, R. A., "Peru's Land Problem," *Americas* (December, 1962), p. 33.
22. PREUSS, W., *Cooperation in Israel and the World*. Jerusalem, Rubin Mass, 1960.
23. MOSHER, A. T., "The Wisconsin Idea and World Agricultural Development." *Land Economics* (May, 1962), pp. 153-68.
24. KARVE, D. G., *op. cit.*, pp. 1981-91.
25. SOLOMON, M., "The Structure of Markets in Underdeveloped Economies," in L. W. Shannon, ed., *Underdeveloped Areas*. New York, Harper & Bros., 1957, pp. 131-40.
26. KLEIN, S., *Pattern of Land Tenure Reform in East Asia after World War II*. New York, Bookman Associates, 1958. Jacoby, E. H., *Agrarian Unrest in South East Asia*. New York, Asia Publishing House, 1961. Froehlich, W., ed., *Land Tenure, Industrialization, and Social Stability*. Milwaukee, Wis., Marquette University Press, 1961. Warriner, D., *Land Reform and Development in the Mid East*. New York, Oxford University Press, 1962. Carroll, *op. cit.* Department of Economic Affairs, *op. cit.* Department of Economic Affairs, *Progress in Land Reform, loc. cit.*, I, 1954; II, 1956. Ladejinsky, W., "Agrarian Revolution in Japan." *Foreign Affairs* (October, 1959), pp. 213-27. Stauffer, T., "Egyptian Land Reform Law." *Economic Development and Cultural Change* (December, 1952), pp. 295-314. Parsons, K. H., "Land Reform in the UAR." *Land Economics* (November, 1959), pp. 319-26. Marii, S., "Agrarian Reform in Egypt." *International Labour Review* (February, 1954), pp. 140-50. Dantwala, M. L., "Land Reforms in India." *Interna-*

tional Labour Review (November, 1952), pp. 419-43. Kristjanson, B. H., "Agrarian-based Development of Iran." *Land Economics* (February, 1960), pp. 1-13. Delwart, L. O., "Land for Venezuelans." *Americas* (August, 1961), pp. 25-30.
27. LADEJINSKY, *op. cit.*, p. 97.
28. *Ibid.*, pp. 95-109.
29. Kaihara, M. in Froehlich, *op. cit.*, p. 143.
30. "Tiny Farms Handicap Japanese Agriculture," *Washington Post,* (August 29, 1963), p. A.5.
31. PARSONS, K. H., "Land Reform in the UAR." *Land Economics* (November, 1959), pp. 319-26.
32. PARSONS, U. S. papers prepared for the United Nations Conference on the Application of Science and Technology for the Benefit of the Less Developed Areas, *Science, Technology, and Development*, Vol. III. *Agriculture* (1963), p. 29.
33. LONG, E. L., "Economic Basis of Land Reform in Underdeveloped Economies." *Land Economics* (May, 1961), pp. 116, 117.
34. Department of Economic Affairs, *Land Reform, loc. cit.*, pp. 59-63. Carroll, *op. cit.*, pp. 171-75.
35. Department of Economic Affairs, *Progress in Land Reform, loc. cit.*, pp. 107-108. *Land Reform, loc. cit.*, pp. 35-36. Gaitskell, A., *Gezira: A Story of Development in the Sudan*. London, Faber & Faber, 1959.
36. ALPERT, P., *Economic Development, Objectives and Methods*. New York, The Free Press of Glencoe. 1963, pp. 121-22.
37. Department of Economic Affairs, *Progress in Land Reform, loc. cit.*, I, 1954, pp. 233-51; II, 1956, pp. 97-108. Preuss, W., *Cooperation in Israel and the World*. Jerusalem, Rubin Mass, 1960. Campbell, W. K. H., *Practical Cooperation in Asia and Africa*. Cambridge, W. Heffer & Sons, Ltd., 1951.

38. CARROLL, *op. cit.,* p. 198.
39. KOOL, *op. cit.,* p. 73. Marcus, *op. cit.,* p. 178.
40. Department of Economic Affairs, *Progress in Land Reform, loc. cit.,* I, 1954, pp. 116-48; II, 1956, pp. 33-48.
41. *Ibid.,* I, pp. 181-207; II, pp. 71-79. (Describes efforts made.)
42. HILL, F. H., and A. T. MOSHER, "Organizing for Agricultural Development." U. S. papers prepared for the United Nations Conference on the Application of Science and Technology for the Benefit of the Less Developed Areas, *Science, Technology, and Development,* Vol. III. *Agriculture* (1963), p. 4.
43. Department of Economic Affairs, *Land Reform, loc. cit.,* pp. 37-43. "Contemporary Problems in the Economics of Agriculture." *International Journal of Agrarian Affairs* (September, 1962), pp. 144-45.
44. Department of Economic Affairs, *Progress in Land Reform, loc. cit.,* II, 1956, pp. 97-108. (A country-by-country description.)
45. FISK, E. K., "Mobility of Rural Labour and Settlement of New Land in Underdeveloped Countries." *Journal of Farm Economics* (November, 1961), pp. 761-78. (Describes the Malayan movement.)
46. Department of Economic and Social Affairs, *Community Organization and Developments.* New York, United Nations, 1953, 1954. (A series of studies of Community Development in various countries.) National Training Laboratories, *Forces in Community Development,* 1961. Public Administration of Community Development, New York, United Nations, 1959. *Public Administration Aspects of Community Development Programme.* London, Oxford University Press, 1962. Department of Economic and Social Affairs, *Community Development,* and National Develop-

ment New York, United Nations, 1963.
47. United Nations, *Public Administration Aspects . . . , loc. cit.,* p. 2.
48. MAYER, A., *Pilot Project India.* Berkeley, Calif., University of California Press, 1958.
49. SUNDARSINGH, JOHN D. K., "Community Development and Economic Growth in India with Special Reference to Kanya-Kumari District in Madras State." Unpublished Ph.D. dissertation, University of Massachusetts, 1960.
50. NEALE, W. C., "The Indian Peasant, the State and Economic Development. *Land Economics* (November, 1962), pp. 287 ff.
51. WALD, H. P., *Taxation of Agricultural Lands in Underdeveloped Countries.* New Haven, Harvard University Press, 1959.
52. Department of Economic Affairs, *Progress in Land Reform, loc. cit.,* I, 1954, pp. 202-207; II, 1956, pp. 114-18. (Gives details of the programs of different countries.)
53. KUZNETS, S., "Economic Growth and the Contribution of Agriculture." *International Journal of Agrarian Affairs* (April, 1961), pp. 70 ff. Ohkawa, K., and H. Rosovsky, "The Role of Agriculture in Modern Japanese Economic Development." *Economic Development and Cultural Affairs* (October, 1960), pp. 61-62.
54. ENKE, S., *Economics for Development.* Englewood Cliffs, N. J., Prentice-Hall, Inc., 1963, p. 148.
55. KOOL, *op. cit.,* p. 149.
56. LINDHOLM, R. W., "Land Use and Land Taxation in Underdeveloped Areas." *Journal of Farm Economics* (May, 1961), p. 242.
57. MALONE, C. C., "Improving Management in Agricultural Development," U. S. papers, *op. cit.,* p. 70.
58. HILL, F. G., "Regional Aspects of Economic Development." *Land Economics* (May, 1962), pp. 85-98.
BAER, G., "Land Tenure in the Hashe-

## ADDITIONAL READINGS

mite Kingdom of Jordon." *Land Economics* (August, 1957), pp. 187-97.

BELOTTI, L. M., "Italian Agrarian Reform." *Land Economics* (May, 1960), pp. 118-28.

BRAY, F. R., "Reflections on Rural Economic Development." *Land Economics* (November, 1955), pp. 289-302.

COOK, H. L., "New Agrarian Reform Law and Economic Development in Venezuela." *Land Economics* (February, 1961), pp. 5, 7.

CRIST, R. E., "Land for the Fellahin." *American Journal of Economics and Sociology* (October, 1957), pp. 21-30; (January, 1958), pp. 157-66; (April, 1958), pp. 295-306; (July, 1958), pp. 413-20; (October, 1958), pp. 83-90; (January, 1959), pp. 193-201; (April, 1959), pp. 313-20; (July, 1959), pp. 415-28; (October, 1959), pp. 81-91; (January, 1960), pp. 207-16; (April, 1960), pp. 311-22; (July, 1960), pp. 427-33; (January, 1961), pp. 115-26.

EDWARDS, D. T., *An Economic Study of Small Farming in Jamaica.* Glasgow, University Press, 1961.

EDWARDS, D. T. "Trends Within the World Cooperative Movement." *International Labour Review,* I (May, 1959), pp. 537-49; II (June, 1959), pp. 643-61.

GITTINGER, J. P., "United States Policy toward Agrarian Reform in Underdeveloped Nations." *Land Economics* (August, 1961), pp. 195-206.

HASHIMI, R., and A. L. EDWARDS, "Land Reform in Iraq." *Land Economics* (February, 1961), pp. 68-81.

MELLOR, J. W., "Process of Agricultural Development in Low-Income Countries." *Journal of Farm Economics* (August, 1962), pp. 700-16.

SAYIGH, Y. A., "Place of Agriculture in Economic Development." *Land Economics* (November, 1959), pp. 297-305.

TINKER, H., "Community Development: A New Philosopher's Stone." *International Affairs* (July, 1961), pp. 309-22.

# CHAPTER

# 5

# *Population*

One of the major issues of today is whether the rise in population will doom the world to a starvation level of living or, at least, will negate any or most of the improvements made in production. If appearance in the literature is any criterion, it would appear that the greater number of economists and other social scientists who write on the issue are viewing the current rise of population with utmost alarm. Several quotations will illustrate this concern: "These relationships [the reciprocal relations between population and the economic and social environment] are among the matters which must be understood if the fundamental reasons for mass poverty, for the wastage of human and physical resources, and for the economic and cultural retardation of many of the world's peoples are to be known." [1] "The population problem has become the most fundamental of all human problems." [2] "One of the major social and health problems of the world today results from the too frequent childbearing of women in all underdeveloped countries." [3]

In general, the fear is that many, whether already living in poverty or not, are doomed to a lifetime of poverty and that the quality of the population will deteriorate, at least with respect to education, training, and health, if not eugenically.* Fears concerning the effects of population growth on society are not new. The problems of population have been discussed in all

* This latter aspect will not be treated in this book.

recorded history,* but the Rev. Thomas Malthus is usually credited with bringing it formally into economic literature in his *An Essay on the Principle of Population* (1798).

Malthus took up the problem of population in opposition to current concepts of the perfectability of man and the view that all men's troubles come from institutions and not man himself. He felt that population increase was the chief cause of mass poverty. He believed that man was able to increase his numbers faster than he could his means of subsistence, and he expressed this by stating that population increased geometrically whereas the food supply increased only arithmetically. He arrived at this conclusion by reasoning from the facts of the physiological possibilities of population increase and the observed fact that there had been relatively little improvement in agricultural methods for some time. He appears not to have taken any thought of the possibilities of technological improvements in agriculture, a perfectly understandable position in view of the slight progress experienced in his immediate past. With little improvement in productivity, the only substantial increases in the production of food that could take place would be by the addition of more workers, and even here Malthus implied what was made explicit by other economists: that the law of diminishing returns would lead to a decrease in the output per worker. The net result, unless the people used preventive checks (that is, celibacy, postponement of marriage, or restraint during marriage, which Malthus did not think likely), would be poverty and misery, with the population held to a subsistence level by the forces of diminishing returns and the positive checks of war, famine, and pestilence.

Malthus' predictions have not been realized in western Europe, for technological revolution in industry, commerce, and agriculture have led to great increases in productivity, and the people seem to have utilized the preventive checks or artificial fertility controls to reduce the rate of population growth. Yet, most economists since Malthus have recognized the underlying threat of a large population increase, and many today see its dire consequences as an imminent reality in many underdeveloped countries. He has many followers today, although they do not hold to the precise Malthusian formulation. As the quotations at the beginning of the chapter indicate, many fear that the increasing growth in population will lead to a decreased scale of living and will bring forth the positive checks of war and an increasing death rate or, at least, a failure to increase the scale of living.

Not all economists are of this opinion; some feel that population will

* For a survey of the views of all theorists on the population problem from early times until the present, see Department of Social Affairs, *The Determinants and Consequences of Population Trends, loc. cit.,* pp. 21-46.

adjust to production possibilities (that is, take care of itself) while others feel that production possibilities will overcome the probable population growth. Various estimates have been made of the maximum population the earth can support, and these range up to twelve billions or more.[4] Most optimistic of all is Colin Clark.[5] He believes that population growth is generally beneficial in that it stimulates economic progress by shaking men out of their established ways and promotes political freedom by making impractical and undesirable the governmental control of economic life. Further, he seems not to be impressed with the probabilities of large increases in the population, for he says, "An average family [born to those who live through the whole reproductive period] of six or seven may provide for some increase in population, but not very much." [6] Also, the world has the capacity to support much larger populations than exist at present. "If all the land suitable for agriculture throughout the world were cultivated in this manner [the Dutch standard] assuming at the same time that the whole world eats as well as the most prosperous countries do now, provision could be made for 28 billion people, or ten times the world's 1960 population." [7] And if the Japanese standards of cultivation and diet were to be followed, three or four times as many could be supported. Moreover, even those standards are being improved. However, such a result would require the free emigration of people in order to adjust population and resources, the opening up of all markets for countries that must industrialize, and external capital assistance for some.

The foregoing comments present an extreme position, which is not widely endorsed but which expresses the judgment that we can increase our production of food to keep abreast of population increases. However, it is of little comfort to estimate that food supplies will do no more than keep pace. What is needed is an increase in the scale of living, and this requires a substantial increase in many areas where the population is now underfed. Nor are we really interested in seeing how many people a country can support at minimum diets. Rather we are concerned with seeing what rates of population growth will best permit a rise in the scale of living.

## The Growth of Population

The fact is that the world's population is growing rapidly. "The time in which we live could be described without exaggeration as the age of the peopling of the earth." [8] Over 50 million are born every year, or almost 1 million each week, or 105,000 a day, or 5,000 every hour.

Population growth was slow in most of the earth's history.[9] Man has existed at least 100,000 years and possibly as long as 1 million. If it is assumed that there were only two dozen people 100,000 years ago, it would have taken a rate of growth of only 20 per 100,000 each year to grow to the present population.[10] At periods, population has grown more rapidly, so that there must have been long periods of stationary or even declining population. Whenever innovations increased the capacity to produce food, such as the domestication of plants and animals or the control of waters (for example, in Egypt and Mesopotamia), there have been growing populations. At the time of the Christian era the world's population was 200 to 300 million. By 1650 this had reached 545 million. Table 5.1 gives the estimated growth of the world's population from 1650. Until 1650 the population had increased very slowly at an approximate rate of 0.04 percent per year. Since then, the rate of increase has become larger until today it is about 1.7 percent. At this rate the world's population would double in 41 years and increase 5.4 times in 100 years.* Sauvy,[11] by applying the principle of compound interest, illustrates the power of rates of growth by citing that one pair of Romans of the Tiberian Age would by now have produced 130 million descendants at a 1.7 percent rate of growth and that the population of the Roman territories, at the same rate, would have resulted in a population today of 6,216,000 to the square mile, or 2 per square yard. This, of course, is unrealistic, but indicates the concern we must have about the current rate of increase of the world's population.

All forecasts indicate a continued high growth for some time. Even at 1 percent a year for 5,000 years, the extent of man's recorded history, there would be 2.7 billion persons per square foot of land surface.[12] W. Vogt,[13] quoting Dr. Harrison Brown, gives an even more fantastic picture of the potentials of growth. Forgetting the problem of food, in 730 years at 18 percent growth per decade, each of us would have 1 square foot of space. In 1,700 years, the population would weigh as much as the earth itself. In 2,400 years, the population would weigh as much as the sun. In 3,300 years, the radius of the earth and the population would equal the earth's orbit. In 5,300 years, the sphere of humanity would expand at the velocity

---

* For other rates of increase, the number of years to double the population and the times of increase each 100 years would be:

| Percent | Years | Times |
|---------|-------|-------|
| 0.5 | 139 | 1.65 |
| 1.0 | 70 | 2.70 |
| 1.5 | 47 | 4.44 |
| 2.0 | 35 | 7.24 |
| 2.5 | 28 | 11.80 |
| 3.0 | 24 | 19.23 |
| 3.5 | 20 | 31.19 |

## TABLE 5.1.

*World's Population (Estimated) and Annual Rates of Increase*

| Period | World Total (millions) | Annual Rate of Increase (%) |
|---|---|---|
| 1650 | 545 | |
| 1750 | 728 | 0.29 |
| 1800 | 907 | 0.44 |
| 1850 | 1,175 | 0.52 |
| 1900 | 1,620 | 0.65 |
| 1920 | 1,834 | 0.62 |
| 1930 | 2,008 | 0.91 |
| 1940 | 2,216 | 0.99 |
| 1950 | 2,476 | 1.12 |
| 1955 | 2,691 | 1.67 |
| 1960 (est.) | 2,910 | 1.58 |
| 1980 (est.) | 3,523 | 0.96 |

SOURCE: Computed from the Carr-Saunders estimates, 1650-1900, *World Population*, 1936, p. 42; and United Nations estimates and published in United Nations, *Determinants and Consequences of Population Trends*,[1] p. 12; and A. Sauvy, *Fertility and Survival*,[9e] p. 19. The annual rates of increase have been recalculated.

## TABLE 5.2.

*Estimated Percentage Rate of Growth of Population by Regions of the World*

| Region | 1900-50* | 1953-57* | 1958-62 † |
|---|---|---|---|
| World | — | 1.6 | 2.0 |
| Africa | 1.0 | 1.8 | 2.3 |
| North | — | 1.9 | 2.3 |
| Tropical South | — | 1.8 | 2.3 |
| Americas | — | 2.0 | 2.3 |
| North America | 1.5 | 1.6 | 1.7 |
| Latin America | 1.9 | 2.4 | |
| Mid | — | 2.6 | 2.9 |
| South | — | 2.3 | 2.8 |
| Asia | — | 1.8 | 2.3 |
| Southwest | — | 2.4 | 2.3 |
| South Central | — | 1.4 | 2.2 |
| Japan | — | 1.1 | } 2.3 |
| Rim of Far East | 0.7 | 1.9 | |
| Europe | 0.7[a] | 0.8 | 0.9 |
| Northwest and Central | — | 0.7 | 0.9 |
| South | — | — | 0.8 |
| East | — | 1.0 | |
| Oceania | 1.6 | 1.6 | 2.2 |
| Soviet Union | — | 1.8 | 1.7 |

SOURCES: "Political and Economic Planning," *World Population and Resources*, Allen & Unwin, 1955, p. 19, taken from Food and Agriculture Organization, *State of Food and Agriculture*, Part II, 1963, p. 13, and United Nations, *Demographic Yearbook*, Table I, 1953.

\* A. J. Jaffe, "Population Trends and Controls in Underdeveloped Countries," *Law and Contemporary Problems* (Summer, 1960), p. 513.

† United Nations, *Demographic Yearbook, 1963*, Table 2, 1964, p. 142.

[a] Including U.S.S.R.

of light. Since this is the ultimate measurable speed, at this point the rate of growth would have to fall. Such figures serve only to indicate that it is impossible for the present rate of increase to continue very long, regardless of the rate of improvement in the ability to produce food. The longer this rate of increase is permitted to continue, the more serious the problem becomes and the more costly it is to solve.

The current rate of growth of the world's population is rapid, but is very uneven throughout the world. Table 5.2 gives various estimated rates of growth by regions of the world for different years. Although different estimates differ slightly, they all confirm the tendency for rates of increase to rise and the fact of variability in growth. In general, Europe has the lowest rates; Japan is next; and the rest of the world, with the exception of Latin America and southwest Asia, is at or slightly above the world average.

Table 5.3 shows that the rapid rates of population increase have been occurring in the underdeveloped areas. Within the major areas, considerable diversity exists in the rate of population growth, as Table 5.4 shows. In Latin America the rate varies from 1.4 percent in Bolivia and Uruguay to

TABLE 5.3.

*Distribution of 125 Countries by Annual Rates of Net Population Increase\**
(Most Recent Year Prior to 1952)

| Continent | Number of Countries | No. under 1% | No. 1-1.9% | No. 2%+ |
|---|---|---|---|---|
| World | 125 | 33 | 49 | 43 |
| Africa | 20 | 9 | 7 | 4 |
| America, North of Mexico | 5 | — | 5 | |
| Latin America | 39 | 1 | 13 | 25 |
| Asia | 17 | 1 | 9 | 7 |
| Europe | 34 | 21 | 11 | 2 |
| Oceania | 10 | 1 | 4 | 5 |

(Average for 1958-62) \*\*

| Continent | No. for All Countries | No. under 1% | No. 1-1.9% | No. 2-2.9% | No. 3%+ |
|---|---|---|---|---|---|
| World | 114 | 20 | 28 | 34 | 32 |
| Africa | 31 | 1 | 11 | 13 | 6 |
| America, North of Mexico | 2 | — | 1 | 1 | |
| Latin America | 21 | — | 4 | 6 | 11 |
| Asia | 30 | 1 | 5 | 11 | 13 |
| Europe | 28 | 18 | 7 | 1 | 2 |
| Oceania | 2 | — | — | 2 | |

Source: \* H. T. Eldridge, "Population Growth and Economic Development," *Land Economics* (February, 1952), p. 3.
\*\* Calculated from Table 5.4.

4.3 percent in Costa Rica. Of the 21 areas in Latin America, 17 have rates of growth of 2 percent or more and 11 of these have rates over 3 percent. Africa had a low rate of 0.5 percent in Sierra Leone and a high of 5.1 in Mauritania. Of the 25 areas, 15 had rates over 2 percent and 5 of these were over 3 percent. In Asia as a whole the variation was from a low of 1.7 in Iran, excluding Japan as a relatively developed country, to a high of 3.8 in Cambodia, excluding Kuwait, which, because of special circumstances,

TABLE 5.4.

Annual Percentage Rate of Population Increase in Selected Countries
of the World, 1958-1962

| Region and Country | Annual Rate of Population Increase | Region and Country | Annual Rate of Population Increase |
|---|---|---|---|
| *North America* | | France | 1.2 |
| Canada | 2.1 | Germany, East | −0.3 |
| United States | 1.6 | Germany, West | 1.3 |
| | | Greece | 0.8 |
| *Latin America* | | Hungary | 0.4 |
| Argentina | 1.6 | Iceland | 1.9 |
| Bolivia | 1.4 | Ireland | −0.3 |
| Brazil | 3.4 | Italy | −0.3 |
| Chile | 2.4 | Lichtenstein | 3.1 |
| Colombia | 2.2 | Luxembourg | 0.9 |
| Costa Rica | 4.3 | Netherlands | 1.3 |
| Cuba | 2.0 | Norway | 0.8 |
| Dominican Republic | 3.6 | Poland | 1.3 |
| Ecuador | 3.2 | Portugal | 0.7 |
| El Salvador | 3.6*a* | Roumania | 0.9 |
| Guatemala | 3.2 | Spain | 0.8 |
| Haiti | 2.2 | Sweden | 0.5 |
| Honduras | 3.0 | Switzerland | 2.1 |
| Jamaica | 1.5 | United Kingdom | 0.8 |
| Mexico | 3.1 | Yugoslavia | 1.1 |
| Nicaragua | 3.5 | | |
| Panama | 3.3 | *Africa* | |
| Paraguay | 2.4 | Angola | 2.4*a* |
| Peru | 2.0*a* | Burundi | 4.9 |
| Uruguay | 1.4 | Cameroon | 1.9 |
| Venezuela | 3.4 | Central African Republic | 1.9 |
| | | Chad | 1.1 |
| *Europe* | | Congo (Brazzaville) | 1.3 |
| Albania | 3.2 | Congo (Leopoldville) | 2.4 |
| Austria | 0.3*a* | Ethiopia | 1.6 |
| Belgium | 0.5 | Gabon | 2.1 |
| Bulgaria | 0.9 | Ivory Coast | 2.2 |
| Czechoslovakia | 0.7 | Kenya | 2.9 |
| Denmark | 0.8 | Liberia | 1.3 |
| Finland | 0.8 | | |

TABLE 5.4. (*Continued*)

| Region and Country | Annual Rate of Population Increase | Region and Country | Annual Rate of Population Increase |
|---|---|---|---|
| *Africa* (continued) | | *Asia* (continued) | |
| Madagascar | 2.8 | Korea, South | 3.3 |
| Mali | 3.9 | Kuwait | 11.3 |
| Mauritania | 5.1 | Laos | 2.5 |
| Mozambique | 2.2ᵃ | Malaya | 3.2 |
| Niger | 3.0 | Pakistan | 2.1 |
| Nigeria | 1.9 | Philippines | 3.2 |
| Ruanda | 2.6 | Thailand | 3.0 |
| Sierra Leone | 0.5 | Turkey | 2.6 |
| Somalia | 3.2 | Viet Nam, North | 3.4 |
| South Africa | 2.6 | Viet Nam, South | 3.7 |
| Tanganyika | 1.9 | | |
| Uganda | 2.5 | | |
| Zanzibar | 1.7 | *Middle East* | |
| | | Algeria | 2.1 |
| *Asia* | | Cyprus | 1.0 |
| Afghanistan | 3.1 | Lebanon | 2.9 |
| Bhutan | 1.9 | Libya | 1.9 |
| Burma | 2.1ᵃ | Morocco | 3.0 |
| Cambodia | 3.8 | Saudi Arabia | 1.6 |
| Ceylon | 2.7 | Sudan | 2.8ᵃ |
| China (Mainland) | 2.4ᵃ | Syria | 4.8ᵃ |
| China (Taiwan) | 3.6 | Tunisia | 1.4 |
| India | 2.3 | United Arab Republic | 2.6 |
| Indonesia | 2.2 | Yemen | 3.2 |
| Iran | 1.7 | | |
| Iraq | 1.9 | *Oceania* | |
| Israel | 3.5 | Australia | 2.1 |
| Japan | 0.9 | New Zealand | 2.2 |
| Jordan | 2.3 | | |
| Korea, North | 2.3 | *U.S.S.R.* | 1.7 |

SOURCES: United Nations, *Demographic Yearbook, 1963*, Table 1, 1964, pp. 123 ff. United Nations, *Statistical Yearbook, 1962*, Table 1, 1963, pp. 22 ff.
ᵃ 1958-61.

had an exceptionally rapid increase of 11.3 percent per year. Of the 25 areas listed for Asia, 21 showed increases of 2 percent or more and 11 of these had increases of 3 percent or more. In the Middle East the range was from a low of 1 percent in Cyprus and 1.6 percent in Saudi Arabia to a high of 4.8 percent in Syria. Overall, 68 of the 114 areas reported had increases of 2 percent or more and 32 of these had increases of 3 percent or more.

Unfortunately, the highest rates seem to be occurring in areas that are already densely populated. The relationship between density of population and economic well-being is not consistent; and density figures themselves

may be meaningless in the absence of data concerning the percentage of
arable land, the fertility of the soil, the climatic conditions, the existence of
subsidiary occupations, and so on. However, an increasing population in
already densely settled agricultural lands would not seem desirable. This
encourages labor-intensive methods and discourages modern techniques because farms must necessarily be small. Also, there is a tendency toward
overcropping, with eventual soil exhaustion and the utilization of unsuitable
lands such as hill areas, which soon deteriorate. The protective forest cover
is removed and erosion results. As shown in Table 5.5, most of Asia and
Middle America have high densities. Low densities exist in South America
and Africa. However, an average for a country can be misleading, for the
population may be concentrated in a few areas, which is the typical situation. The density figures for Indonesia are relatively low, but almost three-
fourths of the people are concentrated on the island of Java, which has one
of the highest concentrations in the world. In much of Latin America the
population is similarly concentrated. Expansion to relatively uninhabited

**TABLE 5.5.**

*Density of Population per Square Kilometer by Major World Divisions, 1962*

| Continent and Region | Density |
|---|---|
| World | 23 |
| Africa | 9 |
| North | 9 |
| Tropical and Southern | 9 |
| America | 10 |
| North | 10 |
| Middle | 26 |
| South | 9 |
| Asia | 64 |
| South West | 73 |
| South Central | 114 |
| South East | 51 |
| East | 74 |
| Europe | 88 |
| North and West | 64 |
| Central | 139 |
| South | 88 |
| Oceania | 2 |
| U.S.S.R. | 10 |

SOURCE: United Nations, *Demographic Yearbook, 1963*, Table 2, 1964, p. 142.

areas is extremely costly and probably not the best way to use scarce capital, as was stated in the preceding chapter.

Such are the statistics of growth. The major cause of this growth is the almost precipitous decline in the death rate, especially among the young, which has occurred since 1930. Death rates have been reduced by one-third to one-half in many areas. Better reporting practices probably result in the declines being even more rapid than the figures show. In the tiny island of Mauritius, the death rate in the postwar period fell from 28 to 12 per thousand (1958) with the birth rate rising from 33 to 41.[14] Thus, the annual rate of population rise from natural causes rose from 0.5 percent to 2.9 percent, a situation that makes their problem very severe. Other examples of decreasing death rates,[15] are given in Table 5.6. This shows a more rapid rate of decline than was ever experienced in the West and came not as a result of rising scales of living, but in spite of the failure of such scales to rise. The primary cause, of course, has been the postwar spread of better medicine, health practices, and sanitary facilities. These things were introduced only slowly in the West and therefore did not reduce death rates so rapidly. Other factors leading to the same result were greater political order and stability, improved transportation which reduced deaths from famine, and some improvements in agricultural techniques.

### TABLE 5.6.
*Decreasing Death Rate*

| Country | Death Rate per Thousand | |
| --- | --- | --- |
| | 1932 | 1950 |
| Chile | 22.7 | 15.7 |
| Costa Rica | 20.5 | 12.2 |
| El Salvador | 21.3 | 14.8 |
| Jamaica | 17.4 | 11.8 |
| Mexico | 26.1 | 16.7 |
| Puerto Rico | 22.0 | 9.9 |
| Ceylon | 20.5 | 12.9 |
| Japan | 17.7 | 10.0 |

At the same time, birth rates did not decline, and in some cases even increased as the health of the population increased. Further declines in the death rate are expected, but no appreciable decline in the birth rate is expected in the near future for various reasons, to be discussed later. Thus, unless something is done or happens to change the trend, even faster rates of growth are probable.

If the production of food or exports to obtain food increased as rapidly, the scale of living would just be maintained. We do not know positively what will happen, but there is grave doubt that production will grow fast enough to raise the scale of living appreciably or that it will in fact succeed in maintaining it. We have already pointed out the difficulties in improving agricultural production. At the present rates of population growth, corresponding growths of food production seem unlikely. The result will be increasing difficulties and a negation of efforts to make the country grow. The relationship between population growth and desired goals will be discussed in the following section.

## Effects of Population Changes

Although there is little likelihood that the world will soon be encountering a lack of standing room, there is definite indication that the present rate of population growth will not permit the underdeveloped countries to grow rapidly, if at all. Therefore, the effects of population growth on the possibilities of growth must be studied in each and every country. There is no categorical solution; each situation must be explored and appraised.

Population growth can at times be an advantage for a country, but only under one or more of the following conditions:

1.   It would result in an increase in the total demand for goods and this demand could be met by increased productivity, either by using unutilized resources or by increasing them at the same time that demand is increasing. Particularly, capital would be available for expansion of productive equipment unless a sufficient quantity were being underutilized. This would be especially true in the case of social overheads.

2.   A growing population would permit a better division of labor while permitting the requisite training and education.

3.   A growing population would afford economies of scale; that is, businesses and social overheads could grow to a more economical size.

4.   The ratio of labor to population would be improved.

5.   The growth of population would act as a shock to get people out of their lethargy and lead them to increase their efficiency, or act as a challenge that would lead them to greater effort.[16]

It is questionable that these conditions will be realized in any heavily populated underdeveloped country or in any in which the population is increasing excessively, even though it is currently "underpopulated" in the sense of having a low density. It is useful to trace the more likely results.

An increasing population in the face of an already low supply of resources and land per capita can only result in diminishing returns in the absence of other changes, such as more capital, better trained labor, and technological innovation. In other words, an increasing population only aggravates an already bad situation.[17] It must be remembered that many countries seem to have low densities, but that this is only illusory because their populations are concentrated. To expand into unoccupied areas is costly and does not take place readily, even though overcrowding already exists. The populations of most countries seem to have expanded to the level set by existing technological levels before the current population growth started. As stated in an important United Nations study,[18] existing theoretical production functions imply that an increase in population and labor force alone would reduce per capita income and that the important consideration is how population growth affects other improvements that are necessary to offset such a decline. This presumably includes those improvements mentioned above, such as the supply of capital, improved training and education of labor, and technological innovation, and all the other factors associated with increasing incomes, to be discussed later. There is a real doubt that increasing the population will affect these favorably. Increasing the population does not even increase the supply of workers for some time, and certainly cannot improve labor skills.

Actually, the usual result is an eventual increase in the quantity of unskilled rural workers. This situation makes for inefficient production methods, for there is a temptation to use labor-intensive methods in production rather than improved methods. Increases in the use of unskilled labor without offsetting increases in capital and technological improvements soon lead to diminishing returns. This is especially true when the labor is employed in one pursuit—agriculture—and not in a variety of occupations. Despite what appear to be popular beliefs to the contrary, the use of low-paid labor and labor-intensive methods is a poor way to try to grow economically. In the long run, more and more pressure is put on the exhaustible resources (which require capital to augment) and forces dependence on agriculture, for it is unlikely that industry can develop rapidly enough to absorb the workers. Thus the surplus is forced back on the farm. The result is a dualistic economy. This means pressure on the land, small plots, the cultivation of inferior areas, and exhaustion of the land from overcropping. Small plots bring little incentive for the spread of modern techniques. The possibility that a growing population will permit better division of labor loses meaning when a given size of population is reached, for at this point no further gains can be expected. On the contrary, increasing numbers may prevent the division of labor because it forces more and more workers back into subsistence agriculture, which Enke[19] calls "population traps."

A second effect of an increasing population is that it increases the need for capital and resources merely to maintain the increasing numbers at the same level of living. It has just been shown that attempting to increase production by adding labor alone would result in diminishing returns and lower per capita output. Capital must also be used to provide the increased production necessary to support the added people. A further increment of capital is needed to supply the necessary social overheads such as transportation facilities, educational and training facilities, and consumer capital goods such as houses. If any improvement in the scale of living is contemplated, the capital requirements are greatly increased. Moreover, it is very doubtful that there would be constant returns to scale of capital at the prevailing density levels; that is, it would take more than a 10 percent increase in the amount of capital goods to increase output 10 percent unless offset by technological improvements. This is probably most true in the case of agriculture (except for a few capital-saving improvements) and the production of energy and mineral resources. Experience shows that the countries with high per capita incomes use more capital per person and per worker than do the countries with low per capita incomes. In the former case at least, technological improvements have been capital-using. The present underdeveloped countries can expect rising capital requirements as they try to raise the average scale of living.*

The amount of capital required to produce one unit of output is usually spoken of as the capital-output ratio. This concept represents an average; that is, on the average a certain amount of capital is needed to create a unit of output. A 4:1 ratio is usually taken as representative. Such a concept is quite indefinite for application to a specific situation and may be misleading for policy determination, for what is important is not the current average ratio but the particular ratio necessary to add additional output—the marginal capital-output ratio, as it is termed.

In any particular case the amount of capital needed would have to be estimated to see how much was needed to offset a population change. It is sometimes possible to find some bargain methods, that is, those with low marginal capital-output ratios; but attempts to get any substantial increase in output or a prolonged increase would soon exhaust these methods. A 4:1 ratio may even prove low if one considers the need for housing, education, and other overheads. If we assume on the average that a 4:1 ratio applies, with a population rise of 2 percent a year (which, as we have seen, is not uncommon), the necessary capital formation would require a saving of 8 percent of the national income just to keep the scale of living steady. This

* N. Coale and E. M. Hoover (*Population Growth and Economic Development in Low Income Countries*, Princeton, N. J., Princeton University Press, 1958, p. 287) in their projections concerning economic development for India estimate that at present fertility rates, India must invest 46 percent of her increased income to get the same rate of growth as with 30 percent invested with lower fertility.

exceeds current rates of saving in some countries; the Indian rate, for example, is 5 to 7 percent per year.[20] Moreover, it takes a long time before some of this investment results in increased productivity (for example, that from education), so that in the meantime the consumption of the rest of the community must suffer unless capital can be obtained from abroad. Unless complementary factors such as trained labor exist, a country may not be able to take advantage of the necessary amount of capital from abroad, assuming it is available.

Leibenstein's critical minimum effort thesis, outlined in Chapter 2, stresses the need for a large effort, including a large use of capital, if growth is to get started. The larger the population growth, the greater the development effort needed. J. J. Spengler[21] has pointed out that western Europe was able to grow with low rates of saving because of its low rate of population growth. This does not seem possible in underdeveloped countries that have rapidly growing populations.

While population growth increases the need for capital, it decreases the ability of a population to save, for several reasons. In the first place, much of the nation's efforts must be devoted to producing food and consumption goods. A nation can devote its efforts to producing more consumption goods for the existing population, to increasing the supply of capital goods, or to feeding more children. Growth occurs only if at least some of the increased effort goes into capital formation. Coale and Hoover[22] show by their estimates for India that an increasing population due to high fertility rates is not likely to lead to a larger potential work force than would low fertility rates for nearly thirty years, and even then the increased size would be small. Thus, the total output is not likely to be quickly increased and would have to be divided among more consumers. The result would be lower standards of consumption and less ability to save.

Another way of saying the same thing is that the immediate effect of present high birth rates and lowered mortality rates would be an increase in the dependency ratio; that is, the number of dependents per economically active worker. Under these conditions there would be more children in the population. It is typical in such countries that the percentage of the population under age fifteen runs 40 percent or over, whereas in the developed countries it is under 30 percent.[23] For example, Kristensen gives the proportion of the population under fifteen years of age as: North America, 28.7 percent; western Europe, 25.4; Oceania, 28.7; U.S.S.R., 31.7; eastern Europe, 25.4; Latin America, 40.5; Middle East, 40.8; Asia, 40.2; and Africa, 41. Dependency ratios are thus high, even though there are usually fewer aged to support than in the advanced countries. For example, the dependency ratio by continent according to one estimate is contained in

Table 5.7.[24] Not all those in the fifteen to sixty-four age groups are economically active. In underdeveloped countries typically, about one-third of the
total population is economically active, whereas in the developed countries,
40 percent is a typical figure.* This means that in the developed countries
each worker must support 1.5 persons besides himself, whereas in the
underdeveloped countries, each worker has two others to support. Thus,
even at the same level of efficiency, the underdeveloped country is at a
disadvantage in savings. The underdeveloped country tries to overcome this
by employing many at ages below fifteen, but the effect is only to maintain
labor inefficiency because the child is then unable to get proper training.

### TABLE 5.7.

Number of Persons Age 0-14 and 65 and Over in Total Population
per 100 Persons, Ages 15-64

| Region | 1950 | 1960 | 1975 (Est.) |
|---|---|---|---|
| Africa | 175 | 179 | 184 |
| North America | 155 | 167 | 163 |
| Latin America | 174 | 180 | 186 |
| Asia | 175 | 176 | 179 |
| Europe | 150 | 154 | 159 |
| Oceania | 160 | 166 | 166 |
| U.S.S.R. | 159 | 155 | 164 |
| World | 168 | 170 | 175 |

SOURCE: *International Labour Review*, April, 1961, p. 386.

Also, a large part of the national income goes to support children who
die before the age of fifteen; these children never replace the amount of
income they consume. Enke[25] states that in India about 20 percent of the
national income is devoted to children who die before the age of fifteen,
compared with 6 percent in the United Kingdom. H. Belshaw[26] quotes Dr.
D. Ghosh as estimating the corresponding figures at 22.5 percent and 6.5
percent. If this extra 14 to 16 percent of the national income could be
devoted to capital formation instead, substantial growth could be expected.
Similar wastage undoubtedly occurs in other countries. Enke[27] analyzes quite
effectively this matter of the economic worth of a birth. Figure 5.1 illustrates the consumption and production of a typical population in the type of
underdeveloped country we are talking about. Of every 100,000 persons
born, a certain number will die each year. Those who live consume goods
each year. For the early years this consumption is not matched by production. Eventually, some number below the original 100,000 reach the productive age and start contributing goods and services. However, some, such
as women, do not enter the labor market and some are unemployed at

* This will be detailed in the next chapter.

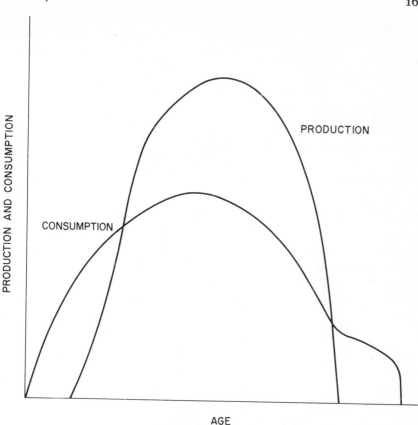

Figure 5.1   Consumption and Production Over
the Life Span of a Given Number of Births

various times. Eventually, some reach retirement age and continue to consume but not to produce. The exact shape of the consumption and production
curves is not known; the diagram here is only illustrative. Unless the production area is greater than the consumption area, standards of living must
fall. High fertility and a sudden increase in population mean a larger consumption in the early years, which is not compensated by an increased production except from other sources.

Actually, it is likely that the result of a high birth rate is decreased production. For one thing, women will be devoting their energies to child bearing and rearing and will have less time to work and less energy. Excessive
child bearing is one of the big health problems of the world. To the extent
that diets are reduced, the male worker will also be less productive. J. J.
Spengler believes a decline in birth rates may increase per capita productivity 15 to 20 percent or more.[28] Moreover, the shortage of capital brought on

by a rising population defers or nullifies programs for improvements in education, public health, sanitation, agricultural improvement, and so on, thus leading to decreased productivity.

One of the advantages presumed to flow from an increasing population is an increase in purchasing power, which acts as a stimulating influence by encouraging investment or leading to the fuller utilization of unused resources. It is possible that this is true of advanced countries in a state of depression, but even this is uncertain. It is less likely, and even unlikely, that this will be the result in underdeveloped countries. Shortages of capital and trained labor are the bottlenecks to increased output, and without increases in these there can be little or no increased output and no increased purchasing capacity. Increasing consumption per head would bring greater incentives for increasing investment. Increasing the number of consumers at the same level of living at best only increases the demand for food and necessities. Increasing consumption per head is the only way to increase the demand for manufactured goods and services.

A further problem of a rapid rise in the population is that eventually there will be a problem of finding employment for an increasing number of workers, and this requires large amounts of capital. A country in this situation must grow rapidly or face unemployment for many of its potential workers.*

Some believe that a rapidly increasing population will increase the role of the state if a country wishes to develop, for it will be impossible to rely on private savings and private initiative. Others believe that attempts to control the population will increase control by the state.[29] It seems more likely that to overcome the effects of a rapidly growing population, such extensive efforts and such sacrifices of the people will be required that there will be need for a vigorous government program. Whether this is good or bad is a matter of individual opinion.

Overcrowded countries and those with a low standard of living are apt to exhibit political instability. Moreover, population pressure has been a cause of international aggression and tension.

Whether all or any of these problems pertain to any one country is a matter for specific determination. A rapidly rising population makes them all possible and, if not reversed, ultimately almost inevitable. At best, such a population change makes development more difficult and, for many of the countries of the world today, almost unlikely. Western Europe was able to

* J. E. Meade ("Mauritius: Case Study in Malthusian Economics," *Economic Journal* [September, 1961], p. 521) portrays the situation of the island of Mauritius in this respect. In a few years, this island faces a 50 percent increase of its working population.

get started on the road to development, even with relatively low savings, because its rate of population growth was low compared with those now being experienced.[30] Countries anxious to grow economically cannot afford to neglect the problem of the rate of their population growth.

Involved in this determination is not only the question of what rate of growth can be met or, rather, more than met by a corresponding increase in productivity, but also the question of the optimum size of the population.[31] This is a somewhat vague concept in that the optimum cannot be stated with accuracy, which can also be said of other commonly used economic terms such as a commodity-demand schedule. However, the concept implies that there is some norm of population size that will maximize income per capita under the prevailing techniques of production. It must be recognized that technologies change and that therefore the optimum may also change. The decision is further complicated in that the population optimum may be different for purposes other than growth, such as for military power.* Despite the difficulties of estimation, countries wishing to maximize their growth efforts must make the best estimate they can of their optimum population and adopt policies best calculated to achieve the desired results. It is only against such a concept of an optimum population that a current trend of population change can be judged. A country below its optimum would have a different view about its rate of population growth than would one already past the optimum.

The optimum depends on the opposing pulls of diminishing returns and the other unfavorable factors detailed above, on the one hand, and the increasing returns also previously mentioned. Gottlieb states what appears to be a correct view when he points out that the optimum is not one exact population figure but more likely a zone or range—and a broad one at that. Moreover, he is of the opinion (although he emphasizes the need for research to verify this) that the optimum size changes only slowly in that innovations usually have a relatively small effect as compared with that of the total situation. If these views are correct, attempts to form population policies with a reasonable chance of being correct do not appear as hopeless as one might suppose.

Not only does population change have effects on the economy, but also changes in the economy affect population changes. For example, increases in the scale of living may at times induce a rise and at other times a decrease in population. The factors that affect population changes will be examined in the following section. At this point, however, one should realize

---

* A. S. Miller (*op. cit.*, pp. 626-27) lists as other objectives: privacy, aesthetics, retention of open and wild land, and the maintenance of democratic values. These are apt to be given little consideration.

that population growth is not a completely independent and uncaused variable. Only by understanding the factors that cause it to change can one approach the possibility of control.

## The Path of Population Change

The usual explanation of the path of population change, following the experience of the West, is that from an original condition of high birth and high mortality rates with a stable population, if the conditions are right, there is first a decline in mortality rates while fertility rates remain high, resulting in a rapid population increase. Eventually, fertility declines until population reaches an equilibrium of low birth and low death rates. The first condition is associated with low-income countries and the last with high-income countries. The important problem is how to change from the former to the latter. Crucial to development hopes is the time lag between the drop in mortality and the drop in fertility. One must explain why mortality decreases, why the fertility decline lags, and why fertility eventually declines. Adelman[32] offers an empirical analysis of the causes.

Population changes are the result of many causes, partly economic but (and possibly to a greater extent) social and cultural as well. Because these factors can work in unpredictable ways, there is no assurance that the present underdeveloped countries will duplicate the history of the West. Cultural conditions and the ease with which they can be influenced will determine this. Current experience gives no ray of hope, with the exception of the Japanese experience, where fertility is beginning to decline.

Mortality declines have been rapid in recent years, as already noted. Many specific reasons[33] can be noted: the improvement in law and order; the introduction of improved medical practice and medical science; the widespread use of insecticides to control diseases and particularly the debilitating diseases such as malaria; the use of cheap and easily diffused public health measures; protected water supplies; improved transport, which reduces famines; better education; an initial rise in incomes, which provides better diets; and improved irrigation and agricultural methods, which reduce crop failures.

The advanced countries also exhibited a decline in mortality as development started, but with the difference that the decline came only slowly and as a consequence of a slow improvement in the scale of living and the slow improvement in medicine and sanitation.[34] In general, it can be said that the decline in mortality was a result of economic development. The situation in the current underdeveloped countries is quite different. The decline in mortality has been precipitous and has occurred before economic development. The decline has come so fast that the fertility lag could well be long enough to permit a population growth that will make development quite unlikely for some time.

Birth rates tend to be maintained for an extended period after mortality rates begin to decline and may even increase because of an initial increase in health. The reduction of mortality is more acceptable to a people than is the decline of fertility and imposes no social obstacles. Not all underdeveloped countries place a high value on births, but generally they do. High birth rates have been necessary to ensure survival because of the high death rates. Those races have survived which have developed incentive systems for numerous births based on prestige, honor, and so forth. The social system, particularly the extended family living together, may induce high fertility. Kingsley Davis[35] describes the reasons why such a system leads to a high birth rate: The economic cost of raising the children does not fall directly on the parents; the inconvenience and effort of child care usually fall on the older women or children while the mother works in the field; the age of marriage is often low because the young husband does not have to support his family alone; the compulsion to marry is strong as a religious or moral obligation and as a means of promoting family alliances; the young wife is motivated to have children early and often to prove her place in the family and to improve her husband's power in the family; and the man is similarly motivated to demand children.* Some societies thus encourage high fertility. Basically, the reduction of the birth rate will occur only after the difficult shift is made from a situation where the major social pressure is the goal of group survival to that where the goal is the furthering of individual welfare and development. It takes time to effect such a basic shift in cultural traits.[36]

In many cases the status of a woman is inferior. She has little role outside the home. Her education is neglected so that she has no independence, no desire for glamour or a career and, in fact, knows no other role than being a wife, a mother, and perhaps a general farm laborer. Marriage occurs at an early age and is almost universal. Her lot and children are accepted fatalistically. When industry begins, it takes some time for her to throw off this role and enter the labor market or take a more active role in society.

Underdeveloped countries are usually agricultural. In such a society children can contribute at an early age, and the cost of their upbringing is low. Development must proceed a long way before the proportion of the labor

* Davis also lists some factors tending to counterbalance these motives, such as the nonremarriage of widows (Hindu), taboo on intercourse for a period after child birth, easy divorce (Muslim), monogamy, and insistence on legitimacy.

force engaged in agriculture is substantially reduced. Thus, the incentive for children in a large part of the economy remains high.

Religion often places great value on high fertility. For example, a son may be necessary to perform the burial rites or to make the prescribed sacrifices at various intervals after death. Because mortality has been high, it is necessary for a family to have many sons to be sure that one will survive. Children may also be a form of social insurance in that they are obligated to support their parents when in need.

Another reason for high fertility is that the methods of contraception known to the masses and economically available to them are crude, unsure, and sexually unsatisfying.

When mortality declines and society begins to change its nature, the necessity for maintaining high fertility disappears. But fertility may remain high because it takes a long time before the mass of the people realizes that the conditions have changed. In the West fertility eventually declined and this is hoped for elsewhere, but it is not certain that this will occur.

Reliance is placed upon economic pressures and social adjustments resulting from them. Major reliance is placed upon the effect of rising incomes on inducing lower fertility. Leibenstein gives this a prominent place in his theory.[37] This happens when the parents weigh the relative benefits and costs of a child. The benefits of a child are as a source of pleasure to the parents, a source of production, and as a potential source of security. The costs of a child are the expenses of maintaining it and the opportunities it forces one to forego, such as physical mobility. As development proceeds and incomes rise, the balance of the benefits and costs changes. There is less economic use for the child (assuming a shift away from agriculture) and the cost of maintenance is greater; mobility is of greater advantage; and security is of lessened value. As a possible general principle, population growth occurs when per capita incomes rise above a certain minimum, and fertility rates drop when per capita incomes rise above a somewhat higher minimum.

A second cause of fertility decline is urbanization, which makes large families inconvenient and more costly, leads to a breakup of the extended family, and wipes out old customs and traditions. Urbanization may also affect the other causes listed. As incomes rise, individual ambitions may rise. Families may desire to give each child a better start. Marriage may take place later in life. The family may substitute consumption for children. In time the woman's status changes. She develops new interests and diversions and may enter the labor market. Her desires receive consideration. Increasing education improves the knowledge of contraception and the economic capacity to use modern methods, which are an improvement over previous methods.

These are possibilities, but they cannot be relied upon in the present underdeveloped countries, for economic development is likely to be slow. Urbanization will occur, but this does not seem a sufficient cause to bring about the desired decrease in fertility. It appears that conscious government policies will be necessary to bring about a decline if it is to occur soon enough to be effective.

## Meeting the Population Problem

The control of population is one possible attack and only part of a general attack on the problem of economic growth and development. Like other matters discussed in this book, an attack on population alone cannot solve the problem of growth and an attack on it requires effort and capital. These must be allocated on the same basis as the allocation to other areas—that is, to whatever makes greatest contribution to the objectives of society.* The role played by investment in controlling population growth as compared to investment elsewhere needs intensive study.[38] Although the general allocation process will be discussed in a later chapter, it should be realized here that capital accumulation and technological change absorb labor but that population growth creates more labor to be absorbed. Rational policy must consider both aspects—increasing the rate of absorption and lessening the number required to be absorbed—with consideration of the relative cost of each course and the interrelations between the progress in one or the other.

Little is known about the cost of an effective program to accomplish a decrease in the rate of population growth, and the total results of such a program cannot be predicted. For example, we do not know what other changes are necessary to make a population control policy effective, such as improved education, increased industrialization, and increased urbanization.† Also, the problem of discounting the value of potential gains is involved, for it takes some time for a reduction in the birth rate to be effective in decreasing the number of workers seeking jobs, whereas it will start decreasing the dependency ratio quickly. It is also possible that an invest-

* These objectives may include matters of morality, religion, cultural change, defense, and so on. Certainly these considerations must be taken into account in determining population policy. One may wish to give up the possibility of increasing the rate of economic growth because the necessary policies have moral objections or interfere with cultural patterns which a nation wishes to retain. However, this is a matter for other than economists, but it should be kept in mind in recommending policy.

† The initial effect of such changes may be to increase the rate of population growth, although the ultimate effect may be to decrease it.

ment in population control may be necessary only until development can get started and may be virtually ignored thereafter. On the other hand, one must consider the cost of not investing in a population policy, for large expenditures of effort and capital may be needed to increase production more rapidly than population and to supply the necessary overheads, such as housing and water supplies. Population policy is thus part of the general policy of how best to achieve economic growth, and requires more intensive study than has hitherto been applied to it.

The problem of a rising population can be met in various ways:

1. Increasing incomes more rapidly than population.
2. Emigrating.
3. Getting more people into the work force at some positive marginal productivity.
4. Improving the quality of the workers.
5. Increasing mortality.
6. Decreasing fertility.

Each way will be discussed in turn.

We have already indicated that it will be extremely unlikely that incomes can be increased more rapidly than population is now increasing. All possible effort should be made to increase incomes, but this seems self-defeating without a successful attack on the problem of an increasing population. Similarly, attacking the population problems without improving economic conditions seems equally self-defeating. Probably both increased incomes and a decreased rate of population growth will occur, or neither will.

It is theoretically possible to lessen population pressure by emigration, but large-scale emigration is no longer likely, for few areas are open to foreign settlers on other than a selective basis. Moreover, any lands that might be made available would require considerable capital for development. The need is too great for this remedy to have more than a marginal effect. Moreover, if there is no change in the birth rate among those who do not emigrate, the natural increase of those remaining in the densely populated areas would soon restore the country to its former population. Those people emigrating to new areas might have the same problem, although it is more likely that new contacts would induce a changed attitude toward family size. Also, unfortunately, those that do migrate are usually the more adventurous and the more skilled—the very ones any country would like to keep. Countries who are receiving immigrants seek the more desired skills and exclude the illiterate, the very poor, the socially undesirable, and even the unskilled. As a matter of fact, if immigrants are properly selected, the receiving country can be the gainer, for it avoids the drain on resources necessary to rear and educate the child, whereas the sending country bears this expense.* Underdeveloped countries should study the possibility of selected immigration, especially to obtain scarce skills quickly.

We have already mentioned the possibility of migration to sparsely settled areas in the same country. It was pointed out that such possibilities do exist but that to carry out such a program, even if the people are willing to go, is probably more expensive of capital than economic improvement would be in the already settled areas. At least there is enough doubt to warrant a careful survey in each country before any such program is undertaken. Such transmigration is probably economic only after development has started in the already settled areas and capital is available to open new areas gradually. One suspects also that transmigration may be more successful if largely confined at first to young single men rather than to entire families, because only in this way can capital be generated in the newly settled area to carry out the economic development.

If more people from the present population could be attracted into the labor force and thus raise the total productivity, some improvement in the scale of living could occur. By and large, the only available unused source in substantial numbers would be women, and in some countries even they are already employed when they are not bearing children. Too many young people are already at work. Unemployment is usually large anyway. Moreover, without additional capital the added output would be low or even nonexistent in many areas. Little hope can be held out for this solution.

It might also be possible to improve the quality of the existing work force. However, this is not something that can be done quickly. It is a long-run remedy, and will be discussed in a later section.

The fifth possible solution is to increase mortality. This, of course, is undesirable, but may be forced upon a country if fertility is not decreased. Voluntary measures are possible as mentioned below, but these are undesirable to most peoples and would not receive popular approval. No government could successfully advocate such measures openly. But, without improvement in the present situation, increases in mortality may occur involuntarily because of the lowered ability of a country to feed its people. Any substantial lowering of current standards would lead to increased deaths from illnesses induced by weakness, epidemics, famines, and wars and revolutions. The Malthusian positive checks are still lurking in the background. In the long run, the control of mortality is not possible without the control of fertility.

---

* A receiving country may also gain by contact with a new culture, by an increased proportion of the population in the work force, and even by some addition of capital.

Suggestions have been made for a phased mortality program.[39] This would involve a temporary emphasis on health among the working group and away from the children and the aged, and a shift of attention from the problem of mortality to that of morbidity; that is, away from the killing diseases in an attempt to lessen the debilitating ones. The advantage of this program would be to increase productivity and to save working groups who represent a great deal of social investment in nurture, education, training, and socialization. The present public health program, which results in more people living at subsistence levels, may not be more humane and may bar progress.

However, it is not possible to think of deliberately increasing the mortality rate. Health and longevity are ends in themselves. If the only alternatives are to decrease the birth rate or to encourage rise of the death rate, the former seems preferable as being more humane. The issue of which is more moral is a complicated one and full of religious implications, but reducing births seems the better alternative from even that point of view. It may be added that increasing the mortality rates will not reduce the current bad dependency ratios unless the increased mortality takes place among the children, the aged, and the unemployed.

The best solution in view of the difficulties of increasing output and the ineffectiveness or undesirability of the other solutions seems to be to decrease the number of births. This is not an easy task and may prove to be as difficult as increasing production, particularly if attempted in a rural area. Three things are necessary to accomplish this: The people must be motivated to want smaller families; there must be knowledge of how this is to be accomplished; and there must be means available for the purpose. Success, in time to help development, will require an all-out government campaign.

We have already discussed the motives for having large families, and these are not easily changed. However, incentives must be sought to make people want fewer children. The best means of controlling births are ineffective if people do not want to use them. On the other hand, if there is a will to decrease births, even crude methods will bring appreciable results. Sociologists are making advances in the science of social change and can do much in instructing countries in how to instill new incentives. Government programs of education, especially if coordinated with appeals of patriotism and nationalism, give hopes of success. Moreover, there is some question whether the mothers in underdeveloped countries do want as large families as they have, and some studies indicate they do want family control.[40] However, many women make no effort to control their families because they do not know how, they accept children fatalistically, they have no will to do so because of their inferior status (domination by the male), or because they are too ignorant to understand the consequences. Improving the status of women and educating them would bring out any latent desire for family limitation. These measures would probably change women's attitudes anyway as they experience a new benefit-cost calculus. That there has always been some motivation is evidenced by the use in primitive societies of measures to control populations, such as taboos on intercourse at certain times, crude efforts at contraception, abortion, infanticide, and abandonment of the economically inferior. Much of this may have had a considerable amount of magical practice intertwined in it, but these do represent efforts to keep populations down.* Monetary incentives, either in the form of payments for small families or the taxation of large ones, may sufficiently raise the costs of bringing up children to provide the necessary incentives. Lessening the hold of the extended family and putting each couple on its own would also be a powerful influence.

Two major obstacles exist. One is the Communist philosophy on population in those countries that have adopted it. The Communists have no moral objection to methods of birth control, but feel that the ills of a people are due to capitalistic exploitation alone and that the way to develop is to install the right institutions. The 1953 to 1957 Chinese population-control campaign was based on protecting the health of mothers and children, letting mothers work and study, and promoting the proper education of the young. Malthusian pessimism was explicitly denied.[41]

The second obstacle is religious beliefs. Most religions do not forbid fertility control, although some place a high value on male survivors. With improved mortality, this is no permanent barrier to fertility control. The Roman Catholic religion is not necessarily opposed to family limitation, but objects to the means used. Approval is given to abstinence from intercourse and the so-called rhythm method, or abstinence during the woman's fertile period, but these are not certain. Artificial means are ruled out as being unnatural and immoral. However, the policies as applied in particular regions are not this clear. There are numerous pronouncements as to the value of large families, and the Church is generally opposed to public programs to discourage fertility on the grounds that this is a personal matter. There are also denials that the problems of underdeveloped countries are population problems, the solutions offered being emigration and help from the more prosperous countries.[42] The suggested solutions and the methods of population control permitted are not practical, especially in the case of

* See K. Davis and J. Blake ("Social Structure and Fertility." *Economic Development and Cultural Change* [April, 1956], pp. 211-35) for an extended discussion of means of population control. It should be noted that primitive societies practiced control over mortality and abortion even more than they did control over conception, probably because of the greater certainty.

uneducated wives. Some further solution is required. The problem was considered at the recent Roman Catholic Ecumenical Council, and some practical solution that does not violate religious belief may evolve from its deliberations. It is not improbable that failure to control the population of Latin America may throw the whole continent of South America into the hands of the Communists.

In addition to the motivation to limit families, there must be knowledge of how to do it. People must be taught not only that limitation is desirable but also that it is possible, and they must be taught how to utilize the methods effectively. This may be difficult in societies with a large amount of illiteracy, but programs can be at least partially effective. After all, one does not have to convince and educate every member of society, but health clinics will not be of much use until people learn to use them. Countries that have instituted programs have seen limited success except in better educated Japan and, for a while, in more closely controlled China. Educating the people and getting them to exercise continuous care is a large undertaking.

Lastly, means must be available. Some means of contraception have been known for centuries in most countries and have been practiced on at least a limited scale. For the most part, these may have been practiced by the upper classes and by prostitutes, but they were not unknown by the lower classes. However, they were crude, uncertain, and sexually unsatisfying. Modern methods are more certain, although not perfect, and more acceptable to the users; but they do require knowledge as to their existence and use and are expensive if compared with the income of the poorer members of society in the underdeveloped countries.

What is needed is a cheap contraceptive, which can be taken orally or by injection and will be effective for a long period of time. Considerable research is being carried on to find an effective method and especially one that can meet the Roman Catholic objections.[43] This search for an effective method needs to be continued. From the point of view of the developed countries, this research may be more productive in the sense of decreasing the need for foreign aid than the investment made in any other project.* There is much discussion of a pill, and apparently this has already been developed and is successful but is too expensive to be feasible. To be entirely fanciful, one might wish for a chemical to be put into the rivers of the overpopulated countries, which, like fluoride for dental caries, might reduce the birth potential.

* For the benefits to be derived from preventing a birth, see Meier, *op. cit.*, pp. 75-88; S. Enke, "Economics of Government Payments to Limit Population." Part I, *Economic Development and Cultural Change* (July, 1960), pp. 339-48; and S. Enke, *Economics for Development*, *loc. cit.*, pp. 368 ff. The proposed bonus schemes are intended to increase the motivation for reducing births.

Birth controls fall into four categories: abstinence, contraception, sterilization, and abortion. Abstinence, either total or periodic, is not acceptable to most people. Delay in the age of marriage can help, but the legal age of marriage has apparently never been set very high anywhere (usually eighteen at the highest). Custom and the need for financial independence may delay marriage somewhat, and these seem to be operating in the underdeveloped countries among the educated women if not elsewhere. Abstention within marriage is not popular and not to be counted on among uneducated couples and women who are dominated by their husbands. Permanent celibacy is usually frowned upon in the underdeveloped countries.

Various methods of contraception are known.[44] These show varying degrees of success and differ in cost, ease of use, acceptability, and so on. Spreading their use is a major problem. Sterilization is the most effective method if people can be induced to accept this. Enke[45] is a leading advocate of sterilization of men through vasectomies. He would pay a bonus to men who undergo this operation, the bonus being based on the expected number of future children and the estimated economic value to the nation of preventing these births. This operation has the advantage of being simple, with little pain and practically no incapacitation; it does not interfere with sexual gratification; it is known and widely practiced; it requires no intelligence or self-control on the part of the subject; its cost is small and incurred only once; and it is positive and irreversible.* The sterilization of women is more complicated and more costly.

Abortion is not usually so acceptable, but is certain and does not require constant attention. Properly handled, it is not very dangerous, but there is some element of danger; and abortion may ultimately affect the physical and mental health of the patient, although there is no conclusive evidence to prove this. It is practiced widely and has been made legal in some countries. Japan legalized abortion as one means of reducing her birth rate until contraception could be more widely practiced, the latter now being used more than abortion. In general, it would appear less desirable than contraception.

Other measures that countries might undertake without adhering to any of the above methods would be to establish birth control clinics, encourage employment for women outside the home,† make payments for nonpregnancy,[46] or tax large families.

A number of countries have made family planning a part of their development policy; examples are India, Pakistan, Japan, Puerto Rico, and Communist China (for a short period).[47] The chief measures are govern-

* Recent evidence throws doubt on its irreversibility.

† A. J. Jaffe and K. Azumi ("The Birth Rate and Cottage Industries in Underdeveloped Countries." *Economic Development and Cultural Change* [October, 1960], pp. 52-63) assert that women employed outside the home have on the average one-half child less than those employed at home.

mental dissemination of information on contraception. Except for Japan, the efforts do not seem to have been permanently effective.

Notestein[48] summarizes the problem and the approach to its solution as follows: It is dangerous to waste the productive power of modern techniques in a social setting calculated to maintain high fertility. He proposes a total program to include:

1. The substitution of a rounded economy for a colonial agricultural economy. This would include industrialization, rationalization of agriculture, and the promotion of international trade.
2. The rapid extension of popular education.
3. The introduction of birth control measures.
4. An emphasis on public health measures.
5. The development of native leadership, which would acquire new values and serve as a medium of diffusion.
6. The breaking down of barriers to the advance of the individual.
7. The encouragement of migration to relieve population pressures.

Population control is thus seen as one part of a rounded program and deserves consideration in the allocation of development funds and efforts.

## Investment in Human Capital

In addition to the problem of the total population and the rate of population growth, which will undoubtedly require the expenditure of effort and funds, the typical underdeveloped country will find it necessary to invest in its human beings by spending money and effort in order to improve them in various ways.

There are many ways in which a country can invest in persons. The most obvious is education, but also important are health, physical development, training in some skill, the development of the attitudes most conducive to the country's objectives, and socialization of the individual; that is, teaching him to take his place in society. Here, only education and health will be discussed at any length. Job training will be discussed in the next chapter, and the process of developing desirable attitudes and social habits has already been discussed in Chapter 3. All these development programs play some part in increasing the productivity of a country, either directly or indirectly. Unfortunately, it is not easy to calculate the return that can be expected from such investment of resources, but an attempt at an estimate must be made if resources are to be allocated, even roughly, for optimum productivity. The investment return from education will be discussed in the next few pages. Similar procedures are necessary in each country for all aspects of investment in human capital.

A major problem is that the returns from such investment may be long delayed and may therefore be neglected in favor of more immediately profitable investments. The returns from investment in education or health may be long delayed, and any reasonable rate of discounting future returns may indicate that the present value of such an investment is zero. Yet, without such investment the extent of development may be seriously limited. The consideration of the merits of such investment must have a time horizon much longer than that of the usual economic decision.

In terms of the amount of capital investment required, if on no other basis, the most important type of human investment is in education. Because the investment is apt to be very large, countries should take special care to see that the amount and kinds of education provided are really productive or conducive to development or other national objectives. Thus, it is necessary that the type and extent of the education provided have relevance to the skills and human development required to promote economic growth.

Investment in education not only increases production but also has its consumption aspects; that is, it increases personal enjoyment and has cultural value in itself. This result is important, but is not the primary claimant for investment funds if economic growth is the goal. Unfortunately, the consumer aspects of education are somewhat of a luxury or side effect that can be indulged in for their own sake only when a nation has less pressing needs for its funds.

If we think of economic growth as using the investment of present resources to produce increased future assets, funds allocated to education must be considered as necessary to future growth, since innovations and changes that are instrumental in realizing economic development are made effective through education. Theodore Schultz,[49] who has been a leader in stressing the value of investment in human beings, points out that people do not have all their capabilities at birth, and that the economic capabilities of man are a produced means of production; except for some differences in inherited abilities, most of the differences in earning ability are due to differences in investment in education.

Galbraith[50] thinks that investment in education may be more productive than investment in some machines. He points out that no illiterate peasantry is progressive and, furthermore, that no literate peasantry is not progressive. A. G. Frank[51] states that much of our increase in productivity is due to the intangibles of technology, the organization of economic activities, and increases in human capabilities, and states that the "investment in the human factor may well have a higher payoff in terms of increased output than does any other input." S. Enke[52] also testifies to the potential productivity of education.

But all education is not equally profitable. The productivity of scientists, engineers, doctors, agricultural experts, and business managers is probably high in the underdeveloped countries. A rigid analysis of various skills might reveal some others that are surprisingly productive. Because capital is scarce, it is necessary to examine the allocation of educational funds carefully.

Research indicates that productivity in the developed countries has increased faster than can be explained by inputs of physical capital and additions to the labor force.[53] It is difficult to establish just how much of the contribution to productivity has been made by improvement in the human factor, but it is essential to establish this, at least roughly, for each country. Schultz[54] estimates this contribution to be one-fifth of the growth in the United States between 1930 and 1957. Various estimates have been made in the United States of the value of a college education, but these are usually in terms of earnings for an individual, whereas the chief concern of a country is the total increase in productivity. At this juncture we can say only that it appears considerable and may have a more worthwhile claim to investment funds than other more directly and immediately productive objects of investment.

The real value of education and learning may lie in the possibility that the actual limit to industrialization and progress lies in technical capacity[55] and not in the supply of capital. For example, after World War II, the European economies speedily grew to their prewar levels and then grew less rapidly. The rapid growth of Japan and Israel can be attributed to the human factor. These examples teach us that if people have the knowledge, they will re-create capital that has been destroyed or is lacking or can utilize what capital can be borrowed. The ability of a country to absorb capital (that is, to use it profitably) rests largely on the supply of trained personnel and the general abilities of its people. Advanced mechanical equipment in truly primitive communities does not have so high a value as it does in progressive countries.

The advantages of education to a country have been ably summarized by B. A. Weisbrod.[56] First, some advantages are realized directly by the individuals educated:

1. Direct financial returns for earnings seem to have a positive correlation with education.
2. An increase in the options or alternatives available.
3. An increase in the ability to adjust to changing situations.
4. Nonmarket returns of culture and ability to enjoy existence and to do things for oneself.*

* The value of being able to prepare one's own income tax is cited as paying for a surprising fraction of the United States' educational bill.

Other gains are realized by the economy as a whole or by other than those directly educated.

1.   Those in the same residence benefit. The current family gains from indirect education and the socialization of the individual. The mother may be able to work. The future family is improved by being born into a better environment.

2.   The neighbors gain through better social and behavioral norms in the children.

3.   The taxpayers gain through less cost for unemployment and crime.

4.   The employer and fellow employees gain from greater productivity.

5.   Society, in general, benefits from the gain in literacy and increased information and better communications. A competitive market economy cannot operate successfully without general literacy. Political democracy depends on the widespread dissemination of information and the capacity of the people to absorb it. Education opens the mind to new ideas and the further advance of knowledge.

If we look on education and training as an investment, each country must ascertain what kinds are needed to meet the needs of the country and must plan the output. Leaving the choice of training to the individual is not likely to lead to the best results. In fact, the favorite personal choice in many underdeveloped countries is in cultural or in legal training. These are useful, but in many countries such people are in oversupply and cannot find employment at tasks they consider suitable. This is often thought of as a major cause of discontent of the intellectuals and of revolutionary movements. It would appear desirable to have some shift toward a more practical training, at least in the early years of development efforts.

What is the proper educational program? One hesitates to lay down a program because it must be specific for each country. But certain common principles may be advanced.[57] First of all, there must be a fairly extensive amount of general elementary education because modern economies require an ability to communicate on a wide scale, which can be done economically only in writing. Moreover, this is the only feasible means of discovering those who can be trained for the more advanced occupations. A general elementary education also promotes social unity in a people and permits the extension of public health programs. Enke[58] stresses the value of a common "national" language and the necessity of overcoming reliance on magic and superstition by the substitution of a sense of science and rationality. He also stresses the value of a knowledge of other peoples and cultures and the strengthening of loyalties and values necessary for a developing economy. However, he raises the question of whether elementary education should be universal or limited to those near cities where the cost would be least. The author feels that this is the place to start, but that the advantages of universal education are so great that universal elementary education should be sought as soon as possible. However, the speed at which this can be accomplished will depend on the particular circumstances in each country, the capital available, the existence of personnel, and so on.

Second, it is advantageous to improve the degree of literacy among adults for the same reasons and, in addition, to form a base for the participation of the people in government and other activities. Even meaningful participation in trade union activity, as it is known in the West, requires some level of educational training. Without literacy the worker's participation is apt to be limited to obeying instructions from the central command. In most underdeveloped countries, illiteracy is high and is a considerable handicap to development. Table 5.8 shows the amount of illiteracy in many countries.

Third, there is need for some advanced education above the elementary level. However, it is hard to say how extensive general education beyond the primary grades should be. General and liberal education can be advantageous to the individual and to society, but only to the extent that a person's mind can be broadened by it and that the stage of economic growth requires an advanced educational level. Some individuals can profit from many years of liberal training and others by only a small amount. At some point a person should leave his general training, or rather, a complete emphasis on it, and should start to learn a specific skill. The point at which this should occur varies with the individual. In the United States we leave the choice up to the individual, with the result that much educational effort is wasted. Conversely, many do not take as much general educational training as they could profit from. The United States is little able to afford such waste, and underdeveloped countries can afford it even less. Prediction of the most appropriate training for each individual is not perfect, but past academic performance is a reasonable guide. However, in the underdeveloped countries the more immediate considerations are the resources available and the types of skills needed immediately to promote economic growth. In the underdeveloped countries' stage of development the advantages of widespread secondary and advanced education of a general type seem to the author less impelling than in an advanced economy. In the underdeveloped countries, there is good reason for a stress on vocational education designed to meet the needs of their economic plans.

Fourth, at the top of the educational pyramid is the university. This is an essential part of the total educational structure, but it is the author's observation that underdeveloped countries are laying too much stress on the extensive development of university training, probably because of prestige

**TABLE 5.8.**

*Illiteracy in Selected Countries, 1962*

| Country | Percent Illiterate | Country | Percent Illiterate |
|---|---|---|---|
| Afghanistan | 95 | Italy | 11 |
| Albania | 40 | Japan | 2 |
| Argentina | 10 | Jordan | 50 |
| Australia | *a* | Korea, South | 35 |
| Austria | *a* | Laos | 80 |
| Belgium | 3 | Lebanon | 20 |
| Bolivia | 60 | Liberia | 95 |
| Brazil | 50 | Libya | 85 |
| Bulgaria | 20 | Luxembourg | 1 |
| Burma | 43 | Malaya | 62 |
| Cambodia | 30 | Mexico | 21 |
| Canada | *a* | Morocco | 90 |
| Ceylon | 35 | Nepal | 94 |
| Chile | 20 | Netherlands | *a* |
| China | 56 | New Zealand | *a* |
| Colombia | 37 | Nicaragua | 60 |
| Costa Rica | 20 | Norway | *a* |
| Cuba | 22 | Pakistan | 81 |
| Czechoslovakia | 2 | Panama | 28 |
| Denmark | *a* | Paraguay | 60 |
| Dominican Republic | 57 | Peru | 58 |
| Ecuador | 43 | Philippines | 36 |
| Egypt | 75 | Poland | 23 |
| El Salvador | 57 | Portugal | 41 |
| Ethiopia | 95 | Roumania | 23 |
| Finland | *a* | Saudi Arabia | 85 |
| France | 3 | Soviet Union | 10 |
| Germany, East | *a* | Spain | 15 |
| Germany, West | *a* | Sudan | 96 |
| Ghana | 80 | Sweden | *a* |
| Great Britain | *a* | Switzerland | *a* |
| Greece | 24 | Syria | 40 |
| Guatemala | 72 | Taiwan | 40 |
| Haiti | 96 | Thailand | 46 |
| Honduras | 60 | Tunisia | 80 |
| Hungary | 6 | Turkey | 65 |
| Iceland | *a* | South Africa | 57 |
| India | 82 | United States | *a* |
| Indonesia | 60 | Uruguay | 15 |
| Iran | 85 | Venezuela | 51 |
| Iraq | 81 | Viet Nam, North | 50 |
| Ireland | *a* | Viet Nam, South | 50 |
| Israel | 7 | Yugoslavia | 25 |

SOURCE: "A World of Facts—How Eighty-eight Nations Compare in Geography, Industry, Government, Living Conditions," The Civil Education Service, 1963, Publisher of *American Observer Weekly News Review.*
*a* Almost none.

considerations. For example, the number of universities reported for Indonesia, starting with the first in 1949, had reached a total of fifty-seven state and private institutions by 1962. The number of students was not clearly stated, but the largest institution had 18,000 students, with 2,200 in the economics faculty. Even more universities were under consideration. In time, this number will be needed, but such rapid growth creates formidable problems of standards, staffing, and financing. From an economic point of view, one suspects that a more selective choice of students in fewer institutions would better meet the country's need for leadership, although political considerations and efforts to avoid discriminatory selection probably require greater opportunity for all. However, mass university education does not appear economical in a country short of capital and short of intermediate skills, in which areas the training is relatively neglected. Conversations with officials of employer associations revealed that the great lack in industry lies in staff skills, foremen, and skilled laborers. Thus, it seems important to lay greater emphasis at early stages of development on establishing technical schools at various levels to train people in such skills as the building trades and machine operators, on up to technical colleges, with a reduction in the amount of university training to a few highly qualified individuals. In time, of course, an expansion of the university system is indicated.* In each country the best proportions of the different types of training are a matter for serious investigation. As the technical level of a society rises, the importance of a universal general education rises and the extent of this general education also rises; that is, in an underdeveloped country with a low technical level, a universal primary education with secondary education for a restricted number plus technical or skill training for another restricted number is preferable. As the technical level rises, universal secondary education becomes desirable and so on.

It may be added that because of the previously mentioned external economies realized from expenditures on education, the provision of such facilities is justified as a function of the state. Similarly, the state is justified in requiring school attendance. In the present advanced countries, further gains in the external benefits of education may be minimal, although it is important to retain those from which we have been benefiting. In underdeveloped countries the public gains are very great, but so are the private ones. On occasion, the university graduate is required to work a certain number of years for the state in order to return some of his private gains to the state.

Similar to the desirability of investment in education is that of investment

---

* One may add that in the United States also, we may well be allocating relatively too much in resources to university training and too little to vocational training.

in health, and in fact the two programs may have to be inseparable, for one depends on the other. Both are joint investments in the same individual. Some health programs depend on education; for example, personal hygiene and sanitation. Illness reduces the effectiveness of investment in education, and educational levels determine the seeking out of health services.[59] Both improve people and yield a continuing return.

Good health has obvious advantages to the individual: better work capacity, a longer life, and a lessened incidence of pain and incapacitation. Sickness results in low productivity, and low productivity means poverty, which is a major cause of sickness. Thus, sickness and low incomes are characteristic of underdeveloped countries.[60] In general, diseases may be classified as debilitating or killing. Malaria and most of the common diseases in underdeveloped countries are debilitating, whereas some of the plagues are examples of killing diseases. Debilitating diseases may well be more costly economically to underdeveloped countries in that the victim continues to consume but has low work capacity. It is important to attack both sickness and poverty on economic as well as humanitarian grounds.

Improved health has important external benefits as well as private ones. Good health in one person reduces the risk of exposure for others. The increased work capacity of the individual is advantageous for society, the employer, and the fellow worker. Good health also increases the number in the work force and extends the life expectancy so that the worker contributes to production for a longer period of time. A health program may also make habitable certain lands that otherwise would not be suitable because of the prevalence of disease. The external benefits are so important that the provision for health cannot be left to the individual but must be a public program.

A health program involves several elements:

1. A public health program, including the improvement of sanitation, providing a safe water supply, and preventing the spread of disease by quarantine; eliminating the sources of infection, as in malaria, mass inoculations, and so on.
2. The establishment of health centers to provide health information, inoculations, information on family planning, and temporary medical care. Essentially, this might be called preventive medicine.
3. Increasing the supply of medical personnel.
4. Providing hospitals.
5. Perhaps establishing means to assure payment for needed medical service.

One would suppose that health protection measures would be readily acceptable and thus easily introduced. For the most part this seems true, particularly in the case of those measures not applied directly to the person, such as treating the waters to reduce the number of malarial mosquitoes. There is greater difficulty in getting individuals to change their own health practices, dietary practices, and so on; in fact, these practices are usually among the hardest things to change. Many continue to believe in their customary medicines or magic rituals, and it will take time and effort to change this. Many in Indonesia, for example, continue to make long scratches on their bodies with a coin, to cure a cold. Moreover, many, even in the most enlightened countries, are apt to take a chance that they will not get sick so as to avoid payment for medical costs. This requires that the government take a firm hand in introducing and carrying out a health program.

## Urbanization

One of the features of economic growth is an increase in urbanization; that is, an increase in the proportion of the total population living in cities. This may be considered a partial test for the degree of development and is usually considered inevitable, even though efforts are made "to bring industry to the countryside." Underdeveloped countries, of course, may have some large cities, but these are primarily commercial, governmental, or religious centers in nature. Growth also brings the industrial city, enlarges the commercial life, and expands the size and number of large cities, at least to a point.

Only the implication of urbanization for economic growth will be considered here. In some ways it contributes to growth and in some ways it hampers it. Its contributions are:

1.  It expands the area of contact with new cultures and leads to the intermingling of different peoples, including different subgroups of its own citizens. This widens the intellectual horizons of the people and brings new ideas and the acceptance of change. The accepted pattern of life is disturbed, and change occurs. Through the city, new ideas are eventually transmitted to the smaller cities and the rural areas.

2.  City living throws a man on his own resources to a larger extent than does rural living and thus has some effect in promoting initiative. The man now must look to his own interests and is apt to throw off the traditions of the past, whether for good or ill.

3.  Urbanization is sometimes thought to be the cheapest way to industrialize because it concentrates the provision of the social overheads, such as power, transportation, and education; but this is a debatable proposition and subject to investigation, since other expenses are involved, as discussed below. Research is needed in each situation to see if the large city is really an efficient method of settlement.

4. The large population may permit greater specialization and division of labor, but again it is debatable how large a city needs to be to give the maximum advantage. The best specialists may be attracted to the larger cities because there are more customers, and a large city may be able to afford better training facilities for specialized jobs, but otherwise its greater size appears to have little advantage over the small city.

5. New service industries can grow in response to the needs of the city and the better market.

6. If the history of the West is repeated, fertility will decline.

But there are difficulties, too, and these include:

1. Change is induced, but the result may be the disturbance of the accepted order without the growth of another order to replace it. The result could be moral confusion until a new code of behavior develops, thus resulting in problems of crime, vice, and political disorder.

2. The very rapidity of growth, which draws its main recruits from the rural unemployed or underemployed of which a large proportion are males and young people, coupled with a failure to plan, has meant that most cities have developed haphazardly. The result has been slum areas and traffic congestion of the worst sort. In time these cities must be rebuilt, and this will be costly. Preplanning could avoid these conditions and therefore seems an activity with a large economic return.

3. Rural unemployment is transferred to the city, where the discontent is concentrated and therefore more explosive.

Thus, the growth of cities has both cost-increasing and cost-decreasing effects. Only a spot study could estimate the balance. Urbanization may be advantageous, but only if the speed of growth can be controlled so as to lessen the worst evils. A preplanned development of the city and a controlled speed of growth may be one of the best potential investments. In general, this means improving the alternatives in the smaller areas. This involves increasing the productivity and incomes, improving the social conditions, providing secondary occupations in the rural areas, and establishing industry in smaller towns. This, too, has costs, and a comparison of the gains and costs is an advisable preliminary step.

## REFERENCES

1. Department of Social Affairs, *The Determinants and Consequences of Population Trends*, Population Study No. 17. New York, United Nations, 1953, p. 3.

2. CHANDRASEKHAR, S., "Population Growth, Socio-Economic Development, and Living Standards." *International Labour Review* (June, 1954), p. 527.

3. NILSEN, STEN S., "Childbearing and the Standard of Life." *International Labour Review* (January, 1954), p. 74.

4. WOYTINSKY, W., "World Resources in Relation to Population," in P. M. Hauser, *Population and World Politics*. New York, The Free Press of Glencoe, 1958, p. 57. (Outlines the best known estimates.)

5. CLARK, COLIN, "Do Population and Freedom Grow Together?" *Fortune* (December, 1960), pp. 136-39. Clark, "Population Growth and Living Standards." *International Labour Review* (August, 1953), pp. 99-117.

6. CLARK, "Do Population and Freedom . . . ," *loc. cit.*, p. 137.

7. *Ibid.*, p. 138.

8. DURAND, J. D., "World Population: Trend and Prospects," in Hauser, *op. cit.*, p. 27.

9. Department of Social Affairs, *Determinants and Consequences . . . , loc. cit.*, pp. 5-20. Hertzler, J. O., *Crisis in World Population*. Lincoln, Neb., University of Nebraska Press, 1956, pp. 9-25. Sauvy, A., *Fertility and Survival*. London, Chatto, Windres, 1961, pp. 17-24. Cook, R. C., "World Population Growth." *Law and Contemporary Problems* (Summer, 1960), pp. 379-88.

10. Department of Social Affairs, *Determinants and Consequences . . . , loc. cit.*, p. 5.

11. SAUVY, *op. cit.*, pp. 22, 23.

12. HAUSER, *op. cit.*, p. 10.

13. VOGT, W., *People, Challenge to Survival*. New York, W. Sloane Associates, 1960, pp. 49-52.

14. MEADE, J. E., "Mauritius: Case Study in Malthusian Economics." *Economic Journal* (September, 1951), p. 521.

15. United Nations, *Determinants and Consequences . . . , loc. cit.*, p. 56.

16. CLARK, "Do Population and Freedom . . . ," *loc. cit.*, p. 139.

17. PEACOCK, A. T., "Theory of Population and Modern Economic Analysis," in J. J. Spengler, *Population Theory and Policies*. New York, The Free Press of Glencoe, 1956, pp. 190-206. Spengler, J. J., "Population and Per Capita Income." *Ibid.*, pp. 207-18.

18. Department of Social Affairs, *Determinants and Consequences . . . , loc. cit.*, pp. 225ff.

19. ENKE, S., *Economics for Development*. Englewood Cliffs, N.J., Prentice-Hall, Inc., 1963, pp. 349ff. and 368ff.

20. ENKE, S., "Speculations on Population Growth and Economic Development." *Quarterly Journal of Economics* (February, 1957), pp. 19-35. Chaudhry, N. K., "Dilemma of Population Planning in India," *Economic Development and Cultural Change* (November, 1955), pp. 68-81.

21. SPENGLER, J. J., "Population and World Economic Development," *Science* (May, 1960), p. 1499.

22. COALE, N., and E. M. HOOVER, *Population Growth and Economic Development in Low Income Countries*. Princeton, N.J., Princeton University Press, 1958, p. 285.

23. "The Race between People and Resources in the ECAFE Region." *Population Bulletin* (March, 1960), p. 36. *Ibid.*, p. 38. Kristensen, Thorkil, and associates, *The Economic World Balance,* Copenhagen, Munksgaard, 1960. Lavell, C. B., *Population Growth and the Development of South America*, Population Research Project. Washington, D.C., George Washington University, 1960, p. 10.

24. See also "The Race between . . . ," *loc. cit.*, p. 38; and Lavell, *op. cit.*, pp. 12, 15, for other estimates by individual country and region. Some individual countries show a ratio of 2 to 1.

25. ENKE, *op. cit.*, pp. 19-35.

26. BELSHAW, H., *Population Growth and Levels of Consumption.* Lon-

don, George Allen Unwin, Ltd., 1960, p. 133.

27. ENKE, S., *Economics for Development*. Englewood Cliffs, N.J., Prentice-Hall, Inc., 1963, pp. 349 ff. and 368 ff. See also Meier, G. M., and R. E. Baldwin, *Economic Development*. New York, John Wiley & Sons, Inc., 1957, pp. 70 ff.

28. SPENGLER, J. J., "Population as a Factor in Economic Development," in P. M. Hauser, *Population and World Politics*. New York, The Free Press of Glencoe, 1958, p. 175.

29. Representative of the first view is Miller, A. S., "Political Economy of Population Growth." *Law and Contemporary Problems* (Summer, 1960), pp. 614-29. Clark, Colin, *op. cit.*, pp. 136-39, represents the second.

30. SPENGLER, J. J., "Population and World Economic Development," *loc. cit.*, p. 1499.

31. GOTTLIEB, M., "The Theory of the Optimum Population for a Closed Economy." *Journal of Political Economy* (December, 1945), pp. 289-316. Enke, *Economics of Development, op. cit.*, pp. 345-49.

32. ADELMAN, IRMA, "An Econometric Analysis of Population Growth." *American Economic Review* (June, 1963), pp. 314-39.

33. Department of Social Affairs, *Determinants and Consequences . . . , loc. cit.*, pp. 47-70.

34. *Ibid.*, p. 58. Habakkuk, J., "Population Problems and European Economic Development in the Late Eighteenth and Nineteenth Centuries." *American Economic Review, Papers and Proceedings* (May, 1963), pp. 607-18.

35. DAVIS, KINGSLEY, "Institutional Patterns Favoring High Fertility in Underdeveloped Areas," in L. W. Shannon, *Underdeveloped Areas*. New York, Harper & Bros., 1957, pp. 89, 90.

36. LEIBENSTEIN, H., *Economic Backwardness and Economic Growth*.

New York, J. Wiley & Sons, 1957, p. 157.

37. LEIBENSTEIN, *op. cit.*, pp. 161ff.

38. RANIS, G., "Allocation Criteria and Population Growth." *American Economic Review, Papers and Proceedings* (May, 1963), pp. 619-33.

39. STYCOS, J. M., "Population Growth and the Alliance for Progress." *Population Bulletin* (October, 1962), p. 124.

40. CHANDRASEKHAR, S., "Prospect for Planned Parenthood in India," in L. W. Shannon, *Underdeveloped Areas*. New York, Harper & Bros., 1957, p. 390. Sauvy, *op. cit.*, p. 164. Nilson, *op. cit.*, pp. 72-76. Meier and Baldwin, *op. cit.*, p. 4.

41. ORGANSKI, K. F., and K. F. A. ORGANSKI, *Population and World Power*. New York, Knopf, 1961, pp. 163-73. Zlotnick, J., "Population Pressure and Political Indecision." *Foreign Affairs* (July, 1961), pp. 688-92.

42. ST. JOHN-STEVAS, N., "A Roman Catholic View of Population Control." *Law and Contemporary Problems* (Summer, 1960), pp. 445-69. Organski, *op. cit.*, pp. 158-63. Zlotnick, *op. cit.*, p. 693.

43. MEIER and BALDWIN, *op. cit.*, pp. 95-.125. (Discusses progress in the field of fertility control.) *Ibid.*, pp. 75-88.

44. TIETZE, C., "Current Status of Fertility Control." *Law and Contemporary Problems* (Summer, 1960), pp. 426-44.

45. ENKE, S., "Gains to India from Population Control." *Review of Economics and Statistics* (May, 1960), pp. 175-81. Enke, *Economics for Development, op. cit.*, pp. 379ff.

46. ENKE, *Economics for Development, loc. cit.*, p. 377. Enke, *Review of Economics and Statistics, loc. cit.*, p. 180.

47. SAUVY, *op. cit.*, pp. 181-210. Organski, *op. cit.*, pp. 180-222 and 169-71. Chaudhry, N. K., *op. cit.*, pp. 68-81.

48. NOTESTEIN, in Spengler, *Population*

*Theory and Policy.* New York, The Free Press of Glencoe, 1956, pp. 470-83.

49. SCHULTZ, THEODORE, "Reflections on Investment in Man." *Journal of Political Economy* (October, 1962), Supp., pp. 1-8.

50. GALBRAITH, J. K., *Economic Development in Perspective.* Cambridge, Mass., Harvard University Press, 1962, p. 49.

51. FRANK, A. G., "Human Capital and Economic Growth." *Economic Development and Cultural Change* (January, 1960), pp. 170-71.

52. ENKE, *Economics for Development, loc. cit.,* pp. 385-90.

53. MUSHKIN, S. J., "Health as an Investment." *Journal of Political Economy* (October, 1962), Supp., p. 129. (Cites numerous sources to this effect.)

54. SCHULTZ, T. W., "Investment in Human Capital in Poor Countries," in P. D. Zook, *Foreign Trade and Human Capital.* Dallas, Texas, Southern Methodist University Press, 1962, p. 4.

55. SAUVY, *op. cit.,* p. 135. Weisbrod, B. A., "Education and Investment in Human Capital." *Journal of Political Economy* (October, 1962), Supp., p. 106. Schultz, T. W., *op. cit.,* pp. 7-9.

56. WEISBROD, *op. cit.,* pp. 108-20.

57. ENKE, *Economics for Development, loc. cit.,* pp. 386ff. (Gives a different concept.)

58. *Ibid.,* p. 387.

59. MUSHKIN, *op. cit.,* pp. 130ff.

60. ENKE, *Economics for Development, op. cit.,* pp. 398ff. (Gives an excellent description of the most prevalent diseases.)

## ADDITIONAL READINGS

CHANDRASEKHAR, S., *Population and Planned Parenthood in India,* 2nd ed. rev. London, George Allen & Unwin, Ltd., 1961.

DAVIS, K., *Population of India and Pakistan.* Princeton, N.J., Princeton University Press, 1951.

DAVIS, K., "The Amazing Decline of Mortality in Underdeveloped Areas." *American Economic Review, Papers and Proceedings* (May, 1956), pp. 305-18.

DAVIS K., and H. H. GOLDEN, "Urbanization and the Development of Preindustrial Areas." *Economic Development and Cultural Change* (October, 1954), pp. 6-26.

HALBWACHS, M., *Population and Society.* New York, The Free Press of Glencoe, 1960.

HAUSER, P. M., "Demographic Indicators of Economic Development." *Economic Development and Cultural Change* (January, 1959), pp. 98-116.

McKELVEY, V. E., "Resources, Population Growth and the Level of Living." *Science* (April 3, 1959), pp. 875-81.

MILLER, H. P., "Annual and Lifetime Income in Relation to Education; 1939-59." *American Economic Review* (December, 1960), pp. 962-86.

OSBORN, F., *Limits of the Earth.* Boston, Little, Brown & Co., 1953.

RUSSELL, SIR JOHN, *World Population and World Food Supplies.* New York, The Macmillan Company, 1954.

SHIMM, M. G., *Population Control.* New York, Oceana Publications, Inc., 1961.

SPENGLER, J. J., and O. D. DUNCAN, *Population Theory and Policy.* New York, The Free Press of Glencoe, 1956.

SPENGLER, J. J., "Population Change: Cause, Effect, Indication." *Economic Development and Cultural Change* (April, 1961), pp. 249-66.

SPENGLER, J. J., "The Population Obstacle to Economic Development." *American Economic Review, Papers and Proceedings* (May, 1951), pp. 343-54.

SPENGLER, J. J., "Population Problem: Dimensions, Potentials, Limitations." *American Economic Review, Papers and Proceedings* (May, 1956), pp. 337-51.

STOCKWELL, E. G., "Relationship between Population Growth and Economic Developments." *American Sociolog-*ical Review (April, 1962), pp. 250-52.

TAEUBER, I. B., "Japan's Demographic Transition Re-examined." *Population Studies* (July, 1960), pp. 28-39.

THOMPSON, W. C., *Population and Progress in the Far East*. Chicago, Chicago University Press, 1959.

# CHAPTER

# 6

# *Labor*

## *The Setting of the Labor Problem*

In United States' universities, the "labor problem" is considered in a particular setting, roughly designated as capitalism. This system is no longer a laissez-faire capitalism, but is best described as a mixed system; that is, one in which government regulation and controls ameliorate the worst excesses of capitalism. We are generally familiar with its outstanding features. Production is carried on to a considerable extent in large factories, although much small-scale industry remains. Production is characterized by the extensive use of power-driven machinery; production is for the general market rather than on order; workers are concentrated in a relatively small space; and the management is hired. Extreme specialization of the worker is the rule; the work is monotonous; and discipline is required in the work place. Workers are interdependent; that is, their jobs and incomes are dependent on employment and spending elsewhere in the economy. Business is dominated by the corporation, and the search for profits is the general rule, although management increasingly recognizes its social responsibility. As a result, labor relations tend to be impersonal. The corporation represents great power, but labor is also strongly organized (at least in some areas). The theoretical base of the business system is competition and individualism; but the guidelines in competition are often quality, service, and salesmanship rather than price, and individualism is often replaced by group action. But competition is still so intense that decisions about labor costs are extremely important to the individual businesses. The controversy between labor and management centers primarily over the division of the proceeds of the business and is conducted by collective bargaining, in which the only solution is group pressure, although certain social and governmental pressures have limiting effects on the group.

The setting of labor relations in the average underdeveloped country is far different. Under the influence of development programs and the money system of exchange, subsistence economies are giving way and a system of hired labor in industry and agriculture is emerging.

The typical employment is in agriculture, trade, small shops, and, increasingly, in government.[1] In the typical underdeveloped country the percentage in agriculture varies (see Table 4.1), a high percentage being a good indicator of the lack of development. The majority of workers may be in agriculture; most of the industry and trade may be carried on in small shops. As countries begin to develop, employment in agriculture and mining tends to decline and that in manufacturing and building and construction to expand. Industry is largely the processing of agricultural products for food and clothing. In many countries, however, there may be considerable employment on large commercial plantations and there may be a few large factories. In Asia, two-thirds of the workers are in agriculture, one-fifth in service, and one-eighth in industry.[2] However, in 1960, the proportions varied greatly, from a low of 13 percent in agriculture in Israel and 40 percent in Japan to 82 percent in Thailand and 75 percent in Turkey. The percentage in services varied from a low of 9 in Turkey and 12 in Thailand to 35 in Japan and 48 in Israel. Similarly, the percentage in industry ranged from 4 in Thailand and 8 in Pakistan to 24 in Japan and 35 in Israel. In the United States, at the same time, 13 percent was in agriculture, 49 percent in services, and 38 percent in industry. Similar variations exist in Africa[3] and other areas of the world. A sample survey in Indonesia[4] gives a more complete picture of the occupational structure in a typical underdeveloped country, as shown in Table 6.1.

The upward mobility of labor, even in socialist underdeveloped countries, is low. The economic barriers to qualifying for the higher jobs by acquiring the necessary education and training are still great. Economic pressure forces the child of the unskilled worker to enter the labor market at an early age. In addition, social and inherited barriers may bar the way. Status brings privileges and preferred position; lack of it may dull one's hopes.

As development proceeds, one can expect a larger proportion of gainfully

## TABLE 6.1.
*Percentages of the Indonesian Labor Force in Different Branches of Economic Activity*

| Economic Activity | Rural | Urban |
|---|---|---|
| Agriculture, hunting, and fishing | 70.18 | 4.58 |
| Mining and quarrying | 0.17 | |
| Manufacturing | 8.35 | 23.28 |
| Construction | 1.09 | 4.20 |
| Electricity, gas, water, and sanitation | 0.04 | 0.76 |
| Commerce | 11.36 | 27.86 |
| Transportation and storage | 1.04 | 8.02 |
| Services | 7.77 | 31.30 |

Occupational Status of the Labor Force (Percent)

| Occupational Status | Rural | Urban |
|---|---|---|
| Employer employing workers | 8.10 | 2.67 |
| Self-employed | 31.19 | 29.39 |
| Worker | 29.10 | 63.36 |
| Unpaid family worker | 31.61 | 4.58 |

Percentages of Work Force in Different Occupations

| Occupational Group | Rural | Urban |
|---|---|---|
| Professional, technical | 0.71 | 4.20 |
| Administrative, executive, managerial | 0.54 | 3.44 |
| Clerical | 0.54 | 10.69 |
| Sales | 12.28 | 26.71 |
| Farmers, fishermen, hunters, loggers | 70.56 | 4.20 |
| Miners and quarrymen | 0.17 | |
| Transport, commerce | 1.17 | 6.87 |
| Craftsmen, production workers not included elsewhere | 8.94 | 26.33 |
| Services, sports, recreation | 3.80 | 16.41 |
| Not classified | 1.29 | 1.15 |

employed at the expense of the self-employed; that is, there will be a shift from agriculture, mining, and personal service to manufacturing, trade, finance, and the professions,[5] and a growth in the skill requirements.

The small factories have much direct competition from large-scale industries, both domestic and foreign, and thus have a low ability to pay wages. In small industry and in agriculture, primitive production methods are the rule. Production methods tend to be labor-intensive, with much hard, physical labor. Usually, considerable unemployment exists.

As a result, labor is in a poor bargaining position and wages are low, often little above subsistence levels for unskilled workers. At the same time, labor is inefficient and wage costs may be high. If labor is inefficient, it is not because of a lack of innate ability but because of poverty; the workers are undernourished, poorly educated, often diseased, and untrained. In general, working conditions are extremely poor. Lighting is bad; temperatures, uncontrolled; the work place, dirty and unsafe.

The individuals and the unions are weak and cannot protect their interests, so the governments usually step in as protectors, partly for political reasons. Because their economic power is weak, most unions look to the government for support, and engage in political action. Many countries have planned economies so that the economic plan is a factor in decisions concerning unions. Balance-of-payments problems also place constraints on actions on behalf of the workers, for a raise in wages or labor costs could result in price increases, which could jeopardize exports or increase imports.

Because of the precarious position of the developing industry, it is likely that the industrial worker is little, if any, better off than before development began. His wages may be a little higher than wages in agriculture, but at the same time the costs of city living are higher, so that he has little left above the level of subsistence. A glance at the cities and farmlands of some countries would convince one that the rural dweller is indeed better off. Moreover, the changes in the modes of living brought about by industrial employment have often caused moral confusion. The transitional stage between an underdeveloped agricultural economy and an advanced industrial one does not seem to be a happy situation for labor. This seems true whether it occurs under capitalism, communism, or socialism. The change requires many adjustments and sacrifices, and one of the major problems in a program designed to induce growth is a decision as to the sacrifices labor may be expected to make for the sake of rapid development. The present underdeveloped countries have perhaps greater problems than the West did in this respect, for they are attempting to make the transition more rapidly.

Many conflicts of interest are due to arise. The worker has his desires, centering largely in increased income or shorter hours, and the employer wants a continuous supply of labor at prices he can afford. The public is interested in the outcome of the relationship between labor and the employer because of the human problems created and the effect on output and the operation of the economy. In underdeveloped countries these varied interests seem currently overwhelmed by the desire for economic growth. The immediate objective is how to get increased productivity from the workers, which involves getting workers to commit themselves to industry, increasing the supply of skilled labor, and increasing the efficiency of others through training and education. The level of wages assumes great importance because of its effect on the savings available for growth and its intimate relationship to individual scales of living. Because of their effect on these matters, labor unionism and labor and social legislation are also important considerations.

Economic growth depends on increasing productivity, but at the same time the workers must be protected against many risks, among which are not only the traditional economic risks but also the social risks that arise because of the effect of industrialization on the traditional social structure.

## Problems of the Work Force

Lack of a proper work force may be the greatest inhibitor in the development of a country. In most cases there is no question as to quantity of labor available; the handicap lies rather in quality of general labor, skilled labor, and the various types of administrative and professional personnel. More economic advances are derived by improving techniques than by multiplying the supply of existing factors, and these require improved personnel. Human beings are the medium through which progress is effected and the capabilities of the personnel available set the limits. Development, then, requires converting rural workers into an acceptable industrial labor force and acquiring the necessary skilled workers and higher-level manpower.

Four processes are involved in the building up of a labor force—recruitment, commitment, upgrading, and security.[6] In the developing countries, hired labor is beginning to emerge. As yet, the proportion of workers in wage-earning employment is relatively low, the proportion varying from 10 to 50 percent, compared with over 70 percent in the United States. The less developed a country, the lower the percentage of workers working for wages. For example, in East Cameroun only 8 percent of the workers are paid and one-fifth of these are in the public sector.[7] The majority of workers will be found in subsistence agriculture. However, as development proceeds, the proportion employed for wages rises and the number of self-employed decreases; in fact, those seeking wage employment can be expected to increase more rapidly than jobs can be created, especially in densely populated areas. Because, in many instances, the available land can support no more people, with current production techniques, much of the increasing labor force migrates to the cities to look for jobs. Only as industry, commerce, and the service trades expand can these workers be gradually absorbed.

Underdeveloped countries, unfortunately, have a low ratio of population in the productive ages to total population, as shown in Chapter 5. Correspondingly, even though women and children may participate to a large degree in the labor force, underdeveloped countries may also have a low proportion of workers to total population, compared with the advanced countries. Tables 6.2 to 6.4 show considerable variation in this respect, the differences being due largely to the extent that women are counted as being in the work force and to differences in definition. Many of the women and children, and even men, may work only part time, so that the effective participation in the work force is less than appears in the estimates. For example, a sample survey in Java and Madura, Indonesia,[8] estimated the rural labor force as 49.96 percent of the total rural population and the urban labor force as 34.31 percent of the total urban population. However, the same survey estimated that in the rural areas only about two-thirds of the available hours were utilized. For most underdeveloped countries, some allowance of this sort must be made. In general, allowing for time actually worked, the dependency ratio appears lower in the advanced countries than in the underdeveloped. This means that a worker's product in the advanced countries must be shared with fewer people. In addition, productivity is low in the underdeveloped areas.

Many women and children work, but at ineffective jobs or for short periods, so that to count them in the labor force overstates the proportion of the population at work. Customs differ as to the participation of women in work outside the home. In many areas it is common for women to help in the fields or to enter domestic service, and therefore they are counted in the labor force. In agriculture this work is often sporadic, commonly being utilized only at planting and harvesting. In some areas, however (for example, Pakistan), it is not common for women to work outside the home, even in the fields.

Nevertheless, over the whole world women have been moving into indus-

### TABLE 6.2.

*Percentage of Economically Active Population to Total Population*
*(Recent Population Censuses, 1946-1959)*

| Region | Both Sexes | Males | Females |
|---|---|---|---|
| World | 42.5 | 58.3 | 27.2 |
| Africa | 35.8 | 56.8 | 14.5 |
| North America | 39.7 | 58.2 | 21.3 |
| Mid-America | 35.2 | 56.6 | 14.2 |
| South America | 35.2 | 57.3 | 13.1 |
| Asia (except U.S.S.R.) | 42.5 | 56.4 | 28.1 |
| Europe | 45.1 | 64.1 | 27.6 |
| Oceania | 40.1 | 61.2 | 18.5 |
| U.S.S.R. | 47.5 | 54.8 | 41.4 |

SOURCE: United Nations, Dept. of Economic and Social Affairs, *Demographic Aspects of Manpower Population Study*, Part I, "Sex and Age Patterns," Population Study No. 33, 1962, p. 3.

## TABLE 6.3.

Percentage of Economically Active Population to Total Population, Africa
(Various Years, 1934-1960)

| Region | Both Sexes | Males | Females |
|---|---|---|---|
| Algeria | | | |
|   Europeans | 36.8 | 58.6 | 15.6 |
|   Moslems | 38.7 | 51.7 | 25.2 |
| Cameroun | 57.9 | 55.3 | 60.3 |
| Congo (Leopoldville) | | | |
|   Nonindigenous | 42.4 | 65.2 | 16.6 |
|   Indigenous | 49.4 | 48.9 | 49.8 |
| Gabon | 59.3 | 61.1 | 57.6 |
| Ivory Coast | 50.8 | 58.8 | 44.4 |
| Malagasy | 47.9 | 52.0 | 43.8 |
| Morocco (Moslems) | 39.0 | 53.6 | 24.5 |
| Mozambique | 29.5 | 55.4 | 5.8 |
| Nigeria (indigenous) | 47.9 | 54.4 | 41.7 |
| Rep. of South Africa | | | |
|   White | 37.2 | 58.1 | 16.3 |
|   Other | 36.0 | 57.1 | 14.1 |
| Senegal | 47.6 | 52.6 | 42.7 |
| Sudan | 37.4 | 66.7 | 7.5 |
| Tunisia | 35.8 | 52.3 | 19.6 |
| Egypt | 29.7 | 53.5 | 6.1 |
| Upper Volta | 55.0 | 54.5 | 55.5 |

SOURCE: "Population and Labour Force of Asia, 1950-80," *International Labour Review* (October, 1962), p. 507.

try and services and out of agriculture, raising new opportunities for them and new social problems, and swelling the numbers seeking employment in the cities. But, with few exceptions, there has been no recent significant rise in the proportion of women employed.[9] Table 6.5 shows the considerable variation in the participation of women in the labor force of different countries.

The large number of children in the population is partially counterbalanced by the fact that more of them work than do those in the advanced countries (see Table 6.6). Age standards for employment are low and are seldom enforced, although legislation is improving. A 1952 United Nations report[10] gave the age of twelve as a common minimum working age. In Lebanon the minimum age is eight, except for mechanical and unhealthful work; and in Egypt, nine-year-olds work in textiles and certain handicrafts. Since then, minimum age standards have been rising, and are now commonly set at fourteen. Most of the children are employed where there is underemployment of adults. Moreover, their work is often quite unproductive; for example, in Indonesia it may consist of herding a few sheep alongside the roadway all day. The worst consequence of this, of course, is the loss of educational opportunity.

# TABLE 6.4.

*Percentage of Economically Active Population to Total Population, Asia*
*(Various Years, 1951-1961)*

| Region | Both Sexes | Males | Females |
|---|---|---|---|
| Japan | 45.8 | 56.9 | 35.2 |
| Indonesia | 47.7 | 56.1 | 39.7 |
| Israel | 35.0 | 51.3 | 18.3 |
| India | 39.2 | 54.0 | 23.5 |
| Ceylon | 37.0 | 53.1 | 18.9 |
| Korea, South | 38.1 | 49.6 | 26.6 |
| Pakistan | 30.7 | 54.6 | 3.8 |
| Thailand | 52.7 | 54.3 | 51.1 |
| Malaya | 34.5 | 50.5 | 17.4 |
| Taiwan | 30.8 | 47.1 | 13.5 |
| Iraq | 27.7 | 54.6 | 4.0 |
| Philippines | 35.8 | 47.2 | 24.3 |
| United States | 40.5 | 55.4 | 25.9 |

SOURCE: "Population and Labour Force of Asia, 1950-80," *International Labour Review* (October, 1962), p. 361.

Despite the improving legislation, such controls as there are over women's and children's work outside of agriculture are difficult to enforce because of the lack of inspectors and the multiplicity of small shops and cottage industries. Enforcement is confined for the most part to the larger factories, and this only drives the women and children to worse places of work.

A second manpower problem is created by the movement to the city. Workers everywhere are leaving the villages to try to find work in the cities, transferring the problem of unemployment from the rural to the urban areas. These migrants are motivated by the pressure on the land, a need for money for special purposes (such as in Africa for the price a man pays for a bride), the attractions of city life, or bad weather conditions such as drought. In most countries these people take up permanent residence, so that the cities have a surplus of unskilled and uneducated workers, mostly unemployed and living under the worst of conditions—even sleeping on the streets when the climate permits.

The African migrations are a special problem. There the individual goes to the city for varying intervals of a few months to several years and then returns to his village. He may make only one or a number of these trips in his lifetime. Thus, rather than a migration to the city, there is a circulation between the city and the village. The worker goes for specific purposes, as mentioned above, or as part of his initiation rite into the tribe, and then returns, although the number of permanent city dwellers seems to be increasing. Ordinarily, the man leaves his family on the farm to secure his rights to the land and in his village. After a few months' work he returns to

## TABLE 6.5.

### Participation of Women in the Labor Force, Selected Countries
### (Various Years, 1947-1954)

| Country | Percent Female Population Working | Percent Women in Total Labor Force |
|---|---|---|
| Egypt | 6.8 | 10.0 |
| Argentina | 16.6 | 19.9 |
| Brazil | 9.6 | 14.6 |
| Chile | 18.1 | 25.0 |
| Colombia | 12.4 | 18.7 |
| Mexico | 8.7 | 13.6 |
| Japan | 33.0 | 38.5 |
| India | 23.5 | 29.2 |
| Pakistan | 3.8 | 5.8 |
| Philippines | 31.0 | 40.1 |
| Thailand | 49.4 | 47.9 |
| Greece | 13.1 | 18.0 |
| Turkey | 44.0 | 43.4 |
| Poland | 42.4 | 44.8 |
| Canada | 16.9 | 22.1 |
| United States | 21.8 | 27.5 |
| France | 29.9 | 34.8 |
| German Fed. Rep. | 31.4 | 36.0 |
| Italy | 20.3 | 25.1 |
| United Kingdom | 27.4 | 30.8 |
| Australia | 19.0 | 22.8 |

SOURCE: "Women in the Labor Force," *International Labour Review* (March, 1958), p. 256.

## TABLE 6.6.

### Labor Force Activity Rates (Males) by Age Groups for Regions of the World

| Region | 10-14 | 15-19 | 20-24 | 25-34 | 35-44 | 45-54 | 55-64 | 65+ |
|---|---|---|---|---|---|---|---|---|
| Africa | | | | | | | | |
| Indigenous | 21.7[a] | 73.6 | 90.7 | 96.2 | 97.3 | 95.9 | 91.3 | 64.9 |
| Nonindigenous | 3.5[a] | 51.6 | 90.9 | 95.9 | 96.1 | 94.2 | 84.3 | 57.5 |
| North America | 3.4 | 57.7 | 91.9 | 95.5 | 95.8 | 93.4 | 79.5 | 38.6 |
| Mid-America | 15.5 | 73.8 | 93.2 | 95.7 | 96.9 | 96.0 | 90.0 | 68.0 |
| South America | 19.5 | 79.3 | 94.2 | 97.2 | 97.5 | 96.1 | 91.4 | 71.3 |
| Asia | 13.6[a] | 66.1 | 89.0 | 96.0 | 97.3 | 96.4 | 88.2 | 58.4 |
| Europe | 8.5[a] | 76.3 | 91.6 | 96.7 | 97.7 | 96.1 | 86.7 | 44.9 |
| Oceania | 1.5[a] | 75.3 | 96.4 | 98.4 | 98.1 | 96.8 | 84.3 | 38.5 |
| Types of Activity | | | | | | | | |
| Industrial | 4.1[a] | 72.4 | 91.5 | 96.7 | 97.6 | 95.9 | 85.6 | 37.7 |
| Semi-industrial | 13.2[a] | 70.3 | 91.8 | 96.2 | 97.1 | 95.9 | 88.9 | 61.0 |
| Agricultural | 23.9[a] | 78.4 | 91.2 | 96.3 | 97.3 | 96.3 | 91.6 | 70.1 |

SOURCE: United Nations, Dept. of Economic and Social Affairs, *Demographic Aspects of Manpower*, Part I, "Sex and Age Patterns," Population Studies No. 33, 1962.
[a] Excluding countries that adopted a minimum age of fifteen years for the enumeration of the economically active population.

take his place in the village. Obviously, this creates social problems both at home and in the city as well as economic problems for agriculture and city industry. Agriculture is disrupted by variations in the labor force, and industry cannot afford to train the workers and so is restricted to primitive technologies. Much time is wasted in the journeys. The circulation is reinforced by both the bad living conditions in the town and the pull of the social security system of the tribe. Better city conditions and greater security would probably increase permanent movement to the city if this were needed.

Really, the great need of underdeveloped countries is to match the flow to the city with the manpower needs so as to prevent both the possible disruption of agriculture and the unemployment in the city with the attendant begging, vice, crime, and even potential revolt. For optimum growth and minimum wastage of capital involved in combating undesirable conditions, some control of this exodus is necessary. The movement might be slowed down in the country by increasing productivity in agriculture, providing secondary occupations, instituting small-scale industries, and by making village life more attractive.* In town it is necessary to provide housing, promote a new set of social values and social relationships, and institute programs of vocational education. In addition, surplus emigrants must be removed to some area where they can be useful. Either to permit free flow of population or to control it is apt to be costly. Only specific studies can determine the appropriate course for a country.

Thus, workers seem to appear in the towns and recruitment is relatively easy. The major problem may be to get them to stay and to work regularly in industry. At the beginning stages of development, countries need to build up a permanent industrial labor force, generally referred to as "getting workers to commit themselves" permanently to industry. As one Indian writer expresses it, "industrial labor in the sense of a stable, reliable, and disciplined group that has cut the umbilical cord connecting it with the land and has become suitable for utilization in factories is not abundant but extremely scarce in a backward country." [11] Workers must often be pushed into industry permanently by land scarcity, taxation, and so on, since they resist leaving their traditional way of life. To do so may mean giving up the social security system of the extended family. Industry requires steady and often monotonous work, so that the individual loses a freedom he is accustomed to. The new occupations do not fit the traditional standards of prestige; for example, promotion is based primarily on merit and not on the

* Improving the economic and social conditions on the farms would not only raise incomes there, but would also lessen the pressure of competition for jobs in the cities and would contribute to raising wages and working conditions there.

customary status symbols such as age and caste. Ordinarily, a lack of housing in the city means that the worker must leave his family behind. The danger of unemployment exists. By going to the city, the worker may endanger his right to land. Discrimination in the factory is sometimes encountered as different tribes or people from different areas mingle. Moreover, in some countries the individual usually looks to the chief or head of the family or the village elders to prescribe his way of life. In the city he loses this direction and is often confused and unable to adjust to new conditions. Because of the surplus of unskilled labor, it is unlikely that wages will afford anything better than a subsistence level of living. Thus, the individual resists staying in factory work.[12]

Because of this in the early stages of industrial development, labor turnover is high. Workers may work only for a specific purpose, as in Africa, or only when seasonal requirements on the farm are low. Many find they cannot stand the work or city life, and return home. However, as industrial work becomes established and the ties of the village grow weaker or become nonexistent, turnover may be virtually nil except for deaths and retirements. Jobs are scarce and highly valued. Because the labor market is poorly organized, finding a new job is very difficult. Moreover, much of the pay may be in periodic bonuses or systems of security built into the job. However, rapidly rising prices seem to increase turnover because the wages of factory jobs are more fixed than the income from selling or self-employment. At least this appears to have been the situation in the recent rapid price rise in Indonesia.

Whether the move to the city will result in the development of a reliable labor force depends in the first instance upon the ability of the worker to make the adjustment to city living. Moving to the city induces a break in old customs or ways of living. If old mores and customs prove strong enough and adaptable enough to permit an orderly adjustment to the new life, a reliable labor force will grow. If they remain too strong, the transition to an industrial life is prevented; if too weak, social degeneration may result. Finding the means to an orderly change to an industrial life is a challenging problem.

Plaguing the underdeveloped countries is the handicap of massive unemployment. Total unemployment is impossible to estimate, but is considerable. Every country has a large reserve of unemployed, plus women and the young and the aged, who are not currently in the labor force. Hence, it is possible to create and expand industry without appreciably affecting wages, except for the cost of moving to cities. As a result, labor is in a poor bargaining position and wages are low. On the other hand, labor at first is inefficient and wage costs may be high.

Employment for wages may become more prevalent during development (although even this is doubtful), but the number seeking employment increases at a faster rate than available jobs so that unemployment grows also. Unemployment may be of four types—visible or open, underemployment, disguised, and potential.[13] Visible unemployment exists when a man has no job at all. This may be total, seasonal, or casual. Total unemployment is usually quite small; that is, almost everyone is doing something, although the individual may not even realize that he is, in effect, unemployed. Many of these are unaware of employment services and do not report that they are unemployed. Furthermore, visible unemployment is essentially a town problem, for the unemployed rural worker drifts to the town. On the other hand, seasonal unemployment may be very great; that is, much time is wasted between the periods of peak labor demands. Hsieh[14] estimates that farmers are idle two to four months of the year in China and India; jute growers in West Bengal are idle nine months; and farm laborers in Burma, seven months; and the idle time is seldom used on other tasks. In Chad[15] the cotton grower works about 150 days a year in the field; the ground-nut farmer, 116; the rice grower, 140; and the herdsman, 92. In East Cameroun,[16] one survey showed men working 105.5 days during the year on farm work, 87.5 days on miscellaneous work not connected with farming, 161.5 days resting, and 9.5 days sick.

Much of the labor is underemployed in the sense that it does not employ all the available hours. In an Indonesian study,[17] open unemployment in the rural areas was estimated at 0.83 percent and in the urban areas at 7.09 percent. However, underemployment in agriculture was found to be large. The total estimated man-hours worked in the rural regions was estimated as 22,352.40 million but, allowing for seasonal unemployment, Sundays, and holidays, the total available hours were 33,604.90 million. Thus, underemployment during the working days amounted to 33.48 percent. United Nations estimates[18] are that underemployment is frequently between 25 and 30 percent. In a West Indies survey,[19] only 74 percent of the workers worked 33 hours per week or more. Underemployment was high in agriculture, domestic service, self-employment, and casual work. A similar situation exists in India, Pakistan, and the Philippines,[20] and probably in most underdeveloped countries. In the latter study, unemployment in India was estimated to be 5 percent and underemployment from 10 to 11 percent. In the rural areas, 24 percent worked under 28 hours a week and 7 percent worked substantially fewer hours than this. In the urban areas, 16 percent worked less than 28 hours and 4 percent were severely underemployed. In Pakistan, unemployment was 3.2 percent, but was 10.3 percent in the large towns of East Pakistan and 6.4 percent in the large towns of West Pakistan.

Excluding unpaid family workers working under 15 hours per week, in East Pakistan 17 percent worked less than 26 hours, and in West Pakistan, 4.7 percent, mostly in the rural areas. In the Philippines, unemployment was 7.2 percent of the labor force. In agriculture, 33 percent worked under 40 hours, and in nonagriculture, 41 percent. Large numbers who worked 40 hours were seeking additional work. The preceding studies show a high rate of unemployment in the large towns, a very high rate of unemployment among young persons and among educated persons, and, as indicated, considerable underutilization of rural manpower.

An especially important problem in some countries is the unemployed intellectual. In many countries the prestige degrees are in the liberal arts and the law, so that there is an oversupply of people in these areas. The surplus is unwilling to accept work below their "dignity" and so remain unemployed, often to become leaders of dissatisfied groups in opposition to existing regimes.

"Disguised" unemployment refers to labor that could be released without affecting production under approximately the same technology. This means that the marginal productivity of such labor is negligible, maybe zero or even a negative amount. Considerable controversy exists over how extensive this is, but it is doubtful that it is as extensive in agriculture as is sometimes supposed. All the labor is needed at the peak seasons and, if labor were withdrawn, the output would suffer. The real problem is that the labor is idle during much of the year or performs inconsequential tasks. In such city occupations as selling, local transportation, household service, or government service, disguised unemployment may well be considerable.

"Potential" unemployment is that amount of labor that would be released by simple technological changes already known; for example, enlargement of farm holdings. This type is undoubtedly extensive, especially in agriculture, street transportation, street and bazaar selling, and in household service. For this reason, development, which can be expected to lead to improved techniques, may not relieve unemployment for some time.

Unless the policy of a country is to create jobs regardless of other objectives, unemployment of one type or another can be expected to characterize the economies of the developing countries for a long time. In fact, it may be possible that efforts to bring about growth may have to center on increasing productivity per worker and may create more unemployment before the expanding economy can begin to absorb additional workers. At the very best, jobs may not increase as rapidly as workers are increasing. Because increasing output will ordinarily be considered a more important objective than increasing employment, countries will probably strive to increase productivity per worker. Thus, unemployment will, most likely, increase for a while. Such countries will find it virtually impossible, even with outside aid, to increase investment on a rapid enough scale to absorb the excess labor of the traditional sector. At the same time, investment in the traditional sector will likely remain stagnant and will not afford additional employment. Excess labor will remain in underemployment on the land or in certain city occupations or be unemployed. Jaffe,[21] for example, believes that output may have to double or triple before there is much increase in employment. This, of course, is a great danger for a country as many see the increasing prosperity but no advantages for themselves.

This leads to the dilemma that a country may have to choose between sacrificing growth and creating jobs. The danger lies in the fact that the development plan may become merely a make-work program. The alternative is to promote the most rapid increase in output and find someplace to "store" the surplus workers until they can be absorbed. Various alternatives are possible as places to store labor: in subsistence agriculture, in an oversupply of labor in factories, on relief, in government service, in household service, in low-paid selling or services, on public works programs, or in the army.* They may be permitted to shift for themselves, to become a burden on friends and relatives, or to engage in begging, vice, or crime. An interesting experiment is that of labor brigades or national civic service battalions similar to the Civilian Conservation Corps in the United States during the Depression.[22] In a number of countries (for example, Togo, India, French Guiana, Niger, Pakistan, East Cameroun) the youth, among whom unemployment is most severe, are drafted into labor brigades if they have been unemployed for six months. Sometimes these are under the military and sometimes under civilian authority. The youths are placed in a camp and are employed on public works or given training or located on rural resettlement schemes. Although conducted only on a small scale and inadequately financed and managed, they seem to have had some success. However, there is always the possibility that these labor brigades may degenerate into systems of forced labor and that cheap labor for the government may become the objective rather than training and reemployment. Under proper safeguards, these seem to be desirable projects. Yet, it will be observed that the funds necessary will compete with investment funds.

Continuing unemployment seems to be the probable result of development. Is it possible for a country to pursue policies of economic growth and full employment simultaneously without sacrificing one or both? Creating economic growth is a big task; trying to provide full employment at the same time is a colossal one. Yet economic growth has meaning only if it

* Because marginal productivity may be zero on the farms is no reason to move people off them, if marginal productivity is zero elsewhere.

increases employment and incomes for the masses. A survey by the International Labour Office has advocated that the two goals be pursued simultaneously.[23] The solution advocated was to restrict the consumption of those with incomes above subsistence so as to provide more capital and to discourage capital-intensive investment. The use of more labor-intensive technologies was suggested, although it was recognized that some capital-intensive industries were necessary. Other methods proposed were to use labor to create capital directly, such as cultivating land more intensively and constructing roads and dams; to use labor in local industries; to encourage new activities, such as animal husbandry, afforestation, orchards, and fisheries; and in urban areas, possibly to introduce multiple shifts. One might observe, however, that if worker incomes are kept low, there will not be a secondary effect derived from their greater spending, at least on industrial goods.

Although labor as a whole is plentiful and is increasingly committing itself to industrial employment, the essential first step in many areas is to find an efficient labor force. Despite unemployment, if economic growth is to take place, it will be necessary to secure increasing productivity and effort on the part of the workers. This means that the worker must not only seek industrial employment, but must also have an incentive to increase his efforts and develop efficiency. For this to happen, the worker must place some emphasis on material values; that is, he must strive to acquire goods. It has sometimes been thought that the worker in underdeveloped countries has no such aspirations and prefers leisure to goods; that is, if he is paid higher wages, he will work fewer hours. This belief seems to have been held in all countries, including the now advanced ones, and is probably no more true of the workers in the underdeveloped countries than it proved to be true in the West. To prove or disprove this contention is next to impossible, but its universal existence seems doubtful.

Incentives will be operative only if they are realizable by the workers themselves. If the result of increased wages is that additional relatives descend on the worker for support or if his income is taken from him in other ways, such as traditional obligations to the family or by exactions of a landlord or creditor, or if no additional goods are available for him to buy, it would not be surprising that higher wages would fail to evoke a response. Efforts to encourage the desire for goods, to protect the worker against the loss of his income from those who would prey on it, provision for advancement by merit, and the elimination of discrimination would be helpful in encouraging increased effort. Under such circumstances one could reasonably expect the workers to respond to incentives and to be encouraged to work harder under the attraction of higher wages. It is understandable, of course, that if a man works twelve hours a day, he will want more leisure instead of an increase in his income, and that there is always a competition between more goods and more leisure. Unless the prospects for economic growth are to be damaged, the worker in the underdeveloped country must understand the necessity for increased productivity as the only means to acquiring more leisure and more goods.

Although labor efficiency in the beginning stages is usually low, this is temporary and due to conditions arising from previous poverty or cultural influences. After some training and with improved income, the workers of all countries are capable of forming an acceptable labor force. But the peoples of many areas are often illiterate, untrained, diseased, and undernourished. The new African worker is reported to be almost without exception the victim of some parasitic disease, malaria, or yaws and to have or have had gonorrhea. Many have syphilis. Often the hemoglobin level is below 65 percent. Most are underfed and have an unbalanced diet. They live under poor conditions.[24] The literacy level of the worker is low. In Indonesia it was reported as 30.27 percent for the rural population and 52.60 percent of the urban population.[25] Because this applies to the entire population, the literacy rate of the working class is probably lower. The rate, even so, compares favorably with that of many other countries. Most new workers lack specific skills because their previous experience has been in self-sufficient agriculture, which does not require any one highly developed specific skill and in which the work habits are such that they cannot be tolerated in industry. Moreover, often the workers remember the injustices that were suffered in industry previously operated by a colonial master, and therefore they remain uncooperative. But education, public health measures, and better diets are capable of transforming most peoples into an acceptable labor force in a surprisingly short time. Industry, once started, helps create its own labor force by providing training and eventually better wages and improved living standards.

Underdeveloped countries have an acute shortage of skilled labor of all types. In fact, this shortage may well be the greatest barrier to development, even greater than the lack of capital. As such, it contributes to the reasons for the surplus of unskilled labor. At first some growth can occur through the use of unskilled and semiskilled workers, but substantial growth can occur only as people with advanced skills become available. As previously reported, studies indicate that a substantial part of the increase of output in the United States over the past fifty years was due to the upgrading of skills (see pages 183 and 184). For example, it is estimated that in twenty years, agricultural output increased 27.5 percent, but inputs increased only 6 percent.[26] In particular short supply seem to be middle-management personnel and supervisors, highly educated professional manpower, subprofessional personnel, such as technicians and nurses, top-level managerial and administrative personnel, teachers, craftsmen, senior clerical personnel, and staff personnel such as accountants, economists, and statisticians.[27]

This shortage can be remedied, but at a cost of capital invested in training facilities or in sending personnel abroad for training. Such investment may be at the expense of investment in factories, but may be among the most profitable that can be made. In Chapter 5 the value of investing in human capital via education and health programs was stressed. To this should be added investment in actual skills. This can be accomplished through on-the-job training, an underworker training plan, apprenticeship programs, employer training programs, government training centers, and technical schools. Many plans of various types are now in existence.[28] In addition, the United Nations and the United States and other countries conduct training programs as part of their aid programs.

The problems encountered are many. There is a lack of equipment, instructional materials, and finances; qualified instructors are scarce; minimum standards are low and even nonexistent; the educational level of the trainees is low; often there is a reluctance on the part of the more able to take technical training because of prestige reasons; and the programs are not always related to needs and the economic plan.

The Indonesian program is typical. Many employers provide on-the-job training in skills; some of the larger ones have formal training programs. In the smaller shops, training is informal under a sort of apprenticeship, or rather underworker, arrangement. Technical schools exist throughout the country, but need better financing, higher standards, and greater prestige, the latter being probably their greatest handicap because many young people seem to consider technical training inferior to academic training. The government has a program for training skilled workers, with training centers located throughout the country. The training is under the supervision of the Directorate of Manpower in the Ministry of Labor. The trainees are selected by the employment service from the ranks of job seekers. The employment service also notifies the manpower directorate of the skills most in demand. The manpower directorate conducts a series of aptitude tests and trade tests, and supervises the training. Currently, the skills being stressed are the building trades, metalwork, motor mechanics, radio and electrical technical work, commercial skills, and agricultural work. When the student completes his course, he is referred back to the employment service for placement. Because skilled workers are scarce, securing employment is usually easy. The biggest problems are in securing trained instructors and in obtaining the necessary equipment. As might be expected, adequate funds are not available to meet the needs of the society. In all, the training centers graduated 4,148 in the five years between 1957 to 1961—a significant number, compared with the existing supply, but a number far short of the need.

Efforts are also made to train supervisors, but there is no agreement as to where to put the emphasis. One central organization is training top or over-all management, feeling that unless such types are developed, trained middle-management cannot be utilized efficiently. The United States technical aid program is emphasizing training for the supervisory level. The middle-management group is relatively neglected, although employer groups seem to feel that this is the most urgent need. As yet, no efforts have been made to integrate government training programs and university education in business management.

In underdeveloped countries there is usually a high proportion of labor to capital and also to land, although there are exceptions. Thus, not only is the capacity of labor low, but also capital to aid the worker. Further, the effectiveness with which capital is used, that is, the state of its technological development and the progress of managerial skills, is inadequate also. As a result of all these factors, the productivity of labor is quite low.

Such labor as there is is not apt to be distributed optimally, for the labor market is poorly organized. Jobs are found largely by personal search or by means of a recruiting agent. Beginnings of labor exchanges exist, but many workers do not know about them, or even understand that they are under-employed, so they do not consult the services. The exchanges are flooded with a large number of unskilled workers for whom there is no work. The large demand is for people with some experience and skill. Transportation is limited and the exchanges, at least in Indonesia, seem to operate only over an area small enough that the worker can walk to the exchange and also walk to any resulting job. The exchanges are also handicapped by a lack of market and occupational information. Labor is quite immobile in most countries and seemingly even more so in underdeveloped countries, if one excludes the migrations in Africa. For example, in Indonesia, labor is poorly distributed. Java is badly overcrowded, whereas there is a labor scarcity on the outer islands. The government has a transmigration program, but finds it difficult to move workers. The reallocation of labor both geographically and occupationally is a universal problem but a difficult thing to achieve.

Such labor problems are not likely to solve themselves. Imperative for economic growth is manpower planning, for improper manpower distribution may well be the greatest restricting force in development. The ability to absorb capital, that is, to use it effectively, depends to a considerable degree on available manpower. Planned development depends on the necesssary manpower to carry out the required tasks. Moreover, it is always important that all national resources be used as efficiently as possible, and manpower is one of the most important resources. Special training programs have been formulated.[29]

The first task in a manpower program is the statistical one of finding information concerning the labor market and complete details concerning the supply of labor. This includes wages, productivity, distribution of manpower, and even details of differences in language and culture, which might make utilization difficult. The next step is to determine the future labor requirements, including quantity, geographical location, and skills. Obviously, this must be related to the economic plan. In other words, a "manpower budget" as well as a financial budget is needed. This includes plans to locate potential supplies and to use labor more effectively, moving it to where it is needed or expanding economic activity where it is available already. Once the needs are known, training facilities must be put to work producing the right kinds of workers. Lastly, the trained labor must be placed in the right jobs, which may require interregional shifts.

The east European planning just mentioned cites the special problems of planning specialists, university graduates, and advanced technicians. These require calculation far ahead. The general technique is to set numbers desired as a percentage allocation to some base, such as doctors to population, engineers to numbers of workers, or teachers per numbers of students.

## Unions and Collective Bargaining

Labor movements are unique in every country, although there are broad regularities. Unions differ because of different levels of economic development; attitudes of government; the nature of union leadership; and different economic, political, and social traditions. For example, most of the Japanese unions, because of the familial tradition, are formed on a company basis and bargain at that level, although wider-range negotiations are increasing.[30] Walter Galenson[31] has arrived at certain generalizations, following studies made of labor movements by various authors, among which is that labor unions will arise and that they will have the following characteristics: Leadership will rarely come from the working class, but will come from the intelligentsia or the political classes. Unions will almost aways be deeply concerned with politics because of the weakness of unions in bargaining and because of unemployment. Political leaders often find that they must encourage unions to prevent the workers from turning to radical

movements. Often unions are blanket in form, that is, they take in all workers regardless of their industry or their job, although industrial unions do
develop where there are well-defined industries. One can almost be certain
there will be a multiplicity of unions representing different ideological, religious, political, or nationalistic views. Unions will almost always lack internal democracy. They will rely heavily on appeals to nationalism. Government activity will have a great influence on unions, and governments may
encourage unions as part of their revolution against foreign interests or as a
symbol of industrialization. In many cases it is doubtful if unions could
exist without the protection of government.*

As mentioned, the unions are often centrally controlled in keeping with
the political structure of the countries. Where a union must fight against
employers for its existence, or where local leaders are scarce, centralized
direction is almost inevitable. The location of power in the unions will depend on the type of union movement, the position of unions in society, and
the political and social development of the people. The power structure of
unions and similar interest groups is an important consideration because of
their influence on the economic and political growth of a country. Some
countries do not favor democratic controls in any form, so that it would be
unlikely that unions would be democratically run in such countries. Moreover, there is a question whether unions can afford to be democratic if they
wish to be successful. At times, strong leadership is needed for self-
protection and to take quick advantage of opportunities. Until the place of
unions in society is determined and recognized, unitary action may be expected.

In centrally controlled unions, the members are generally passive. Most
of the initiative for action comes from the leaders, although local unions
may make recommendations to the central or parent union. The chief functions of the locals may be to transmit orders from the centrals and to rouse
the members to take part in demonstrations of political activity. One of the
big problems for unions is financing, for it is difficult to collect dues from
the members. Enforcing dues collection might only drive union members to
rival unions.

Thus, unions in underdeveloped countries cannot be expected to be like
Western unions. Their centralized control allows the possibility of their use
to promote the interests of political leaders, but probably gives them more
potential power than they would have as simple business unions operating
more or less on a local basis. For this reason governments are tempted to

---

* It is impossible to trace the history of unions in all countries of the world and
to give a complete bibliography. The volumes edited by Walter Galenson[31] describe
a number of these movements.

control them as an instrument of power or as a means of frustrating rival power.

Organized labor faces a number of problems in addition to those mentioned above, such as small size, multiplicity, shortage of good leadership, illiteracy of members, poor finances, the danger of manipulation by political leaders, and the necessity to cope with the newness of urbanism for most of the members. Governments have encouraged unions, but most governments of underdeveloped countries have economic programs designed to aid economic growth, which union activities may adversely affect. Moreover, governments participate directly in the operation of industries in some countries, and so are directly affected by union standards. In turn, government standards have a widespread influence on employment standards through the government's own employment practices. Thus, in newly emerging countries, governments have a closer concern with labor affairs than in the United States and are apt to intervene to a greater extent. Unions, of course, must take this into account when determining their programs.

Also, unions encounter a particular difficulty in adjusting their programs to the balance-of-payments structure—a universal problem of underdeveloped countries. Efforts to improve conditions are circumscribed by the need to keep down production costs sufficiently to encourage exports and discourage imports.

In addition, unions are in a bad position to bargain with employers because of the usual considerable unemployment. Thus, unions face the triple handicaps of weak bargaining power, possible government opposition, and the limitations imposed by foreign trade requirements. At the same time, the members desire more goods and better standards of work. A union that does not make some efforts in this direction will soon lose members to a union that will. Unions thus are caught in a dilemma between the loss of members and influence, and potential increased control by government. The only alternative is to devise some method of operation that will overcome the weakness in bargaining and avoid a government crackdown.

Managers of businesses in underdeveloped countries, like managers elsewhere, prefer a clear hand in making decisions as they see fit. However, they learn to coordinate their decision making with limitations imposed by government, bankers, suppliers, public opinion, and even unions. Business learns to deal with each of these limitations, but learning to deal with unions is usually a bitter experience and one not undertaken voluntarily. Managers in underdeveloped countries do not accept this obligation easily and prefer not to deal with unions. Thus, although unions may be favored by the law in most countries, relatively little progress has been made in collective bargaining, for unions are not strong enough to force the issue and governments are anxious to see that nothing interferes with their plans.

Moreover, the traditional union weapons of the strike and picketing are largely ineffective. Even if such tactics are legal, they are not likely to be successful because of the large amount of unemployment. In other cases, unions may be unable to engage in these activities because they must get governmental permission to strike, or they find the government intervening vigorously to end any strike that does occur. For example, in Indonesia, in the first days of the new country, strikes were considered legal. Today, if one asks if strikes are legal, the answer is usually "Yes," but in fact there have been no legal strikes for three or four years. In 1951 emergency laws forbade strikes in vital enterprises, but "vital enterprise" was not closely defined. Committees of settlement were appointed to handle such disputes as the authorities decided were vital. In 1957 permanent legislation required several steps before a strike could be legally undertaken, including a conference with the employer, mediation efforts by local authorities, and permission by a standing tripartite labor board. Permission has not been granted for several years. Nevertheless, strikes do occur, usually as political demonstrations.

In addition, in some areas the actual relationship between labor and management may best be described as paternalistic. In Indonesia, for example, manufacturing is mainly carried on in small shops with only a few employees, so that there is a close personal relationship between employer and employee or perhaps, more likely, great awe of the employer. As firms get larger, the personal relationship decreases, but custom seems to perpetuate the welfare programs. Late in the Dutch period a system known as the "ethical policy" was introduced. This consisted of providing housing, health care, and social benefits as part of the pay. The custom of considering these part of the wages is strong today and continues, strengthened by labor's desire to be paid in kind so as to offset the inflation. Paternalistic systems fit naturally into the way of life. The individual is in the habit of taking his problems to an elder; for example, his grandfather or the village chief. It is only natural to do the same with his employer. The worker may live in huts around the employer's home or workshop. He may even eat at the employer's house with the household servants. He may work in the home as well as in the shop. The employer pays for most of the medical care; pays a weekly allowance in food, soap, and cooking oil; and on major religious holidays makes a gift of clothing and money. He usually provides burial fees. Wages are low and worth far less than the "free services"; in fact, one inquiry among a group of employers found that "fringe benefits" were 90 percent of the total wage cost. This system is now usually incorporated into the labor contracts.

In a setting of employer strength, government concern, weak unions, and small shops, there can be no real collective bargaining. There may be no overt hostility against unions because unions are protected, but neither is there much bargaining. Yet even with these handicaps, there are signs that collective bargaining may be growing. Because government employment has expanded, government rules and regulations will play a relatively more important role than in the West, but collective bargaining can be expected to emerge in the private sphere as the surplus of labor is reduced. However, the exact form of collective bargaining can be expected to be different in different countries, depending on the political, economic, and social systems. Different degrees of freedom and government control can be expected.

In the West, free collective bargaining seems the accepted pattern, and there has been no really serious threat to its continuance. It is felt that mutually arrived-at agreements are more satisfactory than imposed ones and therefore better adhered to; the possibility of occasional strikes is not so damaging to output as is smoldering discontent, except in public emergency conditions. But collective bargaining has matured in the West and works reasonably well. Collective bargaining is too immature in most underdeveloped countries to be effective, and the results may be too dangerous to the fragile economies for the risk to be accepted. As economic growth takes hold, free collective bargaining may develop, but it will take long experience with some form of bargaining relationship. Much of this background will have to come from experience in settling grievances and small disputes, with (at first) major disputes being taken to government boards. Whether collective bargaining can develop from this will depend on the institutions of the country and the temperament of the people. If a country is to be democratic, it cannot afford not to develop free collective bargaining. Newly developing countries may find that, temporarily, they can afford neither democracy nor collective bargaining.

Few underdeveloped countries today find that free collective bargaining can settle disputes between labor and management. Collective bargaining has proceeded farthest in such countries as Japan, India, Israel, Argentina, Mexico, and Venezuela, but relationships are not always smooth in these areas. Except for India, these countries have advanced relatively far along the development scale, but India has a greater respect for democratic action than most other underdeveloped countries. Even in these countries government pressures have a limiting effect. In many of the underdeveloped countries, systems other than free collective bargaining decide labor issues or are used to supplement it. Many issues may be settled by legislation. Arbitration or settlement by a state officer is widespread. Tunisia has a system of joint consultation backed by compulsory arbitration.[32] Ghana prescribes the number and structure of unions, requires membership, and virtually controls their actions.[33] The Sudan has shifted from a voluntary to a closely controlled system.[34] On the other hand, collective bargaining is growing in Latin America, although there is great reliance on governmental regulation, and the Philippines have shifted from a system of compulsory arbitration to one of collective bargaining.[35]

Thus, some form of compulsory arbitration is practiced in much of the underdeveloped world and undoubtedly interferes with the growth and development of collective bargaining, although it does protect labor standards. For example, in Indonesia, interviews with the leading unions brought forth the view that the system of compulsory arbitration, which permits any union to take a case to the arbitration board, makes for a multiplicity of unions and therefore an inability to bargain. Even grievance cases may be submitted to the board. In the Philippines it was found that compulsory arbitration could not satisfactorily handle disputes over such things as pensions, union shops, seniority, jurisdiction, and representation.[36]

The Indonesian system is an excellent example of a current system of handling relations between labor and management. Compulsory arbitration of all labor disputes is the rule. Other techniques are tried first, but ultimately all cases must be arbitrated if they cannot be resolved in other ways.* The first step is that the employer and the union bargain over the terms of the contract. If they agree, well and good, and the contract is signed. If the parties cannot agree, they have resort to an elaborate procedure, which must be followed before a strike can occur. The first step is to appeal to the local Officer of Industrial Relations, who may suggest voluntary arbitration, or the parties may try this before going to the officer. Less than 1 percent of the cases are handled this way. The decision is reviewed by the Regional Arbitration Board or Committee (discussed below), which may invalidate the award, but only because of incompetence of the arbitrator or because the award is "inconsistent with the public morality or interest."

The more usual course is for the industrial officer to investigate the background and conditions of the dispute, and to try to mediate it within seven days. If he is unsuccessful, the case is referred to the Regional Arbitration Committee. These are tripartite committees consisting of five government representatives, five from labor, and five from the employer, all appointed by the Minister of Labor. If labor intends to strike, or the employer moves to lock out the employees, the anticipatory party must first inform the committee and receive permission from it. Otherwise no strike or lockout can take place. The first step of the committee upon receiving a dispute is to medi-

---

* The procedures are set forth in the Settlement of Labour Disputes Law of 1957, Number 22.

ation. It will negotiate with the two parties and conduct conferences in order to persuade them to make the decisions themselves. If this fails, the committee will suggest an award and attempt to get the two parties to accept it voluntarily. If the parties do not accept the award, the committee may issue a binding award. The award of the regional committee may be appealed to the Central Arbitration Board, also a tripartite board of fifteen members appointed by the Cabinet with the approval of the President. The Minister of Labor may nullify or suspend the award of the central board if it is "not in the interest of the public peace." In order to facilitate its work, the central board may set up a fact-finding board to determine the facts. This board reports to the central board and includes a recommendation of its own. Both original disputes and grievance cases are handled in the same manner.

About 11 percent of the cases reported were settled by management and labor themselves, but these were brought to the industrial officer and then settled before he could act. Some employers say they do not want to be recorded as having a case go to arbitration, and others feel they may do better with a compromise than they would do before the board. This reflects the unsatisfactory state of collective bargaining. Considerably less than half of all disputes are settled by mediation, and the percentage seems to be declining.

According to members of the central board, no central wage policy has been determined. The statement was made that "wage policy is decided case by case." No standards are explicitly recognized except "the interests of the state," and the central board specifically disclaims any need to be bound by precedent.

Under such circumstances of weak collective bargaining and strong government intervention, it is no wonder that the main method by which labor seeks to achieve its ends is usually by political action. Unions often have a close relation to a political party, and in some cases could hardly exist without its support. A large part of the financial support and the top officials may come from the political party, and the economic interests of the worker may be subordinated to the needs of the party. However, political action appears to be more effective than economic action under the circumstances. As indicated, unions do not have much strength in collective bargaining. The structure of unions on a general or industrial basis and along nationalistic or ideological lines makes political action natural. The great influence of the government in the economic field and on wage levels and other labor matters, such as through compulsory arbitration, makes political action essential. Unions operate by seeking favorable legislation on wages, working conditions, social security, job security, and other labor matters, and by trying to influence administrators into making favorable decisions. The important relationship for unions is with government, not with employers.[37]

Unions have considerable potential power and may affect the economy in various ways. They may tie up the economy in strikes. Their wage and other demands have an important effect on the economic objectives of society, not always for the worse. They may affect economic growth by their attitude toward productivity, wage levels, and other labor costs. The prevailing view in most countries is that the greatest need for economic growth is investment and that therefore consumption and wages should be held down. At certain times, although not always, this is true. One is tempted to say unions should act responsibly and should sacrifice member advantages to the nation's economic and social objectives, but the chance of unions' (or the representatives of any other group) acceptance of this "responsibility" remains small. Each group tends to identify its own interests with those of the public. The differences of opinion as to whether wage increases are good or bad are sufficiently numerous for each group to choose the view that benefits it most. Until proper policy for economic growth and other objectives is certain, this will always remain the case. Thus, the real question is: Who is to decide the nation's objectives and the means of attaining them? The controlling group often has its own interests. It is the function of the unions to represent the workers' interests and their point of view in the determination of the country's policies. To the extent that these interests run counter to those of other groups, they will be opposed. The result will depend on the balance of power. Most underdeveloped countries seem to be moving more toward a centralized adjudication of labor issues and a less vital role for collective bargaining. In some areas, labor has a large role in these central decisions, but in others, its views are being subordinated. The matters of wages and other labor costs will be discussed in the next section of this chapter.

It is unlikely that workers can be restrained indefinitely as harmless production machines. Labor must share in the general economic gain or it will not cooperate. What it will consider a "fair" share is unpredictable, but the share may be more than most governments deem desirable. To grant all the demands would be costly and disruptive to investment; to deny them would also be costly in the loss of cooperation, possible strikes, and political opposition.

It has been suggested that what is needed is to develop specific functions for unions, other than their normal ones, that would contribute to growth, or would not deter it, thus directing the purpose of unions toward a common endeavor, but it is unlikely that unions would accept this.[38] Some of the proposed functions are: explaining to members the implication of the economic plan; educating the members in the necessity for restricting consumption and particularly for giving up spendthrift habits; encouraging small savings; increasing labor productivity; inducing members to take training to improve their skills; cooperating with government in enforcing labor legislation; assisting members in making the social adjustment to industry and urban living, and also providing credit cooperatives, housing cooperatives, and literacy training; establishing and maintaining discipline in the plant; and emphasizing and working for better housing, education, and health services. These, of course, would be in addition to their role in representing the workers in the decisions of the state.

Such a program for labor in the underdeveloped countries would be ideal for promoting economic growth and would probably benefit labor in the long run. However, it is too much to expect that workers will voluntarily accept these. One alternative, if the objective is to increase investment, is to force them into at least accepting low wages. Only a Soviet Russia or a Mainland China could do this. Democratic governments would find it impossible. The only course for them is to somehow fit the desires of workers for rising standards of living into their development plans.

## Wage Policy

The wage policy of the workers may be summed up in three objectives.

1. A plea for justice, defined as getting a fair share of any increased productivity of the economy: Thus, as development proceeds, workers expect a rising standard of living. Actually, demands are based often on unfounded notions of how fast the economy is growing so that they are apt to outrun the increases in the output of society. The existence of a few obviously newly rich help produce this effect.
2. Keeping wages at least in line with changes in the cost of living: This is important in those underdeveloped countries where price increases are especially large, a not uncommon occurrence.
3. Hastening development but via the purchasing-power theory of development, as discussed below.

The wage policies of governments must take into account a wide range of conflicting objectives and the final policy must be a compromise among them.[39]

1. The elimination of exceptionally low wages by setting minimum wages: Most nations do this, but the standards are extremely low. Usually they are set industry by industry, with the profitability of the industry a limiting factor.

2. The abolition of malpractices in wage payment, with the aim of seeing that the worker actually receives what he earns: Examples of bad practices are irregular payment and payment at long intervals, unjustified deductions, payment in kind of nonconsumption goods so that the worker must sell them, requiring buying at the employer's shop, and unequal pay for the sexes or the different races.

3. Setting a level of wages that is fair to the worker in relation to the output of the economy: Basically, this must be enough to secure the worker's cooperation and to prevent revolt or political opposition to the government. The proper distribution of income is involved.

4. Protecting the worker against rising prices.

5. Setting a level of wages that will permit competition in the export markets.

6. Setting wages so as to provide an incentive for workers to increase their productivity: Wage increases cannot go beyond productivity without creating inflationary pressure. Usually governments try to hold wage increases below the increase in productivity so as to provide capital for development.

7. Encourage differentials that will allocate labor in an optimum manner: Little is known about the wage structures in underdeveloped countries, which is an unfortunate lack because it is important to attract labor where it is needed most. Little intelligent action can be done without knowledge of the facts. Government wage schedules might be expected to have an influence toward narrowing wage differentials, but what little evidence there is indicates that wage differentials are greater in underdeveloped countries than in the advanced. Whether they are optimally arranged is another matter. Observation indicates that skill differentials in private industry in Indonesia are greater than in the West, the skilled worker getting as much as five times more than the unskilled in some establishments. Payments in kind tend to lessen the differentials between jobs, but widen them among different factories. In a Sukabumi government report,[40] daily rated skilled workers were reported as earning, on the average, 30 to 47 percent more than the unskilled, but this understates the skill premium, for a skilled worker was defined as one whose job required two days or more to learn. Wages in manufacturing were 25 percent more than plantation wages. An International Labour Office study[41] reported wages higher in the cities, with average earnings in agriculture below those of industry. However, the real earnings of the unskilled industrial worker were possibly lower than those of the agricultural worker, particularly under conditions of inflation. Industrial work was less seasonal. Reports on Vietnam,[42] Africa,[43] and Guatemala[44] indicate wide differentials by skill and regions. In Africa, large differentials

existed between the races, and in Guatemala it was stated that the wages of the unskilled were not keeping up with price changes and that the skilled were absorbing all the gains of the increased productivity.

Large differentials are to be expected in view of the shortage of skilled labor and the oversupply of the unskilled, the different rate of development of the regions within each country, and the different profitability of the various industries. Whether the differentials promote the objectives of the country is unknown, but it is important to establish this effect. It should be noted that Soviet Russia has made considerable use of manipulating differentials in order to attract people into the occupations, regions, and industries where they have been considered most needed.

8.   Increase the demand for consumer goods.

9.   Promote industrial investment.

Items 8 and 9 provoke the most controversy and deserve further consideration. The real issue in wage policy is the conflict between the need for capital formation and for consumption. Capital equipment is needed to produce more goods, but increased incomes are necessary to consume the output unless the goods are exported. If incomes are increased without increasing consumption goods, price rises result. Thus, wage increases can be encouraging or discouraging, depending on the circumstances. Wages are both a purchasing power and a cost, and cannot be looked on exclusively from either aspect.

Actually, there are two theories of how to enlarge the total output stream. One holds that it is necessary to have large savings which can be invested in productive capacity, thus increasing in time the flow of goods. The other holds that it is necessary to increase purchasing power so that there will be an incentive to invest. Consumption and investment are competitive in that productive efforts can be used to turn out goods either for consumption or for capital equipment. It is possible for all the output of a country to be consumed—or even more than all the output—but if this is done, capital equipment is not maintained. If capital equipment is to be built up, consumers must refrain from using up all the output. On the other hand, if they do not consume enough, there will be no incentive for producers to turn out goods or to invest in further productive capacity.

Thus, an optimum relationship must exist among total production, investment, saving, and consumption if economic growth is to be maximized. Unfortunately, economic theory has not yet supplied us with an absolute criterion by which to determine the proper relationship, which undoubtedly differs with each situation. There is, of course, some margin of tolerance, but, theoretically, if the relationships get far out of line, difficulties should arise. If either demand or investment falls too low, expansion is likely to be halted.

Most underdeveloped countries have some sort of plan or program for development. If a plan is to be effective at all, a policy for wages must be included. Indonesia is a country with an economic plan calling for overall planning, that is, planning of economic affairs, social and cultural planning, planning for education and health, and for almost every phase of life. As extensive as the plan is, no decision was made as to government policy concerning the wage level. The question of whether the country will try to grow by keeping wages low and encouraging capital expansion, or by utilizing increases in production to raise living standards immediately, or some combination of the two, seems not to have been asked, let alone answered. However, the answer to the question is crucial to this plan or to any other.

By definition, underdeveloped countries are those with a real shortage of purchasing power. Also, savings are low and investment in capital goods is low. Without documentary evidence one can only estimate that savings may be low but that they are in excess of investment. Tales of hoarding, capital flight, and so on bear this out. Attempts to increase savings would be defeating unless in some way it was assured that investment would follow. A government economic plan or direct government investment are two of the answers to this. The reinvestment of private profits cannot be relied upon and compulsory savings invite labor dissatisfaction. However, government investment is uneconomic without a market.

The investigations of E. D. Domar[45] led him to believe that it would be difficult for incomes to grow rapidly enough to support smooth growth. As capital goods are produced, they create the prospect of output. The greater the increase in capital equipment, the greater the potential increase in output, and thus a greater increase in incomes is needed to enable the products to be bought and the necessary savings to accumulate. Investment creates incomes as well as capacity to produce. Also, increased incomes increase the amount of investment needed. Thus, investment and income interact. In countries that are advanced economically, the case seems best for raising incomes as a means of best promoting growth, but not at such a pace as to cause runaway prices or to threaten investments. In such countries, savings are available and production can be expanded readily.

In the underdeveloped countries, both capital and purchasing power are deficient. To increase workers' purchasing power would be inflationary, as the workers would spend it at a nearly 100 percent marginal rate and this would be unlikely to call forth much increased product because the capacity to expand production is just not available. Raising wages without damage to the economy depends on increased productivity, which must come through capital investment or improved techniques, and the latter usually require capital. The best of all possible worlds would have new productive techniques that required no capital and no time period before becoming productive, accompanied by rising wage levels. Examples of this might be the more intensive use of capital, such as in multiple shifts or harder or more efficient work. Lacking this, investment of savings is necessary. Thus, for developing countries, a high-wage policy is not indicated, but neither is a stationary wage level. Modest increases are necessary to increase the markets as increased production becomes possible, and are also necessary for political reasons.

Some underdeveloped countries have a different problem in that they have plenty of capital; for example, the oil-rich countries. In these cases a high-wage policy seems the logical policy.

## Labor Legislation and Social Security

Underdeveloped countries have similar conflicts over objectives with respect to social security and other labor legislation. In the interests of human welfare, such programs are desirable. They may also contribute to productivity and are almost unavoidable after the workers become aware of Western standards. On the other hand, they are costly to businesses, and therefore reduce the ability of business to survive and to compete in foreign markets. Such programs also absorb capital, which might otherwise be used for economic expansion, and may discourage private capital from abroad. Thus, they may be overdeveloped or underdeveloped with respect to their effect on productivity and development.

The attitude of the officials of underdeveloped countries is well expressed by the views of one official at an International Labour Conference[46] when he recognized the desirability of meeting international labor standards but felt that this must yield priority to the problems of poverty, excess population, illiteracy, and disease. There is a growing awareness of the need to tackle all these problems, but also a realization that productivity must be increased in order to do so. In other words, the countries lack the means, not the will. The Japanese appear to have had the same view concerning social security.[47] This view, as reported, is that economic growth must be promoted first and that social security should be improved only after a given level of economic expansion is reached, especially as long as there is less than full employment. It seems that a sound appropriate policy would be one that based labor legislation and social security on their economic effect on productivity and the ability of the society to afford them without sacrificing other more important needs. Such a policy would begin the program by making concessions to social and political needs and then extend other benefits as economic growth occurs.

The social security laws and labor legislation of the underdeveloped countries vary widely from country to country and cannot be detailed here.* The reader may find representative descriptions in the literature.[48] There is a tendency to overdevelop these programs because of the political power or potential revolutionary force of labor. However, administration and enforcement are underdeveloped,[49] and the benefits are not realized.

The laws cover the usual matters of minimum wages, hours of work, working conditions, safety, work of women and children, employment security, and social security. Only a general description of the problem can be attempted.

Minimum wage laws set low standards and are usually established industry by industry, but this modification makes it difficult for some industries to pay them, so that labor is forced into the overcrowded occupations such as agriculture, domestic service, street selling, and the like. Mechanization is encouraged. One suspects that forcing mechanization and efficiency would bring economic growth and eventual increase of employment and wages more rapidly than permitting wages to fall so low that everyone is employed. This could be a way to improve the earning capacity of workers.

The argument for establishing shorter hours for work usually rests on physiological, citizenship, social, and economic gain claims. On each of these bases there may be a different optimum. In the West the first three have had considerable importance, but the most used arguments emphasize the necessity to spread employment when productivity increases so that increased productivity will make it possible for a worker to choose between increased leisure and more goods. Neither of these latter two arguments are applicable to the present underdeveloped countries. Unfortunately, these countries have often copied the legislation that controls working hours in the advanced countries and have even exceeded them, despite the fact that increased productivity has not been realized. For example, hour legislation in Indonesia† sets maximum hours as seven per day and forty per week, except for night work in dangerous trades, where hours are limited to six per day and thirty-five per week. Workers must be given one day of rest per week and are not to work on public holidays "unless the nature of the work precludes interruption." Work at night and on Sundays or holidays must be compensated by double pay, and work on August 17, which is Indonesian Independence Day, at five times the usual rate. All workers are to be given a two-week vacation each year, and after six consecutive years of work, three months' vacation. Time off must be given for the exercise of religious

* Details of specific countries may be obtained from Bureau of Labor Statistic Reports on Labor Law and Practice issued by various countries.
† Law 12 of 1948, Law 1 of 1951, and administrative orders.

duties, and workers are entitled to a break of at least one half-hour after every four hours of continuous work, but the rest period is not included in the total of working hours. Women workers receive three days' menstrual leave each month and three months' confinement leave. If the short hours were used to spread employment, there might be some justification, but the general opposition to multiple shifts results in a lessened utilization of scarce capital and scarce management. The short-hour movement, under such circumstances, interferes with the productivity essential to economic growth. This is particularly true in the case of skilled labor, which could well be used more intensively.

Legislation governing minimum working conditions is usually based on motives of health, efficiency, morale, and worker convenience. In the early stages of industrialization the world over, employers have done little to make their work places clean, sanitary, and pleasant unless forced to do so by government regulation. In many underdeveloped countries the same situation exists. Factories are dirty and poorly lighted, and no effort is made to make the surroundings pleasant. The advanced countries have learned that good working conditions pay off in improved morale, better health, and increased productivity, but this compensatory aspect has not yet become apparent to the underdeveloped ones. In many areas there is extensive legislation but little enforcement. In Indonesia, standards are effectively enforced only in the large factories, for inspection staffs are undermanned and the small shops and cottage industries are too numerous and too isolated for effective control. One glance at the work places is enough to see that the standards are quite low.

Perhaps more important to the worker and to society is the maintenance of safe working conditions. Accidents seem inevitable, no matter how much care is exercised; but experience in Western countries shows that they can be reduced. However, governments must usually take the initiative in requiring safety. From the standpoint of the individual worker and of society, the safety movement is one of the most significant developments in the work place. But it can also be one of the most costly.

Statistics of accidents in the underdeveloped countries are unreliable or nonexistent. One of the first prerequisites to a sound prevention program is the collection of statistical data to establish prevailing rates, the types of accidents, and the causes. A visit to factories in an underdeveloped country would quickly disclose the inferiority of safety standards. Even such an elementary precaution as keeping the floors clear of obstructions so that workers will not stumble and be thrown against machinery is universally ignored. Only the fact that much of the machinery runs at low speed keeps the accident rate from soaring. Modern, high-speed, automatic machinery with existing inferior safety precautions could not help but result in high accident rates. Concomitant with the development of modern industry must come a widespread and thorough safety program. New countries could learn much from the experience of the older industrial countries, for impressive files of accident statistics have been built up and extensive safety programs carried out. The Indonesian safety requirements are a carry-over from the Dutch regime and are out of date and inadequate for modern industry. The inspection staff is too small and poorly trained because of lack of funds and competent instructors. No technical school includes a course on safety.

Regulation of the employment terms for women and children is based on the theory that adverse working conditions have particular effect on their health, efficiency, and general well-being, and bring disease, crime, vice, and low educational standards, thus incurring danger to society and the next generation. Legislation on these matters is improving, and seems advantageous from the viewpoint of growth as well as individual welfare.

Social security coverages include such hazards as old age, unemployment, ill health and hospitalization, home and work accidents, and loss of parents. Most countries throughout the world assume part of the responsibility for such risks and underdeveloped countries are not exceptions. They have more or less developed systems, some going beyond the standard of the United States and others having only the most meager provisions. Such systems can be expensive, but the alternative of starvation, begging, or reliance on relatives is undesirable and is also expensive. It is unknown which alternative is the more costly and whether the cost is chargeable to a country's consumption or to its savings.

Security can be productive by relieving anxiety and restoring people more quickly to employment if they become sick or injured. For underdeveloped countries it is particularly important to take care of the scarce skilled workers, although from a welfare point of view the unskilled require more help. Prevention, of course, pays even more. Untreated disease, for example, tends to be cumulative and may lead to epidemics. To protect society, everyone must have access to medical care. Other kinds of risks have less chance of spreading, although society suffers in other ways if there is no preventive control.

In some areas, particularly South America, jobs are protected by legislation, so that it is difficult to lay off a worker once he is hired. Employment security keeps up morale, but it can interfere with innovations in industry and with proper labor discipline if it is excessive.

Thus, supplying a productive labor force takes capital, not only for training the workers but also for providing them with adequate living and working conditions and a minimum of security. Other labor problems, such as unemployment, are no less a drag on the potential supply of investment funds. Low wages may appear to increase the potential savings, but they also discourage investment. Moreover, labor will insist upon a "fair share" of the gains derived from development. Unions will insist on benefits for labor and are likely to be successful unless curbed by government action. Thus, either granting labor's demands or suppressing them is costly. Such costs must be considered in any plan to allocate a country's resources.

## REFERENCES

1. KUZNETS, S., "Findings on the Industrial Structure of the Labor Force and National Product," in *Six Lectures on Economic Growth.* New York, The Free Press of Glencoe, 1959, pp. 43-68.
2. "Population and Labour Force in Asia, 1950-80." *International Labour Review* (October, 1962), p. 362.
3. "Population and Labour Force in Africa." *International Labour Review* (December, 1961), pp. 499-514.
4. *Report on Labour Force Sample Survey in Java and Madura.* Ministry of Labour, Indonesia, 1961, pp. 22-25, 37-39.
5. "Population and Labour Force in Asia," *loc. cit.,* p. 363. (Shows the progress in Japan.)
6. KERR, C., F. H. HARBISON, and J. T. DUNLOP, "Industrialism and Industrial Man." *International Labour Review* (September, 1960), pp. 236-50.
7. "Economic Development and Employment in E. Cameroun." *International Labour Review* (June, 1962), p. 604.
8. *Report on Labour Force Sample Survey in Java and Madura, loc. cit.*
9. "Women in the Labor Force." *International Labour Review* (March, 1958), p. 255.
10. Department of Social Affairs, *Preliminary Report on the World Social Situation.* New York, United Nations, pp. 111-12.
11. MEHTA, A., "Mediating Role of the Trade Union in Underdeveloped Countries." *Economic Development and Cultural Change* (October, 1957), p. 22.
12. MOORE, W. E., "Primitives and Peasants in Industry," *Social Research* (March, 1948), pp. 44-81. (A discussion of the barriers to and propellants toward such a commitment to industry. This article is a summary of Moore's book by Elizabeth Todd.)
13. HSIEH, C., "Underemployment in Asia." *International Labour Review* (June, 1952), pp. 703-25; (July, 1952), pp. 30-39. "Measurement of Underemployment." *International Labour Review* (October, 1957), pp. 352-53.
14. HSIEH, *op. cit.,* p. 719.
15. "Employment Position and Problems in Chad." *International Labour Review* (May, 1962), p. 506.
16. "Economic Development and Employment in E. Cameroun," *loc. cit.,* p. 607.
17. *Ibid.,* pp. 22-33.
18. "Measurement of Underemployment," *loc. cit.,* p. 350.
19. HAREWOOD, J., "Overpopulation and Underemployment in the West Indies." *International Labour Review* (August, 1960), p. 115.

20. "Unemployment and Underemployment in India, Indonesia, Pakistan, and the Philippines." *International Labour Review* (October, 1962), pp. 369-87.

21. JAFFE, A. J., *People, Jobs and Economic Development*. New York, The Free Press of Glencoe, 1959. Jaffe, "Employment Objectives in Economic Development." *International Labour Review* (November, 1961), pp. 394-411.

22. "Youth Employment and Vocational Training Schemes." *International Labour Review* (September, 1962), pp. 209-34.

23. *Employment Objectives in Economic Development*. Geneva, International Labour Office, 1961. "Employment Objectives in Economic Development." *International Labour Review* (November, 1961), pp. 394-411.

24. DE BRIEY, P., "Productivity of African Labor." *International Labour Review* (August, 1955), pp. 119-37. See also Enke, S., *Economics for Development*. Englewood Cliffs, N.J., Prentice-Hall, Inc., 1963, pp. 366ff., for a discussion of the relationship between calorie intake and energy output and pp. 398ff. for a description of the most prevalent tropical diseases.

25. *Report on Labour Force Sample Survey, loc. cit.*, p. 17.

26. "Human Skills in the Decade of Development." *Department of State Bulletin* (December 3, 1962), pp. 85ff.

27. HARBISON, F. H., "Human Resources Development Planning in Modernizing Economies." *International Labour Review* (May, 1962), pp. 437-38.

28. The following articles describe some of the plans now in existence: Al-Arabi, M., "Modern Apprenticeship Scheme in the U.A.R." *International Labour Review* (December, 1961), pp. 478-98. "Vocational Training and the Establishment of Service Workshops in a Poor Rural Area." *International Labour Review* (February, 1962), pp. 129-47. "National Apprenticeship System in Ghana." *International Labour Review* (June, 1962), pp. 612-21. "Manpower Aspects of the Lower Mekong Basin Development Project." *International Labour Review* (April, 1962), pp. 357-67. Zelenko, H., "Vocational and Technical Training in the U.S.S.R." *International Labour Review* (December, 1959), pp. 489-504.

29. HARBISON, F. H., "Human Resources Development Planning in Modernizing Economies." *International Labour Review* (May, 1962), pp. 435-58. "Manpower Planning in East Europe." *International Labour Review* (August, 1962), pp. 95-127.

30. KIKUCHI, I., "Industrial Relations in Japan." *International Labour Review* (August, 1959), p. 150.

31. GALENSON, WALTER, ed., *Labor and Economic Development*. New York, J. Wiley & Sons, Inc., 1959. *Labor in Developing Countries*. Berkeley, Calif., University of California Press, 1962.

32. LADHARR, N., "Labour-Management Relations in Tunisia." *International Labour Review* (September, 1961), pp. 175-97.

33. RIMMER, D., "New Industrial Relations in Ghana." *International Labour Review* (January, 1961), pp. 206-26.

34. OSMAN, O. M., "Recent Changes in Labor Legislation in the Sudan." *International Labour Review* (September, 1962), pp. 235-46.

35. CALDERON, C. D., "From Compulsory Arbitration to Collective Bargaining in the Philippines." *International Labour Review* (January, 1960), pp. 1-24.

36. *Ibid.*, p. 7.

37. KASSELOW, E. M., "Union Organization and Training in Emerging Labor Movements." *Monthly Labor*

*Review* (September, 1962), pp. 1010-15.

38. STURMTHAL, A., "Unions and Economic Development." *Economic Development and Cultural Change* (January, 1960), p. 200. Mehta, *Economic Development and Cultural Change, loc. cit.* (October, 1957), pp. 16-23. Kasselow, *op. cit.*, pp. 1014-15. Fisher, P., "Economic Role of Unions in Less-Developed Areas." *Monthly Labor Review* (September, 1961), pp. 955-56.

39. *Problems of Wage Policy in Asian Countries.* Geneva, International Labour Office, 1956.

40. *Report on the Sample Survey of Wages, Earnings and Hours of Work in Sukabumi.* Ministry of Labour, 1957.

41. *Problems of Wage Policy . . . , loc. cit.*, p. 16.

42. "Wages in Vietnam." *International Labour Review* (December, 1959), pp. 465-88.

43. "Interracial Wage Structure in Certain Parts of Africa." *International Labour Review* (July, 1958), pp. 20-55.

44. "Minimum Wage Problems and Policy in Guatemala." *International Labour Review* (May, 1959), pp. 459-86.

45. DOMAR, E. D., *Essays in the Theory of Economic Growth.* New York, Oxford University Press, 1957.

46. "International Labour Standards and Asian Countries." *International Labour Review* (April, 1961), p. 304.

47. "Social Security Policy in Japan." *International Labour Review* (October, 1961), pp. 292-301.

48. "Social Security in Asia." *International Labour Review*, vol. I (July, 1960), pp. 70-87; vol. II (August, 1960), pp. 163-83. "Evolution of Labor Legislation and Administration in Iran." *International Labour Review* (March, 1959), pp. 273-95. "Social Insurance in Latin America." *International Labour Review* (September, 1958), pp. 257-83. "Social Security Policy in Japan," *loc. cit.*, pp. 292-301. "Social Security in Africa South of the Sahara." *International Labour Review* (September, 1961), pp. 144-74. Jenks, C. W., *Human Rights and International Labour Standards.* London, Stevens & Sons, Ltd., 1960.

49. GRAHAM, T., "Some Problems of Labor Inspection in Underdeveloped Countries." *International Labour Review* (July, 1954), pp. 547-69. (A description of the problems of inspection.)

## ADDITIONAL READINGS

ALEXANDER, R. J., *Labor Relations in Argentina, Brazil, and Chile.* New York, The McGraw-Hill Book Co., Inc., 1962.

BARBOUR, K. M., and R. M. PROTHERO, eds. *Essays on African Population.* London, Routledge and Kegan Paul, Ltd., 1961. Southall, A. W., "Population Movements in Central Africa," pp. 157-92. Mitchell, J. C., "Wage Labour and African Population Movements in Central Africa," pp. 193-248.

ELKAN, W., "Migrant Labor in Africa." *American Economic Association,* *Proceedings* (May, 1959), pp. 188-97.

ELKAN, W., *Migrants and Proletarians,* New York, Oxford University Press, 1960.

KELBY, P., "African Labour Productivity Reconsidered." *Economic Journal* (June, 1961), pp. 273-91.

KERR, C., F. HARBISON, J. T. DUNLOP, and C. A. MYERS, "Labour Problem in Economic Development." *International Labour Review* (May, 1955), pp. 223-35.

LEWIS, W. A., "Economic Development with Unlimited Supplies of Labour."

*Manchester School of Economics* (May, 1954), pp. 139-91.

MARTIN, L. R., "Research Needed on the Contributions of Human, Social and Community Capital to Economic Growth." *Journal of Farm Economics* (February, 1963), pp. 73-94.

MILLEN, B. H., *Political Role of Labor in Developing Countries*. Washington, D.C., The Brookings Institution, 1963.

MOORE, W. E., and A. S. FELDMAN, *Labor Commitment and Social Change in Developing Areas*. Social Science Research Council, 1960.

SAYIGH, Y. A., "Management-Labour Relations in Arab Countries." *International Labour Review* (June, 1958), pp. 519-37.

TOTTEN, G. O., "Labor and Agrarian Disputes in Japan Following World War I," Pt. 2. *Economic Development and Cultural Change* (October, 1960), pp. 187-212.

VAN EERDE, K. S., "Problems and Alignments in African Labor." *Social Research* (Spring, 1962), pp. 73-100.

WIGNY, P., "Migratory Movements in Underdeveloped Countries in the Course of Industrialization." *International Labour Review* (July, 1953), pp. 1-13.

YESUFU, T. M., *Introduction to Industrial Relations in Nigeria*. New York, Oxford University Press, 1962.

"Production Techniques and Employment Creation in Underdeveloped Economies." *International Labour Review* (August, 1958), pp. 121-50.

"Gradual Extension of Social Insurance Schemes in Latin American Countries." *International Labour Review* (September, 1958), pp. 257-83.

"Economic Growth and Social Policy in Latin America." *International Labour Review* (July-August, 1961), pp. 50-74.

# CHAPTER

# 7

# *Industry*

## *The Motives for Industrialization*

Most underdeveloped countries tend to emphasize the development of industry for a variety of reasons and are making efforts to lessen the industrial gap between them and the advanced countries. Despite great efforts, the gap has been widening, although a few, such as Japan and Israel, have tended to industrialize rapidly. The motives for industrialization are many.

The wealth and power of the Western countries and the impressive performance of Russia—countries with a large degree of industrialization—seem to offer convincing proof of the desirability of industrialization, and this has led to an unwavering belief that industry is the only solution to the problems of the underdeveloped countries. This uncritical acceptance of industry is exemplified by the following statement:

> The importance of industrial development for the general economic progress of the country is revealed by the fact that the richest countries of the world are also industrially most advanced, and the poorest countries are those which are predominantly depending upon the primary sector (mainly agriculture) of their economies: . . . It will appear, therefore, that the road to economic prosperity for underdeveloped countries lies in the direction of industrialization.[1]

That the richer countries are industrialized is an apparent fact, although a country such as New Zealand is somewhat of an exception. It is just as accurate, and probably even more accurate, to say that because countries are rich, they industrialize; that is, as their incomes increase in the primary pursuits, they are encouraged and enabled to shift resources to industry in order to supply wants beyond mere subsistence. Thus, too great an emphasis on pushing industry to the exclusion of agriculture may be self-defeating, since industry may come as a result of general development rather than being the cause of it.

The forced industrialization by the U.S.S.R. and by mainland China has seemed to support the thesis that development depends on emphasizing industry almost to the exclusion of all other sectors. Recent events in those countries, stemming from agricultural failures, seem to indicate a lagging rate of growth imposed by the slower development of other sectors. This must be watched to see if such a lag is an erratic event or the result of overemphasis on industrialization and neglect of agriculture.

Industrialization seems, in some quarters, to be considered a panacea for all ills. The specific circumstances of a country may indicate that industrialization is, indeed, the recommended procedure for development; but it must be justified, after serious reflection, only on the basis that it will contribute to that end better than any other method; and it should be pursued only to the extent that it promotes that end. The exception would, of course, be that other ends were more important.

There is some support for industrialization from considerations of national pride and prestige, modern industry being considered a symbol of a modern state.

The following motives have a more solid reasoning behind them, although each may or may not be applicable to a given situation.

1.  Most underdeveloped countries feel that capital and other resources will be more productive in industry than in other economic sectors, particularly agriculture, and that therefore resources should be shifted toward industry. The productivity of labor in agriculture is low and, as has been noted, there is some belief that shifting people from agriculture into other pursuits will cause little or no loss in productivity in agriculture. That there will be no loss in agricultural productivity is subject to some doubt. The important question for any country to answer is whether the investment in industry will actually result in greater productivity than in agriculture. Moreover, it is necessary that the industrial workers be able to meet their increased demands for food, either by imports or by domestic agriculture; if they cannot, inflated food prices will result, with serious consequences of increased wage demands, which could cripple the rising industry. For most countries it will be necessary for domestic agriculture to improve its productivity. As will be developed later, it is the contention of this author that

the development of no one sector of the economy can be overlooked and that there must be simultaneous development in all areas.* Thus, the fact of low productivity in agriculture does not by itself justify concentrating investment in industry. All indications are that, in the interest of increased productivity, there must be some development of industry. The questions are: How much compared to other activities and of what types?

Even where agriculture is efficient, incomes in agriculture are usually lower than in industry, as is true in the United States where agriculture is very efficient or in Denmark, which is one of the most efficient agricultural countries. As countries develop and incomes rise, the demand for food grows but that for industrial products or for processing services in connection with foods grows more rapidly, thus opening up possibilities for increased incomes for the factors of production. Thus, the promotion of industry, under the right circumstances, is desirable.

2.   Industrial development is looked upon as a means of relieving unemployment in agriculture. It is obvious that, with the amount of agricultural land limited and in many areas already overpopulated, there is little hope for increased employment in agriculture. Moreover, improvements in agricultural techniques can be expected to reduce the need for agricultural labor. On the other hand, as already noted, it is improbable that many can be released from agriculture for industrial employment without reducing output or, at least, preventing the necessary expansion of agricultural output, unless agriculture is simultaneously improved. Unless more food and agricultural materials are made available for the cities, agricultural prices will rise and create problems for industry. Such increased output is unlikely to result without technological change in agriculture, which could very well decrease agricultural employment.

Nevertheless, it is obvious that the advanced countries employ large numbers of their people in industry and in services and only relatively small numbers in agriculture. An increase in manufacturing activities appears logical as a source of increased employment for the immediate future because the peoples of the underdeveloped countries have a desire and need for many material things. However, even though in the long run, as a country develops, its people will spend their increasing incomes on more goods and services, and industry will and must develop and will increase employment opportunities, it is not at all certain that employment opportunities will improve until there has been a considerable increase in industry. The expe-

* This does not mean that "coordinated" development is necessary and that growth cannot be "unbalanced." It does mean that it is not believed that any one sector can be allowed to get too far ahead or to lag too far behind the others. This question will be considered later.

rience in Puerto Rico and elsewhere, as previously discussed, is that the techniques of production chosen are such that total employment does not grow at first. Most underdeveloped countries are hopeful of finding a technology that will economize on capital, increase employment substantially, and maximize output at the same time. Such a development is unlikely. The only other hope for increasing employment by turning to industry is to industrialize very rapidly, but this requires a large amount of capital investment at one time, accompanied by a rapid increase in purchasing power. This also appears unlikely.

Nevertheless, a start must be made to industrialize because unless a start is made, industry will not grow to the stage where it will result in increasing employment. One should not, however, expect too immediate results in increased employment. To use industry as a make-work scheme without regard to productivity would be as self-defeating as to continue to rely on agriculture.

3.    Industry is also desired to lessen the risk arising from price fluctuations for primary products and to overcome deteriorating terms of trade. The export prices of primary products are subject to wide variations depending on the state of business in the importing countries. In the 1930's the depressions of the advanced countries were reflected in low prices of primary products, for supply was quite inelastic and demand dropped drastically. The result was severe economic difficulties for the countries exporting primary products, which included the underdeveloped areas of the world. Foreign exchange tended to be so scarce that many countries increased their own manufactures as it became necessary to meet their own needs by their own devices. Moreover, exporters of primary products are convinced that the terms of trade* are running against them so seriously that it would be advantageous to shift to manufacturing. That the terms of trade have and will be so disadvantageous is not certain, and the available statistics present only averages of many products. Therefore, each country should determine the terms of trade for its own products. In addition, because the terms of trade refer to average selling price only, an analysis of the factor inputs required to produce a unit of the product is necessary. Thus, if the costs have decreased more rapidly than the selling price abroad, a falling terms of trade is not necessarily bad, for the imported goods may cost less factor units. However, if there is reliance on only a few products, a disastrous turn of events leaves little room for adjustment, whereas if a

---

* This term refers to the relationship between an index of the prices of goods exported and an index of the prices of goods imported. Thus, if the export prices of primary products fall and the prices of imported manufactured goods remain the same, the terms of trade are said to run against the exporting country.

country has a diversity of outputs, it may be possible to expand some while others decline. Hence, most underdeveloped countries have a very real interest in diversifying their economies and, in general, do this by increasing the number of products manufactured for export.

4. Closely allied with this motive is the desire for economic independence because of the fear that manufactured imports from the West may be cut off by war, depression, or economic policy. Moreover, modern warfare is dependent on industrial strength, and therefore industrialization is regarded as a military necessity.

5. Because most underdeveloped countries have difficulty in acquiring sufficient foreign exchange for their import desires, they look toward the development of industry as a means of earning exchange or, more likely, reducing the need for foreign exchange by substituting their own production for imports.

6. The introduction of industry is expected to lead to the creation of more and more industries and to the improvement of agriculture—a belief identified with the doctrine of the need for balanced growth. As additional means of livelihood develop, there comes an increased demand not only for more agricultural products but also for more manufactured goods. In a self-subsistent agricultural country, the demand for some products is not great enough to justify the introduction of a manufacturing facility. At some point as demand increases, this does become justified, and as incomes increase further, more and more pursuits become justified. Included will be a demand for better transport, communications, power, and professional services of various kinds. Thus, the growth of one pursuit supports the growth of others. All these lead to a greater utilization of domestic resources and human skills of different types.

Agriculture itself gains in that increased quantities of agricultural products are demanded, opening up the possibilities for a more commercialized agriculture. Industry supplies improved tools and the necessary mechanical apparatus for an improved agriculture. The absorption of agricultural workers into industrial pursuits may also relieve overcrowding on the land and so give rise to the possibility of consolidating holdings into more efficient units. The social life of rural regions may also be improved.

7. Beginning industry is expected to create skills and experience that will promote growth by permitting a more rapid increase in productivity and a more flexible economy. In addition, industrialization undoubtedly means increasing urbanization, which will induce social and cultural change beneficial to the acceptance of further change and growth.

8. There is some expectation that industrialization will result in distributing the benefits of growth more widely, although one might suppose that

the initial effect would be a more uneven distribution of income, particularly if enterprises are privately owned. One of the major motives behind the drive for industrialization in Latin America is reported to be this desire to equalize opportunities and benefits. [2] Thus, much of the impetus behind industrialization is said to come from the disaffected urban groups and working classes, the petty industrialists, and the critical intellectuals.

Thus this increasing emphasis on industrialization has stronger and more solid bases than mere emulation. Whether it is being pushed too much in relation to other activities is a matter for investigation in each specific case. Manufacturing is only one type of economic activity and one way by which people can meet their needs, and there is no evidence that it is always the best way to grow. It is being recognized more and more that increasing the amount of manufacturing is desirable and necessary for most countries, but that the other economic sectors, particularly agriculture, cannot be ignored. The exact proportions of the different possible economic activities that will provide the most efficient allocation of resources and the greatest flow of goods and services and economic growth is unique for each country. In this chapter we will explore only the problems connected with one activity: manufacturing.

## Manufacturing in Underdeveloped Countries

Exact information concerning the contribution of manufacturing to the economies of underdeveloped countries is not possible because of the absence of reliable data. The best measure is the share of the gross national product contributed by manufacturing, but for most countries this can be only an estimate. Indirect measures, such as horsepower used, cement or steel consumption, or imports of capital goods, can aid in the estimate. But even substantial errors in estimate cannot obscure the fact that the share of manufacturing in the total economic activity is quite low. Despite considerable effort, progress in industrializing is slower than most countries desire, and the rate of growth is too low, even lower than that in the advanced countries.[3]

Two characteristics stand out. First of all, there is a high proportion of consumer goods manufacturing, amounting to almost two-thirds of the total in Asia and the Far East, for example.[4] Second, the bulk of the manufacturing is carried on in a large number of small- and medium-sized establishments making a wide variety of goods. Much of the manufacturing is carried on in the home, using family labor. A visit to the workshops ("factory" is too pretentious a word) discloses poorly organized working areas, overcrowding, unsafe and unsanitary conditions, and extremely poor lighting. The equipment is outmoded, even primitive, and is poorly maintained. Much hand labor is used where one might expect simple tools. Thus, labor intensity is the rule. On the other hand, there are usually a few large modern establishments. In Indonesia, such large establishments may be found for the production of cement, sugar, and paper.

The International Bank for Reconstruction and Development (IBRD) has sent many missions to countries to study their economic situation and to make recommendations for a program of development.* Most of these came to the conclusion that industry cannot be expected to make a sizable contribution to the economies for some time, but they do recommend that attention be paid to developing industries, particularly small and medium ones, the exact ones depending on the nation's needs and resources. Usually, emphasis is given to developing agriculture and other phases of the economy as a prerequisite to industrial development.

## The Transformation of an Economy

One important question, which must be asked, is whether all countries must evolve through the same stages, as witnessed in the West, or can move directly into an advanced and modern economy. The author remembers being taught in his elementary economics course that economies move through the stages of direct appropriation, pastoral pursuits, settled agriculture, manufacturing, and finally commerce. Other sequences dealt with the use of mechanical power and the progression of manufacturing for one's own use, through cottage industry, the putting-out system, small workshops, and large factories. As described in Chapter 2, Rostow delineates stages in development.

The reduction of the development process into stages is useful as a generalization, even though it may not be very helpful in determining specific policy for a particular country other than as a general guideline of what one might expect. It may well be possible to deviate from the general pattern set by countries that have developed, but, in the author's opinion, only by marginal amounts, although one can hardly describe this movement as stages. Hollis Chenery[5] has compared developments in many countries and shows that the course of development is substantially the same universally, with deviations that can be explained by certain factors, to be discussed later.

---

* The list of these reports would make a long bibliography in itself. All are valuable and to some extent different, but there are wide similarities, and one would bear reading. A list of such studies was included in Chapter 4.

This, of course, is not proof that other paths cannot be successful and might even be better under intelligent planning. The U.S.S.R. and mainland China, among others, have tried moving directly to heavy industry without following the relatively slow (to them) course of the West. For some time they seemed to achieve spectacular success. However, in 1963 both ran into trouble largely because of the failure of agriculture and consumer goods industries to develop. Whether this is only a temporary misfortune or a permanent defect in the method remains to be seen.

Lest the reader jump to the conclusion that this is necessarily an argument for laissez-faire private capitalism and that there is no room for government intervention in order to hasten development, a disclaimer is in order. As will be seen, government can do much to help development. What is important to remember is that these policies can operate only within certain limits.

Some economies seem to have remained the same for hundreds of years; others have changed or have been transformed. The Western countries have generally gone from a predominantly agricultural economy to one that relies heavily on industry and services, with a relatively minor role for agriculture. All countries seem to develop only through continuous changes in the distribution of resources among the different sectors and subsectors of the economy. This being so, a country's economy must be adaptable to change if development is to occur; that is, it must permit a shift of resources from one pursuit to another.

Assuming that the discussion above is correct, past patterns of development should shed light on the general process of economic development. In the developed countries, industrialization has played an important part, but has been only one part of a much broader process. In these countries, many similarities are apparent, but specific differences exist because of special circumstances. Nevertheless, the uniformity is striking. Chenery[6] lists the following reasons for such uniformity: common technical knowledge, similar human wants, access to the same markets for imports and exports, the accumulation of capital as income increases, and the increase of skills.

Changes in a country's economy occur as a country grows, so that different policies are appropriate at different times. At one time an emphasis on industry may be more appropriate; in another period, some other sector might more profitably be pushed. Thus, economic policy at any one moment would be unique for each country.

The typical pattern of development has been as follows, except as access to export trade has permitted some variance. Before development starts, a country is heavily agricultural, producing mainly for subsistence, with a few craftsmen and small workshops supplying local necessities. For some reason, incomes rise, perhaps from improved productivity in agriculture or the development of an export surplus in primary products. For example, in England, agricultural improvements increased productivity; in Japan, industrial growth came at the same time as agricultural improvements; in the United States, Canada, and Australia, the movement onto new lands yielded a surplus for exports.[7] As surplus production grows, some specialization develops and exchange grows. As incomes rise, the composition of demand changes and countries find it advantageous to produce more manufactured goods, probably as a substitute for imports. Typical early industries are the processing of agricultural and other primary resources and the production of widely used consumer goods, of which textiles are almost a universal example. As manufacturing develops, there is a shift from general agriculture to specialized agriculture, with certain crops (usually the cereals) being moved farther and farther from the urban centers, whereas agriculture in the settled areas becomes more specialized, the chief types being truck, dairying, and fruit culture. Even one of these special types of agriculture may move into specialized areas as transportation improves and refrigeration develops. As manufacturing continues to grow, it draws more workers away from agriculture, so that greater agricultural productivity is required. This necessitates mechanization and the investment of increasing amounts of capital in agriculture.

Industry also exhibits a similar transition. The early industries are associated with direct consumer needs. As incomes grow, new industries develop. It may be said that economic progress is associated more with the growth of new industries to meet new demands than with the steady growth of the old industries. Thus, the ability to innovate is important. Along with the extension of industry, there is an increasing need for public works and public utilities of all kinds, such as transportation facilities, power supply, and city services. Economic growth is impossible without considerable expenditures for these items. As growth continues, industries tend to become more capital-intensive and the engineering type of industries and capital goods industries begin to emerge, while the simpler industries tend to gravitate toward the newer industrial areas. Services seem important in all stages of development, but as development proceeds, more and more specialized service occupations develop, such as the various professions, managers, and those concerned with selling, education, health, recreation, and personal care.

Thus, all sectors of the economy are mutually interdependent, and as one grows in productivity, so must the other. The growth of one aids the growth of the other. Thus, it is necessary to have continuous progress in each. No one sector can lay claim to being the preferred sector; that depends on the situation of the particular country. All sectors must progress for the most effective performance, and a retardation of one will be a drag on the others. As one source puts it:[8] In the short run aid to any one sector is made at the expense of the others, but this may not be true in the long run for the different sectors are interrelated. The best way to encourage industry may be to use more capital in agriculture.

Accompanying this type of development we find growing urbanization; the growth of a wage-earning class; an increasing demand for skilled labor and, in time, the substitution of semiskilled machine tenders for both skilled and unskilled workers, although the process develops a requirement for newer and higher types of skill; greater diversity in the economy; an increasing capital intensity as more and more complicated machines are substituted for human labor; and a tendency for large firms to develop, although small firms do not disappear, particularly in producing special consumer goods and supplying large-scale industries. Seen in this way, industrialization is only one part of a much broader process of economic development.[9]

The process outlined above need not be repeated invariably, for conditions vary in each country. Industry may be retarded because some of its prerequisites are missing, such as an exchange economy or a required level of education and training, or an export of primary products may permit the importation of enough manufactured goods to satisfy the demands of the few with purchasing power. Also, government intervention may change the pattern, as in the U.S.S.R. However, to leap at once to an industrialized pattern requires considerable capital, which is obtained only by rigidly suppressing consumption and the desires of people to have their own enterprises, especially in agriculture. Moreover, the exact proportions of agriculture, industry, and so on will vary according to the national and human resources of the country. In some there will be more manufacturing and in others more agriculture.

The share of the different sectors will vary, but there will be a striking similarity. Hollis Chenery[10] arrived at this conclusion by tracing the share of the different sectors in the economy for fifty-one countries of greatly varying income levels. There were some variations in the proportions of the sectors among countries at approximately the same level of per capita income, but these were explainable by specific factors such as market size, possibly the income distribution, and the resource endowment and foreign export possibilities. As a generalization, the following pattern was postulated as an expectation when per capita income grows. Industry can be expected to produce 17 percent of the national output at a per capita income level of $100 and 38 percent at a level of $1,000. The share of transportation and commerce will also double over this range. Primary production will decrease from 45 to 15 percent, and the share of services will remain almost constant. At $100 income, 68 percent of the manufacturing can be expected to consist of consumer goods; 20 percent, of intermediate goods; and 12 percent, of investment goods. At $600 income, the proportions change to 43, 22, and 43 percent. The specific content of the various sectors would vary. All countries exhibit overall similarities, but each is unique in its economic makeup and must find its own best method for developing. Planning is necessary to get the best and fastest results.*

Other analyses of the changes in the character of industry as development proceeds have been made. One of those cited more frequently is that by W. O. Hoffman, a German writer.[11] He sees the process of industrialization as beginning in the production of consumer goods, particularly those serving the masses' most dominant needs, such as for food and clothing. As incomes increase, other needs are felt and supplied by industry. In time, the manufacturing of capital goods increases rapidly and may dominate. These industries grow in response to the need to supply equipment to the growing consumer goods industries and to provide transportation, communication, and construction. They develop later than consumer goods because they need large amounts of capital, advanced techniques of production, and a skilled labor force. One could also add the need for substantial markets, which must be relatively large in size if efficient production is to be achieved. Eventually, an equilibrium between consumer goods industries and capital goods industries is reached, the proportions and the specific contents of each group depending on the specific demands of the people, the nature of the resources, the foreign demand, and the leadership available. As development proceeds, new industries come to the fore and become the dominant industries. Hoffman states as his thesis that "whatever the relative amounts of the factors of production, whatever the location of the factors, whatever the state of technology, the structure of the manufacturing sector of the economy has always followed a uniform pattern." [12]

S. J. Patee[13] points out that the exact course of development in the advanced countries is an unreliable guide because of differences in resource endowments. However, in all major countries he shows that there has been a continuous decline in the share of consumer goods in total output. For example, the percentage share of consumer goods in total output fell in Great Britain from 52 percent in 1871 to 31 percent in 1946, in France from 65 percent in 1861 to 1865 to 34 percent in 1952, in Germany from

* This has some connotation of being a balanced growth theory, but that balanced growth is necessary or desirable does not follow from the estimate above. Hirschman's argument for unbalanced growth seems to have some validity, if not carried too far. Excessive imbalance wastes capital. Some imbalance may stimulate lagging sectors.

45 percent in 1895 to 23 percent in 1951, in the United States from 44 percent in 1880 to 30 percent in 1947. A similar picture is presented for Belgium, Switzerland, Italy, Japan, and the U.S.S.R. In every case the decline was continuous.[14] In less advanced countries, consumer goods industries comprise about two-thirds of all manufacturing, and in advanced countries this figure shrinks to one-third. This occurs even if countries are varied in natural resources, technical skills, the period in which they began to industrialize, the speed of growth, the attitude toward and the amount of foreign trade and capital movement, the proportion of capital goods output devoted to exports, fiscal policies, and whether industry is financed from private or public sources.[15]

## Obstacles to Developing Industry

The fact is that industry has been slow to develop in the underdeveloped countries to any substantial scale. Cataloging the obstacles as mentioned in the various reports of missions of the International Bank for Reconstruction and Development provides almost a summary of this entire book. Not all are true of any one country, but all appear over and over again in various countries.

The social and cultural attitudes of a people may inhibit industry. For industry to develop, people must be adaptable and willing to accept change in their way of life and there must be a supply of people who can innovate and induce change. Sometimes a low valuation of business or even a preference for a life of leisure, the extended family system, or a wastage of resources on excessive celebrations may be inhibiting factors.[16] Adherence to the traditional customs inhibits industrial expansion.

The educational background of the people and the health conditions under which they live make the labor input unproductive. One report describes this by saying that the country's biggest deficiency is the lack of human experience.[17] Common labor is at times immobile and not willing to move from less productive pursuits into industry. At other times, as in Africa, labor is too mobile. In general, common labor has low productivity because it does not have the proper equipment to aid it. Wage rates may be low, but wage cost may be high because of low productivity. In addition, considerably more labor may be used than in advanced countries.[18] Perhaps the biggest obstacle of all is the scarcity of skilled labor.

The material input also may often have a high cost because of low quality and poor quality control, high transportation costs, and low productivity in the primary and supplying industries. Prices may be unduly high because of heavy taxes or price supports. Imported materials may be costly because of transportation costs and tariffs, or because they are being used in small quantities. Lack of a smooth flow of materials to the factories is discouraging to industry. Most countries have made no survey of mineral resources.

There is often a shortage of effective industrial leadership and administrative ability. A. O. Hirschman[19] lists what he calls the typical shortcomings that undermine the efficiency of firms as: the absence of a "growth mentality," that is, a failure to plow back profits or to keep up with technological progress abroad, and a preference for family control; difficulties in administration, management, and human relations; and difficulty in carrying out functions not directly connected with production, such as planning, accounting, and maintenance. Particularly, there is a lack of middle management and supervision. In addition, the task of the manager is more difficult than in the advanced countries. A United Nations report[20] says the managerial task is more complicated than in advanced countries because demand is less predictable, statistical data are lacking, getting equipment and materials is uncertain, and it is necessary for the owner to carry out most of the managerial functions himself.

Moreover, managements are said to have a high-margin, low-volume complex, which acts as a bar to the growth of industry. H. G. Aubrey[21] insists that this is rational business behavior under the circumstances, for various reasons. The market is too limited to enter without a monopoly. There are uncertainties as to supplies, the continuation of the market, the supply of foreign exchange, the stability of the government, and so on, so that the businessman feels he must recover his investment quickly. In the usual terms, he is forced to have a low time horizon. Moreover, because of the uncertainties, traditional pursuits seem safer than new ones, so innovation is retarded. Until the conditions improve, industrial growth will be hampered.

To complete the picture of a high cost of production because of difficulties connected with a high cost for each factor of production, capital is scarce and expensive. Incomes are low and so savings are low. Any increase in earnings is soon absorbed in increased consumption or increased population. Individual small savings that may exist cannot be effectively mobilized and put into the hands of those who can use them, for suitable financial institutions are lacking. For this reason, businessmen (or their families) must supply their own funds. In some cases private enterprise is discouraged, so that local savings do not result in small industries. Foreign investors prefer a few strategic operations, particularly exportable primary products.

The savings that do exist are apt to go into land, commerce, speculation, or to be invested abroad, for owners of capital fear investing in industry.

Businessmen are often not highly respected. Government interference or even expropriation is always a danger. Labor and welfare legislation may be an onerous burden. The competition of more efficient foreign firms is always a possibility. Inflation is always a threat, so that long-run commitments are distrusted. Inflation also makes the search for foreign markets difficult. The investment requirements may be quite high per unit of output. The use of added capital to compensate for a shortage of skilled labor, inefficient operations, and small size, plus frequent breakdowns, result in low output per unit of capital, making the capital-output ratio as high as that of advanced countries despite using much more labor.[22] Also, inventories must be high, so that working capital requirements are high. Moreover, being remote from other industrial centers may compel an owner to be prepared to make his own repairs to his machinery and often to supply his own social overheads. When all the foregoing hazards are added to the uncertainties previously mentioned, one can understand the reluctance of individuals to invest their capital in industry.

A major problem for the development of industry is the lack of progress in agriculture. For industry to develop, there must be a food surplus to feed the industrial workers, unless the food can be imported. Because it is not probable that industry will be productive enough to compete abroad, the most part of food supplies must be drawn from local sources. As we have seen, obtaining such surpluses without improvement in agriculture or without some device to hold down the peasant's consumption is unlikely. Attempting industrialization without such surpluses is bound to be inflationary since the industrial workers bid for the scarce food supplies. Such rising food prices will push up wages or lead to labor disturbances, both of which hinder the development of industry. Enke[23] gives a more formal presentation of this point.

Industry in underdeveloped countries also suffers from what may be called inadequacies in the economic environment, such as transportation facilities and roads, power, financial institutions, insurance, an established legal system suitable to industry, and the usual urban social services.[24] These require a large investment at one time. As a result, no one firm can afford to develop them except on a limited basis. Thus, this difficulty can be overcome only by government activity. With respect to such environmental conditions, the West was far in advance of the present underdeveloped countries at the time the West started to industrialize.

Industrial technique is deficient and many fail to recognize the importance of improving it. Thus, ancient and inefficient techniques continue and even the nonmodern equipment is not well maintained, resulting in many interruptions to production.

Most underdeveloped countries have balance-of-payments difficulties arising from insufficient exports and a rising desire for imports, especially luxury consumption goods. This makes it difficult to import freely necessary capital equipment and raw materials. To conserve on exchange, imports may be permitted only on license. Seeking licenses means delays. Thus, from the production side, there are numerous and serious handicaps.

From the demand side, there is often little incentive for industry to be developed because the demand for the products is too small. Many countries are just too small in area and population to afford markets within their borders that are sufficient to permit industries to reach a minimum-sized scale for efficient operation. Not only are many countries too small in total size, but also transportation difficulties fragment the market even further. Thus, in many of the smaller countries, industries cannot be economically viable unless they can develop an export trade that will enable the country to import most of its other needs. The prospects for developing an extensive export trade, except in certain primary products, is not to be counted on, and in case such trade does develop, the result is apt to be a dualistic economy.

Reinforcing this deficiency of demand is the low per capita incomes. In the underdeveloped countries even large populations have low purchasing power. What little income the people have is likely to be spent on food, not manufactures. The estimated statistics of per capita incomes even exaggerate the purchasing power because of the usual maldistribution of income. The major difficulty is the failure of agriculture to be prosperous, for the bulk of the people are in agriculture. A general development of industry could overcome this, but it is unlikely that large numbers of small enterprises will start at once in the face of an unprosperous agriculture. Such enterprisers who do start are apt to be of small size and inefficient, making low-grade, standardized products. They are therefore subject to competition from outside factories.[25]

Finally, governmental conditions may be responsible for the failure of industry to develop. If the government is too weak or too inefficient to enforce law and order, to provide the necessary public services, or even to supply adequate statistical information about the economy, industry will find it difficult to get started. Political instability is discouraging to industry. Improper policies may play their part. Examples of such policies are excessive controls and licensing arrangements; extremely favorable labor legislation and excessive factory inspection laws, which raise costs, dishonesty of officials, political favoritism, promotion of uneconomic activities and industries; and total opposition to private enterprise, at least where governments are unprepared to carry out all the economic activities themselves.

## Suitable Industries

A number of important decisions must be made in selecting the amount and types of industry to promote. These include the technology to use, the speed of industrialization, the place of small-scale and cottage industries, the role of government in promoting industry, and selection of the specific industries. In this chapter we present a description of the typical industries that exist in underdeveloped countries or are recommended for them,* the place of small-scale and cottage industries, and the possible role of government with respect to industry. In later chapters the choice of technology, the role of entrepreneurship, and the whole matter of the proper criteria for investment choices will be discussed.

Only the general characteristics of industries that seem suitable for developing countries can be listed. The specific industries within each category are dependent upon the particular circumstances of each country. Therefore, it is necessary for each country to weigh the possible alternatives within the general framework suggested by the categories listed here and the subsequent discussion of investment criteria and planning.[26]

Some general criteria may be listed as placing certain limitations on the choice of industries. First of all, the industry should meet a real need of the people and should meet this better than can any other alternative, such as exporting something else to pay for the imports (barring exceptions for national defense, encouragement of development, and so on). Second, the industries chosen should be based on available local resources, especially raw materials, labor, and power sources. Third, the industries should be within the capabilities of the people. Last, they should be industries that offer a prospect for efficient production so that they can survive possible competition from imports. It is of particular importance not to foster inefficient industries, for these will only be a drain on the standard of living.

Types of industries deemed appropriate are:

1. Those producing consumer goods required by large numbers of people: A primary consideration is the availability of a market as adequate as possible. Therefore, a country should start with those goods bought in the largest quantity or which will be bought as soon as industrial employment increases and incomes increase. If this is not done, inflation will result when the workers search for goods. In addition, each such industry provides a complementary demand for the products of other industries. As previously

* For the latter purpose, the recommendations made by various missions of the International Bank for Reconstruction and Development will be used.

pointed out, the less developed the country, the larger the percentage of industrial output concentrated normally in consumer goods. It is also fortunate that the commonest of these consumer goods industries are suited to labor-intensive methods with modest capital requirements, need only standardized machinery, and use widely spread raw materials.[27] Examples of such industries are food processing, textiles, soap, shoes, utensils, pottery, matches, sugar, salt, sweets, bakery goods, beverages, dairy products, and tobacco.

2. Industries dependent on the processing of primary products, principally agricultural materials: At the start of industrialization most people are engaged in producing raw materials, and these are the basic materials for most of the consumer goods industries. Using abundant local materials avoids tying up large amounts of capital in inventories of imported goods and expands the purchasing power of the masses as markets are created for their agricultural products. In addition, when the materials are shipped abroad, industries are needed to process or semiprocess the materials before shipment. Examples are food processing and preserving, grain mills, vegetable oils, textiles, leather tanning, and coffee roasting. Primary products often processed for export are coffee, tea, rubber, coconuts, cocoa, sugar, tobacco, jute, and minerals and oil.

3. Import-reducing industries: These are important in saving transportation costs and saving scarce foreign exchange. In some cases, where consumer demand is more advanced, a country may save some exchange by assembling imported components; for example, for automobiles, typewriters, and consumer-durable goods. However, this represents a stage beyond the beginning period. Examples could be almost any consumer good, depending on the country's previous pattern of imports.

4. Basic social overhead industries, such as power, transport, communications, irrigation, and the like: These are likely to have a high priority because their scarcity or poor development hampers the growth of other industries.

5. Industries that, because of high transport cost per unit of value, would be excessively high priced if they were not produced locally: In fact, it may be necessary to produce them in various regions of each country. Examples are building materials, cement, glass, furniture, and beverages.

6. Highly perishable goods, such as baked goods and dairy products.

7. Service industries, which must be performed on the spot, such as bicycle repair.

8. Local handicrafts such as pottery, jewelry, and decorations, religious and dance symbols and regalia. Where there is a tourist trade, various handicraft industries may be encouraged in order to sell "typical native products" to the tourists.

9. Simple capital goods to supply the industries mentioned above with intermediate goods such as tools, chemicals, and fertilizers.

A list of major industries in any one underdeveloped region would almost be typical of other countries, depending to some extent on the degree of development, the climate, and the resources available. In Latin America[28] the major industries are food and beverages, tobacco, textiles, tanning, footwear and garments, timber, chemical products, pulp and paper, rubber, cement, glass, ceramics, iron and steel, aluminum, iron and other metal-transforming industries, and building materials.

## Cottage and Small-Scale Industries

One of the major controversies in attempting to develop industry concerns the role of cottage and small-scale industries. This is a confusing situation and one not subject to a categorical solution. As in the case of so many other questions, the answer depends on the circumstances. Thus, we may point out claimed advantages and disadvantages, but only empirical study on the spot will give the answer for a particular country.

A cottage industry is one carried on in the home, wholly or partly by the help of family labor, and often as a part-time occupation. It usually operates with human or animal power. A small-scale industry operates mainly with hired labor in a special shop and employs no more than a given number of workers. Size is relative in the various countries and is dependent on whether machine technology is used, but it is common to regard industries with under fifty employees as small-scale. In some countries, fifty employees might be regarded as a rather large number. A handicraft industry is one that demands a highly developed art and is usually carried on full time.

These small industrial units usually employ the major part of the industrial labor force in the underdeveloped countries.* However, these small units face considerable difficulties and are often unable to survive in competition with modern factories abroad or at home. They have been characterized by primitive technologies, inefficiency, and lack of expert management and marketing. The real question to be answered is whether they have special advantages that make it desirable for them to be encouraged and whether it is possible to make them efficient enough so that they can contribute to the economic growth of a country.

Those who believe that small industries should be encouraged do so for a wide variety of reasons. Perhaps the foremost argument is that they tend to

* For example, in Turkey in 1950, 98 percent of the industrial establishments employed under ten employees and employed 63 percent of the total. (See C. Talas, "Handicrafts in Turkey." *International Labour Review* [October, 1959], p. 338.)

be labor-intensive and so offer more employment than would industry based on large-scale units. This, of course, places employment as the major consideration in policy. The problem of employment and unemployment cannot be ignored, but a concentration on employment possibilities with no consideration of relative productivity would be self-defeating. In fact, concentrating on mere job creation might lessen future employment possibilities. On other grounds, small-scale industry might be advantageous, but there is every reason to believe that it will not be the very labor-intensive, small shop, but one with some degree of modernization and mechanization that will be advantageous for aiding growth. Cottage industries may possibly utilize part-time labor during slack periods in agricultural employment. The purpose is to use labor that would otherwise be wasted and not to draw people out of agricultural employment. The important consideration here is whether the idle time of the meager capital allocated to cottage industries is actually wasteful of capital funds.

A second consideration is that small units can be located throughout the country, especially since the development of small motors and electric power, thus affording some measure of prosperity to all regions and avoiding urbanization with its needs for costly social overheads.[29] Decentralization of industry is looked on as the means for creating markets for local farmers, thus preventing local agriculture from stagnating. One problem is that the rate of progress tends to be slow in small towns, so that such industry may not be efficient. Also, decentralization will require that education facilities be set up in the towns, which may be a slow and costly process.

In addition, the existence of a large number and variety of small industries is said to afford the gains of complementarity; that is, each industry helps support the others. Moreover, where markets are limited and customers have limited means, the small unit has obvious advantages. This is especially true in satisfying local and highly specific demands, artistic tastes, and in providing special services. As demands grow, larger-scale units could emerge. The small unit is thus looked on as part of a transitional stage, remaining only where it can serve a useful purpose in the midst of large-scale enterprises.

Small industry may also attract capital that would not otherwise be available. Capital for large undertakings must be somehow assembled, and institutions to do this are not usually found in underdeveloped countries. Where the industry is small, private capital may be diverted into it and away from investment in land. Rural capital is not likely to be invested in city industry or any distant endeavor, but may find its way into local industry. This rural saving may be substantial.

Small industry can be based on local and traditional skills and with less skilled labor than is necessary for large-scale industry. Expensive and scarce managers, supervisors, and engineers can be avoided as well as skilled mechanics. In the meantime, small industry can afford workers some industrial training. Thus, small industry may be a stepping-stone toward creating an industrial labor force and a group of entrepreneurs. H. G. Aubrey[30] makes the point that urban industry cannot use the traditional skills, but must create new ones. For example, craftsmanship must be replaced by a willingness to obey commands. Also, greater skill in management must be developed. However, it is not at all certain that the workers in the local industries will not stick to inefficient primitive methods. However, developing small industries will be less disruptive of existing habits, yet may act as a good vehicle of change so that workers may become "industrialized." It may be more difficult to create the types of habits and thinking necessary to work in and to operate large industry than it is to find the necessary capital.

The important role of small units in Japan is often cited as evidence of the desirability of promoting such units elsewhere; there, they were used to complement large-scale industry by making parts or performing special services for the larger firms. Similarly, another country might encourage subcontracting some of the parts or operations to small units where these could be made or done more efficiently. Little-used sizes of a product might be more profitably made in a small plant than in a large one, especially if the large one assumes the functions of purchasing materials, marketing the product, controlling the quality, and so on. The success of such a program depends on selecting the proper enterprises and providing the necessary supervision and aid.

Small units are apt to conserve scarce foreign exchange. They may be export producing, but they are more likely to be import saving. Most of their equipment can be produced locally and not imported; they tend to use local materials; and the owners are not so rich that they can import large quantities of luxury consumption goods.

Numerous other arguments for small units appear. Successful small units can grow naturally into large units as demand develops. They are particularly useful in starting new products. Experimentation with a small unit carries less risk of big mistakes. Returns accrue more quickly because long periods are not necessary for productive equipment to be assembled. Their widespread location brings more widespread political support. They produce a larger middle class, which aids internal stability. They are more flexible as conditions change because overheads are low. Large-scale units may mean lack of competition and little incentive to progress.

Lastly, they have proved their value by being remarkably persistent in all countries, including the advanced. As countries grow, the average size of firms will grow, and some will get quite large, but the majority will be small. They will satisfy the occasional and special demands, the artistic desires, specific services, and perform subcontracts for larger firms as well as sometimes compete with them by virtue of their greater efficiency.

On the other hand, there are those who feel that small units, especially the cottage industries, should not be encouraged. The basic reason is that they are apt to be inefficient and wasteful of scarce resources.* It is undoubtedly true that much of present-day, small-scale industry is inefficient, but there is some question whether it must remain that way. Small-scale industry in Japan, for example, is not inefficient. Current inefficiencies in other countries are due to various things. Management is inexperienced. Technological standards are low and equipment is primitive and ill-maintained. Much of small-scale industry is part-time work, and so uses capital inefficiently and wastes motion. Workers are poorly trained and often so lowly paid that their work capacity is impaired. Purchases of materials are small and marketings small, which makes for low bargaining power and inefficiency. Credit is difficult to get, and expensive.

It may be added, however, that large-scale industry is not usually so efficient in the underdeveloped countries as in the advanced. Work forces are not so adequate and mistakes and damage take place more often. Repairs take longer and there may be much idle time waiting for parts. Thus, downtime, which cannot be tolerated in large-scale units if efficiency is to be maintained, is a chief cause of high costs. Capital is scarce and expensive, and transportation is expensive and difficult. High-salaried managers and skilled labor must often be imported. Large urban costs should also be a charge against such units. Thus, it is necessary to weigh the costs of each sized unit in each situation to judge the relative advantages. The fact that current, small-scale units in underdeveloped areas cannot compete against the large-scale units of advanced countries is not conclusive evidence that large-scale units are desirable for the underdeveloped areas.

There is considerable debate whether large-scale or small-scale units use more capital per unit of output; that is, have a larger capital-output (K/O) ratio. Various studies give contradictory results.† In each instance, the

---

* B. F. Hoselitz ("Small Industry in Underdeveloped Countries." *Journal of Economic History* [December 1959], p. 609) presents statistics to show that labor productivity is lower in small-scale industry than in large (in Norway and Japan) and is even close to the productivity in agriculture.

† A report including data of India ("Production Techniques and Employment Creation in Underdeveloped Economies." *International Labour Review* [August, 1958], pp. 121-50) asserts that the K/O ratio for small plants in ten industries proved to be higher than in the large plants. K. Grunewald and J. O. Ronall (*Industry in the Middle East.* Council for Middle Eastern Affairs, 1960, p. 114) state that several studies show the K/O ratio to be lower in small plants. A report on the Punjab, India ("Development of Small-Scale Engineering Industries in the Punjab."

truth must be determined, with allowance for the capital required for social overheads.

Other objections to small-scale industry are numerous. The product is apt to be of low quality, unstandardized, and unreliable. Once started, such industries will build up a group of people interested in protecting themselves so that there will be a group with a vested interest in inefficient methods. Such industries, located in the smaller towns, will not have the influence that urban living has on cutting the rate of population increase. They do not provide the strong psychological lift and the symbol of achievement that are characteristic of the more spectacular large-scale projects. Working conditions are usually poorer, and government is less able to enforce labor laws that control safety measures, working conditions, minimum wages, and social security measures. They generate less surplus and thus do not permit as much reinvestment as would large-scale enterprises. Eventually, they will have to disappear so that resources invested in them will be wasted.

Lastly, there are those who believe that growth will be more rapid if there is a disequilibrium type of growth; that is, units with excess capacity should be built so as to encourage development of other industries that will utilize the excess capacity.[31]

There can be no valid generalization for all countries as to the role of small-scale industry, other than that they do seem to have a role to play, although not an exclusive one. Each country must determine for itself the part to be assigned small industry in the total industrial picture and whether it can be efficient as a producer and under what circumstances. A major consideration  is that it be efficient, for underdeveloped countries need productivity in order to develop. The role of small-scale units must be a continuous study as a country grows, for as development occurs, it is to be expected that some small-scale enterprises will be absorbed in the large units and others of the same size will spring up to replace them.

The important consideration is that all projects should contribute to economic growth and that the encouragement of any activity should not be at the expense of the general welfare. Only if it is determined that small industries can become efficient producers should they be protected against outside competition and should aid be extended to them. The major problem is to select the most appropriate types to help. Many countries are not willing to make a choice, and so waste funds by helping all.

In any event, if it is decided that some small-scale enterprises are to be

---

*International Labour Review* [June 1962], p. 595) states that the output-capital ratio is smaller than in large factories; that is, the K/O ratio is larger. H. G. Aubrey ("Small Industry in Economic Development." *op. cit.,* p. 296) asserts that small plants use less capital and require less social capital.

encouraged, they should be helped to become efficient. In particular, they must be aided in improving their standards of quality, their productive efficiency and technical knowledge, their purchasing and marketing techniques, their social and sanitary conditions, and credit must be made available to them on reasonable terms. Suitable buildings for rent might be provided. To survive, small-scale industry must become modernized, and this is what must be encouraged where conditions warrant it. Fortunately, with the development of electricity and the internal-combustion engine, productive efficiency can be developed in small enterprises.

Cottage industries are too difficult to develop on an efficient basis and probably should be neglected, unless a country is concerned with providing employment on a make-work basis rather than promoting economic growth, or there is a strong export demand for specialties, such as for Thai silk.

Similarly, it is probably too difficult and expensive to start new handicrafts where they do not exist. A limited number of handicrafts might be encouraged if they are already established and there is a demand for their products from tourists, residents, or for export. If they are to be effective, they need all the help previously mentioned. Handicraft centers to serve as outlets and to train workers have proved helpful. A batik institute, for example, exists in Indonesia to train workers and to aid in the marketing of batiks.

It may be that some intermediate form of organization would be suitable. One method is the Japanese system of large-scale industry with subcontracting of certain parts and services. Under this system there is a consulting service to give technical help, and a kind of broker or middleman supplies the raw materials and markets the product, thus improving the efficiency in those areas. This system is feasible only when distances are short and transportation is adequate.

Another method is the industrial estate, which has been used in India, Puerto Rico, and other areas. The state, or some development agency, provides factory space and facilities common to a number of potential small firms, such as metalworking facilities and power and transportation facilities. Some technical advice may also be provided.

The most usual device to aid small business is the cooperative. These organizations develop sources of supply, grant credit, do the marketing, and give technical advice. A feature of Indonesian small industry is its concentration in and around small villages, such as leather work near Magelang, umbrellas in Djuwiring.[32] Numerous other examples could be given. This concentration makes the development of cooperatives more feasible, one of their major difficulties being the widespread nature of small industry in many countries. However, cooperatives, to be valuable, must be efficient and well-managed, and this does not occur merely by forming them. Training officials for cooperatives is a major prerequisite for developing successful small enterprise.

## The Role of Government

Without government aid, industry is not apt to progress in the underdeveloped countries. For some reason, impetus is lacking, and governments must seek ways to provide it. One deterrent may be the position of **private enterprise** in relation to government control, operation, or planning **(to be discussed later)**. In this section, we will consider only the minimum incentives necessary to encourage industry, assuming that there is some sphere to be allotted private enterprise and that the government will not conduct all economic enterprise.

First, and as an absolute necessity, there must be large government investment in social overheads, such as power, transportation, communications, education, and health.

There must be provision for training skilled labor because no firm can be sure of keeping any man it trains and therefore cannot afford an extensive training program. In addition, there should be managerial training, especially middle managers and foremen.

Credit supplies of all types should be encouraged or supplied by the government, including long-term credit and credit for working capital. Development banks are usual devices for providing the necessary capital.

Technical aid and the establishment of various research institutions would be extremely helpful. There must be continuous research to find the most appropriate technical possibilities, economic opportunities, quality, potential markets, and so forth.

Incentives to persuade individuals to establish businesses are probably desirable, but considerable care needs to be exercised so that the right enterprises will be established and firms will not be oversubsidized. Numerous possibilities exist.[33] Providing a flow of reliable economic data, furnishing information about the economy, and publicizing opportunities are most helpful. Providing suitable buildings, for purchase or rent, and industrial sites may be necessary to attract firms short of capital. The industrial estate is a device that can attract a number of small enterprises to a locality and, by judicious location, can spread industry throughout a country. It may be necessary to assure a steady flow of imports that may be required. Tax concessions are a familiar device to attract industry to many areas, including regions within the advanced countries. There is a real question whether this is advantageous for small localities because of the loss of tax revenues, and therefore the possible reduction of essential services. There is more excuse for using it in the larger areas, however; there, the loss of revenue is relatively less, and this may be offset by the economic gain stemming from the new industry. Even so, care should be exercised to promote only needed industries and not just any industry, many of which will not prove viable. Moreover, it is preferable to promote new industries and not subsidize old ones, to avoid regional competition, and to make the concessions for only a limited number of years. In order to be selective, subsidies may be superior to tax concessions.

Tariff protection is a time-honored device to aid industry, but again caution should be used. Protection should be on a selective basis so that only economically desirable industries are promoted. The danger is that all industries will seek protection. Moreover, protection should not be so excessive that it permits monopolistic pricing and should not be permanent.

If any private enterprise is desired, there must be a favorable economic and political climate for it, including reasonably sound standards with respect to taxation and fiscal policy, regulations on business, administration of business regulations, inflation, expropriation, political favoritism and reprisals, foreign exchange regulations, the legal system, and political stability. It is very essential to eliminate uncertainty as to the scope of public enterprise. In particular, excessive labor protection would have to be avoided.

Governments may have to create and operate industries themselves if private enterprise is unwilling. It is not difficult for any government to discourage private enterprise, and therefore if it is government policy to encourage such enterprise, the authorities should first make sure that their restrictions do not really make it unlikely. Moreover, governments must judge the economic worth of the industries encouraged, if not in profitable production, at least through the effect on increasing development in other areas. If capital is available and an industry is potentially profitable, one could well be suspicious if private enterprise did not take advantage of it, although there may be other valid reasons for hesitancy. Because the biggest problem is capital and because engaging in too many economic activities would burden inexperienced governments, public enterprise should normally be restricted to a few relatively large and vital undertakings. Pilot plants may be effective in starting an industry and permitting research into new technologies.

Lastly, the other areas of the economy must be developed and aided so that industry can have a market.

# REFERENCES

1. AKHTAR, S. M., *The Economy of Pakistan.* Lahore, Publishers United, Ltd., 1961, pp. 1-2.
2. FELIS, D., "Industry and Stabilization Dilemmas in Latin America." *Journal of Economic History* (December, 1959), p. 586.
3. *Processes and Problems of Industrialization in Under Developed Countries.* New York, United Nations, 1955, pp. 127ff. United Nations, *Patterns of Industrial Growth, 1938-58,* 1960, pp. 153ff. Chenery, H. B., "Patterns of Industrial Growth." *American Economic Review* (September, 1960), p. 632. Kuznets, S., "Quantitative Aspects of the Economic Growth of Nations," II, "Industrial Distribution of National Product and Labor Force." *Economic Development and Cultural Change* (July, 1957), Supplement.
4. Economic Commission for Asia and the Far East, *Formulating Industrial Development Programs.* New York, United Nations, 1961, p. 3.
5. CHENERY, *op. cit.,* pp. 624-54.
6. *Ibid.,* p. 626.
7. BRAND, W., *The Struggle for a Higher Standard of Living.* New York, The Free Press of Glencoe, 1960, pp. 62-66.
8. BAUER, P. T., and B. S. YAMEY. *Economics of Underdeveloped Countries.* Chicago, Chicago University Press, p. 235.
9. *Processes and Problems . . . , loc. cit.,* 1955, p. 2.
10. CHENERY, *op. cit.,* pp. 624-54.
11. HOFFMAN, W. O., *Growth of Industrial Economies,* trans. by W. O. Henderson and W. H. Chaloner. Manchester University Press, 1958.
12. *Ibid.,* p. 2.
13. PATEE, S. J., "Rates of Industrial Growth in the Last Century, 1860-1958." *Economic Development and Cultural Change* (April, 1961), pp. 316-30.
14. *Ibid.,* p. 322.
15. KUZNETS, S., "Quantitative Aspects . . . ," *op. cit.* (Presents statistical data on the composition of the various sectors in the economies of many countries.)
16. *Processes and Problems . . . , loc. cit.,* pp. 18ff.
17. International Bank for Reconstruction and Development, *Economic Development of Nigeria.* Baltimore, Johns Hopkins Press, 1955, p. 348.
18. BHATT, V. V., *Employment and Capital Formation in Underdeveloped Economies.* Bombay, Orient Longmans, 1960, p. 46.
19. HIRSCHMAN, A. O., *Strategy of Economic Development.* New Haven, Yale University Press, 1958, p. 136.
20. Department of Economic and Social Affairs, *Development of Manufacturing Industry in Egypt, Israel, and Turkey.* 1958, p. 83.
21. AUBREY, H. G., "Industrial Investment Decisions." *Journal of Economic History* (December, 1955), pp. 335-59.
22. BHATT, *op. cit.,* p. 6.
23. ENKE, S., *Economics for Development.* Englewood Cliffs, N. J., Prentice-Hall, Inc., 1963, pp. 133ff.
24. *Processes and Problems . . . , loc. cit.,* pp. 11-13.
25. *Ibid.,* p. 14,
26. Economic Commission for Asia and the Far East, *op. cit.*
27. Economic Commission for Asia and the Far East, *Economic Survey of Asia and the Far East.* New York, United Nations, 1958, p. 89.
28. *Economic Survey of Latin America.* New York, United Nations, 1957, pp. 75-93. (For other countries, see the studies of the International Bank for Reconstruction and De-

velopment or the *Statistical Year-book* of the United Nations.)

29. BRAY, F. R., "Reflections on Rural Economic Development." *Land Economics* (November, 1955), pp. 289-302. (An argument for developing the rural areas.)

30. AUBREY, H. G., "Small Industry in Economic Development." *Social Research* (September, 1951), p. 297.

31. LEIBENSTEIN, H., *Economic Backwardness and Economic Growth*. New York, John Wiley and Sons, 1957. Hirschman, *op. cit.*

32. RAO, K. N., "Small Scale Industry and Economic Development in Indonesia." *Economic Development and Cultural Change* (January, 1956), pp. 159-70.

33. JAFFE, A. J., *People, Jobs, and Economic Development*. New York, The Free Press of Glencoe, 1959. Stead, W. H., *Fomento: the Economic Development of Puerto Rico*. National Planning Association, 1958. Perloff, H. S., *Puerto Rico's Economic Future*. Chicago, University of Chicago Press, 1950.

## ADDITIONAL READINGS

AGARWALA, A. N., *Some Aspects of Economic Advancement of Underdeveloped Countries*. Kitab Mihal, 1958, pp. 27-34, "Cottage Industries."

AUBREY, H. G., "Deliberate Industrialization." *Social Research* (June, 1949), pp. 158-82.

CHENERY, H. B., "Role of Industry in Development Programs." *American Economics Review, Proceedings* (May, 1955), pp. 40-57.

HIRSCHMAN, A. O., "Investment Policies and 'Dualism' in Underdeveloped Countries." *American Economic Review* (September, 1957), pp. 550-70.

KUZNETS, S., W. E. MOORE, and J. J. SPENGLER, *Economic Growth: Brazil, India, Japan*. Durham, N.C., The Duke University Press, 1955.

LALOIRE, M., "Small-scale Industry in the Modern Economy." *International Labour Review* (October, 1961), pp. 246-68.

# CHAPTER

# 8

# *Technology and Entrepreneurship*

## *Meaning of Technological Change*

One of the most striking features of underdeveloped countries is the low level of technology and technical practice.* In many countries there has been no change in the technique of production for centuries. In the meanwhile, the technology of advanced countries is changing so rapidly that the gap between that of the advanced and underdeveloped countries is becoming increasingly wider. In many of these countries there may be a few technologically advanced plants but such better methods have not spread far. Also, the habit of thinking in terms of change and improvement is not characteristic of such societies.

Technology has been defined in terms of industry. However, in the eyes of economists this is too restrictive a term. It should be expressed in terms of the entire process of production, the latter itself being interpreted broadly. It is concerned with processes of producing existing goods, the creation of new products, the improving of old ones, finding new uses for

* *Webster's New International Dictionary* defines technology as "industrial science; the science or systematic knowledge of the industrial arts."

old products, changes in business organization such as the introduction of the corporation, changes in the technique of management and marketing. E. D. Domar[1] has defined technological change as the sum of the influences on output above the quantitative inputs of capital and labor. As such, this includes: economies of scale; external economies; improved health, education, and skill of the labor force; better management; and changes in the product mix. It is concerned with industrial fabrication, agriculture, distribution, and every other phase of the process of transforming goods from the elemental state to the form for ultimate consumption. In general, at first, most innovations may be in the fabricating process or the process of actually forming or growing physical products. Later the emphasis is on the less tangible processes of production, managerial techniques, organization, labor relations, marketing, and so on.

In this sense, then, technological change refers to any change in the methods by which materials are transformed and brought to consumers. Technological change is sometimes thought of as synonymous with invention, but it implies more than this. Invention is only one stage in the whole process of effecting a change in production processes, and may not even be the most difficult stage. Various stages have been distinguished:[2]

1.  Discovery of a basic scientific principle or law of nature, including human behavior.
2.  Invention, or the application of this basic principle, or a combination of basic principles, to a particular problem.
3.  Development of this invention into a workable practice; that is, fitting it into a specific technology. This stage is given the name of "innovation" and is likely to be the most difficult and expensive stage. This stage is the sphere of the entrepreneur.
4.  Imitation by the large body of producers.
5.  Constant improvements and adaptations to increase efficiency.

Actually, there is usually a long lag between the conception of an idea and its realization in actual practice. This can be illustrated by many examples, but the automobile may serve as well as any other. Dreams of a self-propelled vehicle apparently existed before the Christian era and had resulted in crude steam vehicles in the early 1800's in England. Although automobiles date from the early 1890's in the United States, their practical use can be dated from around 1910, when Ford began to produce them on a mass basis, and from the 1920's when they became popular with the masses.

Technological change is often associated with major new processes, but this also appears to be too limited a view. Perhaps just as important or even more so for our purposes are the myriad of small improvements in the productive processes that occur constantly in a progressive society. Only when a people are constantly on the alert for such small improvements will technological change be an effective instrument for economic growth.

Also, perhaps more important than the introduction of an idea from the standpoint of economic development is the process of imitation by the bulk of the producers in a country. Innovations have very little advantage until many producers follow suit and are forced to pass the benefits of the innovation on to the public. If only one producer adopts an improved technique, he is apt to retain the benefits for himself. One of the objections to monopolies is that, even though they may become efficient, they do not pass any savings on to the public. As far as underdeveloped countries are concerned, there is little need for invention. They have available to them many alternative techniques, which are already in practice somewhere in the world and from which they can choose. The real problem is to select the most promising, adapt it to the country's own peculiar situation, and see that it is utilized widely. This will require, however, considerable effort and considerable research.

It is surprising how slowly people imitate others unless they are forced into it by one means or another. Competition has been a potent force for requiring imitation, but its effects (even in the supposedly competitive United States economy) are not so compulsive that all industries are forced up to the best level of technical efficiency already in effect. The innovator has not usually pressed his advantage, preferring to leave the price alone and not force the issue too greatly.

Imitation in the underdeveloped country is even slower to take place, for competitive pressures are not great, the innovation is not widely known, and change is not usual. To get a substantial amount of imitation, it is necessary that there be a widespread knowledge of the new technique; an absence of artificial hindrances, such as monopoly; a supply of people willing to take the risks of innovation; and a willingness of the people to accept change. None of these is a usual situation in underdeveloped countries.

Changes that occur may be of various types.[3] They may be classified as cost saving, product improving, or novelty introducing. Or they may be classified as capital saving or capital using, labor saving or labor using, skill saving or skill using, and the like. An innovation may be both capital saving and labor saving; that is, it may increase output with respect to both factors. An innovation may be capital saving (or labor saving or skill saving) with respect to the particular instance of innovation, but it may be capital using (or labor or skill) for the economy as a whole. For example, the introduction of a modern plant may actually be economical of capital in relation to output, but may require large capital costs for urbanization, social overheads, and the like. The exact effects of the innovation are important to establish in any plan for development, and research must be directed toward those types most advantageous for the particular economy. For example, if capital is the scarce factor, innovation might well be capital saving, unless other considerations, to be discussed later, are more important.

## The Role of Technological Change in Development

If one were to survey all the writers on economic growth for their opinions as to the most essential ingredient for growth, one would undoubtedly find the major emphasis being given to capital accumulation, technological change, or entrepreneurship, or some combination of these. Actually, it would be hard to make a choice among them, for all three must come together for the most effective results. Capital accumulation by itself can bring some improvement in output, but the gains are limited. Some technological change, for example, the reorganization of work space, can be effected without increasing the amount of capital, but technological change normally requires at least some new capital investment. Finally, someone must be the decision maker who effects the technological change. Thus, the three are virtually inseparable. All are of great importance and essential for development. It is important to have more capital with which to work, but it is even more important to have better capital and better managerial methods. Technological change has probably been the central fact in the development of the advanced countries.[4]

J. A. Schumpeter[5] made innovation the central feature in his theory of economic growth. Essentially, he saw innovation as a discontinuous process, being concentrated in certain periods that gave spurts to growth so that the economy would grow by leaps and then, so to speak, consolidate its position after an ensuing business cycle. Discontinuous "large" innovations have been important (for example, the canal, railroad extension, and the automobile) and have provided spurts to development. However, one should not overlook the value of the continuous "small" improvements in production which take place at all levels of endeavor. What underdeveloped countries need most of all is an attitude conducive to the search for such minor improvements in all phases of life because of the need for general development and because of the shortage of capital.

Technological change plays various roles in the development process. In addition, it creates problems, but these will be discussed later.

1. It increases productivity, as cited above. Merely increasing the supplies of the factors of production, including capital, ultimately results in diminishing returns unless the factors are improved or combined in a more

effective way. As development proceeds, it is usual that more and more capital is combined with labor and land, so that one would expect the rate of return per unit of capital to decline as diminishing returns set in. Instead, in the advanced countries, technological change has resulted in rising returns to both capital and labor; that is, productivity has increased by more than the amount of capital and labor added. The obvious result has been the possibility of a rise in living standards.

2.  It relieves the scarcity of resources by enabling a country to tap new sources of raw materials such as: deeper oil wells; use of inferior grades; and use of new resources such as silicon, which was once largely waste. In effect, it enlarges the supply of resources by making them more productive and by economizing in their use. It seems obvious that if incomes are to rise, the factors must be used as efficiently as possible.

3.  By reducing costs it makes added savings possible. Only by increasing the productivity of the country's resources can surpluses be created and thus the necessary goods be made available to provide both for increased consumption and for a growing quantity of capital goods. It should also be borne in mind that technological change, in permitting greater output with the same amount of resources, can result in unemployment unless purchasing power keeps pace or capital investment takes place rapidly enough to absorb the displaced labor. Thus, technological change can be a danger, but only under improper economic arrangements.

4.  It stimulates demand and new investment by developing new products and processes. It thus creates and satisfies new wants.[6] It is not possible, except at the lowest levels of living, to expand demand very far without introducing new products. Thus, the appeal of new products is important for development, especially after the initial stages of development have begun. As one writer puts it, "in the place of one blade of grass or a single pig, the world now needs a juicier blade plus a fatter pig plus a shirt plus a book plus a piece of music."[7] This desire for new goods may compete with the need for savings, but it acts as a spur to development. If one had to wait for the development of existing industries, growth would be quite slow. The creation of new industries provides a much more powerful stimulus to growth.

5.  It affects human dignity in different ways. It eliminates the most backbreaking of work and thus enables man to escape being a physical drudge in both agriculture and industry. On the other hand, the first changes in industrial machinery threatened to turn man into an automaton and a slave to the machine. Recent changes in the field of automation have begun to eliminate this for many and require greater human skill and ingenuity, making man a director of the production process and not one whose

every action is dictated by the pace of the machine.* It would be hard to say why human slavery has been eliminated, but included among the complex causes would be that changes brought in production by machinery and managerial improvements made slavery no longer profitable.†

6. It acts as a balancing factor between labor and capital in the conflict over the distribution of income. If labor becomes expensive relative to capital, innovations will tend to be labor saving, and vice versa. Technological change thus acts to prevent the gains of the productive process from being excessively absorbed by any group for a long period of time.

## Factors Affecting the Rate of Technological Change

Many factors affect the rate at which technological change takes place.[8] The larger the number of people who make decisions, the greater will be the opportunity for innovations because there will be more new ideas. Thus, the more centralized and dictatorial the decision making (whether this comes about by the decision of an individual or by custom), the less chance of widespread improvements, for the one leader or the few cannot think of everything and also may find change a risk and uncomfortable. Free enterprise has been conducive to change, but has had to be restrained by government action in its tendency to overrun the small man's rights. Thus, a modified free enterprise system seems most likely to produce a dynamic society. This does not, however, preclude government planning of a society, but does indicate that considerable attention should be given in the planning to promoting suggestions from a wide range of people and to improving the opportunities for private enterprisers to start new businesses, for new firms are apt to be the ones that undertake the new ideas.

Free enterprise has the advantage of offering a powerful incentive in private profit, providing a compulsion to improve in the form of competition, and of diffusing initiative and decision making. However, to be most effective, this system requires among other things a high general level of education and skill, a respect for the rights of others, and a general acceptance that a man is to be judged solely by his own ability and efforts. Moreover, the individual must be able to enjoy the fruits of his own ideas. Therefore, it may not be the most appropriate system at all times and among all peoples.

From the experience of the United States, the existence of large-scale enterprises seems most conducive to rapid technological change, but only if

---

* However, those who "watch" the automated machines may find their jobs even more monotonous than did the machine tender. Other problems are created, but these should not be unsolvable.

† It may be argued that it never was profitable.

competition remains, since competition is necessary to ensure that all are forced to adopt the improved techniques. Thus, for the most rapid advance, the market must be large enough to support several large firms. Where there is no great pressure for innovation, the hierarchy of officials may tend to "play it safe" or may have a hard time agreeing on a change. Moreover, the large firm may be committed to an existing technology because of its sunk investment, and so may be reluctant to change unless forced. Today in the United States, research is associated with the large-scale enterprise, the government, or the university, which are organized for research and have the funds to support it. Individual inventors are still active, but such autonomous invention is becoming more and more rare, yielding to organized research.

However, much of industrial research may be of a defensive nature; that is, designed to produce changes merely to forestall competition. Fundamental innovations are often more associated with new firms. Thus, only fairly large firms can afford the necessary research, but it is necessary to have many firms in order to get optimum introduction. Neither pure competition of many small firms nor one large monopolized firm has been the optimum situation for innovation, for the former are too small and the latter are under no pressure to accept it. Perhaps what is needed is a larger number of firms with government-supported, centralized research available to all. For underdeveloped countries it is not likely that large private firms will bring rapid change for some time. Their place seems further along on the development road. At early stages, it seems, the government needs to do most of the research, although individual enterprises promise the most rapid utilization of any findings that might be made.

Perhaps more important than any other factor in determining innovation is the attitudes of the people, especially a supply of innovating entrepreneurs and a people willing to accept change. As pointed out in Chapter 3, the people's attitudes and the institutional arrangements must be right for change to take place.[9] The people must hold values conducive to change and must want the change. For example, W. A. Lewis says that man must be curious and experimental, for this is the way knowledge grows.[10] He says that the most important inventions have been writing (because each generation can build on preceding knowledge) and the scientific method or questing mind.* Underdeveloped countries may be literate but prescientific, and so not progressive. He adds that the questing mind is encouraged where

* W. J. Hull ("Growing Pains of International Technical Cooperation." *International Labour Review* [October, 1961], pp. 223-45) describes an "efficiency barrier" which develops on the road to economic prosperity. This develops from a lack of materialist tradition, which does not permit the development of modern scientific techniques, and from a failure to be productivity- and efficiency-oriented. He then discusses how to get past this efficiency barrier.

religion is competitive; where political and economic power are widely diffused; where there is a diversity of experience, such as is afforded by urbanization, outside contact, and diverse pursuits; in a young and ambitious nation; where artisans can retain the fruits of new ideas; and where knowledge is not monopolized. The necessity for the development of rationality and a scientific frame of mind cannot be overemphasized. Its growth depends fundamentally on widening the education of the people. Perhaps a third requirement should be added: Society must be productivity- and efficiency-oriented. Unless this is an integral part of the people's mental makeup, innovation will be delayed. However, proposed changes cannot be too alien to the culture, nor can technological advance be more rapid than the people's rate of comprehension.

E. E. Hagen[11] stresses the importance of a deviant group in introducing change. If some unrecognized group can acquire status by economic success, and this can be attained through innovation, they are apt to make such changes, afterward trying perhaps to acquire the traditional symbols of status.

The attitudes of the people may also be conditioned by the attitudes of the governmental authorities. If government encourages change and innovation and ties them to a national purpose, changes are likely to be accepted, as appears to have happened in Soviet Russia.

In addition to these positive actions, certain negative barriers must be razed if innovation is to grow. Poverty discourages change because people on the edge of starvation cannot afford to undertake the risks of a new technique; the necessary capital is not likely to be available; disease and malnutrition sap desire; and illiteracy makes innovation unlikely. Thus, in the early stages, innovation may have to be introduced from above by government. Only after some advance can much innovation be expected from individuals. Other barriers may be social custom, prevailing legislation, religious prohibition, or the opposition of vested interests. The extended family system gives little scope for initiative and encourages population, and therefore poverty. Economic institutions such as land tenure, credit facilities, and marketing may be deficient. Thus, a whole complex of social and institutional changes may be necessary before innovation will be forthcoming and accepted.

Technological change depends on the existence of a science base and a spirit of research that can adapt known principles to practical use. For underdeveloped countries there is no immediate need to concentrate much effort on pure science or in developing technologies that are new to the world, for there are plenty of techniques and practices already in existence which are superior to those now being used in such countries. The major problem is to adapt existing technologies to the country's needs; for example, developing improved strains of seeds and discovering the best agricultural techniques. Thus, underdeveloped countries need applied science rather than pure science, although this will come eventually. Much can be done by practical men with little knowledge of pure science. In addition, there is a great need for government-sponsored research programs, for as development proceeds, organized research will have to replace the more "practical" improvements. The establishment of a series of such research institutes would seem to be a good investment. Just as important is the establishment of facilities to see that discoveries are made available to the decision makers, perhaps similar to the agricultural extension workers in the United States or the industrial advisory services offered by some universities.

Economic growth itself promotes technological change, for as markets grow, it becomes profitable to increase investment. As new investments are made, it is likely that more modern equipment will be used. Moreover, as opportunities expand, better executives are likely to develop. Hagen[12] lists two factors as being essential for technological change, although neither will in itself initiate it: market expansion* and a flow of savings. Only a growing economy offers these in any substantial fashion and leads one to the oft-repeated conclusion, "Nothing induces growth like growth itself." Not only does growth widen markets and increase savings, but the fact that change is occurring is conducive to further growth, for change has a cumulative effect.[13] As scientific and technical knowledge grows, it induces further growth; the scientific attitude spreads; the hold of tradition and custom weakens; and poverty and the conditions associated with it begin to disappear. As change and development become general, a discovery in one area can be utilized in others or may have a favorable widespread effect and thus become more feasible. For example, improvements in transportation, energy sources, or social overheads become more profitable as they serve a wider range of activities.

Technological change may be limited by a shortage of any factor, such as capital, technically trained people, or energy sources. Any innovation that improves the supply of these, such as credit institutions, improved tax structures, changes in income distribution and savings habits, or training centers for needed skills, is a major force that spurs technological change and so permits an economy to exploit favorable opportunities and move in different directions.

Necessity plays a role in inducing technological change. If it is easy to get additional resources, particularly labor and raw materials, there will be lit-

* Some technologies may require worldwide markets to make them practicable.

tle incentive to improve methods. Where labor or resources are scarce, there is an incentive to introduce techniques that will use them economically. Labor-short communities are the most likely to advance technologically and therefore the most likely to experience a rise in their standard of living.

Y. Brozen[14] believes that the choice among various alternative techniques is important in determining whether there will be any substantial further advance. He feels that certain types of technology will lead to the centralization of decision making, both economically and politically, and so slow further growth. Techniques that require large quantities of capital for single enterprises and which urbanize a people fall into this category. Even though this may immediately provide more output, the effect or rather lack of effect on the masses of the people may, in Brozen's view, warrant a slower advance via less advanced techniques.

Of great importance to underdeveloped countries is the rate at which any successful technological advance is imitated. It does very little good to have a few very modern factories or farms if the bulk of the economy retains primitive methods, producing a dualistic economy.* There is always a gap between the best currently practiced techniques and those used by the majority of the producers, but efforts should be made to narrow this as much as possible. Anything that reduces the pressure to imitate will slow growth. Examples are numerous.[15] A shortage of capital, misuse of the patent system, overuse of tariffs, excessive union restrictions, the lack of competition, ignorance of the best practices, adherence to the family system of management, and a social structure that hinders incentives, such as insecure tenure in agriculture, are a few of the many obstacles to imitation.

The report of the International Bank for Reconstruction and Development's mission to Ceylon[16] cites Mexico's experience in trying to improve technological change as an example of what can be done. The responsible agency was the Bank of Mexico. It first made a "technological audit," which set forth methods to improve existing production through known or new technologies and which listed the new industries, activities, and resources suitable for development. It applied practical scientific research to problems that were hindering development. To do this, it set up an independent research institute, with an outside director, and recruited young Mexican scientists and engineers. The institute carried out research where needed or sent Mexican personnel abroad to give them experience and to find solutions for problems. Advice was given to individual production units. The essential bases were research in areas where needs were found

---

* This does not mean that all large-scale enterprises are inappropriate, but rather that improvements should take place generally and in all sectors of the economy.

and an independent research agency that private enterprisers would not hesitate to use. Some similar system might be a good investment for any underdeveloped country.

## The Transferability of Technology

There is a tendency for technology to spread from country to country even in the face of opposition from the exporting country. Familiar examples are the transfer of cotton textile machinery from England to the United States, rubber seedlings into Southeast Asia, and clove production from present Indonesia. Borrowed technology has been one of the primary factors in the past development of many areas. For example, that the United States borrowed heavily from England and Japan from the West are prime instances of advance through imitation.

Today, few artificial barriers exist to the spread of technology. In fact, as will be described below, the advanced countries have organized deliberately to teach improved technologies to the underdeveloped parts of the world. In addition, business firms with foreign branches have been agencies for transmitting new technologies, and capital-equipment producers are eagerly looking for markets.* However, one of the major forms of transmission—emigration—is now quite limited. In its place are technical-aid programs, student programs, and objective governmental research institutes.

Successful transmission depends on a variety of conditions. First of all, it depends on the reception given to the new methods. It is just not possible to introduce changed methods without regard for the social situation; technological change may produce vast social changes, but conversely, the social structure may limit its acceptance or may even reject it. The knowledge of new techniques is worthless unless accepted, absorbed widely, and used. This requires that new techniques be adapted to old habits and have some compatibility with them. Acceptance is easiest if the change is an improvement on local practices and can be fitted into prevailing beliefs, but it is most difficult if the change is very radical, requires a series of succeeding changes, affects individual living habits closely, upsets existing power relationships, is introduced by unpopular groups, requires initial adoption by large numbers of people, requires large amounts of capital, or can be appropriated by a small group.[17]

Second, successful transmission depends on being able to communicate

---

* One of the problems of this type of transmission is that too advanced techniques may be transferred and do not spread beyond the original factory or plantation, resulting in a technological dualism.

the new technique to the thousands of small units in agriculture and industry where improved methods are most needed and which are most tradition-minded. This requires facilities for communication and an improved level of literacy. One of the greatest needs for development is improvement in our methods of contacting these units, for the written word may not be a useful instrument without a long and costly education process. Particularly, experimentation in demonstration techniques is necessary. It does very little good to set up modern large-scale farms or factories, for these are alien to the world of the small farmer and entrepreneur and are completely beyond his understanding and means. Demonstration must be at the level of the operator to be effective, and the improvements must be within his means and not too alien to his accepted beliefs.

Third, the new technique must be economic, or reasonably so, under the circumstances of the receiving country. Many techniques that are highly successful in the advanced countries are not yet economical in the underdeveloped areas because they require, among other things, too large a scale of operation for the market available; the resource and factor situation is not favorable; or the skill level is too low. The advanced countries tend toward capital-intensive projects, which are not always indicated for underdeveloped countries,* for capital may be expensive and skills in short supply, and their adoption may increase unemployment. This would require repression of labor and individual opportunity to enter business. On the other hand, reliance on old techniques may limit advance. It may be that a compromise between the best level of technology and the immediately most economic level would be best. This would have the advantage of lowering the cost of obsolescence and giving some impetus to improvement in society.

Fourth, successful transmission depends on the supply of complementary factors, such as entrepreneurs, capital, and appropriate skills. A transfer of techniques is ineffective unless the process of transfer is complete and the complementary factors, including attitudes favorable to further experimentation, are improved. Thus, there is a necessity to increase the absorptive capacity for new ideas and processes.

Lastly, there is a need to determine the person or groups most appropriate to introduce the innovation. This will be discussed later.

It is easy to transfer knowledge of scientific principles but not particular techniques, for they can rarely be introduced in unmodified form. The latter must be fitted into the conditions of the country, including the relative supply of the factors and the social conditions prevailing. The problem is to

* They should not be automatically adopted, but neither should they be automatically ruled out.

decide what to borrow as a basis for adaptation. For example, one usually cannot transfer directly into one region a strain of seed developed in another. Even if it were to grow and produce well, it might require other adjustments such as further processing or a change in eating habits. Thus, each transfer has its special problems.

This means research on the spot if new technologies are to be most effective. Thus, what really must be transferred is an attitude of rationality and of guided experimentation so that the most suitable of alternative techniques can be selected. Fortunately, there is a wide range of technologies from which to choose as a start. It is probable that no specific kind is exactly right, but much of the cost of developing the most appropriate one can be avoided. Developing new technologies is expensive because of much wasted effort, but this developmental stage has been passed through in some area of the world for a wide range of technologies. Starting from such a known base can also shorten the time interval between the recognition of a problem and finding the appropriate solution.

Out-and-out imitation may be a good way to get started, but advance will lag unless experimentation is carried out to improve practices under the current operating conditions. Once a practice is initiated, the innovator must be constantly alert so that, as resource availabilities change and conditions change, the technologies are adapted to the stage of development.*

If experimentation is necessary to adapt foreign technologies, it is almost certain that it will have to be carried out under government auspices. Private enterprises in the underdeveloped countries usually do not have the resources or personnel; even if they do, they will not experiment unless they can get a monopoly for the use of the technology. Government research institutions would seem to be a wise choice for investment funds.

## The Most Suitable Type of Technology

Selecting the most appropriate technology is an important decision for underdeveloped countries. This concerns the choice between capital-intensive and labor-intensive technologies. Also involved may be the question of large-scale versus small-scale units, but this is not necessarily the case, for small-scale industry or agriculture can be capital-intensive or labor-intensive although the latter is usually the case. Large-scale industry is al-

---

* J. Baranson ("New Technologies for Developing Areas." *Bulletin of Atomic Scientists* [September, 1961], pp. 275-77) proposes that underdeveloped countries find brand new technologies especially suited to their needs. For example, he suggests the use of dirigibles to bypass the need for roads.

most always capital-intensive, but this can be a matter of degree and any operation can be more or less capital-intensive.

There is no approach equally applicable to all countries and all situations, since each must be tailored to the specific case. One of the prerequisites for most effective development is investigation by each country as to the most feasible technology in the light of its own situation and own set of goals.

The choice of a goal is an important consideration. Availability of many different methods of production, of varying degrees of capital and labor intensity, affords much opportunity of selection. But there are also a great variety of possible objectives, which complicates the selection.[18] The choice of objective will influence the choice of the appropriate technology. Some of the possible objectives* are:

1. Lowest per unit cost of production.
2. Maximum output per unit of capital or of labor.
3. Maximum employment.
4. Optimum effect on the country's capacity to grow.
5. Maximizing the accumulation or attraction of capital.
6. Time and cost required for people to learn the requisite skills.
7. Time for the output to become available (gestation period).
8. Ability to use domestic materials and to save on them.
9. Effect on the scale of operations.

The first of these objectives is the lowest per unit cost of production. In seeking this, one obviously has to consider the scale of operation, for if the purpose is to minimize current costs, it would be poor policy to set up facilities for producing more quantities than can be disposed of, merely to get low unit costs. The objective is better stated as "obtaining the lowest cost per unit for the desired output."

Minimizing cost is the usual criterion in a privately operated business and is generally recommended for business operated by the government. Only by minimizing costs are resources considered to be allocated in the most efficient manner. However, this assumes as the objective the maximization of profits for the individual firm, which may not be what a developing society wants for there may be other objectives, as listed above. For a developing country, returns from the employment of factors must be considered more broadly than immediate economic profit taken on a firm-to-firm basis.† Long-run returns and the effect on development must be con-

---

* Many of these are similar to the criteria used to determine the kinds of enterprises in which to invest, which will be discussed in Chapter 14.

† In the advanced capitalistic economies, firm-by-firm considerations are expected to yield an optimum social allocation by the shift of factors to the most profitable pursuits. That this actually occurs in these societies is doubtful because competition is not perfect. This is even less true for underdeveloped societies.

sidered. Much of the answer to the question of the degree of capital intensity depends on whether the country strives to maximize returns on existing resources or to maximize other longer-run objectives. However, if the output faces foreign competition, it must be produced at comparable costs (unless subsidized), and this requires close attention to costs.

To minimize cost, the rule is to economize on the most costly factor as long as factor substitution is possible. Figure 8.1 illustrates the situation in which only two factors, capital and labor, are involved. The output line is an ordinary isoquant, which shows the various combinations of capital and labor that can be used to produce the desired output. The line $C_1L_1$ is an equal outlay line, which shows all the combinations of capital and labor that can be purchased for $100. Outlay lines calling for a greater or lesser expenditure would be parallel to this line. For example, line $C_2L_2$ shows all the combinations of capital and labor that can be purchased for $75. The combination of capital and labor to be chosen is found where the output line just touches the lowest possible outlay line. This is point $P_1$ on line $C_1L_1$. If, as we have assumed, capital costs $25 per unit and labor costs

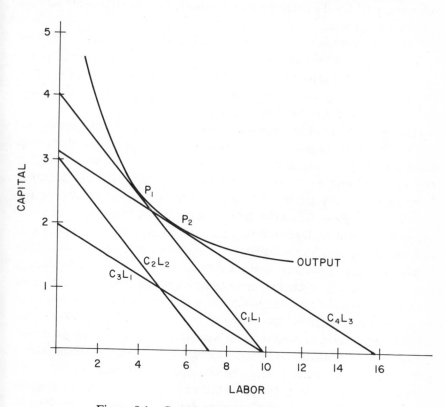

Figure 8.1    Combinations of Capital and Labor
Producing the Highest Output at the Least Cost

$10 per unit, slightly over two units of capital would be used and somewhat over four units of labor. No other combination could produce this output more cheaply.

Now suppose capital increases in cost to $50 while labor remains at the same price. The outlay line would now have a different and flatter slope. Outlay line $C_3L_1$ would show all combinations of capital and labor that could be bought for $100. Now the required output would not meet the equal outlay line at all; that is, such an output could not be produced for $100. Either a smaller output would have to be produced or a greater expenditure would have to be made for inputs. The latter would be shown by the equal outlay line $C_4L_3$. The new minimum cost would be at $P_2$. In this case, the output would be obtained by employing a little less than two units of capital and a little over five units of labor, at a total cost of approximately $160. Because of the increase in the price of capital, the same output would cost more, but less capital and more labor would be employed. The use of the factors thus depends on the relative cost of the factors and the shape of the output isoquant; that is, the substitutability of factors. The higher the price of capital (or the lower the cost of labor), the less capital-intensive an operation is apt to be.

If more factors are considered, the principle remains the same. The rule is to economize on the most expensive inputs. In the underdeveloped countries, the scarcest and most expensive factor is usually taken to be capital. If this is true, and immediate low cost or large profit is wanted, the labor-intensive alternatives are the best choice.

However, it may not be true that capital is the scarcest and most expensive factor. There is a general assumption, at least by the masses, that cheap labor is practically unlimited; but this is not true for industry, although it may be for agriculture. Workers may be cheap in unit price, but industrial labor may be costly for the individual employer[19] and especially for the economy as a whole. The individual producer is faced with costs of training, low productivity, high turnover, labor union pressure, and high standards of factory and social legislation. Legislation may require an excess number of workers and may make it difficult to dismiss them. Efficiency is low, so that more workers may have to be employed than in the advanced countries. Capital-intensive technologies may make better use of labor because machines determine the pacing of the worker and the timing of his actions, and thus act as substitutes for management in controlling the activities of the new industrial workers. Moreover, the existence of capital with a given capacity sets a performance goal as a guide for management.[20]

In addition to the cost to the individual employer, developing an acceptable industrial labor supply involves large costs for society, as described in

Chapter 6. Because capital goods are already in existence and can be obtained through purchase, it seems more convenient, quicker, and cheaper to use these than to try to develop a labor force. Urbanization costs are said to be large for labor-intensive industries.* However, even though the direct effect of capital-intensive industry may be the hiring of less labor to produce a given product, the indirect effect is usually the urbanization of the population. Modern capital-intensive industries require specialized labor and services and a better-trained labor force. These are more likely to be found in the larger cities. Moreover, large-scale industries must usually seek exports, and therefore must locate in the seaports. The result is a growth of large cities and heavy urban costs. The more labor-intensive industries are apt to be of smaller scale and more amenable to being scattered throughout a region, although they, too, gain advantages from concentration. Nevertheless, industrialization usually means increasing urbanization and its consequent costs. Educating and training labor, improving its health, and creating the necessary environment for industry, all increase society's cost for labor.

Capital may even be relatively cheap compared with the cost of some other factors, such as skilled labor, because of the sale of raw materials, particularly oil, or because of foreign grants or low-interest loans, which may never be collected.† Countries may form development banks to make capital available at easy terms, and large firms may control their own banks. The actual interest rates,** which may represent a subsidy from society, may not be any greater than in Europe or Japan, according to one writer.[21] On the other hand, capital may be used no more efficiently than labor.

Thus, there is no universal solution. The effect of capital intensity on costs depends on many factors. Moreover, the real scarcity may be skilled labor of various types, which would require a special technology to economize this resource. It may be more important to have quality control for competitive purposes than to obtain the lowest possible cost, which could be provided by modern capital-intensive industry. Thus, despite appearances to the contrary, some degree of capital intensity may be needed. One

* R. L. Meier ("Automation and Economic Development," in L. W. Shannon, *Underdeveloped Areas.* New York, Harper & Brothers, 1957, pp. 232-40) advocates automation for underdeveloped countries for various reasons, such as lessening the migration of the labor force into industry.

† Capital is never so abundant that it need not be allocated carefully and put to its best use. The allocation of investment capital will be discussed in Chapter 14.

** From a social point of view, subsidies that lower interest rates may result in a misallocation of resources. For the individual making an investment decision and who is faced with such artificially low rates, the best decision would be to make his enterprise more capital-intensive than would otherwise be the case.

report[22] says that despite cheap labor and high interest rates in Asia, there is some evidence that the most advanced methods with high capital requirements give the lowest unit cost and highest profit rate; that is, the savings in labor cost are greater than the capital cost.

It is possible to divide the problem in each firm by making some operations capital-intensive (usually the direct production processes) and others labor-intensive, especially the subsidiary tasks such as materials handling.[23] Thus, there needs to be considerable study to determine the most effective way to produce goods.

A second objective may be to maximize immediate physical output from the use of given resources. Certainly, the most abundant factor is labor, and it may seem that labor-intensive production is desirable. However, this is true only up to a point. All employment requires some capital unless it is to be very inefficient; for example, catching fish with one's bare hands. To try to utilize all labor may result in using capital so inefficiently that the output will be less than that obtained by using relatively more capital-intensive projects. For example, in India, considerable emphasis has been put on encouraging textile production on a cottage industry basis. Although statistical evidence is lacking, it is questionable that there has been as great an output as would have been obtained if the capital had been invested in more modern facilities, to say nothing of better quality. The same question applies to pedicabs and bazaar selling. The point is that labor-intensive methods usually result in low labor productivity. Harvey Leibenstein[24] comments that any increase in production would lead only to a population increase. According to him, a large unit increase in output is needed in order to overcome such a trend. Again, the answer is uncertain, but a much greater use of labor than of capital is almost certain to result in diminishing returns.

A third objective could be to maximize employment. If this is chosen as an objective, labor-intensive methods will provide the most immediate employment, although output may be too low. In the long run, it is questionable whether technological change reduces total employment, although it may cause specific unemployment. In fact, the weight of opinion would undoubtedly be that it has resulted in the ability to employ increased numbers in the advanced countries. It would be disastrous economically to make the development program a make-work program. On the other hand, it could be disastrous politically to ignore the employment situation. Some compromise is necessary. It is not unusual to introduce capital-intensive projects and then lose advantages by requiring extra labor.

The preceding objectives have had immediate concerns: cost, output, and employment. All are important. However, any development program must forecast the long-run effects on these objectives. The real purpose is to optimize these quantities over a period of time, but not over too distant a future. For example, if maximizing employment currently results in a failure to develop, some compromise must be made. Moreover, more than economic outputs must be considered in the desired returns. Much of the discussion over the degree of capital or labor intensity centers on the preferences for immediate and economic returns or long-run and somewhat broader goals. Long-run results and noneconomic returns, such as cultural and political considerations, are important.

Many argue for capital-intensive industries on this basis. Outstanding is Hirschman's doctrine of unbalanced growth, described in Chapter 2, which postulates that the characteristic growth pattern is rapid growth in a few centers and industries. This, in turn, results in opportunities for development elsewhere as excess capacity is made available or shortages appear in the supplying industry. The overdevelopment of social overheads illustrates the former and a modern textile mill the latter. Investment in these makes further investment possible elsewhere. Eventually, the poorer sectors will be drawn into the development stream. Thus, capital-intensive industry in a few areas may lead to much more industry, perhaps even of a labor-intensive nature. On the other hand, to copy advanced techniques may be so costly that other projects are unlikely to start. In the meanwhile, much capital equipment may be unused and wasted.

Other economists may favor capital-intensive industries in order to avoid the wastage of capital. It is argued that when development is finally realized, industry will be capital-intensive. To introduce labor-intensive industry at the early stages because it appears to be economic involves a wastage of capital as methods change and also creates barriers to later modernization. Small-scale industry and the workers may resist future changes. The former fear is not serious, for capital does wear out and must be replaced. Moreover, modern technologies require rapid advance to remain modern and require constant scrapping of machinery. The fear of the resistance of vested interests is a real one. All economies, advanced or underdeveloped, have this problem and must learn to cope with it.

Other analysts say that capital-intensive industries with impressive outputs can have a large psychological effect on a people and serve as a symbol of achievement. Gradual improvement does not meet most people's expectations and so leads to unrest and political instability. A growth period is a period of heavy sacrifice and will be endured only if there are some obvious evidences of growth, a strong nationalistic feeling, or strong leadership.

On the other hand, it could be argued that capital-intensive industry has little effect on local purchasing power and little educational and training advantage. A few capital-intensive industries may create a problem of transportation and power development, and these facilities are also usually capital-intensive. A possible result is the creation of a dualistic economy when all effort is placed on these few projects. Capital-intensive projects also require a great change from local tradition and ideology.

Another premise is that modern capital-intensive industry, especially large-scale industry, can generate and attract more financial capital and so result in an increased volume of investment. This is based on the belief that profits will be higher and that the resulting income will go to people with high savings habits, so that greater reinvestment will occur.[25] This leads to one criterion for investment policy: equating at the margin the discounted value of the general reinvestment stream, including investment in social overheads and human improvement. This, however, assumes that the wealthy have a higher propensity to save or pay taxes than lower-income people can be forced to assume through taxation and that they will use these savings for reinvestment in productive enterprises. It is probably easier to attract public foreign capital for a few large modern projects than for a general program that develops small-scale industry. Such projects are more likely to attract foreign private capital. However, many countries do not welcome such capital.

On the other hand, proponents of small-scale operations in the rural areas believe that much local capital will be made available for small industries, which require little capital. This, otherwise, would not be available. Even small-scale, capital-intensive industries may be too large for this kind of capital.

It is not certain which type of industry requires the longer time and greater cost to teach the requisite skills. Primitive industry of the type already in existence, of course, requires no more training than is currently given, but neither does it bring progress. To improve techniques requires time and effort. Labor-intensive industries require the training of large numbers in industrial habits, simple machine skills, and business management. A few capital-intensive projects require teaching to a few (or importing) the fairly advanced work and managerial skills. The former require expanding the educational system fairly extensively; the latter can utilize the relatively few who are already being educated, supplemented by selective-skill training. The disadvantage of the latter is that the few who are trained may use their privileged position to reap most of the benefits of development. As described in Chapter 7, it seems unlikely that one can start with an advanced industrial society, but rather that long historical processes are necessary and that a country must start with simple techniques and advance to more complicated ones as capital becomes available, labor is trained, skills develop, and markets grow.

Labor-intensive projects release their products more quickly than capital-intensive ones, and therefore involve less of a waiting period. Investment is thus less apt to be an inflationary force, for the new products absorb the increased purchasing power released by the investment.

Labor-intensive industries are usually better able to use local materials, especially those produced in scattered quantities or of varying quality. The heavily mechanized plants have difficulty operating without highly standardized materials. The machine is less able to adapt to variables than are human beings.

Some planners propose technologies that will promote the development of small-scale industry for various reasons, mentioned previously.*

Thus, the diverse approaches emphasize the importance of analyzing the various industrial and agricultural projects a country wishes to undertake, to find the best techniques or combination of techniques to accomplish what is most desired. For developmental purposes it is probably best to use capital-intensive projects where necessary to get low costs and high output, but to substitute labor-intensive techniques wherever possible without sacrificing too much efficiency and output. As previously stated, it seems best to accelerate the improvement in technology in order to stimulate the economy. The ideal would be output-producing techniques that are capital saving, employment creating, low cost, development-oriented, and with whatever other characteristics that are desired. This is undoubtedly not realizable, but research should be directed toward the best compromise.

## Technical Assistance

One of the outstanding developments of the postwar era is the emphasis placed on transmitting to the underdeveloped countries the skills and techniques known in the advanced countries. A conscious effort to transmit skills is not new, for there had been much previous action by missionaries and for military and rehabilitation purposes. However, only after World War II, with President Truman's Point 4 as the focus,† was technical aid given on a massive scale and in an organized and more or less coordinated manner. The United States program has been followed by a wide variety of

* For example, Y. Brozen ("Technological Change, Ideology and Productivity," *loc. cit.*) would promote small-scale industry so as to discourage centralized decision making.

† Point 4 was the fourth proposal in the inaugural address of January 20, 1949, in which President Truman declared that the United States would participate in efforts to raise the standard of living of underdeveloped countries and would make available our store of technical knowledge.

programs by other countries. The U.S.S.R., France, United Kingdom, and Japan are among those with aid programs. The United Nations has an extensive program,[26] as have such regional organizations as the Organization for American States for Latin America and the Colombo Plan for Southeast Asia. Private organizations, including the foundations and philanthropic groups, religious organizations, and private business firms, carry on programs. In fact, the involvement of so many agencies may tend to hinder assistance and make it haphazard and uncoordinated.

Technical assistance is given over a wide variety of activities. The major ones, however, are government administration, agriculture, education, health, manpower training, and transportation and communication. Many examples of individual projects in different countries are given in the literature.[27]

It is difficult to unravel the motives behind such a rapid expansion of technical assistance programs as we have seen. There is no question that they have had a broad humanitarian appeal and are motivated by a sincere desire to be helpful. Unfortunately, assistance can also serve the interests of the lending nation, and there is always the danger that the first consideration will be given to this rather than the need to help. Examples of advantages to the lending nation are exports, particularly of capital goods; investment and market opportunities; friendship in the struggle for world leadership; and military partnership.

Because there is a possibility that national interests may intrude, there are advantages to providing aid through a multinational body.[28] Such aid could draw on the resources, physical and human, of many nations. It would be politically more acceptable, for the recipient would be a member of the organization and the obligation would be less direct and more general; mutuality and cooperation would be strengthened; greater continuity would be possible; projects that concerned several countries simultaneously could be coordinated; and less competition between the great powers would result. However, multinational aid could also have its problems: there might be squabbling among the nations for priority in receiving aid (for example, there is a problem of coordination of projects among the numerous organizations within the United Nations), and funds might be less than those available through individual country efforts. It is probably best to continue aid on a dual basis, although efforts should be made to coordinate programs and to base the aid on actual need rather than international competition.

Those who have participated in aid projects report[29] certain necessary procedures and policies and the avoidance of certain actions. First, they report the necessity for making increase of efficiency and productivity the chief aim. As stressed previously, this need not mean an emphasis on direct production, but may often more properly be aimed at such indirectly productive measures as improved education, health, and governmental efficiency. A second requirement is that the efforts should involve the mass of people who are to use the technique and not just a selected few. For this reason the techniques cannot be too complex or too costly. As an illustration of this, the so-called Japanese method of rice culture may be cited. This method is more productive than the native Indian method, but requires more capital. Even though the increased production may more than pay for the increased capital, it is unlikely to be adopted by the Indian peasant because he cannot obtain the capital.[30] Other guiding principles are: it should fit into the country's needs, economic situation, and plans; there should be a coordinated plan of new techniques. One isolated improvement is of little benefit.

Likewise, there are certain obstacles to overcome. A major one is getting the people to accept the new practices, for there is great reluctance to adopt new ideas. The new practice must be fitted into local needs, culture, and institutions so that it will be accepted and at the same time increase production. At least, the new technique cannot be strongly contrary to established beliefs. This requires a knowledge of the habits, practices, and beliefs of the recipients.* It is also necessary to get results quickly enough so that the people will follow the practice and possibly be led to more fundamental changes.

In addition to changing the attitudes mentioned, there is the decision to be made concerning the best techniques to use. Primarily, one can say that these must be tailored to the circumstances, but, by and large, there is general agreement that the best technique is to train and educate native personnel to be the leaders of their fellows. In this way, training is more likely to be carried on after the experts leave, and instruction tends to be more acceptable. Opinion is divided as to the value of model demonstration projects and pilot plants. The model cannot be very far beyond current practices or too costly, or it will remain only a curiosity and not imitated.

The United Nations, which extends aid through a variety of subagencies,† operates in various ways. It provides survey committees or missions to study conditions, resources, and needs. It sends advisory missions to promote plans and operations. It sends people for specific training activities and may grant fellowships for nationals to travel abroad for training.

* This was discussed in more detail in Chapter 3.
† These include the Food and Agricultural Organization (FAO), World Health Organization (WHO), UN Educational, Social and Cultural Organization (UNESCO), International Labour Office (ILO), International Civil Aviation Organization (ICAO), and UN Technical Assistance Administration (UNTAA).

An interesting and valuable device is the productivity and vocational training center. Israel has its own Institute of Productivity,[31] controlled by representatives of government, employers, workers, and associations of engineers and architects. This institute conducts a large number of training courses and makes studies to determine the most efficient methods. From small beginnings this has expanded to more fields and more skilled administration, including top management. The International Labour Office[32] recommends such centers to undertake productivity studies; organize practical courses; apply modern methods in selected plants as demonstrations; promote the adoption of cost accounting and statistical techniques; study human relations; and give advice about systems of wage payment, design and layout, health, safety, welfare, and so on.

Particularly, all projects must be approved by the government and local officials. Unless the leaders want to bring improvements, and transmit this desire down the line, little will be accomplished. Vested interests may block reform. Local officials who feel downgraded because they have to receive assistance may be uncooperative unless they are allowed to take the credit.

A thorny problem is finding suitable personnel, which is not easy. Incompetent personnel are resented. Competent ones from donor countries must be paid salaries far out of proportion to those of their native counterparts. The living standards may then be far different. On an amateur basis, the Peace Corps overcomes some of these difficulties. Important also is the necessity to avoid being a spokesman for any ideology or taking sides in a political dispute. To be successful, the "expert" must identify himself sufficiently with the host country so as to serve its needs.

## Problems of Technological Advance

Technological advance brings benefits but it also arouses fears. First, and most feared, is that unemployment may result. Technological unemployment has been known and feared from before the Industrial Revolution of the eighteenth century. Now, in the United States, in the form of automation, it induces great apprehension. There is no reason to believe that technological change will pose any less of a threat to employment in underdeveloped countries. Western economists have accepted the idea that technological change may cause specific unemployment; that is, certain skills, certain persons, and certain places will experience unemployment. However, in the long run, increased employment is expected to result. Increased incomes lead to increased demands, especially in the services, and these in turn call for more labor in sales and in designing, and in making and servicing machines.

The speed of absorption of the displaced workers depends on the adaptability of the workers and the price-cost-wage relationships that develop. In fact, it might help to focus our attention on the weak spot if we did not talk of technological unemployment but of wage-price unemployment. That underdeveloped countries can escape the problem seems unlikely, for neither factors of production nor prices and wages are very flexible.

It is clear that some traditional skills will be dispensed with and the work transferred to the factory; for example, the manufacture of cloth. Some handicraftsmen may continue, for specialty needs or the tourist trade, but many will be forced to shift their employment. Also, improved agricultural techniques will release many from the farms. Similarly, surplus labor will be released from household service, marketing, and transportation. There is no question but that many will be required to shift and will have to rely on developing industry and services for jobs. Existing workers may remain unemployed because they do not have the necessary qualifications for jobs in the new factories. One of the costs of the new technology will be increased costs for educating and training workers.

Improved technology may even reduce the total need for workers temporarily. The remedy for technological unemployment is an increasing level of demand for goods and thus for labor. As demand increases, one can expect further technological change, which will slow the reabsorption of labor. Thus, demand may have to increase to a large extent to keep total employment rising. Demand may be for consumer goods, which requires increased purchasing power, or for increased capital formation, which requires increased savings. Too great a diversion of total income to either consumption or saving could create difficulties.* The former reduces the possibility of capital formation and so the possibility of increased production. The latter reduces purchasing power, so that if the increased saving is invested, there will be no markets for the product except possibly in foreign countries. The proper balance for optimum development is not easy to ascertain.

Absorption of unemployed labor depends on a rapid rate of growth. If new investment and increased output take place in a relatively localized sector of the economy, some workers get increased income and look around for someplace to spend it, usually on food and other essentials. Unless increased supplies of these goods are available, prices will rise and workers will demand higher wages. As a result, savings may decline, and further expansion will be halted or slowed. Thus, increased output will be necessary in a number of areas, particularly agriculture. Because it can be assumed that technological change will tend to replace labor in those areas,

* See the theory of Harrod-Domar, Chapter 2.

total demand must also rise fairly rapidly if unemployment is to be avoided.

Not only workers but other people also will be hurt as technology improves. Existing capital will become obsolescent; less efficient firms will go bankrupt; some cities will lose business; and the power and prestige of traders and landowners may be threatened. These interests, including the workers, can be expected to try to protect themselves by slowing change and acquiring privileged positions or monopoly. Such obstruction will be an obstacle to development.

As discussed in Chapter 3, technological change may also bring cultural dislocation; that is, alter the pattern and structure of people's lives. Cultures comprise interrelated units, and change at one point causes change elsewhere.[33] That is, there is a relationship among economic production, the political system, religious beliefs, social life, and ethical attitudes, and a change in one affects the others. There is no assurance that material progress will bring adverse cultural changes, but it will bring change as man adapts to the new technology, and the change may not be wholesome. The automobile brought undoubted benefits, but also made crime prevention more difficult, among other things. The elevator contributed to urban congestion. Technological changes have increased the optimum scale of industry and thus promoted large organizations of businessmen, unions, and government. Established systems of values, goals, and sanctions may disappear and new ones may not be established quickly enough to restore a harmonious order. Many of the problems of city life have been due to the breakdown of such sanctions. The faster the change, the greater is the maladjustment and the more difficult is the reintegration. Thus, one must consider the social and cultural situation when new technologies are to be introduced. It may be necessary to find new values, and this will be one of the costs of development.

Another problem is that the gains of the new technology may not be shared equally. A few may reap all the benefits, as seems true of Latin America, with the result that the maldistribution of income increases. In such a situation political stability may be jeopardized. Furthermore, there may be psychological problems arising out of the dependence on other countries for technical aid or capital funds.

As technology improves, people are drawn more and more into the orbit of commercial life and competition. One innovation does not suffice for a lifetime, so that the businessman or farmer must constantly try to improve. In a subsistence economy there is no such pressure. In a commercial one there is, and life cannot remain calm and peaceful.

## The Role of Entrepreneurship in Development

It has been mentioned earlier that entrepreneurship is considered one of the three prime requirements for economic development. The entrepreneur is, in general, the initiator and operator of an enterprise. As such, his functions are to initiate the enterprise, introduce new ideas and innovations for its operations, assume the risks of the enterprise, obtain the necessary capital and other factors required to operate the business, and coordinate their use, especially in new combinations. In any one enterprise the initiator or entrepreneur can be several men or, over a period of time, a series of men. A well-conceived enterprise must experience a series of innovations and have a series of innovators if it is to continue to grow.

Today, in the West, the functions of the entrepreneur have been increasingly subdivided. Three aspects stand out: the supplier of funds, the manager, and the initiator.[34] The funds are supplied by the capitalist. The management supervises and coordinates the operations. The entrepreneur proper is the planner, innovator, and ultimate decision maker. He deals with the new and the untried, the uncertain. It is in this sense that we are concerned here with entrepreneurship as a special requirement for growth. Although these functions are increasingly separated in the West, in the underdeveloped countries all functions are usually combined in one person.

Not only are the entrepreneurial functions increasingly separated in the West, but they are also even subdivided. The capitalist, or supplier of funds, is really many persons, representing owners of various types of securities. For the most part he has hardly any function except supplying funds, for he rarely chooses to exercise an active interest in the business. Management is increasingly professionalized, specialized, and bureaucratized. Instead of personal guesswork, management relies on accounting, statistics, methods systems, and standards. Advisory staffs of trained specialists aid management; for example, personnel, labor relations, safety, time-and-motion studies, and factory layout. Managerial techniques have improved greatly, and we have witnessed a great increase in our ability to supervise and coordinate, although the art of management is still in its infancy. Unfortunately, management tends to become routinized and adverse to change. The manager is to be distinguished from the entrepreneur who introduces innovations and upsets routine management.

The basic challenge is to increase the supply of entrepreneurs in the planning, innovating, and decision-making sense. Directors of business have been classified[35] as innovators, those who see and put new ideas into effect;

as imitators, those who are quick to adopt innovations made by others; as fabians, those who exercise great caution and change only when it is safe; and as drones, those who refuse to change.

For a country to advance, the first two groups must predominate. For the underdeveloped country, it is probably sufficient in the first stages if there are plenty of imitators. In time, innovators will be necessary if a country is to continue to advance. A major fear and obstacle to growth is that innovators may grow scarce.

Just what is the role of the entrepreneur in development? In keeping with J. A. Schumpeter's view,* the major role of the entrepreneur is that of being an innovator. It has just been pointed out that development comes from many sources, but most certainly it must be accompanied by successful innovations that increase productivity, introduce new products or new outlooks, and so forth. Someone must make the decision to innovate, and he must take the risk that the innovation may be a failure. New techniques or ideas do not introduce themselves. They must be introduced by someone who sees an opportunity and is confident that his way of exploiting this opportunity is the best one. Enterprising people can usually find ways to surmount the obstacles that prevent growth.

In the United States we usually think of this innovator as a private person seeking his own gain, but there is no reason government officials cannot be innovators. However, unless the top officials are development- and innovation-minded, this is not likely. The governments of many underdeveloped countries, however, believe that they must concentrate at least major investment decisions in a central plan and thus are the major innovators of new lines of endeavor.

Entrepreneurs are not only the prime movers of change, but they are also the selectors of the techniques of change and economic growth, and perhaps even the direction. In the latter case, they are more likely, if private enterprisers, to follow the best profit opportunities as they judge them. To the extent they judge correctly, they tend to be successful.

To survive in a competitive world, the economic activity of a nation must be flexible; that is, resources must shift as the best opportunities shift. It is the entrepreneur who must foretell the necessary changes and initiate the appropriate action.

* J. A. Schumpeter (*The Theory of Economic Development, loc. cit.*) made the innovator the prime mover in development. He was undoubtedly thinking more of developed countries than of underdeveloped ones, and concentrated on the major innovations. Nevertheless, his exposition remains the most famous expression of the role of innovators.

## Entrepreneurship in Underdeveloped Countries

One of the greatest problems in underdeveloped countries is a shortage of dynamic entrepreneurs to utilize any available resources or to introduce new ways of doing things. As just pointed out, without entrepreneurs to make such changes, development will be virtually impossible, for growth comes by increasing efficiency, which is brought about by innovations.

Not that the businessmen in underdeveloped countries are averse to making money! In fact, they are often among the most acquisitive in the world, but usually their profits are made not through engaging in productive enterprises or by risking their capital in relatively permanent investments as in industry; instead, their philosophy is one of large profit on small volume based on a monopoly position. This is not the stuff of which expanding businesses are made. Operating in a competitive market on small margins and relying for profits on superior quality or greater productive efficiency is the way to develop, but is not the usual pattern of business in underdeveloped countries. The usual pattern is rational but not conducive to development.

Instead of production, businessmen go into trade, speculation, or land purchase. Here the returns are safer, quicker, or more respectable. Y. A. Sayigh[36] describes the requirements for such activity, which fit more into the conditions of underdeveloped economies, as immediate high profits; less and shorter-term investment, based on the idea of transactions and not a continuous process; little advanced technology; not much teamwork or complex organization; high liquidity; and secrecy of affairs. Industry, on the other hand, requires long-range planning, a willingness to undertake long-range investment, the acceptance of low-profit margins, advanced technology, organization, coordination, and teamwork.

Industrial entrepreneurs are short of supply in the planning, innovating, and decision-making areas particularly, for various reasons.

1.   In many countries it is degrading to work with one's hands. This is necessary in small businesses.

2.   In the past, industry was largely in the hands of the foreigner, so the potential local businessman gained little experience.

3.   Engaging in industry may be in disrepute because it is associated with foreigners and colonialism. In the days of colonial domination, the foreigner was the initiator and operator of the major business firms, many of which were established primarily for the export business and were considered by the native population as exploitative. Often wages were low,

which did not enhance the popularity of the businessman. Nor does Marxian doctrine add to his prestige.

4.    The task of operating a business is much more complicated in the underdeveloped country than in the developed one.[37] Demand is less predictable and often limited; statistical data are lacking; getting equipment, materials, and repair services of the right quality and at the right time is uncertain; skilled labor is short and the labor force unpredictable; the foreign exchange position may be precarious; governments are often unstable, not always impartial in administering the laws, and may intervene closely in the operations. Above all, the enterpriser must carry out all the managerial functions by himself, for he has no trained staff to rely upon and usually must supply his own capital. It is no wonder that the enterpriser discounts future returns heavily and relies on short-term commercial gains or speculates in land. People start businesses only if they think they can overcome the uncertainties that inevitably face every businessman. The greater the uncertainties, the less likelihood of finding people who will attempt to overcome them. For this reason, government itself must often be the innovator and the operator of the business enterprises. At the very least, government must supply the social overheads.

In most underdeveloped countries it will be necessary to have centralized planning with major investment decisions in government hands, at least until development has proceeded far enough so that the necessary interrelations among the various sectors of the economy have been established and a price system is operating well enough to serve as a guide and incentive to private enterprisers.* In the long run, central governments cannot expect to carry out all business decisions by themselves. They must find some device to decentralize these, and one such device is private enterprise. In the author's opinion, the developing countries would do well to shift to private hands as much of the decision making as possible, keeping such controls as necessary to prevent decisions contrary to the public interest and perhaps operating those industries most essential to the proper functioning of the economy. Examples of these are the utilities, such as electric power, transportation, communication, and perhaps steel. But, in the first instance, innovation may have to be by government in order to break tradition, as in agricultural practices or to get industry started, because it does not represent a good risk until a later stage of development has been reached.

* The role of government and private enterprisers will be considered more fully in Chapter 13.

## Factors Affecting the Supply of Entrepreneurs

An interesting question is how to increase the supply of entrepreneurs in the planning, innovating, and decision-making areas.[38] Potential entrepreneurs undoubtedly exist in all societies, but they may be suppressed because of the lack of opportunities or the values held by the society.

The first suggestion for increasing the supply is to give individuals the opportunity to make decisions. This means, for example, that children must be given the responsibility for making decisions of their own and must be encouraged to take as much responsibility as they are capable of. In many underdeveloped countries, children are brought up to be excessively obedient and subservient to their elders. This may be easy on their parents, but it reduces the supply of innovators. American children are much more encouraged to take responsibility, and, although they may be difficult to live with, are more apt to develop as decision makers. Participation in sports, which requires decision making on the spot, may well be good practice for later innovation of a more economic sort. Unfortunately, too much of the decision making in United States sports is being centralized in the coach in the interest of winning. This, to the author, seems to be a mistake.

Further, the system of education is outstandingly important in the type of person it turns out. Too often the student in the traditional societies is required to do little more than memorize, and is completely discouraged from questioning the professor and the texts or from bringing forth his own ideas. To have a plentiful supply of future entrepreneurs, education must be research-oriented and students must be encouraged to investigate new ideas and to form opinions of their own. A universal system of education will enlarge the potential supply of entrepreneurs and make it easier to discover such talent. Just as important, it will enlarge the knowledge base, thus increasing the possibility of new ideas. McClelland[39] has investigated the role of the usual children's stories in making individuals achievement-oriented. Where the stories are achievement-oriented, as in the well-known "The Little Fir Tree" of Hans Christian Andersen, the readers of these stories may be expected to be more achievement-oriented. In the Indonesian tales, one finds a struggle between the "goods," represented usually by royalty, and the "bads," represented by giants and "outsiders." As in our own cowboy stories, the "goods" consistently lose at first and are in danger of being overwhelmed. At the end, in Indonesian stories, the "goods" win, not by their own efforts but by the intervention of the gods or by magic, a result not likely to encourage individual initiative.

The populace must be change-oriented and achievement-conscious if innovations are to occur and be accepted. Otherwise, the managerial type of businessman will predominate and routine operation will prevail. The hardest job in getting development started is to break the hold of tradition. Once this is done and innovation is accepted, development becomes possible. McClelland[40] emphasizes this in his analysis of how to accelerate economic growth. His major recommendation is to "pay attention to the effects your *plans* will have on the values, motives, and attitudes of people because *in the long run* it is these factors that will determine whether the plans are successful in speeding economic development." [41] He summarizes his recommendations as: Break the orientation toward tradition and increase other directedness; increase achievement motivation; and provide for a better allocation of achievement-motivated resources. To do this, he recommends stressing new types of interpersonal relations; increasing communication and contact; conducting an ideological campaign, using the appeal of national pride, religion, or even Communism for those so inclined; adopting a free press; emancipating women; getting the children to participate in group play and activities; producing outside the home; decreasing parental dominance; altering the children's stories; and giving management more prestige. He cites also the influence of reform movements in religion.

The businessman and the innovator must be given status and social prestige if the best and most creative people are to be attracted into business.[42] The innovator, whether a government official or a private enterpriser, must be able to look forward to rewards. In a private enterprise system, this will be accomplished through an opportunity to make profits. In government, it must come through promotion, salary increases, awards, and honors. The top official must be innovation-minded and must encourage it at all levels.

Entry into business or other new activities must not be limited by any personal criterion other than ability. Whenever people who may have ideas are eliminated through institutions of class, caste, or other discriminatory treatment, or advancement comes primarily through favoritism, a loss of potential ideas occurs. Discrimination against any able minority retards a country's advance. To get continuous innovation, there must be a constant entrance of new entrepreneurs, for there is a tendncy for many to try to protect a previous innovation and resist further change or encroachment on it. Schumpeter,[43] for example, felt that innovations were most apt to be made by the new firm and the new man.

There must also be financial institutions to make capital available to men with ideas and such adequate supporting facilities as roads, communications, and power. In other words, the business enterpriser is limited by his economic environment. To improve this requires government action and proper planning. In addition, government policies must promote and not destroy the incentive of businessmen to become entrepreneurs. Government cannot compete too actively with new enterprises nor can it tax them too heavily. Governments can help by supplying information, especially about improved technologies, by protecting property and contract rights, and by providing a sound monetary and tax system.

Some analysts[44] have stressed the necessity for promoting a new emerging class, especially a disadvantaged one or one just below the ruling elite, on the grounds that they will be interested in promoting change, whereas the *top* elite will be more often satisfied with the status quo. Examples of such vigorous groups have been the Jews in various countries, the Armenians, and the Chinese in Southeast Asia. This principle may be called "the law of the subordinated group" or the "creative minority." In addition, incentives to innovate may be provided by the temporary importation of foreign entrepreneurs. The experience of Sears, Roebuck and Company[45] in promoting industry in Mexico illustrates this.

Growth itself increases the supply of entrepreneurs. As development proceeds and the expectations of profit improve, one can expect a rise in the quantity of entrepreneurs. The desire for gain exists everywhere, and it would probably be surprising how fast entrepreneurs would develop if the opportunities existed and some began to be successful. To speed this, there should be opportunities for small-scale enterprise, especially the availability of capital and credit and research into improved technologies suitable for small-scale enterprise.

## REFERENCES

1. DOMAR, E. D., "On the Measurement of Technological Change." *Economic Journal* (December, 1961), p. 709.
2. MACLAURIN, W. R., "The Sequence from Invention to Innovation and its Relation to Economic Growth." *Quarterly Journal of Economics* (February, 1953), pp. 97-111.
3. BROZEN, Y., "Determinants of the Direction of Technological Change." *American Economic Review, Proceedings* (May, 1953), p. 289.
4. ALLEN, F. R., and W. F. OGBURN, "Technological Development and Per Capita Income." *American Journal of Sociology* (September, 1957), pp. 127-31. Ogburn, W. F., "Technology and the Standard of Living in the United States." *American Journal of Sociology* (January, 1955), pp. 380-86. Enke, S., *Economics for Development.* Englewood Cliffs, N.J., Prentice-Hall, Inc., 1963, pp. 93, 94.
5. SCHUMPETER, J. A., *Business Cycles.* New York, McGraw-Hill Book Co., Inc., 1939. Schumpeter, *The Theory of Economic Development.* Cambridge, Mass., Harvard University Press, 1934.
6. DUESENBERRY, J., "Innovation and

Growth." *American Economic Review, Proceedings* (May, 1956), pp. 134-41.

7. FISHER, A. G. B., "Implications of Material Progress." *International Labour Review* (July, 1935), p. 18.

8. GILFILLAN, S. C., "The Prediction of Technical Change." *Review of Economics and Statistics* (November, 1952), pp. 368-85. Maclaurin, *op. cit.*

9. HAGEN, E. E., *On the Theory of Social Change.* Homewood, Ill., Dorsey Press, 1962, Chaps. 11 and 12. Belshaw, H., *Population Growth and Level of Consumption.* London, George Allen & Unwin, Ltd., 1960, Chaps. 9 and 10.

10. LEWIS, W. A., *Theory of Economic Growth.* Homewood, Ill., Richard D. Irwin, Inc., 1955, Chap. 4.

11. HAGEN, *op. cit.*, pp. 185ff.

12. *Ibid.*, p. 238.

13. BELSHAW, *op. cit.*, p. 153.

14. BROZEN, Y., "Technological Change, Ideology and Productivity." *Political Science Quarterly* (December, 1955), pp. 522-42.

15. BROZEN, Y., "Invention, Innovation, and Imitation." *American Economic Review, Proceedings* (May, 1951), pp. 239-57.

16. International Bank for Reconstruction and Development, *Economic Development of Ceylon.* Baltimore, Johns Hopkins Press, 1953, pp. 799ff.

17. HOSELITZ, B. F., *The Progress of Underdeveloped Areas.* Chicago, University of Chicago Press, 1952.

18. "Production Techniques and Employment Creation in Underdeveloped Countries." *International Labour Review* (August, 1958), pp. 121-50.

19. ROSEN, G., *Industrial Change in India.* New York, The Free Press of Glencoe, 1958, pp. 147ff. Bhatt, V. V., *Employment and Capital Formation in Underdeveloped Economies.* Bombay, Orient Longmans, 1960, pp. 45ff.

20. HIRSCHMAN, A. O., *Strategy of Eco-*

*nomic Development.* New Haven, Yale University Press, 1958, pp. 145-55. (Develops this idea extensively.)

21. ROSEN, *op. cit.*, p. 156.

22. "Production Techniques . . . ," *loc. cit.*, p. 124.

23. HIRSCHMAN, *op. cit.*, p. 151. Bhatt, *op. cit.*, pp. 42, 48.

24. LEIBENSTEIN, HARVEY, *Economic Backwardness and Economic Growth.* New York, John Wiley & Sons, Inc., 1957, pp. 94ff.

25. *Ibid.*, pp. 264ff.

26. Department of Economic Affairs, *Technical Assistance for Economic Development.* New York, United Nations, 1948. (Gives a full description of the original types of aid provided.)

27. Department of Public Information, *I Saw Technical Assistance Change Lives,* 1957; *Techniques for Tomorrow,* 1956; *Sharing Skills,* 1953. New York, United Nations. Teaf, H. M., and P. G. Franck, *Hands Across Frontiers.* Ithaca, N.Y., Cornell University Press, 1955.

28. MEIER, G. M., and R. E. BALDWIN, *Economic Development.* New York, John Wiley & Sons, Inc., pp. 415ff.

29. Public Administration Clearing House, "Experience of Personnel of United States Voluntary Agencies." *Economic Development and Cultural Change* (June, 1954), pp. 329-49. Franck, P. G., and D. S., "Implementation of U.N. Technical Assistance Programs." *International Conciliation* (February, 1951), pp. 61-80. Teaf and Franck, *op. cit.* "I.L.O. Productivity Missions to Underdeveloped Countries." *International Labour Review,* vol. I (July, 1957), pp. 1-29; vol. II (August, 1957), pp. 139-66. Hull, W. J., "Growing Pains of International Technical Cooperation," *International Labour Review* (October, 1961), pp. 223-45. Goldschmidt, W. R., "The Interrelations Between Culture Factors and the Acquisition of New Technical

Skills," in B. F. Hoselitz, *op. cit.,* pp. 149-51.

30. SUNDAR SINGH, JOHN D. K., "Community Development and Economic Growth in India (Kanyakumari District)." Unpublished Ph.D. dissertation, University of Massachusetts, 1960, pp. 83ff.

31. "I.L.O. Productivity Missions . . . ," *loc. cit.,* pp. 14ff.

32. *Ibid.* (August, 1957), pp. 139ff.

33. GOLDSCHMIDT, *op. cit.,* pp. 135-51.

34. RADLICH, FRITZ, "The Business Leader in Theory and Reality." *American Journal of Economics and Sociology* (April, 1949), pp. 223-37.

35. DANHOF, C. H., "Observations on Entrepreneurship in Agriculture," in A. Cole, ed., *Change and the Entrepreneur.* Cambridge, Mass., Harvard University Press, 1949, pp. 22-24.

36. SAYIGH, Y. A., *Entrepreneurs of Lebanon.* Cambridge, Mass., Harvard University Press, 1962, p. 26.

37. Department of Economic and Social Affairs, *Development of Manufacturing Industry in Egypt, Israel and Turkey.* New York, United Nations, 1958, p. 83. *Processes and Problems of Industrialization in Underdeveloped Countries.* New York, United Nations, 1955, p. 31.

38. MCCLELLAND, D. C., *The Achieving Society.* Princeton, N.J., D. Van

Nostrand Company, Inc., 1961. Hagen, E. E., *op. cit.* Sayigh, *op. cit.* Williamson, H. F., and J. A. Buttrick, *Economic Development.* Englewood Cliffs, N.J., Prentice-Hall, Inc., 1955, Chap. 6. Brozen, Y., *Entrepreneurship and Technological Change.* New Haven, Yale University Press, pp. 196-241.

39. MCCLELLAND, *op. cit.,* pp. 75ff.

40. *Ibid.,* pp. 391ff.

41. *Ibid.,* p. 393.

42. GERSCHENKRON, A., "Social Attitudes, Entrepreneurship and Economic Development," in L. H. Dupriez, ed., *Economic Progress.* Louvain, Institute of Economic and Social Research, 1955, pp. 307-29. (Discusses the social attitudes necessary to create entrepreneurs.)

43. SCHUMPETER, J. A., *Business Cycles,* vol. I, *loc. cit.,* p. 96.

44. HAGEN, *op. cit.* Kerr, C., J. T. Dunlop, F. Harbison, and C. A. Myers, "Industrialism and World Society." *Harvard Business Review* (January-February, 1961), p. 114.

45. WOLF, C., JR., and S. C. SUFRIN, *Capital Formation and Foreign Investment in Underdeveloped Areas.* Syracuse, N.Y., Syracuse University Press, 1955, p. 28.

## ADDITIONAL READINGS

AUBREY, H. G., "Industrial Investment Decisions." *Journal of Economic History* (December, 1955), pp. 335-50.

BASTER, J., "A Second Look at Point Four." *American Economic Review, Proceedings* (May, 1951), pp. 399-406.

BROZEN, Y., "Research, Technology, and Productivity." Industrial Relations Research Association, *Industrial Productivity* (December, 1951), pp. 25-49.

CARLIN, E. A., "Schumpeter's Constructed

Type, the Entrepreneur." *Kyklos,* Fasc. I (1956), pp. 27-43.

DALTON, G., "Traditional Production in Primitive African Economies." *Quarterly Journal of Economics* (August, 1962), pp. 360-78.

ESPY, W. R., *Bold New Program.* New York, Harper & Bros., 1950.

HOSELITZ, B. F., "Entrepreneurship and Economic Growth." *American Journal of Economics and Sociology* (October, 1952), pp. 97-110.

HUSAIN, A. F. A., *Human and Social Impact of Technological Change in*

*Pakistan.* Pakistan, Geoffrey Cumberlege, Oxford University Press, 1957.

MEIER, R. L., *Science and Economic De-*velopment. New York, John Wiley & Sons, Inc., 1956.

"Technical Assistance." *International Conciliation* (January, 1950), pp. 1-48.

# CHAPTER
# 9

# *Financing Economic Development— Domestic Sources*

## The Need for Capital

Previous chapters have indicated the need for considerable investment in many areas. Large amounts of capital goods* are needed if a country is to produce the large amounts of goods and services required to meet the needs of rapidly growing populations experiencing modern development. Some improvement can take place by increasing the productivity of existing factors of production (for example, by improving agricultural techniques), but

---

\* Capital goods, or simply capital, as the term is often used, are most simply defined as man-made instruments of production. This includes such things as factory buildings, machines and other tools, and equipment; social overheads, such as roads, harbors, and school buildings; irrigation projects; residential and office construction; and inventories. Today, more and more, investment in human beings is also being considered as capital. Investment in any durable good or service that makes a population more productive can be considered as capital creation. Capital goods are to be distinguished from financial capital, or the funds used to procure capital goods. Unfortunately, the simple word *capital* is usually used to refer to both.

for significant improvements a country must add to its resources of capital and land.

Capital goods are so important for development that there has been a tendency to emphasize the need for capital accumulation beyond the need for other changes. It is important, but it must be remembered that capital accumulation is not the sole requirement for development. Technological change, entrepreneurial development, and social and cultural changes, among other things, must accompany capital formation. All must occur together. Nevertheless, it is important to emphasize separately the need to accumulate capital equipment and the problems involved.

Capital equipment contributes much to economic development by raising the productivity of the economy. Productivity can be increased within limits by using additional quantities of the same kinds of capital (capital widening), but for extensive development, not only more but better capital (capital deepening) is required. The use of capital equipment gives the worker more power, more speed, and greater accuracy, and thus permits better quality. It permits worker specialization, allowing the more gifted to devote their talents to the more demanding tasks and the less gifted to perform the routine operations. Capital equipment permits greater productivity in a smaller space, and so allows better control of operations and requires less transport of goods. It permits man to operate higher in the air, deeper in the earth, and on and under water. Moreover, technological change, which has been pointed out as the great need for increased productivity, can take place usually only as new capital goods are created.

One of the major problems of many underdeveloped countries is that they have lacked sufficient capital goods. As a result they have had to use a much larger proportion of labor in their production activities. The result, of course, is diminishing returns per worker.

Thus, the inability to provide the proper kinds and amount of capital equipment can limit economic development; it is no wonder that the accumulation of capital has usually been stressed by writers on development. As population grows and development proceeds, more and more capital is required. Even if each additional unit would yield the same output as preceding ones, population increases would require large amounts of new capital. Capital itself is just as subject to diminishing returns as any other factor, so that capital must be accumulated even faster than the rate of population increase, except as offset by capital-saving technological improvements. However, it appears that, on balance, technological improvements are capital using, and therefore even faster rates of accumulation seem necessary. Since capital is such a limiting factor, it is generally assumed that there would be more production if there were more capital.

The usual situation in underdeveloped countries is one of a scarcity of capital goods. A country cannot consider a development program without considering the means of financing it. Paying for the development program may be a major problem.

Capital goods are created as a result of saving, or of expending effort on the creation of goods that are not consumed immediately but which produce other goods. One can produce capital directly: for example, the primitive fisherman might devote some of his time not in attempting to catch fish with his bare hands but in making a spear or a net. Or a farmer might use part of his time to dig an irrigation ditch. The process of saving is thus one of devoting positive effort to the making of producer goods. Today, however, people generally save by putting aside part of the money they have acquired by their productive efforts. They do not usually invest; that is, utilize these funds to buy materials and hire laborers to produce capital goods. For the most part, different people save and invest. The investor may use some of his own savings, but usually he relies on utilizing the savings of others. Thus, several things are necessary for the creation of capital goods. Some workers must refrain from spending all their money on consumption goods. There must be institutional arrangements by which these savings are made available for would-be investors. There must be people willing to make investments, which implies an economic environment suitable for investment. Most underdeveloped countries experience difficulties in each of these stages.

Thus, it is important that there be sources to finance the purchase and creation of capital equipment. The usual sources are domestic savings and foreign borrowings. Characteristic of most underdeveloped countries is a shortage of domestic savings, for various reasons, which will be discussed later. Because domestic savings are low, there is a tendency to rely on foreign borrowing or grants. Possible exceptions to this are the oil-rich countries. However, even in such countries the needs for development are so great that the large oil revenues may not be adequate for financing all the needs. Thus, there are probably no countries, including the most advanced, which do not need to make conscious efforts to develop their savings.

However, as we shall see, foreign aid is quite limited and is inadequate to finance the world's needs. If development is to proceed rapidly (to the extent capital is the limiting factor), the funds will have to come from domestic sources. Because voluntary savings, at least at first, are not apt to be great because of low incomes and low investment opportunities, other means must be found, including involuntary savings. These will be examined in turn.

The crucial period of development is at its beginning, for it is at this time that the capacity to save is lowest. As development proceeds, more can be saved (and also probably more borrowed). E. M. Bernstein[1] says that foreign investment can develop a modern sector in an underdeveloped country but that much more is needed to develop an economy. A national economy requires a widespread development of the local economy, and this requires domestic savings and domestic entrepreneurship. The real problem is usually government's unwillingness to persuade people to divert their funds from consumption to investment, for this may involve heavy taxation or other unpleasant measures.

However, A. K. Cairncross[2] believes that the principle of capital accumulation is greatly overemphasized. He says that capital cannot bring growth by itself, and the growth of capital can account, in fact, for only about one-fourth of the recorded rate of economic progress. Other things, he says, are more important, particularly technological innovation or new and cheaper ways of doing things. However, it usually takes capital to introduce technological innovations, and usually there are enough known uses for funds at any one time so that capital is the limiting factor. Nevertheless, it is important to recognize that other factors have an important role to play and that the difficulty of providing for them in some circumstances may be greater than that of accumulating capital. Besides technological innovation there must be a development of entrepreneurship, a general development, so that there is an incentive to invest as well as a scale of values conducive to saving, investing, and innovating, among other things. Wolf and Sufrin[3] say that the accumulation of capital is not so much one of scarce resources as of competing values. In addition, for development to proceed satisfactorily, there must be an optimum allocation of the country's resources and especially an economy in the use of government funds, for large amounts of potential savings may be wasted in extravagant expenditure and excessive personnel.

This need for complementary factors and conditions has given rise to the concept of "the ability to absorb capital." Theoretically, there is no limit to the amount of capital a country can absorb if it is willing to import foreign personnel, hire an army of people to compel obedience to government decrees, provide the necessary purchasing power, and so on. But the concept of ability to absorb capital refers to the amount that can be profitably employed under existing conditions. This amount depends on a number of factors, such as the quantity and quality of complementary resources; facilitating conditions, such as the existence of social overheads; monetary and legal institutions, and the existence of markets; and the rate of population growth.

How much capital do the underdeveloped countries require? The exact amount is subject to debate and is estimated at widely varying quantities. Whatever the right amount is, one can be sure of one thing: It is larger than the funds likely to be readily available to these countries. The most widely quoted figure is $19 billion a year, of which about $14 billion would have to be obtained by foreign aid, if national incomes are to be raised 2 percent a year.[4] Paul Alpert[5] says this is now thought to be too high, for it is based on an investment of $2,500 per employed industrial worker, which is based on the experience of advanced industrial countries where industry is apt to be more capital-intensive than in the labor-surplus, underdeveloped countries. Also, an incremental capital output ratio of 7.5 was used in arriving at the estimate, but this ratio is larger than that actually experienced. Alpert also reports a 1953 estimate by Everett Hagen of $9 to $12 billion, with foreign aid requirements of $4 to $7 billion.

These figures are deduced by estimating each country's needs, as each country must do in formulating its own development program. The amount required depends on the objectives, the rate of population increase, and the productivity of capital and other factors. As population grows, capital must be added just to keep the standard of living stationary. If population is growing by 2 percent a year and the marginal capital/output ratio is 4:1, it would be necessary to add capital equal to 8 percent of the national income just to increase total output by the 2 percent necessary to offset the population increase. If, in addition, there is a desire to raise living standards by, say, 2 percent a year, slightly more than an additional 8 percent of the national income must be raised.

Too much should not be inferred from this illustration. The assumed population-increase figure is quite realistic, and even low in some cases, but there is uncertainty as to the proper marginal capital/output ratio to apply to individual countries. In some cases it may be below and in some above, especially in the case of countries that require large investments in activities which will yield increased productivity only over a long period. The ratio may vary for different countries and at different times. Even at very low ratios, the amount of capital formation required to raise living standards for the rapidly rising populations is beyond the low levels of savings of most underdeveloped countries.

Another need is to establish balance among saving, investing, consumption (spending), and production. As a country starts to develop, expenditures for development will exceed the increase in output (the capital/output ratio is more than 1:1). These expenditures are made to purchase materials and to pay people, so that many have funds to spend and generally do spend them on consumption goods, mostly necessities. If the supply of the necessities they wish to buy is inelastic, which is usually the case, there is pressure on prices. Unless savings increase (which is unlikely) or the excess purchasing power is siphoned off in imports (which will not be permitted because of import restrictions), government taxation must be utilized to reduce this inflationary gap. As we shall see, instituting good tax systems is not an easy task. As a matter of fact, most governments find that the amount of funds they need for their current expenditure and their development program is more than they can comfortably raise; therefore, the governments contribute to the inflationary gap through deficit spending.

The proper amount of saving and consumption is a problem for any country. Underdeveloped countries need all the savings they can muster to construct the capital equipment they need. But they also need all the purchasing power they can get in order to provide an incentive to invest. Unfortunately, savings are both a source of investment and a drain on purchasing power. Balancing these is one of the major problems in economic planning. The ideal is that total savings cover all investment and that total incomes minus savings equal the supply of goods and services. Achieving this is no easy task.

Thus, countries need to take into account in their investment plans the amount of savings—voluntary and involuntary—that is available to them. This will determine how much can be spent for development purposes without upsetting the country's financial stability. This means surveying the different sources, as will be done below. The relative desirability of the different methods will vary from country to country and must be related to the specific situation. However, the general character of each source can be examined. For the most part, for the reasons stated previously, considerable effort should be made to finance domestically as much as possible of the development.

## Making Use of the Unemployed

One possible way of creating capital is to put to work the unemployed and the disguised unemployed. The theory is that these workers must be maintained anyway and that they contribute little or nothing to output, so they might just as well be put to some useful work, particularly on projects that require little capital. Actually, most construction does use local labor, the first problem being to find projects for which the skills of the unemployed are suitable. This does not make available a wide range of suitable projects. Probably the most suitable are simple roads, irrigation ditches, and perhaps simple schools. India has used this technique to construct roads between villages. Indonesia has constructed school buildings and other village facilities through a process of mutual self-help. This is a different concept than that of having the state employ the unemployed, but one that could well be developed elsewhere. The U.S.S.R. appears to have used many of its subjects as virtual slave labor gangs to build roads and improve farms.

There is no question but that much potential manpower goes to waste in underdeveloped countries, as described in Chapter 6. Wolf and Sufrin[6] estimate that India wastes each year as many gross man-years of labor as are contributed each year by the labor force of the United States. Maintaining such idleness is a great drain on potential savings.

Using these unemployed seems an easy way to compensate for capital scarcity, and this may be of some help, but it is unlikely that it can contribute very significantly because of the limited skills of the workers. Also, the practice assumes that there are large numbers of unemployed or disguised unemployed and that the diversion of their efforts would not reduce production elsewhere. True, large numbers of workers (the potentially unemployed) could be released if simple new techniques were introduced in many areas (such as agriculture, selling, street transportation, and household service), but these changes require some capital, and it is always a question whether this may be the most effective use of a country's capital. It is also true that during much of the year there is disguised unemployment on the farms, but workers cannot be drained off permanently, for production would suffer at certain seasons when all workers are needed. Such workers could be useful on off-season projects, but, otherwise, their contribution to capital construction would be at the expense of farm production. Longer-range projects might prove wasteful of capital because irregular attendance would force capital to remain idle at times.*

Moreover, the worker, unless forced, which would require paid guards, would usually demand some compensation above that obtained when not working. As new roads or irrigation ditches are built, there must be an investment in other facilities to make them useful. Moreover, these projects might not result directly in increased output, so that if increased wages were paid, there would be a further addition to the inflationary pressures.

Thus, such projects are seldom costless, and so should be weighed carefully when a country is considering its investment alternatives. H. Belshaw[7] says, for example, that it makes more sense to put the money into fertilizer or other agricultural projects that would increase production quickly and help the farmer directly. Nevertheless, the use of the unemployed should be considered. It is likely that there are many worthwhile projects that require little capital and use much local labor, but it is not certain that this will

---

* This is based on the premise that most projects will require the use of some capital.

necessarily be so. The best results from using otherwise idle labor are apt to be realized from individuals working on their own properties or by community mutual-aid projects adapted to the Indonesian model.


## The Sale of Resources

Primary materials such as agricultural products, minerals, and oil may be sold abroad and the resulting foreign exchange used to import capital goods.* In particular, the oil-rich countries find this a good way to acquire the means to purchase capital goods, even though they may use the funds otherwise. Other primary products can serve the same purpose, but few products have the ready market that oil enjoys.

However, there are problems, and it is doubtful if any country, except one favorably situated with respect to markets or the possession of a particularly desirable product, can rely on this to a large extent. Because the markets for most primary products are expanding slowly, there is not much hope for great expansion of this source of capital, although there are, of course, resources yet to be discovered or not readily accessible at present.

In the first place, the markets for most primary products are unstable, so the foreign exchange earnings are unstable also. A sudden drop in earnings may disrupt a development plan. The markets for most primary products are expanding slowly, if at all, and there is a growing competition with synthetics. Thus, this is an uncertain source at best, except for a possible few countries. However, no country is likely to abandon a product it already sells unless it can slowly substitute a more favorable one. Expansion of output, especially in competition with other underdeveloped countries, holds very little promise.

Second, there is often resentment against the presence of foreign firms and personnel and a belief that they take out an undue share of the proceeds. Hence, exploitation of primary products by foreign firms ordinarily conflicts with a country's nationalistic pride.

Third, the old role of the underdeveloped country under colonialism was as the supplier of raw materials to an advanced country already industrialized. Hence, there is a presumed relationship between the production of primary products and dependency and between industrialization and independence. Therefore, many people resent the implication of dependency and underdevelopment and do not wish to advance primary production.

---

* The same could be said for any export. However, facilities to produce a marketable manufactured product involve many problems and markets are more difficult to develop. Foreign capital and personnel are usually available to develop the minerals, oil, and plantation products.

Lastly, reliance on primary products too often has not led to development but to a dualistic economy. If the returns go to a few who spend their incomes on luxury imports or invest abroad, little benefit is derived by the local economy. On the other hand, if the local production of necessities is inelastic to the extent that added incomes do go to local citizens and is not taxed away, inflationary pressures are exerted.

One variant has been the operation[8] of marketing boards for agricultural products as a means of capturing rising incomes for government use and for stabilizing prices. The farmer sells his crop to the board at a given price and the board markets the product. Various arrangements are possible for the distribution of the proceeds, but a common one is for the government to hold the profits. In poor seasons, the government continues to pay the farmer the fixed price and recoups its losses from any accumulated surplus. Unless the prices paid are realistic, output is apt to suffer.

## Domestic Private Savings

In the long run, a country must do its own saving. Loans must ultimately be repaid or credit will be stopped. Grants cannot be expected to be continued forever. Outside aid may be necessary to help a country get started, but ultimately domestic saving must take over the job of providing the necessary capital. The willingness of a country to promote domestic saving may be the best test of whether a country will make the total effort necessary for growth.

It would be preferable to finance development by using a country's own resources. Outside interests would not be involved, so that foreign private investors or foreign governments would not be in a position to exert an influence on the government's program. Financing capital accumulation through domestic saving is less inflationary than foreign borrowing. If foreign borrowing is used to pay for imported capital goods, local labor and materials will have to be used with this capital, and payments to these will be spent on necessities that are apt to be in inelastic supply. Unless these wages and other local expenditures are offset (until finished products result) by savings, either public or private, inflationary pressures will arise. This in itself may discourage further savings. Unfortunately, foreign loans are not usually available for small enterprises but only for a few large isolated projects where products may be long delayed. This is the difference between developing a modern sector in an underdeveloped country and developing an economy. In other words, for an economy to develop there must be a substantial amount of local enterprise, which requires domestic saving.

However, underdeveloped countries do not save and accumulate capital in large quantity, which is one of the major reasons why they are underdeveloped. The institutions and attitudes of the people are often such that saving is not popular, and much of the saving that does occur does not go into productive capital goods. For such countries to develop, a conscious effort must be made to increase savings, either from existing incomes or by capturing a major share of the rising incomes that result from inducing greater effort and productivity or from securing outside funds.

The capacity for underdeveloped countries to save is usually thought to be relatively small for various reasons. Standards of living are low, the typical situation being one of low productivity, low incomes, and a necessity to spend all one's income in an effort to survive. As incomes rise, there is a tendency for families to grow as larger numbers of children are enabled to survive. The masses, under the influence of contact with the peoples of the richer countries, are insisting on rising consumption standards. Political instability and inflation also discourage saving.

Saving is usually thought of as being typically about 5 percent of national income, an amount far too low to provide rising standards of productivity. However, estimates show a marked divergence in the rate. A United Nations study of the Far East[9] estimated the following rates of net domestic saving (percentage of gross national product): Burma, 13.6; Ceylon, 10.4; mainland China, 10.3; Taiwan, 3.9; Malaya, 17.5; India, 8.5; Indonesia, 2.8; Japan, 20.9; South Korea, 1.2; Pakistan, 2.5; Philippines, 2.0; and Thailand, 9.3. Only Japan and Malaya had net domestic savings of 15 percent, and Malaya, according to the same report, invested half of her savings abroad. Several others reached 10 percent, the amount designated as necessary for the takeoff in Rostow's concept. In another report[10] the net domestic savings of thirty-seven countries was estimated. Three saved 15 percent or more: Venezuela, 16; Congo, 16; and Malta, 15. Eight others saved between 10 and 14 percent, and ten saved between 5 and 9 percent. Thus, the savings picture is not bright.

It is not certain that the capacity of the underdeveloped countries to save is as low as sometimes supposed. Some countries obviously do fairly well and others might match this if given the right incentives. Some of the poorest have numerous expensive temples, as evidence of the capacity to save. In some cases there are net capital outflows that are held or invested abroad. The Latin American countries, for example, hold large assets abroad. It was mentioned above that half of Malaya's savings are invested abroad. Two-thirds of the public savings in Nigeria between 1950 and 1952 accumulated abroad.[11]

The Japanese experience shows that it is possible for a country in its poor stage to save large amounts. Japan received a relatively small amount of foreign capital during its developing period and relied largely on voluntary savings. The Japanese have a high propensity to save, and most families seem to try to save some of their incomes. Exploitation of the farmer and the laborer played its part, as well as a willingness to introduce advanced techniques rapidly, thus increasing profits. Adequate savings institutions were introduced early and political conditions were quite stable. As development has proceeded, some of these conditions are disappearing, but the propensity to save out of rising incomes seems to be increasing,[12] and there has been a sharp rise in the rate of government investment. This experience holds hope for other underdeveloped countries if guided by the right policies.

In every underdeveloped country there are a few people with very large incomes who might be expected to have considerable savings. However, they tend to spend lavishly on luxury living, to invest abroad, to buy land and buildings or jewelry, or to speculate in trade. None of these transactions adds productive capacity unless the receiver of the funds invests, which apparently does not happen. Alexander[13] points out that there are normally four groups of savers: landlords, merchants, higher government officials, and professional people. He says landlords prefer buying land and shun manufacturing as being socially degrading. Merchants sometimes start manufactures, but are usually interested in quick profit margins. Government officials are interested in putting their money where it is safe and cannot be confiscated. Professional people do tend to invest in industry once it gets started.

The problem is that there is little incentive to invest in productive facilities, for markets are limited in the absence of a development program. It is likely that as investment opportunities begin to appear, savings will rise also and be invested in such undertakings.

However, even if the rich were to have a high savings potential, there would be a limited amount of savings. If a country is to have sufficient savings, much of it must come from people with medium and low incomes. The majority of the people have very low incomes and do not appear to have much capacity to save, but the fact is that they spend large amounts on tobacco, liquor, and amusements[14] and divert surprisingly large sums to various ceremonials or contributions to the temples. These latter may be more desirable than saving for development for noneconomic reasons, but they do compete for potential savings. Despite these things, many still manage to save a little. Unfortunately, these savings are likely to be in the form of hoarded cash or jewelry.* Moreover, as incomes have risen, there does not appear to have been any increase in the propensity to save, caused by larger

* Governments could compensate for this hoarded cash without adding to inflation by issuing an equivalent amount of paper money.

families and the demonstration effect. It is possible for the low-income people of the underdeveloped countries to contribute much more in savings than they do. The problem is how to increase the motivation and how to collect the savings so as to make them available to industry.

In advanced countries the great bulk of the savings is done by businesses, especially corporations. The lack of established businesses is the largest handicap of underdeveloped countries in their efforts to increase savings. As businesses develop, they most certainly will save and improve the savings outlook for these countries. Until this happens it is unlikely, except in exceptional cases, that underdeveloped countries can develop by relying entirely on voluntary personal efforts. To come closer to having a satisfactory savings ratio, governments must take a hand. As previously stressed, many steps must be taken in order to promote development, but one of the most important is the increase of savings.

From the standpoint of one who feels that it is desirable to have as much individual freedom as is consistent with other objectives, the most desirable effort is in the direction of encouraging voluntary savings. To the extent this fails to meet the desired objectives of development, it would then be necessary to force savings in one way or another.

One possible solution is to increase the inequality of incomes, for it is general experience that it is the rich who save the most. However, as pointed out previously, in underdeveloped countries there is a strong tendency for the rich to spend on luxury living, to import heavily, and to invest in other than domestic productive facilities. The result is that inequality does not assure a high rate of effective saving and investment. With proper incentives, however, their savings might become directed into production. Inequality of income is very high already, and too little savings have been forthcoming. To try to increase the inequality of incomes in the light of existing attitudes would be grossly unfair, would be politically impossible except under strong dictatorship, and would hardly be an effective way to accomplish the desired objectives. The more usual solution is taxation of the wealthy to lessen inequality.

W. A. Lewis[15] says that the way to increase savings from 5 to 12 percent is to encourage the emergence of entrepreneurs, who, he says (with good reason) are thriftier than other groups, either public or private. This need not mean increasing maldistribution of income, for communities where profits are large do not have the greatest inequality. For one thing, rents may be a smaller proportion of total income. Entrepreneurs save because this is their road to power and status. Such a capitalistic sector can be encouraged by providing security of investments against expropriation and arbitrary raids; increasing the profitability of investment through cheap labor, technological progress, improved communications, and so on; and promoting the entrepreneurial type of businessman. However, development must be on its way before this takes place.

In view of the improbability that entrepreneurs will develop until initial savings are used to get development started, and the probability that taxation will be used to lessen inequality of incomes, there must be an effort to encourage in the majority of the people a desire to save. This will be difficult because of the universal desire for rising standards of living. The alternative, however, is an autocratic government that forces contributions from the people and devotes these savings to whatever purposes seem desirable to the government.

In the long run, the supply of savings is institutionally determined. It is influenced by such factors as the desire for security, for power, for certain living standards, for social emulation, and by the rate of growth and level of new things to buy, by one's concern for his children, and so on. Thus, people must acquire attitudes that make them want to save. The Weber-Tawney thesis[16] held, for example, that a major reason why the early Protestant countries developed was that the early Protestant doctrines taught the virtue of plain living and saving. It can be added also that ostentatious church buildings were discouraged among some, thus making savings available for industry and trade. The taking of interest was also made respectable. Wolf and Sufrin[17] say that the failure to accumulate capital is not so much a matter of scarce resources as of competing values, and that these must be changed, at least marginally. Values that stress production must be substituted for those that stress the maintenance of status.

An autocratic government may induce development faster, at least in the initial stages, for such a government can hold down living standards while drawing off the excess income. The U.S.S.R. and mainland China have practiced this to a considerable degree. Such governments can hold off such large drains on capital as housing and luxury consumption. They can be more selective in expenditures for education, transportation, and so forth.

If a government decides to force savings, the first decision it will have to make is who is to be asked to give up purchasing power over consumer goods, which is what saving requires. Various people have been called on in the past, either through government action or the lack of government action, the farmer and the worker being the usual targets. R. J. Alexander[18] points out that in England, the farmer paid heavily by the enclosure movement and the repeal of the Corn Laws and the worker was penalized through long hours and low pay. The profits of the slave trade also helped. In Soviet Russia, the peasants, the workers, and the former aristocrats and capitalists were singled out. In the United States, those who were most affected were the foreign investor, immigrants, and the agricultural population. The workers contributed to some extent, but never to the same extent as those in England or Russia. Japan taxed the farmer heavily while enter-prisers exploited the worker. Present underdeveloped countries find it more difficult to exploit the worker and the farmer, even with dictatorial govern-ments. The agricultural landlord seems to suffer most. Thus, the exploita-tion theory of development seems difficult to apply. Only the communist governments that are in firm control espouse it openly. However, neglecting justice, savings will be maximized if those who save the most (for example, entrepreneurs) are encouraged and others (such as farmers) are discouraged by being taxed to prevent increased output from resulting in large families, and wages are kept low to encourage greater surpluses for industry.

If democratic government is desired, strong efforts must be made to in-crease voluntary savings. Unless this can be accomplished, there will be either dictatorial governments or litttle or no development.

Populations can be expected to increase their savings under the right circumstances. One deterrent is the lack of familiarity with banking institu-tions. Others are the lack of security and liquidity in investments, in gen-eral. There must be education to show the relationship between savings and development, and particularly to show their contribution to large projects. A program through the schools should be instituted. If coupled with a patri-otic drive or connected with a specific development plan that the public supports and on which it is fully informed, some progress should result, particularly if other steps are also taken.

1.  The creation of an atmosphere of general confidence and stability, including the avoidance of inflation, will lessen the greatest of savers' fears.

2.  Of special importance is the creation of various financial institutions that can collect and disburse the savings, since one of the features of eco-nomic development is the need for large projects, which require the concen-tration of the savings in a few locations. Otherwise, savings will be held in small, isolated pockets and will not be available where they are needed. These institutions must be of the type readily available to all the people and able to carry government guarantees of immediate liquidity and ensure against loss of value. High interest rates, including higher rates for time deposits, are helpful. Various types of institutions are needed in order to attract different types of savers and to serve different types of borrowers. The effect on savings depends on the number and accessibility of the finan-cial institutions, plus their safety, liquidity, and interest payment. Examples of institutions needed are cooperative credit agencies, particularly those that serve agriculture, small industries, small traders, fishermen, and so on; postal savings banks; development banks;* and the regular commercial and savings banks with which we are familiar in the advanced countries.

* Discussed later in this chapter.

In the long run, a capital market will have to develop if large businesses are to develop. As yet, such markets are deficient and people are not accustomed to buying securities. In order to promote security buying, it will be necessary to develop new types of securities in small denominations, which would offer security and liquidity. Attaching a lottery feature most likely would prove attractive.

3.    The necessity to create opportunities for profitable investment has already been mentioned. This requires a rising home market, which can come only by increasing productivity in all areas as the only feasible way of raising incomes generally. At least at first, the outlet for domestic savings will have to be in local industries. Only as these are encouraged can there be a real incentive to save.

4.    There must be controls to prevent savings from going into undesired forms; for example, exchange controls to prevent capital flight and control of speculation in excess inventories and land.

5.    Governments may increase capital formation by borrowing and investing themselves. The effect on savings depends on where the funds come from. Unless the money it raises would otherwise have been spent, no increase in savings will result. The aim is to persuade people, who would otherwise have spent savings, to lend the funds for investment. Unfortunately, fear of inflation and lack of confidence in many governments hinder this, so that governments who wish to borrow usually turn to the banks.

If the government borrows from the banks, it is apt to be highly inflationary, as banks may simply create credit for the purpose. The farther down the income scale that bonds are placed, the more likely is spending to be displaced. Thus, the big effort must be toward attracting low-income buyers. Recommendations include small denominations; convertibility at par; a higher rate of interest the longer the bond is held; possible compensation for price-level changes; and perhaps a lottery feature. Bonds for specific purposes (for example, land reform) are likely to be more popular than general bonds.

## Taxation

In the beginning stages of development it will be impossible for underdeveloped countries to rely on voluntary savings for their development needs. Despite the utmost encouragement, voluntary savings are apt to be low until development is fairly well along. In addition, all governments must undertake certain investments such as roads, water supply, and schools, at a very minimum. If capital needs are to be financed domestically, it must be done through taxation. This, of course, will result in the government being heavily involved in the economy, a different kind of economy than is known in private enterprise systems like that of the United States.* An almost unavoidable feature of attempts at development is this large role for government. In fact, one of the limiting factors in development is the ability of the country to raise funds through taxation.†

Unfortunately, attempts to finance development through taxation encounter certain problems. In the first place, taxation has many purposes, and the imperfectly developed tax systems found in underdeveloped countries make it difficult to get a proper balance among them. Among the possible purposes are to finance current expenditures, raise development funds, maintain economic stability and prevent inflation, reduce inequities in wealth and income, and maximize incentives for increasing productivity. The major conflicts are between revenue needs and justice and incentives. These create special problems.

We usually think of just taxation in terms of ability to pay, which implies progressive taxation. Unfortunately, most underdeveloped countries cannot afford this principle of taxation, for it would sharply curtail tax revenues. Most tax systems tend to be regressive. Dr. Richard Goode[19] lists the conditions necessary for a modern tax system:

1. The existence of a predominantly money economy.
2. A high standard of literacy among taxpayers.
3. Honestly and reliably maintained accounting systems.
4. A large degree of voluntary compliance on the part of taxpayers.
5. A general political belief in progressive taxation, for which free political democracy is the most conducive.
6. Honest and efficient administration.

Few underdeveloped countries can meet such tests. The indications are that the only feasible tax systems will be far more regressive than most economists would prescribe for the advanced countries. Income taxes are very difficult to impose. In many cases, the rich (for example, the landowners in Latin America) have great influence in the government and are not anxious to increase their own taxes. Only a few citizens may have incomes large enough to make the tax productive. Books are inadequately kept. Since the majority of the people are poor and illiterate, they cannot prepare returns. Much of their income is in kind. There is also the possibility that new enterprises will be discouraged.

Thus, the usual situation is the widespread use of product taxes, especially on imports and exports. One advantage of these is that the goods go

* This problem will be discussed in Chapter 13.
† Tax systems will be discussed in Chapter 12.

through relatively few hands, which makes collection easy. Import duties can be used to limit luxury consumption and to reduce unnecessary imports, but to use them as a major source of revenue could discourage capital imports. Thus, they must be selective. Care must also be used in the case of export taxes so that domestic enterprise will not be injured in international competition and thereby endanger foreign exchange earnings. In order to raise sufficient revenue, the general sales tax will undoubtedly have to be used. Real estate taxes may also help to break up large estates and force idle land into use. However, these taxes are difficult to establish and administer.

Efforts should be made to tax large incomes, luxury consumption, speculative profits, and so on, but despite the best of efforts it will be necessary to place a large burden of the taxation on low-income people. There are just too few rich to be able to provide all the funds needed. Most of the people are poor, but if development is to be brought about, they must help finance it even though the resulting tax structure is defective by Western standards. From the standpoint of justice, taxes should be as progressive as possible without discouraging enterprises, but taxes on the poor are inevitable. Discouraging the use of increases in income for consumption purposes is a necessary policy for development. The standard of justice between individuals may have to yield to the pressures of expediency and to the desired effect on the economy. R. J. Chelliah[20] lists five canons of good taxation in underdeveloped countries:

1. Taxes should absorb economic surpluses, wherever they are found.
2. Each person should contribute in accordance with his ability to contribute to economic development.
3. Taxes must prevent consumption from increasing proportionately with income.
4. As incomes rise, the share of taxation in total income should rise.
5. Taxes should be equitable among different classes of people and equal among taxpayers of the same circumstances.

If the tax systems suggested appear regressive, they would probably be less so than inflation, especially where wages and agricultural prices are controlled. They would probably be less damaging to equity than reliance on measures to increase personal savings, which would, without doubt, result in considerable maldistribution of income. If taxes were administered capably and honestly and loopholes in existing taxes were closed, there would be considerable improvement in their equity.

Using taxation as a means of raising funds is, in a sense, an alternative to encouraging savings. The purpose is the same—to dry up some part of consumption so that productive effort can be released and devoted to capital formation. The choice between the two depends on which is more effective. It should be borne in mind that increasing taxes can dry up voluntary savings and thus shift funds from private industry to government-owned industry. Taxation effectively promotes development only if it diverts funds from consumption to capital formation or from a less desirable to a more desirable spending or investment. Thus, good judgment must be exercised before instituting a tax program.

Moreover, one must take into account a proper balance between capital formation and consumption. One cannot dry up consumption excessively without making investment unproductive or bringing about political repercussions. W. A. Lewis[21] believes that 20 percent of the national income should be taken by taxation for development to proceed satisfactorily, 12 percent to be spent on public services, and 8 percent on capital investment. This would be added to the 5 percent devoted to capital formation from personal savings. Actual tax levels are somewhat below this. U. T. Wai[22] shows that in 1959, countries with per capita incomes above $500 collected 25 percent (median) of the national income in taxes; those with incomes between $200 and $500, 15.2 percent; and those with incomes below $200, 13.7 percent. However, the amounts collected varied greatly within each group. Thus, according to Lewis' standard, the funds collected are insufficient to promote development. The taxable capacity of countries undoubtedly varies with the conditions, including the height and distribution of income, the capacity of the government, and so on. The exact capacity of each country must be established by economic research.

Inherent in the effort to increase capital formation through tax funds is the necessity to curtail unnecessary government expenditures for current uses, especially the hiring of excessive personnel. Political expediency breeds the temptation to increase such expenditures when funds are at hand. Thus, governments need a rigorous control of their current budgets, which they have not achieved to any successful degree. Moreover, there must be a well-conceived economic plan for investment so that the results will be maximized.

One fear is that the use of taxation will result in the centralized control of industry in government hands and that the industries will be run inefficiently. It is not at all certain that raising capital through taxation must result in nationally operated industries. Methods should be devised to afford the possibility of placing such funds in private hands for management. Possible methods are allocation of the funds to a development bank, which can lend to private industries, or leasing government-built plants to private interests or ultimately selling them to private owners, as Japan has done.

To the extent that governments do own the new enterprises, they must follow a price policy that will aid development and accomplish other growth purposes. In some cases, operating at a loss may be the best policy if this will encourage other industries or other activities, but this is always a dangerous policy, for special interests are apt to seek such favorable treatment. Governments the world over, for example, subsidize industry and private users by providing free roads, except for some special toll roads. The schools and the post office are other examples of subsidized industry. Similar subsidies might be considered in the sale of electric power.

Price policy may be used to capture the gains from other development. For example, irrigation charges might be used to draw off some of the increase in agricultural productivity. Consumer goods industries such as sugar or tobacco might be used to gather investment funds by charges designed to make a profit. The U.S.S.R. finances itself mainly by this method.

A major obstacle has been the need to secure efficiency in the operation of such industries. Inefficiency is not inevitable, but it must be carefully guarded against. For political reasons, excessive and inefficient personnel are not unusual.

## Inflation as a Means of Financing Capital Expansion

Inflation is sometimes considered a possible means of diverting funds from consumption to capital formation, and judging by current practice, it is almost a traditional means. The theory is that governments, by issuing paper money or borrowing bank-created deposit currency and using the funds to invest, will have reduced the public's ability to buy consumption goods as prices rise under the pressure of the competition between the government and consumers for goods and services and factors of production. Thus, factors are diverted to the production of capital goods. If such inflationary measures could actually and successfully create the requisite amount of investment, there is much that could be said for such a course. There is, however, considerable doubt that it does, in the long run, result in increased investment.

It is not certain that deliberate inflation will result in greater investment, but it is virtually certain that a high rate of investment will inevitably be accompanied by inflation because savings are seldom sufficient to meet the needs. A major influencing factor is the inelasticity of supply of local products such as food, so that rising incomes brought about by increased investment expenditures will result in excess bargaining for the limited supplies. Coupled with this are a high propensity to consume and an immobility of resources.

Thus, creating excess money tends to raise prices except under special circumstances. The public is left with the same number of monetary units and the government is armed with a new supply. The two compete for the scarce goods. Rising prices would be avoided only if the newly created purchasing power merely matched the public's hoarding, or if unemployed factors would be drawn into production and could match the new money with an equivalent output of goods. Output, however, is not likely to be easily expanded in most underdeveloped countries. Also, the new investment has some gestation period, so there is no immediate output to match the money. Unless excess purchasing power is saved or taxed away, rising prices seem inevitable. In time, as output results, it is hoped that a brake will be put on the rising prices. However, it is more likely that the initial inflation will generate further monetary creation and more inflation.

A small amount of inflation may result in some capital creation by inducing people to work harder to try to maintain their incomes and by depriving them of purchasing power, but experience seems to indicate that it is unlikely that price rises can be held to small amounts. Output is much too rigid. The results of investments in roads, power, education, and other public facilities may be long delayed. Rising prices lead to increased government expenditures and so to increasingly large deficits to be financed by credit. Most governments of underdeveloped countries are poorly equipped to fight inflation.[23]

In the long run, rising prices, and especially rapidly rising prices, are apt to discourage saving and capital formation, for various reasons.[24]

1.  Rising prices lead possible investors to turn to speculation, especially in inventories.
2.  The flight of capital into foreign investment is encouraged.
3.  Holders of funds buy up tangible property, especially land, avoiding the problems and uncertainties caused by rapidly changing material prices, labor dissatisfaction, etc.
4.  Private foreign capital is discouraged.
5.  Export industries find it hard to compete and their profits are reduced as internal costs rise.
6.  Saving is discouraged, at least in the fixed-dollar types such as insurance and savings accounts.
7.  Because tax systems are relatively inflexible, government revenue does not rise so much as prices; hence the government will be soon getting a smaller part of the national output unless it creates even more money, thus promoting greater inflation.
8.  On the other hand, money seems easy for the government to get, so there is a great temptation toward government extravagance.

Other problems are encountered. As prices rise, there will be balance-of-payment problems when exports fall off and the tendency to import increases. This will act to deter the purchase of foreign capital equipment.

Moreover, inflation is really a tax on the poor and those with fixed incomes, and causes social discontent. Inflation favors speculators and black marketeers. Wage earners find their incomes lagging, but redouble their efforts to keep wages up with prices. Peasants might be expected to gain, but often their prices are controlled; for example, in Indonesia, they must deliver a given proportion of their crop to the government at a fixed price. Lastly, production is apt to shift in favor of producing luxuries, for inflation favors the wealthy, especially the speculator.

Thus, it does not appear that deliberate inflation is a proper policy for underdeveloped countries. It may appear as part of the development process, but efforts should be made to keep it in check. The real solution for inflation is to increase the supply of goods available for purchase. This, however, is not possible without financing. Diverting purchasing power and not increasing it seems the more logical way, but this means increasing taxes. Eventually, as investments are made, they will become productive and so soak up purchasing power. A big push on capital investment at one time is the danger. A coordinated development of long-term projects and short-term projects would soften the inflation.

## Expropriation

Some governments seem to feel that seizing foreign enterprises with little or no compensation, or with payments that are soon wiped out by inflation, is one way to increase the potential savings. Mexico, Cuba, Egypt, and Indonesia, for example, have expropriated foreign properties. Another and perhaps stronger motive for seizing properties, nationally as well as foreign owned, is to remove foreign influence or the influence of the rich, as in the U.S.S.R. and mainland China.

This policy may have more political than economic value.* Whether it promotes capital formation depends on circumstances. Initially, of course, it adds no real capital, for only ownership of existing physical assets is transferred. But such ownership avoids later repatriation of profits and principal to foreign countries. If the properties continue to be profitable, such surpluses can be used for investment. Such earnings that do exist can go to investment instead of to the luxury consumption of the rich (although governments have been known to engage in their own luxury spending).

Expropriation, however, may have bad effects also, which could offset

---

* M. Bronfenbrenner ("The Appeal of Confiscation in Economic Development." *Economic Development and Cultural Change* [April, 1955], pp. 201-18) discusses the economics of confiscation and defends it as increasing savings.

any possible gain. For one thing, expropriations can seldom be large enough to be really significant in the total picture of development. Foreign investors may lose their confidence and fail to invest new capital in the country. Foreign governments may cut their loans and grants and even impose trade sanctions. Lastly, there is always a question whether proper personnel are available to maintain production and profits. The Mexican oil wells retrogressed after expropriation, as have the Indonesian rubber plantations and sugar mills. The value of expropriation depends on whether the resulting operating surplus is larger than the foreign investor chose to reinvest in the country. The result can be verified only by experience.

The removal of foreign influence, however, may be a more important consideration. It would be desirable to arrive at universal rules of fair compensation or have the United Nations buy out foreign-owned enterprises when a country so desires and then lease, sell, or give them to the host country.

## Development Banks

A highly useful device, which serves at the same time to increase domestic savings and to attract foreign capital, is a relatively new type of institution called a development bank.[25] These banks are established to help provide capital to new industries, both private and public, and to assist them in their problems of getting started.

These banks take a wide diversity of forms. Some are entirely government owned; some, private; and some, both. Some can lend only to government enterprises; some, only to private; and some, to both. Some have broad planning functions; some can only lend; some can buy stock; and some can start their own businesses. Some are general and some are confined to a particular economic sector, such as industry or agriculture or cottage industry or handicrafts.

A number of functions are performed by such banks, although individual banks may be restricted in their activities. They may grant loans to worthwhile enterprises. They may provide managerial and technological advice. They may make nationwide industrial surveys. They may develop a capital market by selling their own securities or underwriting private issues. They may start industry in neglected areas.

Development banks operate with more flexible criteria than regular banks, taking into account not only profitability but also the proposed project's contribution to national objectives, such as its total impact on national income, its foreign exchange savings and earnings, its influence on other industries, and its utilization of domestic materials. This combination of criteria is the "distinguishing mark of a development bank." [26] Such banks, on the other hand, may turn down "bankable" projects because they serve no development objective. They can and do consider projects with a long payoff period. For this reason they are likely to require some participation by the government in their financing.

These banks offer considerable advantages in other ways. They can grant considerable flexibility in terms. They permit the joint participation of public and private capital. They may aid in the creation of an investment habit by offering their own securities in small denominations. They permit the assembling of foreign capital for small investments. The International Bank for Reconstruction and Development, or other United Nations or governmental organizations, often cannot lend to private industrial projects. The development bank can. It can receive the loan and conduct an investigation of the individual projects. Even private foreign investors may find it feasible to forego the necessity for making local investigations by lending to the Bank. Such investments may even be more protection against expropriation than direct investment, so that private investment will be attracted. Countries or groups of countries would be well advised to start such institutions.

## REFERENCES

1. BERNSTEIN, E. M., "General Problems of Financing Development Programs." *Journal of Finance* (May, 1957), p. 170.
2. CAIRNCROSS, A. K., *Factors in Economic Development.* New York, Frederick A. Praeger, Inc., 1962, Chaps. IV and V., pp. 75-97.
3. WOLF, C., JR., and S. C. SUFRIN, *Capital Formation and Foreign Investment in Underdeveloped Areas.* Syracuse, N.Y., Syracuse University Press, 1955, p. 16.
4. *Measures for the Economic Development of Underdeveloped Countries.* New York, United Nations, 1951, Table 2, p. 76.
5. ALPERT, PAUL, *Economic Development, Objectives and Methods.* New York, The Free Press of Glencoe, 1965, p. 135.
6. WOLF and SUFRIN, *op. cit.,* pp. 13, 14.
7. BELSHAW, H., *Population Growth and Levels of Consumption.* London, George Allen and Unwin, Ltd., 1960, p. 121.
8. BAUER, P. T., *West African Trade.* London, Cambridge University Press, 1954, pp. 263-346.
9. Economic Commission for Asia and the Far East, *Economic Survey of Asia and the Far East, 1961.* Bangkok, United Nations, 1962, p. 43.
10. *World Economic Survey, 1960.* New York, United Nations, 1961. Part I, Chap. 2, Table 2-2, p. 61.
11. International Bank for Reconstruction and Development, *Nigeria.* Baltimore, Johns Hopkins Press, 1955, p. 130.
12. OKITA, S., "Savings and Economic

Growth in Japan." *Economic Development and Cultural Change* (October, 1957), pp. 32-41.

13. ALEXANDER, R. J., *Primer of Economic Development.* New York, The Macmillan Company, 1962, pp. 88ff.

14. WOLF and SUFRIN, *op. cit.,* p. 13.

15. LEWIS, W. A., *Theory of Economic Growth.* Homewood, Ill., Richard D. Irwin, Inc., 1955, pp. 226ff.

16. WEBER, MAX, *The Protestant Ethic and the Spirit of Capitalism,* trans. by T. Parsons. London, Allen and Unwin, 1930. Tawney, R. H., *Religion and the Rise of Capitalism.* London, John Murray, 1937.

17. WOLF and SUFRIN, *op. cit.,* p. 16.

18. ALEXANDER, R. J., "Who Bears the Cost of Economic Development?" in R. A. Solo, *Economics and the Public Interest.* New Brunswick, N.J., Rutgers University Press, 1955, pp. 286ff.

19. GOODE, RICHARD, An address before the Forty-fourth Annual Conference of the National Tax Association, 1951, contained in the *Proceedings* of that Conference, pp. 213-15.

20. CHELLIAH, R. J., *Fiscal Policy in Underdeveloped Countries.* London, George Allen & Unwin, Ltd., 1960, pp. 66-67.

21. LEWIS, W. A., "Some Reflections on Economic Development." *Economic Digest* (Winter, 1960), pp. 3-5. Reproduced in Meier, G. M., *Leading Issues in Development Economics.* New York, Oxford University Press, 1964, pp. 95-98.

22. WAI, U. T., "Taxation Problems and Policies of Underdeveloped Countries." *International Monetary Fund Staff Papers* (November, 1962), p. 429.

23. LEWIS, *op. cit.,* pp. 217-25. (Discusses the problem of minimizing inflation.)

24. DORRANCE, G. S., "The Effect of Inflation on Economic Development." *International Monetary Fund Staff Papers* (March, 1963), pp. 1-47. United Nations, Economic Commission for Asia and the Far East, "Inflation and the Mobilization of Domestic Capital in Underdeveloped Countries of Asia." *Economic Bulletin for Asia and the Far East,* vol. II, No. 3 (1951), pp. 22-25.

25. DIAMOND, WILLIAM, *Development Banks.* Baltimore, Johns Hopkins Press, 1957. Boskey, S., *Problems and Practices of Development Banks.* Baltimore, Johns Hopkins Press, 1961.

26. BOSKEY, *ibid.,* p. 50.

## ADDITIONAL READINGS

BRAND, W., *The Struggle for a Higher Standard of Living.* New York, The Free Press of Glencoe, 1960, Chap. 4, pp. 51-93.

BUCHANAN, N. S., and H. S. ELLIS, *Approaches to Economic Development.* New York, The Twentieth Century Fund, 1955, Chap. 3, pp. 51-73.

ELLIS, H. S., and H. C. WALLICH, *Economic Development for Latin America.* New York, St. Martin's Press, 1961, pp. 82-109.

International Bank for Reconstruction and Development. *Basis of a Development Program for Colombia.* Washington, D.C., Government Printing Office, 1950, pp. 37-60.

KUZNETS, S., W. E. MOORE, and J. J. SPENGLER, *Economic Growth: Brazil, India, Japan.* Durham, N.C., Duke University Press, 1955, pp. 179-228.

NURKSE, R., *Problems of Capital Formation in Underdeveloped Countries.* New York, Oxford University Press, 1953.

ROSENBERG, N., "Capital Formation in Underdeveloped Countries." *American Economic Review* (September, 1960), pp. 706-15.

United Nations: Department of Economic Affairs, *Domestic Financing of Economic Development,* 1950. *Methods of Financing Economic Development in Underdeveloped Countries,* 1949. Economic Commission for Asia and the Far East, *Mobilization of Domestic Capital,* 1953 (Columbia University Press). *Mobilization of Domestic Capital in Certain Countries of Asia and the Far East,* 1951 (Bangkok, United Nations). Technical Assistance Administration, *Taxes and Fiscal Policy in Underdeveloped Countries,* 1955.

# CHAPTER

# 10

# *Financing*
# *Economic Development—*
# *Foreign Sources*

### The Role of Foreign Capital

It seems apparent that underdeveloped countries can achieve little, if any, economic growth on the basis of the amount of domestic savings they are likely to develop in the near future. If any appreciable growth is to be experienced, it must be through the medium of foreign capital or improved export trade.* However, exports probably cannot be developed rapidly enough to provide the foreign exchange necessary to pay for the capital goods needed for development purposes, including the expansion of the export industries needed to acquire the foreign exchange in the first place. Thus, foreign capital seems an essential ingredient for growth, at least in the early stages of development.

Estimates referred to in the preceding chapter showed a need for from $9 to $14 billion a year of foreign capital if growth rates were to be satisfac-

* See the next chapter for a discussion of the role of foreign trade.

tory. Other estimates may place the need as greater or less, but no one seems to disagree that the needs are greater than the current levels of aid.

The most important function of foreign capital is to aid in getting started. As we have seen, under stagnant conditions the hope of developing enough savings to start incomes rising, and thus increasing the ability to save, is quite remote. Equally remote is the possibility for the underdeveloped countries to produce modern capital equipment until their economies have developed considerably beyond their current levels. These goods must be imported. If exports to pay for them are lacking, foreign capital must take over. Foreign aid thus enables underdeveloped countries to acquire these necessary capital goods and even consumer goods to meet rising demands.

Moreover, as countries grow, bottlenecks are apt to develop. Outside capital is a means of breaking these more quickly than domestic efforts alone could.[1] A. O. Hirschman[2] sees foreign capital as a means of starting out on the path of unbalanced growth by enabling countries to undertake the large indivisible investments he sees desirable. Large sums may be needed to provide the expensive social overheads necessary for development.

Nurkse[3] sees one advantage in using foreign funds as lessening the need for autocratic governments, assuming that only autocratic governments can force the necessary domestic savings. Unfortunately, foreign capital thus far has been so limited that it is impossible to assess its effect in promoting democracy. Nurkse also points out[4] that this is a means of improving the distribution and use of the world's resources.

One thing must be kept in mind: the ability to absorb capital. This is not really a question of the amount that can be absorbed, but is one of obtaining the right kinds of capital and in the right order. Unless the proper complementary industries, materials, and skills are available, any imports of capital will be inefficiently used at best. This is a matter of making proper investment decisions and programming the development plan correctly. Needless to say, with foreign capital in short supply, the utmost efficiency in its use is essential. Also, domestic policies must be such that development is actually promoted. Using foreign capital efficiently is the great problem in the whole realm of international capital flows. One suspects that the past degree of efficiency has been rather low.

For the underdeveloped countries there are two major disadvantages to using foreign capital. One is the possibility of foreign pressures to affect the country's program, a fear of a neocolonialism based on investment. Or, lacking such direct pressure, there may be at least a feeling of obligation. The other disadvantage is that if the capital is made available in the form of loans, these must be paid back ultimately. Unless such loans produce outputs before they are due, growth will be handicapped because other domestic materials will have to be used for repayment. In this connection, borrowing for military purposes creates serious problems. Similarly, borrowing for projects based on a long payoff period, unless on a delayed repayment basis, can be quite awkward.[5]

Foreign capital can come from either private sources or governments. Each has its own advantages and problems for the underdeveloped countries.

## Private Foreign Investments

Before World War II, private foreign investment was a large source of development funds and certainly more important than government transfers. Particularly during the nineteenth century there was considerable movement across country borders. Large sums flowed to the United States and to countries on the Continent, especially from Britain, whose overseas investments were very large compared with her income.[6] This investment yielded an income, secured a supply of raw materials, and supplied a market for British exports. Britain gained and the developing countries also gained through accelerated development. There is a temptation to believe that the same situation would hold true today, that foreign investment would be to the advantage of both the investing country and the receiver, and that it would start the process of development. A. K. Cairncross,[7] however, does not believe that foreign investment will be so significant in developing the present underdeveloped countries. For one thing, domestic savings are not so large, compared with the capital flows, as they were in the present advanced countries, and therefore the foreign capital does not find so favorable a complementary economic setting as it did when the receiving economies were already expanding, so that aid did not initiate the growth but pushed it along. Also, the borrowing countries were relatively large and were higher above the level of subsistence; there was a market in the lending country; and there was no problem of transferring funds. In other words, there was considerable development before capital flows became important.

After the 1930's, and continuing after World War II, private foreign investment dwindled, especially when one considers the growth in the world's economy. In recent years net private capital flows have been only about $2 billion a year, mostly from the United States.[8] Net flows run about $2 billion per year and gross private investment is probably in the vicinity of $5 billion, although there seems to be no reliable figure. For example, in 1956 net outflow was $2.76 billion.[9] Retained earnings raised this to an estimated $3.96 billion; and investment of depreciation reserves increased it to around $5 billion, of which $1.7 billion was in underdeveloped countries. By 1943 United States investments abroad[10] had totaled $8 billion and by 1953 this had risen to $16 billion, $6 billion coming after 1949. By 1961 total private investment abroad was $55.5 billion[11] with government credits and claims raising this to $77.36 billion. However, foreign assets and investments in the United States were $50 billion. Illustrating the relatively minor role of private foreign investment, N. S. Buchanan and H. S. Ellis[12] state that from mid-1945 to 1952, United States private foreign investment was $5.5 billion,* whereas the United States Government transferred nearly $41 billion. The amounts sound impressive, but private flows were no more than the private capital flows in the 1920's and were far less in real terms and as a percentage of the national incomes of the lending countries, although more went to the underdeveloped countries. By the 1950's the reinvestment of earnings was rapidly becoming the dominant source of private funds.†

The problem is that the underdeveloped countries need capital at a time when there is a world shortage of capital, and they must compete for it against more profitable investments in the relatively more developed countries. In this competition the underdeveloped countries have not fared well, the bulk of the investments going to the relatively more advanced, such as Canada, Australia, Brazil, and Mexico. For example, of the United States investment from 1946 to 1952, 40 percent went to Canada, 30 percent to Latin America, 15 percent to west Europe, and 15 percent to the others.[13] In recent years[14] half of the flows, excluding those to Canada, have been to Latin America (and concentrated in the richer areas). Africa received between one-fifth and one-third, and Asia received less.

In addition, those investments that have been made are concentrated in the extractive industries, mainly oil, minerals, and plantation products for export. Thus, they have not met what the underdeveloped countries consider to be their greatest need: investment in manufactures. The small percentage of capital directed to manufacturing has been largely in the relatively more developed regions like Canada, Australia, Brazil, and Mexico. Capital does not seek manufactures, for domestic markets are poor, social overheads are not well developed, and export markets are virtually closed.

To complete the picture of capital scarcity is the tendency of foreign

---

* C. Wolf and S. C. Sufrin (*Capital Formation and Foreign Investment in Underdeveloped Areas*. Syracuse, N. Y., Syracuse University Press, 1955, p. 53) place private investment, including reinvestment of earnings, at $9.3 billion for this period.

† A study by J. N. Behrman ("Promoting Free World Economic Development Through Direct Investment." *American Economic Review, Proceedings* (May, 1960), p. 272) of the policies of 115 large American companies with investment abroad bears out this statement.

firms to invest directly in branches of the parent company, with portfolio investment declining. The study by Behrman[15] showed that American corporations prefer wholly owned operations abroad or at least those in which they have majority control. Particularly, investment in foreign government bonds virtually disappeared after the wholesale defaults in the 1930's. The policy of direct, wholly owned investment has allowed only minimal opportunity for domestic participation, which is disappointing to the underdeveloped areas. It has, however, been advantageous in leading to the reinvestment of earnings, the dominant source of new investment, and for which no fixed repayment is required as in the case of loans.

Why do private funds move less readily than they did in the past? Many impediments are known to exist. The long list given below does not apply, of course, to all countries and to all times, but each has operated from time to time as a barrier to investment. Underdeveloped countries are becoming aware of these, and progress has been made in lessening them to some degree. Nevertheless, sufficient impediments still exist, and private investment is much lower than expected and is far from taking over the job of supplying the needs of underdeveloped countries.

An imposing number of possible impediments are discussed below.

1. Government aid itself may be an impediment: Presumably, government aid was intended as a stopgap measure to get countries started so that private capital would find the opportunities attractive and gradually take over the burden. But the borrowing governments may find government loans and grants more attractive in that they give the officials more control and prestige and fit in with the preference in many countries for nationalized industries. In other words, the "competition" is somewhat unequal.

2. There is a world shortage of capital for which the underdeveloped countries must compete: The advanced countries where capital funds exist also have a great need for capital; for example, for automation and modernization of factories in the United States and automation plus rapid growth in Europe. Capital that does leave its country of origin is apt to go to those countries who have started on their way to advancement. Private capital goes where returns are the greatest, allowing for risk and other factors mentioned below. The rate of return on investments in the underdeveloped countries has not, on the average, been so great as expected. Some undertakings have been enormously profitable, but the average returns do not seem to be attractive. The best chances for profits seem to be in raw materials and not in manufacturing because domestic markets in underdeveloped countries are weak. As development proceeds and more profitable opportunities arise, more capital will be attracted.

3. Private investors have a number of fears that, if realized, lessen or

eliminate any possible profits: There is a fear of war or outside aggression, especially in areas close to the U.S.S.R. or mainland China, or of internal rebellions, as in the Congo and Southeast Asia. Investors fear possible expropriation without adequate compensation or, possibly, general harassment; for example, extra taxation and other special restrictions that may amount to gradual expropriation. There is the possibility of exchange controls, resulting in possible losses or the inability to repatriate profits and capital when desired. Exchange controls may also make it difficult to finance imports essential to the continued operation of the enterprise. There is also the wariness in dealing with strange legal concepts, business practices, and customs.

4. On occasion unwelcome restrictions lessen opportunities; for example, investment in certain operational areas may be forbidden. Examples are ownership of land and social overheads such as power facilities, publishing, communications, domestic aviation, banking, and insurance. There may be restrictions on discharging employees and employment quotas that require excessive personnel. Advanced and costly social legislation is not uncommon. Profits may be limited and there may be a legal obligation to reinvest a certain percentage of the profit.

5. The attitude of the host country toward foreigners and foreign investment may not be favorable: Marxian doctrine treats private investment as a new form of colonialism leading toward ultimate control of the host country's economy. There is usually a sufficient communist minority to see that this is given wide publicity. There is often a belief, inherited from colonial times, that foreign countries exploit the raw materials and the people. In many countries, national ownership of industry is the ideal, so any private industry, especially foreign, is subject to suspicion. Government officials concerned with such industries cannot be expected to welcome private firms. Thus, there is plenty of play for antiforeign propaganda and foreign companies are favorite targets for attack by politicians.

6. Increasingly popular is the requirement that a certain percentage of the managerial and skilled staffs should be host nationals: Some investing companies prefer importing their own staffs because they know its abilities. Whatever the result on long-run efficiency, it is possible that immediate efficiency may be sacrificed by a requirement to employ host nationals. Closely allied may be a requirement that a certain percentage of the business be owned by nationals.

7. In some cases profits may not be earned for some period of time: It takes time to organize the necessary labor, raw materials, and markets. Social overheads may be insufficient. Complementary industries may have to be encouraged. Thus, returns may be too remote to be attractive.

8.   Our own tariff and import practices and those of the West work against investment in anything but raw materials.

9.   Much of our savings are in forms that cannot legally take the risks of foreign investment: For example, insurance companies and banks are generally prohibited from lending abroad on a long-term basis.

According to S. C. Sufrin,[16] the conditions needed for private investors to be attracted into the foreign field are profitability, convertibility, and stability of the receiving country. The impediments discussed previously indicate that these tests are not always met sufficiently to attract large amounts of foreign capital.

Many, especially those brought up in a private enterprise system, feel that there are considerable advantages to an underdeveloped country in permitting and encouraging the inflow of private capital. United States policy, especially as expressed repeatedly in Congress, is to encourage private investment rather than aid. The hope seems to be that private investment will ultimately supplant governmental loans and grants. Business interests, of course, proclaim the superiority of private investment. The presumed advantages to underdeveloped countries are:

1.   Foreign public capital is just not sufficient to meet the needs of the underdeveloped countries. Private capital is potentially much greater in amount. Without it as a supplement to government aid, growth is likely to be retarded.

2. Private investors who are setting up branches can be expected to accompany the investment with skilled management and technicians. The technology introduced is likely to be in advance of that in the receiving country. Also, new developments in the advanced countries will be known and made available more rapidly than in any other circumstances. Productivity, the basis of development, is greater because of this access to skilled personnel, and is likely much greater than in locally owned firms or government-operated firms. To the extent that productivity is improved, foreign exchange may be earned or saved and national income raised. Successful industries are the best sources of tax revenues and may be the largest supplier of government funds. Such firms may exert an impact on every aspect of a country's life. In the short run, they may open up new frontiers, lead to resource discovery, create social capital, train workers, rouse the spirit of enterprise, and improve the managerial know-how.[17] They may thus be the catalysts that transform the economy.

3.   Private investors are apt to establish an enterprise on a "sound business basis"; that is, in the most profitable areas and on the most profitable basis. That maximizing relatively short-run profit is the best way to bring development is debatable, but flagrant wastes on showy and prestige projects are more likely to be avoided.

4. Private investments do not have to be repaid on a fixed schedule, and to the extent that they are profitable, provide their own means of repayment. During depressed times, profits are apt to be low, whereas fixed-interest payments on public loans might prove an intolerable burden.

Whether such advantages will be realized is the decision each country must make when private foreign investment is available. A. Y. C. Koo[18] suggests the following criteria for testing the contribution of private enterprise to a nation's economy: the percent of local payments per sales dollar, the proportion of local sales to total sales, the rate of plant replacement, and the ratio of inflow to outflow of funds. These criteria are based on the assumption that the major contribution is the amount of local purchasing power generated. These are limited criteria, but do serve to indicate whether the firm is fitting advantageously into the local economy or is simply an appendage to a foreign country that reaps the benefits and absorbs the profits.

Capital exporting countries also may look kindly on private investment. The burden of foreign aid is reduced. Moreover, the government can avoid the necessity of choosing between competing claimants for aid, and thus making enemies.

However, underdeveloped countries have mixed feelings about such capital and often feel it is harmful or, at best, contributes little.[19] It is obvious to them that private foreign investments have been concentrated on primary products for export, such as agricultural products and industrial raw materials, and only to a limited extent in manufactures. Therefore, the projects do not fit into the development schemes of most countries, which are anxious to replace primary production by manufactures. Private investors are guided by monetary returns and not the long-run development of the country. This policy of investment to earn immediate profit does not contribute to the permanent needs of the country. Moreover, investment is apt to be sporadic as profitable situations ebb and flow, especially during cycles of prosperity and depression in the purchasing countries. Little concern is likely to be felt in developing the country's social overheads except those immediately useful to the firm, such as transportation facilities to the seaport, harbor facilities, and the like. In short, there is a general belief that primary production has few "spread" or "multiplier" effects on the economy. The projects are too large to encourage imitation on the part of local producers and, even more apparent, local businessmen may be driven out because they are unable to attain the same efficiency. Few people are affected and most of the increased incomes generated go to a few favored people who spend much of it abroad.[20] Moreover, by specializing in such products, the economy is subject to considerable fluctuations, especially in foreign exchange earnings. These products are also believed to be subject to

decreasing terms of trade.* Much is made of the exploitation of local resources and local labor for foreign benefit.

There is a fear of foreign domination through the pressures exerted by
the companies on government officials and by foreign countries seeking to
"protect" their nationals. Past investors have interfered in politics and have
asked extensive favors. Officials have been bribed. The Latin Americans
still remember the landing of the United States Marines. Recent United
States policy toward Cuba is not seen solely as a reaction against a Communist take-over. Thus, suspicions still exist. Particularly for this reason,
there is reluctance to have foreigners control vital economic activities.

Balance-of-payments problems may arise. In time, net outflows of profits
may exceed new investments, thus using scarce foreign exchange. Of course
the new industry may have created more than enough in extra production to
meet these demands, but there is still resentment over the use of scarce
resources for such purposes since they compete with very pressing needs.
Moreover, there is a belief that such companies make exorbitant profits
while contributing little to development. A United Nations study[21] of foreign investment in Latin America reported that increased postwar earnings,
averaging 11.2 percent of book value in 1945 and 21 percent in 1948,
had a wide range from industry to industry. Earnings were reported as 31.1
percent in petroleum from 1948 to 1951 and 28.1 percent in distribution,
but only 2.9 percent in public utilities. The average return on investment
was estimated as 4 to 9 percent higher than it would have been in the
investor's own country, and if petroleum were excluded, the spread would
have been much narrower. After adjusting book value to replacement cost
and taking into account tax differences, there is a question whether the
profits earned were worth the extra risks taken by the investors. Although
statistics are lacking and some companies do make large profits, the average
returns are not believed to be very high. Otherwise, there would be a rush of
private capital abroad. Nevertheless, the belief of excessive profits and an
unfair division of these persists.†

Many countries are socialistic and resent private enterprise except in
small undertakings.

The foreigner himself, although he may not be quite an "ugly American,"
has a different culture which, in some aspects, may arouse disfavor. For

* These views will be developed in the next chapter.

† D. Seers ("Big Countries and Small Countries." *Kyklos*, No. 4 [1963], pp. 599-
608) expresses the belief that small countries are not collecting as much in taxes as
they could where one or a few big companies dominate the export business. Transfers
of materials at fixed prices among branches, excessive charges of central office
overhead, sales to branches in "tax havens," and the corruption or inefficiency of
tax administrators—all contribute to the lessening of taxes.

example, the drinking of alcohol in Muslim countries or the more independent behavior of Western women may cause resentment. This is especially so when the foreigner lives in enclaves and mixes little with the local people. His higher standard of living also arouses envy.

Because of these beliefs, some countries have set up obstacles to private investment. Certain projects may be declared off limits. The company may have to hire a certain percentage of local people. Some percentage of ownership (up to two-thirds in India) may have to be held by nationals. Prices and wages may be controlled. Thus, private investment does not find the way easy. Yet, under the right circumstances, such investment can be advantageous to both the underdeveloped country and the investing one.

In order for private capital to be welcome, the investors must conform to certain modes of behavior.[22] They must seek to fit their project into the development plans of the country, become "national" by bringing in local people and using local raw materials wherever possible, be moderate in their demands for foreign exchange, and obey the laws of the country, especially as to labor conditions and wages, social security, and taxation. In fact, they probably will have to set superior standards. They must not become involved in local politics and must not ask for special privileges over local firms or attempt to get them by influencing government officials. Lastly, foreign personnel must learn to adapt themselves to the customs and habits of the local people and associate more with them as equals.

Underdeveloped countries can do much to encourage foreign capital, yet fit it into their development needs.[23] One of the first measures to adopt is a program to avoid inflation. Some price increases are undoubtedly inevitable, but efforts should be made to hold them within reasonable bounds. A. K. Cairncross[24] believes that private capital will come into a country and into manufacturing if there are markets. Therefore, the need is for general development and the raising of incomes, especially in agriculture, and the provision of necessary social overheads. The country must also give evidence of internal security and political stability and also avoid involvement in external aggression.

More specifically, there should be an effort to fit private investment into the local development plan. To do this, the sphere of private enterprise should be carefully laid out so that firms will have a reasonable knowledge of what is expected of them. No nation can be expected to guarantee against eventual nationalization, but guarantees of fair compensation if properties are taken over would allay the major fears of investors. Joint ventures between government and private investors or between domestic and foreign investors would provide some assurance of continuity. Countries could also provide information about investment opportunities, borrowing facilities for local currency needs, and perhaps buildings that might be bought or rented. Taxation should not be discriminatory. Generally, it should be the same as that for nationals, and to avoid double taxation, agreements should be made with the countries from which investments are expected. Similarly, other controls should be no greater than those on nationals. Many countries might well consider revising their controls, even on local businesses, to make them less burdensome, where it can be done without sacrificing essential principles of justice.[25] Firms will need the right to bring in a certain number of managers and technicians, although they should also be willing to undertake the training of local personnel for all important positions. Agreements should be reached as to the conditions for the remittance of profits and dividends. Efforts should be made to improve the general climate of friendliness.

A favorite device to attract capital has been tax concessions. Although effective in some cases, this is a doubtful policy because of the effect on government revenues and ultimately on government services. Even firms that receive the advantages should be cautious, for the economic climate might not improve enough to make their operations profitable.

If private investment is to increase, the lending countries must try to encourage it. The United States, in particular, has adopted a policy of promoting private investment, although the actual administration of the policy seems to have fallen short of expectations. The basic policy was expressed in the Foreign Assistance Act of 1961, which required the President to carry out programs of assistance through private channels wherever appropriate.[26]

Available to foreign investors are a number of aids. First, there are tax advantages. Partly, the privileges given have been extended to prevent double taxation, but the concessions seem to have gone beyond this. Examples of advantages are: offsets against the domestic income tax for foreign income taxes paid abroad; elimination of taxes on reinvested foreign incomes; offsets against domestic profits for losses abroad; exemption for American citizens resident abroad, under certain conditions, from Federal personal income taxes; and the granting of liberal depreciation allowances. Concessions beyond eliminating double taxation seem of doubtful value because they benefit only a favored few large corporations who are in a position to make foreign investments.

The United States helps in a second way by providing an insurance program against most losses except normal business losses. Protection against expropriation, war risks, and inconvertibility of exchange are examples. This applies to new investors, so that old investors are discriminated against. Moreover, only limited use has been made of this insurance, probably because this would involve a government review of the operations. The U. S. Government also helps in supplying information on investment conditions; for example, by providing financial assistance in making surveys.

Lastly, the United States has entered into treaties with other countries to prevent discrimination against United States capital. The treaty with Uruguay is an early example and a good model.[27] This treaty gives our nationals the right to engage in commerce, manufacturing, construction, and cultural activities on the same basis as host nationals; provides most-favored nation treatment in exploring and developing minerals; gives our nationals equal treatment in holding property and in access to the courts; grants companies an absolute right to import specialized personnel; provides for the same taxes as for host nationals; and provides for assurance against unreasonable or discriminatory measures. Other countries are not willing to go this far, but treaties setting forth the terms of entry would eliminate a large measure of uncertainty. Recipient countries cannot be expected to give foreign capital a free hand and must protect themselves against exchange difficulties, foreign domination of vital industries, and the exclusion of training for their citizens.

## Foreign Public Loans and Grants

Underdeveloped countries have three methods of getting from abroad the capital equipment they need in their development programs: increasing their exports, borrowing the funds from private sources, or receiving aid in the form of public loans or grants. In calculating the reliance to be placed on each of these methods, we seem to have a process of successive residuals; that is, the amount of foreign aid needed is determined by first estimating total needs to meet given objectives and then deducting the trade balance and the private investment. Similarly, private investment on the trade balance may be treated as the residual. In actuality, it is necessary to calculate the capital needed to obtain the objectives and then plan the best way to acquire it. One means is through public loans and grants. Resort to these should be fitted into a coherent overall program, including the amount of domestic capital formation. On a short-term basis, loans and grants may be used to offset deficits in the balance of payments.

Foreign aid may be made available in a number of forms: long-term loans repayable in one of the widely acceptable currencies, so-called hard loans; long-term loans repayable in the currency of the recipient country, so-called soft loans; outright grants of money; and sale of surplus products for local currency. Technical assistance may also be included as aid, and short-term credits are sometimes considered as aid. The amount of interest varies from the market rate to a nominal rate. Repayment may be made over a long period of time, and the beginning of repayment may be delayed for some period.

Total foreign aid given each year is difficult to estimate, for there is dis-agreement as to what is aid; what is investment for defense purposes; and what is to be used for building up military strength. The flow to under-developed countries is only a relatively small amount and far short of what they want and short of what they need to meet their quite optimistic objec-tives. The *Economist*,[28] using United Nations figures, gives foreign aid as about $2.5 billion for an annual average from 1953 to 1956 and $3.4 billion from 1957 to 1959. Tables 10.1, 10.2, and 10.3 show the source of the aid, the percentage of aid to the donor's gross national product, and aid received per capita by certain countries. The latter two, especially, show how small foreign aid is. P. N. Rosenstein-Rodan[29] estimates total capital inflow in 1961 from the free world as $3.65 billion. Adding private invest-ments and Soviet aid brings the total to $5.15 billion.

The purpose of foreign aid is to accelerate economic development to the point at which the receiving country can achieve self-sustaining growth. Foreign aid, as economic aid, is justified only when it leads to an increase in the productivity of a country. A given amount of aid may create specific facilities, but may not bring development. More is needed than mere capi-tal. For development to proceed, the economy must be transformed; the people must be encouraged to work harder; entrepreneurs must develop;

**TABLE 10.1.**

Sources of Foreign Aid, 1953-1956 and 1957-1959
(Annual Averages in Millions)

| 1953-56 | | 1957-59 | |
|---------|---|---------|---|
| Source | Amount | Source | Amount |
| Multinational | $200 | Multinational | $400 |
| Other | 20 | Other | 40 |
| CANZ[a] | 60 | CANZ [a] | 105 |
| United Kingdom | 115 | United Kingdom | 185 |
| France | 640 | France | 775 |
| United States | 965 | United States | 1665 |
| | $2400 | West Germany | 40 |
| | | Japan | 90 |
| | | Soviet bloc[b] | 140 |
| | | | $3440 |

SOURCE: "Aid in Perspective," *Economist* (August 26, 1961), p. 788.
  [a] Canada, Australia, New Zealand.
  [b] Estimated.

## TABLE 10.2.

### Aid as a Percentage of Donor's Gross National Product, 1957-1959

| | |
|---|---|
| France | 1.39 |
| United States | 0.38 |
| Japan | 0.32 |
| Australia | 0.30 |
| United Kingdom | 0.29 |
| Netherlands | 0.26 |
| Canada | 0.18 |
| New Zealand | 0.18 |
| West Germany | 0.14 |
| Belgium | 0.11 |
| Sweden | 0.01 |

SOURCE: "Aid in Perspective," *Economist* (August 26, 1961), p. 790.

## TABLE 10.3.

### Aid Received per Capita, 1957-1959
### (Not Including Soviet Aid)

| | | | |
|---|---|---|---|
| Jordan | $36.30 | Pakistan | 1.91 |
| Libya | 31.64 | Burma | 1.59 |
| Israel | 24.61 | Afghanistan | 1.54 |
| Korea | 14.13 | Indonesia | 1.24 |
| Formosa | 9.14 | Sudan | 1.24 |
| Bolivia | 8.52 | Brazil | 1.05 |
| Chile | 7.69 | India | 0.74 |
| Colombia | 5.83 | Iraq | 0.58 |
| Iran | 3.92 | Ethiopia | 0.43 |
| Ceylon | 2.30 | U.A.R. | 0.41 |
| Mexico | 2.04 | | |

SOURCE: "Aid in Perspective," *Economist* (August 26, 1961), p. 790.

and many other changes previously discussed must take place. Foreign aid is thus a means to help development, but not a sure cure for development problems. A. K. Cairncross[30] says foreign borrowing is justified only if it permits a higher rate of domestic investment than domestic savings alone would support. If foreign aid is used as a substitute for domestic savings, a country will not get very far. Also, of course, it must be used efficiently, to be advantageous, and not wasted on poorly conceived projects or luxury consumption for a few. The real test of its value is whether it induces the people to put forth additional effort. It may well be that a showy or prestige project, although not economic in itself, may be justified if it leads to an increase in the people's efforts because of national pride.

Although foreign aid may not bulk large in the total picture of capital formation, it can be crucial for development. It may be the catalyst that moves an economy off center. Even though it is small compared with total national income, it may provide a large share of a country's foreign exchange and be a significant addition to its capital funds. For one thing, it may be the only source for the financing of costly social overheads and other long-term projects. It may remove temporary bottlenecks that block growth. It can fit more readily into the overall plan than do private investments because it is to a considerable extent directed by the government. Moreover, being largely in government hands, the funds can be used to support agriculture and small business, which is difficult for private foreign capital. Much of the help from abroad must be public, for much of the investments will be made by governments.[31] As noted previously, private investors have become wary of foreign government bonds and prefer direct investments.

Why do the advanced countries make grants or lend to underdeveloped countries at below-market interest rates and stipulate repayment in inconvertible currencies? There are various motives; undoubtedly immediate self-benefit plays a role, and perhaps an overwhelming one. If it does, the advanced countries are pretty sure to be disappointed, for the benefits are likely to be rather remote and indirect. Russian propaganda has stressed the exploitation inherent in aid and a resulting increase in the disparity of incomes of advanced and underdeveloped countries.* An overstress on the supposed gains to the advanced countries, probably made necessary to get legislative support for such aid, has some tendency to support the Russian charge and so make our aid suspect in the underdeveloped countries and less effective than it might otherwise be.

Just what are the supposed gains? Increased markets may be a motive, since we see that the richer the country, the better the market it is. Loans and grants may be extended as credits to be used for buying American goods. Financing one's own sales seems hardly a way to benefit except for certain producers and except for the possibility of curing an unemployment problem, which could be done in other ways than through foreign aid. In time, as development proceeds and incomes rise, advanced countries can expect to sell more goods and to buy more goods. Whether a particular country gains relatively will depend on how it meets world needs. Attempts to tie credits to purchases from one's own producers only increases resentment. Thus, immediate benefits are unlikely unless the country's competitive condition is good. Increased sales may ultimately result, but not all the industries of the advanced countries will benefit. Some markets will be de-

---

* V. Rymalov ("Economic Competition of the Two Systems and the Problem of Aid to Underdeveloped Countries." *Problems of Economics* [December, 1960], pp. 43-52) portrays this view and claims that socialist aid has no strings attached and that its only motive is speeding up development.

stroyed, probably in the light consumer goods field. For example, textile production is shifting to the less developed countries. Shifts in exports will have to occur as development proceeds, the advanced countries relying on the sale of capital goods, complex consumer goods, and technical services. Both advanced and underdeveloped countries stand to gain in the long run.

A second motive may be to get necessary raw materials and perhaps even to control the sources of strategic ones. It is not certain that the advanced countries' interest in obtaining these materials will be served by helping the underdeveloped countries industrialize. Such development may use the very raw materials desired.

A third motive is political in nature. There may be a desire to forestall authoritarian governments and the spread of Communism. The assumption is that, if aid is not provided, countries may choose the course of the U.S.S.R. or mainland China because democratic governments will be unable to raise the needed funds domestically. Only a dictatorship is presumed to be able to command the necessary sacrifices. Actually, there is little assurance that economic development will result in political stability and free economic institutions. Development creates internal conflicts, and power struggles may develop. This makes democracy, as we know it, difficult to maintain. Nevertheless, it is equally easy for a people to trade personal freedom, which is meaningless in poverty, for a promise of more goods under Communism. It is often assumed that people turn Communist because they are poor. They often do, but there are also relatively well-to-do Communists in the more advanced countries. The degree of correlation between democracy and height of the national income is not high. The best weapons against Communism are justice, equal opportunity, and intelligent propaganda to demonstrate the advantages of freedom. However, preventing the economic collapse of a country may lessen the opportunity for a Communist take-over.

It may also be hoped that a political advantage will accrue in that aid will lead to friendship, so that the receiving nation will line up on the lender's side in international disputes. This objective is a losing one at best, for countries cannot be bribed with a few dollars. Moreover, two can play the same game, and there has been a tendency for underdeveloped countries to play off one side against the other and obtain aid from both. If this were the aim of aid, countries with wavering friendships and a vocal Communist minority would have the best chance of getting aid. It must be recognized that aid will not enable us to control other countries, to get them to vote with us, or make us popular, although aid may be used as a lever to retain control of former colonies, as seems possible in the aid activities of the French.

Two motives seem more legitimate. One is of a purely humanitarian nature: Aid can save lives and help people to lead happier lives. The other is related but has more economic implications: a sincere desire to help people who are making a real effort to help themselves. This would indicate that the sole question in granting aid should be: Does it help development? Military and political considerations and short-run gains would play no part. Surprisingly, following this rule may be the way to attain the ends of friendship and cooperation.

There is some sentiment, especially among underdeveloped countries, that the advanced countries have a moral obligation to extend aid because of their fortunate position[32] or because they have exploited much of the underdeveloped world as former colonies or through reaping all the gains from foreign trade.

Although, in the case of the United States, most people seem to approve of foreign aid for one reason or another—mainly because of supposed military advantages or the weakening of Communism—some naturally are opposed. An example of the reasons for opposition are those given by the Citizens Foreign Aid Committee.[33] Aid is used for socialist purposes; increases our national debt; promotes philosophies akin to Communism, for example, nationalization. Aid results in a heavy gold loss, which may weaken the dollar. The use of aid to buy our products is inflationary. Aid will build up competing industries abroad. The funds are used inefficiently and not accounted for properly. Aid is a crude attempt to buy allies, but the United States has become the most disliked nation. Apparently the general public, however, as represented in Congress, believes the advantages of aid outweigh these alleged objections. Nevertheless, a mere recital of these negative arguments again raises the question of whether advanced nations stand only to gain. It is time that this be given at least a second look.

Various problems are encountered in the giving and receiving of foreign aid. The first question concerns the manner in which the limited funds are to be allocated—whether loans are to be extended by a single country or by a multinational agency. As the statistics on aid indicate, past aid has been spread very thin, with the result that improvements traceable to foreign aid have been relatively meager. That spreading aid thinly is the best way to bring development is debatable. It is conceivable that channeling aid to a few countries that have the best chance of achieving self-sustaining growth and then moving on to another few or aiding one regional grouping could be the best way of enabling the world to develop. But in this political world, such progressive policy is not possible, and decisions must be made as to how to divide the limited funds among all claimants.

Unfortunately, political and military considerations have played a large part in past decisions. Such criteria yield seemingly strange decisions and are based on relatively short-run advantages. Latin American countries seem to feel that they have been slighted and have not gotten their full share of aid from the United States because it is believed that their friendship is assured, whereas countries whose friendship wavers, or where there is a threat of a Communist take-over, seem to be courted with aid. For example, Indonesia and Egypt have been anything but friendly to the United States, but have received considerable United States aid. If such a claim is true, the very aim of cultivating friendship would seem to be negated. On the other hand, basing aid on demonstrated friendship would lay a country open to charges of trying to dominate the recipient's policies. In addition, political friendships have a way of changing almost overnight. Using political considerations as a basis for extending aid is a losing game and one that has yielded few advantages in the past. At best, one might draw the line at aiding one's outright enemies.

Nevertheless, C. D. Kindleberger[34] says that the process of rationing aid is clearly a political one and that there is no scientific basis for rationing it. Evidently, political considerations produce no clear-cut answer and seem less desirable as an aid policy than some attempt to apply economic considerations. Applying political considerations may mean that impact or show are more important than real needs. The U.S.S.R. seems to use aid for impressive undertakings such as steel mills and military equipment. The author's own belief is that the U.S.S.R. is not concerned with projects that are economic but prefers those that are uneconomic as a means of hastening national bankruptcies and political upheavals from which they might benefit. If this is not their policy, it would be an ideal one for their purposes.

Military considerations designed to bolster sagging governments have been important and perhaps necessary to protect constitutional governments against subversion or against attack from without. The danger lies in protecting governments that do not truly represent the people. As a guess, most economists would like to see military aid and economic aid separated so that experts in each field would have a better chance to make intelligent decisions. Obviously, the policy of one should not be used to offset that of the other. Presumably, the first decision should be on an economic basis. This could then be modified to the extent that political and military considerations were to be taken into account. In the past, economic considerations seem to have had too little weight.

In applying economic tests, one immediately thinks of the usual means in a free economy of allocating scarce resources—the use of price. This would require that aid be given in the form of loans with interest charged at whatever rate the market would need to balance supply and demand. Because the supply of public loanable funds would presumably be determined on bases other than the interest that could be gained on loans, the interest rate would merely ration the available supply among the various claimants. As interest rates rose, nonessential projects would be discouraged. This, unfortunately, would not meet the real problem, for need is not correlated with ability to pay. In fact, the more underdeveloped the country, the less its ability to pay, at least in the short run. The purpose of aid is to promote long-run growth, not to measure short-run profitability.

A widely used method of testing is to finance the direct foreign exchange requirements needed to purchase the capital goods for any approved project. Capital requirements to be produced locally, and any direct or indirect increases in consumption imports or imports of raw materials, are required to be financed domestically. This, of course, does not directly allocate the funds going to any one country except roughly on the basis of the ability and willingness of each country to finance its share of the project. Again, this works against the needs of the most underdeveloped countries. Because the needs are great, such countries are encouraged to resort to inflation in an effort to finance their share, a course not well calculated to aid development. In actuality, however, adopting this rule probably cuts down on the total claims for aid, but in itself provides no basis for judging among the various claimants.

Closely allied to this is the test of the ability of a country to service its loans; that is, to meet payments of interest and principal. This does have some relation to the productive use of aid, but is also influenced by the level of development. It is likewise possible that this test would be better used as a criterion for determining the type of aid (loan or grant) and the terms of repayment, such as interest paid and the timing of repayments.

A better criterion than these, and one that has some economic basis, is a judgment on how much a country needs aid to further a well-conceived development project and on how well the country has used any previous loan. One basis for such a judgment is the increase in the nation's productivity resulting from the projects financed. However, this may be too narrow a basis, for the optimum use of the funds may be in laying a base for future production; for example, by promoting education and health. The impact of these on productivity may not be felt for some time. Therefore the decision would have to allow for the contribution to ultimate development or for the degree to which the projects were fulfilling the development plan. Alternatively, a judgment would be required of the extent to which present progress would be stopped if future aid were denied. This would be no easy task and certainly not one based on precise and measurable data. But a rough ranking of the most deserving countries would be possible.

Rosenstein-Rodan[35] uses as a criterion a judgment as to the efforts of a country to aid itself. To him, the purpose of international aid is to accelerate economic development to the point where a country can have self-sustaining growth. Unless the country makes an effort to help itself, outside aid is wasted. Thus, the purpose of aid is to provide a positive incentive for maximum national effort. Aid is ideally allocated when it has the maximum effect on national effort and not on maximum income created per dollar. Evidence of this is given when the marginal rate of saving is higher than the average rate. Other criteria include: increase in the volume of investment; the capacity of the overall administrative and development organization; and total national productivity, not individual project productivity.

Chester Bowles[36] says that realistic criteria for the distribution of aid would reflect three factors: (1) the basic objective must be to help those who are prepared to defend their independence and are increasingly willing to work with us (a political consideration); (2) the changes effected must affect the lives of all the people, particularly the rural, and not just a few; and (3) a new outlook must inspire the people. He then adds a variety of specific tests, such as per capita income and distribution, the competence of the government and its sensitivity to the needs of the people, the existence of a well-conceived and long-term plan, adequate distribution and collection of taxes, priority for citizens in rural areas, existence of a favorable climate for foreign and domestic private investment, control over the use of foreign exchange for luxury living, and a government rooted in public support.

One can quarrel with specifics of such proposals, but it seems incontrovertible that the general idea for the test of distribution of loanable funds must be based on a judgment of the overall effect on development, including political considerations.

A second problem of aid is whether it should be made outright to a country or made only for specific projects. If the foregoing argument is sound, aid should be made outright, and the individual country should be left free, under whatever investment criteria it chooses, to decide how the funds can best be used. Current practice does not follow this principle. Instead, the lending countries must approve the specific project and have some review as to how effectively the funds will be spent. Presumably, approval depends on whether the proposed projects fit into the objectives of the granting country or conform to its view of the best way to develop. P. Alpert[37] points out that the United States prefers to assist agriculture and the building up of the infrastructure, and frowns on heavy industry. The U.S.S.R., however, has been willing to accede to the desires of underdeveloped countries for such industries. Assistance should be given to countries

in devising intelligent development plans and in drawing up a list of appropriate projects, but insistence on particular ones or against others may have
serious political repercussions. In the long run, the decisions must be made
by the borrowing country, and they must stand or fall on their own decisions. After all, one of the major contributions aid can make to growth is to
encourage intelligent decision making and planning.

In the long run, the decision whether to continue aid depends on the
judgment of the proper way to develop; but the decision, as recommended
above, must be based on overall performance and not on specific projects.
If a nation restricts its aid to approved projects, it is only fooling itself into
believing that it is exercising substantial control over the development plan.
All the borrowing country has to do is to shift its own funds from projects
for which it can get loans to those for which it cannot. True, there are limits
to this, but actually countries can do pretty much as they wish. When political considerations also enter, it is just as well to make outright loans not
tied to any specific project and thus avoid the charge of interfering.

It follows that tying too minute conditions to foreign aid is a dangerous
practice. Examples of conditions that may be attacked are: the borrower
must spend the funds in the lender's country; the lender must be permitted
to supervise the use of funds; the lender must have a veto over projects to
be started; or that certain reforms, such as fiscal reform or land reform,
must be carried out.

These seemed designed to yield short-run gains to the lender or to interfere with the sovereignty of the borrower, and are particularly resented by
the borrower. General conditions, such as insisting on the submission of a
sound development plan, are less resented, for the implication is that the
borrower is the beneficiary and not the lender. It seems doubtful that more
specific conditions than this, such as detailed supervision of the expenditures, can be imposed without offending nations jealous of their newly won
sovereignty. Insisting on supervision lays one open to the charge of neocolonialism; failure to do so may mean an inefficient use of funds or appropriation for personal benefit. Neither course seems desirable, but less specific
supervision seems preferable. At best, a joint board with the borrower having majority control and the lender having minority representation is indicated. This was tried in Libya (apparently successfully), although even this
was abandoned, or rather allowed to die of neglect. In such an arrangement
the borrower retains control, but the lender is in a position to know what
use has been made of the funds and can be guided accordingly on future
loans. Any check a country wishes to exercise, if the aim of aid is to secure
good will, seems best exercised via granting or refusing future loans based
on overall past performance. Specific conditions and inspection might better

be left to multination agencies in which the underdeveloped countries are represented.

The condition that the borrower buy from the lender is particularly obnoxious to the underdeveloped countries, which are anxious to get the best bargain they can. This seems to place the lender's interests first. The lender need not lose sales anyway, if it has exportable capacity, for the exchange earned by the seller is most useful, only if spent again. By freeing purchases, exports should develop along natural lines and not be forced artificially. If aid is given in the form of grants, there is more justification for tied conditions. Underdeveloped countries (for example, India) often seem to prefer loans to grants, perhaps for this reason.

A problem for both lender and borrower is that of the "return flow," that is, payments of interest and repayments of principal. The two together may be called servicing costs. Eventually, if the loan is to be repaid and interest paid, the borrower must export and the lender must expect an import balance, unless it keeps lending at an increasing rate. Permitting an inflow of goods and services is not always acceptable to the lender, for some industries and the people connected with them will be affected and can be expected to ask for protection. If a country wishes to be repaid, it must have a commercial policy that permits import.

The borrower has the problem of repayment and so must secure the resources from somewhere and earn foreign exchange with them. Presumably the aid will result in increased productivity of the economy as a whole and thus provide the resources. The need for ultimate repayment (unless the country expects not to have to repay) should serve as a warning to use aid efficiently. Some projects, such as improved education, may be necessary for development, but may yield their returns only after considerable time. Unless repayment is postponed, difficulties will arise. Repayment terms thus must take into account the expected timing and nature of increases in the country's output. Repayment can be scheduled for the most appropriate times and may even be specified in certain commodities so that the borrower has an assured market.

Just how much a country can safely borrow is difficult to determine. The servicing capacity depends on the balance of payments, and this, in turn, depends on the future course of imports and exports. There is some critical ratio between servicing costs and export earnings, but no one seems to have arrived at an acceptable figure. Each situation is likely to be different. The less stable a country's export earnings, the lower will be the ratio. In each case, servicing payments must be programmed against expected payments balances.

Because repayment may be difficult for both lender and borrower, aid may best be given in the early stages of development in the form of grants rather than loans. Loans are most appropriate for self-liquidating projects, and grants for other projects. However, the distinction is virtually meaningless, for a country can merely shift its internal capital. As development proceeds and a country's general repayment capacity improves, loans would seem the preferable form.

Aid for defense purposes where the lending country's interests are being served is best given in the form of grants. Defense preparations are apt to add little to national productivity, and repaying such loans might so interfere with development that the objective of defense would not be met. For example, military aid from the U.S.S.R. to Indonesia, given largely in return for repayment in specific commodities after (usually) ten years, will handicap a country already struggling against considerable odds.

As previously mentioned, total aid is short of the needs of the underdeveloped countries. One of the reasons has been that the bulk of the aid has come from two countries and that of France has been largely restricted to her former colonies. As large as United States aid seems, it is only a small fraction of the national output. In recent years the United States has been urging other countries to increase their aid, with only slight success. Rosenstein-Rodan[38] suggests a standard of one-half of 1 percent of a country's gross national product as its share of aid. The statistics given in Tables 10.1 and 10.2 show that, to meet this standard, all countries except France would have to increase their aid. This seems a reasonable goal to strive for, but one unlikely to be attained.

Because of the many problems connected with aid from individual countries, there is some sentiment for having all aid channeled through international bodies. Multinational aid has certain advantages.

1. There is less suspicion of the objectives of the aid.

2. A multinational body in which underdeveloped countries are represented can impose conditions not possible for an individual nation.

3. Aid from such an organization maintains the self-respect of the underdeveloped country, for they are members of the lending body. As members, they could check on one another's extravagant claims.

4. Multinational bodies can draw on a wide variety of experience and technical personnel.

5. More countries are enlisted, so theoretically more funds are available. However, countries may be more willing to give aid directly because of the supposed political advantages.

6. Aid from the individual countries is totally uncoordinated. Various countries offer duplicate aid, and some underdeveloped countries are not averse to playing off one lender against the other. The result is likely to be

an imbalance in the relative shares. Moreover, under national aid programs, each country is faced with an almost impossible variety of programs. Harlan Cleveland[39] lists the foreign aid activities in Indonesia in 1957. Omitting the less significant ones and the international loan agencies and bilateral agreements, forty-one different projects were under way, aided by eleven different agencies.

7. Political considerations are minimized, although politics do appear in the multinational bodies.

There appears to be considerable merit in distributing aid in this way. However, it does not appear likely to be brought about, for individual countries are not willing to give up what they believe to be the advantages of an aid plan. Giving aid through such a body would be a good test of whether a nation's objectives were really to further the welfare of the underdeveloped or to promote their own interests.

## United States Foreign Aid

Although as a general policy the United States Government prefers private foreign investment as the means of supplying the capital needed by the underdeveloped countries, the United States extends more foreign aid than any other nation. It has done this through a variety of programs, to be outlined below. In addition, the United States has been the chief contributor to international agencies that supply aid.

The United States has a long history of aid. Prior to World War I, aid was given largely to meet specific emergencies such as famine, but these loans were quite spasmodic. During World War I, loans were made to our allies for military purposes and to support their wartime economies. A large portion of these were never repaid because the countries were unable to earn enough dollars to meet their payments. During World War II, aid was given our allies to enable them to carry on their military operations. The postwar objective was first to rebuild the European economies so as to restore an international trading relationship. Later on, aid turned to military and defense assistance and to aiding the economic development of underdeveloped countries.

Thus, the objectives of our aid have been relief of distress, rehabilitation of war-devastated economies, military aid, and long-run development assistance.

What the motives were behind this aid are difficult to assess. Political and military considerations have seemed extremely important because these have been stressed as a means of getting public support for the effort. Undoubtedly, there has been the belief that helping poor countries would keep them from becoming Communist. It may even be that there has been some thought that the prospect of losing economic aid might deter nations from turning left. If these motives have been behind the aid program, the results are disappointing. There is also support for aid on the grounds that as other nations develop, all nations will gain from the expanded trade. Those producers who export capital goods undoubtedly have thrown their support behind foreign aid. The aid program could not have been continued without public support, which has generally been given on the basis of the foregoing considerations plus a surprisingly widespread belief in the obligation of the country to help others. Although perhaps not the "Number One" motive, there is considerable concern for others hidden in what seem to be economic, political, and military endeavors. Thus, the motivation is mixed.

United States policy at first leaned toward grants rather than loans, especially for technical assistance programs. As time passed, grants dwindled and the official policy became that of making loans, although many have been made on favorable terms and for repayment in the recipient country's currency, which ultimately may turn out to be equivalent to a grant. What the policy toward repayment of loans will be as world pressures mount remains to be seen.

It is almost impossible to separate economic aid from military aid, so one is forced to present a picture of total aid with as much breakdown as possible. Between July 1, 1940 and June 30, 1958, "gross utilized foreign aid" given by the United States was $120.8 billion.[40] In addition the United States' share in international organizations was $3.4 billion. The $120 billion was divided as shown in table 10.4, only a small amount being aid to underdeveloped countries.

**TABLE 10.4.**
*United States Foreign Aid, 1940-1958*
*(in billions of dollars)*

| | |
|---|---|
| War Period, July 1940 to June 1945 | |
| Gross grants, lend-lease | $46.7 |
| Gross grants, other | 1.4 |
| Utilized credits and loans | 1.1 |
| Total | $49.2 |
| Postwar Period, July 1945 to June 1958 | |
| Gross grants | $55.0 |
| Utilized credits and loans | 16.5 |
| Total | $71.5 |

SOURCE: *United States Foreign Aid*, House Document No. 116, 86th Congress, 1st Session, GPO, 1959, pp. 3 ff.

The same source, quoting the report of the Committee on Foreign Relations, divides the aid between 1948 and 1958 as $22.6 billion for economic aid and $20.4 billion for military purposes. However, much of the economic aid was designed to help weak economies of countries to which we were giving extensive military aid, and therefore can be considered as "defense support" aid.

Although one can obtain different figures for the amount of aid each year, depending on what one chooses to count as economic aid, since 1958 the United States has continued to aid other countries to the extent of $4 to $5 billion per year. The *World Almanac* lists the total of foreign aid for these years as: 1958, $4.66 billion; 1959, $4.40 billion; 1960, $4.07 billion; 1961, $3.92 billion; 1962, $5.13 billion; 1963, $5.06 billion. Over 90 percent of this was bilateral aid. From 1961 to 1963 a little over one-third was in grants and about one-fourth called for payment in the recipient's own currency.[41] In 1963 about one-third of the total was classified as military grants.

An extended description of the various agencies through which aid has been given by the United States is not in order in this book. However, a short summary may be useful. A full description is available in the literature.[42]

The first extensive aid after World War I was made through lend-lease. With the war going badly against our future allies, President Roosevelt decided to aid these countries to the fullest extent. To avoid postwar repayment problems, materials needed by the Allies were loaned or leased against repayment after the war in returned supplies or other goods or services to be agreed upon. All countries except the U.S.S.R. made satisfactory settlements, the bulk (representing war materials used up) being canceled.

The first postwar aid was channeled through the United Nations Relief and Rehabilitation Administration (UNRRA), which gave necessary goods to war-torn nations that could not acquire these abroad. This was really the first multilateral aid program, to which the United States contributed $2.67 billion. At the same time, the United States made greater aid contributions directly.

Postwar Europe needed greater aid than UNRRA could supply, and the United States found it necessary to extend aid on a large scale. First, in 1947, it came to the aid of Greece and Turkey to keep them from coming under the control of the U.S.S.R. Similarly, it became necessary for security reasons to prevent the collapse of the western European economies. On June 5, 1947, Secretary of State Marshall outlined his plan, which became the European Recovery Program and was popularly known as the Marshall Plan. This plan was designed to bring about a recovery of the economies and was to be given only after the countries had made satisfactory recovery plans. The Economic Cooperation Administration (ECA) was set up to administer the plan. Total aid from 1948 to 1952 was $13.15 billion.

In 1949 military aid to Europe began under the Mutual Defense Assistance Act, administered by the Mutual Security Agency (MSA); a small amount of aid was allocated to non-European countries, but this increased when difficulties arose in China, Korea, and Southeast Asia. In 1951 this program was replaced by the Mutual Security Act and by a similar act in 1954. This provides military assistance to any country that is deemed important to the security of the United States. In 1958 military aid was being given to over forty nations, most of them outside Europe.

In 1948 various economic aid programs were started, apparently based on the success of the Marshall Plan. Aid went first to China, Korea, and then to other Asian countries. The Mutual Security Act of 1951 authorized material help and technical advice to the underdeveloped nations, but indicated much of this would be for defense support. Such aid has been continued by annual appropriations from Congress and carried out by a number of different controlling agencies, the current one being the Agency for International Development (AID). MSA was succeeded in 1953 by the Foreign Operations Administration (FOA), and in 1955 by the International Cooperation Administration (ICA). However, the United States has a wide variety of programs,[43] including technical assistance programs.

Two government-created banks extend loans for development purposes. The Export-Import Bank was created in 1934 primarily to stimulate United States exports, and so help relieve unemployment, by providing loans for foreign purchasers when regular banking facilities were unavailable. Postwar loans have increased for capital purchases by underdeveloped countries, to facilitate their development. Most of the loans are now made in underdeveloped countries and may be considered development loans. The chief purpose, however, is still the promotion of United States exports. Loans are generally for the amount of the foreign exchange requirements of a project, and purchases are required to be made in the United States. Interest is charged and the Bank has operated at a slight profit.

In 1957 the Development Loan Fund was established in response to increased requests to obtain loans rather than grants. This institution makes loans, for economically sound development projects, to governments or private interests where funds are unavailable through regular channels. Interest rates are low and loans may be repayable in local currencies, which is a considerable advantage to the borrower in that it eases his problem of acquiring foreign exchange in hard currencies.

The United States may also extend aid through the sale or grant of surplus agricultural products.[44] These may be sold for local currencies and the proceeds used for extending loans or grants to the receiving country. Also, the products may be given outright. Most are sold for local currencies. During the period 1954 to 1958, $6.8 billion were exported in this manner.[45]

Such aid has considerable advantages for countries where agricultural output cannot be expanded rapidly enough to keep up with the expansion of demand that accompanies development efforts, where food imports seriously endanger the balance of payments, or where it is desirable to divert most of the capital formation into industry or social overheads rather than agriculture. Thus, such aid serves a major role in lessening the inflation that comes from competition for food and raw materials, which the country cannot otherwise acquire. On the other hand, such a policy creates several problems. First, such sales and grants may be at the expense of sales by friendly governments.* A second danger is that receiving governments may be led to delay improving their agriculture. Lastly, such sales plus other loans for local currency have given the United States a claim on large quantities of currency in various countries (such as India). An effort by the United States to utilize these funds could be quite inflationary. Also, these funds may not be expended carefully (for example, high living for visiting dignitaries), and so divert local resources to uses not consistent with development. In actual practice the United States holds most of the funds and does not expend them. Nevertheless, they remain a temptation for unnecessary expenditure.

The United States also contributes to various multinational regional development organizations such as the Inter-American Development Bank (Latin America), the Alliance for Progress (Latin America), The European Economic Community Development Fund (mainly African aid), and the Colombo Plan (Southeast Asia).

## Foreign Aid from Other Countries

Other nations engage in foreign aid through contributions to the United Nations agencies and through bilateral or multinational programs of their own. Except for France, aid is on a much smaller scale than that provided by the United States. Western European aid has gone largely to nations with which there are close political ties. The United Kingdom aid is largely to former colonies and to Southeast Asia through the Colombo Plan. French air goes largely to former colonies in Africa; Belgian aid went to the Congo; and the Netherlands' aid went to Indonesia before the split in rela-

* A possible solution is for all agricultural exporters to pool their surpluses and distribute them where needed.

# ECONOMIC GROWTH AND DEVELOPMENT

tions. Much of western Europe's aid is coordinated by the Organization for Economic Cooperation and Development, to which belong Belgium, Canada, Denmark, France, the Federal Republic of Germany, Italy, Japan, the Netherlands, Norway, Portugal, the United Kingdom, and the United States.

A significant plan is the Colombo Plan.[46] It was started in 1950 as a Commonwealth Plan, but was soon extended to other countries. The original non-Asian members were the United Kingdom, Canada, Australia, and New Zealand as contributors of financial aid and technical assistance. The United States joined a year later, and Japan has entered since then. The original Asian members were Ceylon, India, Pakistan, and Malaya; Burma, Indonesia, Nepal, Cambodia, Laos, and Vietnam joined later.

Each country has its own programs, and loans and aid are made on the basis of bilateral agreements. There is a central consultative committee of all members to discuss the plans of the various members. No control is exercised over individual countries or projects, the role of the central council being to exchange information and opinions. In providing aid, the emphasis has been on economic overheads such as electric power, water, and transport, and on social overheads such as education and health, training of workers, and agricultural development.

U.S.S.R. economic aid is a new factor in the aid picture.[47] Much of this aid is devoted to military buildup or a few large projects, and consists of credits and not grants. No facts are available to estimate the amounts.\* The U.S.S.R. emphasizes "no strings attached" and states as its objectives: maintaining the independence of the recipients, rapid development, and world peace. Aid is given without a survey, which leads to resentment against the West's "interference." Projects that attract public attention are favored, even though they may contribute little to economic development. As mentioned previously, this could be a deliberate policy. Western observers doubt the disinterested nature of such aid and believe it is designed to woo friends or at least decrease Western influence. The military aid makes the countries dependent on the Communist bloc for spare parts.

*Business Week*[48] estimates Communist bloc credits less repayments as only $200 to $300 million annually although in 1961 there were $4 billion in credit outstanding. Although much less than American aid, the same source credits Communist aid as generating more good will because it is

---

\* The statistics given here are broad estimates made by the United Nations, Department of Economic and Social Affairs, in 1964. Bilateral economic assistance of the U.S.S.R. is estimated as: total prior to 1960, $1,880 million; 1960, $584 million; 1961, $555 million; 1962, $233 million. For all centrally controlled economies for the same periods, the estimates were: $2,327 million, $893 million, $1,168 million, and $444 million. The aid is thus considerably below that of the United States.

given in the form of credits, not grants, repayable in local currency to be used for imports over twelve years at low interest. These arrangements give the impression of imposing no conditions. Moreover, the form of the aid in credits cuts down on the number of requests and so lessens the number of refusals.

## United Nations Aid

The United Nations extends aid in a variety of ways and through a host of agencies with very little central coordination.[49] The major agency has been the International Bank for Reconstruction and Development, but aid is also dispensed through the United Nations Technical Assistance Administration, UNICEF (Children's Fund), ILO (International Labour Office), WHO (World's Health Organization), ICAO (International Civil Aviation Organization), FAO (Food and Agricultural Organization), and UNESCO (United Nations Educational, Scientific, and Cultural Organization). During the postwar period, the United Nations Relief and Rehabilitation Administration dispensed aid for war-torn countries.

The International Bank for Reconstruction and Development was authorized in 1944 with a capital fund of $10 billion, later increased to $21.6 billion, pledged by such countries as chose to join. However, only 20 percent was required to be paid in and 90 percent of this could be in local currency and used only with the consent of the member. The Bank's purposes were to assist in reconstruction and development by facilitating the investment of capital, promoting private foreign investment by guaranteeing such loans, and promoting long-range balanced growth of international trade. Since it cannot compete with private lending agencies, it makes relatively few loans out of its own resources. Its chief activity is to guarantee private loans. Most of the loan funds come from guaranteed securities that are sold in all the capital markets of the world. Loans are made to governments or are guaranteed by governments only where the borrower does not have access to ordinary sources under reasonable conditions.

Underdeveloped countries have been disappointed in the Bank, for they had hoped for larger direct loans for general purposes. Instead, the Bank lends for specific projects and appears to them to be too conservative in selecting projects and in the amount it lends for each project. The Bank lends only after a thorough survey and a judgment as to the repayment possibilities of the specific project and the extent to which it will contribute to the productivity of the economy. Loans are generally limited to the direct foreign exchange requirements of each project. This means that the local economy must meet other costs and any indirect increase in foreign exchange requirements. This limits expansion seriously and handicaps the less financially able countries. Such loans are unsuitable for long-range projects such as education, which do not create a specific repayment prospect. Because loans must be self-liquidating, the least developed countries may have difficulty justifying certain large projects that will be profitable only at a later stage of development but which may be necessary for development.

In order to meet the needs for such things as public service projects, the underdeveloped countries urged an International Development Authority to make grants and soft currency loans. A special organization to be known as SUNFED (Special United Nations Fund for Economic Development) was proposed for this purpose, but was opposed by the nations who would have had to supply the funds. In 1957 the International Finance Corporation was established to lend directly to private industries without government guarantees.* It aims to increase private investment, especially portfolio investment. It can buy securities on its own and sell its own holdings or its own securities as a last resort. Unfortunately, its authorized capital is low.

Finally, in 1960, the International Development Authority was established as a substitute for SUNFED, the difference being that the lending nations had more control. It is authorized to make long-term, low-interest loans for social development projects that are not self-liquidating, and for local currencies. It is thus designed to finance activities that underlie successful development but which in themselves do not have repayment possibilities.

# REFERENCES

1. REUBENS, E. P., "Foreign Capital and Domestic Development in Japan," in S. Kuznets, W. E. Moore, and J. J. Spengler, *Economic Growth: Brazil, India, Japan.* Durham, N.C., Duke University Press, 1955, pp. 179, 210.
2. HIRSCHMAN, A. O., *Strategy of Economic Development.* New York, Oxford University Press, 1963, p. 205.
3. NURKSE, R., *Problems of Capital Formation in Underdeveloped Countries.* New York, Oxford University Press, 1955, p. 141.
4. *Ibid.,* pp. 129, 130.
5. NURKSE, *ibid.,* pp. 132ff. (Problems of the "return flow.")
6. MEIER, G. M., and R. E. BALDWIN, *Economic Development.* New York, John Wiley & Sons, Inc., 1957, p. 207.
7. CAIRNCROSS, A. K., *Factors in Economic Development.* London, George Allen and Unwin, Ltd., 1962, pp. 41ff.

* Both the International Development Authority and the International Finance Corporation were set up as affiliates of the IBRD.

8. MEIER, G. M., *Leading Issues in Development Economics.* New York, Oxford University Press, 1964, p. 149.
9. COLLADO, E. G., and J. R. BENNETT, "Private Investment and Economic Development." *Foreign Affairs* (July, 1957), pp. 631-35.
10. STASSEN, H. E., "The Case for Private Investment Abroad." *Foreign Affairs* (April, 1954), p. 408.
11. *Survey of Current Business* (August, 1962), p. 32.
12. BUCHANAN, N. S., and H. S. ELLIS, *Approaches to Economic Development.* New York, The Twentieth Century Fund, 1955, p. 343.
13. WOLF and SUFRIN, *op. cit.,* p. 53.
14. MEIER, G. M., *op. cit.,* p. 149.
15. BEHRMAN, *op. cit.,* p. 272.
16. SUFRIN, S. C., "Foreign Investment." *Foreign Policy Bulletin* (September, 1963), pp. 5ff.
17. KOO, A. Y. C., "A Short Run Measure of the Relative Economic Contribution of Direct Foreign Investment." *Review of Economics and Statistics* (August, 1961), p. 269.
18. *Ibid.,* p. 270.
19. VERNON, R., "Saints and Sinners in Foreign Investment." *Harvard Business Review* (May-June, 1963), pp. 146-61. (Discusses reasons for distrusting private investment.)
20. SINGER, H. W., "Distribution of Gains Between Investing and Borrowing Countries." *American Economic Review, Proceedings* (May, 1950), pp. 473-85.
21. Department of Economic and Social Affairs, *Foreign Capital in Latin America.* New York, United Nations, pp. 13, 14.
22. ALEXANDER, R. J., *Primer of Economic Development.* New York, The Macmillan Company, 1962, p. 113.
23. GRUNWALD, K., and J. O. RONALD, *Industrialization in the Mid East.* New York, Council for Middle Eastern Affairs Press, 1960, pp. 95ff. (Gives a description of the investment laws in the Mid East.)

Lewis, W. A., "Report on Industrialization and the Gold Coast," (1953), reproduced in G. M. Meier, *Leading Issues in Development Economics.* New York, Oxford University Press, 1964, pp. 163-66. (Lists the issues to be decided by the governments wishing to attract private capital.) Benham, F. C., *Economic Aid to Underdeveloped Countries.* London, Oxford University Press, 1961, p. 80. (Suggests a World Investment Code.)
24. CAIRNCROSS, *op. cit.,* pp. 62ff.
25. MEIER and BALDWIN, *op. cit.,* p. 419. (Lists some of the controls businesses face.)
26. CLUBB, B. E., and V. W. VANCE, JR., "Incentives to Private United States Investment Abroad Under the Foreign Assistance Program." *Yale Law Journal* (January, 1963), pp. 475ff.
27. BROWN, W. A., JR., "Treaty, Guaranty, and Tax Inducements for Foreign Investments." *American Economic Review, Proceedings* (May, 1950), pp. 486-94.
28. "Aid in Perspective." *Economist* (August 26, 1961), pp. 788-90.
29. ROSENSTEIN-RODAN, P. N., "International Aid for Underdeveloped Countries." *Review of Economics and Statistics* (May, 1961), p. 116.
30. CAIRNCROSS, *op. cit.,* p. 59.
31. LEWIS, W. A., *Theory of Economic Growth.* Homewood, Ill., Richard D. Irwin, Inc., 1955, p. 260.
32. BENHAM, *op. cit.,* p. 87.
33. *Congressional Digest* (May, 1959), pp. 141-47.
34. KINDLEBERGER, C. P., *Economic Development.* New York, McGraw-Hill Book Co., Inc., 1958, p. 300.
35. ROSENSTEIN-RODAN, *op. cit.,* pp. 107-109.
36. BOWLES, CHESTER, "Foreign Aid: The Essential Factors for Success." *Department of State Bulletin* (June 17, 1963), pp. 939-45.
37. ALPERT, P., *Economic Development, Objectives and Methods.* New York,

The Free Press of Glencoe, 1963, p. 293.

38. ROSENSTEIN-RODAN, *op. cit.*, p. 110.
39. CLEVELAND, HARLAN, "The Convalescence of Foreign Aid." *American Economic Review, Proceedings* (May, 1959), p. 226.
40. *United States Foreign Aid*, House Document No. 116, 86th Congress, 1st Session. U. S. Government Printing Office, 1959, pp. 3ff. (The amount of aid to individual countries is given.)
41. *Development Assistance Efforts and Policies, 1964 Review*, Organization for Economic Cooperation and Development, September, 1964.
42. *United States Foreign Aid, loc. cit.* Pentony, D., ed., *United States Foreign Aid.* San Francisco, Chandler Publishing Co., 1960. *Congressional Digest* (May, 1959), pp. 129-60.
43. CLEVELAND, HARLAN, *op. cit.*, pp.

216-30. (Describes the complexity of the programs.)
44. DAVIS, J. H., "Agricultural Surpluses and Foreign Aid." *American Economic Review, Proceedings* (May, 1959), pp. 232-41. (A discussion of the value of this form of aid.)
45. *Ibid.*, p. 232.
46. BENHAM, F., *The Colombo Plan.* Royal Institute of International Affairs, 1956.
47. BERLINER, J. S., *Soviet Economic Aid, The New Aid and Trade Policy in Underdeveloped Countries.* New York, Frederick A. Praeger, Inc., 1958.
48. *Business Week* (January 27, 1962), pp. 88-90.
49. BOTTING, D. C., "New Concepts in Economic Assistance for Underdeveloped Countries." *Western Political Quarterly* (June, 1961), pp. 496-516.

## ADDITIONAL READINGS

ASHER, R. E., *Grants, Loans and Local Currencies, Role in Foreign Aid.* Washington, D.C., The Brookings Institution, 1961.
BENVENISTE, G., and W. E. MORAN, JR., *Handbook of African Economic Development.* New York, Frederick A. Praeger, 1962, pp. 81-104.
ELMAN, R., *Asian Experiment.* Toronto, Ryerson Press, 1961.
Department of Economic Affairs, *International Flow of Private Capital, 1946-52.* New York, United Nations, 1954.
GOODMAN, B., "Political Economy of Pri-

vate International Investment." *Economic Development and Cultural Change* (April, 1957), pp. 263-76.
MIKESELL, R. F., "America's Economic Responsibilities as a Great Power." *American Economic Review, Proceedings* (May, 1960), pp. 258-70.
ROSENBERG, N., "Capital Formation in Underdeveloped Countries." *American Economic Review* (September, 1960), pp. 706-15.
United Nations, "The Colombo Plan." *International Labour Review* (March, 1955), pp. 498-515.

# CHAPTER
# II

# International Trade and Economic Development

## The Role of International Trade

Controversy exists over whether engaging in foreign trade can help an underdeveloped country grow. The traditional view is that foreign trade can contribute to a country's growth by permitting it to increase its productive efficiency through specialization and by acting as a transmitter of growth from one expanding sector to the rest of the economy and from one expanding center to the rest of the world. Others, especially the underdeveloped countries, see foreign trade in its current pattern as being a drag on growth.

One obvious rationale for engaging in foreign trade is its usefulness in accumulating funds for purchasing capital goods that otherwise could not be acquired through domestic savings and foreign borrowing or grants. This presupposes, of course, that the foreign exchange earned will be used to import capital goods. The real question is whether foreign trade is an economic way to acquire such goods or, in reality, may prove to be a drain on the productivity of a country. In quantitative terms, foreign borrowings and grants cannot be expected to provide the exchange necessary to import the capital goods required for any development effort. Foreign exchange earnings are significantly larger and in the long run must be the source of payment for imports.* The relationship between the costs of producing the exports and what is obtained in return is an important one for underdeveloped countries. The more their exports buy, the better. Also of importance is the question of whether exports can bring in a steady flow of the necessary goods.

Generally, underdeveloped countries prefer to get their foreign exchange through trade rather than through aid or foreign investment.† For one thing, exports will ultimately be necessary to repay loans or return investment, for such large obligations can hardly be paid off in gold. Secondly, fewer strings are attached to foreign exchange earnings than to loans or grants. Loans and grants may be made for specific projects only, or only after the adoption of an approved development plan. They may be made contingent on some supervision. Annual negotiations are often embarrassing and give the receiving country the feeling of having an inferior status. Loans and grants may arouse suspicions of neo-colonialism.

Yet underdeveloped countries seem to be trying to discourage exports, especially on the basis of the existing pattern of trade which they feel (1) is unfair to them, (2) leaves them too dependent on external forces, and (3) is a pattern carried over from the dictates of the colonial system.

As countries strive to develop and draw plans toward that end, they must decide the role that international trade is to play in such development. There is no single solution that applies to all countries. In some cases, expanding international trade may be an all-important consideration. In others, producing their own needs or at least a relatively large share of them may be indicated. Undoubtedly, all countries will find some role for international trade. Even the United States and the U.S.S.R., despite their great size, find it desirable to import some goods and must, of course, expect to pay for them and for the foreign services they use. Others, especially small countries without a variety of resources and with small internal markets, will have to rely heavily on international trade to meet their requirements if they are to do so economically and have a rising scale of living. Some may choose to limit their trade more severely than economic considerations would indicate for political or other reasons. The choice is a complex one. The following discussion indicates the type of considerations to be taken into account.

* According to W. Butler ("Trade and the Less Developed Areas." *Foreign Affairs* [January, 1963], p. 372) in 1960 total exports from underdeveloped countries were $31 billion, and financial assistance (including private foreign investment) totaled $8 billion.

† "Trade Not Aid" became a popular slogan following the publication of Willard Thorp, *Trade, Aid or What?* Baltimore, The Johns Hopkins Press, 1954.

The classical view of the value of international trade to a country was that it led to economic advancement by promoting economic efficiency through division of labor. This view was based on a principle called the "law of comparative advantage," and supposedly operated to extend the benefits of technological advance in one area to others by various indirect effects. The theory of domestic trade, which assumed there were no barriers to the movement of the factors of production and customer preferences, held that the prices charged for any one product would become equal, except for transportation costs, and the returns for identical factors would also become equal. Differential returns among the different kinds of factors would be determined by their relative marginal productivities. In their view of international trade, the Classicists recognized barriers to free movement, but still saw returns being equalized except for certain costs such as transportation. This would occur through trade, which would be conducted in accordance with the principle of comparative advantage. Imbalances in trade would result in monetary flows, which would affect relative price levels and thus tend to restore a balance of trade and offset any tendency for factor returns to depart far from their relative marginal productivities. Trade was thus a substitute for factor movements. To these arguments could be added the view that tying the nations together in trade would make war impossible and thus promote peace.

In accordance with this view, it was to the economic advantage of each country to produce according to its comparative advantage, which might shift continuously as relative resources, costs, and demands changed. Thus, the pattern of trade might be continuously modified, but the principle by which production was determined would remain the same. The law of comparative advantage is based on the demonstration that where productive abilities differ, a country can get indirectly more goods with the same quantity of productive resources by concentrating them in certain lines and trading the surplus for other goods in which another country specializes. This is illustrated by the following example.

Assume that Country A, using its resources, could produce either $80P$ or $100M$, while Country B could produce either $60P$ or $60M$. Country A has an absolute advantage in each; that is, can produce both $P$ and $M$ more cheaply than can Country B. Yet it pays Country A to concentrate on $M$ and Country B to concentrate on $P$, each exchanging its surplus with the other. A can produce 1⅔ times as much $M$ as B, but only 1⅓ times as much $P$. It is said to have, therefore, a comparative advantage in producing $M$, and B has a comparative advantage, or least comparative disadvantage, in producing $P$. The maximum that B will pay for $1M$ is $1P$, for it could divert labor from $P$ to $M$ and produce its own $M$ for that amount. The least that A will take for $1M$ is $0.8P$, for the same reason. The price at which trade could take place would be anywhere between these points, the exact point determining the distribution of the gains from trading. Let us assume that $M$ exchanges for $0.9P$. For $40M$, A can obtain $36P$, and therefore it has $60M$ and $36P$ while B has $40M$ and $24P$. If each country had to meet its own requirements, A could produce $60M$ but only $32P$ with the remaining labor, and it would be $4P$ worse off. Similarly, B could produce its $24P$ and use the remaining labor to produce $M$. However, it could only produce $36M$ and would be $4M$ worse off. If the price were $1M$ for $1P$, Country A would reap all the gains from the trade, and if the price of $M$ dropped to $0.8P$, Country B would reap all the gains. If we let $M$ stand for manufactures, $P$ for primary products, $A$ for advanced countries, and $B$ for underdeveloped countries, we have a very simplified model of current trade as the underdeveloped countries see it. As we shall see, they believe the price of $P$ has dropped and that therefore they have not gained from trade, all the gains going to the advanced countries. As long as both obtain some gain, however, trade is advantageous, even though the gains may not be equal.

A typical illustration of this law is the case of a lawyer who also happens to be the best typist in town. Yet it pays him to hire a typist and devote himself to his law practice, for he has a comparative advantage in that profession. This assumes that he can be kept busy at his law practice. If he cannot find enough law practice to keep busy full time, it would be to his economic advantage, disregarding all other considerations, to dispense with the typist and do his own typing.

In a more complicated situation the advantages of producing more or less of many different commodities must be compared with the gain from importing more or less of any of the many different kinds of commodities produced by other countries. The law of comparative advantage does not imply that one country will produce all of one commodity or several commodities while a second produces all of one or more other commodities. Both countries would likely produce some of each. Otherwise, one would have to say that the least efficient producer in one country can produce a product more efficiently than the best producer in the other country, allowing for transportation costs. This may be the case with respect to some commodities that are produced everywhere and do not enter international trade because they are too bulky or too costly to transport, such as building materials or the services of a barber. Others are traded widely because their production is localized, such as bananas. Others are traded in greater or smaller amounts as relative costs change. The lower the transportation cost, the easier for a commodity to enter or leave trade as relative advantages change. In any event, at any one time, production in a country will be optimized when no additional goods can be obtained more cheaply through trade than by producing them at home.

This is a long-run and a static view; that is, at any one time, given the supply and character of the factor resources, full employment of the factors, and constant production functions, there is one best division of labor among countries, and it is toward this norm that factor allocation tends. Nothing is said as to future shifts in trade. The emphasis is on current economic efficiency based on the most efficient allocation of resources. With each change in costs or in the world's demand and supply conditions brought about by other events, the optimum allocation of resources may change. This theory merely shows how any country should adapt to such a specific change. Given the conditions assumed, it is easy to prove that production would be maximized if the principle were followed. It should be remembered that the argument is a purely economic argument and takes no account of such things as political considerations.

Although the doctrine of comparative advantage is thus a static argument, many believe that maximizing current output is the best way for an underdeveloped country to develop. The most important steps, to them, are to maximize current savings and raise current incomes in order to create a better market. These cannot be done, so the view goes, by using resources inefficiently. Provided the greater output is used effectively, this course would contribute most to development.

This would be especially true when a country's resources were not varied and labor and management were not equipped to carry out a wide variety of tasks. A country well along the road to development, with varied resources and adaptable people, might "get by" if it avoided trade to a large extent. But a small country with small internal markets, undeveloped resources except for a few special ones, and a labor force with low adaptability stands to benefit greatly from trade, exchanging the few specialties in which it has a comparative advantage (usually raw materials and agricultural products) for the manufactured goods, especially capital goods and the more complex consumer goods in which it is inefficient. This classical view is based on the assumption of unequally located resources and differing factor efficiencies and incomes. It is only on this assumption that trade makes sense. Each country would use relatively more of its most abundant factors. The marginal return from each resource would become equal in all industries and all prices would be equal (except for transportation and similar costs) if the optimum allocation were realized. This doctrine is the backbone of the free-trade argument. According to this view, any interferences with trade will result in lessened efficiency.

The later macroeconomic techniques have revealed how trade may change the relative situation of a country so that its comparative advantage may change through time and its growth may be affected. The important considerations here are the interrelations that develop among producers, consumers, and investors in the economy and how the social and political situation adapts to new impacts on the economy. The favorable effects are termed the "spread" effects of trade and are to be distinguished from their opposite, the "backwash" effects, or growth-inhibiting effects. As the first countries industrialized and later ones joined in, exports of primary products from the underdeveloped countries grew. Sometimes these countries developed and sometimes they remained static. The reason for the difference lies in whether or not the gains of trade were transmitted to the internal economy. For growth to occur, it is necessary for markets to grow and for changes to occur in the quantity and quality of the factors of production.

Various spread effects can be cited.[1]

1. Trade brings increased incomes to a number of residents. Profits are earned in the export trade, although where foreign interests own the export industries, these may not accrue to local people. Wages are paid and raw materials purchased. To the extent that this income is spent in the underdeveloped countries (and foreign managers do spend part of their incomes), internal trade is encouraged and new businesses may arise. Business can spring up to supply the new export industry or to process its by-products. Widening markets bring possible economies of scale. The possibilities for awakening the domestic economy exist. The real question is whether the opportunities will be seized and new commercial life stimulated. As we shall see, the underdeveloped countries feel that such incomes are insulated from the local economy and provide little stimulus for development.

2. New export industries introduce new skills into a country. Managerial techniques are improved, labor is trained, and skilled laborers developed. A commercial spirit may be encouraged and improved commercial techniques developed. New technologies are introduced, particularly if the expanding export business is a branch of a foreign-owned progressive business. These new techniques may stimulate innovation in domestic industry. This effect on technology may well be the most valuable impact of trade on an economy.

3. Investment is attracted, so foreign capital pours in.

4. Dormant or idle resources may be brought into use.

5. Certain goods can be obtained more cheaply by imports. If these are raw materials or capital goods, industry may be stimulated.

6. Imports of consumer goods can "spy out demand."[2] In time the country can replace these imports as volume exceeds the minimum quantity

needed to attract efficient industry. Thus, outside industry can stimulate domestic demands. Unfortunately, the more advanced a country, the stronger are likely to be the spread effects; and the less advanced it is, the weaker will be these results.

It is not seriously questioned that trade played a substantial role in the development of countries in the nineteenth century. Britain developed as the leading industrial center, from which growth was transmitted to other countries through trade. The United States, Canada, Australia, and New Zealand, for example, developed partially because of European demand for their foodstuffs and raw materials, although this was not the only factor in their development. Other countries with leading export sectors were Sweden after 1880, Denmark, Switzerland, and the Low Countries.[3] Foreign trade was also a propulsive factor in the case of Japan where, as in the other countries, the expansion of export trade was accompanied by improved agriculture, which afforded improved domestic markets and became the vehicle for spreading the benefits of trade. Trade, in these other countries, has been described by D. H. Robertson[4] as an "engine of growth."

During this period, the underdeveloped countries in the temperate zone had an advantage in food grains and other materials, and were faced with rapidly expanding markets as Europe industrialized. Not only did demand expand but the new producers were able to replace the domestic farmers in the industrialized centers. Technological progress in supplying these materials was encouraged. The internal situations of the emerging nations was such that the internal economies were stimulated and industry developed in turn. For one thing, the standard of living was already relatively high, so wider domestic markets developed quickly. The United States had other advantages such as favorable government policies; favorable economic, legal, political, and social institutions; growth consciousness of the American people; resources of excellent quality, quantity, and location; scarce labor, which acted as an incentive for innovation; a large number of entrepreneurs willing to take risks; a large unhampered market; and an emphasis on building economic and social overheads.[5] Ragnar Nurkse[6] says that as these countries started to grow, they attracted capital and investment. "The first law of development" is "to those who have shall be given."

The essential requirements, if trade is to act as an "engine of growth," are an increasing and steady market for products in which one has an advantage, and an internal economic, political, and social situation that allows the spread effects to dominate. The oil-exporting countries meet the first condition today. Uranium and copper have at times been heavily demanded. Unfortunately, the effects have not always spread to the rest of the economy, as will be indicated in the next section. Expanding markets must be accompanied by sound development efforts. Growth depends not only on growing markets but also on growing supply. The results seem disappointing today, but A. K. Cairncross[7] believes that trade still operates as an engine of growth, and he cites the experience of Argentina, Africa, and India. The failure lies in internal conditions and policies, although conditions for expanding trade may not be so favorable as in the nineteenth century.

This is not to say that growth cannot occur without international trade, but it takes special circumstances for this to happen. The country must have adequate resources of most types, adequate entrepreneurship, labor, and a developing agriculture; in short, it must have all the favorable conditions for development that have been described up to this point. Probably only large countries can develop adequately in this way. The U.S.S.R. is trying it. That other countries, including such large ones as mainland China and India, can follow the same path is doubtful. For one thing, their living standards (and therefore markets) are below those of the U.S.S.R. when she started her program. Few, if any, countries are endowed with the necessary resources and other factors. It is also possible that the U.S.S.R. might have developed faster by permitting more international trade.

## The Trade Situation of Underdeveloped Countries

Underdeveloped countries are generally characterized as exporters of primary products and importers of manufactured products, and advanced countries are pictured in the reverse. Although this is essentially true, qualified description is necessary. Advanced countries, for example, although they export more manufactured than primary goods, still are large exporters of the latter. Underdeveloped countries, although not large exporters of industrial products, still do not have to import the bulk of their needs.

The trade pattern of the world is an unbalanced one.[8] Exports of industrial countries to each other are 43 percent of total trade (excluding the Soviet areas); industrial countries to nonindustrial, 26 percent; nonindustrial countries to industrial, 22 percent; and nonindustrial countries to each other, 9 percent.

Underdeveloped countries do export a much larger percentage of primary products than industrial. However, they do not import all their manufactured needs. Such countries import only about one-third of their manufactures, and this proportion is falling; their imports today are largely capital goods and base metals to support their expanding industries, and foods. Nine-tenths of their food output is consumed at home and one-tenth is exported. Two-fifths of their fuel and raw materials and nearly 100 percent of their oil is exported.[9] Underdeveloped countries import half as much primary products as they export.

Advanced countries import one-tenth of their food and one-fourth of their raw materials, but are, at the same time, the largest exporters of agricultural products.

Most underdeveloped countries seem to have trouble with their balance of payments, except for the oil-rich ones. Some of the problems come from the earnings side, which will be discussed in the next section. Sluggishness of demand for their products, a possible deterioration in their terms of trade, and rapidly fluctuating prices are the major problems discussed there.

However, the problems of their balances of payments do not all spring from the earnings side. It is typical for countries to push their development programs as hard as possible, thus constantly crowding against foreign exchange limits as capital goods and raw materials imports rise. As development proceeds, increasing incomes lead to a desire for imports. Relative neglect of agriculture and rising populations has meant that food must be imported. Inflation has made imports attractive. India's experience is illustrative.[10] As national income growth increased from 2 to 5 percent, new capital goods imports increased probably by 9 percent, but total imports increased 40 to 50 percent of the total of exports.

## The Experience of the Underdeveloped Countries

The underdeveloped countries believe that their past and present role in the international distribution of trade, that of suppliers of primary products, has not contributed to their economic growth, but in fact has detracted from it and promises to do no better in the future. In other words, they believe the backwash effects are stronger than the spread effects. Coupled with this are the failure of trade in primary products to grow rapidly, a worsening of the terms of trade,* and violent fluctuations in the price of primary products. Perhaps the leading proponents of this view are Raul Prebisch,[11] and H. W. Singer.[12] Support of this view is given to a certain extent by G. Myrdal[13] and Ragnar Nurkse.[14] The limitations of this view are well pointed out by G. M. Meier.[15]

The law of comparative advantage is recognized as valid, the only objection being that what is important is not current efficiency or maximizing current output but maximizing economic growth. Production of primary products for exports does not have this effect, according to this view, and

* The price of exported goods relative to the price of imported goods.

what is needed is industrialization. It can be argued that most countries need more diversification and flexibility in their economies but that establishing industry indiscriminately for industry's sake may not necessarily do it.

The first problem is that the backwash effects of trade in primary products is said to be strong, arising in several ways.

1. Foreign investment is not being attracted to underdeveloped countries. In the past, investment was attracted to export industries, primarily raw materials and foods, in response to the investing country's own demands. This is declining, for the various reasons discussed below. Investment is not attracted to manufactures because of the lack of purchasing power in the domestic market. In other words, the engine is running down and no longer exerts a strong tendency toward spread effects.

2. The rise of purchasing power as a result of exports of primary products has, in fact, little effect on stimulating domestic industries. Much of it is spent on foreign goods and the "demonstration effect" leads to an emphasis by the people on foreign goods, thus inhibiting savings. The country then tends to live beyond its means, and so encounters balance-of-payments difficulties, perhaps necessitating the curtailing of essential imports. Foreign industries drive out what little domestic industry exists, forcing these people into unproductive agriculture or trade. H. W. Singer[16] believes that the multiplier (spread) effects really take place in the investing country. That country gets added income, employment by processing the materials, capital, technological knowledge, external economies of production, and so on. This is another way of saying that where economies are not ready for industrialization, the spread effects from trade are weak.

3. Production of primary products for export usually results in foreign enclaves and a dualistic economy. The techniques and skills introduced are far in advance of those already practiced and, as such, are not readily copied. For one thing, the new techniques tend to be capital-intensive and so are not available to local entrepreneurs. Moreover, the small amount of local entrepreneurial talent may be absorbed in the export sector, leaving the domestic sector with weakened leadership. Few domestic workers are hired and supplies and raw materials are bought abroad, so that little employment is afforded the rising population. More and more of the people are forced back into subsistence agriculture, in which the country may have a comparative disadvantage but no alternative. Heavy concentration on a few products leaves a country few alternatives and little flexibility. Factors have the choice of being employed only in the few export industries where employment is limited or in subsistence agriculture or poorly remunerated services.

The export industries become more capital-intensive, and modern and domestic industry become more labor-intensive, primitive, and unproductive. Wages in the export industries remain low, for labor is in great oversupply and almost inexhaustible at the current low wage. Even considerable expansion thus has little effect on raising incomes. When unskilled labor is emphasized and the more skilled workers are imported, labor training is almost nil. Labor turnover is great, so that what work experience is available is not long continued. Peasant output and methods may prove unadaptable to a market economy, especially where there is a surplus population, and so they are allowed to remain relatively untouched by the outside contact. Thus, an emphasis on primary product exports does not condition a country or the factors of production for development.

One wonders whether foreign trade in primary products produces a dualistic economy (that is, prevents the domestic market from growing) or whether a failure of the domestic economy to accept change and to grow prevents the favorable effects of trade from operating. The author inclines toward the latter view. Trade can help, but economic development is primarily a domestic problem. If a country's trade, even in primary products, continued to grow vigorously, its effect would eventually be felt in the domestic economy. Domestic policies could speed or slow the process. A sluggishness of trade is another story.

One of the major concerns of underdeveloped countries is that there is a slow growth in the trade of primary products, which make up the great bulk of the trade of those countries. Except for oil, the share of the underdeveloped countries in world trade is declining as a percentage of total trade, although total trade is expanding. But the expansion does not seem to be sufficient to promote development in the face of all other obstacles that exist. Individual commodities find the same sluggish markets. Seven items make up three-fourths of the total exports of primary produce from underdeveloped countries: petroleum, beverages, textile fibers, base metals, sugar, oilseeds and fats, and rubber.[17] Only the exports in oil and some of the metals seem to be expanding. The exports of tea, coffee, cocoa, cotton, jute, wool, sugar, ground nuts and other oils, and rubber are all at a low point. Individual countries may show satisfactory gains in sales, but this is generally achieved at the expense of other countries.

One hundred years ago the trade in primary products was increasing very rapidly. Then the underdeveloped countries were in the temperate zones, as were the industrial nations. Demand for food and raw materials increased in the industrial nations as populations and incomes rose, but, just as important, the newer countries also replaced the output of producers of primary products in the industrial centers.

Today's conditions are quite different. With few exceptions the growth in trade for primary products is very slow. Thus, trade with the advanced countries cannot operate so effectively in transmitting growth. For example, the lag explains, in part, the lack of interest on the part of investors in advanced countries to make investments in underdeveloped countries. At the same time, populations and labor forces are growing and require employment. This slackening of the rate of growth is occurring for various reasons.[18]

1.   The income elasticity for food products is so low that demand in any given country increases less rapidly than total income. As a result, the share of food in trade is declining. Income elasticity is undoubtedly no less than it was one hundred years ago, but (as just pointed out) at that time, food producers not only met the needs of increasing populations with increasing incomes but also replaced the production of domestic producers. Underdeveloped countries today produce mainly tropical products, and so are meeting an entirely different sort of demand, an addition to the varieties of food. Expansion of sales here depends on rising populations and rising incomes. The effect of the latter is thought to be small because of low income elasticities. Moreover, the countries compete with one another for these sales.

2.   Primary agricultural raw materials are doing no better. For one thing, synthetics (in rubber and fibers, for example) are replacing some of them. The discovery of new synthetics is progressing rapidly, although one might suppose there would be little incentive unless prices of the natural product were high. Importing countries also are making progress in finding substitutes for imports; for example, vegetable oils are being produced domestically by many countries. Progress is also being made in economizing in the use of materials and scraps. Also, complex consumer goods have a low material content compared with selling price. In the advanced countries there is an increasing share of services in the total output, thus holding the increase in materials usage below the increase in total output. On the other hand, new materials become important from time to time; for example, uranium, newsprint, aluminum, and other metals.

3.   Agricultural protectionism in the advanced countries is reducing opportunities for trade.

4.   Internal inflations, which seem to accompany development efforts, have hurt exports. In addition, some countries can raise revenue only by taxing commodities that move in trade. High taxes on exports may injure sales.

Moreover, new countries are entering into competition for this business. For example, exporters of cotton, coffee, and cocoa have multiplied. It seems strange that new countries would enter such seemingly unpromising lines, but this may be what their resources are suited for. When prices have been high, as during the Korean incident, there has been a tendency for production to expand, the expansion sometimes being effected after the boom was past. Unfortunately, it is hard to leave a particular kind of production, once it has been started, especially in the case of tree crops like rubber. Hence, many products are in oversupply, with little prospect that demand will soon catch up at reasonable prices. The scope for further expansion is limited by this oversupply.

However, the foregoing comments apply in general terms. Some countries and some products undoubtedly are doing badly, but others may be doing well. To recommend industrialization or other diversification for a nation on the basis of a general situation is not sound. To forecast the outlook of any particular nation, one would have to look at its exports specifically. Each country must decide its export future on the basis of its own specific situation.

Moreover, future action should not be decided on the basis of past events. Because sales have declined in the past, it does not mean they will in the future, although the general presumption of declining rates of growth for primary products seems general. Each commodity should be analyzed separately, based on population increases, income elasticity, substitutions, and the like.[19]

The sales prospects of the underdeveloped countries appear dim, and these countries believe that the terms of trade for their primary products have been declining and will continue to decline in the future. The best known proponent of this belief is Raul Prebisch of Argentina, whose reasoning will be explained below. Many countries, especially those in Latin America, seem to accept this thesis.

This belief was originally based on two studies of the long-run terms of trade in the United Kingdom,[20] which showed that the terms of trade improved remarkably from 1873 on. From 1873 to 1937 the apparent increase was over 40 percent. From this it was inferred that the terms of trade for the primary products bought by the United Kingdom fell correspondingly. Kindleberger[21] reviewed the terms of trade of European countries for the same period and found contradictory results. Theodore Morgan[22] also reviewed these and other data and found no conclusive proof of falling terms of trade for primary products. He throws doubt on the purely factual conclusions. He points out that only the years 1876 to 1938 were used, whereas data are available from 1801 to 1953. These show an unfavorable trend for British exports from 1801 to the 1860's or 1870's, when the long-run improvement began. By 1953 the terms had turned unfavorable again because of rising prices for primary products due to the Korean incident.

Since then the prices of primary products have dropped sharply and their terms of trade as well. B. A. Balassa[23] says that from 1928 to 1961 there was a slight decrease in the terms of trade for primary products, but that this was due to the fall in the export prices for Australia and New Zealand, which are quite advanced countries.

Thus, the facts are in dispute, and one can prove almost anything by picking the right beginning and ending dates. The producers of primary products seem to look on the high prices of the early 1950's as the normal level, just as stockholders seem to think of normal profits as the highest profits their corporation ever earned. Even more difficult is predicting what the future terms will be.

If the facts are in dispute, how do the rival sides explain what they think has happened? Those who contend that the terms of trade have declined and will continue to decline present four arguments.

1. The major blame for this state of affairs is placed on a great increase in agricultural production in the face of a demand that is inelastic as to price and income. For manufactured goods, demands are considered elastic as to income, if not as to price, so that increased supplies have been and will be met with a demand that is rising more rapidly than that for primary products. Therefore, such products fare reasonably well. Because the demand for primary products has not been rising rapidly and because the demand is inelastic as to price, the increases in supply have been thought to have and will continue to have a disastrous effect on price. In the case of manufactured products, supplies are fairly readily adjusted to price changes, so no wide price swings can take place. In the case of primary products, supplies cannot be adjusted readily, especially for the tree crops, which take some years to become productive but then produce without replanting for many years. When prices are favorable, competitors rush in, but when they are unfavorable, there is no ability to shift to other lines. The problem of the terms of trade is thus immobility of supply and inflexibility of the economy, which prevents a shift to more favorable lines.

2. Perhaps the most used argument is the Prebisch thesis.[24] This view starts with the statement that in the international division of labor, the underdeveloped countries (the periphery) drew the task of supplying food and raw materials, whereas the advanced countries (the center) were to furnish the industrial products. The primary producing countries were supposed to share in the benefits of technological progress through international trade. As technological progress was experienced, the prices of industrial products should have fallen so that some of the gains would be spread throughout the world. Historically, so goes the view, industrial technological progress has been greater than that of primary production in the underdeveloped coun-

tries. Therefore, the prices of industrial products should have fallen relative to those of primary products. However, the reverse has taken place. The reason for this has been the bargaining power of the factors of production in the centers. The factors have forced their incomes up more than the productivity increases, thus resulting in price rises. In the periphery, the bargaining power of the factors has been weak, so that incomes have increased less than productivity, with the result that prices have declined. Because of this, the centers have retained the whole benefit of their own technological development and part of that of the underdeveloped countries as well.

Singer[25] adds to this argument by asserting that the export facilities of the underdeveloped countries never really became a part of the economic structure of those countries, but remained merely as outposts or appendages of the economies of the advanced countries. The processing, servicing, and so on were done in the advanced countries, so that any multiplier effects were felt there and not in the underdeveloped countries.

3. A further reason for the decline lies in the weak bargaining position of the primary producing countries.[26] Few of the primary producers supply more than a small portion of the total world crop, and so have no ability to influence its price but must compete with others who are equally anxious to sell. The countries must export, for the foreign exchange that is necessary for their essential imports depends on exporting this one crop. Moreover, their financial position is too weak to carry over surplus stocks, even if this would have some influence on price.

4. The fact of poverty may be cited as proof of this view, but this is hardly valid. Many underdeveloped countries have taken much of their increased productivity in the form of more children and not in higher incomes. Moreover, there are many reasons why nations have low per capita incomes. The poorer countries are mainly primary product exporters, but not all primary product exporters are poor; for example, Australia, New Zealand, Denmark (although now more industrial than agricultural), and some of the oil-producing countries. In the United States, Iowa is an agricultural state, but a prosperous one. Countries with a large proportion of industry may have higher incomes, but they are able to maintain this high ratio of industry because they have a prosperous primary product sector. As previously suggested, it could be that countries have industrialized because they were prosperous and not that they have become prosperous because they have industrialized.

The contention of declining terms of trade and the conclusions drawn from it have been questioned. Representative criticisms are cited.[27]

1. As already mentioned, the alleged proof has been challenged. More-

over, even if the terms of trade of the United Kingdom have been improving, this does not mean that the terms of trade of all underdeveloped countries have been falling, for various reasons. In the first place, the terms of trade are an average among many exports and many imports, so that the terms for any one other country would be unlikely to be exactly the reverse. Second, quality changes in the products exported and imported have taken place and are not reflected in the statistical calculations of the terms of trade. By and large, greater improvements have taken place in manufactured goods than in primary products. Third, the composition of exports and imports has changed over time, many new ones appearing while others disappear. This also is not accurately reflected in the calculations. Fourth, and most important, no correction is made for the fall in transportation cost. The United Kingdom values its imports at the landed cost and its exports as they leave its shores. It is entirely possible that the United Kingdom could have paid less for its imports and the exporting countries received more because of the rapid fall in transportation costs which occurred. The same, in reverse, could be said for the exports of the United Kingdom.

2.   A comparison of selling prices by themselves is no proof of good or ill fortune. Everyone would, of course, like as high prices as possible for his products, but of equal importance is what it costs to produce the goods. If productivity has increased so that fewer factors are used to produce a given output, one would expect the price to go down. The country exporting such a product would suffer, only if the use of a given quantity of factors would buy less than at some previous time. This is known as the factoral terms of trade as distinguished from the previously discussed commodity terms of trade, and would be the more valid comparison. Unfortunately, there are no direct comparisons to show whether the factors employed in producing primary products are earning more or less imports than previously.

A third term-of-trade concept is the income terms of trade.* Meier[28] says that the factoral terms and the income terms have improved for many poor countries, although their commodity terms of trade may not have. These would be more significant measures for judging the effects of trade on welfare.

Conversely, the mere existence of improving commodity terms may not mean that a country is better off.[29] Falling import prices may ruin domestic industry. An increased price of exports necessitated by increased inefficiency, assuming competitors are equally affected, is no advantage. Falling

---

* The income terms of trade equal the price of exports times the quantity of exports, divided by the price of imports. This represents the capacity of a country to import, based on exports.

terms due to increased efficiency may be an advantage. Prices may fall, but the factors may receive more. Thus, one cannot make a blanket statement that falling terms are responsible for the present position of underdeveloped countries. The exact situation must be analyzed for each country.

3.  There is doubt that the terms of trade will inevitably run against primary products. As more countries industrialize and populations and incomes increase, demand should increase despite a low-income elasticity; and supplies of primary products may shrink, making more favorable terms for primary products. Also the law of diminishing returns can be expected to lead to increased prices for primary products. Opposing these forces is technological progress, which has eliminated scarcities of raw materials in the past and will continue to do so in the future. What the outcome will be is not certain. Certainly, no one can be positive that the terms of trade will inevitably turn against primary products. This seems to the author, however, to be the more likely prospect, but not to the extent that improvements in producing the primary products will not overcome the trend and make it profitable to produce them and even to expand production.

4.  It should be kept in mind that advanced countries are also primary product exporters; in fact, they export slightly more than do the underdeveloped countries.

By and large, it has not been proved that terms of trade shifts are such as to require a shift to industry. Nor have the critics demonstrated that the view is false. The argument as a generalization for all underdeveloped countries is faulty. Many products show unfavorable price trends and sluggish demand. Others seem to be doing well. Each country must analyze its own prospects, but certainly it should not pursue or force a losing business. Nor should it abandon a profitable one just for the sake of industrialization.

Perhaps a problem for countries that are exporters of primary products, which is more important than either sluggish demand or declining terms of trade, is that such products are vulnerable to violent short-term price fluctuations. Such fluctuations in purchasing power are particularly significant for underdeveloped countries because they are highly specialized in exports of primary products. A change of 5 percent in average export prices equals the whole flow of private and public capital and government grants.[30]

Most underdeveloped countries depend for their exchange earnings on a few primary commodities. Tables 11.1 and 11.2 illustrate this dependence. Thus, a major swing in price for these commodities can cause a major swing in exchange earnings. That the swings in price have been substantial, there is no doubt. Year to year fluctuations in Asia and the Far East, in both price and quantity sold, have been remarkable, as Table 11.3 shows.

A more extensive United Nations study[31] of 25 commodities for the pe-

**TABLE 11.1.**

*Commodity Exports of Various Countries*

| Country | Product | Percent of Exchange Earnings* |
|---|---|---|
| Venezuela | Oil | 92 |
| Colombia | Coffee | 75 |
| Brazil | Coffee | 61 |
| Burma | Rice | 74 |
| Egypt | Cotton | 72 |
| Pakistan | Cotton, jute | 70 |
| Malaya | Tin, rubber | 73 |
| Ghana | Cocoa | 62 |
| Chile | Copper | 68 |
| Rhodesia | Copper | 54 |
| Australia | Wool | 50 |
| Uruguay | Wool | 50 |

SOURCE: International Labour Office, *Employment Objectives in Economic Development*, Geneva, 1961, p. 124.

* NOTE: The years to which these percentages were applicable were not given.

**TABLE 11.2.**

*Exports of Asian and Far Eastern Countries, 1948-1956*

| Country | Product | Percent of Exchange Earnings |
|---|---|---|
| Brunei | Oil | 96 |
| Burma | Rice | 78 |
| Malaya | Rubber, tin | 83 |
| Ceylon | Tea, rubber | 80 |
| Thailand | Rice, rubber | 75 |
| Taiwan (1950-56) | Sugar, rice | 74 |
| Pakistan | Cotton, jute | 74 |
| Indochina (1948-54) | Rubber, rice | 71 |
| N. Borneo | Rubber, logs, lumber | 66 |
| Indonesia | Rubber, oil, tin | 70 |
| Philippines | Copra, oil, sugar, abaca | 69 |

SOURCE: United Nations, Economic Commission for Asia and the Far East, *Economic Survey of Asia and the Far East*, 1957, p. 113.

riod 1901 to 1951 shows the same wide variations. The average year-to-year price fluctuations for these commodities was 13.7 percent, with a high average of 21 percent (rubber) and a low of 5 percent. The average cyclical swing was 12.8 percent on the upswing and 13 percent on the downswing, with the maximum swings a +22 percent (shellac) and a −21 percent (silk). The average within-a-year variation was 26.7 percent, with a high of 37 (rubber). This study also found that volume fluctuated more than price.

In a ten-year period, coffee prices varied from 75 percent above average to 50 percent below; cocoa, from almost double the average to almost 50 percent below; and sugar, from 50 percent above to 25 percent below.[32]

## TABLE 11.3.

*Fluctuation of Export Prices, Quantities, and Proceeds of Principal
Primary Commodities, 1948-1956*
(*in percent*)

| PRODUCTS AND REGION | AVERAGE YEAR-TO-YEAR FLUCTUATION | | | LARGEST YEAR-TO-YEAR FLUCTUATION | | |
|---|---|---|---|---|---|---|
| | Proceeds | Price | Quantity | Proceeds | Price | Quantity |
| Rubber | | | | | | |
| ECAFE Region | 32.2 | 29.4 | 5.6 | 59.0 | 53.4 | 19.4 |
| Cotton | | | | | | |
| Pakistan (1948-56) | 24.3 | 18.7 | 20.8 | 46.0 | 35.4 | 49.6 |
| Jute | | | | | | |
| Pakistan (1949-56) | 21.6 | 15.5 | 17.7 | 40.2 | 31.5 | 43.2 |
| Hemp | | | | | | |
| Philippines | 21.8 | 14.2 | 18.6 | 38.9 | 37.3 | 38.7 |
| Sugar | | | | | | |
| Taiwan | 23.9 | 13.1 | 32.1 | 35.0 | 35.1 | 53.4 |
| Philippines | 16.8 | 4.8 | 15.6 | 54.0 | 7.1 | 47.7 |
| Copra | | | | | | |
| Philippines | 22.6 | 18.9 | 13.6 | 42.0 | 39.7 | 24.8 |
| Tin | | | | | | |
| Malaya | 13.8 | 11.0 | 11.1 | 24.1 | 30.3 | 33.5 |
| Petroleum | | | | | | |
| Brunei | 15.3 | 8.8 | 9.9 | 59.8 | 50.3 | 19.7 |
| Indonesia | 12.7 | 8.2 | 12.3 | 33.7 | 26.1 | 32.3 |
| Rice | | | | | | |
| Burma (1950-56) | 11.0 | 15.7 | 17.0 | 24.0 | 25.0 | 33.0 |
| Thailand | 14.7 | 11.0 | 14.9 | 35.2 | 24.8 | 33.2 |
| Tea | | | | | | |
| Ceylon | 10.9 | 11.3 | 3.1 | 26.5 | 26.4 | 8.0 |

SOURCE: United Nations, Economic Commission for Asia and the Far East, *Economic Survey of Asia and the Far East*, 1957, p. 113.

The reasons for such fluctuations can be found both in sudden changes in demand and variations in supply; there is little agreement, however, as to which factor is more responsible for the difficulties that underdeveloped countries face. Demand fluctuates with such conditions as prosperity in the customer countries and war. When depressed conditions occur, prices drop drastically because supplies cannot be adjusted rapidly. Boom periods cause high prices for the same reason. The essential problem, thus, is widely fluctuating demand with low elasticity of supply. Because demands are largely inelastic, sales do not increase greatly as prices fall.

Supply variations are due to irregularities in the weather, political instability, inflationary pressures, changing domestic demands for subsistence crops, changes in tariff policies and taxes, and government domestic price policies. For example, the government may require deliveries of certain quantities of a product at fixed prices. If the price is set too low, the producers may shift to other crops. This seems to have been the case with the Indonesian price on sugar, resulting in diversion of the lands to rice production. New suppliers can increase quantities from time to time. Surprisingly, price and supply fluctuations have not been inverse, but have actually supplemented one another so that income swings have been greater than price swings.[33] As previously mentioned, supplies are more elastic upward than downward, although the speed of reaction varies from product to product.

International trade for the underdeveloped countries is generally large compared with total national product, so that fluctuations have considerable effect on the total income. The ratio is usually around 20 percent,[34] but does run higher. For example, from 1949 to 1953 the exports of the Federation of Malaya were 51 percent of gross domestic product, and from 1948 to 1955 those of Ceylon were 34 percent.[35] Boom periods have often meant increased incomes, which have led either to inflation because domestic output of consumer goods could not be expanded quickly, to an import of consumer goods, or even to a shift of consumption to luxury goods. These add little to development. For example, one would not recommend luxury industries as a basis for development. The gains from increased export prices usually go to people not interested in real capital formation; for example, foreign firms, exporters, and locally based aliens. Little may be transmitted to native producers.[36]

On the other hand, depressed conditions seriously affect the primary-product exporting countries, which rely heavily on their foreign exchange earnings to obtain the capital equipment necessary for development and often for essential consumer goods. Export taxes may also supply a considerable part of government revenues. If receipts drop, the budgets of the underdeveloped countries may be disrupted, and cuts may be required in government undertakings and imports unless the country has large foreign exchange reserves. Either essential foods or machinery imports may be cut. Development projects already started may have to be postponed, with a resulting waste of the previous investment. Domestic undertakings such as public works, which are a precondition to development, may be included in the postponed projects or may be financed by inflationary means. Many countries have little margin over subsistence, so a sudden drop in export earnings may have serious consequences and certainly will reduce savings. Fluctuation makes a steady government policy difficult.

Exchange instability causes frequent changes in the tightness of import controls and thus affects the internal economy through fluctuating costs, disrupted business, and so on. Instability also gives a mentality of a "large killing" in raw materials and therefore prevents needed shifts to other lines.[37]

## Proposed Remedies

Various proposals for aiding the trade positions of the underdeveloped countries have been offered, ranging from making the present trade profitable to compensating for losses sustained, changing the pattern of trade, and dropping out of trade to a large degree. The solutions do not account for the possibility that the interests of the underdeveloped countries and those of the advanced nations may not coincide. An acceptable solution must be satisfactory to both sides. In effect, it is largely a question of how far the advanced nations are willing to go to aid the underdeveloped countries. The advanced nations are interested in full employment for their workers and do not appear willing to open their markets to unrestricted imports of primary products or simple manufactures. Nor does it seem that they wish to subsidize the producers in underdeveloped countries along the lines of the United States agricultural policy. The alternative may be increased aid in some form or increased barriers to trade. The solution must also depend on a compromise among the various objectives of nations, such as economic development, full employment, a favorable balance of payments, price stability, and national defense.

There is much that the underdeveloped countries can do for themselves and this should be attended to at once. Unfortunately, some of the necessary actions require time to work out, so that other expedients are necessary also. But the underdeveloped countries should do what they can. Much of the difficulty lies in the fact that their economies are so inflexible that production cannot shift away from the unprofitable lines to more profitable ones. This is a problem of the low state of development. The problem of foreign trade, in other words, arises from a failure to provide for development, rather than the other way around. Activities that promote general development will lessen trade problems. These include provisions for economic and social overheads, improving agriculture, establishing industry where possible, and all the other things already discussed. As development proceeds, income from trade will aid in transforming the economy. The real problem is a lack of carry-over from trade to the rest of the economy. Activities that promote efficiency would also help.

The underdeveloped countries must control inflation to the degree possible so as not to weaken their export capacity or to encourage imports. Excessive export taxes should be avoided. These countries must also learn that during export booms, investments and consumption must be restrained to a level that can be sustained over a long period. This means insulating the economy from part of the boom-time income, building up foreign exchange reserves to finance imports during emergencies, and taking steps to level out the expendable income of consumers. To do these things, various actions are possible: The central bank can hold or release foreign exchange reserves; state marketing boards may pay a stable price to peasant producers to assure them a steady income, accumulating profits during booms and sustaining losses during dull periods; and export and other taxes may be varied. It will also be necessary to prevent the dissipation of exchange in unnecessary consumption imports and to allocate it to those goods that will promote domestic development and raise productivity. Also, agriculture should be improved so as to lessen the need for food imports. These steps will not be easy, but they are essential. Without internal reforms leading to development, other measures will not prove effective.

It often seems that underdeveloped countries favor cutting down on their traditional exports, or at least refusing to expand them, chiefly on the grounds that they are considered inferior. It may be good policy to do just that in specific cases, but only on the basis of a thorough investigation of the specific facts and not in general. These exports still provide the most reliable markets for underdeveloped countries, and these countries will have to rely on them for some time. It is in these products that the underdeveloped countries probably have a comparative advantage. Other remedies should be sought, but opportunities in the old lines should not be neglected. Trade in these should be expanded to the extent that markets do expand. Where such trade is actually unprofitable, investment should be withdrawn in as orderly a manner as possible. The first step is to try to raise the productivity in these export industries. The second is to try to expand or stabilize these markets or to develop new products. One possibility is to serve the markets of newly developing countries. Such efforts will not bring a permanent solution unless market trends change more favorably, but they can help until more fundamental reforms bear fruit.

Underdeveloped countries might industrialize for home consumption. This is part of the solution recommended by Ragnar Nurkse;[38] he also suggests expanding traditional exports where possible and seeking industrial exports. Nurkse believes that investment has been attracted only to export industries because of the lack of a domestic market, which in turn is due to a failure to have balanced growth. Thus, it is necessary for underdeveloped countries to develop a variety of domestic industries so as to generate local purchasing power and to serve as a market for each other's products. Because individual investors will not be willing to undertake a new industry in the absence of a wide variety of industries, it is necessary to start through public investment. It is not necessary, however, to promote all industries, no matter how inefficient. It is sufficient to promote a wide variety as long as they are efficient. Therefore there is plenty of room for both specialization and balanced development. Costly and inefficient industries should not be promoted, for they would be a drag on growth. This program of balanced growth also requires a comparable advance in agriculture, if domestic purchasing power is to be increased. Moreover, such a program does not preclude exports of primary products or of those manufactured goods that can find markets, especially in other underdeveloped countries.

Raul Prebisch[39] bases his argument for the promotion of domestic industry on the assumption that exports, especially of primary products, cannot be expanded rapidly enough to provide the necessary imports and that comparative advantage at the margin favors import-saving commodities. Therefore, it is necessary to develop import substitutes, especially for consumer goods, which he feels can be developed with no detriment to productivity, although with some initial "inconvenience." He does not feel that import-substitute industries for industrial materials and capital goods can be developed as effectively.

A. K. Cairncross[40] advocates that underdeveloped countries widen their range of exports and develop domestic sources of the simpler manufactures as a means of breaking away from dependence on one or a few primary product exports and thus avoiding all the dangers risked by extreme specialization.

As previously mentioned, increased incomes stimulate a diversified economy more than a specialized one. The income effects of increased trade are more likely to be realized in increased production than in increased prices. Highly specialized economies are apt to remain dualistic in nature, whereas diversified and flexible ones are not. One cannot help but be impressed by the fact that as Mexico has developed, her exports and her internal production have changed constantly, although her exports remain mostly primary products.[41] Less rapidly developing countries show no changes in exports or domestic production.

Promoting import-substitute consumer goods may not solve the problem of an unfavorable balance of payments, however, for their development may increase the demand for imports of capital goods and raw materials. In this case a country must increase its exports or develop its own capital goods industries. An attempt at too wide a diversification, especially for small countries, may result in great inefficiency. Few, if any, existing underdeveloped countries could justify such wide diversification by becoming practically self-sufficient. They must continue to export and import. To adopt diversification merely for the sake of diversification is poor policy, since the probable result will be inefficiency because the supply of factors is inappropriate or the market does not permit some industries to reach the minimum size necessary for efficiency. Inefficient output will only hinder growth. Capital should be invested only where it is most advantageous economically, unless there are compelling political and social reasons to do otherwise.

Inescapably, all countries must export in order to get necessary or desirable imports. Because underdeveloped countries feel that concentrating on primary-product exports is poor policy, they may try to develop exports of manufactured goods. This would have the advantage of earning foreign exchange in an area where demand is presumably expanding rapidly, thus giving considerable opportunity for growth. If successful in increasing their exports, this would eliminate the necessity for improving productivity in all fields. For example, it might be possible to bypass the need to improve peasant agriculture and to import the necessary food.*

Entering into foreign trade with manufactured articles that compete with those of existing producers is no simple task. Assuming no artificial barriers such as tariffs, it still would not be easy. For one thing, it would be necessary to overcome the habits of customers who prefer to maintain established connections because they are a known quantity. Therefore, new exporters must develop their selling techniques, and here they are at a disadvantage with the older exporters. Or, they must offer a superior product or a similar product at a lower price. Again they are at a disadvantage, for the advanced countries have developed better quality controls, have developed the techniques for increasing efficiency, and have the technical knowledge to effect constant improvements in their products or even to develop substitutes. Even if a country succeeds in finding a market, it is not always easy to keep it. Maintaining one's position requires constant innovation, both with respect to one's product and to the techniques of production, and this takes business and technical leadership. Relying on exports of manufactures may prove a precarious business, especially since there are a large number of underdeveloped countries trying to do the same thing or, at least, trying to produce their own requirements. Each country might find that it was trading specialization in a few primary products for specialization in a few manufactured ones, with much the same hazards. Japan managed to break into world markets by flooding the markets with salesmen, offering extensive credits, cutting prices, and paying great deference to consumers' demands. Breaking into world trade takes boldness and resoluteness, especially since so many countries are trying to follow Japan's example.

Underdeveloped countries seem to have a natural advantage in producing

---

* Obviously, not all countries could do this; food prices would rise and make the development of agricultural exports attractive.

the simpler manufactures, especially articles of everyday use. The textile industry, for example, is usually one of the first to develop in a country. The techniques are simple, and low labor costs are an advantage. For this reason it may be called a "frontier industry," just as wheat and sheep raising are frontier agricultural industries; that is, other forms of agriculture prove more profitable in the more developed areas and push them to the newer or frontier regions. The same thing might be expected to happen in the case of textiles and other simple manufactures, whereas the advanced countries concentrate on producing capital goods and the more complex consumer goods.

But developing efficient industries in most underdeveloped countries is not a simple matter and will take time. Internal inefficiency and inflation will prove to be potent obstacles. Domestic markets are too small to allow economies of scale, so that it will be difficult to develop low costs. Labor may be cheap, but not in terms of unit costs for industrial purposes because of its inefficiency and because of inexpert management. Until such industries are established locally and gain some experience, they will have difficulty in getting a foothold in foreign markets. This will require social overheads, labor training, and other measures previously mentioned, including agricultural development in order to provide markets. Because it is difficult to get started locally, underdeveloped countries have advocated one-way protection; that is, protective tariffs at home for their new industries, but free trade in the advanced countries where they hope to find markets.

Moreover, the types of industries that the underdeveloped countries might be expected to develop are ones for which total demand is not expanding rapidly.[42] Growth will depend on replacing domestic producers, and the advanced nations may not be willing to face the problem of letting such industries die and shifting resources to the more technically advanced ones. That this would be advantageous in the long run is probably correct, but economic policy in democracies is not always based on long-run considerations.

Thus, for the underdeveloped countries to shift to exports of manufactures depends to a considerable extent on a lenient commercial policy in the older industrial countries, and this is not to be counted on. Even if unrestricted imports were permitted, there is no assurance that this would be continued. Underdeveloped countries might then be more at the mercy of the trade policies of other countries than they now are. If the advanced countries did remove their tariffs on light manufactures, exports for the underdeveloped countries would grow, but there is a real question whether they would grow rapidly enough to meet the needs of all the countries that are trying to develop. Not only would the advanced countries have to lower their protective barriers, but they would also have to provide financing and technical and managerial advice. The establishment of branch factories by firms from advanced countries might be the answer, but this would introduce another situation the underdeveloped countries would not like. If the underdeveloped countries were successful in expanding their sales rapidly, the resulting unemployment in the importing countries would be almost certain to cause a reversal of policy.

What underdeveloped countries need is preferential treatment in a given market and not free trade because of the potential intense competition among them. The British Commonwealth, with its close political ties, seems suited to this policy as the United States has been with Puerto Rico. Few advanced countries seem likely to be willing to open their ports to all countries. Perhaps regional trading areas, to be discussed below, are the answer until the industries of the underdeveloped countries can get established. The most promising area of expansion is with other underdeveloped countries, but this will require some sort of preferential arrangement.

One way in which the advanced countries could help immediately, but are not likely to because of domestic pressures, would be to reduce their barriers to agricultural imports, such as sugar and meat in the United States. Also, heavy consumption taxes in Europe on such products as coffee, tea, and tobacco affect consumption adversely. Some modification of these could help.

The best chance for these countries to break into trade is for them to increase their output of goods for the home market. Eventually, each country will discover those industries with the best opportunity for success;[43] first of all this will require general economic development, including agricultural development.

The underdeveloped countries have been trying to reduce trade barriers, without great success. The General Agreement on Tariffs and Trade (GATT) has effected slight concessions to textiles, but the underdeveloped countries have been dissatisfied with the progress and feel that GATT is too well controlled by the advanced nations. They prefer a new organization in which they have a greater voice. In response to this, a large and long conference, called the United Nations Conference on Trade and Development, was held in Geneva from March 23 to June 16, 1964. The seventy-seven underdeveloped countries participating in the conference[44] insisted on a new international division of labor based on increasing industrialization in the underdeveloped areas. The achievements of this conference have been listed as follows:

1. A tremendous amount of detailed study and identification of problems and suggestions for their solution.

2. Establishment of a Trade and Development Board.
3. The beginning of a general economic charter for trade and development.
4. Acceptance of the principle that commodity prices can no longer be left to the market but that export earnings should be assured.
5. Industrialized countries were advised not to extend trade barriers on the main commodity exports and to reduce internal taxes on tropical products.
6. The principle was accepted that the advanced countries would study the feasibility of trade preference in manufactures and semimanufactures to the underdeveloped countries.
7. The principle of industrial transformation was accepted; that is, that simple industries would be transferred eventually to the newer industrial countries.
8. Industrialized countries were asked to give 1 percent of their gross national product to foreign aid.

Whether anything develops remains to be seen. The major requirements are improved efficiency on the part of the underdeveloped and a willingness to cooperate on the part of the advanced, despite temporary economic maladjustments.

A frequent proposal has been to stabilize the price of individual commodities by various means. The problem is to prevent temporary wide fluctuations in exchange earnings, yet permit supplies to adjust to long-term trends. Unfortunately, it is hard to discover the latter, so the former goal tends to predominate. International agreements have been in effect for wheat, sugar, tea, rubber, tin, coffee, and other products. Various devices have been used or proposed.[45]

One possibility is for the primary producers to control output, and therefore price, but this has been unsuccessful. The problems are financing the storage of surpluses and getting all the possible competitors to agree. When the British tried to control rubber production and Brazil attempted to stabilize coffee prices, other countries increased their share of the market. Moreover, this is unworkable when the importing countries can produce synthetics, as in the case of rubber, or can produce substitute supplies such as vegetable oils, or can produce the commodity itself, such as tobacco. Only when all producers can be controlled and no closer substitutes can be found do the underdeveloped countries have any opportunity for control, and past performance does not indicate much hope for success.

Multilateral agreements, including both producer and consumer countries, might have a chance for success if all parties could agree. The wheat agreement was designed to keep prices within certain limits. Buying countries agreed to buy unlimited quantities at the minimum price, and exporters agreed to sell at the maximum price. Unfortunately, it has never been possible to get all producers and all consumers in one agreement, so there has been a temptation to break the agreement; producers sell above maximum prices when the opportunity is offered and buyers seek prices below the minimum. Simple price setting without quantity restrictions does not seem workable. Regulation of production would require an expensive control mechanism and interferences few countries would care for.

International quota agreements such as those that have prevailed for sugar are a third possibility. This method provides for a fixed quota of exports into the major markets by each of the producing countries. The objective is to prevent excessive competition and to secure orderly reduction in an overdeveloped industry. Unfortunately, this stabilizes price by restricting production and freezes a pattern of production and exports that does not reflect changing production costs.

A fourth method is the use of international buffer stocks, which was used, in part, in the tin program. Under such a scheme there would normally be an international administering authority, which would buy surplus supplies when prices were low and sell them when prices were high. It would have the advantage of not interfering with production and individual country exports, but it would present the problems of financing the storage of surpluses and of finding the right price and price trend around which to stabilize. The underdeveloped countries want "fair prices," and the result might be large and growing stocks. One could also expect pressure not to release stored stocks when prices were rising.

Bilateral agreements, whereby a country agrees to buy certain quantities on long-term contracts, gives some stability, but only to a limited degree. This probably means government trading. The major difficulty is that surpluses become concentrated on the noncontract markets, greatly depressing the prices there. The U.S.S.R. now uses this device extensively, but requires that payment be made in her own goods, which may not turn out to be much of a bargain. Nevertheless, the stability offered seems to have gained her good will.

A last proposal is to adopt a commodity currency scheme. This would establish an international currency backed 100 percent by a combination of primary products. Each product would be represented in the monetary unit in proportion to its value in world production, adjusted periodically. Producers could thus always sell a unit of commodities for international currency or buy back units as they chose. This is similar to a gold standard except that different commodities and a combination of them would be used. However, it would present more problems of storage, if production became excessive. The monetary value of the commodities would remain stable, but their purchasing power in other goods could fluctuate as the supply of currency increased or decreased.

Stabilizing individual prices does not seem very feasible, as the United States experience with agricultural price supports shows. Other stabilizing devices seem necessary. These have as their objective the stabilization of total exchange receipts for a country or total receipts from a specified list of commodities rather than receipts from any individual commodity. The prices of these would be allowed to fluctuate freely. Thus, the emphasis in stabilizing production would be on a country's importing power, and not on the fortunes of the individual producers.

Three types of proposals have been made.[46] One would provide loans, on a bilateral basis, by the advanced countries to compensate for decreases in their purchases of certain commodities. The advanced countries would make available a certain amount of foreign exchange each year, based on the amount earned in a prior period (for example, the preceding year or an average of the previous three years). In years of good exchange earnings, the loans would be repaid. A second proposal would have the International Monetary Fund (IMF) make up for shortfalls in foreign exchange, particularly if caused by a depression in a major industrial country. This would involve loan limits for IMF in excess of those permitted today and for much longer periods. This would have the advantage of not being based on bilateral agreements, which might embarrass a given nation, and would introduce an established agency that could carefully scrutinize applications for loans, always assuming that such loans would not be made automatically, as underdeveloped countries apparently prefer. The third plan is a development insurance fund into which all nations would pay, the advanced economies contributing a larger share, presumably based on national output. Countries that would experience a given fall in exchange receipts would be compensated up to a certain percentage of some fixed or moving average base. The benefits could be in the form of either outright claims or repayable loans. Actually, this amounts to an aid plan rather than an insurance plan.

Such proposals appear deceptively simple. They seem to have the advantage of leaving prices free to fluctuate and to adjust around long-term trends without having to agree on a price at which to stabilize or to project a price trend. The need for periodic revisions to correct inaccurate predictions would be avoided. However, there would be disagreements over the period to use as a base, the exact commodities to be covered, and the percentage of loss to be compensated. They do act directly to accomplish what is desired, that is, to protect countries against sudden large falls in exchange earnings. At the same time, they permit gradual adjustment to changing trends. Advanced countries would find such stabilization beneficial, for the underdeveloped countries could maintain in large measure their imports of capital and other goods.

But all these proposals encounter difficulties. They compensate not only for losses of exchange that arise from demand instability, but also for those that arise from supply instability, including national policies of the countries involved. For example, a country could cut its exchange earnings by curtailing its production, by requiring that it be consumed at home, or by instituting tariffs that would provoke retaliation or lower customers' exchange earnings. Moreover, there is less assurance that the funds would be used more constructively than in the case of the alternative of foreign loans and grants, which can be withheld from undesirable projects.

Despite their limitations, these proposals, if properly safeguarded, show more promise as a means of solving the problem than do efforts to stabilize the prices of individual commodities.


## Underdeveloped Countries and Protection

Underdeveloped countries, in general, see protection as a means of increasing wealth by promoting industry, which is equated with growth and wealth. They feel that free international trade works to the advantage of the advanced nations and tends to prevent the industrial advance of the underdeveloped. They point out that the free trade argument is based on the gains from efficient allocation of resources through the operation of the principle of comparative advantage. This principle works only under static conditions, and its value for promoting growth is suspect.

Two general means of protecting industry are used: tariffs and exchange controls. Either may be used, or both may be combined. The case for protection is based on a number of standard arguments.[47] Perhaps the favorite argument is the "infant industry" argument, familiar in the history of the discussion of Western tariffs. This holds that, with protection, there is an incentive for domestic investment to enter industry, which is a prerequisite to development, and that some industries (the infant industries) offer enough promise of future success that they could, in time, stand on their own feet and provide an industrial base. The greatest fallacy of this argument is that it offers no way to identify the true infant industries, nor does it suggest when protection should be withdrawn, once the need is past. Because it is difficult to recognize the true infant industries, the tendency is to promote a wide range of industries, with little analysis of their growth prospects.* There is some value in picking out a few of the most promising

---

* The International Bank for Reconstruction and Development reports on Venezuela (1961, p. 207) and for Ceylon (1953, p. 149) give examples of this and express fears and beliefs that inefficient industries with low-quality products have been promoted.

industries to protect, but general protection can lead to the inefficient use of resources and leave the country worse off. J. Viner[48] rejects this whole argument on the grounds of probable irrational selection, wide extension, failure to provide domestic competition, the tendency toward permanence of protection, and the cost imposed on other industries during development. Subsidies are probably superior to protection for the purpose of promoting specific industries.

In addition to the infant industry argument, an "infant economy" argument is used. This is based on the need to develop economic and social overheads and train the people for industry before any industry can become competitive. Until some industrial experience is gained, all industries are vulnerable to foreign competition, and the country is prevented from developing any industry. In other words, industry can get established only by getting started. Protection is necessary to establish those industries that will affect the level of skill and technology and change habits, particularly by providing employment outside agriculture. This, in effect, avoids (or at least postpones) identifying the true infant industries. However, if too many inefficient industries are protected, and if other countries retaliate against the exports of a country following such a policy, a serious decrease in total productivity may result. If resources are not ready to move into industry, the result will be rapid price rises for the protected goods and a glut of the exported products.

The "inferiority of agriculture" thesis holds that labor and capital are more productive in industry than in agriculture, and that industry promotes social change and possesses more external economies and linkage effects. Because of this, it pays to develop manufactures even at some temporary sacrifice. If the assertions were true, it would pay to shift to industry. However, the facts have not been established and must be investigated for each country. There will be little gain in shifting a man from agriculture where his marginal productivity is low to an industry where it is even lower. Moreover, a strong agriculture helps form a strong industrial base, so that the two must progress together. The trouble is not agriculture itself, but inefficient methods of agriculture.[49]

The supposed unfavorable terms-of-trade situation and the fact of fluctuating prices are used as arguments for protection. In the first place, the ability to impose a tariff and to divert resources to industry, thus cutting the supply of exports, is said to increase the country's bargaining power in international trade. This is doubtful unless the country is an important consumer and (or) controls the major part of the supply of the product it exports. In such a case it would probably have adequate bargaining power anyway. Secondly, when the economy is diversified by promoting balanced internal development, including industry, the necessity to exchange primary products for industrial products is avoided. Only if the new industries use labor and capital effectively will there be any possible gain.

Protective measures may be employed to protect the balance of payments, especially during depressions abroad, when the demand for primary products falls sharply. Raising tariffs or, more likely, varying exchange requirements will make imports more expensive, thus cutting them down and preventing too unfavorable a balance. It is easier to seek a balance by decreasing imports than by increasing exports, but this may not be favorable for growth if restrictions on imports affect production. The restriction of unnecessary imports (for example, of consumption luxuries) is desirable in such situations, but care must be exercised to use protection on a selective basis. General protection is likely to hurt total output, at least temporarily, cause a possible loss of exports, and especially if other countries retaliate, at least make it difficult to meet foreign indebtedness. Unless the fundamental causes of an unfavorable balance are removed, general protection is not likely to improve the situation.

Protection is also thought to result in increased direct foreign investment when foreign industries attempt to avoid tariffs by establishing branches. Unfortunately, this occurs only where there are substantial domestic markets, so that only the relatively more developed areas can benefit.

Protection may also be used to insulate economic plans against international trade disturbances. Only the imports necessary to meet the objectives of the plan or to offset deviations from the plan would be allowed, as is the policy of the U.S.S.R. This, again, is successful only if the country has plentiful and varied resources. Moreover, there is no reason why international trade cannot be incorporated into an economic plan.

Of all the foregoing arguments the only one that carries much weight is the infant industries argument. It is very doubtful that protection, unless highly selective and restrained, really aids an underdeveloped country; instead, it may be a drain on its potential real income unless the country has a real industrial capability and follows a program designed to facilitate development. In other words, protection unaccompanied by real reform efforts will not be effective. When protection is used, it cannot be excessive. When home markets are small, developing local industries may result in lower productivity for local labor. What is needed is general development, including more or less industry as the country's situation warrants and a removal of economic, social, and political institutions that prevent a carry-over from international trade into domestic production. Selective protection will be helpful where there are true infant industries, but general protection, except in the countries with large and varied resources and an adaptive people, appears to be inefficient and wasteful.

Instead of using protective tariffs, it is possible to control trade and save exchange by means of exchange controls and import restrictions. Typical forms are multiple exchange rates, different buying and selling rates for foreign exchange, bilateral trade balance agreements, exchange devaluation, quotas, and licenses.

By multiple exchange rates a country can impose various buying rates for exchange, depending on the type of product that it wants to import. The rate, for example, may be higher for luxury consumption goods than for necessities or capital goods, or higher for one industrial product than for another. Such rates can thus be used to influence the pattern of imports and to protect certain industries. In effect these rates act as a variable tax on imports. This device has the advantage of selectivity, which may be desirable if wisely chosen or which may have an unfavorable influence on the direction of investment if arbitrarily chosen. Changes in the rates, however, may lead to problems of favoritism and of uncertainty.

The purposes of different buying and selling rates are to obtain protection from foreign competition by making imports expensive, prevent capital flight, affect the impact of foreign exchange earnings on local incomes, obtain more favorable terms of trade by lessening the demand for imports, and encourage the diversion of local purchasing power from imports to savings or domestic purchases. The results are not always as intended. Exporters may be discouraged. Imports may become, even to a greater extent, items of conspicuous consumption, and smuggling may be encouraged if there is too great a deviation in rates.

Bilateral agreements often establish a balance in the payments between two countries, thus lessening the problem of imbalance. This, of course, can create a balance, but it distorts trade from normal channels and at the expense of limiting exports and preventing buying in the cheapest market.

The exchange rate may be devalued, thus making goods cheaper in terms of foreign money, with probable increasing sales. This amounts to general price cutting, which may or may not be profitable. Also, unless the underlying causes of poor trade are remedied, such as inefficiency and inflation, the devaluation will not help for long.

Direct prohibition against specific imports can be effective in shutting them out, except for smuggling, and thus seems a way to save exchange for other imports. However, demand may only shift to other items unless more positive steps are taken or domestic capital can be diverted to producing the prohibited goods. This is similar in effect to a prohibitive tariff and is justified only for defense or if the product is a true infant industry.

Instead of total prohibition, quotas or licensing requirements may be imposed to restrict the amount of exchange used for nonessentials or to direct trade to or from certain countries. This has all the defects of direct prohibition and opens the way to graft and favoritism. In addition, the effect is to raise the price of the restricted goods.

Thus, none of the devices for restricting trade is without problems. If any one is used, it should be adopted only after intensive study of the consequences.

## Regional Groupings

It is apparent that it is not easy for the usual underdeveloped country to shift from primary production to industry because the domestic market is small and it is difficult to break into the export business in industrial products. The cost of self-sufficiency is also prohibitive. The solution may be in finding a sheltered market large enough to permit economical operations and the acceleration of specialization so that resources can be allocated more efficiently. Puerto Rico found such a market through her special relationship with the United States. This type of sheltered market could conceivably be found in some form of regional customs grouping, either on a free trade or preferential tariff arrangement. The most noted example is the European Common Market. To aid the underdeveloped economies, attempts have been made to form some type of common market by the Arab Union, the Central American republics, Latin American countries, and various groupings in Africa.[50] None of these is fully operative and the prospects for effective operation seem meager and distant.

The theory is that such groupings, if correctly chosen, can support a wide variety of efficient economic undertakings by permitting greater economies of scale. The potential gain would then offset the temporary losses from protection. But just as for the individual country, care must be taken to see that only truly infant industries are protected and that protection is not excessive. Otherwise all that is created is a high-cost trading area. The problem of discovering true infant industries is the same, but the range of choice may be wider. Furthermore, as industry gets established, outside trade is expected to grow as regions specialize in products for which they have developed a comparative advantage. There is also some hope of improved bargaining power through possible control of supply, and with this the hope of better terms of trade.

It is hoped also that, with a bigger market, foreign investment will be attracted. This will occur only if the investor is convinced that the region is an economically sound one and that the political ties are so strong that the group will not disintegrate and so restore the old unprofitable situation.

There is no question but that protection imposed by a region against the rest of the world, unless lower than the previous tariffs imposed by the individual countries, will support inefficient and high-cost enterprises and will result in some loss of trade with the outside. On the other hand, some trade will arise among the participating countries. Whether trade reduction will outweigh trade creation must always be a consideration and will depend on the level of the tariffs, the transportation facilities available, the efforts to promote development, and so on. Unfortunately, the result is difficult to forecast.

How large must a region be to produce favorable results?* According to those who investigated this problem, with the exception of a few industries the maximum efficiency can be achieved by moderately sized firms. Certain industries such as auto, aircraft, locomotive, and heavy machinery are found only in large countries. The larger the country, the more specialization within industries. In small countries all lines are produced in the same plant. The conclusion was that most of the economies of scale could be obtained by a population of 50 million and that any advantages beyond a population of that figure appear to come from increased competition and specialization, although better government policy and better resources might also play a part. Thus, there is little economy in integrating markets when population is more than 50 million. At the same time, there are no apparent diseconomies beyond that figure as long as the larger grouping of countries conducts its affairs with equal efficiency.

The first requirement for a successful grouping is that the countries be complementary and work together. Political affinity is important, and it may be better to group countries on the basis of political ties rather than geographical proximity. The British Commonwealth, for example, appears to be a more logical unit from a trading point of view than are many contiguous areas. One of the problems of grouping nearby countries for economic purposes is that they may be too alike to help one another substantially. If all have similar exports, especially of primary products, and have no experience in trading with one another, gains will be slow in appearing. In Central and Latin America, for example, there is competition in current production and the transportation ties between the various countries are meager at best. It may be added that the territory included must be potentially productive and offer a sufficient market, if the desired results are to appear.

Getting agreement on a region is not a simple matter. Each country will probably want the industry and choose not to be the primary producer.

* The discussion here is based on E. A. G. Robinson's summary of the deliberations of a number of writers in his book *Economic Consequences of the Size of Nations,* London, The Macmillan Company, 1963, pp. xiii ff.

Industry is likely to gravitate toward the one relatively most advanced country, creating a problem of income disparity within the region, something that even regional planning may not solve. Latin American experience indicates the difficulties of getting an agreement to permit specialization.[51]

Thus, regional groupings may help overcome the trade problems of underdeveloped countries, but this result cannot be guaranteed. Such groupings will have to be approached with caution.

## REFERENCES

1. For discussions of how trade affects economic development see: VINER, J., *International Trade and Economic Development.* New York, The Free Press of Glencoe, 1952. Myrdal, G., *Rich Lands and Poor.* Harper & Bros., 1957. Cairncross, A. K., *Factors in Economic Development.* New York, Frederick A. Praeger, Inc., 1962, pp. 190-229. Hirschman, A. O., *Strategy of Economic Development.* New Haven, Yale University Press, 1958, pp. 183-201. Nurkse, R., *Equilibrium and Growth in the World Economy.* Cambridge, Mass., Harvard University Press, 1961, pp. 282-336. Haberler, G., "International Trade and Economic Development," from National Bank of Egypt Fiftieth Anniversary Commemoration Lectures, Cairo, 1959, reproduced in T. Morgan, G. W. Betz, and N. K. Choudhry, *Readings in Economic Development.* Belmont, Calif., Wadsworth Publishing Co., Inc., 1963, pp. 240-49. Chenery, H. B., "Comparative Advantage and Development Policy." *American Economic Review* (March, 1961), pp. 18-51.

2. HIRSCHMAN, *op. cit.,* p. 120.

3. KINDLEBERGER, C. P., *Economic Development.* New York, McGraw-Hill Book Co., Inc., 1958, p. 246.

4. ROBERTSON, D. H., *Essays in Monetary Theory.* London, P. S. King & Sons, Ltd., 1940, p. 240.

5. MORRIS, B. R., *Problems of American Economic Growth.* New York, Oxford University Press, 1961, pp. 30ff.

6. NURKSE, *op. cit.,* p. 288.

7. CAIRNCROSS, *op. cit.,* p. 192.

8. NURKSE, *op. cit.,* p. 293.

9. CAIRNCROSS, A. K., "International Trade and Economic Development," *Economica* (August, 1961), pp. 247ff.

10. REDDAWAY, W. B., *Development of the Indian Economy.* Homewood, Ill., Richard D. Irwin, Inc., 1962, p. 31.

11. PREBISCH, RAUL, "The Economic Development of Latin America and Its Principal Problems," *Economic Bulletin for Latin America* (February, 1962), pp. 1-22. Prebisch, "Commercial Policy in the Underdeveloped Countries." *American Economic Review, Proceedings* (May, 1959), pp. 251-73.

12. SINGER, H. W., "Distribution of the Gains Between Investing and Borrowing Countries." *American Economic Review, Proceedings* (May, 1950), pp. 473-85.

13. MYRDAL, *op. cit.*

14. NURKSE, *op. cit.*

15. MEIER, G. M., *Leading Issues in Development Economics.* New York, Oxford University Press, 1964, pp. 371-76.

16. SINGER, *op. cit.,* p. 475.

17. CAIRNCROSS, *op. cit.,* p. 225.

18. NURKSE, *op. cit.,* p. 294-95.

19. BALASSA, B. A., *Trade Prospects for Developing Countries.* Homewood,

Ill., Richard D. Irwin, Inc., 1964. (Covers this for a variety of products.)

20. *Industrialization and Foreign Trade.* Geneva, League of Nations, 1945. *Relative Price of Exports and Imports of Underdeveloped Countries.* New York, United Nations, 1949.

21. KINDLEBERGER, C. P., *The Terms of Trade.* New York, John Wiley & Sons, Inc., 1956. Kindleberger, "Terms of Trade and Economic Development." *Review of Economics and Statistics* (February, 1958), pp. 72-85.

22. MORGAN, THEODORE, "The Long Run Terms of Trade Between Agriculture and Manufacturing." *Economic Development and Cultural Change* (October, 1959), pp. 7-23.

23. BALASSA, *op. cit.,* p. 9.

24. PREBISCH, "The Economic Development of Latin America . . . ," *loc. cit.* Prebisch, "Commercial Policy . . . ," *loc. cit.* Singer, "Distribution . . . ," *loc. cit.,* pp. 473-85. (Supports and adds to Prebisch.)

25. SINGER, *op. cit.,* p. 474.

26. SWERLING, B. C., "Some Interrelationships Between Agricultural Trade and Economic Development." *Kyklos,* No. 3 (1961), p. 382.

27. MEIER, *op. cit.* Morgan, *op. cit.* Meier, G. M., "Export Stimulation, Import Substitution and Latin American Development. *Social and Economic Studies* (March, 1961), pp. 42-62. Haberler, G., "Terms of Trade and Economic Development," in H. S. Ellis and H. C. Wallich, *Economic Development of Latin America.* New York, St Martin's Press, 1961, pp. 275-307.

28. MEIER, *Leading Issues . . . , loc. cit.,* p. 373.

29. BENHAM, F., "Terms of Trade." *Economica* (November, 1940), pp. 360-76.

30. *Employment Objectives in Economic Development.* Geneva, International Labour Office, 1961, p. 124.

31. *Instability in Export Markets of Underdeveloped Countries.* New York, United Nations, 1952.

32. BUTLER, W. D., "Trade and the Less Developed Areas." *Foreign Affairs* (January, 1963), p. 377.

33. Economic Commission for Asia and the Far East, *Economic Survey of Asia and the Far East.* New York, United Nations, 1957, p. 117.

34. *Measures for the Economic Development of Underdeveloped Countries.* New York, United Nations, 1951, p. 71.

35. Economic Commission for Asia and the Far East, *op. cit.,* p. 112.

36. REUBENS, E. P., "Commodity Trade Export Taxes and Economic Development." *Political Science Quarterly* (March, 1956), p. 51.

37. WALLICH, H. C., "Stabilization of Proceeds From Raw Material Exports," in H. S. Ellis and H. C. Wallich, *Economic Development of Latin America.* New York, St Martin's Press, 1961, p. 348.

38. NURKSE, R., "Some International Aspects of the Problem of Economic Development." *American Economic Review, Proceedings* (May, 1952), pp. 571-83. Nurkse, *Equilibrium and Growth in the World Economy, loc. cit.,* pp. 221-336. Nurkse, "International Trade Theory and Development Policy," in H. S. Ellis and H. C. Wallich, *Economic Development of Latin America.* New York, St Martin's Press, 1961, pp. 234-74.

39. PREBISCH, RAUL, "The Structural Crisis in Argentina and Its Prospect of Solution," in E. Nelson, *Economic Growth.* Austin, Texas, University of Texas Press, 1960, pp. 104-26. Prebisch, "Commercial Policy . . . ," *loc. cit.*

40. CAIRNCROSS, "International Trade . . . ," *loc. cit.,* p. 249.

41. International Bank for Reconstruction and Development, *Economic Development of Mexico.* Baltimore, Johns Hopkins Press, 1953, pp. 111-47.

42. NURKSE, *Equilibrium and Growth . . . , loc. cit.,* p. 311.

43. Reddaway, *op. cit.,* p. 29.
44. "United Nations Conference on Trade and Development." *Far East Trade and Development, Supplement* (July, 1964).
45. General Assembly, *Committee of Experts on Commodity Trade and Economic Development.* New York, United Nations, 1953. Economic Commission for Asia and the Far East, *loc. cit.,* 1957, pp. 132ff. Alpert, P., *Economic Development.* New York, The Free Press of Glencoe, 1963, pp. 208-27. Swerling, B. C., "Problems of International Commodity Stabilization." *American Economic Review, Proceedings* (May, 1963), pp. 65-74. Mikesell, R. F., "International Commodity Stabilization Schemes and the Export Problems of Developing Countries." *American Economic Review, Proceedings* (May, 1963), pp. 75-92.
46. General Assembly, *Committee of Experts . . . , loc. cit. International Compensation for Fluctuations in Commodity Trade,* New York, United Nations, 1961. *Stabilization of Export Proceeds Through a Development Insurance Fund.* New York, United Nations, 1962. *A Development Insurance Fund for Single Commodities.* New York, United Nations, 1962. Mikesell, *op. cit.*
47. Meier, G. M., and R. E. Baldwin, *Economic Development.* New York, John Wiley & Sons, Inc., 1957, Chap. 19.
48. Viner, J., *op. cit.,* p. 59.
49. Meier and Baldwin, *op. cit.,* p. 400.
50. Mikesell, R. F., "The Movement Toward Regional Trading Groups in Latin America," in A. O. Hirschman, *Latin American Issues.* New York, The Twentieth Century Fund, 1961, pp. 125-61. Allan, R. L., "Integration in Less Developed Areas," *Kyklos,* No. 3 (1961), pp. 315-36. (Discusses the merits of regional groupings.)
51. *Study of Inter Latin American Trade.* New York, United Nations, 1957.

## ADDITIONAL READINGS

Bauer, P. T., and F. W. Paish, "Reduction of Fluctuations in the Incomes of Primary Producers." *Economic Journal* (December, 1952), pp. 750-80; (December, 1954), pp. 704-29, and comment pp. 730-43 by B. M. Niculesco.
Frank, I., "Issues Before the U.N. Conference." *Foreign Affairs* (January, 1964), pp. 210-26.
Harding, J. E., "Dynamic Trade Theory and Growth in Poor Countries." *Kyklos,* No. 3 (1963), pp. 371-94.
Maizels, A., "Effects of Industrialization on Exports of Primary Producing Countries." *Kyklos,* No. 1 (1961), pp. 18-43.
Myint, H., "Classical Theory of International Trade and Underdeveloped Countries." *Economic Journal* (June, 1958), pp. 317-37.
Meier, Gerald M., *International Trade and Development.* New York, Harper & Row, Publishers, 1963.
Ranis, G., "Trade, Aid and What?" *Kyklos,* No. 2 (1964), pp. 179-96.
"Symposium on the Quest for a Stabilization Policy in Primary Producing Countries." *Kyklos,* No. 2 (1958), pp. 141-265.
"Symposium of Stabilization and Development of Primary Producing Countries." *Kyklos,* No. 3 (1959). (Entire issue.)
United Nations: Economic and Security Council, *Commodity and Trade Problems of Developing Countries,* 1963. Department of Economic and Social Affairs, *Latin American Common Market,* 1959. Conference on Trade and Development, *Towards a New Trade Policy for Development,* 1964.

# CHAPTER
# 12

# The Role of Certain
# Institutional Arrangements

Attention is usually focused on improving a country's direct productive efforts, but changes in certain institutions may contribute as much or more to growth, and are therefore necessary to make increased production possible. Changes in these institutions, such as the monetary and banking system, the fiscal system, marketing, transportation and other economic overheads, and legal systems require special attention.

## Money, Banking, and Credit

Some underdeveloped countries are hardly in the money economy and others are plagued by inflation.[1] Still others have a substantial monetized part of the economy but also have large areas still in the barter stage. Money exchange must develop before production can become efficient. Barter exchange is too cumbersome to encourage producers to specialize, which is essential for efficiency. With the development of a money freely acceptable in exchange, it becomes feasible for producers to specialize and to exchange their surpluses for the goods they want. Until exchange develops extensively and peasants enter into a commercial life, food and materials are unlikely to be available at a scale necessary to meet the needs of industrializing cities. Unstable money systems are perhaps better than no monetary system for such purposes, but to the degree that a money is unstable, it creates uncertainties that are bound to interfere with economic decisions and productive efforts.

As nations develop, the use of money is replaced more and more by credit. This is an efficient means of effecting payments and permits temporary and permanent savings to be directed where others can use them. Commercial enterprises and production units all need credit for various purposes. Short-term credit is necessary to meet peak needs for inventories and payrolls, unless a firm is to keep in reserve this required capital, using it only at such times and letting it remain idle at other seasons. This would be an inefficient use of a scarce resource. Peasants need credit to buy seed and durable equipment and to finance themselves while crops are maturing. Business firms need credit for working capital and for longer-term equipment needs. Thus, credit of various types is necessary to promote production.

To supply credit requirements, banking institutions must be established. These have developed in many areas, but not all sectors of the economies have them.* In the former colonial areas, these are usually commercial banks, and are branches of large foreign banks. These were set up to meet the needs of foreign trade and large estates, and now tend to maintain the same kind of business. For example, in 1960 in Thailand (although not a former colonial area), 40 percent of the credit to the private sector went to finance foreign trade, 15 percent to domestic commerce, and 8 percent to construction.[2] The remainder is probably handled by village moneylenders, whose charges are usually regarded as being excessive.[3] Thus, the greatest credit deficiencies exist for the farmer and the small businessman, on whose progress economic development depends. Thus, channeling savings away from local firms has in effect made underdeveloped countries become capital exporters.[4]

Particularly scarce are funds for long-term loans. Capital markets are absent or poorly developed, and specialized banking institutions such as agricultural banks and insurance companies are just beginning. Commercial banks prefer short-term loans to merchants or loans on town real estate. Firms must get long-term funds through a succession of short-term loans or must supply all the funds from a single family's capital. One of the major controversies in underdeveloped countries is whether commercial banks

---

* For a detailed description of the banking systems in a number of countries, see the various studies of the International Bank for Reconstruction and Development.

should be permitted to make such loans, contrary to generally accepted commercial banking practice. Moreover, too much of the credit goes for consumption purposes; for example, to finance weddings or funerals.

Now domestic commercial and savings banks are developing, but there is a distinct shortage of them. People do not have the check-writing habit, so that checking accounts are virtually limited to government and business firms. As much as 50 percent of the total transactions may be settled with currency, whereas only about 10 percent in the United States are settled with cash. Also, there is a hesitancy on the part of people to put their money in banks, although, with the aid of postal savings, this is increasing. Thus, banks are limited in accumulating resources. The greatest problem, however, may be the shortage of trained bankers.

Almost all countries have central banks as a matter of prestige and as a sign of a modern nation, if for no other reason, but most of these have not developed effective control over the credit system and often seem to exist only to create credit to loan to the government. However, the central banks are undertaking credit control increasingly and are engaging in efforts to promote the economic objectives of their countries.

Thus, there is a great need to provide a stable purchasing media, to control credit creation, to establish appropriate credit institutions, and to channel savings into desirable investments. Such activities are a concern of the central banks.

The usual functions of central banks in advanced countries are to curb credit extension by commercial banks so as to stabilize the monetary system and the economy; to see that commercial banks remain liquid, by providing facilities for them to exchange their loan instruments for cash or deposits; to act as a fiscal agent for the government; to hold the bank system's reserves so that banks will not overextend themselves; to conduct clearings; and to issue currency.

The underdeveloped countries give a wide variety of functions to their central banks, including the traditional ones and adding others. The following functions as well as the traditional ones may not be performed by all central banks, but the expected roles are generally wider than, say, in the United States. Three functions assume much more importance than in the United States and most other advanced countries. First, it is necessary for the central banks to moderate the effects of fluctuations in foreign exchange earnings. The banks, in addition, administer the exchange controls. As previously noted, exchange earnings may fluctuate widely. Banks use these exchange earnings as reserves. Thus, in prosperous periods, banks accumulate large reserves and have a high capacity to extend loans. In poor times, credit contraction may be necessary. To flatten out these swings, central banks may have to keep large holdings of foreign exchange out of the system's reserves on some occasions and release them at other times. Although this may be considered a form of credit control, its exercise has special significance for underdeveloped countries.

Second, the central banks must undertake the responsibility for developing new banking institutions, improving the existing inadequate ones, and starting capital and money markets. This will be discussed below.

Third, and most important, is the necessity to promote economic development. As one might expect, the various functions or objectives of the central banks conflict, so that choices must be made among them. The promotion of economic development is usually the principal objective and one that is not likely to be sacrificed in favor of the more traditional goals. Because of this, underdeveloped countries are prone to inflation, and especially so because current economic philosophy urges government and private enterprise to push investment even further than the amount of voluntary savings. From such a viewpoint the traditional functions seem of less significance than in advanced countries, although they cannot be ignored.

E. Nevins[5] describes three ways by which central banks can aid economic development. First, they can increase investments through their own resources, including the excess of reserve deposits and currency backing not necessary to keep credit liquid or to perform its other functions. That is, using these resources would turn excess reserves into productive investment. Generally, this is done by buying securities of specialized institutions such as industrial development banks rather than by direct loans or purchase of industrial securities. Second, by applying selective credit controls and offering credit guarantees, they can direct investment into the most needed areas. Third, they can build up the financial system (for example, local money and credit markets), ensure sound commercial credit, and supply investment advice and information about the economic system. This means that they must extend the maximum credit consistent with the need to prevent inflation, and at minimum cost. It seems obvious that choosing development as the primary objective almost automatically invites an easy credit policy.

This raises the question of the degree to which the central bank is to be independent or controlled by the government. The usual practice in the advanced countries is to establish central banks as independent agencies, but with a great deal of direct or indirect government influence. For example, the Federal Reserve System of the United States acts independently of the Treasury, but the Board is appointed by the President. The Treasury has large powers to affect the supply of currency and credit, so that the Treasury and the Federal Reserve can offset the actions of the other. This induces at least attention to one another's problems, if not active cooperation. Because governments in the underdeveloped countries are more closely concerned with development plans than is the United States Government, it appears inevitable that they will have a more intimate relationship with the central bank.* Yet a large degree of freedom of action for the central bank seems to be desirable to prevent undue credit inflation that would be injurious to development. The issue of credit control is thus an important one.

Inflation is the usual situation in underdeveloped countries and results, if carried too far, in a decrease in total savings because of speculation, the flight of money abroad, conspicuous consumption, foreign exchange deficiency, a stoppage of foreign investment, and a reduction of export possibilities, as previously explained. Inflation amounts to a tax without regard to who bears the burden. For example, it is usual for wages to rise more slowly than prices. This puts great pressure on low-income people.

Inflation arises because nearly every country has a development program and is usually impatient with the financing available from voluntary savings. Large amounts of capital are required by the government for social and economic overheads, and taxation is not adequate. Impatience for development and political pressure leads to attempts to get funds by issuing currency or borrowing from the central bank. Individuals also wish to borrow for productive purposes or for speculative purposes, or they have become aware of higher living standards and try to acquire more output than can be provided. Many bottlenecks exist in the economy, so rising incomes do not call forth greater production.

If inflation is to be avoided, consumption spending must be limited to the level of output available for consumption at present prices, that is, of total product less investment. Or, alternatively, tax receipts plus voluntary savings must match government expenditures and investment plus private investment. Savings, however, are low, tax systems are not so productive as desired, and government needs are great. As a result there is a great temptation to transfer more resources to the government via the borrowing route. The issue is the extent to which credit is to be controlled at the expense of government investment programs. Most underdeveloped countries are willing to take a chance on rising prices, but there is a need to keep the rise within limits. At the very least, unessential borrowing should be controlled. Thus, central banks are often equipped with wide powers to control credit. Yet their ability to control credit extension is limited, for some of the powers are ineffective and political pressures may prevent the use of the powers

---

* L. V. Chandler (*Central Banking and Economic Development*. Bombay University Press, 1962, p. 7) states that most of such central banks are dominated by the central governments.

that might work. Beyond this there are few trained bankers and administrators, which makes control difficult even with the best of intentions.

The most usual control devices in the West are open-market operations, rediscounting operations, and changing reserve requirements. The use of an open-market policy, that is, the buying and selling of government or other securities to affect credit, is virtually denied the underdeveloped countries because there is seldom an organized capital or money market. Government securities are not widely held, so the ability to buy and sell them is distinctly limited. Moreover, the market is so narrow that even minor efforts may result in widely fluctuating prices for securities. The power to change rediscount rates is usually given to the central banks, but this, too, proves ineffective. Banks seem to have excess reserves, and foreign banks replenish their reserves from the parent offices abroad. Interest rates also are quite inflexible, so that changes must be very large to have any appreciable effect.

Setting and changing reserve requirements is usually regarded as a crude method of credit control, for it affects all banks alike, including those that have been following conservative policies. However, in the absence of other effective powers, it may be necessary for underdeveloped countries to employ this strategy. Because this may be a hardship for some banks and not others, an alternative method is to alter the reserve requirements only on increases in deposits, thus affecting credit extension by all banks equally.[6]

Two other control devices may be utilized by the central banks, and these seem superior to the more usual techniques just mentioned. One, which operates on much the same principle as open-market operations by drying up or building bank reserves, is to transfer government deposits from the central bank to the commercial banks (or the reverse). This, of course, to be effective, implies a statutory reserve ratio. If deposits are transferred from commercial banks to the central bank, the commercial banks will tend to lose reserves; on the other hand, if deposits are transferred from the central bank to the commercial banks, the central bank will tend to gain reserves.[7]

The second device consists of selective controls so designed that credit is used in accordance with government plans or in an approved fashion and is not used in certain sectors such as real estate speculation.[8] This can be done by specifying the purposes for which loans may be made or by varying the rate and eligibility of loans of different types for rediscounting. Or margin requirements may be varied by types of loan or by requesting particular forms of collateral, such as real estate or inventories.[9] Advance deposits may be required on imports so as to reduce them.* Installment credit

---

* Having to make such advance deposits involves interest costs and so increases the cost of imported goods, thus tending to make them less attractive.

terms may be controlled to reduce consumer borrowing, but this is of value only where installment credit is widely used.

The Japanese central bank is able to operate largely through moral suasion.* However, this is an exception rather than the rule.

The second "must" for the new central banks is to create financial institutions so as to increase savings that will be channeled into the appropriate fields. A big handicap in underdeveloped countries is often the lack of a suitable place in which savers can put their money. Savings are small, often are kept hidden, and are not deposited in banks where they could be loaned for investment purposes. A major goal of development policy should be to encourage the banking habit. One step toward this is the establishment of suitable deposit institutions. Postal savings banks have had some success and credit cooperatives offer some attraction, although their operation needs to be improved. Savings banks or savings departments of commercial banks also have their place.

Just as important as collecting savings is seeing that they get into productive investments. Commercial banks are not really equipped for making long-term loans. It is necessary for them to remain liquid so that they can safely devote only a small part of their resources to long-term loans, which are badly needed by agriculture and industry. Desirable institutions to serve such neglected areas are industrial development banks, agricultural banks, banks for small industry, and so on. These have the advantage of being able to become very familiar with the problems in a given sector. They can attract resources, which might not otherwise be available, by serving as an investment outlet for surplus funds of commercial banks, especially if the central bank affords such securities special rediscounting privileges. These institutions must be government banks, for the areas to be served are underdeveloped and the amount of business is relatively small and scattered. For this reason private banks are not usually attracted. Yet these areas must develop, if the economy is to develop.

Also, capital markets are needed in order to enlarge the market for government securities and to give government bonds greater marketability and hence make them more attractive to purchasers. Likewise, stock exchanges may be ultimately helpful in developing a securities market, and so, in time, encouraging investment in industrial securities. However, in the early stages of development when accounting records are unreliable, government controls are weak, and the number of securities is small, the danger of fraud and speculation is great. The stock exchange appears to belong to a somewhat later stage of development.

Thus, a sufficient quantity and variety of financial institutions are major

* For a description, see the *Economist* (March 31, 1962), pp. 1261-62.

requirements for growth. These require capital and trained personnel, and so must compete with other uses for their share.

## Tax System

It has been previously indicated that much of the funds for economic development must come from tax sources, for savings are usually inadequate and not easily channeled into the investments a developing country needs. Furthermore, much of the investment must be undertaken by government because of the nature of the investment (such as the economic and social overheads) or because there is a shortage of private innovators, which in turn may be due to a lack of investment opportunities in the absence of such overheads. Nearly all countries have a development program, and the tax system is a major determinant of the level of investment that forms the core of such a program. The funds needed for successful development are a relatively large proportion of the national income, but the tax amounts collected in the underdeveloped countries are usually low compared with those in the more advanced countries.*

However, the tax systems of most underdeveloped countries are poorly developed, generally unjust, and yield inadequate amounts. A study by U. T. Wai,[10] summarized in Table 12.1, shows the low level of tax receipts. Of the fifty-two countries presented, India raised in taxes the lowest percentage of its national income, 7.7 percent. The same report showed that countries with per capita incomes above $500 collected 25 percent (median) in taxes; those with incomes between $200 and $500, 15.2 percent; and those with incomes below $200, 13.7 percent. In general, the lower the income, the lower the percentage collected in taxes, despite the great need for investment.

Wai lists the reasons for this low level of collection: Countries do not feel they can impinge too heavily on low living standards; the size of the monetary economy is smaller; and conditions such as illiteracy, lack of systematic accounting, inefficient tax administration, tax evasion and avoidance, social codes of behavior inimical to voluntary compliance, and political influence make collection difficult.

---

* A United Nations study (*Economic Survey of Asia and the Far East*, 1960, p. 67ff.) reports government expenditures as a share of total product in 1957 or 1958 as follows: Burma, 28 percent; Cambodia, 14; Ceylon, 26; Taiwan, 33; Malaya, 19; India, 16; Indonesia, 20; Japan, 26; S. Korea, 24; Pakistan, 15; Philippines, 11; Thailand, 14. Public investment as a share of total investment ranged from 26 percent in the Philippines and 28 percent in Malaya to 73 percent in Taiwan and 71 percent in India. The share of investment in governmental expenditure ranged from 20 to 40 percent, except for Indonesia, which had 9 percent.

## TABLE 12.1.

*Central Government Taxes as a Percent of National Income, 1959*

| Over $500 Per Capita | | $200-$500 Per Capita | | Below $200 Per Capita | |
|---|---|---|---|---|---|
| Austria | 32.9 | Ireland | 26.1 | U.A.R. | 23.7 |
| New Zealand | 31.4 | Italy | 22.7 | Ceylon | 22.4 |
| United Kingdom | 30.8 | Chile | 21.9 | Burma | 20.6 |
| Finland | 29.6 | Greece | 20.9 | Iraq | 19.8 |
| Venezuela | 27.1 | South Africa | 18.8 | Peru | 19.3 |
| Israel | 26.6 | Malaya | 18.7 | Korea | 16.7 |
| Netherlands | 25.8 | Costa Rica | 16.2 | Syrian Rep. | 16.1 |
| France | 25.4 | Portugal | 15.7 | Guatemala | 15.9 |
| Norway | 25.0 | Panama | 14.8 | Ghana | 13.9 |
| Australia | 24.0 | Lebanon | 14.7 | Ecuador | 13.7 |
| Germany | 23.2 | Spain | 13.2 | El Salvador | 13.6 |
| Sweden | 22.9 | Japan | 12.9 | Thailand | 12.9 |
| Denmark | 20.6 | Argentina | 11.1 | Honduras | 12.1 |
| Belgium | 17.7 | Brazil | 10.1 | Pakistan | 11.6 |
| Canada | 17.6 | Colombia | 8.3 | Philippines | 10.5 |
| United States | 17.1 | Mexico | 8.1 | Indonesia | 10.4 |
| Switzerland | 8.1 | | | Haiti | 9.9 |
| MEDIAN | 25.0 | MEDIAN | 15.2 | Turkey | 9.9 |
| | | | | India | 7.7 |
| | | | | MEDIAN | 13.7 |

NOTE: For qualifications see Ref. 11.

For this reason major attention must be paid to improving the tax system and the means of handling public funds. Unless the tax system diverts a substantial amount of purchasing power away from consumption, investment must be either curtailed below the amount desired or financed by credit, most of which is of the inflationary type. As previously mentioned, inflation brings numerous difficulties, including speculation, competitive spending, and balance-of-payments difficulties.

The question is whether fiscal systems can be made adequate and can even approximate the goal of diverting funds to the government to the extent necessary to induce development. Coupled with this must be the utmost attention to government economies; for example, avoiding lavish expenditures for display purposes and reducing unnecessary employees.

There is a heavy reliance on consumption or property taxes, so the systems are regressive, although heavy taxes on luxury goods somewhat lessen the effects. Of these taxes, there is a heavy reliance on taxes on foreign trade (import, export, and exchange taxes). Wai reports[11] that high-income countries rely on such taxes for 9 percent of their revenues (median); medium-income countries, 23 percent; and low-income countries, 30 percent. The reasons given were that international trade is a higher percentage of national income and collection and administration is relatively easy, for the goods pass through few ports and hands.

Income taxes play a relatively small role, although their use is increasing. However, more of such taxes fall on salaries and wages than in the advanced countries, thus somewhat reducing their progressive effects.[12] Former British colonies place relatively more reliance than do other countries on simplified income taxes.[13] The high-income countries rely on direct taxes for 43 percent (median) of their revenues; the medium-income countries, 29 percent; and the low-income countries, 20 percent.[14]

Numerous examples of this type of structure can be given from all over the underdeveloped world. As one example, over half of the countries in Latin America obtain over 50 percent of their revenues from indirect taxes, and two of these reach 70 and 85 percent. With one exception the remaining governments raise over 33 percent in this way.[15] The Asian pattern is similar, as shown in Table 12.2.

Heavy reliance on indirect taxes is probably inevitable in view of the present state of tax administration and the need for revenues. Such taxes tend to be regressive except as softened somewhat by excise taxes on commodities used more by the rich and medium-income classes. These classes also tend to consume most of the imported goods, so that import duties are not so regressive as they would be in the United States. Those living in the subsistence sector are not affected by such taxes, but these people, of course, are the poorest.

## TABLE 12.2.

### Components of Government Revenue
#### (percent of total revenue)

| Country | Year | Taxes on Foreign Trade | Internal Transactions | Income and Wealth | Profits of Government Enterprises | Other |
|---|---|---|---|---|---|---|
| Afghanistan | 1958 | 39 | 13 | 19 | 3 | 26 |
| Burma | 1958 | 41 | 21 | 25 | 1 | 12 |
| Cambodia | 1958 | 30 | 49 | 7 | | 14 |
| Ceylon | 1958 | 53 | 13 | 23 | 1 | 10 |
| Taiwan | 1958 | 14 | 55 | 10 | 10 | 11 |
| Malaya | 1958 | 53 | 10 | 16 | 4 | 17 |
| India | 1958 | 10 | 43 | 25 | 5 | 17 |
| Indonesia | 1958 | 43 | 25 | 22 | 1 | 9 |
| Iran | 1958 | 76 | 7 | 10 | 5 | 2 |
| Japan | 1958 | 4 | 42 | 47 | { 7 } | |
| S. Korea | 1958 | 19 | 35 | 26 | 4 | 16 |
| Laos | 1958 | 53 | 31 | 10 | 4 | 2 |
| Pakistan | 1957 | 20 | 24 | 22 | 5 | 29 |
| Philippines | 1958 | 26 | 36 | 18 | | 20 |
| Thailand | 1958 | 49 | 35 | 7 | 4 | 5 |
| Viet Nam | 1958 | 23 | 57 | 9 | 3 | 8 |

SOURCE: United Nations, *Economic Survey of Asia and the Far East*, 1960, p. 87.

The most important of these taxes are usually taxes on foreign trade. These are used not only to produce revenue but also to restrict unnecessary imports, to encourage import-substituting industries, and to impound gains when export prices and trade are favorable. In addition to usual import and export taxes, some countries tax the purchases of foreign exchange; for instance, the Philippines levies a 25 percent tax, and others use multiple exchange rates. For example, Indonesia in 1962 sold foreign exchange, for which the official rate was 45 rupiahs for $1.00 at varying rates up to 200 rupiahs for $1.00, depending on the type of purchase. Some countries, instead of taxing exports, exercise a monopoly of exports of certain commodities such as Burma and Thailand in rice, Taiwan in sugar, and Indonesia in copra.[16] Export taxes are relatively easy to administer, yield large revenues, help prevent excessive importing, and tend to offset cycles in foreign exchange earnings.

Taxes on internal transactions are also of numerical importance, although more difficult to apply than foreign trade taxes. The reasons for this are that selling units are small and numerous, many sellers are illiterate and lack accounts, barter is still of importance, and the unit of sale may be very small (for example, one cigarette).[17] For administrative reasons, consumption taxes must be imposed where a large part of the output passes through few hands (such as at the wholesale level). Unfortunately, this results in the pyramiding of the tax, thus increasing the burden on the consumer. General excise taxes run into the difficulty that there are many small manufacturers and the small sales make such taxes relatively unproductive. Although no study seems to exist, collections must be haphazard, with many sales being made without the tax.

An alternative has been to rely on selective sales taxes placed on tobacco, liquor, gasoline, motor cars, and entertainment. These are easier to administer than general sales taxes and, if rightly chosen, can lessen the regressivity of consumption taxation. Many countries are extending the list of taxed commodities and are raising the rates.

It is almost unavoidable that the poor must pay most of the taxes, and consumption taxes are the means of reaching them. For one thing, there are too few rich, although efforts should be made to tax them more heavily than is usually done. Moreover, it is necessary to lessen consumption so that resources can be devoted to producers' goods. Actually, because people are often so poor that any attempt to reduce their meager scale of living would have unfortunate results on their survival, the usual objective is to prevent increases in consumption. Because consumption taxes are relatively crude tools for this purpose, such taxes are bound to reduce the living standards of many, even though the objective is to take for the government a share of any increase in incomes. For the present, excessive spending by the rich can be reached by selective taxes on luxuries and by income taxation. Direct taxes on expenditures are also a possibility.

Because land is the most common productive resource, one might expect to see extensive taxation of land. Land taxes of widely varying types are used. H. P. Wald[18] lists a variety of such taxes: those based on land area at either a uniform or classified rate; those based on a rental value concept such as an assumed annual rental value or capital value; those based on an income concept such as the tithe, gross yield, gross income, net income, or total marketable produce; and special purpose taxes such as taxes on incremental value, penalty taxes for nonuse or wrong use; and special taxes on certain natural resources. Some countries substitute a separate income tax on agriculture. However, the yields are low and of decreasing importance.*

Land taxation has some disadvantages. There must be proven ownership based on surveys, which are often nonexistent and which would be expensive to undertake. Assessment is either difficult to determine or arbitrary. The yield is relatively inflexible, for assessments are not kept up to date even though the general price level is rising. In some areas, especially Latin America, the wealthy landowners have such political power that taxing land has proved to be very difficult.

Despite these difficulties, Meier and Baldwin[19] and Richard Goode[20] believe that efforts should be made to make taxes on land and agriculture more productive. Such taxes offer certain advantages. Speculation in land would be discouraged. Some of the socially created increase in land values would be recovered for the public. Some of the special benefits that development projects (such as irrigation schemes) create would accrue to the public. Farmers would have to make larger amounts of food available to the cities in order to meet such taxes. Land is easily observed, so escape from taxation is less likely than in the case of some other taxes. Moreover, because land is the largest producer of wealth, it seems natural that it should bear a fair share of the taxes. Lastly, such taxes are the only way to reach the subsistence sector, which would otherwise escape taxation.

The Japanese experience shows that land taxes can be important, yielding large revenues, bringing food supplies to urban areas, and promoting agricultural efficiency.[21] Study of ways to improve this type of taxation seems a worthwhile endeavor.

The development of income taxation has lagged, although many coun-

---

* H. P. Wald (*Taxation of Agricultural Lands in Underdeveloped Economies.* Cambridge, Mass., Harvard University Press, 1959, pp. 10ff.) states that seven countries raise 20 percent of their revenues from such taxes, seven raise 10 percent, thirteen raise 5 percent, and eight from 1 to 4 percent.

tries have instituted such taxation. Actual tax systems show wide variations. Some systems tax all incomes at the same rates, and others tax different types of income at different rates and exempt some altogether (for
example, income earned abroad, or capital gains). Some tax only a few types
of income while others tax rather widely. The rationale of such classification is ability to collect at the source and supposed differences between
earned and unearned income. The Brazilian system illustrates such a classified system:[22] The taxpayer pays 3 percent on interest from Brazilian government bonds and 6 percent if they are bearer bonds; 10 percent on other
interest; 21 percent on nongovernment bonds in bearer form; 1 percent on
salaries and wages; 2 percent on professional fees; 3 percent on rentals of
land and buildings; no tax on dividends and profits of enterprises, foreign
source income, profits of farming, livestock raising, and processing of one's
own products; and 5 percent on all other income, including rentals for pat-
ents and subleases. The taxpayer computes his tax and deducts his payments
for interest and life insurance premiums, losses from natural calamities,
charitable contributions, fees for medical care, and personal exemptions. He
then computes a complementary tax on the remainder at progressive rates.

The Ceylonese tax of 1959 represents the more universal type,[23] although
it affects only a few and the yield is quite low. The taxable unit is the
family and all incomes must be aggregated. However, the income brackets
are multiplied by a family quotient, the husband counting 1.5 and the wife
and children 0.5, with a maximum quotient of 4. Personal exemptions are
high, being in 1959 eleven times the average per capita income for a family
of four (in the United States this was 1.1. times). Rates ranged from 5 to
60 percent. The top rate is applied to incomes that are 57 times the national
per capita figure for single persons and 113 times for married couples (in
the United States in 1959 this was 10.5 and 21 times, respectively). Deductions from income were allowed, but these were limited in the case of travel,
entertainment, and advertising. In addition, there was a wealth tax, an expenditure tax on personal consumption expenditures, and a gift tax. This
was expected to be a "self-checking" system, but is complicated. It gave
great weight to family size (up to four children) and encouraged the
wealthy to adopt dependents.

The former British colonies in Africa have a simplified direct personal
tax,[24] which is called a hybrid between a poll tax and an elementary income
tax. The tax varies from country to country, but almost everyone pays a
minimum tax. There is some progression by income brackets, income being
assessed by local committees without the filing of returns. Assessment may
be on the basis of such external criteria as amount of land owned. Often the
tax is on assessed gross income without exemptions.

The taxes paid are relatively low. Table 12.3, taken from United Nations' sources,[25] compares income taxes paid in selected advanced and underdeveloped countries. But there is much tax evasion. Prest[26] says that, commonly, less than 3 percent of the people pay taxes and only 5 to 20 percent of the total income is taxed, whereas in the United Kingdom 75 percent of income is taxed. There appears to be a possibility of greater revenue from income taxes as systems improve and conditions become more appropriate.

Income taxes are difficult for underdeveloped countries to use. Accounting and other records are not sufficient for enforcement. Much of the income is not in the form of money. The incomes of many are so low and so close to the level of subsistence that the tax is virtually limited to a few and is therefore not highly productive. The income tax requires an administrative authority that is honest, efficient, and technically competent, but qualified administrators are in short supply. Income taxes require an attitude on the part of the taxpayers that induces almost unanimous voluntary compliance. Otherwise it is just too difficult to find out how much income a man has. The crying need of underdeveloped countries is for savings, and high rates of income taxation are thought to discourage savings and thus the

## TABLE 12.3.

Burden of Income Taxes Paid by a Married Couple with Three Children in Relation to National per Capita Income, 1958-1960, Selected Countries

| Country | Maximum Nontaxable Income (Multiples of Per Capita Income) | Taxes as Percent of Earned Income (Various Multiple of per Capita Income) | | | |
|---|---|---|---|---|---|
| | | 10 | 20 | 50 | 100 |
| Underdeveloped Countries | | | | | |
| Mexico | 1.9 | 2 | 4 | 9 | 17 |
| Argentina | 7.7 | 3 | 16 | 34 | 43 |
| Malaya | 9.8 | — | 4 | 12 | 21 |
| India | 11.5 | — | 2 | 8 | 21 |
| Ceylon | 12.5 | — | 2 | 9 | 23 |
| Philippines | 15.6 | — | 1 | 10 | 19 |
| Burma | 19.0 | — | — | 4 | 11 |
| AVERAGE | 11.1 | — | 4 | 12 | 22 |
| Developed Countries | | | | | |
| Australia | 0.7 | 30 | 43 | 55 | 59 |
| United States | 1.3 | 23 | 35 | 54 | 69 |
| Canada | 1.9 | 19 | 32 | 45 | 55 |
| United Kingdom | 1.9 | 28 | 44 | 67 | 78 |
| France | 2.1 | 13 | 23 | 35 | 45 |
| Germany | 2.2 | 20 | 28 | 39 | 46 |
| Japan | 3.4 | 11 | 19 | 31 | 39 |
| AVERAGE | 1.9 | 21 | 32 | 47 | 56 |

possible start of new enterprises, although there is no assurance that private savings will actually go into productive enterprises. Moreover, if the national economic plan is reasonably sound, diverting savings from private hands into public investment need not be disadvantageous. Income taxes also require a high degree of literacy because they are based on self-assessment and the filing of forms. All in all, the use of the income tax poses many problems. R. Goode[27] lists six necessary conditions for income taxes to be efficient: existence of a predominant money economy, a high standard of literacy, prevalence of honest accounting records, a large degree of voluntary compliance on the part of taxpayers, no group with considerable political power, and an honest and efficient administration.

Nevertheless, income taxes are needed for equity in view of the regressive nature of most types of other taxes. As development proceeds, income, corporation, and business taxes can be expected to become more important and should be more important. Also, even though yields may not be high in the early stages of development efforts, it may be necessary to institute income taxes (if for no other purpose) to lessen political and social tensions. Moreover, they can serve the valuable function of capturing a large share of rising incomes as development proceeds, for, because of progressive rates, collections increase faster than incomes.

It seems desirable, thus, to foster such taxes as soon in the development effort as feasible. If experience in the various countries is a good indication, the systems cannot be copies of Western systems but must be adapted to the peculiar conditions of each country. This will require considerable thought and effort.

Corporation taxes also pose a dilemma. On the one hand, the grant of the corporate form is a valuable privilege for which some return should be made to the state. Moreover, many are foreign corporations, and countries like to tax foreigners wherever possible. In addition, they are large and relatively few in number and they are likely to have good accounting records. Thus, administration is relatively easy and compliance problems are reduced. On the other hand, the corporate device is the best means, other than through government, for concentrating funds for large ventures. For this reason, care should be exercised not to discourage the corporate form or the expansion of business, nor to repel foreign capital. Tax concessions for selected new industries may be used to soften such possible effects of the corporation tax. Like the income tax, however, such taxes undoubtedly must eventually become a part of every tax system.

In addition to the taxes discussed above, one should probably add the progressive inheritance or estate tax as a means of counteracting any tendency toward an unequal distribution of income and the regressivity of the

rest of the tax structure. Another problem in many tax systems is the existence of a host of small nuisance taxes, which are quite unproductive. These
should either be dropped in the interest of efficiency or made more productive.

Aside from the national tax revenues, local finance must also find sources
of support. The locality may not have any one adequate source of revenue,
and hence will try to rely on numerous unproductive taxes or on duplicating
central government taxes. A system of shared taxes may be necessary. Dividing taxes between the central and local government is always a problem.
The solution depends upon the precise allocation of governmental functions
and the tax sources and administrative abilities available. Local governments can better handle those taxes requiring administrative discretion,
such as assessing land or taxes collected in kind or labor.

Several interesting proposals for tax systems have been designed to be
self-enforcing. Each provides a series of taxes so designed that evasion of
one leaves the taxpayer subject to heavier payment of another tax; or the
information given by one taxpayer serves as a check on another. Examples
are a proposal by B. J. Higgins,[28] the system of Ceylon, described by R.
Goode,[29] and a proposed system for India.[30] These are ingenious, but it has
not been proved that they can make the tax structure self-enforcing.

The tax system must, of course, reflect certain objectives or meet certain
criteria. There are many different possible criteria, which may conflict and
have to be reconciled. In the United States we usually think of the dominant
criterion as justice as between individuals, and we define justice in terms of
"ability to pay." However, in actual practice we depart from this because of
expediency and the desire to accomplish other objectives. Nevertheless, we
tend to emphasize the criterion of justice.

In underdeveloped countries it is very difficult to develop a just tax system based on ability to pay. In addition, this may not be the most desirable
criterion. For the time being, a country may not be able to do more with
respect to justice than to avoid cutting incomes below a minimum standard.
The first and primary objective in most underdeveloped countries is economic growth, and the tax system must reflect this. To bring about growth,
resources must be available for investment and personal expenditure must
be cut. In other words, taxes must be productive and must at least prevent
consumption from rising even though they may not diminish it. Taxes that
accomplish this in the early stages of development are apt to bear heavily
on the poor and hence would not be in accordance with ability to pay.

Other criteria, in addition to the usual ones of convenience to pay, easy
to understand, low cost of collection, and so on, which seem most pertinent
to underdeveloped countries, also align with systems that bear heavily on
the poor. Some of these criteria are:

1. Taxes should not discourage productive investment or productive activity unduly and should even be designed to encourage it. For example, heavy profits taxes could discourage investment in new enterprises. On the other hand, land taxes payable in money may encourage commercial agriculture.

2. The tax system should direct resources toward the desired sectors and out of the undesired; that is, the system should be functional by contributing to the economic plan. For example, heavy taxation on speculative activity seems desirable, or, on occasion, if used judiciously, tax exemptions or subsidies may be worthwhile. The system should, if possible, promote the characteristics most needed for development, such as the willingness of people to accept risks.

3. The system should restrain inflation, which means that it should curtail consumption and raise sufficient funds to meet government expenses, including the investment program. In other words, it should balance aggregate demand and aggregate supply.

4. The ease of collecting and administering the system must be given prominent consideration.

5. Where the benefits from development projects are measurable (as in the case of irrigation projects and electrification), the tax system should try to recover some of this benefit.

But justice, in the sense of distributing the tax burden on the basis of ability to pay and reducing excessive inequality in the distribution of income, remains a desirable goal in the minds of most people. For this reason and for political reasons, as much justice should be built into the system as possible, while still seeking the other objectives. As development proceeds, tax systems should shift to a more just form. The indication is that progressive and direct taxes should replace the regressive and indirect ones to the extent that they become feasible.

A source of increased revenues perhaps more important than adding new taxes is the collection of the existing ones. Tax evasion is widespread. A characteristic story is that given for Latin America.[31] This source estimates that tax evasion in Latin America amounts to 50 to 60 percent of potential revenue. Auditors are underpaid, which is always an invitation to bribery; they moonlight for private companies and may audit their own reports. Administrative law has not developed sufficiently to permit proper enforcement. Smuggling is common, often with the connivance of the customs officials. There are too many taxes to keep track of. The problem lies in untrained and low-paid administrators and in complex tax systems. A training school in tax and public administration seems a worthwhile investment.

One of the major administrative obligations is to make sure that the proceeds of the revenue system are actually used for essential government services and for development purposes. Especially must there be a guard against overdevelopment in spectacular projects and against lavish displays. In other words, the expenditure side of public finance is as important as the revenue side. The government budget is thus a vital part of the whole development process. This can be the weakest aspect of government finance. The report of the International Bank mission to Thailand is representative.[32] According to this report, the spending units did not always adhere to budget appropriations. Various sources of public revenue were not even included in the budget; these included the lottery, some income-producing operations, and eighty or more quasi-independent government organizations such as the railways. The accounting and fiscal reporting functions were considered inadequate. In preparing the annual budget, agencies seeking funds gave no justification and usually padded their requests. These were insufficiently screened because of a lack of personnel, the result being haphazard cutting and excessive budgets. This could be called the "bargaining" budget. Government expenditures should be as carefully planned as the whole process of development, and every effort should be made to make government operations as efficient as possible.

Unfortunately, many governments use government service as a make-work project and carry many unessential people on the payroll. The author's experience in getting permission to use the municipal tennis courts in an Indonesian city illustrates this. A permit had to be obtained at the city hall each time one wished to play; no monthly or yearly passes were available. To obtain this permit, someone had to go to city hall, where twelve copies of the permit form had to be filled out and nine different signatures obtained. The whole process took from one to two hours, depending on whether the officials, who cannot delegate the task, were busy. The fee was insufficient to pay the salaries, and perhaps not even enough to pay for the paper. Naturally, one hired someone to spend the time to get the permit. The same situation exists elsewhere.

Budgeting would be facilitated if there were good public accounts and an adequate review of all expenditures. And it would help if the expenditure budget and capital investment budget were kept separate, for this would afford a better check on government operations.

The extent of the government development effort depends on the ability of the government to raise revenue. Thus, an important consideration is the limit of the ability of the government to tax; or, in other words, the taxable capacity of the country. At any one time this is, of course, difficult to determine, and increases in the rate of taxation can be approached only marginally. Groups who are taxed exert great pressure to pass on their taxes or to avoid taxes. Much of the tax effort may merely end up in rising prices.

Moreover, heavy taxes may dull incentives and so reduce total effort. On the other hand, increased governmental expenditure may increase economic activity and taxable economic capacity. The optimum level varies, depending on the preferences of the citizens, the administrative competence of the government, the present condition of economic overheads, and whether the taxes fall on productive or unproductive resources.

The less developed a country, the lower the proportion of the national income (see Table 12.1) that can be raised through taxation.[33] In actual practice, underdeveloped countries typically take about 12 percent or slightly more of the national income in taxes,[34] although this varies considerably from country to country. Many feel this could be raised a little but that it would be difficult to push this quickly above 15 percent. However, only a small increase would greatly increase the funds available for development purposes, assuming current governmental costs were kept under control. In time it is certain that taxable capacity will grow, particularly as incomes rise. Even in the short run, more revenues could be obtained, if the reports of the various missions of the International Bank are correct. Every effort must be made to bring about this increase, provided incentives are not affected.

It has already been said that it is necessary to increase the flow of credit and to provide more revenue for the governmental development effort. However, monetary and fiscal policies may be used for purposes other than raising revenues, including stabilizing prices, promoting full employment and economic growth, redistributing income, and so on. The effects of credit policies on prices has been discussed. Is it possible to adjust monetary and fiscal policies so as to encourage greater production, as seems feasible in the advanced countries? One theory, not shared by all economists, is that a major deterrent to full employment and economic growth is the lack of purchasing power, and that as long as there are unemployed resources or resources that can be drawn into production at no great increase in cost, putting extra purchasing power into the economy would not increase prices but would result in the greater employment of resources. Would the same be true for the underdeveloped countries?

Superficially, the conditions seem ideal for increasing bank credit, thus injecting more purchasing power into the economy, in the hope of calling out unemployed resources. Resources are unemployed in large numbers, and purchasing power is low. The problem is, however, that there are so many barriers to increasing production that production cannot be increased quickly. The result of trying to force production by increasing total spending would be largely a rapid increase in prices, which would raise other problems. Until the economies become more flexible, reliance on monetary and fiscal policies will not be sufficient. Until then, governments will have to intervene more directly in the economic system than do those of the more advanced countries. The most that can be expected of monetary and fiscal policies is that they may be used to avoid deflation and to attempt to prevent runaway inflation. In practice, much of the effort now has to be directed toward restraining price increases, with a possible restraining effect on investment. Even this is difficult because the credit controls and tax systems are poorly developed.

## Marketing

As countries develop, the number of people engaged in marketing seems to grow. However, this is largely illusory, as P. T. Bauer has shown.[35] In the underdeveloped societies there are few marketing specialists, but much time is spent in marketing, probably more than in the advanced countries. The producer or his wife markets the family production and the cost involved is large, at least in time spent.

Little attention seems to be paid to market structures in underdeveloped countries, as most of the attention is focused on industry and economic and social overheads. Many countries do not tamper with existing systems because they absorb many people who would otherwise be unemployed.[36] The result is that consumers subsidize large numbers, which they can ill afford to do.[37]

Yet, the development of an efficient marketing system is essential for development for various reasons:

1.    Efficient marketing permits specialization and division of labor and larger-scale production, thus reducing costs. Specialization can exist only when the market is sufficiently large for the producer to exchange his entire production for his other wants. With specialization and markets, the people can be integrated and made interdependent. A widening of markets can bring an escape from regional isolation and so promote national unity.

2.    Marketing is a good training ground for entrepreneurs and is often the starting place for the accumulation of capital.

3.    Efficient marketing reduces the need for individual inventories.

4.    Efficiency in marketing releases labor for industrial work, since marketing is one of the major areas of excessive underemployment.

5.    Marketing is a creator of new small businesses, for it opens up the demand for new products. It thus increases the alternatives available to the people. This gives greater scope for the use of productive capacity, much of which is currently wasted.

6.  By establishing a price system, marketing sets up a set of price signals that serves to attract or repel supply, thus directing resources to where they are most desired, and to perform the other allocative functions of a price system. Thus, the need for direct controls is lessened.

Marketing practices differ in detail from country to country, but most are roughly similar. Often there is a specialized structure for export products, particularly plantation products. The marketing boards in various African countries are examples of such specialized agencies. On the other hand, there is little development of the local marketing structure.

The usual system of retail distribution consists of many bazaars with little interconnection, hordes of street peddlers, and many small specialized shops. Standardization and grading are nonexistent, weights and measures are inaccurate, and cleanliness is practically ignored. Trade is in small surpluses, the bulk of the rural people being largely self-sufficient. Most of the trading is done by women, and many walk surprising distances to sell small quantities. One study by students in Indonesia reported for one day 4,000 sellers in the bazaar and only 12,000 customers. Many sellers attempt to dispose of small quantities of identical merchandise, the visitor being surrounded by many sellers, each trying to dispose of her small supply. On the streets, one encounters large numbers of sellers who carry their wares, which are often of considerable weight. The bargaining system generally prevails, which is time consuming and costly, but time appears to be of little value. Bargaining is based on maximizing the return from each individual transaction. It also makes it impossible to expand one's business by hiring clerks because there would be too many opportunities for dishonesty. Thus, the size of the selling unit is limited to the size of the immediate family. The merchant thus prefers large gains on a limited volume rather than small gains on a large volume, which is essential for mass marketing and which in turn seems essential for a growing economy. The marketing system is thus costly. It results in much waste, spoilage, and great duplication.

Storage facilities are scarce and transportation facilities inadequate, so that wide price variations exist seasonally and among the various regions of a country. Wide price variations among neighboring towns is common, especially for fresh vegetables, as local supplies vary. It is said that each supplier goes to his customary market regardless of price conditions, mainly because he has no access to market information.

The staples, such as rice or wheat, are grown largely by peasants who have little surplus and must sell in the local markets. They may have to give up much of their crop to the landlord or the village moneylender, who may act as the local wholesaler. It is usual for the wholesale trade to be in the hands of foreigners who have used their monopoly position in the local market to exploit the peasant. The peasant is forced to sell when everyone else is selling, and so is easily taken advantage of by one or more of the few buyers.

Manufactured goods are usually sold by the craftsmen themselves and only over a narrow area. Normally the craftsman waits for customers to come to the shop, sells at the bazaar, or sells to a small-shop owner. If small-scale industry is to survive, considerable improvement will be necessary in the marketing structure. The craftsman needs credit, efficient purchasing, and efficient marketing. These may come through an efficient wholesale system or producer cooperatives. However, preventing exploitation, on the one hand, and training efficient administrators, on the other, face formidable obstacles.

The present marketing systems must be considered inadeqate for economic growth, and their improvement must have a vital role in any economic plan. Economic growth involves greater commercialization, and this requires a large increase in the amount of goods marketed. Supplies and customers must be coordinated, or surpluses and deficits will exist side by side, resulting in waste. Goods are not fully produced until they reach the final buyer, so efficient marketing can be considered part of an efficient production system.[38] Goods will not market themselves, and present systems are too time consuming and costly for the job needed. Setting up efficient procedures of marketing must accompany improvements in agriculture and industry.

## Transportation and Communication

As previously mentioned, anything that reduces costs is a potential contributor to economic growth and development. One International Bank report[39] has this to say: "Transportation, communications and power have one important element in common. They all provide auxiliary services important to the development of agriculture, industry, mining and domestic and foreign trade." Inadequacy of these services constitutes one of the greatest barriers to economic development.

Transportation improvements are important in many ways. They reduce costs between the producer and the customer, permitting goods to be delivered to the customer more cheaply with even, on occasion, increased prices to the producer at the same time. The decreased costs widen the market and thus make specialization possible, opening new areas for industrial and agricultural development. This is the familiar case of expanding the possibilities of division of labor, thus eliminating subsistence economies. One estimate for Turkey[40] is that production could be increased 75 percent if incentives for marketing through adequate transportation were created. Similarly, for Mexico,[41] transportation development is credited with stimulating the extension of cultivation, the commercialization of agriculture, the growth of markets, increased exports of cotton and winter vegetables, and a growth of the tourist trade. In theory, when transportation facilities develop and become cheaper, individuals (or governments) should begin to develop new industries as they are able to exchange their surpluses for their needs. This is what happened in the United States and other developed areas, but has not always happened in other lands. Thus, transportation development is a necessity for development, but not always a sufficient cause, and so must be coordinated with other measures.

Transportation development brings other advantages. It reduces spoilage. The report on Turkey cites a survey, which shows that 10 percent of the annual wheat production is lost through spoilage because of inadequate transportation facilities. Inadequate transportation can result in undesirable concentration of economic activity. Investment in transportation can play a leading role in stimulating an economy, as in the United States. Easy transportation, along with communication, is vital for social progress and political stability. Isolation and backwardness tend to disappear, people mingle with stimulating results, traditions and customs feel the impact, and education and health measures can spread.[42]

Various agencies supply the necessary transportation services, such as railroads, roads, airplanes, and waterways. Each has its own advantages and disadvantages. None is superior in all types of terrain, so coordination is necessary and the proper combination must be studied firsthand for every country. Costs are heavy and resources are inadequate to provide all the desired services, so careful planning is most essential. The first function of the economic planner is to establish priorities, first for the areas to be served and secondly for the type of service to establish.

It is possible to set up an ideal typical sequence of transport development[43] as follows:

1. At first there is a scattering of small ports along the seacoast, with little lateral connection and a limited hinterland.
2. Major lines of penetration are extended to the interior, to expand the hinterland.
3. Feeder lines develop as the major ports begin to pirate the territory of other ports.
4. Nodes develop along the major interior lines to serve as focal points for feeder networks. Thus, interior concentration begins.
5. Interior centers begin to link up.
6. The development of national trunk-line routes or "main streets" and the development of high-priority linkages are effected.

Taafe *et al.*[43] also say that the most important phase of transportation history is the first major penetration line to the interior. In general, the first step is to connect the most important producing and consuming regions (often export ports), for where there is heavy traffic, there is a high return on investment. Where there are no heavy concentrations, such as in Africa where distances are great and the populations scattered, careful planning is necessary to see that the best potential areas are connected and the costs of extending transportation lines are minimized. In addition, even in areas where there are existing concentrations, one could well consider supplying transportation to areas with current low-traffic densities but with large potential for development. These, however, should be made only after careful surveys.

After the major penetration lines are chosen, feeder lines have a high claim for priority. In many countries the major lines were already built at the end of the colonial period, made largely for the military purposes of the occupying powers, if nothing else. In these countries the greatest deficiency is in the feeder lines. A further problem, which cannot be neglected, is that of municipal transportation where congestion is a major consideration. Lastly, particular attention needs to be given to minor roads between villages, on social as well as economic grounds. Use of local labor on a labor-intensive basis may be indicated here.

The second step is to determine the best type of transportation to develop in each specific area. Transportation facilities should be planned as a coordinated whole, with each type of transportation rendering the service it is best suited to provide. No one means has a general advantage over all kinds of terrain, so this problem must be investigated in each case.[44]

Railroads are very expensive to build and maintain, and skilled people are required for operation and maintenance. On the other hand, once they are built, they can be economical to operate, at least for long-distance hauls. They need supplementing, of course, for door-to-door delivery. Because they require so much capital, care should be exercised in not overbuilding them, and other transportation means should be coordinated with them. Vairous International Bank studies of underdeveloped countries report the major problems in connection with railroads to be poor management, high maintenance costs, lack of modernization, and surplus staff. Inferior management means not only higher operating costs but also higher construction costs. The International Bank study of Nigeria[45] indicates that better management of rail traffic would reduce the need for double tracking. Better management and modernization can result in heavier loads, faster speeds, better scheduling, better maintenance, better labor relations, and improved safety. Unfortunately, it is usually not possible to expand railroads a bit at a time, although lines can be extended from a central system.

For a railroad to be economical, a system of a certain size must be built as a complete unit. A railroad must also be built before it is actually needed. This means that rail lines should probably be reserved for the most obvious areas and should be supplemented by feeder auto roads.

Roads are relatively flexible in that they can be extended a little at a time and can be built relatively quickly. With developments in automotive facilities, road transportation deserves high priority in the underdeveloped countries. Roads do need to be planned and coordinated, with special emphasis on location, design, traffic regulations, and maintenance standards.

Air lanes are important in developing an area. They offer a relatively cheap, from a capital point of view, way of opening up an isolated area, especially where the terrain is too difficult for land travel. Not all air traffic is profitable, but it is surprising how much can be carried profitably when planes are specially designed for specific products. This is also an aid to the tourist trade. Developing an external air service is another matter. There is great glamour in having an international air line, but it is of doubtful profitability.

Internal waterways may be a useful supplement where rivers and lakes are suitable, for water transport is relatively cheap. Adequate ports and coastal shipping should not be forgotten. The major problems here are terminal handling, storage, and transportation to the interior. Good port management is important to prevent port congestion and excessive storage.

The third step is to get economies in construction and operation by better administration and maintenance. The various International Bank studies mention such things as an unusually large number of personnel for the methods employed, especially overhead personnel, improper road design, and lack of control of weight limits and speed. Proper road design is important. Excessive standards for the traffic involved bring about waste in construction costs. Inferior standards mean excessive maintenance. Thus, road design must be related to the traffic involved. Particularly, local governments need help in locating roads and determining road standards. As traffic increases, more appropriate roads can be built. A country probably never finishes improving and extending its road facilities.

Maintenance standards are usually low and often neglected because funds are not provided, appropriate personnel are not available, and equipment is misused. The result of the latter is rapid deterioration of equipment and an accompanying high cost of operation. Lack of enforcement of weight and speed limits also results in excessive wear and increased maintenance costs. A major problem is the large amount of slow road traffic, bicycles, oxcarts, and so on. In areas of greatest traffic density, special roads of less high standards for this traffic would appear economical.

A fourth step relates to the matter of competition between transportation companies, especially truck and bus lines. Two extremes seem unsatisfactory. One would be to accord monopolies to carriers between given points, which would result in excessive charges and possible attempts to influence the controlling authorities. The other extreme would allow unlimited competition, which would result in cutthroat competition, depreciating equipment, a low regard for safety and other controls, and eventually poorer service. Finding a compromise between these policies is one of the key problems to be faced. A related problem is the charge to be made the user, especially in the case of roads.

Cheap power is fundamental to a developing industry, whether industry be large or small scale. Nonhuman power, which usually means electric power, increases human power and is a fundamental factor in increased productivity. Energy is also fundamental to welfare as a consumer good. Unfortunately, power projects are apt to require a heavy capital investment and have a high foreign exchange component so that mistakes can be serious. Even the final use of electricity is foreign exchange-intensive, as most electric equipment must be imported. The International Bank reports reveal serious defects in power systems. In Venezuela[46] the report indicates that growth has been haphazard and plants badly located, distribution facilities have been neglected, different governmental regional systems and private companies have not been coordinated, and most economical size has not been considered.

Important factors are the degree and constancy of use and the regularity of supply. Low-load factors are common. Large hydro-projects require expensive transmission and are subject to fluctuating output as the wet and dry seasons alternate. There appears to be considerable need to study the feasibility of small diesel units as an interim measure, especially for isolated villages, as a means of reducing transmission costs. However, the less the interconnections among systems, the greater the problems of peak-use periods. It is reported in Jordan[47] that inconstancy of supply leads industries to develop their own facilities, so central facilities exist mainly for domestic purposes. The result is that peak loads are high and of short duration and the load factor is extremely low. Intensive study is necessary to determine the most appropriate way to develop the power system.

Poor communications, including telephone, telegraph, post office, radio, and TV broadcasting are an impediment to development. Modern industry cannot tolerate the delays of slow communications or the lack of information that results from difficult transmissions. International Bank surveys report poor administration of the telephone systems, lack of coordination, and an imbalance in the systems, which cause a low-load factor, especially when attempts are made to extend telephone lines beyond the thickly settled areas. The report for Venezuela,[48] for example, recommends a limited approach to extension outside the major areas until there is an increased capacity to operate the system; or, one could add, until the load factor is high.

Water, sewage, and waste disposal are important for urban survival. These lag because they require heavy investment. Nevertheless, they must be given high priority for health reasons.

## Legal Systems

Law must provide an elementary framework of order, security, and purpose.[49] Investment is discouraged if property is not protected, and savings are kept in liquid form or exported abroad. Extremely detailed legal and administrative restrictions hinder trade and slow down initiative. Different sources of law result in conflicts, and so confusion and uncertainty, thus forcing business plans to be very short run. Institutions that no longer serve an economic function survive, and these, such as land tenure, inheritance, and transfer regulations, may result in excessive fragmentation of land. Legal systems in underdeveloped countries are often primitive, a combination of indigenous law and imposed law, or are based on inflexible customary procedures so that modern business practices are handicapped and development is slowed. Because of this conflict with modern business practices, it is necessary that legal processes be reformed. Actually, traditional law does change under the impact of development, but law is notoriously slow to adapt and represents a drag on economic change. Laws need to be codified and national legal systems created out of the present heterogeneity of regulations into legal systems consistent with each country's philosophy.

### THE CORPORATION

In the advanced nations the corporation is now taken for granted, but it took some time to develop. In many underdeveloped countries the corporation is still in its infancy. Its growth is a necessary adjunct to the growth of the large-scale enterprise. The corporation is the best-known means of gathering together in one enterprise large sums of money.* Its full development depends on the general population acquiring the willingness to buy shares and so trust their funds to strangers, the existence of security markets, and a willingness of businessmen to enlarge their businesses by hiring

---

* It has other advantages of unlimited life, limited liability, likelihood of scientific or at least specialized management, and transferability of shares.

personnel from outside their immediate families. Without the corporation private enterprise is unlikely to be a vehicle for rapid development.

## The Tourist Trade

For some countries the tourist trade offers great advantages as an immediate earner of needed foreign exchange.* For very few can this be considered a major reliance for development funds, but Switzerland has done very well with her tourist trade. It can, however, be a useful supplement on occasion. Care does have to be exercised that the capital cost of the necessary equipment (hotels, restaurants, transportation facilities, and so on) are not out of line with the return. For some countries, the prospects of a large amount of tourist trade are so small that trying to attract tourists would be uneconomic. Thus, this activity must be as carefully scrutinized as any other activity in the decision to allocate funds. One advantage is that it requires less government assistance than other sectors. The International Bank reports for Libya, Tanganyika, and Jamaica[50] describe the prospects in those countries and the problems involved. Each has its own peculiar attractions, as has every country. Jamaica, for example, is considered to have her greatest comparative advantage in the tourist trade.

The usual problems are the need to develop modern hotels and restaurants with trained personnel, beach resorts, transportation facilities, facilities for local excursions, sports facilities and amusements such as local music and dancing, skilled guides proficient in different languages, and tourist agencies. Even gambling is recommended as a good revenue raiser. The development and maintenance of antiquities and museums is also cited. For many countries, special problems exist in complicated entry and exit formalities and internal travel permits. The writer can testify to this in Afghanistan, which requires internal travel permits. Since he wanted to go back into the country, a visit was made to the proper office after many misdirections. A permit was duly entered on the passport in the Afghan language and the trip was made subsequently without incident. After returning, a visit was made to the same office for an exit visa, only to receive the information that this had already been granted. At the airport a German national, who also knew no Afghan, and who had appeared at the same time at the visa office, was informed that he could not leave because he had no exit visa. His passport carried only an internal travel permit! One wonders where the two Russians, who also had similar language difficulties in the visa office, ended up.

* Tourist trade, of course, hardly classifies as an institution, but is important enough to be mentioned in a work on development.

The general recommendation is that a country cater to middle-income tourists by arranging low-cost package tours, rather than cater to the luxury trade, as the most profitable possibility.

## REFERENCES

1. BOHANNAN, P., "Impact of Money on an African Subsistence Economy." *Journal of Economic History* (December, 1959), pp. 491-503. (An account of a semideveloped monetary system.)

2. AMATAYAKUL, R., and S. A. PANDIT, "Financial Institutions in Thailand." *International Monetary Fund Staff Papers* (December, 1961), p. 477.

3. MOORE, F. J., "Money Lenders and Cooperators in India." *Economic Development and Cultural Change* (June, 1953), pp. 139-59. (An account of these operations in India.) Bottomley, A., "The Structure of Interest Rates in Underdeveloped Rural Areas." *Journal of Farm Economics* (May, 1964), pp. 313-22.

4. NEVINS, E., *Capital Funds in Underdeveloped Countries, Role of Financial Institutions.* New York, St Martin's Press, 1961, p. 50.

5. *Ibid.,* pp. 40ff.

6. BLOOMFIELD, A. I., "Monetary Policy in Underdeveloped Countries," in C. J. Friedrich and S. E. Harris, eds., *Public Policy* (Harvard University Press, 1956), reproduced in T. Morgan, G. W. Betz, and N. K. Choudhry, *Readings in Economic Development.* Belmont, Calif., Wadsworth Publishing Co., 1963, p. 374.

7. NEVINS, *op. cit.,* p. 357.

8. *Ibid.,* pp. 63ff.

9. CAIRNCROSS, A. K., *Factors in Economic Development.* New York, Frederick A. Praeger, Inc., 1962, p. 164.

10. WAI, U. T., "Taxation Problems and Policies of Underdeveloped Countries." *International Monetary Fund Staff Papers* (November, 1962), pp. 428-48.

11. *Ibid.,* p. 434.

12. KALDOR, N., "Will Underdeveloped Countries Learn to Tax?" *Foreign Affairs* (January, 1963), p. 412.

13. HELLER, W. W., "Fiscal Policies for Underdeveloped Countries," in *Taxes and Fiscal Policy in Underdeveloped Countries.* New York, United Nations, 1954, p. 19.

14. WAI, *op. cit.,* p. 431. (The percentage for individual countries is given.)

15. KYBOL, E., "Why More Taxes?" *Americas* (April, 1962), p. 12.

16. Economic Commission for Asia and the Far East, *Economic Survey of Asia and the Far East.* New York, United Nations, 1957, pp. 88ff.

17. PREST, A. R., *Public Finance in Underdeveloped Countries.* London, Weidenfeld & Nicolson, 1962, p. 74.

18. WALD, H. P., *Taxation of Agricultural Lands in Underdeveloped Economies.* Cambridge, Mass., Harvard University Press, 1959, pp. 10ff.

19. MEIER, G. M., and R. E. BALDWIN, *Economic Development.* New York, John Wiley & Sons, Inc., 1957, pp. 388-90.

20. GOODE, RICHARD, "Reconstruction of Foreign Tax Systems," in *Proceedings of the Forty-fourth Annual Conference of the National Tax Association,* 1951, reproduced in G. M. Meier, *Leading Issues in Development Economics.* New York, Oxford University Press, 1964, p. 126.

21. KALDOR, *op. cit.,* p. 413.

22. CROCKETT, J. P., "Tax Pattern in Latin America." *National Tax Journal* (March, 1962), pp. 97, 98.

23. GOODE, RICHARD, "New System of Direct Taxation in Ceylon." *National Tax Journal* (December, 1960), pp. 329-40.

24. DUE, J. F., "The African Personal Tax." *National Tax Journal* (December, 1962), pp. 385-98.

25. WAI, *op. cit.,* p. 433.

26. PREST, *op. cit.,* p. 28.

27. GOODE, quoted in Heller, *op. cit.,* pp. 20, 21.

28. HIGGINS, B. J., *Economic Development.* New York, W. W. Norton, 1959, pp. 524-44.

29. GOODE, "New System . . . ," *loc. cit.*

30. FROOMKIN, J., "A Program for Taxation and Economic Development— the Indian Case." *Economic Development and Cultural Change* (January, 1958), pp. 129-42.

31. "T-men Join the Alliance." *Business Week* (February 23, 1963), pp. 68ff.

32. International Bank for Reconstruction and Development, *Public Development Program for Thailand.* Baltimore, Johns Hopkins Press, 1960, pp. 198-207.

33. See also Heller, *op. cit.,* p. 6.

34. Economic Commission for Asia and the Far East, *loc. cit.,* p. 85.

35. BAUER, P. T., *Economic Analysis and Policy in Underdeveloped Countries.* Durham, N.C., Duke University Press, 1957, pp. 67-72.

36. HOLTON, R. H., "Marketing Structure and Economic Development." *Quarterly Journal of Economics* (August, 1953), p. 345.

37. WESTFALL, R., and H. W. BOYD, JR., "Marketing in India." *Journal of Marketing* (October, 1960), pp. 11-17. (Describes the marketing system in India and its defects.)

38. COLLINS, N. R., and R. H. HOLTON, "Programming Changes in Marketing in Planning Development." *Kyklos,* No. 1 (1963), p. 123.

39. International Bank for Reconstruction and Development, *The Economy of Turkey.* Baltimore, Johns Hopkins Press, 1951, p. 121.

40. GRUNWALD, K., and J. O. RONALD, *Industrialization in the Middle East.* New York, Council for Middle Eastern Affairs Press, 1960, p. 83.

41. International Bank for Reconstruction and Development, *Economic Development of Mexico.* Baltimore, Johns Hopkins Press, 1953, p. 93.

42. AKHTAI, S. M., *Economics of Pakistan.* Lahore, Publishers United Limited, 1961, vol. II., p. 171.

43. TAAFE, E. J., R. L. MORRILL, and P. GOULD, "Transport Expansion in Underdeveloped Countries: A Comparative Analysis." *Geographical Review* (October, 1963), pp. 503-29.

44. International Bank for Reconstruction and Development, *The Economic Development of Syria.* Baltimore, Johns Hopkins Press, 1955, p. 431.

45. International Bank for Reconstruction and Development, *The Economic Development of Nigeria.* Baltimore, Johns Hopkins Press, 1955, p. 458.

46. International Bank for Reconstruction and Development, *The Economic Development of Venezuela.* Baltimore, Johns Hopkins Press, 1961, p. 281.

47. International Bank for Reconstruction and Development, *The Economic Development of Jordan.* Baltimore, Johns Hopkins Press, 1957, p. 31.

48. *Ibid.,* p. 310.

49. Discussion in this section is largely based on the following works: "The Legal System and Economic Development of Greece." *Journal of Economic History* (June, 1959), pp. 173-98. Baade, H. W., "Foreword," *Law and Contemporary Problems* (Autumn, 1962), pp. 537-44. Fallers, L., "Customary Law in the New African States."

*Law and Contemporary Problems* (Autumn, 1962), pp. 605-16.

50. International Bank for Reconstruction and Development, *The Economic Development of Tanganyika*, 1961, pp. 295-300; *The Economic Development of Libya*, 1960, pp. 208-21; *The Economic Development of Jamaica*, 1952, Baltimore, Johns Hopkins Press, pp. 90-95.

## ADDITIONAL READINGS

ADLER, J. H., *et al.*, *Public Finance and Economic Development in Guatemala.* Stanford, Calif., Stanford University Press, 1952.

BAUER, P. T., and B. S. YAMEY, "Economic Progress and Occupational Redistribution," in B. Okun and R. W. Richardson, *Studies in Economic Development.* New York, Holt, Rinehart and Winston, 1962, pp. 219-28.

BERNSTEIN, E. M., and I. G. PATEL, "Inflation in Relation to Economic Development." *International Monetary Fund Staff Papers* (November, 1952), pp. 363-98.

BERNSTEIN and PATEL, "The Role of Transportation in Economic Development," and papers by H. Heymann, Jr., J. H. Kaufman, and W. Owen, *American Economic Review, Proceedings* (May, 1962), pp. 386-415.

BOHANNAN, P., and G. DALTON, eds., *Markets in Africa.* African Studies, No. 9. Evanston, Ill., Northwestern University Press, 1962.

CHELLIAH, R. J., *Fiscal Policy in Underdeveloped Countries.* London, George Allen & Unwin, Ltd., 1960.

DEWEY, A. G., *Peasant Marketing in Java.* New York, The Free Press of Glencoe, 1962.

DEWEY, "African Law." *Law and Contemporary Problems* (August, 1962), pp. 537-652.

JACOBY, N. H., "Taxation in Laos: Policies for a New Country with an Underdeveloped Economy." *National Tax Journal* (June, 1961), pp. 145-62.

# CHAPTER

# 13

# *Control of*
# *Economic Decisions*

### The Problem

All the actions and decisions thus far discussed must be carried out through the institutional structure and the value system of the economy. Economic activity goes on in any society, and a system of control, or order-inducing arrangements, is necessary. In general, there are three types of control: social, cultural, and religious influences; more or less "automatic" economic institutions such as the free operation of market forces; and government control, which can range from regulation of abuses, economic planning of various degrees of completeness, government operation of key industries, and democratic socialism to autocratic Communism, and all stops in between. The three types of society can be designated as traditionalist, private enterprise, and consciously controlled. Thus, there are a number of solutions to the question of control.

Actually, few if any instances of a pure form of any of the three types have existed, except for the traditionalist. Laissez-faire private enterprise has never really been laissez-faire, but has always been modified by some degree of government intervention, even in the early days of the Western countries. Similarly, no country has ever relied on 100 percent government controls. In actuality, all countries exhibit some controls of each type, although each may emphasize one or the other. Thus, we can say a society is traditionalist if it has an unusually large area of control by custom and such influences. Private enterprise societies are those with a relatively large sphere for private enterprise. Other countries with a large sphere for government action may be classified as socialistic or communistic. All countries seem to have a combination of the three types of control. The exact combination varies from country to country, with varying results. The optimum combination undoubtedly varies, depending on the circumstances, including the competence of the particular government. It does appear that a heavy reliance on traditions is not conducive to economic growth. A very real concern for underdeveloped countries today is whether it is better for them to rely primarily on private enterprise or government direction and the choice of the optimum combination of the two. One should not expect any particular country to pattern itself exactly after the Western private enterprise economies, for their situations differ. Nor should they blindly follow the Russian pattern. This requires serious study, and it is hoped that from the efforts of the underdeveloped countries new and fruitful ideas on the organization of societies will evolve.

One fact is inescapable today. There has been a great increase in the role of government in the economic life of all countries, regardless of the dominant ideology, and this has come about for many reasons, to be discussed later.

Traditionalist societies are very apt to be unprogressive, for innovations are discouraged. Improvements in production methods may be scorned. Much time is wasted on ceremonials or in excessive leisure. One's status in life is apt to be determined by the conditions of his birth and not by individual achievement. Work may be looked down upon and the occupations of religion, war, and government may hold the highest prestige. The authority of the rulers is often supreme, and all activity is ordered according to their whim and usually to their advantage. Often a man's product is distributed according to a fixed rule within the family, and decision making may be a family affair. Thus, there is little incentive for individual initiative or for innovation. The innovator may even find himself a social outcast. The central problems of the traditionalist society are thus the curse of conformity and the failure to progress.

This is not to say that custom and tradition have no place. It is necessary that there be some resistance to change or else there will be haphazard change, which would be wasteful of effort. In other words, there must be enough retention of custom and tradition to force a proposed change to prove its worth. What is bad is that tradition may be so strong that even worthwhile change, which could bring growth, is inhibited.

Once economic development starts, traditions tend to be swept away and some new order-inducing arrangements must be substituted. The question before underdeveloped countries is: What type? A major problem for many has been the efforts of the Western colonial powers to change the lives of the local people economically and to substitute much of the institutional arrangements of private enterprise.[1] The result has often been confusion and a collapse of old values, with no unifying substitute to take the place of the old traditions. Traditional obligations have been weakened and a pseudoprivate enterprise has developed, which practices exploitation in various forms, more often than not by the country's own nationals. The consequence is a job of major proportions in instituting economic and political controls of a suitable type.

## Private Enterprise or Government Controls?

There is a wide range of views as to how economic decisions should be made, ranging from a completely laissez-faire system of markets and private enterprise through various degrees of government intervention such as regulation of private enterprise, operation of economic enterprises of varying degrees and extent, and economic planning of varying degrees of thoroughness. All alternative systems perform certain economic functions and all have their social and political trappings and their social and political consequences. Economically speaking, humans must be motivated to perform economic acts, and these acts must be coordinated. Each economic system has its own means of doing these things, and the methods employed affect the lives of individuals.

The Western world seems anxious to transfer its more or less free economic system and accompanying institutions to the underdeveloped countries. The Soviet bloc countries are trying just as hard to transfer their controlled system. It is likely that neither can be transmitted in the exact form in which they exist in the transmitting countries. Extensive modification may be necessary to fit the situation. Nor does either group exhibit a uniform system. The economic systems of the United States, the United Kingdom, and the continental European countries all differ by degree, and in fact, some of them are considered socialistic. Within each country there is disagreement as to the exact proportion of private enterprise and government intervention. Similarly, the controlled economies also differ. Soviet Russia, mainland China, and Yugoslavia, for example, have varying economic structures.

Actually, the argument, as it is carried on between the advocates of an uncontrolled market system and various varieties of controlled systems, is quite unrealistic. Those who favor the laissez-faire price system tend to explain how their system works in theory, the result being that decision making is optimized and the greatest good for all is brought about. They tend to contrast this theoretical best with the actual operation of a government-controlled or planned economy in all its practical imperfection. The advocates of government intervention do the same in reverse. At their theoretical best, both systems would result in well-functioning societies that would accomplish the aims of the people. Undoubtedly the people would be indifferent to which system prevailed. But a comparison of the theoretical best of both is sterile, for neither works out to its theoretical optimum, but falls far short. The only valid comparison is between their operating realities in the situation that is being faced. This is the choice which underdeveloped countries must make.

Neither camp has a clear-cut claim on the basis of past experience. Some free enterprise areas have grown rapidly and others have not. The same is true of controlled areas. No positive correlation seems to exist between economic success and the structure of the economy. Each has its individual champion, and the argument is usually framed in reference to two countries, the United States and Soviet Russia. The United States, under a somewhat modified free enterprise system, has been highly successful in its economic growth. Soviet Russia, with extensive government controls, has had a phenomenal rate of growth but over a much shorter period. It is beyond the scope of this work to examine why growth has occurred in each case, but underdeveloped countries should examine this closely, particularly as to the extent the economic and political structures were responsible for the growth.

There is also a tendency to argue in terms of all black or all white. The contrast is made between pure laissez-faire and totalitarian and complete planning. In actuality there has never been either extreme and both are likely to be quite unthinkable. Laissez-faire private enterprise has always been modified by some role for government. Planning can be democratic and can be less than complete with considerable sphere for private decision making. Thus, government controls and private enterprise can exist together and in fact may well be improved by each other's presence. The real concern is the proper sphere for each under the particular circumstances which a country faces.

It must be emphasized that there is no universal answer to this problem. What is suitable for one country may be unsuitable for another. The exact mix of private enterprise and government intervention depends on the exact circumstances and may even change as the circumstances of the country change. For example, there is the possibility that the role of the government in underdeveloped countries may be very great during the time the country is striving to get the development process started. At a later time, when economic conditions are more favorable, it may be possible to rely on a greater amount of private enterprise.

Moreover, the question of what is expected to result from the decision making must always be asked. Just how does one test the efficiency of an economic system? The early economists used the test of efficient allocation of resources so as to maximize total profit and with it current production and consumer satisfaction. Other goals may be desired, such as greatest long-term growth, maximum defensive strength, optimum distribution of income, or self-sufficiency. Different types of societies may be necessary to bring about different combinations of desired goals. These, too, are not universal, but must be determined by each country for itself.

The laissez-faire free enterprise system in theory is an efficient way of coordinating economic activity. It rests on the assumptions that the consumer wishes to maximize his satisfactions and has the requisite knowledge to choose wisely among competing goods, and that the producer wishes to maximize his profits and is able to move from good to good as profits are greater or smaller. Because the producer is interested in accumulating income, he will go to where consumers are spending their money, or casting dollar votes, as it is often termed. Through offers of goods, on the one hand, and purchases on the other, prices are influenced, demand adjusted to supply, and profits equalized in all fields. Similarly, resources compete for employment and producers compete for suitable agents of production, thereby bringing wages, rents, and interest into line with productivity so that everyone gets what he deserves, based on his contribution to productivity. Resources are thus allocated to their most effective use and consumers maximize their satisfactions. In this way, through the search for profit and maximum satisfactions, individual efforts and decisions lead to the optimum social advantage.

Because private offers and demands were presumed to accomplish these ends efficiently, little if any role was accorded to government in the laissez-faire economy as originally conceived. At best, government was to limit itself to improving the private sector and supplying certain things necessary for the successful operation of the private sector; these obligations of government were to be confined to maintaining peace and order, courts of justice, a monetary system, weights and measures, and certain social overheads that private enterprise seemed loathe to undertake or that private enterprise could not conveniently operate, such as roads or flood control or similar projects for the common good where charges could not be conveniently assessed to the user.

The major emphasis in this system was on efficiently allocating resources and maximizing current production of desired goods. Actually, economic development was presumed to follow as producers, seeking to increase their profits, introduced cost-saving innovations and their competitors followed, thus decreasing price and expanding demand. The desire for goods would also serve to motivate the factors of production to greater effort in order to increase their incomes, assure their employment, and improve their scale of living. The right of private profit and personal reward through the right of free enterprise, plus the guarantee of the right to private property, thus would afford the most potent incentives for action that could be devised. Competition would coordinate the efforts and assure that individual efforts would lead to maximum social welfare.

It is to be noted that the aim was social welfare and not individual profit or self-interest, but that the latter was to be used to accomplish the social aims and that individual ends were to be pursued under well-defined rules of competition. The motivating force was to be the lure of private profit as apportioned by the price system. Individual actions were to be coordinated by competition. Thus, the competition of producers for profits and customers for maximum satisfaction would harmonize all interests and promote economic growth. Government regulation would be unnecessary and even harmful.

Such a system as that described has never really existed. The assumptions under which the posited results were to obtain—mobility of the factors of production, large numbers of buyers and sellers, homogeneous commodities, reasonable knowledge of economic conditions and values on both sides of the market, and active competition—are not true today and were not even true when the theory of the laissez-faire private enterprise system was formulated. The economic system has been characterized in the West, and perhaps even more so in underdeveloped countries, by large-scale industry or semimonopoly, inequality in economic power, rigidities of economic movement, and (in the West) rapid changes to which the sluggish mobility of the economic system could not accommodate itself with great efficiency. Too many vested interests have chosen not to play the game according to the rules of competition. They have set up roadblocks to competition by attempting to create monopolies (or at least organizations of sufficient size to influence the market); they have used salesmanship and advertising rather than price to overcome competition; they have restricted entry of competing products to the market; and they have even resorted to unfair methods of competition.

These practices could not help but raise difficulties, and there was no assurance that individual interest and social interest would coincide as has been assumed. Therefore, each country has had to introduce modifications, usually through government intervention, to assure that the social interest would be served. The private enterprise system (or capitalism, as it may be termed) differs among the Western countries in the varying degrees of government intervention. Much of Europe has advanced social welfare schemes, an increasing amount of government ownership and operation of enterprises, and economic planning to various degrees. In the United States, government intervention has always been present, even in the earliest days, and in the recent past has seen such stages in social development as the New Deal of Roosevelt, the Fair Deal of Truman, and the New Frontier of Kennedy. The basic system of private enterprise has been retained, but it has been modified in various ways to eliminate some of the worst abuses under a system that is generally referred to as a "mixed economic system." Thus, most Western countries, including the United States, rely heavily on the guidance of the state to assure that economic interest will not operate to the detriment of society's welfare.

The state has been important in promoting economic development in all countries in the West.[2] Even in the United States the government has encouraged and aided various industries. For example, extensive use has been made of the protective tariff, and in the early days the introduction of machinery was promoted, railroad building was encouraged later, and so forth. Thus, no country has, in practice, considered economic development as a natural and self-regulating process that calls for any further social, political, or administrative action other than setting up a private enterprise economy. Private enterprise systems have had to be facilitated by government intervention. In fact, the introduction of free markets increased the need for government regulation and intervention, and economic development was not "natural," but deliberately induced and continuously protected.[3]

Yet, in the West, the major sphere of decision making in economic affairs has been allocated to private enterprise. This system is credited with bringing a number of favorable results, not perfectly but in larger degree than any other system.

1. It has been highly creative and flexible and has allowed for a maximum of individual initiative and innovation. In fact, it forces people to effort and innovation.
2. It has afforded, at least legally if not in practice, a maximum of individual freedom. The chief virtues of the private enterprise system may well be not economic but an emphasis on the worth of the individual man and the opportunity it has afforded to many to advance through personal initiative and ability.
3. It has provided for an impersonal selection of winners and losers in the economic struggle, which may not always be a blessing, and avoids centralized direction. The dispersal of economic decision making avoids the inefficiencies of an overgrown bureaucracy.

4. It has brought to many countries, but not to all where it has been tried, great increases in wealth and leisure, although the gains to the masses were somewhat delayed. Moreover, the variety of goods and occupations has been multiplied as wealth has increased.
5. When accompanied by political democracy, it has broadened the base of political power.
6. It has permitted vertical mobility, economically, socially, and politically, and thus has continually refreshed the controlling elites.

But, private enterprise has also presented its followers with many problems. In private enterprise where government intervention has been minimized, the following have often been experienced:

1. The emphasis on material wealth and economic considerations has led to a neglect of noneconomic values. For example, the United States in the past was often accused of neglecting cultural pursuits.

2. Collective ends such as education and other social and economic overheads are relatively neglected because of the difficulty of imposing taxes.

3. The future good tends to be neglected; for example, resources are not conserved or the effects on future supplies of factors are ignored. As an illustration, education and training for creating specific labor skills are given relatively little consideration compared with the attention given to general education. Also, private investment neglects the prospects for external economies.

4. Social costs are overlooked; for example, hills may be lumbered with little regard for soil erosion or resulting floods, or mills may belch out smoke to the detriment of people's health and the cleanliness of homes.

5. Business cycles have been magnified as private interests strive to take advantage of rising prices in the upswing of the cycle and to protect themselves in the downswing. In addition, there have been individual insecurities of many kinds, including unemployment and unattended disease.

6. As enterprises have had to become large scale in order to get low costs under the influence of complicated technologies, firms have not been so adjustable and flexible as expected. Economic and political power have become concentrated, and large special-interest groups have applied pressures to introduce government measures for their benefit and protection. Economic operations have tended to degenerate into centralized private controls, characterized by artificial restraints on competition. Modern technologies and the conditions under which business must be carried on have evolved beyond the capacity of uncontrolled private enterprise to meet the aims of the masses and even to allocate resources optimally.

7. Incomes and economic opportunities have been unequal and real freedom has been limited through this inequality of economic means. For

example, at one time the sons of the poor found it difficult to advance because they lacked the economic means to qualify for superior positions through expensive education and training. Large-scale enterprise has limited the ability of small enterprisers to start a business. Unwarranted inequality leads to a feeling of frustration and discontent as well as to inequality of opportunity, concentration of political power, and social inequality. This has meant a lack of real personal freedom and democracy. Regional and national inequality have also become greater.[4]

8.   Preference is given to the desires of those with money. As a result, it can be seriously questioned whether maximum individual satisfaction obtains. In underdeveloped countries, especially under private enterprise, economic activity caters to the wealthy who have the buying power. In the search for maximum private gain, economic activity has been devoted to a few luxury industries and the export of raw materials, with little effect on development or local initiative. The small number of enterprises has resulted in monopoly and a tendency to restrict output in favor of large profit margins.

9.   The social conditions of industrialism have often been poor because the pressures of competition hinder their improvement; for example, inferior working conditions, unsafe factories, monotony and uncreativeness of work, impersonality of man, urbanization and speed of life, family disruption, and the growth of crime and vice.

Because unregulated market systems have not been effective in producing economic development in underdeveloped countries, and because the fear persists that any development that might result would have undesired consequences, as just listed, many leaders of underdeveloped countries feel that governments should play a major role in promoting economic progress. Many writers seem to share this view.

Explanations of why private enterprisers are unwilling to expand production and so promote development are as varied as the theories summarized in Chapter 2. Among these are: a deficiency of markets because of a lack of balanced growth (Nurkse); a lack of capital because people are too poor to save and because appropriate credit facilities are not available; a disposition to seek large profit margins on small turnover; the ineffectiveness of the price system to perform the essential economic functions because the economies are not flexible; the necessity for a "big push" (Hirschman); or a "minimum critical effort" (Leibenstein). A. Eckstein[5] says that economic growth is the widening of the range of alternatives open to society and that in underdeveloped countries there are few alternatives for people and thus a limited scope for individual choice and decentralized decision making. V. V. Bhatt[6] blames the failure of underdeveloped countries to grow naturally on the fact that such states failed to fulfill their economic functions.

P. A. Baran's explanation[7] is in terms of the failure of capitalism to sweep away all preceding systems. He explains that capitalism broke the feudal regulations but succeeded only in freeing the ruling classes from their obligations to the ruled, leaving the rulers free to exploit the masses. The reaction against the resulting system was not really a reaction against private enterprise but against the remaining feudalism represented by the power of a privileged few while the masses had no opportunity. He says further that a country can advance by capitalism (or private enterprise) only when there is a striving middle class that identifies itself with the common man and not with the ruling class and privilege. Lacking this leadership, the masses tend to turn to foreign ideological movements. In this situation, industry is not apt to develop and the country must rely on government to institute the conditions necessary for private enterprise to function. Even then, private enterprise is hesitant. Because private enterprise is not apt to take the lead, development decisions must be undertaken by government. But once industry is started by government action, private enterprise is not apt to develop unless special attention is paid to its encouragement.

The conclusion must be that a private enterprise economy can be successful only under certain conditions. There must be available a supply of capital, labor, and other resources; economic and social overheads must be reasonably well supplied; entrepreneurs and others must be responsive to economic opportunities; and there must be demand sufficiently above the level of necessities so that there is a prospect for a new enterpriser to drain some of it off to his own product. Furthermore, even under the best of circumstances, government must exercise many functions such as preventing private monopolies and appropriation of power, relieving unemployment, providing a minimum living standard for the unfortunate, and supplying the necessary economic and social overheads. These are not characteristic of underdeveloped countries.

The essential ingredient of the foregoing explanations is that private enterprise cannot in itself start development in the stage of underdevelopment and that government must force the issue. Government action is desirable for various reasons.

1. The major advantage of private enterprise, as it is practiced in the West, is in innovation and the development of advanced technologies and skills, but these are not essential in underdeveloped countries in the early stages because there is plenty of opportunity to innovate by imitating what is being done elsewhere. Government is capable of doing this and has the advantage that it can obtain large amounts of capital and can invest without regard to short-run monetary returns and in favor of long-run developmental gains.

2. Development requires rationing and priorities, and these must be a

function of government. In the typical underdeveloped country, the economic sectors are disintegrated and only a large decision and planning center can establish the necessary growth relations.[8] Imbalances are great and require a concentrated attack on a centralized basis.

3.   Of great importance is the matter of speed.[9] Underdeveloped countries cannot wait for private enterprise to bring development, but must try to hasten it in order to overcome the population growth, to avoid economic dependency, and to satisfy populations desirous of better standards. These countries are in a hurry, and private enterprise does not produce results rapidly enough, especially in the first stages of development.

4.   Social questions are also involved in development; for example, raising substandard levels of living for the masses and providing a minimum of security, which private enterprise is apt to overlook.

5.   Military considerations and balance-of-payment difficulties also indicate the need for government intervention.

6.   Private enterprise looks on investment and other matters in the light of its own needs, whereas governments can look at economic activity as a whole and make decisions on that basis.

7.   Governments also are the only agencies in a position to force a change in the social and cultural *status quo*.

The need for government intervention is seldom disputed; arguments are more frequently concentrated on how far it should enter into economic decisions at any particular stage of development. It seems likely that the less developed a country, the more need for government intervention. A. Eckstein[10] indicates a greater tendency to push for state intervention when a greater range of ends and a higher level of attainment are sought; when the time horizon is short; when the factor endowments are unfavorable; when the institutional barriers are many; and when the economy is relatively backward. These have been summed up as follows: The importance of the state is "an increasing function of the degree of relative backwardness of a country and the magnitude of the effort necessary for it to catch up with the other advanced countries." [11] Yet, government intervention is not without its difficulties.

1.   There is always the possibility that a government may not be interested in promoting development but only in protecting a privileged class, such as the landed aristocracy or government officials, or in providing positions for political favorites or relatives. Pressure groups are certain to attempt to turn decisions to their own advantage. Public administrators may not be qualified* and may even be dishonest. Planning by inefficient personnel may be worse than no planning.

* J. J. Spengler ("Public Bureaucracy, Resource Structure, and Economic Develop-

2. Governments may be tempted into showy and monumental consumption expenditures of their own, including expensive governmental buildings, stadia, and large military establishments. Also, investments in certain locations may be favored for political purposes.

3. Extensive controls may lead to centralization, with a possible loss of individual freedom and democracy, and a large and often unwieldy bureaucracy that involves costly delays in reaching decisions. Managers of enterprises may be subject to detailed rules and regulations. Moreover, government action is just as subject to diminishing returns as any other activity. A government may be able to carry out a particular function better than if it were left in private hands, but if this function is piled on many others, the ability to perform it more efficiently may not actually be realized.

4. The ability of governments to carry out long-range growth policies when these conflict with the short-run objectives of the people may be open to question, especially in a democracy. Individuals are largely concerned with their personal interests in the immediate future and become impatient when efforts are designed to benefit the general public or even themselves or their children in the future. The lower the current standard of living and the higher the expectations that have been aroused, the more this is likely to be so. Development efforts led by government may thus perforce have to be undemocratic ones, if they are to be effective.

5. Governments can also be wrong and make improper decisions. Such mistakes may be small and inconsequential, but they may also be very big mistakes with magnified effects.* A possible example is the strong emphasis India has placed on the development of cottage industries. The final analysis of this experiment has yet to be made, but the writer's view is that it will not aid economic development. It may provide a meager living for many and pacify them politically, which could be the major objectives and a necessity under the circumstances, but it does not appear to be a policy calculated to speed development. Attempts of nations to be self-sufficient may also hamper growth.

6. Government taxes, induced inflations, forced reforms, and occasion-

---

ment," *Kyklos,* No. 4 [1958], pp. 459-89) discusses this problem of management. He states that one of the major deterrents to development is a shortage of managerial and entrepreneurial skills. Although many feel that the state can provide such skills, Spengler believes that the growth of the public sector reduces the supply of entrepreneurs and subjects the managers to rules and politics. The state, moreover, may require particular attributes of its managers, which are not related to the economic function (such as belonging to the right party), and may exclude some on irrelevant grounds (such as nationality or color). His conclusion is that the role of the state is limited by the capacity of the bureaucracy.

* The increased efficiency of computers and the use of input-output models make very large mistakes less likely.

ally expropriations may discourage private enterprises, thus leaving the whole job to government.

7.   Government-operated industries may not be as efficient as private enterprise because standards for comparisons of efficiency may not be available. Nor may they develop new lines so readily as private firms, at least not in the later stages of development where innovation becomes more precarious.

The conclusion seems to be that neither an absolute laissez-faire free enterprise system nor an absolute government-controlled and -operated system offers the ideal solution to the problems of development. Government must undoubtedly do much to promote development, but it also seems desirable to take some of the load off government by encouraging private enterprise in those areas where it can accomplish the desired ends. Neither is all good nor all bad. Private enterprise is not always efficient, productive, and progressive, nor is it always selfish and irresponsible. Governments are not all-wise and completely devoted to the public interest, but neither are they always wasteful, corrupt, and unprogressive. No matter at which extreme a country starts, one can expect that ultimately there will be a trend toward a compromise or mixed system. Today this appears to be happening in both the United States and in the U.S.S.R. A considerable amount of government activity and private enterprise can exist side by side under the proper conditions.

The ideal, to the writer, seems to be governmental economic planning in which private enterprise is assigned a prominent role. The goal should be to retain private enterprise and individual decision making as much as possible while government sets up programs and rules to see that social values are optimized, steps in to fill any vacuum that develops, and provides the necessary economic and social overheads and those key industries that private enterprise is unable and unwilling to tackle. This means that government must determine the overall objectives and goals, and must exercise enough leadership to see that individual decisions are led in the right direction.

The big question is: Under what conditions can private enterprise and state planning work side by side? E. Staley,[12] in talking about the more advanced countries, lays down the following appropriate rules:

1.   There must be enough overall planning in monetary management and the relation of savings to investment to prevent a cumulative, contracting process.
2.   Planning must be positive rather than restrictive; that is, it must promote change and stimulate adjustments that work rapidly and smoothly. It must work with, rather than against, market forces.
3.   The planning means used by the state should operate by price rather than by direct quantitative controls. It might be better, however, to add the phrase, "wherever possible."

4. In the market sector, competition must prevail.
5. The methods of controlling monopoly power (and other evils of private enterprise) should be carefully chosen.

At any rate, the government must create, among other things, a congenial environment for business, including suitable economic and social overheads, a suitable legal system, satisfactory monetary and credit facilities, and an assurance against sudden government competition in the sphere allotted to private enterprise.

The most appropriate combination of government and private enterprise will differ from country to country, and each must analyze its own peculiarities. Copying exactly the practices of another country is seldom successful, as can be seen in those countries that have copied directly either Western democracy or Russian dictatorship. Each people has its own mixture of economic and noneconomic values and must seek its own way of doing what it wants done, compatible with its own culture. The proper proportion of investment to be made by the public and private sectors will depend on how well the private sector in each country responds to the development efforts. In some countries, government investment should be relatively small; and in others it should be large.

Under current circumstances, when the emphasis in underdeveloped countries is on government planning and operation, it seems desirable to stress the advantages of as much private enterprise as possible, as long as it operates within the limits of the economic plan. The objective stressed is not laissez-faire, but a private enterprise that will complement governmental efforts. This can be expected to be relatively low as a country tries to develop, but as development proceeds, the sphere for private enterprise can be expected to grow.

Private enterprise of the dimensions suggested can be expected to yield these benefits:

1. It can relieve government of tasks that might otherwise be burdensome. It is desirable to utilize all the talent available, especially letting individuals decide minor issues. For government to make all decisions, including the minutest, would be costly indeed and would embroil a country in red tape and bureaucracy. Also, getting people accustomed to making decisions promotes entrepreneurship and innovation, which are two of the major cornerstones of growth.

2. Noneconomic values such as democracy and freedom and a sense of individual involvement on the part of many are more likely to be realized. The base of political power is broadened, although this may be a disadvantage to efforts in the early stages of growth when individual sacrifices are vitally necessary.

3. Greater flexibility can be expected, for a large bureaucracy may be

unwilling to change an existing pattern. At first, governments may have to play a relatively larger role to assure larger supplies of essential goods, but as purchasing power expands and people have a choice in spending beyond the level of necessities, flexibility in meeting changing wants will have to be provided. The search for profitable opportunities by many individuals will make available, in time, a wide variety of new products.

4. There is a great need for cost and efficiency consciousness, which is better enforced in a well-functioning price system than under government operation. Government, however, must see that the price system functions properly by eliminating discrimination and favoritism, eliminating monopoly, providing adequate information and complementary services, and so on.

But inevitably the government must take a larger hand in economic affairs than we are accustomed to in the West. Just how much government does will depend on the ability and willingness of private enterprisers, the exact economic condition in the country, and the ability of the government.

Representative functions of government are to:

1. Provide appropriate social and economic overheads such as education, public health, basic communications, and power.

2. Institute tax programs that will divert purchasing power from nonessential consumption and investment into productive investment. Particularly, the government must supply capital for those enterprises requiring large-scale operation for efficiency, and must make credit available to agriculture, smaller enterprises, and commercial undertakings. To the extent that private investment is allowed, governments should influence the use of resources to prevent their waste on unnecessary or harmful activities.

3. Start key economic enterprises when private enterprise is unwilling to lead the way; or encourage private enterprise by providing the proper atmosphere in which it may operate. Many enterprises will have to be started by government because of a shortage of private capital or of entrepreneurs. Where properly selected to yield large external economies, such investment may even encourage private enterprise.

4. Carry out the general governmental control functions of removing the most pressing economic injustices, preventing runaway inflation, and the like. Land redistribution and the protection of workers against the hazards of industrialization are likely activities.

5. Formulate some plan or strategy of action for development. There may be a question whether this economic planning should be centralized and detailed, should be a set of certain targets or guidelines, or should be merely the determination of the essentials necessary for the functioning of a private enterprise economy. However, underdeveloped countries must plan so as to maximize the use of their scarce resources.

6.  Above all, instill in the people a desire for development and values that are basic to development, such as the habit of making decisions and innovating.

A. O. Hirschman[13] gives government two general functions, an initiating one and an equilibrating one. The first is usually emphasized; that is, to provide the prerequisites for further development. The second is a pressure-relieving function. As shortages, including injustices, are revealed, the government must take steps to relieve them.

Government action is apt to be not only more pervasive than in the West but also more direct. The indirect controls of tax, monetary, and credit policies are not so effective as in the advanced countries because of their lesser quantitative importance and, more likely, because of the rigidities in the economic systems, which produce bottlenecks and a tendency toward inflation. Direct controls such as government ownership, operation of industrial enterprises, and economic planning are the more suitable tools. Economic planning is an almost universal characteristic of the efforts of underdeveloped countries to develop.

## Economic Planning

Underdeveloped countries consider, seemingly correctly, that economic planning is essential in order to maximize the use of scarce resources and, at the very least, to decide what the government and private enterprise should and should not do. Economic planning is a device for coordinating national policy. It is because economic growth has not occurred that the governments of most underdeveloped countries have decided to take positive steps to stimulate growth. These steps are the content of the economic plan. If near unanimity of practice indicates the correctness of the desire to plan, economic planning has a large vote of confidence, for most underdeveloped countries have economic plans of one sort or another.[14]

There is a tendency to think of economic planning as a system for rigidly controlling practically every aspect of the economy, generally on the model of the U.S.S.R. or mainland China. This is, of course, a possibility, but various types of economic planning exhibit varying degrees of control and rigidity.

The first type is the comprehensive planning just mentioned, which may be called "blueprint" planning, in which activities are controlled down to the smallest detail, control is centralized, and the objectives are centrally determined.

The second type is planning by coordination, in which objectives are centrally determined and governmental activity and private enterprise are coordinated toward that end. Planning in this sense is really a strategy for development, a framework for investment and programs. In contrast with blueprint planning, in which the government has large powers of enforcement, much of the activity expected in this type of planning must depend more on elicited response and public support, with some help from government undertakings. Instead of engaging in activity itself, government may promote institutions or activities aimed at stimulating private enterprise; for example, making credit available, improving communications, and providing statistical data. In this type of planning, the government has predetermined ends and an overall program that includes a more or less generous sphere for private enterprise, depending on the situation in the country involved. If governments did not draw up such programs, the various agencies might well work at cross purposes and would be more likely to work toward short-run rather than long-run goals. Then private enterprise would have no incentive to initiate action. Such planning works through fiscal and monetary policy, control of the amount of savings, direction of investment, establishment of priorities, and governmental activity to break bottlenecks, such as offering skilled labor and technical research and providing incentives where private enterprise is loathe to go. In effect, planning involves determining what is necessary to be done to bring development; that is, making the best policy decisions and seeing that these are enacted by some combination of direct and indirect means. These decisions are remade periodically, the favorite period being five years.

The third type is bottleneck planning, in which the government acts to break bottlenecks as they arise. Obvious examples of bottlenecks are shortages in capital, skilled labor, and foreign exchange.

In the fourth type planning may consist of simple projections of what is expected to happen, which serve more or less as guidelines to individual decision making. The Japanese plan is of this type.

The final type comprises planning of the wishful-thinking variety, in which a country projects what it hopes to attain without any real basis for the projection. There seems a tendency to go from the last step toward the bottleneck type and then to the coordinating plans as information and techniques improve.

It should be stressed that economic planning is not synonymous with communistic or dictatorial programs. Dictators do plan, but democracies also plan. Private enterprise economies can gain by having a well-conceived government program. A market economy can exist side by side with planning, unless plans are of the blueprint type. The crucial point is the quality of the planning and the type of atmosphere created. France and Norway combine planning and large private sectors along with democratic systems of government.

The question is not whether or not to plan, "but *what* to plan for, *how* to plan, and *where* to plan"; that is, determining the proper scope and effort of government and of free enterprise.[15] Underdeveloped countries must use every device possible to mobilize all available resources and knowledge, including those of both private enterprise and government.

Actually, it is now easier to coordinate economic activities centrally than ever before, thanks to the computer, better communications, improved methods of large-scale management, better statistical information, and improved techniques of analysis (such as input-output analysis, linear programming, and other mathematical techniques). Although central planning has been made more feasible as a result of these techniques, the considerations for democracy and economic freedom may stop planning short of the blueprint stage. The desirable goal seems to be the coordinating type, when the necessary techniques and data become available, because it can mobilize resources and concentrate them in the areas most essential for achieving developmental objectives. In particular it can provide for a high level of capital formation. Both the theory of the "big push" and that of balanced growth are consistent with this ability to direct the use of resources.

Coordinated planning can also provide for a wider range of objectives than we have been able to pursue hitherto; for example, economic growth, full employment, greater equality of income, and military strength. In other words, it can be welfare-oriented as well as material-oriented. Particularly, it can account for social objectives that may be neglected if the economy is allowed to find its own way through the efforts of private individuals striving to achieve their own ends. A specific activity may not be immediately profitable for a private enterprise in the short run, but may yield such social gains or external economies that it is socially profitable and may lead to growth in other areas. The building of a railroad is an example. The receipts from the sale of freight and passenger services may not justify building the road, but the increased value of the surrounding land and the contribution of the industries and agriculture encouraged by it may justify the costs involved. Similarly, the social costs arising from an activity can be taken into account.

Economic planning can consider a longer time horizon than fragmented decision making; that is, it does not consider merely the return in the short run but takes account of the effects of an investment over a period of years. Thus, the return on investment in education may not pay off for many years; yet, without it, economic growth may never occur. Thus, planning may be necessary to take the "great strides." [16]

Underdeveloped countries are in a hurry, and private enterprise does not move rapidly enough for them at the early stages of development. Economic planning can more rapidly make the necessary adjustments to the changes that must be introduced to bring about growth. Growth involves many changes, including technological change and much labor displacement. As productivity increases in agriculture, say, labor is released and must be reabsorbed elsewhere. In the West it was reabsorbed, but only after tremendous cost in unemployment and wasted lives. Although economic planning cannot prevent all such hardships, it can alleviate them. For example, provision for a rapid training of new skills is much more feasible, and new projects can be deliberately started. Governments can plan to increase the supply of resources while leaving their use largely in private hands.

Planning, of course, is not without its problems; those discussed below indicate some of the difficulties to be overcome if planning is to be successful.

First, it is essential as a prerequisite to planning that the innovating agency have accurate information and a concept of what is necessary to achieve the desired objectives. Early planning may well have to be largely of the bottleneck-breaking type because of the scarcity of data. The strategy for development must be worked out for each country on the basis of the principles outlined previously.

Second, the plan must be programmed so that proper time sequences are maintained in order to match needs and supplies continuously. When a given industry is constructed, there must be available to it the materials and labor necessary for it to produce and a reasonable market for its product. To construct a steel mill only to find no iron ore or no steel-using industries would be a waste of capital. Economists are generally agreed, and the U.S.S.R. has shown, that sequence programming can be done reasonably well.

Third, the people must be willing that the plan be carried out and be willing to submit to the necessary sacrifices; otherwise the government must be strong enough to enforce the sacrifices. The latter method may suffer from lack of cooperation. To have such willingness the people must be united in a common purpose and the major power centers must accept the plan.

Fourth, planning that involves extensive governmental operations may have difficulty proceeding when it is necessary to develop entirely new ideas and new lines. However, this is not really a problem in underdeveloped countries because activities in other countries can be imitated. However, the U.S.S.R. has not been lacking in inventiveness or technological advance. It does seem likely that the more advanced a nation, the more advantageous it is to leave more and more decisions to individual enterprises.

Lastly, the government itself must be efficient and honest, administratively capable, and have the people's interests at heart. The administrative problems are tremendous, as the following administrative implications of an economic plan indicate.[17]

1. There must be appropriate central and regional planning organizations to gather and process needed statistical information. There must be a two-way flow of information even to the lowest levels. Incompetent, inefficient, or corrupt administration at any level weakens the plan.
2. The plan must be formulated; that is, objectives decided on, priorities determined, coordination achieved, and resources obtained.
3. The plan must be implemented and its progress watched over and reformulated, if necessary. Particularly, duplication must be avoided. The actual operation of the plan will usually be in the hands of the regular governmental departments, which must cooperate with the planning authorities.
4. If the government operates enterprises itself, capable managers must be secured.
5. Various reforms, such as agricultural reform, will be necessary and these may demand considerable administrative skill.

Thus, planning demands considerable administrative talent. The less developed a country, the more necessary it may be, yet the least possible. It seems most desirable to start with bottleneck planning and to work toward coordinating planning as the necessary administrative skills develop. As growth proceeds and entrepreneurs expand the areas for private enterprise, an overall plan still seems to be called for.

## Administrative Problems of Underdeveloped Countries

In many of the previous chapters it has been pointed out that certain functions will have to be carried out by the government of underdeveloped countries because there is no likelihood that private enterprisers will have the initiative, resources, or willingness to undertake them. All of these functions make up a truly staggering burden for any government to undertake, let alone a newly formed and inexperienced one. Thus, development may get only as far as the quality of governmental administration can carry it, and economic planning may fail because of lack of proper administration. Even though most governments of underdeveloped countries do not have the administrative experience, they must cope with these tasks— otherwise they will not get done. A major effort must be made to improve the administrative skills of governments.

The governments of many underdeveloped countries leave much to be desired from an administrative point of view. This is due partly to lack of training and experience, and partly to the low-pay scales that fail to attract and hold qualified personnel. Considerable investigation[18] supports this observation.

The most commonly cited problems are discussed below.

1.   Instability of Governments: A tradition of a peaceful change of tenure is not always fully developed, resulting in tension and discord (at the very least) when an administration changes. Recent peaceful transfers of power in Mexico and Venezuela were unusual enough to excite repeated comments in the newspapers. After the first flush of unity achieved through the struggle for independence, power struggles may arise or splinter groups may move off in pursuit of their own interests, unless there is some unifying force to bind them together. Nations may split along ethnic, linguistic, religious, or tribal lines. The Congo, for example, has fallen into tribal warfare, and other countries are held together by tenuous strings such as the maintenance of continual opposition to supposed recolonialism practiced by President Sukarno of Indonesia. The resulting drag on development may well be less undesirable than a political breakup of the nation. Various devices may be necessary to serve as a unifying force.[19] Pakistan uses a common religion as a unifying force. Others emphasize cultural features or press for an indigenous language. Using capital for national symbols may help: monuments for national heroes, as for Gandhi in India and Ataturk in Turkey; impressive public buildings such as Olympic stadia; or impressive industrial complexes such as a steel mill or power facilities. The showy project may, after all, be economic if it holds the nation together through pride. Yet many governments remain fragile and unable to carry on an adequate development program.

2.   Public Welfare: Some governments seem uninterested in the general welfare and are more concerned with showy projects, protecting the personal interests of the leaders or enhancing their personal power by building up a following of government employees, as the past records of leaders illustrate only too well.

3.   Administrative Inexperience: There is a shortage of trained administrators at all levels. A rapid shifting of senior personnel is a common occurrence. Not only the competence but also the honesty and devotion of government officials to their duties have been often questioned. Salaries are so low that employees must seek outside jobs, often with firms whose activities they must control. Nepotism is widespread.

4.   Distribution of Responsibility: There is a tendency to concentrate all decisions and not delegate responsibility or allow the subordinate any initiative. Elaborate manuals of procedures control every detail, with many successive levels checking each detail of the operation. Excessive checks

and balances are installed to prevent errors or dishonesty. Higher officials are so tied down by detail that they have little time for policy making. Their desks are piled high with papers to be personally signed, thus delaying decisions that may be urgently needed. The official cannot delegate authority. If he is away from his desk, nothing gets done, even in response to urgent requests. The biggest task facing underdeveloped countries may be the retraining of civil servants who are accustomed to this system.

5.   Inept Local Administration: Even where some success is achieved at the national level, administration at the local level may be intolerably bad. As one writer states, local government in underdeveloped countries is so "hopelessly enmeshed in red tape, corruption and maladministration" that it cannot provide the basic services.[20] The tasks required are great and the resources are low. For example, in India, local governments are called on to help frame economic goals, raise the standards of cultivation, serve as a channel for government assistance, spur the voluntary contribution of labor for local improvements, and enforce tenancy and land regulations, among other things.[21] With the low salaries and low prestige, talent adequate to such demands could not be expected to be exceptional. Local governments are apt to be overstaffed but untrained and tied up in excessive red tape. As an illustration, permits in Indonesia were at one time required for assemblies of five or more people, so that if one were to hold a party, a permit would be necessary. Usually, this was turned over to a servant, but once the present writer decided to go through the procedure himself. The result was an impressive document with numerous signatures and stamps, obtained after spending four hours of time!

Thus, a prerequisite to development is to build up the public administration of a country, both in efficiency and in a tradition of service. Success or failure in development may depend on the ability to establish an effective system of public administration. As one author argues,[22] improvements in public administration may yield higher returns than added investments in specific industries.

## The Form of Government

Government is a device to accomplish the objectives of a people, and should be organized to carry out these objectives most competently. The problem is that there are many objectives, among which economic growth is only one. If this were the only objective, a fully democratic government might not be the answer, at least in certain stages of development. If maximum individual freedom were the only objective, a democratic governmental structure would be ideally suited. Underdeveloped countries have many objectives, but above all they have a desire to grow rapidly economically and to modernize. For this reason they are apt to shy away from democratic forms of government in favor of more autocratic forms that promise a more rapid rate of development.

The choice of government is often put in the form of the democratic United States model or the dictatorship of the U.S.S.R. Actually, there are all degrees of alternatives on both sides; for example, on the democratic side, the United States, United Kingdom, France, or the Scandinavian countries. Among the dictatorships loosely termed Communist are such different forms as the U.S.S.R., Yugoslavia, Poland, and China.[23] The most appropriate governmental institutions will differ from country to country. Each country must analyze its own needs and not just copy another structure blindly. Each country has its own economic and noneconomic values and must devise structures consistent with these.

We in the West tend to believe that only a democratic government like one of the Western models is satisfactory from the standpoint of both economic growth and human values. Others, of course, favor the Soviet type, which, incidentally, also believes in democracy but of a type differently defined. Growth has occurred in the Western democracies, but it has also occurred in the Communist countries, sometimes on a spectacular basis.

The Communist model seems to have a special appeal to the peoples of underdeveloped countries, and Communist propaganda exploits a number of themes to strengthen this appeal. The following quotation is a good, succinct example.

It is well known that imperialism adheres to the principle of domination and subjugation, oppression of the weak by the strong, in relations between countries. Socialism offers in opposition to imperialism a new type of international relations based on peace, equality, the self-determination of peoples, respect for the independence and sovereignty of all countries.[24]

Strong governments are required, and this is generally considered synonymous with dictatorship on the Communist model, although strong and at least semidemocratic governments with popular backing are possible; for example, India under Nehru. Nevertheless, those who favor Communism exploit the theme that only their form of government is capable of accomplishing the needed reforms and actions. They support their claim with the following points.

1.   They make much of the point that where there was a colonial power, it was usually a Western country, generally with a democratic government and free enterprise. They play on the resentment against the colonial power and connect its institutions to past indignities. By implication, their own

institutions are pictured as eliminating all such evils. The current efforts of the West are usually pictured as neo-imperialism based on financial domination.

Actually, colonialism does have much to answer for.[25] The colonial economies were given a lopsided development and directed toward international trade, which made them vulnerable to cyclical fluctuations in the world market and encouraged dualistic economies. A few residents were favored while the masses remained in poverty and illiteracy and were often treated with contempt. On the other hand, the colonial powers did contribute to the development of the economies. They made investments of considerable size, mostly in primary production and economic overheads. Productivity was increased, but this only permitted more to live at the traditional level. The countries were united politically. The ambition to modernize was instilled. Moreover, the profits were not particularly great. Unfortunately, all the ills of underdeveloped countries are blamed on exploitation by the colonial powers, whether true or not.

2. The Communists have tended to identify themselves with popular reforms such as land reform to appease the land-hungry peasant, higher incomes for industrial workers, and industrialization and large projects, even though the latter two are not consistent in newly developing countries and even though they have not followed all these reforms themselves.

3. The success of the U.S.S.R. in developing rapidly, economically, and in achieving political independence and power is suggested as a motive for adopting the Communist model. However, it is seldom suggested that conditions in the underdeveloped countries may not be the same.[26] For example, the foundations for development were further advanced in the U.S.S.R. than in most underdeveloped countries, population size and rate of growth were not threats to economic growth, the country was large enough and rich enough in natural resources to permit virtual self-sufficiency and to avoid balance-of-payments problems, and the standard of living was high enough to permit substantial saving. Moreover, growth was achieved at the expense of rigid controls and considerable personal sacrifice.

4. Democratic governments are pictured as slow-working and inefficient. The U.S.S.R. offers a model of rapid industrialization and prestige projects, whereas the United States' policy of aid has been that of a slower initial rate of growth via improved education, training, health, agricultural methods, and gradual industrialization. Underdeveloped countries are anxious for rapid industrialization and may choose the form of government that advocates active governmental intervention and control to achieve it.

Economic development does require heavy personal sacrifices, and these may not be voluntarily assumed by the voters. Consumption must be curtailed, increased effort put forth, and positions of wealth and power abandoned. Cultural bonds must be broken and new habits established. It is questionable if democracy can effect these sacrifices, especially at low levels of development, because the necessary measures just do not get the necessary consent.[27] Workers want higher incomes and more security. Consumers want more goods, especially foreign goods. Unemployment is apt to grow and cause discontent. Land reform cannot satisfy the total demand for land. The total wants are more than the economy can provide, and some demands must be denied. The opposition raised induces many leaders to seek a form of government that permits them to make the necessary decisions without getting the direct consent of the people, and which promises early results that will attract support.

The Communist model has weaknesses and high costs, largely along human lines, and has no monopoly on rapid growth, as has been demonstrated in West Germany, Japan, and for some periods in Mexico. Individuals have been suppressed and small enterprisers eliminated. Collectivized agriculture has not been a success. Consumption has been kept low, and housing in particular has been neglected. Red tape and bureaucracy are common. There seems much to condemn in the Communist method, yet the West has been ineffective in presenting its weaknesses, perhaps because of its own former ill-favor and perhaps because the West has exhibited little interest in helping devise some practical alternative halfway between totalitarianism and a completely free economy.

In the short run, at early stages of development, autocratic governments can probably speed development, but in the long run, democratic governments are commended for their emphasis on human values, which seems more likely to channel human efforts toward reaching various goals, including growth. Democratic governments may seem to generate friction and lose much time in discussion, but they do release human energies. An autocratic government may be necessary at first to break the bonds of custom and ready the people for democracy, but ultimately, to the Westerner at least, the latter appears to offer greater advantages.

But the choice is not necessarily between dictatorial Communism and liberal democracy. Alternatives between these extremes can generate the necessary power while resting largely on the consent of the people and offering better opportunity for replacement by a more truly democratic government when conditions are ripe.

Current governments may be classified into three groups.[28] First are the traditional, aristocratic, authoritarian, or dynastic monarchies. These aim to preserve the traditional society, may have little interest in progress, and are motivated by loyalty to family, religion, or tradition. They may include some modern elements and even democratic symbols, as in Ethiopia, Jordan, and Iran.[29] The leading members of these dynasties seem to be trying to bring about some development, but opposition is too great within the ruling elite for these efforts to be effective.

Second are oligarchies based on adherence to either nationalist leaders in the fight for freedom or to the revolutionary intellectuals. Some of these governments (such as Pakistan, Burma, and Thailand) may be of the type that Millikan and Blackmer[28] call "transitional oligarchies," where there is no genuine national political process and no peaceful way of changing leadership. Control is impossible to retain under democratic processes, so authoritarianism is the rule. Efforts are made to obtain the cooperation or performance of the masses by emphasizing nationalism and perhaps creating continuous emergencies, undertaking large-scale development projects, advocating land reform, directing the educational process, and exercising various controls. Much of the activity is carried on by the state. The problems are devising an adequate national plan, getting the people to cooperate actively, and finding the necessary number of capable administrators. Some immediate growth is possible, but internal dissension and lack of cooperation may be limiting factors.

Lastly, there are "actively modernizing oligarchies" with broadened leadership and an effort to maintain and operate modern institutions. Millikan and Blackmer classify Turkey, Brazil, Mexico, Malaya, India, and the Philippines in this category. More effort is made to meet the people's desires, and they are given more voice. However, only a strong minority may participate in the political process, and the state may retain considerable powers and even operate large segments of the economy.

As development proceeds, a strong middle class is built up, illiteracy is greatly reduced, and greater democracy may be possible. With mass illiteracy and a small middle class, democracy may result only in chaos. The modernizing democracies are always threatened by mass movements and always in danger of converting to authoritarian government.

The first requirement for economic development is political stability; the second, a government actively working for development. Constant rebellions may discourage growth, as will inefficient, dishonest, or traditionally minded governments. For each country the particular conditions may determine the best type of governmental structure for it. Unfortunately, in many cases, economic and political influences force another type of structure on a country.

## REFERENCES

1. BARAN, PAUL A., "On the Political Economy of Backwardness." *Manchester School* (January, 1952), pp. 66-84. (The effects of the capitalist system on the traditional societies.)

2. AUBREY, H. G., "Deliberate Industrialization." *Social Research* (June, 1949), pp. 158-82.

3. KAPP, K. W., "Economic Development, National Planning and Public Administration." *Kyklos*, No. 2 (1960), pp. 175, 176.

4. MYRDAL, G., *Rich Lands and Poor*. New York, Harper & Bros., 1957. (Lays great stress on the effect of the competitive system in increasing national inequalities.)

5. ECKSTEIN, A., "Individualism and Role of the State in Economic Growth." *Economic Development and Cultural Change* (January, 1958), pp. 81-87.

6. BHATT, V. V., *Employment and Capital Formation in Underdeveloped Economies*. Bombay, Orient Longmans, 1960, p. 118.

7. BARAN, *op. cit.*

8. ELLIS, H. S., and H. C. WALLICH, *Economic Development for Latin America*. New York, St Martin's Press, 1961, p. 118.

9. AUBREY, H. G., "Role of the State in Economic Development." *American Economic Review, Proceedings* (May, 1951), pp. 266-73.

10. ECKSTEIN, *op. cit.*, p. 83.

11. BHATT, *op. cit.*, p. 116.

12. STALEY, E., *World Economy in Transition*. Council on Foreign Relations, 1939, pp. 179-87.

13. HIRSCHMAN, A. O., *Strategy of Economic Development*. New Haven, Yale University Press, 1958, pp. 202-203.

14. Perhaps the best-known plan is that of India, but for a description of several others see E. E. Hagen, ed., *Planning Economic Develop-ment*. Homewood, Ill., Richard D. Irwin, Inc., 1963.

15. STALEY, *op. cit.*, pp. 196-97.

16. GALBRAITH, J. K., *Economic Development in Perspective*. Cambridge, Mass., Harvard University Press, 1962, p. 35.

17. KAPP, *op. cit.*, pp. 177ff.

18. For a number of descriptions of personnel and administrative problems encountered, see the following: Corpuz, D. D., *The Bureaucracy in the Philippines*, 1957, Institute of Public Administration, University of Philippines, pp. 237ff. Sulton, J. L., ed., *Politics and Administration in Thailand*, 1962, Institute of Training for Public Service, Indiana University. International Bank for Reconstruction and Development, *Economic Development of Iraq*, 1952, pp. 72-86; *Economic Development of Jordan*, 1957, pp. 35-40, 424-36; *Economic Development of Libya*, 1960, pp. 75-99; *Economic Development of Guatemala*, 1951, pp. 244-64; *Economy of Turkey*, 1951, pp. 195-206; *Public Development Program for Thailand*, 1960, pp. 208-28. Baltimore, Johns Hopkins Press.

19. VORYS, K. VON, "Some Political Incentives for Economic Development in India, Pakistan, Burma and Ceylon." *Western Political Quarterly* (December, 1959), pp. 1065ff.

20. RIGGS, F. W., "Development and Local Government, Philippines." *Economic Development and Cultural Change*, vol. I (July, 1960), p. 389.

21. THORNER, D., "Village Panchayat as a Vehicle of Change." *Economic Development and Cultural Change* (October, 1953), pp. 209-15.

22. KAPP, *op. cit.*, p. 200.

23. GALBRAITH, J. K., "Economic Development: Rival Systems and Comparative Advantage." *Department*

of State Bulletin, July 2, 1962, p. 13.

24. NETRUSOV, A., "Development of Economic Relations Between Countries with Different Social Systems." *Problems Economic* (February, 1962), p. 54.

25. WATNICK, M., "The Appeal of Communism to the Peoples of Underdeveloped Areas," *Economic Development and Cultural Change* (March, 1952), pp. 22-36. Tinbergen, J., *Shaping the World's Economy*. New York, The Twentieth Century Fund, 1962, pp. 19-23. Ward, Barbara, *The Rich Nations and the Poor Nations*. New York, W. W. Norton Co., 1962, pp. 112-17.

26. BOWLES, W. D., "Soviet Russia as a Model for Underdeveloped Areas." *World Politics* (April, 1962), pp. 483-504.

27. SCHWEINETZ, K. DE, JR., in "Industrialization, Labor Controls, and Democracy," *Economic Development and Cultural Change* (July, 1959), pp. 385ff. Schweinetz, "Free Enterprise in a Growth World." *Southern Economic Journal* (October, 1962), pp. 103-10.

28. MILLIKAN, M. F., and D. L. M. BLACKMER, *The Emerging Nations, Their Growth and United States Policy*. Massachusetts Institute of Technology Center for International Studies (1961), pp. 79-86. Kautsky, J., ed., *Political Change in Underdeveloped Countries*. New York, John Wiley & Sons, Inc., 1962, p. 4. "New Theory of Growth, Leaders Set the Pattern." *Business Week* (October 29, 1960), p. 128.

29. MILLIKAN, M. F., and D. L. M. BLACKMER, *op. cit.*, p. 79.

## ADDITIONAL READINGS

BASTER, J., "Development and a Free Economy—Some Dilemmas." *Kyklos*, No. 1 (1954), pp. 1-17.

BRAIBANTI, R., and J. J. SPENGLER, *Administration and Economic Development in India*. Durham, N.C., Duke University Press, 1963.

ELIAS, T., *Government and Politics in Africa*. New York, Asia Publishing House, 1963.

GORDON, L., "Private Enterprise and International Development." *Harvard Business Review* (July-August, 1960), pp. 134-38.

HICKS, U. K., *Development from Below*. Oxford, Clarendon Press, 1961.

LAMPARD, E. E., "The Price System and Economic Change." *Journal of Economic History* (December, 1960), pp. 617-37.

MALENBAUM, W., and W. STOLPER, "Political Ideology and Economic Progress." *World Politics* (April, 1960), pp. 413-21.

MASON, E. S., *Economic Planning in Underdeveloped Areas*. New York, Fordham University Press, 1958.

MYRDAL, G., *Beyond the Welfare State, Economic Planning and Its International Implications*. New Haven, Yale University Press, 1960.

SPENGLER, J. J., "Economic Development: Political Preconditions and Political Consequences." *Journal of Politics* (August, 1960), pp. 387-416.

VAKIL, C. N., and P. R. BRAHMANAND, *Planning for an Expanding Economy*. Institute of Pacific Relations, 1956.

# CHAPTER

# 14

# *Investment Criteria and Programming*

## The Need for Investment Decisions

Thus far we have mentioned many activities that seem essential if development is to occur. All require the investment of capital to a larger or smaller degree. The needs for capital are great and the supply of capital is too small to cover all the legitimate needs. Because capital funds are scarce, they must be allocated very carefully if growth is to be optimized. Making the correct choices is the essence of development planning. Determining the correct priorities is a difficult task and a necessary one. It is relatively easy to ascertain that certain activities are necessary or desirable. Choosing among them is the hard task. Making the correct choices involves establishing investment criteria by which alternatives can be judged. To discuss these is the purpose of this chapter.

Various problems are involved in drawing up an investment plan. In the first place, one must decide how much of the nation's resources are to be devoted to capital investment and how much to consumption. In private enterprise economies, this is decided by individual decisions to save, consume, borrow, or invest. Various factors affect individual decisions, including the distribution of income, the interest rate, the marginal efficiency of capital, the outlook for changes in personal incomes and business activity, and many others. In planned societies the amount to invest is apt to be the result of a value judgment on the part of the planning authorities. This may be decided on the basis of how much purchasing power can be wrung from the inhabitants and the amount of foreign aid or foreign loans that can be obtained. The basis for the decision is thus more or less arbitrary and involves only remotely a calculus of the costs involved in giving up consumption as compared with the gains of increased future productivity.

Assuming that this matter has been decided, there are two other problems: deciding what is to be produced and how it is to be produced. In a free enterprise society, the first problem is presumably determined on the basis of consumer dollar votes. The producer, anxious to make profits, shifts resources to making those things the consumer is willing to spend his money on. It is recognized that the producers exercise considerable influence on what the consumer will want, but essentially the decision to invest is related to the prospects of profitability. In a planned society the criterion of profitability and consumer preference may not be followed, and other criteria may be substituted, as will be discussed below.

The question of how to produce is a complicated one, involving various separate decisions. The producer must decide by what techniques the goods and services are to be produced. One choice is between more or less capital or labor-intensive techniques. Thus, there is a choice as to what resources to use. The producer must also determine the regional location of productive activity and the size of the firm or industry. His fourth decision involves the time dimension of production; that is, whether to sacrifice current production for increased future production. In a private enterprise economy, all these decisions are guided by one objective—the search for maximum individual profit. In a more planned society, efficiency principles, although calculated on a different basis than in a private enterprise economy, can be used to decide the "how to produce" questions. Value judgments will decide the "what to produce" problem.

A further question may be: Who is to make the investments, private industry or government? Whether government or private industry can make the more correct decisions is a value judgment and depends on what one looks upon as the goals of an economy. In underdeveloped countries the decision is likely to be in favor of a larger quantity of government investment, for two reasons: (1) the belief that private investors are not attracted in sufficient numbers because of structural deficiencies in the economy that make investment unprofitable, and (2) decisions by private investors, although correct from the point of view of maximizing personal profits, will not maximize social benefits.

It seems obvious that, by any rational criteria, there is no set pattern for development which all countries must follow. Each must make its decisions based on the criteria it thinks important and the facts of the case. Thus, development planning is not a set of rigid formulas but a process of thought in which all pertinent objectives, criteria, and facts are considered. These may be reduced to a formula when the elements can be quantified, but the formula will be uniquely applicable to the country being planned and specifically characteristic of the agency doing the planning. Such a formula will reflect the judgments and preferences of the planners and cannot be considered as something independent, inviolable, and based on scientific law.

## Investment Decisions Under Private Enterprise

According to the traditional economic theory that is standard in most college textbooks, economic efficiency is reached through the process by which individual firms seek to maximize their profits. A producer will maximize his profits if he equates marginal costs and marginal revenues; that is, if he continues to add units of output just as long as the added units bring in more revenue than they cost. In the short run, this involves adding variable costs to existing fixed assets and thus does not involve investment. However, if the producer is to survive in competition, assuming perfect competition, he must produce at minimum cost, and this means finding the best combination of the factors of production for the size of output he deems most desirable. He must compare the returns and costs of producing different-sized outputs in the appropriate-sized plant, and he must do this for various locations. Having made these decisions, he will minimize his costs when he so combines the factors that the last dollar spent on each type of factor yields the same return; or, put in another way, so that the ratio of the marginal revenue product of each factor to the price of each factor is equal.*

However, this is not the end of the story. If profits are higher in one industry than in another, capital will flow to the industry with higher profits until the marginal product of capital will be the same in all pursuits. Investment will continue until the marginal return of capital in all its uses is equal to the rate at which funds for capital investment can be borrowed. All excess or pure profits will then have disappeared. At this point, the economy is in equilibrium, and there is no incentive for changes to take place in the pattern of investment unless some outside change (like a new invention or a change in wage rates) upsets the equilibrium and starts a new process of seeking a new equilibrium position. Such a state of equilibrium is defined as

---

* The yields are, of course, obtained over a number of years; to obtain present value, they must be discounted by an appropriate interest rate.

constituting economic efficiency, for all goods would be produced at minimum cost.

The efficiency of this method for determining the optimum investment decisions has been questioned, especially in connection with investment decisions in underdeveloped countries. In the first place, it is questioned whether, even assuming that the rule of equalizing marginal products is correct, that private decisions can in fact bring about such a result. Economic theory proceeds as though marginal products can be calculated accurately, but this is extremely doubtful even for short-run time periods. Marginal productivity can be estimated only within very wide limits. As previously mentioned, investment decisions have many dimensions, including what to produce and how to produce. Along with these are the subdecisions as to the proper combination of the factors, the size of the firm, the location of the industry, and so forth, all based on anticipated prices and demands. Calculating all these and arriving at even an approximate answer is an almost impossible feat. The longer the time horizon of the investment decision, the more unlikely a correct decision will be made. It is true that there may be a constant effort to correct mistakes by marginal changes, but recovering from initial mistakes is no easy task.

Moreover, an exact operation of the theory assumes a perfect divisibility of the factors so that fine gradations can be made in order to reach the optimum combination of factors and amount of investment. In truth, investments are often lumpy; that is, a unit larger than one that would meet the marginal equating condition may be necessary in order to get a practical operating unit. A railroad is the classic example. The main line between two points must be built in its entirety or not at all. Some adjustments can be made, such as single tracking instead of double tracking, but a complete line must be built even though the marginal principle is temporarily violated.

Moreover, the investor faces constant changes in his economic environment, and so must continuously make changes in his investment pattern. No one should expect perfection, but the impression is given too often that only private investors, following the lure of profits, can be expected to make correct investment decisions. Our texts make private decisions look easy and government or group decisions difficult. The assumed perfection of private investment decisions is decidedly misleading.

A second objection is that the marginal criterion is a purely static concept. It portrays how a man would make investment decisions in a given institutional and economic structure and under certain known or predicted conditions. It has nothing to say concerning the effects of decisions on changing the entire structure of a society, as is the intent and effort of many of the underdeveloped countries. Also, investment decisions are expected to maximize returns for the individual on the basis of what other firms are currently doing, or might reasonably be expected to do, and says nothing about desirable sequences of investment. If A makes a given investment, it may be profitable for B to make a certain investment. However, if B had made his investment first, A might have made a far different and, for society, a superior investment. Let us say that B's investment is an electric power source. Without it and without other industries that might be encouraged by the existence of a source of electric power, A might have established, following the maximizing principle, a small-scale manufacturing establishment, using an inferior source of power such as human power or a small steam engine. Other firms might have done likewise, ultimately leading B to establish his electric power plant. However, if the power source were developed first, different-sized plants could have been established, using different factor combinations. The point is that nothing in the marginal principle ensures that the optimum sequence of investments will be established.

Private investment decisions do not take into account social costs and social benefits. A traditional example of this failure to take into account a social cost is that of the steel mill which neglects the problem of the smoke damage its operation inflicts on the community. The price system fails to cover this cost that is avoided by the steel company to the detriment of the community's residents. Another example is the case of the elevator. The elevator is a wonderful thing. It has enabled men to build high buildings and to conserve space. Elevators are installed when the direct monetary gains to the investor exceed his costs. But the elevator has encouraged crowded cities and the large costs of urban congestion, none of which are paid for by the investor.

Similarly, some investments bring social benefits that cannot be recovered by the original investor. The building of a railroad may increase land values for owners other than the railroad. In fact, it is conceivable that such a railroad might not be built privately because the expected profit from carrying freight and passengers might not be profitable. However, if the builder could capture all the external economies created by building the railroad, such as increased land values, the railroad might be profitable to build. The railroad is desirable from a social point of view but not from an individual investor's point of view. An even more classic case is that of education. Many people gain from the education of the young—their families, their neighbors, their employers, and society in general. If education were left as a purely private venture, fewer individuals would undertake the cost and would tolerate inferior training, and society would suffer. Therefore, society subsidizes education and even compels students to go to school, thus violating the presumed efficiency principle.

The margin-equating rule assumes perfect competition. Where monopoly elements or lack of mobility exist, investment decisions will not reflect the efficiency rule.

Investments that yield their returns only after a long period would most certainly be neglected because the discounting process would not value their future products highly. However, it may be just this expenditure, such as expenditure on health or education, that may make development and future investments by others profitable.

The marginal principle effects efficiency only on the basis of acceptance of the current distribution of income, which has considerable influence on the demand for different commodities and on the propensities to save and consume. A different distribution of income would require a different distribution of resources to conform to the efficiency principle. It may be argued (but this is a doubtful position) that the income distribution is the result of payment to the factors on the basis of their respective productivities and thus meets the efficiency criterion.

No one should expect absolute precision in this process of investment. The real question is whether equalizing of the marginal productivity principle is the most efficient standard available. Society has recognized that in some instances it is not, and has modified its operation by government action. Government provision for economic and social overheads, government control of monopolistic practices, and prohibition of certain investments, as in the manufacture of narcotics for general sale, are cases in point.

Once a country has developed to a considerable degree, the marginal principle seems to work reasonably well. It permits a country to get along and even to grow, just as the crude Newtonian physics of a hundred years ago permitted us to develop a reasonably advanced machine economy. The marginal principle works fairly well in such circumstances because the investor can count on a supply of all the factors of production he needs. The economic and social overheads are in place. There is plenty of demand above the minimum of subsistence, which may be diverted to the new producer. His effort is only a small part of the total economy. The principle seems to work, but there is no assurance that it brings about the maximum growth possible or accomplishes whatever other objectives a country has. Advances in physical science have increased our physical productivity and enabled us to do new things. Perhaps new ideas in investment theory will do the same for economic growth. The modifications discussed below show promise, but cannot yet be said to have proved their superiority. Improving our investment decision making is one of the largest tasks facing economic theory today.

Even though the marginal principle seems to work in the advanced countries, it cannot be counted on for the underdeveloped countries. The individual investor cannot count on a supply of materials and labor. Economic and social overheads are lacking. Demand is low. Competition exerts little pressure for choosing the optimum combination of the factors. What is needed is not marginal improvements in efficiency but a complete structural change of the economy, and in this process the marginal principle has no application.

## The Criterion of Social Marginal Productivity

In 1951 A. E. Kahn[1] introduced a modification to the marginal principle with a concept called "social marginal productivity." This was an attempt to indicate the elements to be included in any assessment of the total contribution of the marginal unit to national product, rather than the amount of productivity recoverable by the investor. Further contributions, to be discussed below, have virtually destroyed the marginal concept as the sole method of determining investment in a newly developing country.

According to this concept, deviations of actual prices from true social costs would be compensated for by setting "accounting" or "shadow" prices. These prices would make allowance for all social costs and benefits, for the deviations of monopoly or understated prices, and presumably for any other conceivable social cost or benefit, including intangible ones such as political or social benefits. Subjective judgment would thus play a large role in the determination of investments. With all the possible adjustments it would be difficult (and in some cases, such as an allowance for structural changes, meaningless) to calculate the margin. As a result, investments would be chosen on some other basis, probably a ranking basis. It would be possible to rank projects in a fairly consistent order of priority.

However, the proposed modification did not answer the real question—how far to carry one type of investment before beginning another. That is, it may be clear that investment A is superior to investment B. But the millionth dollar invested in A may not be more important than the first dollar invested in B. Equating the decreasing importance of extra dollars invested in A with the importance of some dollars invested in B is the essence of the marginal principle. This cannot be left out in developing any program.

The attempt is to make investment decisions conform to the totality of a country's objectives, including economic, social, and political welfare,

. rather than being based on individual profit calculations. It adds many dimensions to the discussion and so makes the decision more difficult, albeit more satisfactory from a social point of view. Harvey Leibenstein[2] comments that all the word "social" does is to warn us not to accept the private evaluation of productivity. But putting a money value on social costs and social benefits does have a value in making the necessary value judgments explicit and forcing them to be defended.

The succeeding discussion should indicate the values and difficulties of this approach.


## The Objectives of Investment Decisions

The marginal method of determining investments highlights the objective of producing outputs at the least cost through the efforts of individuals to maximize profits. Not only is there doubt that this goal can be actually achieved under the conditions existing in either advanced or underdeveloped countries, and especially the latter, but there is also doubt that this is a sufficient goal. For this reason, developing countries have favored planning bodies to determine rational investment programs, the first step of which is to determine the country's basic objectives.

There are many possible objectives a country can pursue. None is superior to the other in the sense that it offers definite standards that can determine which values a country should favor and in what combination. There are an infinite variety of combinations of objectives, each with its own optimum investment pattern.[3] Because all goals are not obtainable simultaneously, choices must be made and priorities established before an investment plan can be formalized. Some of the possibilities are discussed below.

1. Maximizing total product or per capita product either over a relatively few years or over some longer time span: This will involve decisions as to the division of the product between consumption and investment, both temporarily and in the long run. This has a major influence on answering one question: how much to invest?

2. Achieving a more equal distribution of the benefits of development, both among individuals and among regions: The latter is basic in determining the question of where investments shall be made.

3. Full employment: This will influence the degree of capital and labor intensity of projects.

4. Self-sufficiency of the economy in order to protect it against external influences.

5.   Freedom of individuals from state control.

6.   Political considerations, including the ability of the government to survive the decisions it makes.

Decisions as to investments must, then, maximize some combination of various possible objectives and must, furthermore, be made under some limitations such as the supplies of foreign exchange and the availability of capital and labor. The determination of objectives is political and not subject to marginal considerations. A country, when planning, may choose one objective as paramount, usually economic growth, and try to optimize this. However, this primary selection may be subject to minimum standards for other desired objectives, such as a rise in consumer expenditure, the distribution of income, the amount of individual freedom, the foreign exchange balance, and employment.

Having determined the objectives, or having been given these by the political heads, the planning authorities are ready to apply any of various possible criteria for selecting the appropriate investments, as will be outlined in the next section.

## Possible Investment Criteria

A number of criteria have been suggested as aids in making investment decisions.[4] These may all be subsumed under the social marginal productivity rule, if we can conceive of this rule as including all the factors that must be taken into account in order to achieve the objectives a country sets for itself. No agreement exists as to the relative value of each criterion or the way in which it should be combined into an integrated policy. Certainly, making corrections of actual prices to accommodate even one of them cannot be very precise, although this imprecision is certainly an improvement over neglecting any one criterion altogether. All that we shall do here is to introduce a number of possible criteria from which choices can be made. Planning authorities show no evidence, however, of using well-defined or consistent guides.[5] Because there are so many alternatives, there is great scope for the value judgments that are applied less systematically through government regulations in a private enterprise economy.

Each criterion may be considered in finding answers to the fundamental questions of what to produce and how and where to produce, with probably different weights assigned to it for each question. The marginal productivity criterion can be useful in determining the combination of factors to use in producing a given product, after the product has been chosen with the aid of other criteria. However, even in this case, the marginal criterion may have to be modified for various reasons, such as maximizing employment and the effect on developing and training workers.

The value of this process of listing and considering many criteria, tangible and intangible, economic and noneconomic, is twofold. First of all, investment decisions will be made on the basis of the total advantages and disadvantages of alternative decisions, the entire complex of economic, political, and social factors. Second, the basis of the decisions can be made explicit and thus be more subject to rational discussion and debate.[6]

Conflicts are possible among the criteria. For example, in order to maximize employment opportunities, labor-intensive techniques would be utilized, but to maximize reinvestment possibilities, capital-intensive projects would be indicated.[7] The solution would depend on the objective that had priority and the strategy for development that is being pursued.

The first step in selecting the criteria after the objectives have been determined and ranked is to decide on a strategy for development and growth, a matter about which economists differ. Three general types of strategy exist:[8] (1) concentrate on affecting the cultural and political character of the people; (2) develop key groups of people—technicians, administrators, elites, entrepreneurs, and decision makers; and (3) accord most importance to savings and investment. The latter, subject to some modifications on the basis of the other two, is favored by economists. With the criteria selected on the basis of the accepted strategy, and with a list of limitations, a model for development can be determined and even reduced to a mathematical formula. Using this guide, general allocations of investment can be made, after which the specific projects can be selected. Project formulation has not been reduced to an exact formula, largely because of the lack of an accepted theory of development and an inability to quantify accurately all factors to be considered. But decisions can be improved, even though the exact composition of investment must proceed on a more or less trial-and-error basis, of which a simplified description will be given in the next section.

The specific criteria suggested are described below in no order of importance or relative weight.

A criterion of major importance is that of supplying a minimum quantity of consumer goods necessary for the welfare of the people. A certain amount of food, clothing, shelter, transport, and so forth must be supplied. For this there is no choice, and investment funds must be allocated to this purpose. The real question of choice is how much consumer goods will be provided above the necessary minimum; that is, the level of consumption and investment. For the rapid growth of productive capacity, only the most urgent needs would be provided, although consumption would have to grow as productive capacity grew so as to provide a market for the potential production.

Maximizing external economies or social benefits and indirect effects and minimizing the social costs of investments should be taken into consideration. This criterion requires investment in economic and social overheads, especially transport, power, education, and health. The major difficulty involved is in calculating the direct and indirect effects of these on ultimate productivity. The decisions must be made on a more or less intuitive basis, since our current level of knowledge of the ultimate effects of such investments is incomplete. The values of transport and power are more clearly recognized than many others, but the value of health and education is becoming more greatly appreciated, although the exact nature of the best program for these is debatable. Even such investments as those for recreational facilities and a cultural atmosphere may affect productivity, but their value is extremely difficult to assess. O. Eckstein[9] recognizes the value of the indirect effects of investment. He includes in his concept the external economies and the effect of a given program on the abilities of a people, and wishes to substitute for the narrower social marginal productivity concept what he calls the "marginal growth contribution" of an investment. These indirect effects may be more important than the direct production resulting from an investment. Examples of indirect effects are the training afforded managers and workers, effects on the motivations and cultural traits of the people, the effect on population growth, possible political and social tensions, and the tendency for innovations to spread outward from the original point of innovation.

A much discussed criterion is that of the minimum marginal capital/output ratio. This is the amount of capital necessary to produce an additional unit of output. The concept may be used in two ways. First of all, an overall capital/output ratio for the economy as a whole may be used for estimating total production possibilities, or conversely, if a given increase in output is desired, to estimate the amount of capital required. For example, if the capital/output ratio is 4:1 and 12 percent of the national income is invested, national income would increase 3 percent. Or in reverse, if the desired rate of growth is 3 percent, the required investment would be 12 percent. Secondly, it can be used to estimate capital requirements in each sector of the economy or in each project. The values to be assigned this ratio can be estimated on the basis of past experience, the experience of other countries, or by input-output analysis where the data are available.

The capital/output ratio is also suggested as a criterion for determining what to produce and the type of technology to use, the rule being to pick the projects with the lowest capital/output ratios on the assumption that capital is the scarcest factor. The objective is to maximize the return on the scarcest factor and to spread its use as far as possible. Maximizing the return on capital bears some resemblance to the marginal principle, but in fact it assumes the costs of the other factors to be zero. The marginal principle would indeed indicate a sparing use of capital, if it were actually the cheapest factor, but the lowest cost would be obtained when the ratio of marginal revenue output to the price were the same for every factor.

A. E. Kahn[10] suggests that minimum capital use is safer except where there are obvious bottlenecks, for there is less risk of mistake and obsolescence and such projects are apt to conflict less with social values and customs. But this may not be valid because changing values and customs may prove to be a way of growth.

In addition, although there may appear to be advantages in using capital-intensive methods of production, it is difficult to realize the advantages in practice.[11] Labor may be inefficient, repairs may be slow and costly, management may fail to use the equipment properly, complementary industry may fail to meet its needs, and so on.

Various objections have been raised to using this principle as a solitary rule. As does any single criterion, it leaves out important matters such as the possibility of external economies or costs, or indirect effects. Other fundamental objections are raised. First, it makes no proper allowance for the length of life of the physical capital. Projects with the lowest capital/output ratio in the short run may be expensive of capital in the long run, if they must be replaced often. Second, maintenance costs must also be considered. Capital-intensive methods may on occasion be cheaper because they require less maintenance, a very important consideration in countries where repair facilities and spare parts may be in short supply. Third, specific projects may require heavy supplementary investments such as economic overheads, urbanization costs, and labor training. Thus, what may at first glance seem to involve low capital costs may turn out to be expensive of capital. The substitution of labor for capital is not costless, for it must be induced to move to the city, trained, and housed.[12] Fourth, capital may not in fact be the scarcest resource. This doubtful honor may go to skilled labor or business managers, for example. Also, wages may be low, but labor efficiency may also be low, resulting in high wage costs per unit of output. Lastly, a labor-intensive technique may result in inferior merchandise, which would limit its salability abroad. Some industries have had to compromise. They may use capital-intensive methods in that part of the operations where precision and quality control are vital, and use labor-intensive techniques where such things are not so important, as in materials handling. Thus, an industry does not have to be all modern or all labor-intensive. Research as to the best combination seems desirable. It is also pointed out that when it is important to compete with foreign modern factories on the bases of quality and perhaps cost, a factory may have to "start modern" or not at all, and this may be more important than factor proportions.[13]

Despite these objections, care does have to be exercised to conserve capital to as great an extent as possible. This also is true of any other scarce factor.

W. Galenson and H. Leibenstein[14] have developed a criterion, termed the "maximum reinvestment quotient." The objective is to maximize output at some future time, rather than immediately; or: How can we attain the largest possible output in 1986 and not the largest in 1966? The obvious answer would be to provide for the largest possible increase in the creation of productive facilities, material and human, and this means maximizing savings. This would require maximizing profits from which most savings are expected to come. The investment rule would be to equate the "marginal per capita reinvestment quotient." This would presumably indicate capital-intensive projects, which would have the further advantage of not encouraging rapid population increases.

It will be recognized that this conforms essentially with the practice of the U.S.S.R., except that that country does not rely on savings out of profits but taxes the earnings of people above the allowable level of consumption. It is an exploitative theory.

The objections are three: First, objection is raised to the exploitative nature of the criterion. Increases in current consumption may be very important for reasons of justice as well as economic efficiency and political reasons. It is conceivable that growth can be speeded up by diverting production from consumption to investment, but accomplishing this through large profits and a maldistribution of income seems particularly unjust. The rewards of growth should not go to only a few. Second, at some point, emphasis on reinvestment must stop and attention must turn to producing consumer goods, which, after all, is the purpose of work and effort. Lastly, diverting incomes to those who save does not assure that the savings will be reinvested. This criterion has only limited applicability at a certain stage of development when savings are insufficient and must be increased at all costs if growth is to begin.

A major objective of an investment program may be to increase employment, giving rise to a "maximum employment absorption" criterion. Because unemployment is a major problem, there is a natural desire to relieve it quickly and directly. The application of this requirement would, of course, mean labor-intensive projects, and following this criterion could lead to inefficiency and a lower level of output than could otherwise be

attained. The employment of labor is subject to the law of diminishing returns and its use can be carried too far. When carried too far it is simply a
make-work policy rather than a production policy, which can only result in
preserving inefficient work methods and dimming all hopes of improving
labor productivity.

It is also possible that adopting more productive methods today, even
though not so much labor is absorbed at the moment, may permit a higher
rate of investment, which will induce growth and increase employment
later.[14] It may also be said that maximizing current output, even at reduced
employment, could permit higher living standards for all, but of course this
would require the maintenance of the unemployed, presumably by government payments. Employment effects probably must be secondary to output
and productivity effects, but they cannot be neglected completely.

The effect of an investment program on the balance of payments is an
important criterion, for the supply of foreign exchange can be a critical
factor in a country's economic life. An increase in economic activity is almost certain to increase the pressure for imports and usually to a greater
degree than the increase in domestic production. In the first place, an expanding investment program in many cases will require the import of capital equipment (especially for countries just beginning to develop) and of
raw materials. Second, as incomes rise, there is a tendency for consumers to
increase their demands for imported consumer goods. Something can be
done by rationing the use of whatever exchange is available to a country,
but the pressures will be eased if some attention is given to the "foreign
exchange criterion" for investments.

This criterion favors projects that will either provide exportable products
or projects that are import reducing. If capital goods must be imported, less
capital-intensive techniques may be used. Products that use domestic materials may be favored.

There is a danger that this criterion may be overemphasized to the detriment of maximum productivity. Concentrating on goods in which a country
has a comparative advantage can increase total productivity, provided, of
course, markets are available. But the hazards of foreign markets are great
and many countries prefer the route of import substitution, with the result
of less production but more security.[15] The smaller the country, the more
this criterion is likely to lead to uneconomic production decisions. Yet it
cannot be neglected, for the foreign exchange situation is a fact of life with
which a country must live. Tied up with this criterion is the question of
balanced growth or the concentration of investment in a few sectors. This
will be discussed in the next chapter.

The time period in which the output of an investment is realized must also be considered. Different investments take different periods of time before their products are realized (the gestation period). Many investments in agriculture, such as the increased use of fertilizer or pesticides, yield their results relatively quickly. Investments in handicrafts and (generally) in labor-intensive consumption goods projects have short gestation periods. Investments in power supplies yield their returns only after some time; investments in human capital, even more slowly.

Too long a time period cannot usually be endured at the beginning of development. The act of investing produces consumer incomes, which puts pressure on the limited supply of goods and so exerts an inflationary force. Yet, too great attention to short-yielding projects may slow ultimate advance. Thus, a judicious mixture of all types is indicated. Concentration on the quick-yielding investments will raise consumption immediately at the expense of more rapid growth. Concentration on projects with long gestation periods may optimize growth, but will be at the expense of improved standards for the present generation. Once, however, there is a large volume of projects, some of which are beginning to yield in each year, this criterion fades in importance. Unless the output of some investment is postponed, the supply of new products acts as a deflationary force. Thus, the problem of advanced countries may be in finding a sufficient volume of current investment. Their solution lies in increasing consumption. The problem of the underdeveloped countries is in curtailing consumption while productive facilities are being built up.

A. O. Hirschman[16] emphasizes the "linkage effects" of investments. Investments may induce other investments, either by affording a market for the outputs of other industries (backward linkage) or in supplying inputs for others (forward linkage). Investments selected by this criterion should be centered on those projects that afford the greatest amount of linkage effect. Investments in excess of present needs may create additional pressures by making supplies for later-stage industries cheaper and may increase the potential market for prior-stage industries. The amount of linkage can be estimated by input-output analysis.

There is something to be said for this view, provided the facilities are not built too far in advance of actual needs, which would needlessly waste capital in unused facilities.

The problem lies in finding the right industries. This involves another criterion based on the proper time sequence in which industries are to be introduced. In underdeveloped countries this may be quite important. The more industry that already exists, the less this becomes a problem because supporting industries and markets are available. This is not the situation in underdeveloped countries.

The first consideration should be given to removing obvious bottlenecks or shortages. If a particular product is in short supply and holding up other industries, investment (or imports) is advisable. Or, the bottleneck may be caused by a lack of skilled labor or entrepreneurs. Whatever the deficiency is, efforts should be made to repair the shortage.

Other time sequences are important. The nature of the capital in place at a given time can affect the cost of any other given investment. The total cost of producing a given combination of outputs may differ, depending on which parts of the combination are built first. Investment in economic overheads has high priority for early investment, for this reason.*

Also, some industries may serve as leading "growth centers," as did the railroad in the United States or textiles in England. These are industries that have great possibilities for growth, either in serving the domestic market or the export market, or in providing investment or consumption goods opportunities. Their growth supplies income and investment funds and encouragement to other industries.

Political considerations may affect investment decisions.[17] Military considerations may outweigh economic ones. The country may wish to avoid aiding the previously dominant foreign interests. Spectacular or prestige-building projects may be favored to attract popular support. Similarly, the effect on the distribution of income can be important for political as well as welfare reasons. Even dictators must seek a certain degree of public acceptance and thus may try to have everyone share in the benefits. For similar political reasons, regional balance may be sought, even though this may have economic disadvantages. On the other hand, there is also the possibility that regional balance will be economically desirable in itself because of economies in transportation or the avoidance of transferring people to one center.

Investment projects may be picked because they will attract foreign capital.[18] The international agencies, for example, concentrate on large economic overhead projects. Another consideration in choosing investments is to maximize the use of domestic materials and resources in plentiful supply or a product that has been encountering price fluctuations on the world market. Shortages of materials impose obvious limitations on investments unless they can be imported, thus bringing into play the balance-of-payments criterion.

Thus, many criteria can be and have been devised. This rather lengthy description illustrates a groping for ideas that can lead to a satisfactory set of investment criteria. There is widespread dissatisfaction with the tradi-

* One recognizes the resemblance of this criterion to the external economies criterion.

tional standard, but the foregoing discussion shows that economists have not come up with a clear-cut and acceptable substitute. Such description does, however, make explicit the types of judgments that must be made.

## Programming Investments

The elaboration of criteria to be applied in determining investment priorities is the first step to be taken in a development plan, but the actual planning can be completed only with a program of action. Early techniques were crude and mostly on an *ad hoc* basis, but techniques have improved greatly so that countries with adequate personnel and statistical data can formulate reasonably efficient plans and programs. The description of programming techniques given below is quite simplified and is intended to cover only the basic procedures and problems.[19] Elements of good planning include determining the objectives of the plan, establishing an effective planning machinery and securing adequate personnel, and carrying out or implementing the plan. These will be assumed and will be neglected here, although they are important matters. Thus, only the procedure and problems of programming will be considered.

Because capital is usually necessary to carry out any reform, programs have become essentially investment programs. The problems are (1) how to use scarce capital as efficiently as possible to maximize progress toward the country's desired goals and (2) how to increase the supply of capital to the level necessary for the desired rate of growth.

To be successful, a program of investment must ensure that individual projects are consistent, that is, correctly integrated with one another and efficient in that they are produced at minimum cost. By various techniques, consistency can be secured reasonably well. However, this does not assure an optimum rate of growth or even efficiency. Special attention must be given to these objectives. A country's sights cannot be too high or too low, or economic difficulties will arise. Determining the optimum rate of growth is often a matter of judgment or a comparison of alternative programs.

Almost every underdeveloped country has a plan of some sort, for this is the symbol of modernity even if ineffective. Some, such as India and Pakistan, have quite advanced plans. Others have plans that are little more than expressions of national aspirations or predictions of the course of development. Others embody actual directives for action, although they are not necessarily based on any specified objectives. Theoretical techniques have gone far beyond the capacity of most underdeveloped countries to carry out. Elaborate mathematical models have been constructed and elaborate mathematical formulas have been introduced to aid in formulating the programs. However, in most underdeveloped countries, the absence of staffs capable of constructing models specific to the conditions of the country and the lack of adequate data make cruder methods necessary. Nevertheless, techniques are improving and simple methods are available that permit reasonable results. Whatever the degree or lack of sophistication, a plan gives some guidance to governmental decision making.

Highly sophisticated plans are probably not suitable for most countries in the present stage of their development. However, countries should move toward integrated and consistent plans with as much speed as their capacities permit. Unless private enterprise is doing the job—and the lack of development indicates it is not—the government must undertake structural changes to induce development and accomplish its other objectives. Planning is simply a way of attempting to do this with as much speed and efficiency as possible under the circumstances.

The first type of plan may be one that merely expresses national aspirations or hopes. No effort is made to coordinate activities and little is known about the physical capability of reaching the goals. Such plans seem to serve very little use, but in fact they do have value. They force decision makers to concentrate on the country's objectives, arouse the people's enthusiasm and evoke their active support, and give recognition to the role of government and of planning in promoting development.[20]

A second type of plan may be one designed to remove bottlenecks. Studies may indicate activities whose absence is hindering development. Resources are allocated to these areas, usually without any effort at coordinating all national activities and sometimes with little analysis of the indirect effects on other activities. Typical bottlenecks are the supply of capital, foreign exchange, transportation, skilled labor, and urban overheads.

The third type of plan, which is probably the most widespread, is simply an aggregate of individual projects proposed by the individual ministries or departments without any attempt at integration. These may be selected roughly on the basis of the investment criteria discussed previously, or through the political influence of the individual ministers. They will be directly influenced by governmental policy decisions, typical examples of which will be discussed in the next chapter. Some projects are clearly recognizable as high priority items, and pushing them appears to help. However, a failure to integrate them into an overall plan may lead to difficulties such as projects built to the wrong size, in the wrong location, or at the wrong time. Unless coordinated, they may be built too soon and so produce at less than capacity, or they may be built too late and so hold up other projects. Their production may be delayed because essential materials and labor are not available. The result is a waste of scarce resources.

Almost by definition this type of approach is simply a government investment plan with little attempt to coordinate with private investment. Ministers propose their plans and make their budget requests. Unless the planning authorities extend their influence into the ministries, the quality of the projects and the priority rankings may vary in soundness from ministry to ministry. Moreover, the total allocated to any one sector may depend more on the minister's political influence than the necessity for the projects he proposes. The costs of the projects requested are totaled and compared with the available capital. Budget requests are trimmed and allocations are made to the ministries, who are then free to undertake their projects in any order they see fit.

Nevertheless, when more complex and consistent plans are not available, much can be done by this method, but only if there is a competent central planning board with some authority over timing and regional allocations. At the very least, public expenditures must be planned so as to have as large an effect as possible.

The fourth type of planning is forward or projective planning. This type of plan bears some resemblance to project planning in that it starts with the existing situation and bases its plans on attaining the maximum progress with what is currently available. It differs in that it is based on some theory or model of growth; that is, on some preconceived strategy for development, which may or may not be expressed in a mathematical model. Allocations of resources are made within the framework of this model. For example, the strategy may be to increase basic food production at a rate based on projected population growth and the rise of incomes, and to expand industry at as rapid a rate as possible so as to absorb a projected work force. Projections of trends may reveal a shortage of capital or any other resource, requiring efforts to increase its supply or reducing the demands by cutting out certain projects. Projects are phased (that is, started according to appropriate schedules based on their gestation periods) and are coordinated with one another to assure needed supplies and needed outlets for the resulting production. Goals are determined for each sector, based on the predetermined strategy. The ultimate total output is not predetermined except as a projection.

In short, there is a plan and not a collection of projects or even simply a forecast. There is implied an effort to change basic conditions so as to maximize progress toward certain predetermined objectives. In particular, there is an effort to ensure sufficient capital formation and its proper allocation so as to optimize the efforts of the country to reach its objectives.

The first step is a survey of current assets, including capital, manpower, and present production facilities. Surveys will also be made to assess advantageous lines or industries for development and the possibilities for different regions.

Next, projections of key variables are necessary. These include population, manpower, and such economic variables as gross national product, the consumption of various classes of goods, savings, private investment, foreign exchange, and the funds available for capital investment. These projections can be made under various assumptions concerning the choice of products to promote, the regional distribution, and so on. The projected gross national product will depend on assumptions as to the capital/output ratio and the amount of savings available. The totals must then be broken down by major sectors, whose interrelationships must be calculated and coordinated. Finally, individual projects within each sector must be decided upon.

The projected growth in incomes will, of course, affect the types and quantities of products consumed. Working forward from assumed investments and backward from changes in incomes, adjustments will be made until proper phasings and regional locations are balanced year by year. Bottlenecks will be determined in this way so that efforts can be made to relieve them.

The fifth type of plan is backward, or target, planning. Instead of starting with the existing resource endowments and planning forward, this type of planning draws a picture of what the economy should look like, in terms of consumption standards, government services, private investment, international trade, and so forth, at the end of a certain number of years. It then plans backward to see what resources need to be developed in order to bring about the desired final production. Final output goals may be determined on the basis of complete freedom of consumer choice as to content and proportion of spending relative to income, or on the basis of government restrictions as to content or amount, or both. Actually, a number of different future economies may be assumed, with varying degrees of economic progress so that the maximum feasible rate of growth may be chosen. The minimum rate of growth to be chosen is one that would retain the same scale of per capita output as at present. Above this, various levels can be selected, usually expressed as different percentage rates of growth in per capita incomes. As planning proceeds backward, various shortages will appear. The possibility of relieving these must then be assessed. If they cannot, the proposed goal is not feasible, and a new and lower goal must be tried. The final choice of goal or target is essentially a political one because it involves not only economic feasibility but also political feasibility. The latter is primarily a consideration of how much sacrifice the people can be induced or forced to accept. Thus, economic feasibility depends in part on political feasibility.

The first step is to set the output standard in overall terms at the end of a specified number of years. Utilizing overall capital/output ratios, one can work backward to find the amount of capital formation required and the permissible consumption rate per year. A rough estimate of feasibility can thus be made. In theory, any other ratio, such as labor/output, can also be used. However, capital is considered the scarce factor that sets the limit on growth.

Second, the final output is broken down into consumption and investment, and these are further broken down among broad sectors of the economy. Aggregate consumption is broken down by sector (for example, agriculture, industry, services, imports), based on budget studies or on estimates of income elasticity of demand. Sector capital/output ratios, manpower requirements, foreign exchange needs, and so forth are calculated to reveal possible shortages and determine feasibilities. Sectoral interrelations are calculated by input-output analysis or by successive approximations. A tentative order of preference or phasing of main projects can be established.

Next, the sectors are broken down into individual projects: primary, intermediate, and final production necessary to meet the final needs. Capital and other resources are then allocated to the projects. With these allocations, necessary new projects to meet production needs can be determined and the phasing of all projects worked out.

This planning cannot be put neatly into a compact whole according to one all-inclusive formula. Successive approximations will have to be made until a reasonable balance is determined. Even this will not be perfect, and constant adjustments will have to be made. In effect, what happens is a combination of backward and forward planning until a workable balance and phasing is worked out.

Both methods of comprehensive, or integrated, planning involve a number of problems and require specific kinds of determinations. One decision to be made is the length of the plan period. Three different length plans are common: long-run perspective plans of twenty or more years, intermediate plans of four to six years, and annual plans. Four- to six-year plans, and more frequently five-year plans, seem favored. This period is short enough that basic economic variables will ordinarily not change substantially, so that calculations are easier; yet it is long enough to permit some basic changes in the structure of the economy and the development of scarce or nonexistent resources. However, a time horizon limited to such a period would not maximize growth, for many projects, such as specialized manpower requirements, have a much longer lead time. Furthermore, one five-year plan leads into another and cannot be considered a separate and distinct period. If the second five-year period is to proceed smoothly from the first, some capital starts must take place in the first period. The smoothest transitions would be made if new five-year plans were made each year and were based on longer projected goals, but the calculations would be burden-some.

Thus, there is need for long-term goals or perspective planning against which the intermediate plans can be assessed, and which are long enough to permit structural changes to be considered. The Indian system[21] is to make long-term plans for each sector, based on anticipated needs and technological changes. These plans are not coordinated, nor are financial plans made. The plans are strictly engineering ones based on physical production possibilities. Resource needs can thus be anticipated, and five-year plans can be formulated against the background of the perspective plans in each sector. Constant reviews are necessary as new technological possibilities arise.

Annual plans are a necessity, for no group of planners can identify all contingencies or make perfect allocations even if they could foresee them. Planning is thus continuous even within the annual plans, which may be broken into quarterly and monthly estimates. Constant revisions are necessary as shortages or surpluses appear and as new conditions appear, such as unexpected bad weather conditions in agriculture or a breakdown in an essential industry.

The longer the time horizon, the more possible to plan for given goals, but also less gains will be enjoyed by the present generation.[22] For political reasons some gains in consumption must be initiated as soon as possible, especially in democratic countries. Hence, intermediate plans are the most popular because they set goals that the present generation can hope to realize. The more quickly consumption is allowed to grow, the more the present generation benefits, but also a slow rate of growth is more likely. If consumption increases can be postponed, all growth in resources can go toward increasing basic production resources, which can be fed into producing more productive facilities and intermediate products and eventually into a greater stream of consumption goods. But only a strongly entrenched government can postpone consumption indefinitely and even such governments have limitations. In one sense, planning attempts to alter the time horizons of the people, which, in underdeveloped countries, is usually very short. Incomes are immediately spent on consumption and little savings occur.

The basic outline of procedures has been described and the overall problem of the length of the plan period discussed here. Some of the problems and procedures involved in the various steps deserve somewhat fuller attention if the complexity and nature of the planning procedure is to be realized. These problems and procedures are necessary whether forward or backward planning is used.

As previously stated, some sort of model or strategy for development is necessary and this may be expressed mathematically. The model must include the objective, the variables to be considered, and the relationships among the variables. J. Tinbergen and H. C. Bos[23] contend that interdependencies can be solved best by the use of a mathematical model. These models, they say, must satisfy certain conditions. They must be complete, that is, not overlook any important variable. They must be correct, that is, assign values that correspond with reality. The coefficients must be more or less known. The models must be manageable by those who will use them and must be understandable to those who will use their results. To list these requirements indicates the difficulty in applying complex models to most underdeveloped countries. Tinbergen and Bos indicate that some current models violate one or more of these requirements, and so are not usable in practice. They advocate planning in stages, by which they mean determining a few of the most important variables and later adding others as they become known. Whether or not the strategy is reduced to a mathematical model, the relevant relationships must be made explicit, such as the effect of investment in economic overheads on other sectors or the effect of investment in given industries on imports.

Another essential is the initial survey of current assets. No plan can start except from the position in which a country finds itself. It must know, therefore, as much as possible about the resources and potentials of the country and what the barriers to development are. This necessary information should be not only made available initially but also collected on a permanent basis. The types of information that should be collected are legion, and most of them are usually lacking at the time a country starts thinking about planning. Among the types of information desirable are:

1.  Present and potential physical resources, including agricultural production, minerals, manufacturing facilities.
2.  Economic overheads such as transportation facilities, power, water, irrigation projects, sanitary arrangements.
3.  Social overheads such as hospitals, educational facilities, housing.
4.  Economic institutions, including marketing facilities, banking, and credit.
5.  Consumer equipment and needs.
6.  Population and its composition, distribution, trends, mobility, educational and skill endowments, and its availability as manpower.
7.  Exports and imports and the country's access to foreign exchange.
8.  Political, social, and cultural patterns, and legal practices to determine if any barriers to development exist.
9.  Financial estimates, including national income estimates and its distribution among consumption, investment, government expenditure, and foreign trade; expenditure and savings patterns, and the distribution of income; sources of investment funds and their present disposition, including private savings, taxation, foreign borrowing and grants; current and potential governmental operating costs.

10. Surveys of land use and tenancy, soils, geological and mineral formations, and existing and potential roads, railroads, and other forms of communication.
11. Market surveys, both domestic and foreign.
12. Present and expected activities of private enterprises.

A number of projections are basic, and information and techniques must be developed in order to make them. An estimate of total population and its composition is necessary both for an analysis of demand changes and for potential manpower supplies. Demographers have worked out these projection techniques quite satisfactorily. Short-run changes have been reasonably accurately estimated, but long-run changes have not been. It can almost be said that whatever the estimate, it will turn out to be too low. Manpower is an important constraint on development, and projects to remedy deficiencies may require a long lead time, so that projections of needs and supplies are important. Projections of aggregate needs may be made by use of a labor/output ratio or a labor/capital ratio, making an allowance for technological changes that alter the labor content of production methods. Allowances must be made for the effects of policies on immigration and emigration, retirement, the participation of women, school attendance, health programs, hours of work, and so forth. This overall estimate can be used to predict unemployment and suggest methods for eliminating it. In addition to aggregate estimates, needs for specific skills must be estimated, perhaps on a basis of a given percentage of total manpower, derived from experience in other countries with a similar level of technology. Such needs as physicians can be put on a per capita basis.

Other projections relate to personal income and expenditure patterns. Per capita personal income may be estimated from total growth estimates and its division among the sectors of the economy. The consumption and savings function must be estimated as incomes rise, and future tax policies must be allowed for. On the basis of personal incomes and production needs, total demand must be projected. Consumption trends can be estimated by studies of income elasticities of demand, the experience of other countries, or family budget studies supplemented by estimates of population change, changes in the distribution of income, and the effects of urbanization. Some consumption may be controlled by the government, but unless all output is rationed, the element of private choice must be estimated. Fortunately, especially above the level of necessities, one consumer item can, within limits, be substituted for another. Because consumers will usually spend their money on a substitute product, if a desired good is not available, errors in estimating original demands for individual projects may not be realized. Government consumption in the form of operating expenditures can be controlled in part, but also in part may be dictated by the projects that are necessary for development. The determination of the demands for intermediate goods and capital goods will be discussed later.

Determining the amount of investment capital needed is perhaps the basic projection, for all other shortages may ultimately be resolved into this one. For example, shortages in manpower can, in time, be relieved by investments in training facilities. Even cultural traits can be changed by a sufficient investment in education, means of consumption, and so on. The basic concept used is the capital/output ratio, which simply expresses the amount of capital used to produce one unit of output. The relevant ratio is the marginal capital/output ratio. Estimates have been made on the basis of the overall experience of other countries or of the average of the country's own recent past. This overall figure may not be accurate for a country undergoing rapid change and having conditions different from those in the country used as a norm. The composition of investment may be very different and the initial conditions entirely incompatible with respect to the capital already in place. To be realistic, a country needs to project a separate capital/output ratio for each sector, and it would be even better if it could be done for each product. The importance to be given each sector and the interrelations among all sectors must then be determined to permit the assigning of relative weights to each sector. The interrelations are particularly important, for the indirect effects of an investment may be very great. For example, locating a given factory in one area may require transportation facilities, power, and urban costs. Moreover, some reasonable percentage of operation below 100 percent capacity must be assumed because of inevitable delays in supplies, breakdowns, failures of markets, and so on. It is quite likely that marginal capital/output ratios will tend to be larger than estimated.

The foreign exchange balance is also a constraint on development, so that demands for exchange and sources of supply must be estimated. Imports arise from consumer demands and to meet production needs. Both may be controlled to some extent. Consumer imports have a high-income elasticity and, if unrestricted, will grow rapidly, introducing exchange difficulties. One problem of projection is lessened if imports are strictly reduced to necessities or to any surplus exchange remaining after production needs are met. Production may require imports of capital goods and raw materials. These must be estimated on the basis of the planned production and the degree of introduction of import-saving industries. Import needs must be matched against estimated exports. Projections of existing exports can be made on the basis of income elasticities of demand in the importing countries, and efforts should be made to increase these or other exports. A large element of judgment enters here, for other countries will also be attempting to increase their exports. Only an expert in the field can hope to be reasonably accurate. Estimation of exports may be the most uncertain of all the projections. In addition to estimating physical quantities of trade, price levels and exchange rates must be predicted. This is particularly difficult for the prices of raw materials, which are very erratic. Lastly, other items of the balance of payments may be important, such as capital flows, the services of shipping, insurance, and banking, and all must be considered.

Another major area for calculation is that of determining the interrelationships among segments of the economy, as well as regionally, in order to get internal consistency in the program. The aim is to make sure that the right goods are produced at the right time and the right place so as to avoid shortages or excess capacities. Historically, the first method was the "method of balances" used by the U.S.S.R. as a necessary process in the absence of sufficient data to apply more advanced techniques, which the U.S.S.R. is now introducing. The method of balances is one of successive approximations.[24] A target of outputs is selected and the need for intermediate and capital goods is computed by index numbers or ratios, step by step from the highest to the lowest stages.* By summing these, the total of all inputs required to produce the final output is arrived at. If the total required does not match the available supplies, the targets are changed, or changes are made in the technology or the allocation of inputs, or efforts are made to increase the resources until a physical balance is achieved. Shortages can also be compensated by importation, but this is not part of the normal policy of the U.S.S.R. A major balancing device can be the reduction of low priority targets, which, in the case of the U.S.S.R., are consumer goods.

A more refined type of balancing is carried out by input-output analysis.[25] The input-output model shows for each industry its sales to and purchases from every other industry. These tables may be very complex where data are available, but most underdeveloped countries are restricted to fifteen or twenty production sectors and a few final use sectors at best. Under this method, aggregate production is broken down by sectors, giving a less aggregated picture of flows throughout the economy. In addition, because coefficients of inputs can be inserted and can be made specific for each sector, a more realistic approximation of the necessary inputs can be made. Coefficients for such inputs as capital, manpower, imports, raw materials, fuel,

---

* The input requirements were first calculated as the average for each industry and then were set somewhere between the average and the best realized, or at a point determined by scientific studies. Gradual changes might be introduced in order to improve efficiency.

power, and transport, can all be calculated by this method. Usually, constant coefficients are assumed. To be realistic, technical coefficient data need to be developed.

The great value of this method is that the indirect effects of an investment or the secondary and tertiary waves of changes that must be made to complete an initial investment can be traced through and are not so likely to be overlooked. One disadvantage is that this method normally shows the relationship as of one time, that is, it is a static concept. It shows the necessary relationships at the end of some period or any period in between, but does not demonstrate the phasing of the projects; consequently, there are repeated calculations for different time periods. This method also assumes constant input coefficients and linear relationships. To the extent that these are not valid (and they may not be with economies of scale and will not be with technological change), an element of error is introduced. Also, the balancing methods can bring about a reasonable physical balance, but this in itself cannot assure the planner that he has chosen the most efficient balance. This is another disadvantage. Regional input-output models show the relationships among the various regions of a country.

Another method for securing balance is to establish reserves of resources, but this is wasteful of resources. These methods are designed to achieve physical balances, of which there are a number. Production and use must be coordinated. This could be done through price changes, but such a process would be inflationary or would defeat the purposes of planning. Similarly, there needs to be a balance between productive facilities and the uses made of their product. The products of one stage must meet the needs of the succeeding stage and not be in surplus supply. But there are other kinds of basic balances: manpower, financial, foreign exchange. To get all these balances and efficiency at the same time is the real goal of planning. Incidental to this goal is the allowance made for the private sector. The actions of private persons can be encouraged or discouraged through a price system, taxation, rationing, and so on, but estimates of individuals' effects on the plan always remain less than certain.

The manpower balance is a basic need and one that requires considerable lead time to solve. The first requisite is enough general education to permit easy technological instruction. Beyond this is the need for advanced education for some and special training for many types of workers. The very fact of the need for a wide variety of skills makes planning for manpower very complex. Often, specific manpower needs are the scarcest resource at any one particular time. In addition to quantity balances of labor, there must be regional balances, or provision must be made for mobility of labor. In most of the underdeveloped countries the most likely situation will be one of a large amount of unemployment after all the capital is employed. The problem will be what to do about it.[26] The technical structure could be changed to be more labor-intensive, but this may hinder progress. Wherever output is sacrificed only a little, this method may be used. Otherwise, surplus labor may be used where no capital is required, such as household service, assuming that housewives have the necessary household capital. Or they may be crowded into other services, or onto subsistence farms, or supported by the state in idleness. Reducing output in order to have full employment is not a method designed to bring growth.

Financial balance is also necessary in order to prevent price instability, which could wreck a plan. Consumers' incomes less anticipated savings and taxes must equal the total price tags put on consumer goods, particularly the necessities. Otherwise, prices will rise or fall and shortages or surpluses will appear. A rising price for necessities may lead to wage demands and upset all calculations. Prices might be allowed to rise on luxuries, if necessary, and so drain off some surplus purchasing power, but there is no assurance that the surplus will not seek out the scarce necessities instead. Of special importance is the government price and wage policy, for this is the major determinant of the consumers' incomes and the total price tag for consumer goods.

Total savings, whether privately or governmentally centered, plus foreign borrowing, must equate with planned investment. In a private enterprise economy, actual savings always equal actual investment, as explained by the Keynesian macromodel. In a planned society, the effort is to make savings and investment equal before actual operations begin, in order to prevent unwanted adjustments.

The government budget must be balanced, except to the extent that consumer savings can be channeled to the government by borrowing. Unbalanced budgets, especially if the shortage of government purchasing power is compensated by issuing paper money or obtaining bank credit (unless there are offsetting delays or cessation of spending elsewhere), are inflationary.

Total output must be broken down into a number of more or less related sectors such as agriculture, industry, services, and foreign trade, and even finer divisions must be considered. Industry must be divided into consumer goods, capital goods, economic and social overheads, and so on, and each of these broken down still further into individual industries and then into projects. The model will tell something about the relative emphasis to be placed on each. This must be supplemented by analysis of the interrelations among the sectors. None can be considered in isolation, for each sector uses products of the other.

Eventually, individual projects must be selected. Possible projects in each sector must be screened in the light of final output targets. The preliminary plan may have specified a certain amount of consumer goods, which is then divided among food, clothing, and so forth. Project allocation involves choosing the particular type of food or clothing to produce and how to produce it. Consumer preferences may be followed or government may simply choose the output it wishes. In the case of the capital goods sectors, alternative projects may meet the same need and choices must be made.

Thus there are alternative projects and there are alternative ways of producing each output. It is at this point that efficiency criteria are needed and that the choices must be made on the bases of the investment criteria outlined in the beginning of the chapter. Choices as to phasing, product design, the quality of the product, the scale of the factory, the location of the factory, and the technology to be used must be made. Accounting prices, making allowance for social costs and benefits and the use of foreign exchange, may be utilized to select the project. The factory is faced with certain constraints of materials, capital, and labor, and also faces prices for inputs, which may be freely determined or imposed by authority. It is the manager's job, who now takes over from the economist, to combine the factors so as to reach his goals, which may be to maximize profits in a private enterprise economy or to reach his production targets in a controlled economy. As now introduced into the U.S.S.R., the manager has an incentive to maximize his profits, which means getting the most efficient combination of resources or skimping on the quality of the product where he can. The use of a price system is useful in aiding decisions at this level. After these decisions have been made, a rebalancing of resource, financial, and manpower requirements may be necessary.

It has previously been mentioned that the usual economics text makes production, investment, and price decisions look easy in a private enterprise economy. In fact, they are not, and inefficiencies creep in, maximum growth may not be achieved, price stability is unusual, and less than full employment prevails. Government intervention attempts to remedy the worst of these defects, but in the absence of an overall plan it may fall short of the goal and may even make things worse.

It is not intended here to imply that making production, investment, and price decisions in a planned economy is easy and 100 percent efficient. Present procedures are such that planned societies usually fall far short of their goals, and especially so where a large amount of individual freedom is allowed in economic affairs. Where data are unavailable and administrators inexperienced, planning may well be less efficient than that of private enterprise. But planning can choose the objective a country wants and be more effective in leading a country toward a complex of goals than if they were left to the mercy of chance. Also, planning techniques are improving and give promise of achieving greater efficiency as well as reaching other objectives. To the present, mathematical models have not been devised and data are not plentiful and accurate enough that the planners can put them into a computer, punch a button, and see a complete, thoroughly integrated, and efficient list of projects and activities come out. Human judgment and estimation are still necessary, and human judgment is susceptible to error.

## REFERENCES

1. KAHN, A. E., "Investment Criteria in Development Programs." *Quarterly Journal of Economics* (February, 1951), pp. 38-61.
2. LEIBENSTEIN, HARVEY, "Why Do We Disagree on Investment Policies for Development?" *Indian Economic Journal* (April, 1958). Reproduced in T. Morgan, G. W. Betz, and N. K. Choudhry, *Readings in Economic Development*. Belmont, Calif., Wadsworth Publishing Co., 1963, p. 138.
3. LEIBENSTEIN, *op. cit.*, p. 132.
4. The discussion in this section is based on the following works: Ahumada, J., "Investment Priorities," in H. S. Ellis and H. C. Wallich, *Economic Development for Latin America*. New York, St Martin's Press, 1961, pp. 366-98. Enke, S., *Economics for Development*. Englewood Cliffs, N.J., Prentice-Hall, Inc., 1963, pp. 277-97. Hirschman, A. O., *Strategy of Economic Development*. New Haven, Yale University Press, 1958, pp. 76-97. Meier, G. M., *Leading Issues in Development Economics*. New York, Oxford University Press, 1964, pp. 229-49. Sen, G. R., *The Strategy for Agricultural Development*. New York, Asia Publishing House, 1962, pp. 99-122. Belshaw, M., "Operational Capital Allocation Criteria for Development." *Economic Development and Cultural Change* (April, 1958), pp.

191-203. Bohr, K. A., "Investment Criteria for Manufacturing Industries in Underdeveloped Countries." *Review of Economics and Statistics* (May, 1954), pp. 157-66. Chenery, H. B., "Patterns of Industrial Growth." *American Economic Review* (September, 1960), pp. 624-54. Chenery, "The Role of Industrialization in Development Programs." *American Economic Review, Proceedings* (May, 1955), pp. 40-57. Chenery, "The Application of Investment Criteria." *Quarterly Journal of Economics* (February, 1953), pp. 76-96. Dosser, D., "General Investment Criteria for Less-Developed Countries." *Scottish Journal of Political Economy* (June, 1962), pp. 85-98. Eckstein, O., "Investment Criteria for Economic Development and the Theory of Interpersonal Welfare Economics." *Quarterly Journal of Economics* (February, 1957), pp. 56-85. Galenson, W., and H. Leibenstein, "Investment Criteria, Productivity, and Economic Development." *Quarterly Journal of Economics* (August, 1955), pp. 343-70. Kahn, *op. cit.*
5. BELSHAW, *op. cit.*, p. 191.
6. International Labour Office, "Some Aspects of Investment Policy in Underdeveloped Countries." *International Labour Review* (May, 1958). Reproduced in Meier, *op. cit.*, p. 242.

7. MEIER, *op. cit.,* p. 229.
8. PAPANEK, G. F., "Framing a Development Program." *International Conciliation,* No. 527 (March, 1960), pp. 312ff.
9. ECKSTEIN, *op. cit.*
10. KAHN, *op. cit.,* p. 51.
11. BRAND, W., *The Struggle for a Higher Standard of Living.* New York, The Free Press of Glencoe, 1958, p. 87.
12. KAHN, *op. cit.,* p. 41.
13. BYE, M., "The Role of Capital in Economic Development." in H. Ellis and H. Wallich, *Economic Development for Latin America.* New York, St Martin's Press, 1961, p. 117.
14. GALENSON and LEIBENSTEIN, *op. cit.*
15. SCITOVSKY, T., "Growth-Balanced or Unbalanced?" in M. Abramovitz, *et al., Allocation of Economic Resources.* Stanford, Calif., Stanford University Press, 1959, pp. 207-17.
16. HIRSCHMAN, A. O., *Strategy of Economic Development.* New Haven, Yale University Press, 1958.
17. DOSSER, *op. cit.,* p. 93.
18. *Ibid.,* p. 95.
19. This discussion is based on the following works: Bettelheim, C. O., *Some Basic Planning Problems.* New York, Asia Publishing House, 1961, pp. 1-34. Central Treaty Organization, *Conference on Development Planning.* CENTO, 1960. Chenery, H. B., and P. G. Clark, *Interindustry Economics.* New York, John Wiley & Sons, Inc., 1959. Hirsch, H., *Quantity Planning and Price Planning in the Soviet Union.* Philadelphia, University of Pennsylvania Press, 1961. Lewis, J. P., *Quiet Crisis in India.* Washington, D.C., The Brookings Institution, 1962, pp. 114-36. Meier, *op. cit.,* pp. 464-564. Tinbergen, J., *The Design of Development.* Baltimore, Johns Hopkins Press, 1958. Department of Economic and Social Affairs, *Analysis and Projections of Economic Development.* New York, United Nations, 6 vols., 1957-59. Committee for Asia and the Far East, *Formulating Industrial Development Programs—Asia and the Far East.* Bangkok, United Nations, 1960. *Programming Techniques for Economic Development.* Bangkok, United Nations, 1960. Wagle, S. S., *Technique of Planning for Accelerated Economic Growth of Underdeveloped Countries.* Bombay, Vora, 1961. Walensky, L. G., *The Planning and Execution of Economic Development.* New York, McGraw-Hill Book Co., Inc., 1963. Chenery, H. B., "Development Policies and Programs." *Economic Bulletin for Latin America* (March, 1958), pp. 51-77. Papanek, *op. cit.*
20. Economic Commission for Asia and the Far East, United Nations, "A Decade of Development Planning and Implementation in the ECAFE Region." *Economic Bulletin for Asia and the Far East* (December, 1961). Quoted in Meier, *op. cit.,* p. 424.
21. SEN, *op. cit.,* pp. 74ff.
22. ROSENSTEIN-RODAN, P. N., ed., *Capital Formation and Economic Development.* Cambridge, Mass., The M.I.T. Press, 1964, pp. 71ff.
23. TINBERGEN, J., and H. C. Bos, *Mathematic Models of Economic Growth.* New York, McGraw-Hill Book Co., Inc., 1962. Quoted in Meier, *op. cit.,* pp. 480ff.
24. HIRSCH, *op. cit.,* pp. 23-43.
25. LEONTIEFF, W. W., "Input-output Economics." *Scientific American* (October, 1951), pp. 15-21.
26. BETTELHEIM, *op. cit.,* pp. 15ff.

## ADDITIONAL READINGS

ARNDT, H. W., "External Economies in Economic Growth." *Economic Record* (November, 1955), pp. 192-214.

BALASSA, B. A., *Hungarian Experience in Economic Planning*. New Haven, Yale University Press, 1959, pp. 44-91.

BARNA, T., ed., *The Structural Interdependence of the Economy*. New York, John Wiley & Sons, Inc., 1956.

BJERVE, P. J., *Planning in Norway, 1947-56*. Amsterdam, North-Holland Publishing Co., 1959.

BLITZ, R. C., "Capital Longevity and Economic Development." *American Economic Review* (June, 1958), pp. 313-32.

GOLAY, F. H., *The Philippines: Public Policy and Economic Development*. Ithaca, N.Y., Cornell University Press, 1961, pp. 346-75.

HACKETT, J., and A. M., *Economic Planning in France*. London, George Allen & Unwin, Ltd., 1963.

HIRSCHMAN, A. O., "Investment Policies and 'Dualism' in Underdeveloped Countries." *American Economic Review* (September, 1957), pp. 550-70.

KOOPMANS, T. C., ed., *Activity Analysis of Production and Allocation*. New York, John Wiley & Sons, Inc., 1951.

KUMAR, B., *Introduction to Planning in India*. Calcutta, Bookland, 1962.

MONTIAS, J. M., *Central Planning in Poland*. New Haven, Yale University Press, 1962.

REDDAWAY, W. B., *Development of the Indian Economy*. Homewood, Ill., Richard D. Irwin, Inc., 1962.

SPULBER, N., ed., *Foundations of Soviet Strategy for Economic Growth*. Bloomington, Ind., Indiana University Press, 1964.

WATERSTON, A., *Planning in Yugoslavia*. Baltimore, Johns Hopkins Press, 1962.

WATERSTON, "Investment Policy in Underdeveloped Countries." *International Labour Review* (May, 1958), pp. 389-416.

# CHAPTER
# 15
# *Typical Policy Decisions*

Any summary of the problem of economic growth must take note of the fact that all underdeveloped countries differ and that the exact program for each must differ. A. O. Hirschman[1] emphasizes this and says that some complain because there is no theory of development in the sense that one can cite a "single and unbroken chain of causes and effects" which would explain or promote development. But he believes this to be a credit to economists that they have not developed such a theory. Although the exact programs and sequences of growth will differ, all countries must make a number of typical decisions. These include:

1. A choice of the extent to which growth is to be pursued relative to other goals.
2. The major types of attack to follow.
3. Who is to bear the cost and who is to get the gains.
4. Whether to invest primarily in things or humans.
5. Whether to rely on exports or self-sufficiency.
6. Whether development can be brought about gradually or will require the "big push."
7. Whether growth should be balanced or unbalanced.
8. Whether growth should be concentrated in a few areas or be promoted generally.
9. Whether investments should be capital- or labor-intensive.
10. Whether the active agent of development should be government or private enterprise.

The answers given will vary with the circumstances and will evoke different patterns of development and possibly faster or slower rates of growth.

That all, or even a substantial number, of the present underdeveloped countries will actually grow and develop is problematical. One hesitates to make predictions as to whether the many decisions will actually turn out to be the correct ones for the circumstances, for predicting what the world will be like in, say, fifty years, would be hazardous indeed. One would like to be optimistic and believe that growth will be great. Although the possibilities exist for most, if not all, to grow economically, it is easy to be pessimistic about any significant decrease in the disparities of income among the world's peoples or even about the possibility of any substantial improvement in the scale of living of many. The major obstacles appear to be excess population growth, political uncertainty, an unwillingness to undergo the necessary sacrifices, and a failure of governments to place national growth ahead of personal power and prestige. As uncertain as economists are up to the present time concerning the best means to grow, the major obstacles do not seem to be economic but political and social. If man has the will, and has a little help in the right places, he can increase his output on the basis of present knowledge, almost anywhere on this earth. Physical resources are no longer so basic to development as they once were. A plentiful supply makes development easier, but it is possible to overcome poor resources and to develop. But the political and social conditions must be right, and these appear to be the major deterrents faced by the underdeveloped nations. Moreover, changes in these existing climates are partly preconditions for development and partly its consequences. Because of this interrelationship, growth may be slow at first and accelerate as development occurs.

## The Choice of Goals

The first requisite is that a people must choose to grow economically and must be willing to make the necessary sacrifices, as discussed in Chapter 1. It was pointed out there that economic growth is only one of many possible goals and that these goals may conflict, especially those of economic growth and increased leisure. One hopes that the pursuit of material wealth will not be a single-minded objective of any nation. Other important values should be preserved; that is, a place should be found among traditional values for a satisfactory amount of growth, and diversity in culture and tradition should be maintained. A completely materialistic world would be a sorry place. The leading powers, the United States and the U.S.S.R., place great emphasis on material wealth, and their example may induce others to do so. Unfortunately, both countries also lay great stress on national power, and can afford to do so at the expense of some economic growth. It would be unfortunate if this policy were to be copied by the emerging countries, for it would be to the detriment of both power and economic growth. Similarly, the movement toward shorter working periods, if carried too far before productivity is increased, or toward social security in advance of ability to pay, may hinder economic growth, although these are desirable objectives in themselves. It would make things much easier if one could pursue economic growth without considering other values, but unfortunately for economists this cannot be done.

Thus, countries must make a choice of what they want and be willing to work toward those ends. What, in the last analysis, is meaningful in a country's accomplishments is whether the masses of the people attain what they want—more goods, more security, more leisure, or more of something else.

Countries must thus decide how hard they wish to work and what sacrifices they are willing to make in present consumption and in customs and traditions. These are difficult choices, but they must be made because they are fundamental to the development they seek. All too often leaders have promised all good things at the same time and in a hurry. Unfortunately, no one has yet discovered a quick and easy way to accomplish this and such promises do not materialize. The result can be disillusionment and rebellion and a transfer of cause to outside forces. A full and complete realization at the outset that the road to economic growth is long and arduous and full of choices and sacrifices is desirable and conducive to faster growth in the long run.

## The Major Areas of Attack

Almost without exception economists agree that the essential ingredients or critical factors for economic growth are more capital, technological improvement, better entrepreneurship, and better and harder work. It is easy to add many others, as discussed throughout the previous chapters, such as better political administration, improved foreign trade, and improved markets. All are ultimately essential, but the first four factors seem to be stressed the most. It is easy to say that each of these should be developed, but the supplying of each one has a whole host of problems in its background. Although the foregoing variables are economic in nature, their supply is a composite of economic, social and cultural, and political considerations. Thus, one must be concerned not only with each part of the problem but also with the total picture.[2] There must be a sound overall development strategy, applicable to the particular situation of the country. That is, the pieces must fit together, and each piece must be studied and improved before it fits the pattern. The appropriate strategy relates directly to the circumstances in which the country finds itself at this particular time in history. Unfortunately, countries and people want simple rules that they can apply, but these are not available. There just is no simple explanation for development, no generally accepted theory, and no unique process.

Thus, stating that emphasis must be placed on capital, technology, entrepreneurship, and labor habits is misleading. As stressed in Chapter 3, the problem of economic development goes much beyond economic issues and must be considered in the context of a whole social and cultural environment. Yet, economic considerations cannot be ignored either. Development is the result of a whole complex of interacting changes. The economist soon feels helpless without the help of the anthropologist. The anthropologist soon finds he cannot get very far without the economist. And both together soon realize that reforms must take place in political administration. The full explanation of development requires study of the entire structure of society and cannot be a matter for isolated specialists. The resulting institutional arrangements must encourage the development of the proper attitudes that lead to more capital, improved technology, better entrepreneurs, harder work, a better labor force, improved governmental administration, proper population policies, and so on.

Things get done through people, so that as much or more stress must be put on the development of human beings as on direct productive equipment. Capital comes into being only through the actions of human beings, positively by savings or passively by submitting to taxes. Unless there is proper motivation with an understanding of the gain involved and unless education provides the necessary foresight, attempts to increase capital may be very difficult. Many things are necessary to increase savings, including proper financial institutions, increased incomes, security of property, and, not least, social attitudes that make thrift respectable and frown on ostentatious display and ceremony.

Technological improvements take place only through people, either because they can appreciate the advantage of borrowing ideas already practiced elsewhere or because they can perceive new ideas themselves. It takes a special type of person to be an innovator, as seen in Chapter 8. It also takes a special type of person to think up new ways of doing things. The development of the right attitudes is a very special problem of development, one which may well be outside the scope of the economist. In addition, the people as a whole must be receptive to new ideas and change.

Entrepreneurs are people, but of a very special type. They must be achievement-motivated, daring, have foresight, and be willing to accept opposition because of the changes they introduce. But, even if entrepreneurial types exist, they cannot fight too great an opposition; that is, the attitudes of the people must be such as to accept change, even if grudgingly. Also, such things as credit must be available, markets sufficiently available to act as an incentive, and adequate transportation, communication, and other overheads available to make enterprise feasible. Similarly, hard work requires a certain attitude toward life and personal qualities similar to that of the entrepreneur, even if somewhat subdued.

What is being stressed in the preceding discussion is that promoting institutions and arrangements that will produce the kinds of people who will bring about growth is at least equal in importance with producing the necessary economic equipment. If people have the know-how and the right attitudes, they will supply the essential economic ingredients and will bring about growth, as shown in the example of much of devastated Europe after World War II. However, unless both social and cultural patterns and economic growth occur at the same time, neither is likely to occur. A change in one feeds on changes in the other.

Thus, economic changes, social and cultural changes, and personality changes must all occur. The big problem is where to begin. One change may be the key, although more likely one change without other necessary changes may be wasted. For example, merely an increase in capital with no corresponding change in attitudes may lead only to a temporary increase in well-being, which is soon absorbed by a greater population or declines when capital equipment falls into disuse because of a lack of markets. Planning is one way of organizing society's efforts so that all the necessary steps will be taken in the proper sequence, so that the best results will be achieved at the least cost. The exact plan, however, must be specific to the country's circumstances. In every country, in its specific situation, there will be major deficiencies that lead to a shortage in the critical factors. Planning is designed to find the shortcuts to relieve these so that growth will proceed. Finding the key may not be easy.

Certain minimum preconditions seem necessary for growth, such as: the maintenance of law and order, good government administration, adequate transportation and communication, minimum educational standards, improved health and sanitation practices, credit facilities, improved labor skills, and a source of cheap foodstuffs. These areas are good starting places for development. Promoting these may not produce quick and spectacular results, but without them rapid and sustained growth seems unlikely. It thus is obvious that the author believes, using Rostow's terms, that the precondition stage is much more important to emphasize than the "takeoff." The preconditions cannot be circumvented. According to this reasoning, economic growth is a long and arduous process and not a rapid and spectacular event.

## *Who Is to Bear the Costs and Reap the Gains?*

Whatever the strategy for development, funds will be required; for the most part, these will have to come from the incomes of citizens, except for those fortunate few countries that can sell off a natural resource such as oil. Even in this case, funds that might otherwise be available for consumption must be diverted into investment. Therefore a decision must be made as to how much consumption shall be sacrificed for investment and which citizens are to be asked to give up the purchasing power. Similar decisions must be made as to who is to secure the ultimate gains of growth in the form of increased consumption, security, and so on.

The first decision concerns the level of investment. Increasing total investment and thus the speed of growth requires the sacrifice of present consumption, unless some foreign sources can be persuaded to supply the necessary capital equipment. This, however, can never be more than marginal, so that most of the savings must be acquired domestically. The more present consumption is sacrificed, the greater can be the rate of growth that will ultimately provide more goods and services. In private enterprise economies the level of investment is determined by individual decisions as to savings and investment, and is a result partly of the distribution of income and profits. Essentially, only the rich have a capacity to save and invest at low levels of development. The poor, collectively, do save substantial amounts, but because of the lack of appropriate financial institutions, they do not make the funds available to industry. Moreover, with a lack of markets, surplus incomes are not apt to be invested in industry but in trade, speculation, luxury living, or in industry abroad. Thus, complete reliance on private enterprise in the underdeveloped countries is not likely to bring about development. Government investment does have the advantage of permitting investment in direct and indirect productive facilities in advance of profit prospects, so that savings do in fact get invested. How far governments should go in directing all investments is another matter, to be discussed below.

If one institutes policies to eliminate extremes in the distribution of incomes, voluntary savings cannot be relied upon to provide the savings necessary for a positive rate of growth, for the masses lack goods that contacts with other peoples lead them to desire. In such circumstances, the size of the development effort must be a political decision and will depend on the willingness of the people or on the power of the government to enforce compliance. This is not an economic decision. The rate at which consumption can be prevented from increasing* and the amount of economic security to be given depend on the amount of sacrifice that can be imposed on or accepted by the present generation for the benefit of future generations. Justice demands that people not be asked to sacrifice in order to finance unproductive investments. One may glory in palaces, cathedrals, stadia, large armies, or unproductive showpiece factories, but these are built at the expense of present and future consumption standards.† Thus, there must be a choice between present individual and governmental consumption, on the one hand, and the amount of investment and its related rate of economic growth on the other. That rapid economic growth is necessarily the right choice is far from being an established fact, but people should be aware of what the choice is and of the consequences of choosing a particular alternative.

Whatever the speed of growth to be pursued, a decision must be made as to who should bear the burden of the necessary sacrifices. The Japanese placed the burden on the peasant through heavy taxation and on the worker through low wages. The U.S.S.R. has exploited the peasant and has kept the living standard of the worker low. In western Europe, low wages placed much of the burden on the worker. In the United States, the exploitation of natural resources lessened some of the sacrifice, but the urban workers also received only a slow gain in the general advance during the period of growth. In some areas the landlords and minority groups have had their wealth taken away in total or in part. By forcing requisitions of food from peasants at low prices, it has been possible to keep down their incomes, and industrial wages have been generally low. Thus, almost universally, the peasant and the industrial worker have been the major bearers of the burden of development. The new industrialist or the government administrator, and those with a few scarce skills, seem to be the ones who gain. The usual result is a large and probably not decreasing inequality in the distribution of income. Undoubtedly, the masses must sacrifice for development. It would seem, however, that more effort could be made to equalize the burdens and that one of the objectives of economic policy must be to improve the well-being and security of the masses. Otherwise, it is difficult to conclude that an emphasis on economic growth is a desirable objective.

Social justice requires that the benefits of economic growth be widespread, even if they must be deferred. All too often foreign aid has resulted in the rich getting richer and the poor gaining little, if anything. Lending countries, unfortunately, are not in a good position to prevent this, for there

---

* Standards of living are usually too low to permit consumption to be cut.

† An exception to this would occur when expenditure for one of these would so unite a people or increase their cooperation that additional sacrifices could be endured.

would be an immediate cry about interference in a country's internal affairs. On the other hand, one must recognize that scales of living cannot be permitted to rise too rapidly; otherwise, development will not proceed rapidly. A rising scale of living for the masses must be postponed, and this is difficult because of the "demonstration effect." Only as productive equipment is built up and business firms (or governments) are taking care of the necessary savings and investment can consumption be allowed to rise substantially. At this point more attention needs to be devoted to consumption, social justice, and economic security. Strong dictatorial governments, such as the U.S.S.R., have been able to postpone consumption; at the same time, however, these governments condemn worker exploitation in noncommunized countries. Because the masses want increased consumption, only secure governments can force the postponement of consumption. Governments face a real dilemma. Economic growth must proceed, if the people are to support the government, but efforts to speed up growth by restraining any increases in consumption may similarly lead to revolt. It is little wonder that democratic governments find it hard to survive. At all events, one of the first objectives should be to eliminate substandard levels of living, education, health, and so on. Beyond this, the extent to which standards can be allowed to rise will depend upon the speed at which the country wishes to develop and how long it will postpone enjoying the benefits of growth.

## Balanced or Unbalanced Growth

In previous chapters the dispute over balanced and unbalanced growth has been mentioned. Nurkse represents the first position and Hirschman, the second. Choosing the approach to follow is an important decision.

Those who favor balanced growth do so because they believe it is necessary to provide a wide supply of goods in order to absorb the increased purchasing power and so prevent its concentration on a few goods, primarily agricultural goods, in which a rapid price rise would ultimately affect wages and disrupt the plan. It is obvious that those who hold to this premise do not believe that consumption and other needs can be met through foreign trade; that is, that the surplus outputs of a few industries can be exchanged readily for the necessary variety of goods. A realistic appraisal would support the view that the opportunity to export is limited and that it would be difficult for most countries to achieve balance through trade. The view holds that once industries are started, those with export prospects would grow and engage in foreign trade. But, in the beginning, a country would have to produce most of its own needs.

It is not intended that all industries would grow equally because of differences in the income elasticity of different goods. Obviously, as spending patterns change, supplies of the various goods would have to keep in step, assuming there were no imports. Efforts would be concentrated on those industries whose supply lagged, and no sector would be allowed to hold other sectors back.

It is possible also to talk of balance in a more limited sense as merely that practice of establishing a number of mutually supporting industries.[3] It is difficult to dispute this limited concept as a principle, but it is not usually what is meant by balanced growth.[4]

On the other hand, those who favor unbalanced growth point out that balanced growth requires large investments because many industries must be started at once. Moreover, each is apt to be on a relatively small scale at first and thus inefficient and not yielding the full economies of scale. A wide variety of skills in large quantity would be required, but the necessary personnel would not be likely to be available. Trying to develop rapidly on all fronts would result in labor bottlenecks, creating wage pressures and high costs. Labor cannot be drawn rapidly from agriculture and be given sufficient training. Also, the balanced growth method involves extensive government control of the investment pattern in that it is assumed that industries will not develop through voluntary response unless many of them are started at once.

A further objection[5] is that, carried to its extreme form, advance must take place on a wide front, including the customary consumption goods; productivity must first be increased in existing industries until incomes are raised sufficiently to justify new industries. This is not looked on as feasible, especially when one considers the difficulty of introducing change into traditional industries.

The advocates of unbalanced growth propose pushing certain lines in advance of their current requirements in order to get better economies of scale and in order to evoke voluntary responses from other lines in supplying the necessary materials and in using the resulting product. Attention would be concentrated on investments, which would make the economy more flexible and thus able to respond to new opportunities. Surplus capacity would make materials cheap for other domestic industries or would result in surpluses that could be traded for needed imports. These imports would show the way for local industries, which would then be led to try to capture a proven market, provided local resources made such a venture feasible. Obviously, appropriate areas for concentration would have to be selected. Thus, instead of relying on domestic industries eventually growing efficient and moving into foreign trade, this method would start with efficient-sized industries that could engage in foreign trade, with domestic industry growing up where feasible. This is the real distinction between the plans of balanced and unbalanced growth.

Scitovsky[6] shows that England's growth came from concentration on a few sectors, in accordance with the law of comparative advantage. This required reliance on foreign trade for markets and raw materials. As efficiency increased, the released resources were used to expand existing industries or develop new ones. But, Scitovsky continues, unbalanced growth is out of fashion today because of political uncertainties, balance-of-payments difficulties, and high competition in world markets. Countries fear that markets may be suddenly withdrawn, leading to economic difficulties. They therefore seek a large degree of self-sufficiency, which is used as an argument for balanced growth. If one is determined to be self-sufficient, balanced growth seems necessary. Modern arguments for unbalanced growth, however, are not based on arguments of comparative advantage but on technological considerations; that is, industries should be built to economical size even though this may require the uncertainties of entering international trade. Temporary imbalances are accepted in order to get later balance at low cost.

Thus, the decision whether to rely on exports or internal self-sufficiency is tied up with the balanced growth controversy. Self-sufficiency can be contemplated only where internal resources are plentiful and varied, where markets are large enough to permit an economical size of industry, or where external markets are lacking or too fluctuating to be relied upon. Few countries can look forward with confidence to such a course. Come what may, they must rely to some extent on imports, and this requires developing export capacity. This, in turn, requires that the export enterprises be efficient enough to compete, even if they must be large scale and capital-intensive.

The balanced growth method obviously assumes that the necessary resources for all industries will be available and that not too much output will be sacrificed by attempting to be virtually self-sufficient. That this is possible in a large country with diversified resources and some purchasing power above that required for necessities is likely. In small countries or in those with poor resources, an attempt at balanced growth and economic self-sufficiency would be economic suicide. Regional groupings with a sufficient variety of resources, materials, and personnel could conceivably use this method, although there always would be some sacrifice of the advantages of international trade.

As mentioned, the method of balanced growth requires government control of the entire investment program and requires calculations of needs well in advance so that the right industries will be selected. This government control can be avoided if a country is quite far advanced, the bulk of industries are in place, and materials and personnel are readily available. Under such circumstances, investment decisions can be left to the marginal decisions of private investors with a reasonable expectation that balanced growth will result. The advocates of unbalanced growth hope to avoid extensive government controls and to rely on private response to new investment opportunities. Like the balanced growth theory, this assumes some degree of development, at least of the personal element. In most underdeveloped countries it would seem necessary for the government to create the key industries and try to encourage private industry to pick up the others. Some reliance on foreign trade to meet temporary shortages would seem necessary.

Some imbalance seems desirable, but this cannot be done to excess without wasting capital. What really matters, however, is the proper sequence of industry for most rapid development, and not balance or imbalance per se. In countries that are small, economically speaking, concentration on a few lines for export appears the only feasible means of getting a variety of goods cheaply; hence, the interest of underdeveloped countries in getting the advanced countries to protect them against temporary deficits in their balance of payments and against fluctuations in the prices and sales of their exports, especially primary products. From the standpoint of these countries, the best help that could be given them would be this protection, plus aid in the form of investment in human capital and economic overheads and in technical aid. The author tends to believe that this would be a good program for development, provided population growth were controlled and political stability assured.

A special case of balanced growth is the relationship between the industrial sector as a whole and the agricultural sector as a whole. Some planners would concentrate investment wholly on industry; some, on agriculture; and some, on a combination of the two. Each country must decide on the relative emphasis to be placed on each of these within the total strategy of development. By and large, the tendency, as pointed out in Chapter 4, is to neglect agriculture in favor of industry.

An extreme all-or-none position is desirable only under special conditions. It would pay to concentrate entirely on agriculture only if the country had a comparative advantage in agriculture and could find assured profitable outside markets for enough output to keep its labor force employed, and could be assured of being able to import its manufactured needs, except for those that would voluntarily spring up in the country in response to the rising purchasing power. Commercial agriculture would have to be widespread, and the entire society would have to be drawn directly or indirectly into dependence on external markets. Few, if any, countries are likely to have these favorable conditions.

Likewise, it would pay a country to concentrate on industry if it had a comparative advantage in enough industry to employ all its labor, could find profitable outside markets, and could be assured of importing the needed food at favorable prices. It could also concentrate on industry if agricultural output would respond to the probable rise in prices by voluntarily expanding to meet the need for food. This, also, is unlikely for very many countries.

The issue boils down to the emphasis to be placed on agriculture and industry. On a relative basis, greater emphasis must be placed on industry in the long run if standards of living are to be raised, except for those countries with extremely favorable agricultural conditions. Increases in the consumption of foodstuffs is limited. Rising incomes will seek new products, largely manufactured goods and services.

Nevertheless, agriculture cannot be neglected because it is necessary that food supplies be increased, labor released, and domestic markets provided. Exporting manufactured goods to buy food cannot be relied upon until a country gains manufacturing experience and competence. If agricultural producers responded readily to price incentives, and if output increased as prices rose and was marketed instead of being consumed on the farm, there would be no need to worry about priorities. However, response is not likely to be quick enough and sufficient enough to keep agricultural prices from rising unduly, so that specific attention must be paid to increasing agricultural output.

However, a country must be careful not to develop industries merely for the sake of having industry. Inefficient ones developed at the expense of agriculture cannot prove beneficial. Moving labor with a low or zero marginal productivity in agriculture into industries where its marginal productivity is just as low or lower does not make any sense. Unfortunately, there is great danger that this will be done, since it is believed that any industrialization is better than agriculture and that productivity can be increased more rapidly in industry than in agriculture. This is often true, but not universally so. Development plans must not be based on generalizations but on the facts of the case. The question of which sector is more important is quite pointless. Under different circumstances one or the other might be stressed. The difficulties the U.S.S.R. has recently been having because of its agricultural problem is a case in point.

A good rule would be to invest just enough in agriculture to meet the pressure of the increased demand that will accompany industrial development. Otherwise, resulting price rises could cause labor unrest and economic and political difficulties for the development program. One recognizes that in the beginning stages of development, most of the increase in demand is likely to go to agricultural products. This would mean a relatively stronger emphasis on investment in agriculture in the earlier stages of development rather than in the later.

Another problem of balance is that between investment in productive equipment and investment in human development. The temptation is to devote as much investment as possible to factories and machinery, which are the visible means of production. The expectation is that one investment will lead to others, either to supply materials or to use the finished product, as outlined by those who favor unbalanced growth, or that investment will be spread widely, directly via the doctrine of balanced growth. Unfortunately, both theories take for granted that the proper personnel will be available and the proper institutional arrangements, such as markets and law, will be in place. Investment in things assumes an appropriate response from people, but unless the people are also developed, the desired response is not likely. Education, training, new attitudes, and the scientific approach are necessary to make growth self-sustaining. If these are not widespread, the government, if it has people with the necessary abilities, will have to take the responsibility for every move and change.

If there is to be any imbalance, the author believes it should be on the side of investment in human capital. Such investment will yield its returns only over a long period, but it is likely to be more productive in the long run because it will permit the responses necessary to make material investment profitable and self-generating. Of course, not all investment in human beings is equally productive, and care must be taken to select the most appropriate education, training, health practices, and so on.

## Gradualism or the Big Push?

A plea for a concentrated effort, or "big push," seems popular, especially in the countries that are trying to develop. This belief gives rise to hopes for sudden advances and certainly cannot help but be more attractive than the view that economic growth not only can but also must be gradual to be long lasting and not detrimental to other values.

The argument for the "big push" is fourfold. First, there is a tendency for small gains to be immediately overwhelmed by a rising population or a desire of people with substandard diets to increase their consumption. In either case, not only is added savings prevented but the increase in demand is along the lines of existing demands, largely food and other necessities. No incentive is thus given to new industries considered essential for development. Only if the rise in incomes is relatively rapid will increased incomes be devoted to new products and thus serve as an incentive for new industries. The balanced growth concept is based on the need for creating more purchasing power and a variety of industries to absorb this purchasing power, and so requires the "big push."

Second, the realization of "external economies" may require the "big push." Certain activities such as the training of labor or the construction of economic overheads must be carried out on a large scale to be efficient and to yield the maximum of stimulating effects to the economy. It is the "lump-iness" of this investment or the need for large concentrations of capital that requires rapid growth, if there is to be any.[7]

Third, a similar argument is that modern production methods in industry require large-scale operations. Thus, for maximum efficiency, large-scale units must be developed. This, in turn, will require large-scale markets. These may be provided either by following the advice of the balanced-growth advocates or by resorting to foreign trade and unbalanced growth. The former must be based on the "big push"; the latter, not necessarily so.

Fourth, many reforms are needed for a country to get started, as outlined in previous chapters. There must be changes in institutions and attitudes, provision for social and economic overheads, increased productivity in agriculture and industry, a solution to the foreign trade problems, govern-mental reform, and many others. Without a large effort, only token changes can be made in these. Small changes cannot hope to break the hold of custom or bring the structural changes necessary to reorganize the society. Obstacles to growth may resist small efforts and can be pushed aside only by a massive effort.

On the other hand, there is opposition to this view. Those who are afraid of extensive government control likewise oppose the idea of the "big push," which requires much government planning and direction. Such concentrated effort requires large savings, which are likely only if forced by the govern-ment. Likewise, it is feared that heavy government taxation will be difficult in a democratic society, especially in one where added consumption has a relatively high importance to the majority of the people. The alternative, it is feared, is totalitarianism. There is little doubt that private enterprise capi-talism will not be able to start underdeveloped countries on the way to growth without extensive government aid. Thus, a rapid rate of growth in-dicates a much larger role for government than many would like.

Second, the "big push" argument is seen as being based on a mistaken preoccupation with industry and a neglect of agriculture. An emphasis on agriculture would permit a more gradual approach.

Third, there are limits to the speed with which change can be effected. Human beings do not seem capable of making complete reversals in their mode of behavior overnight. New institutions cannot be developed in an instant. Thus, at any one time, there is a limit to the ability to absorb large quantities of capital. At low stages of development, this may not be great. Moreover, if change is imposed too quickly, existing social bonds may be shattered and social integration destroyed. If change is too rapid for reintegration to take place, the resulting problems may be too high a price to pay for development. The "big push" argument, in this view, would be applicable only after a long preparation of the human factor.

To the author, the view that growth must be gradual in the early stages of development seems the more reasonable one. It is difficult to visualize underdeveloped countries growing rapidly for some time. Much preparation is necessary in the people's education, training, attitudes, and socialization— in the sense of learning to live in an industrial society. Large efforts in these and other directions are desirable and preferable to small efforts, but a country should not be discouraged if large investments in industry are not immediately available. When the population is ready, a "big push" would seem desirable to get self-generating growth started.

## The Choice of Capital-Intensive or Labor-Intensive Techniques

The problem of the degree of capital or labor intensity is an important one and one on which economists disagree. Traditional theory says that production agencies should use relatively more of the cheaper factor, which in the case of underdeveloped countries implies an emphasis on labor-intensive techniques. However, R. S. Eckhaus[8] points out that the correct rule is that each resource "make the same relative contributions to output in the various types of production." He cites as an example that capital-intensive methods in producing electric power and labor-intensive methods in agriculture may be consistent in the same country. The answer lies not only in cost but also in contribution to output. In other words, the technological conditions are such that to get the same output of electric power, one would have to substitute so much labor to replace the capital used under usual techniques that the cost would be far greater. The real test, thus, is whether a substitution of one factor for the other really pays. It is not a foregone conclusion that because labor is cheap, it always pays to substitute it to the extent that each industry will be labor-intensive.

That labor intensity is desirable has been disputed for various reasons. In the first place, labor may not be the cheapest factor. Wage rates for unskilled labor are undoubtedly low. However, efficiency is also low, turnover is often high, absenteeism may be great, and inexpertness may be damaging to equipment and wasteful of resources. As a result, wage costs per unit of output may be high. Also, the indirect costs of hiring large quantities of labor may be great. Labor must be trained and industrialized, that is, acclimated to an industrial life; and labor must be brought to the city, thus creating large costs of urbanization. Only a careful study of the particular enterprise would reveal the correct situation. Moreover, skilled labor is scarce and may be the most expensive factor. Accordingly, it would have to be used as effectively as possible.

Second, although the use of labor-intensive techniques may be the cheapest at the moment, using them may not be conducive to the fastest growth for various reasons. To have growth, it is necessary to have increased output per capita. Trying to increase output rapidly by labor-intensive techniques shows little promise. Only as new and better capital and more efficient management are combined with labor will output rise substantially. Moreover, an emphasis on labor-intensive techniques is apt to degenerate into a make-work program in the interest of seeing that everyone is employed. The important consideration for economic growth is increased total output over time. Introducing advanced techniques that would increase productivity per worker would not only make more goods available immediately but would also induce or serve as an example in other areas where people could be trained in improved techniques. Also, capital-intensive production creates a break with local tradition, which may be helpful in creating an improved atmosphere for industry. Such spread effects arising from the introduction of improved methods are important for growth.

Third, if there are to be export sales, the industry must be able to compete not only in cost but also in quality. Labor-intensive techniques often fail to provide high and uniform quality. Similarly, where the product is used in other industries, as are the products of the capital goods and intermediate products industries, uniformity of product may be very important and result in lower costs in the user industry, even though the purchase price may be somewhat higher. The important consideration is the cost of obtaining a desired quality, which may often require capital-intensive techniques.

Fourth, if a plant is modern, outside capital may be easier to obtain, thus increasing the total quantity of capital available to the country. Also, capital-intensive techniques will probably result in greater savings, for the major portion of profits can be expected to go only to a few and a relatively small amount of the total will go to labor. In the case of labor-intensive techniques, a larger share of the receipts will go to labor and will be spent on consumption.

Yet, the employment effects of the development effort cannot be disregarded. Considerable skill must be employed to restrict capital-intensive techniques to uses where it is cheaper, where the product must be superior, and where the effect on other industries is most important. Labor-intensive techniques should be used where there is no great sacrifice of cost or quality. In almost every industry there are operations that could advantageously be made labor-intensive, with other, more critical operations made capital-intensive.

Other problems may be encountered with capital-intensive techniques. Extensive reliance on these probably means greater government control and fewer opportunities for small enterprisers to enter business, with a consequent loss of individual initiative. Too great a reliance on modern capital-intensive methods may create the dualistic society that economists would like to avoid. Few workers would be affected, and there would be little addition to local purchasing power. Even the raw materials might be imported in order to assure uniform quality, for modern capital-intensive methods have a low tolerance to quality differentials in their inputs. The owners and most workers may prefer imported goods. As a result, little would be spent locally and local enterprises would not be stimulated, and thus would have no incentive to change from their traditional methods. Moreover, few would receive industrial training that might carry over into local pursuits. Some large-scale efficient industries (and agricultural units) may be necessary to provide sufficient output to support development and to act as a spur to industrial advance, but there must be enough gains to a sufficient number of local people so that advance can be supported by increased internal purchasing power and general industrial training.

Neither extreme of capital intensity or labor intensity seems to hold the answer. The optimum combination has seldom been discussed. An intermediate pattern of some capital-intensive and some labor-intensive operations would appear to be the best approach, but the approach must fit the exact circumstances of the country in question.

The general purpose is to maximize the returns from investment funds and other resources, but the returns must be considered more broadly than just immediate economic outputs. The effects on employment, future savings, changes in attitudes and skills, and so on must also be considered.

## General or Concentrated Growth

A. O. Hirschman[9] raises the question whether the pattern of investment should be dispersal, concentration of growing areas, or development of backward areas. He says it is most common to disperse funds among a large number of small projects scattered widely. This is done to get widespread political support and is not based on considerations of efficiency or maximizing growth. Efforts to help truly backward sections and remote areas at the expense of more efficient enterprises may be even more uneconomic.

Hirschman himself is an advocate of concentrated growth. He feels that growth is not likely to proceed at the same pace everywhere and that efforts should be concentrated on the growing points. In such a case, interregional inequalities would be inevitable. Eventually, poorer sections might gain as materials were demanded, the example of the progressive sector taken up, or as manufacturers migrated to the poorer sections in search of cheap labor, as is evidenced by the shift of manufacturers toward the southern sector of the United States. But this will not happen unless the people are prepared to seize the developing opportunities. The way to improve the poorer sections is through improved agriculture, education, and transportation, and not by trying to introduce industry prematurely.

Much of the solution depends on the relative costs of providing the economic and social overheads and on the optimum scale of operation. Concentrated industry lessens the cost of some overheads, such as power and transportation, but increases the costs arising from urbanization. Scattering industry may lessen urbanization cost, but may raise the costs of transportation, communications, and power. Large countries with thinly scattered populations would find dispersal inefficient unless the optimum scale of operation of the production units were small. Where economies of scale are large, concentration is indicated. Where the best scale is small, greater dispersal may be practiced.

## *Private Enterprise or Government Operation?*

Lastly, a decision must be made whether the major responsibility for investment decisions should be governmental or private. The inclination, for one raised in a private enterprise system, is to favor as much private enterprise as possible. There are undoubted advantages to private enterprise where conditions are such that private enterprise can work.

Some of these advantages are: It allows greater freedom for the individual, although certain antisocial actions such as unfair competition may have to be restrained. It is thought to make for more democracy, although large industry does not present a picture of democracy and there is no reason that a country in which the government operates a given industry cannot also be democratic. Greater progress is considered probable because competition promotes technological change and new products. Much of this innovation may be applied to nonessentials, such as an attractive package, but along with this there are also increases in quality and serviceability. For the underdeveloped country, however, the problem is not so much creating something new as imitating something already known elsewhere. Governments are not so handicapped in this as in creating the new, although there is the possibility that government servants may not have so much incentive to introduce the new as would private enterprise under the right conditions. This, however, is not a universal experience.

As previously stated, for private enterprise to work reasonably well there must be available a supply of capital, labor, and other resources; economic and social overheads must be reasonably well supplied; entrepreneurs and others must be responsive to economic opportunities; and there must be sufficient demand above the level of necessities so that there is a prospect for a new enterpriser to drain some of it off to his product. Furthermore, even under the best of circumstances, governments must exercise many functions, including preventing private monopolies and appropriation of power, relieving unemployment, providing a social minimum living standard for the unfortunate, and supplying the necessary economic and social overheads.

In the beginning stages of development, private enterprise has considerable difficulty inducing growth. One can expect that there will have to be a larger amount of government action to promote development than is found in the United States, at least until conditions are improved. Governments have certain advantages. They are able to mobilize savings through the tax power. Investments can be made with a longer-range objective than that of short-run profits. Full account can be taken of the proper sequence of investments, the social benefits and external economies, and even for social costs. Governments can plan for overall social objectives. They can initiate social and cultural as well as technological change. Centralized government industry may even be able to economize scarce entrepreneurial skills.

This cannot be an all-or-none proposition. Jan Tinbergen,[10] states that neither of the extreme economic systems, Communism or laissez-faire private enterprise, has been particularly effective in creating well-being. Neither one is optimum and, he says, mixed systems are better. However, the nature of the mixing needs study. Governments simply cannot do everything and must allow some scope for private enterprise; if nothing else, for such personal services as barbering and shoe shining. At least these do not seem suitable for government monopolies. Going beyond this, there seems to be room for the advantages of private enterprise, such as individual initiative and resourcefulness and flexibility, as well as those of government planning. The real question is: How much government and how much private planning?

It is the author's belief that in the early stages, government in an underdeveloped country will have to do more than that in an advanced one. It is to be hoped that as much as possible will be turned over to private hands and that the private sector will be encouraged to grow as the country develops, with its bad features being controlled. This will require a conscious policy on the part of the government, for government ownership and operation of many industries may make businessmen wary lest any business they start may be the next to face direct government competition or expropriation.

There is much that governments can do to encourage private enterprise besides making clear their intention to promote it, including supplying adequate statistical information, supplying economic and social overheads, and providing credit institutions. Japan had considerable success in starting new industries and ultimately turned them over to private enterprise. Puerto Rico[11] has shown considerable ingenuity in promoting private enterprise through tax concessions, providing information about the economy, constructing buildings, and so forth, although it also had such advantages as open access to the United States market, United States protection, and tax concessions. To aid private enterprise effectively, however, governments must be efficient, honest, and stable. At the moment, this seems perhaps the most difficult goal to attain.

Many reforms have been proposed. It seems more and more obvious that there is no one method, no magic formula, which will bring development, although certain common problems exist. Each country and its problems are unique. Different obstacles to development exist and different opportunities to overcome these are available. A specific program must be tailor-made for each country, and this can only be effective more than marginally after full study of the country's economy, social and cultural background, and political traditions and goals. A further need is to recognize all the potential problems and policies. Pointing these out has been the aim of this book. Putting the pieces together and evolving a plan of attack is a complicated matter, which is merely outlined in Chapter 14 and which requires far more study and "expertise" than is given in that chapter.

At this point in time, the specific information at our disposal concerning every phase of the underdeveloped countries needs to be multiplied many times. Comparative studies of different economies will discover likenesses and differences, and especially how these are affected and affect different policies. In the absence of such information, many of our conclusions and suggestions can be only tentative and should be taken as such. The development of a theory of economic growth is only at its beginning. There is much to be done before scientific guidelines can be formulated.

## REFERENCES

1. HIRSCHMAN, A. O., *Strategy of Economic Development*. New Haven, Yale University Press, 1958, p. 50.
2. GALBRAITH, J. K., *Economic Development in Perspective*. Cambridge, Mass., Harvard University Press, 1962, p. 4.
3. NURKSE, R., "International Trade Theory and Development Policy," in H. S. Ellis and H. C. Wallich, *Economic Development for Latin America*. New York, St Martin's Press, 1961, p. 249.
4. SINGER, H. W., "The Concept of Balanced Growth in Economic Development: Theory and Practice," in E. Nelson, *Economic Growth*. Dallas, Texas, University of Texas Press, 1960, pp. 71-86.
5. *Ibid.*, p. 77.
6. SCITORSKY, "Growth Balanced or Unbalanced?" in M. Abramovitz, *et al.*, *Allocation of Resources*. Stanford, Calif., Stanford University Press, 1959, pp. 207-17.
7. For a description of this belief and arguments for it, see Rosenstein-Rodan, P. N., "Notes on the Theory of the 'Big Push,'" and comments in H. Ellis and H. Wallich, *Economic Development for Latin*

*America*. New York, St Martin's Press, 1961.
8. ECKHAUS, R. S., "Technological Change in the Less Developed Areas" in *Development of the Emerging Countries. An Agenda for Research*. Washington, D.C., The Brookings Institution, 1962. Quoted in G. M. Meier, *Leading Issues in Development Economics*. New York, Oxford University Press, 1964, p. 244.
9. HIRSCHMAN, A. O., "Investment Policies in Underdeveloped Countries." *American Economic Review* (September, 1957), pp. 550-70.
10. TINBERGEN, JAN, *Shaping the World's Economy*. New York, The Twentieth Century Fund, 1962, p. 181.
11. JAFFE, A. J., *People, Jobs and Economic Development*. New York, The Free Press of Glencoe, 1959. Stead, W. H., *Fomento: The Economic Development of Puerto Rico*. National Planning Association, 1958. *Annual Reports,* Puerto Rico Industrial Development Co. *The Commonwealth of Puerto Rico*. Office of the Commonwealth of Puerto Rico, 1962.

## ADDITIONAL READINGS

ADELMAN, I., *Theories of Economic Growth and Development*. Stanford, Calif., Stanford University Press, 1961.
ADLER, J. H., "Policy Problems in Economic Development." *Economic Development and Cultural Change* (January, 1961), pp. 111-19.
BLACK, E. R., *Diplomacy of Economic Development*. Cambridge, Mass., Har-

vard University Press, 1960.
BRUTON, H. J., "Short Run Problem of Growth in Underdeveloped Countries." *Kyklos,* No. 3 (1957), pp. 281-98.
Department of Economic Affairs. *Measures for the Economic Development of Underdeveloped Countries*. New York, United Nations, 1951.
FRANK, A. G., "Hirschman's Strategy."

*Economic Development and Cultural Change* (July, 1960), pp. 433-40.

LEWIS, J. P., *Quiet Crisis in India*. Washington, D.C., The Brookings Institution, 1962.

LEWIS, W. A., "Consensus and Discussions on Economic Growth." *Eco-nomic Development and Cultural Change* (October, 1957), pp. 75-80.

MYRDAL, G., *Rich Lands and Poor*. New York, Harper & Bros., 1957.

SINGER, H. W., "Trends in Economic Thought on Underdevelopment." *Social Research* (Winter, 1961), pp. 387-414.

# *Index*